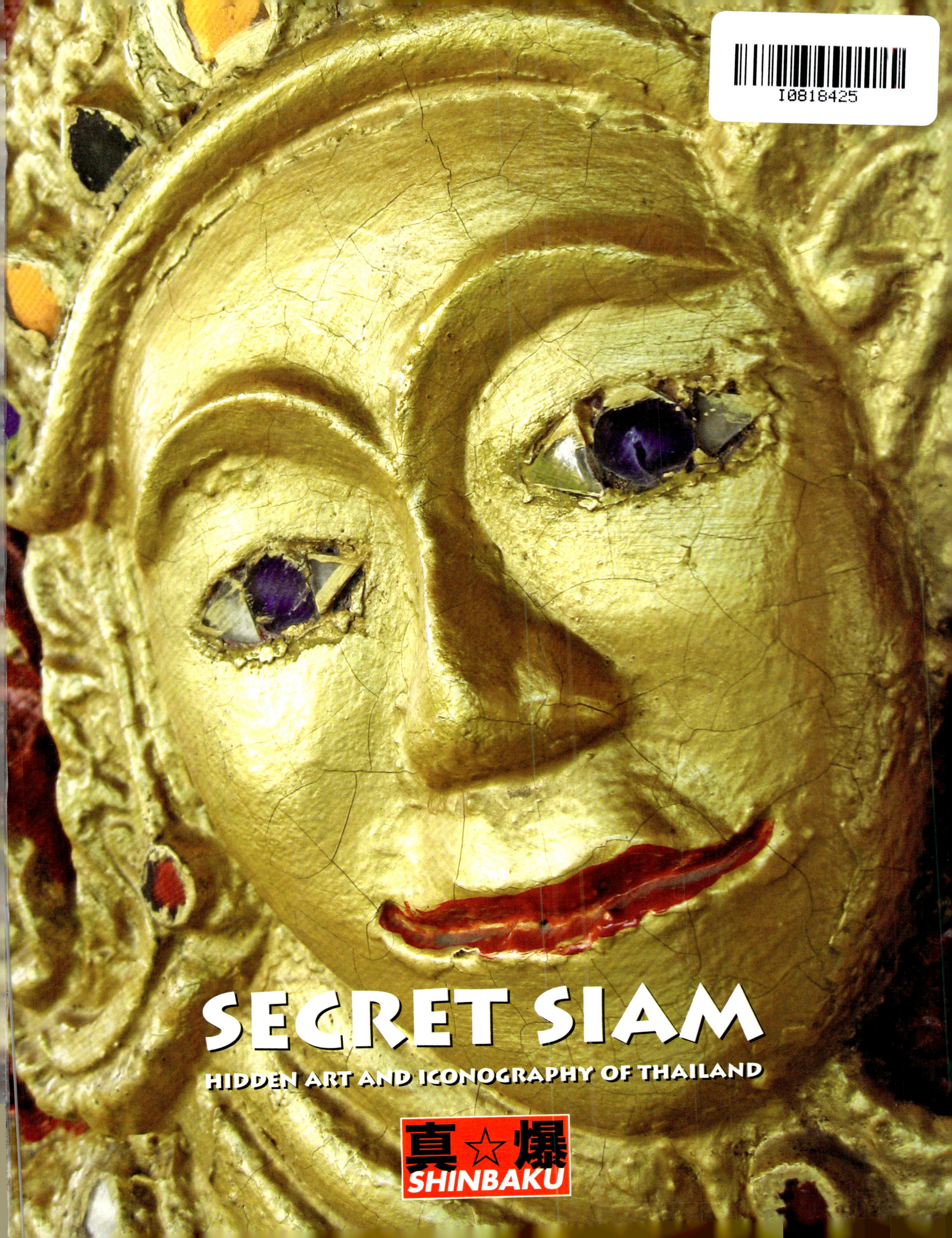

I0818425
SECRET SIAM
HIDDEN ART AND ICONOGRAPHY OF THAILAND
真☆爆
SHINBAKU

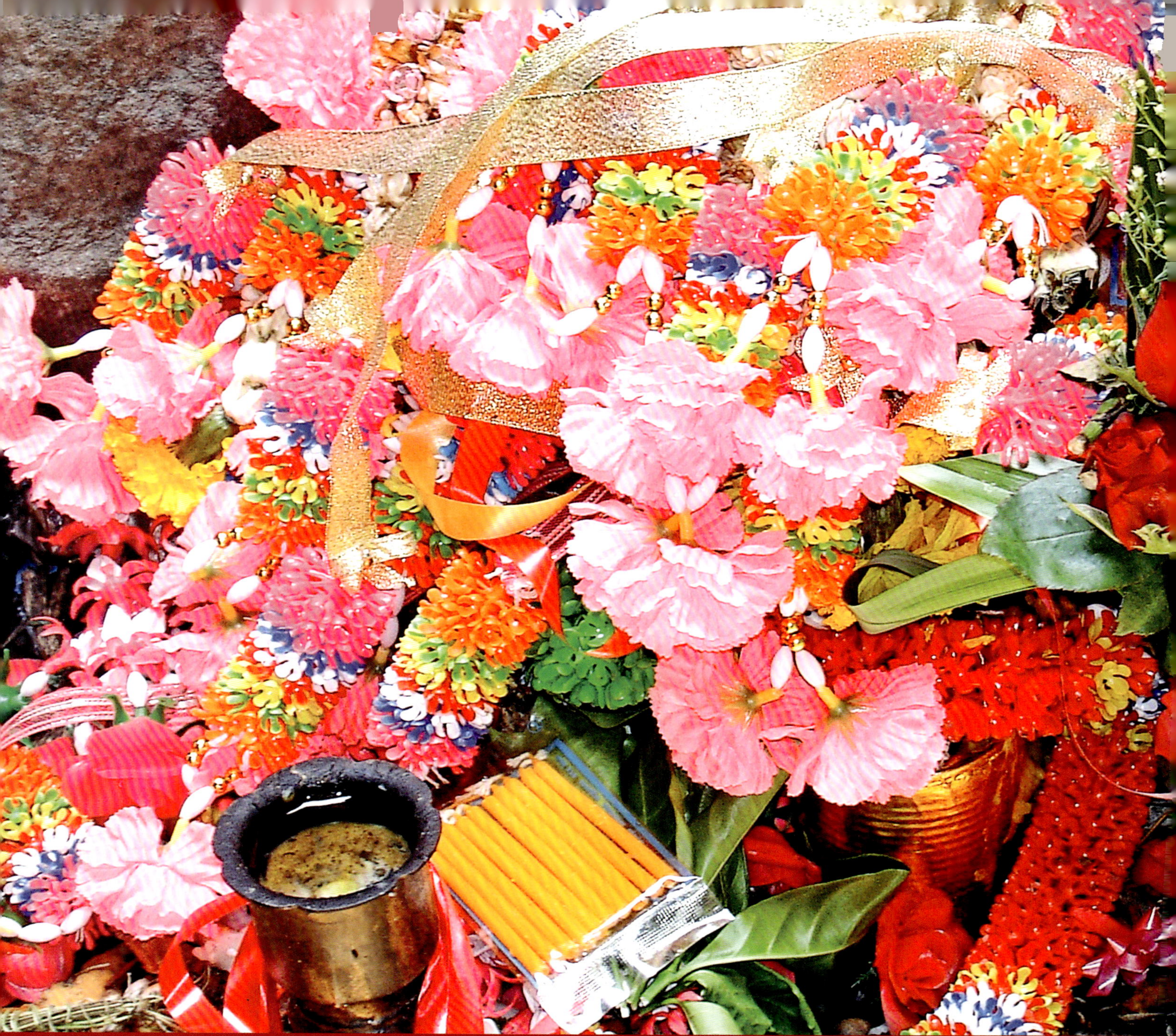

SECRET SIAM

Hidden Art And Iconography Of Thailand

Photography and text by Mark Hejnar

Published 2014 by Shinbaku

ISBN 978-1-84068-330-1

Design by Broken Fang Cryptography

Rights management: www.krystall-korp.com

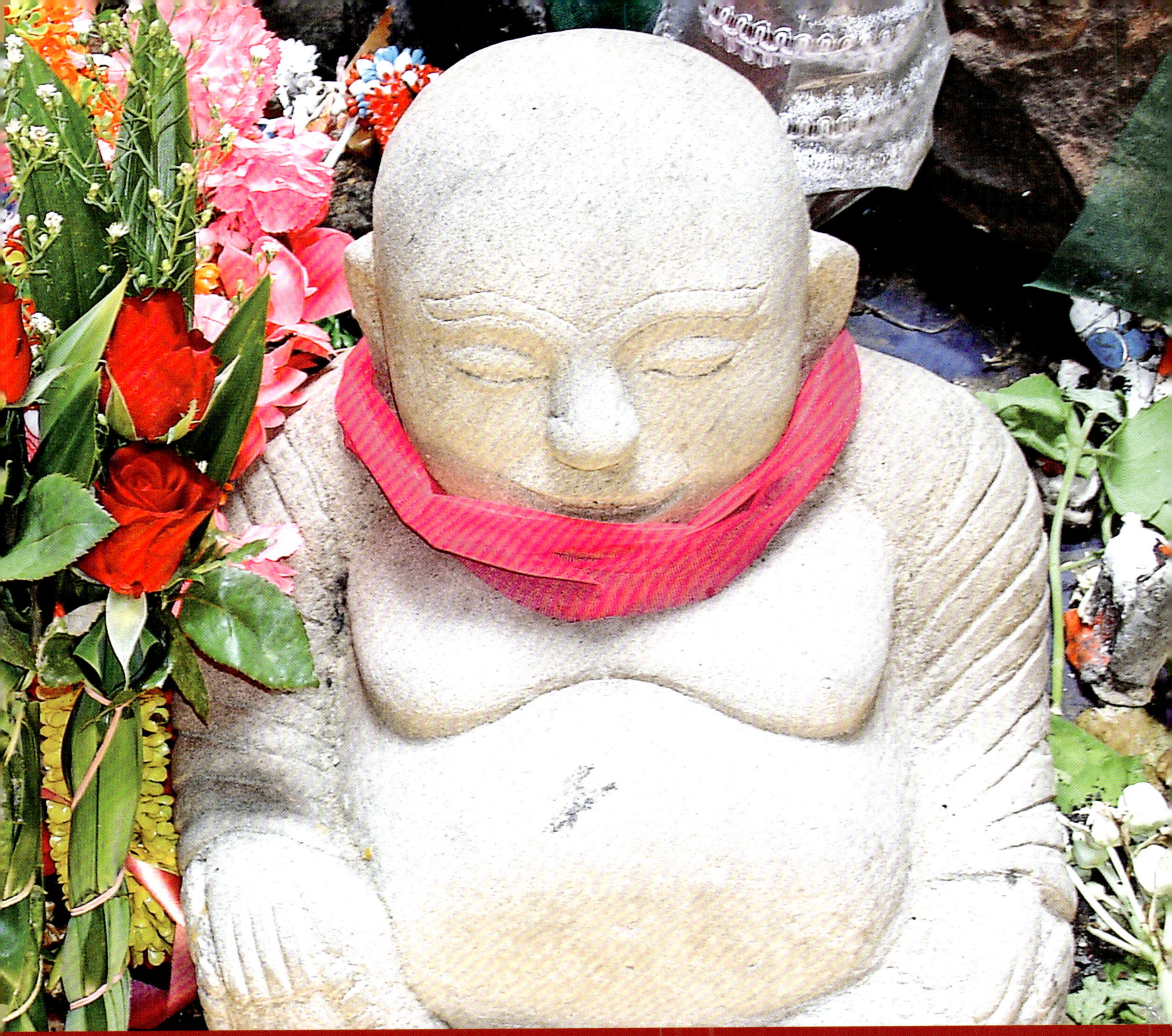

CONTENTS

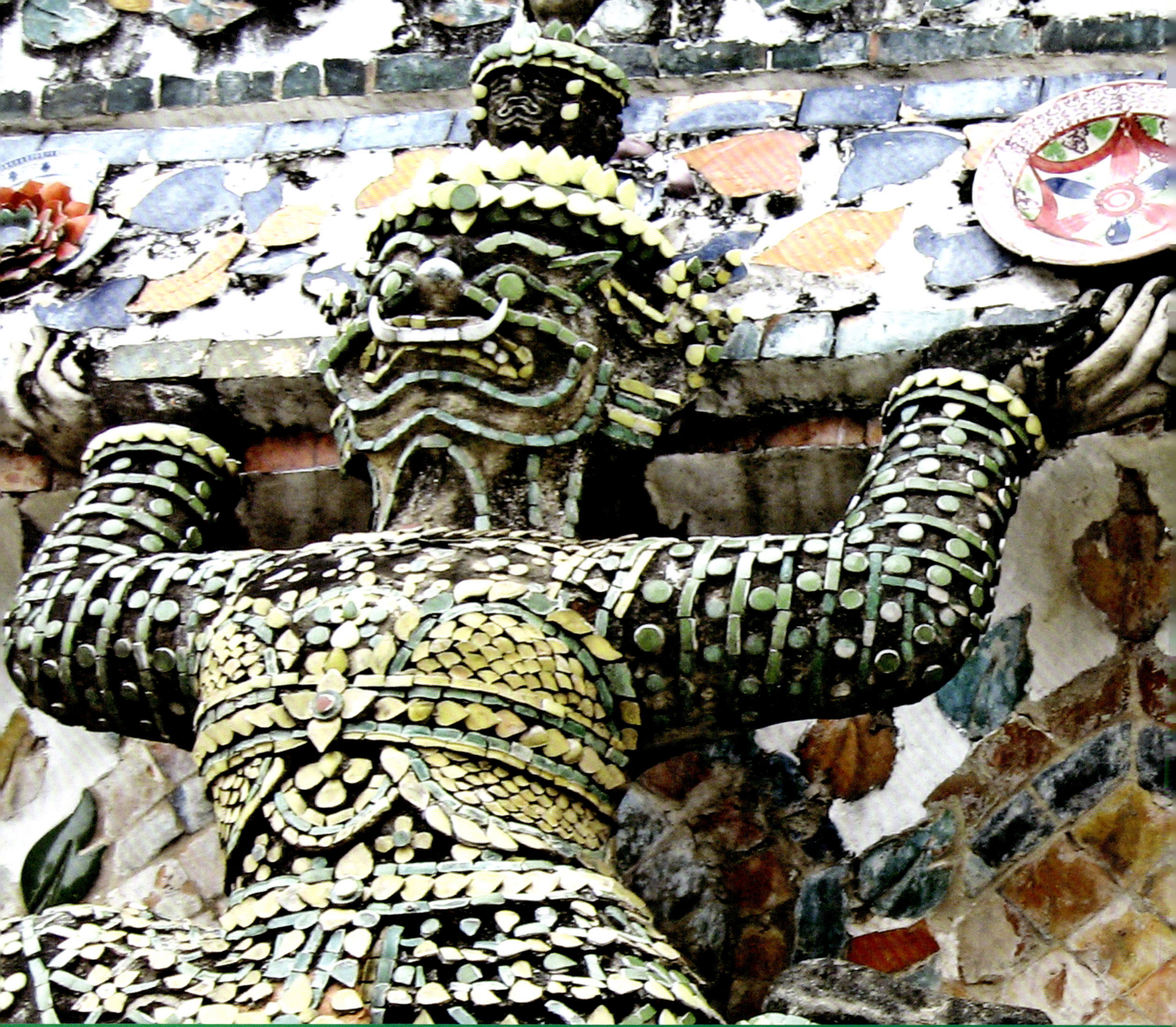

FOREWORD

There is a Thai term, *prathap jai*, which translates as "stamp heart" (Moore, 1992, p. 45), meaning to leave a deep positive impression. I have great *prathap jai* for Thailand. I was lucky enough to live there for four years, following two years traveling back and forth from the U.S. During that time, I traveled throughout the country and took thousands of photos and hours of video trying to capture what was hidden just beneath the surface: the icon in the middle of a busy intersection, the broken spirit houses left by a tree, and the folk art rendition of a serpent with the Buddha.

Influences on Thai art come from numerous sources, initially Chinese and later Indian civilizations, as adapted by the Mon and Khmer people (Krairiksh, 2012, p.28). Elements of ancient Hinduism, Brahmanism, Buddhism and Animism coexist in Thai art, religion, and daily life. Over 90% of Thailand is Buddhist, either Theravada or Mahayana, the balance made up of Muslim, Hindu, Animist and Christian. Thai art should be considered the servant of religion, and its radiant temples are everywhere, serving as focal points of community life and religious meditation.

Perhaps this ability to absorb elements of other cultures rather than to separate and exclude, while maintaining a Thai essence has kept Thailand from prior colonization. The mythological *Ramakien*, as written by King Rama I in 1807, is the Thai

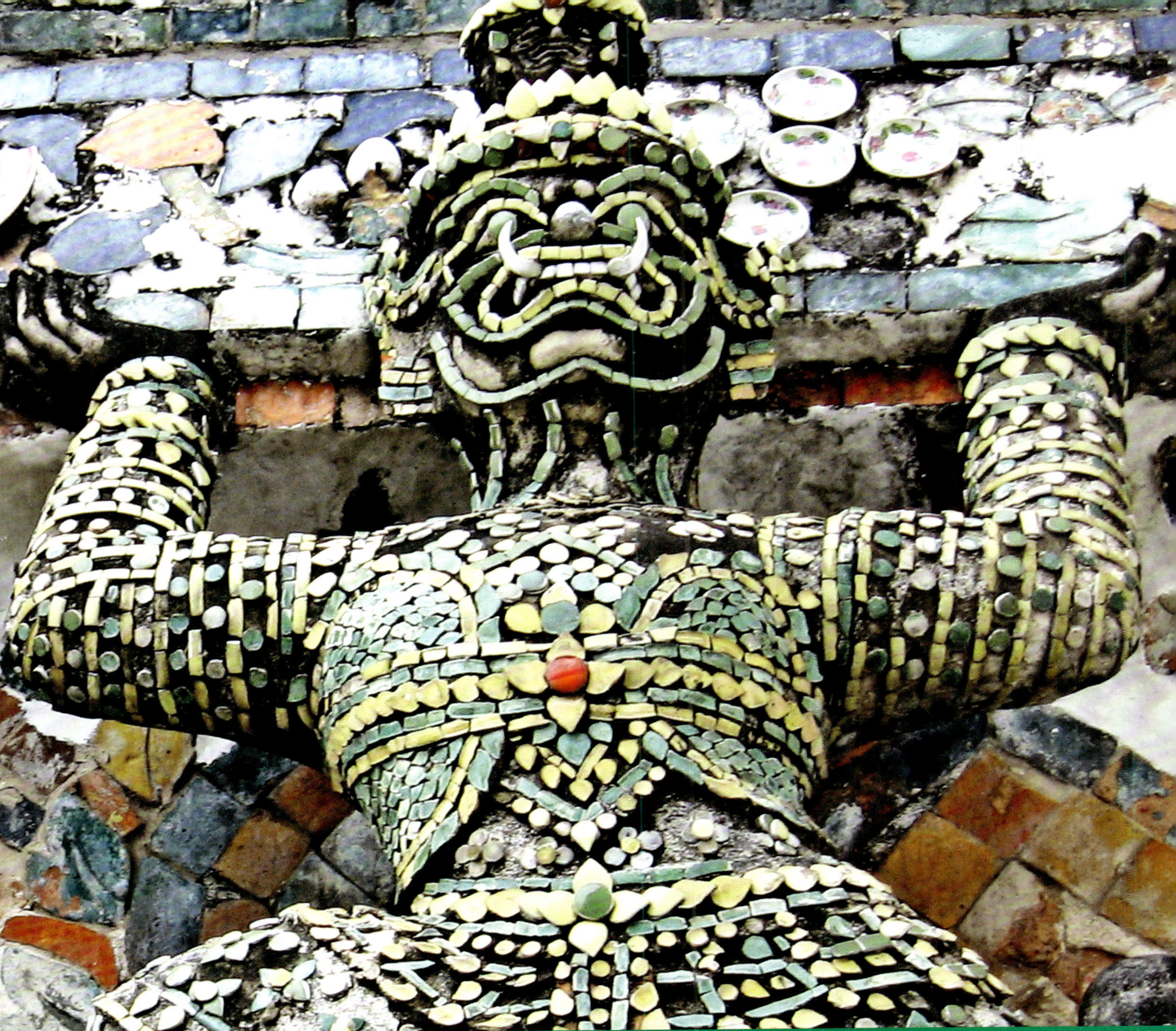

version of the 2000-year-old Sanskrit *Ramayana*, depicting the victory of man over evil as assisted by the gods. It has been assimilated and modified to reflect Thai beliefs so no Thai would consider it foreign (Jumsai, 2002, pp. 2-4). Its story is depicted on the walls of the Temple of the Emerald Buddha, and its creatures, the *naga*, and the *garuda*, protect Thailand's temples and banks. Temple paintings reveal rural village life or show the *Jataka* stories (in Thai: *chaddock*), some of the earliest known Theravada Buddhist texts, detailing the previous lives of the Buddha.

Folklore and superstition play a key role in Thailand's art and belief system. Every shopkeeper has a *nang kwak* figurine, the beckoning lady, for good luck. Spirit houses are everywhere in Thailand: if one erects a new building, an alternative house must be built for the displaced spirit of the land, as it is the rightful owner of the place (Freeman & Shearer, 2000, p. 35).

Thais, however, seem to hide in plain sight. For an outsider, an examination of the art of Thailand leaves one with more questions than answers, but this is acceptable as the journey merits the investment. For the people of Thailand, art is the tie that binds.

–Mark Hejnar, Moscow, September 2013

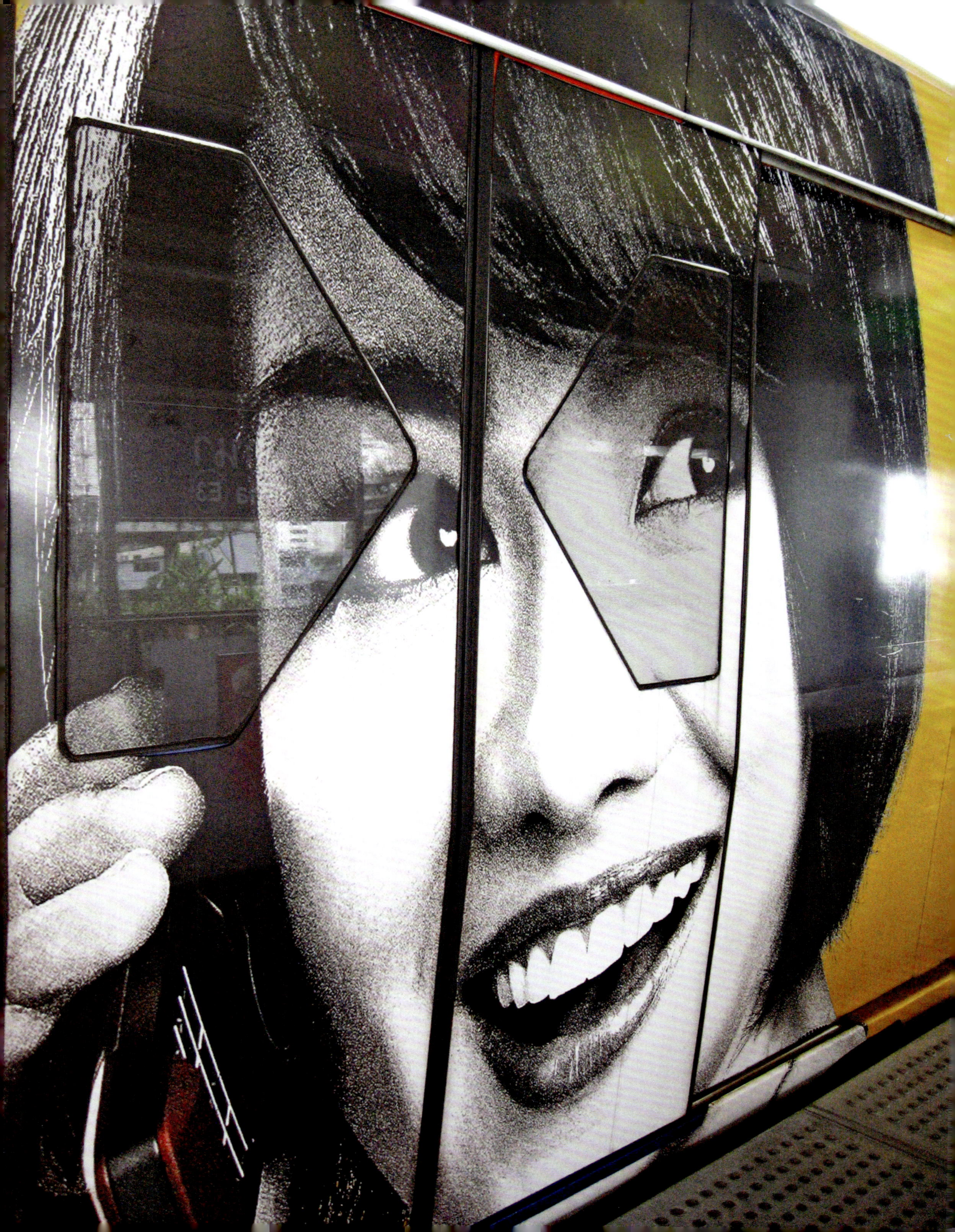

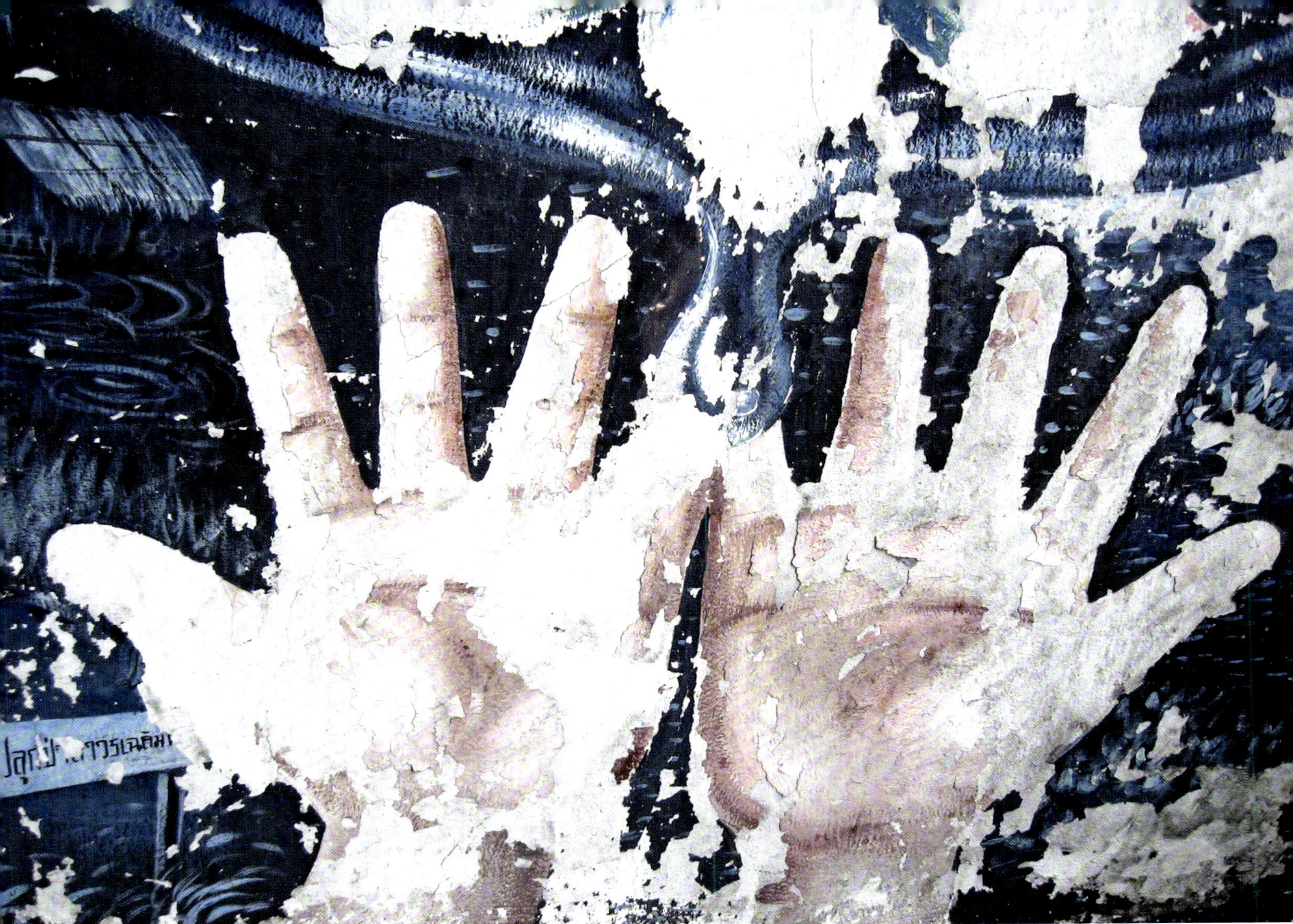

1. BANGKOK

There is no place like Bangkok, juxtaposing the mythic and the modern, evolving while silently protecting its distinct identity. Beginning as a small trading village in the fifteenth century during the time of the Ayutthaya kingdom, Bangkok became Thailand's capital in 1782; today the city has more than nine million residents. It boasts the world's longest official name, abbreviated in English to Khrung Thep (meaning the "City of Angels"). Situated on the Chao Phraya River, a network of canals was the primary source of transportation until modern roads were built in the late nineteenth century.

At one of the city's busiest intersections, hundreds of people, tourists and locals alike, make daily offerings at a shrine to Brahma. Not far away stands a larger-than-life Ronald McDonald, bent in a *wai*, the Thai gesture of respect. Modern commercial art covers the exterior of the BTS Skytrain, and futuristic plastic bulbs shelter hi-so shoes by the escalator. From the Skytrain, one sees an ancient temple in the shadow of the Emporium Mall: each Thai *wais* the temple as they pass. A migrant worker sells fish-balls on a stick and soda in a bag next to a 50-foot plastic hand holding a mobile phone. Formerly, a trip to Bangkok was not complete until an elephant walked by the bar. Shortly after sunrise, barefoot novice Buddhist monks collect their daily alms from Bangkok residents, given as a form of *tam boon*, or merit-making. Later in the day, the same novice might be playing a video game or talking on a mobile phone. When elections are held, Bangkok's street poles are crammed with competing party posters. On December 5th, the King's birthday, tremendous banners depicting King Bhumibol Adulyadej hang throughout the city. This King is believed to be a reincarnation of Vishnu: no Thai home is complete without his portrait hanging in a place of honor. Few Thais make a major life decision without first consulting a fortuneteller or astrologer. Amulets and religious tattoos called *sak yant* protect the wearer and bring good fortune. Thousands of spirit houses are visible in Bangkok, next to schools, construction sites, apartment buildings and empty lots. Resembling dollhouses or miniature Khmer temples, they reflect indigenous and animistic superstitions still important in modern daily life. Bangkok remains a city of superstition and tradition, offering constant contradiction, innumerable obstacles, unanswered questions and endless enjoyment.

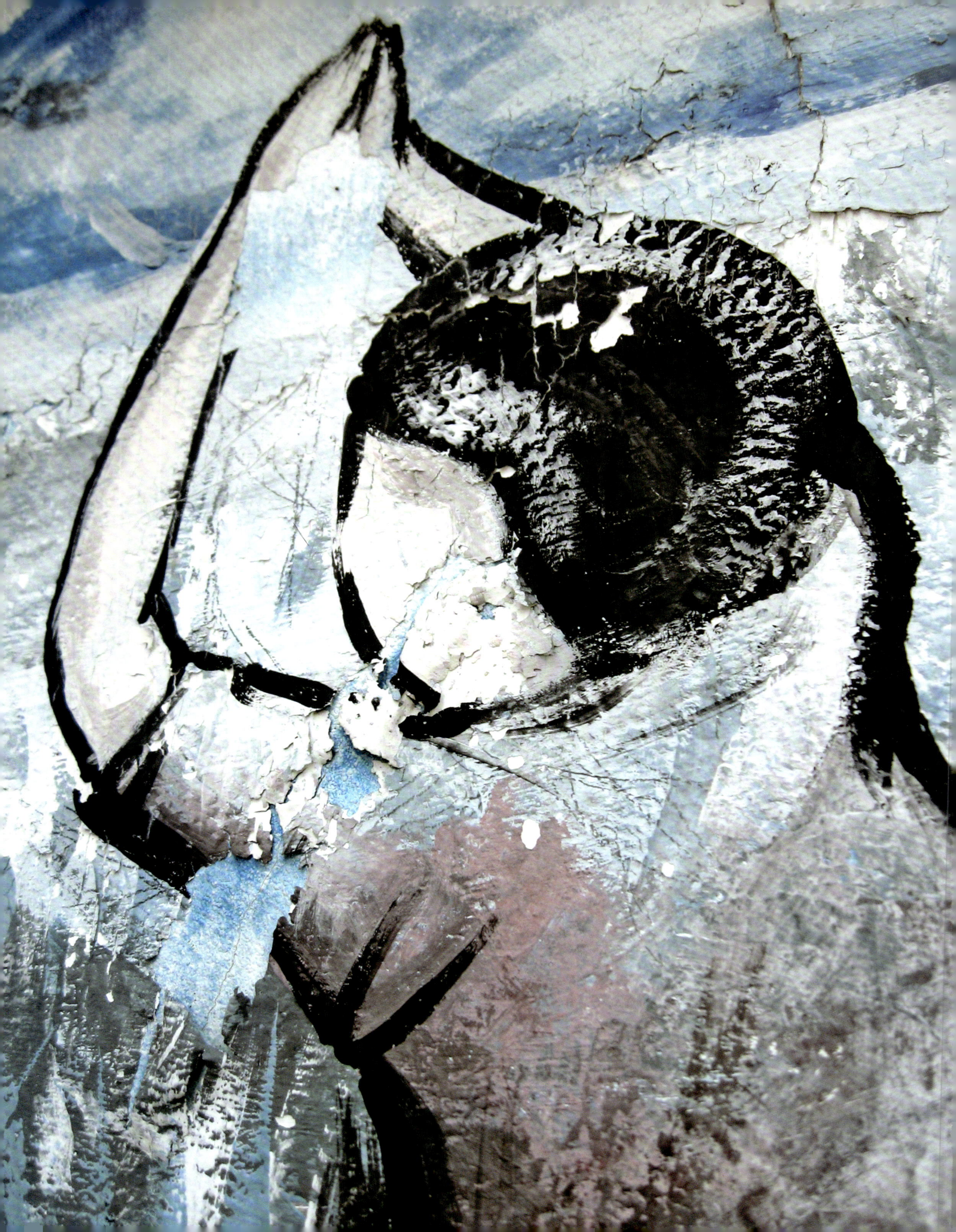

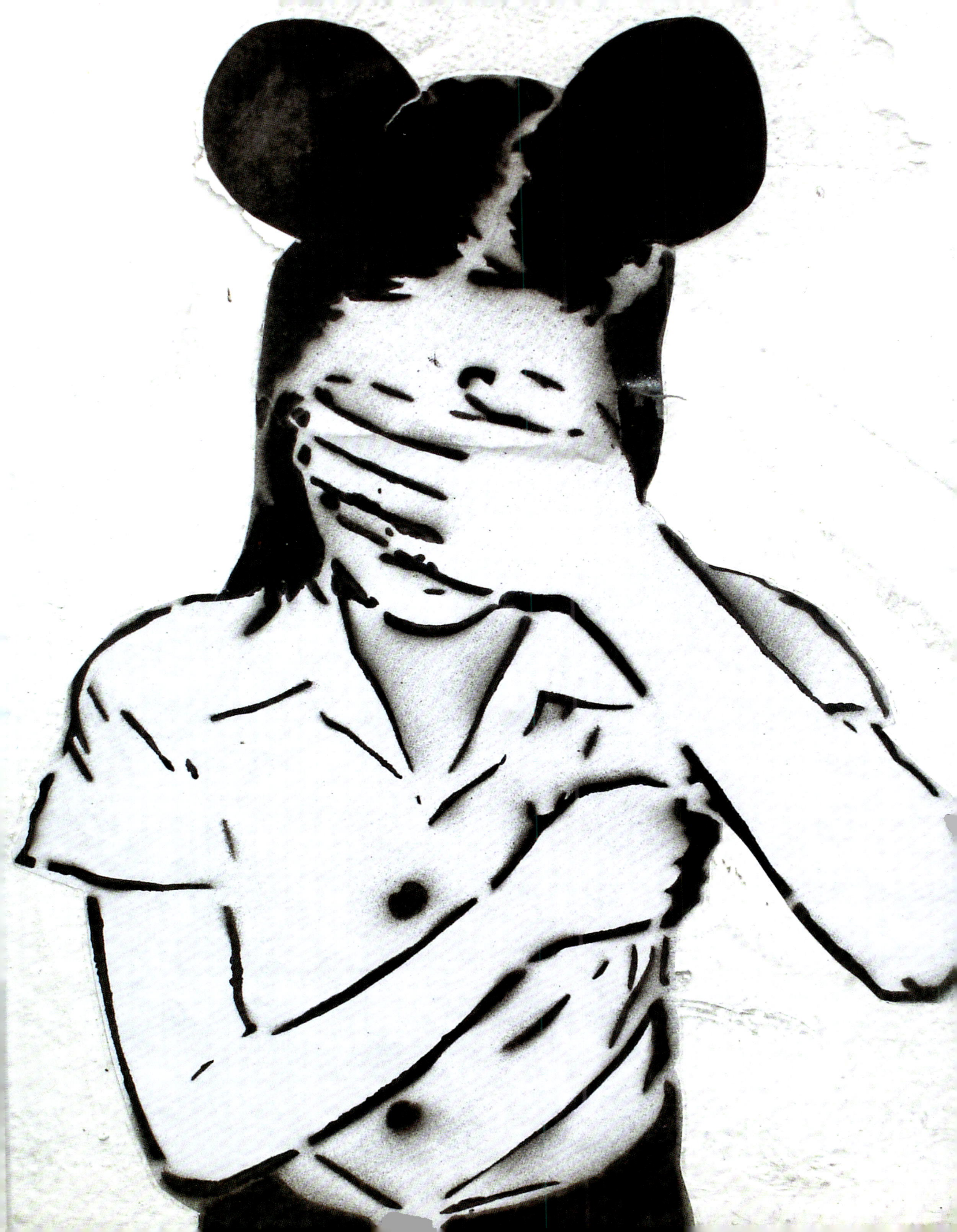

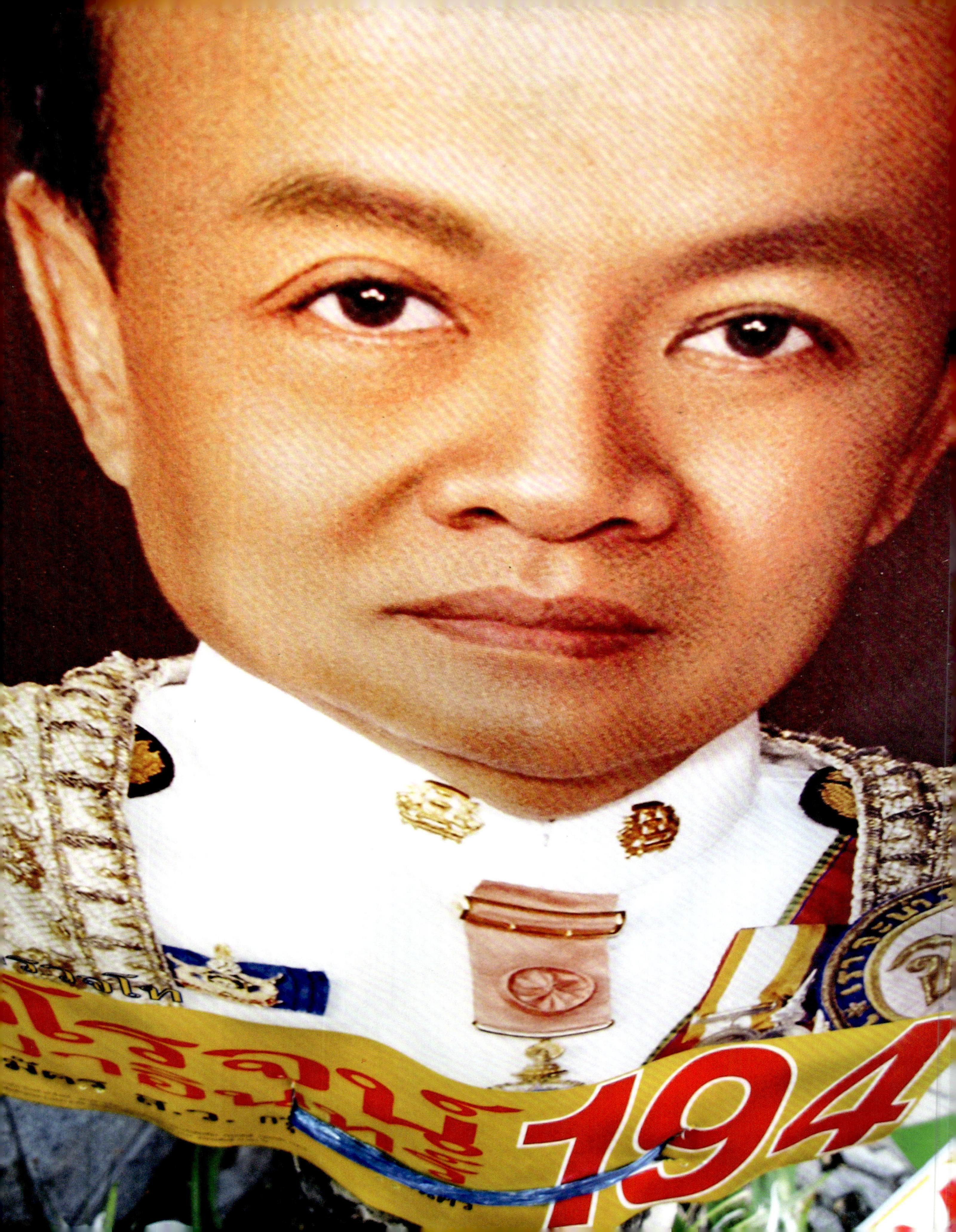
194

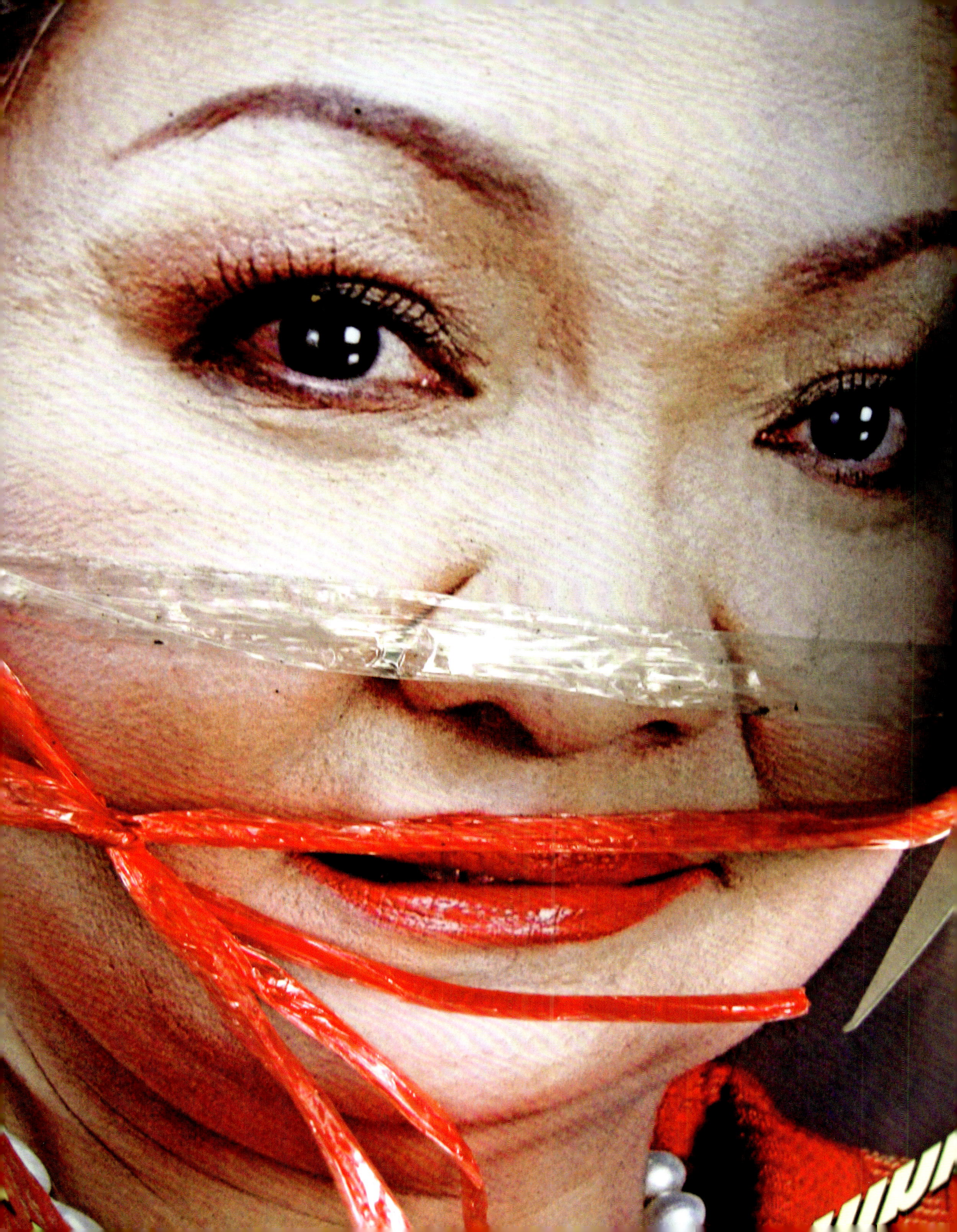

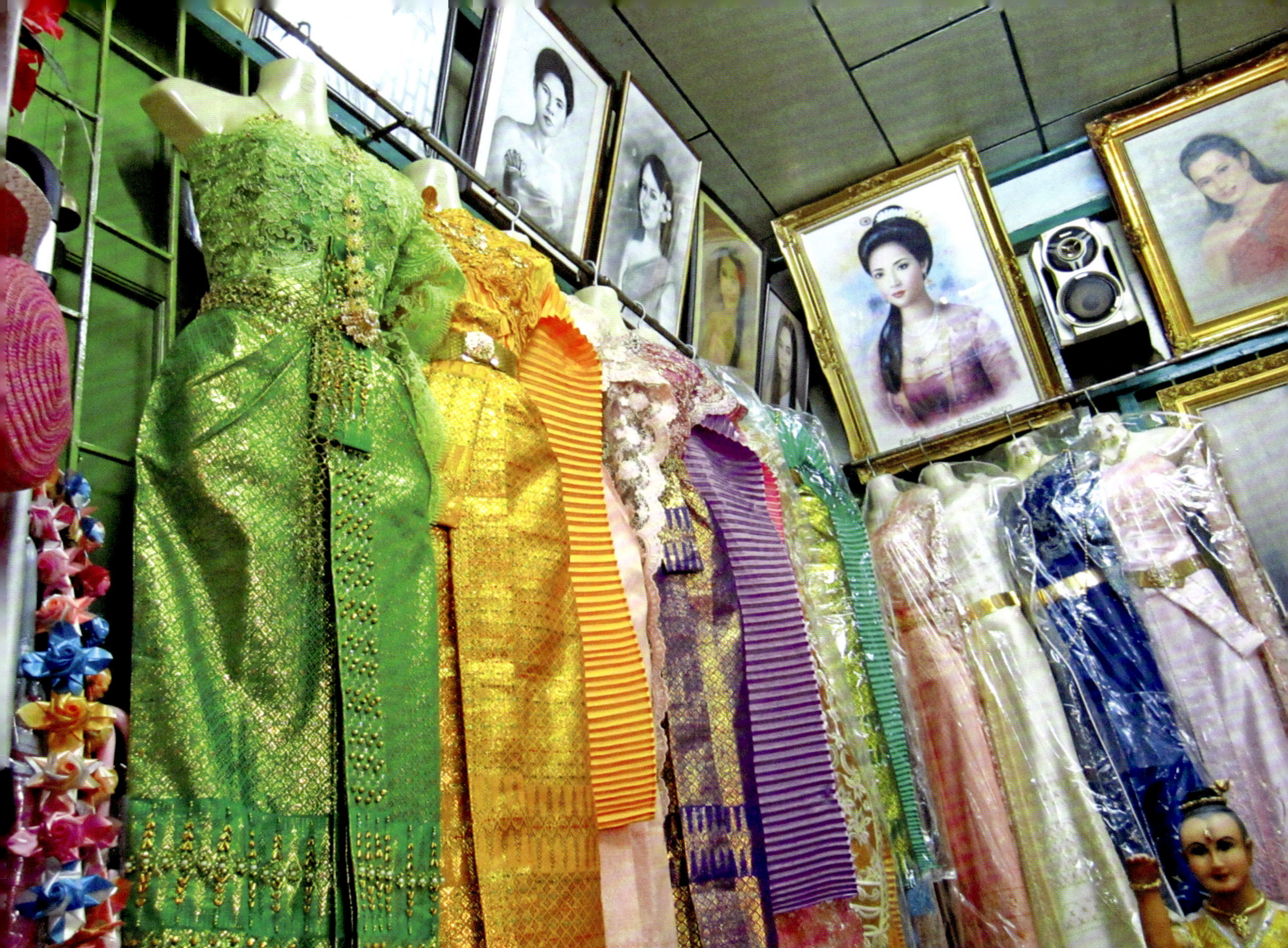

MAE NAK

Every Thai knows the story of Mae Nak, the woman who loved her husband so much she refused to accept death. Variations aside, Mae Nak and her unborn infant die in childbirth while her husband, Nai Mak, is away fighting in battle. Her death unbeknownst to Mak, he is overjoyed to find mother and child waiting upon his return, albeit alarmed they are so cold to the touch. Traditional Thai homes are built on stilts due to the seasonal rains. One day, while making *som tam*, Mae Nak drops a lime. A terrified Mak stares in disbelief as Mae Nak extends her arm all the way to the ground to retrieve it, even more so when his laughing baby flies up onto the ceiling rafters. Mak hides at Wat Mahabut, for his wife, having suffered a painful death in childbirth, has become a *phii phrai*, the fiercest of spirits, destroying everyone in her path. Challenging the sanctity of the temple, her dripping footprints appear on the *viharn*'s ceiling: Mae Nak demands Mak's return. A gifted novice lures her tormented soul into a ceramic pot, which is then ceremoniously sent to the bottom of the river. Her skull is made into a belt buckle for the monk. Tragically, dutiful wife has become malevolent ghost and then miraculously transformed into the protecting deity of Phra Khanong, where Mae Nak's bones are buried beneath a *takian* tree. Her shrine receives daily adoration in a section of Wat Mahabut.

The sacred tree is wrapped in colorful fabrics, its bark smooth in spots as visitors rub for winning lottery numbers, gifted from another female spirit residing there. The figure of Mae Nak and two babies sit on a bench at the rear of the shrine, behind a glass cabinet full of *baht* notes, cosmetics, figurines, sweets, baby clothes and a bowl of bracelets. Paintings of her likeness cover the walls, racks of beautiful dresses hang all around, a television mounted on the wall opposite a constant companion. Attendees regularly change her dress, wigs and jewelry, removing the *baht* notes left as offerings from her waist sash. Devotees pray and make requests, burn incense and candles, leave red and pink roses, offer gifts and place stamp-sized gold leafs on the baby and her mother for good fortune. Expectant mothers do not normally visit, but young men awaiting conscription call-up do, praying for her assistance.

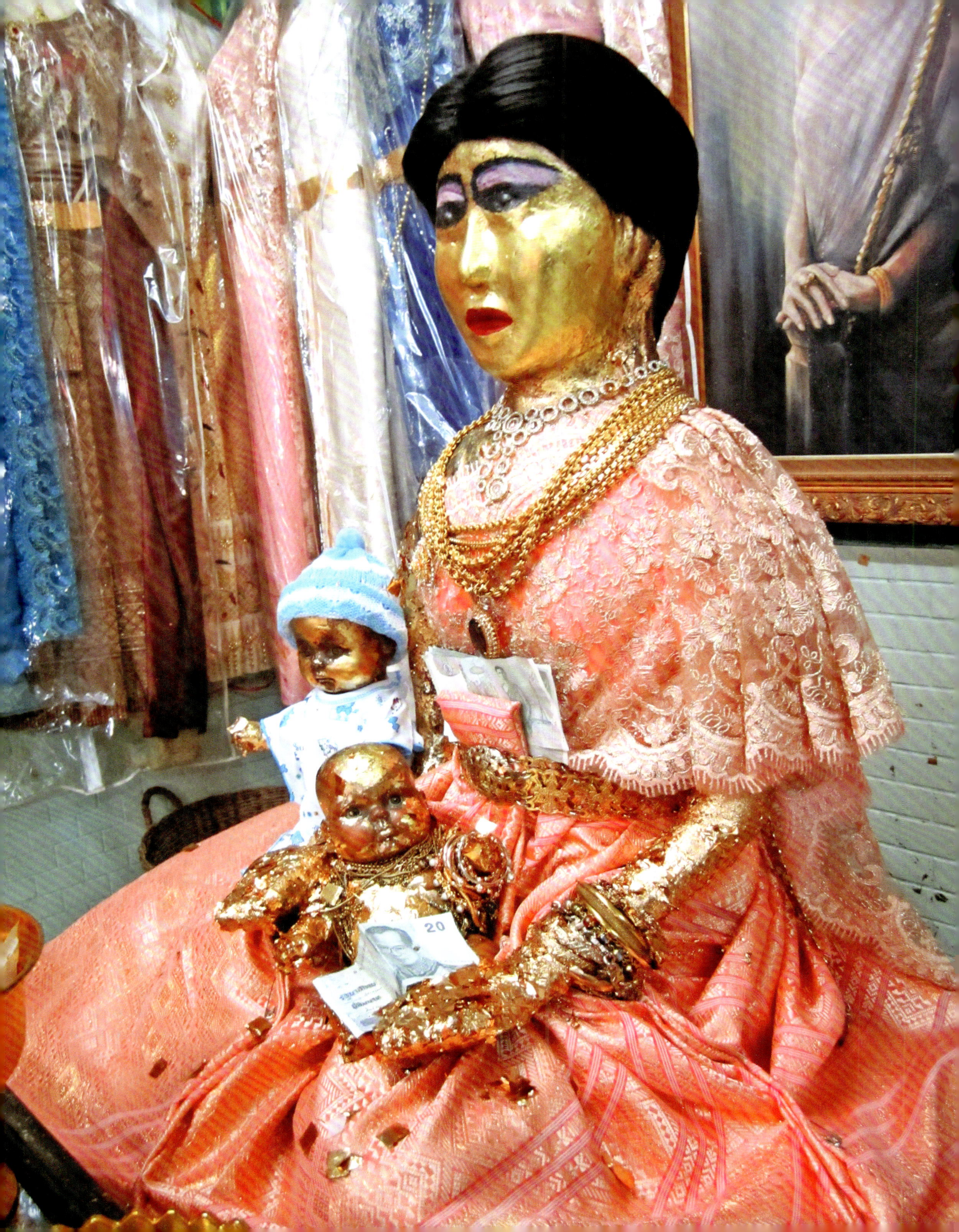
20

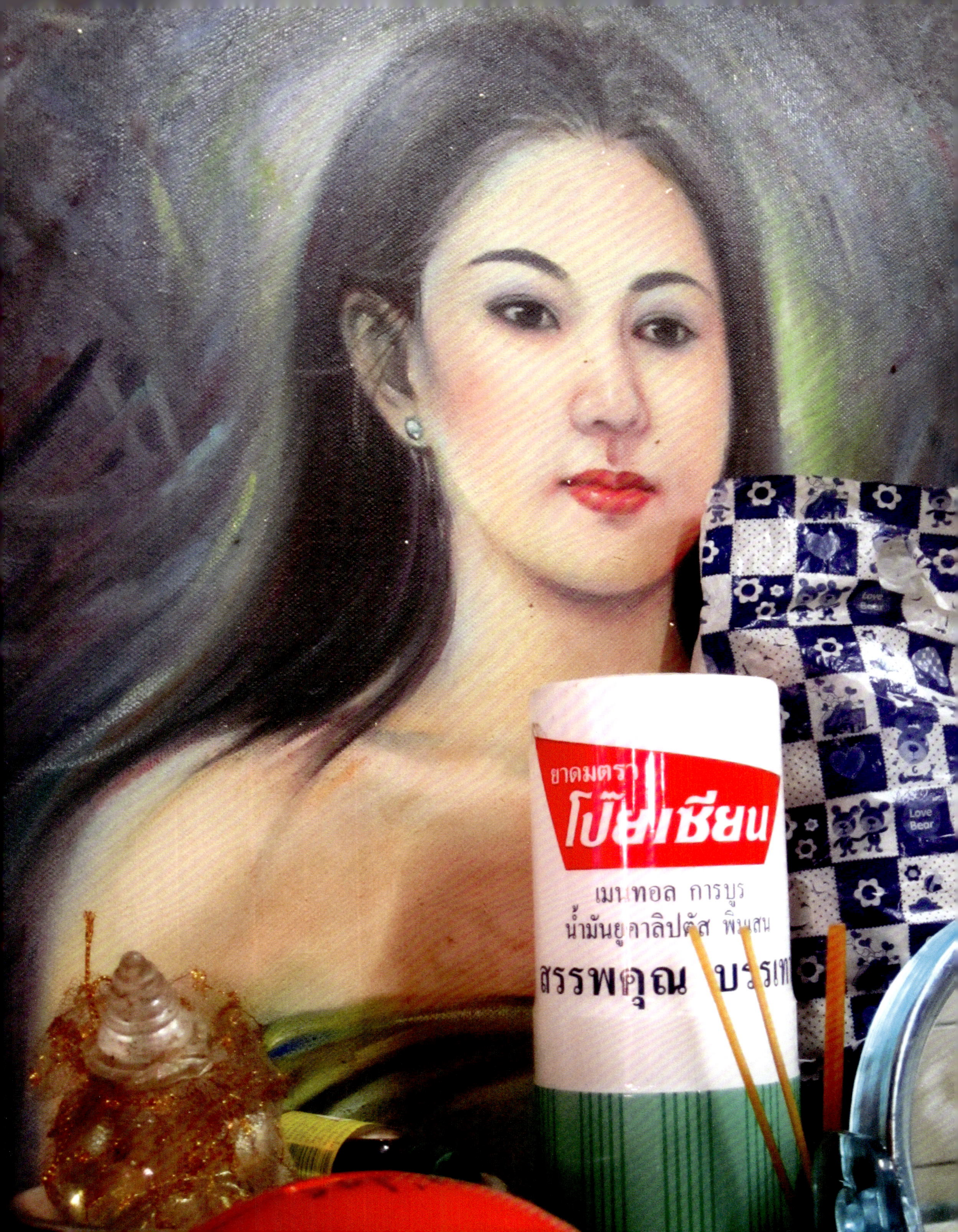
ยาดมตรา
โป๊ยเซียน
เมนทอล การบูร
น้ำมันยูคาลิปตัส พิมเสน
สรรพคุณ
Love Bear

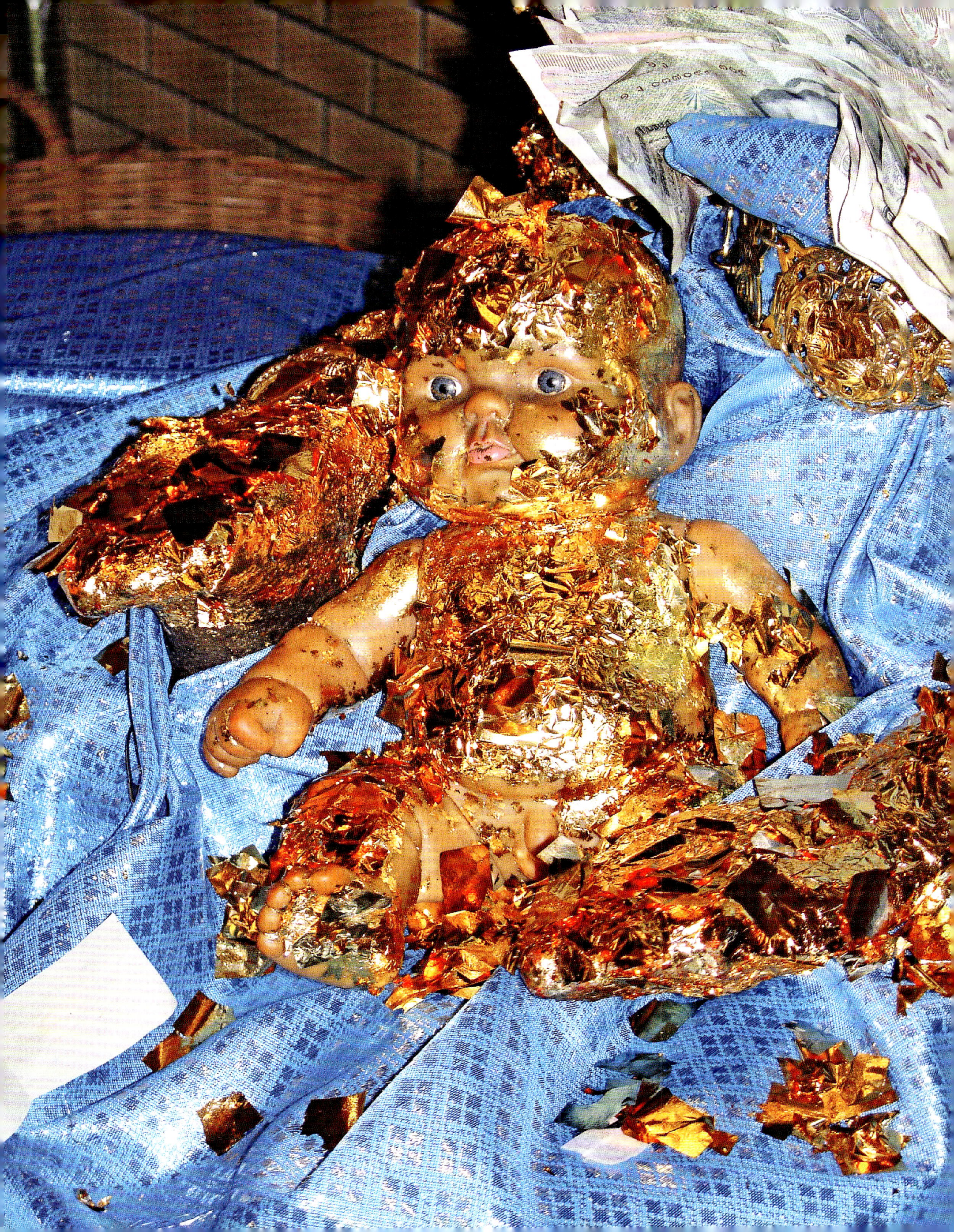

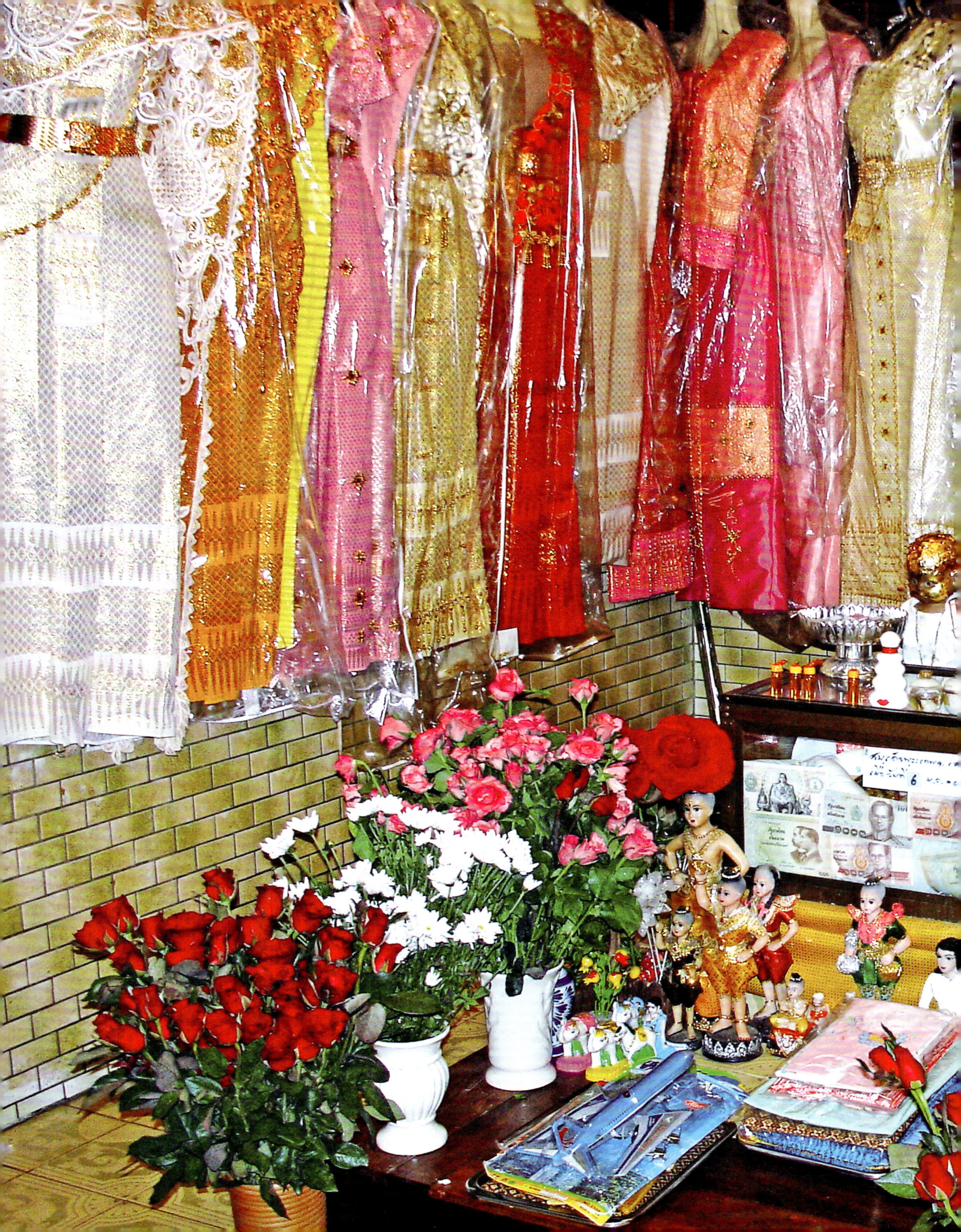

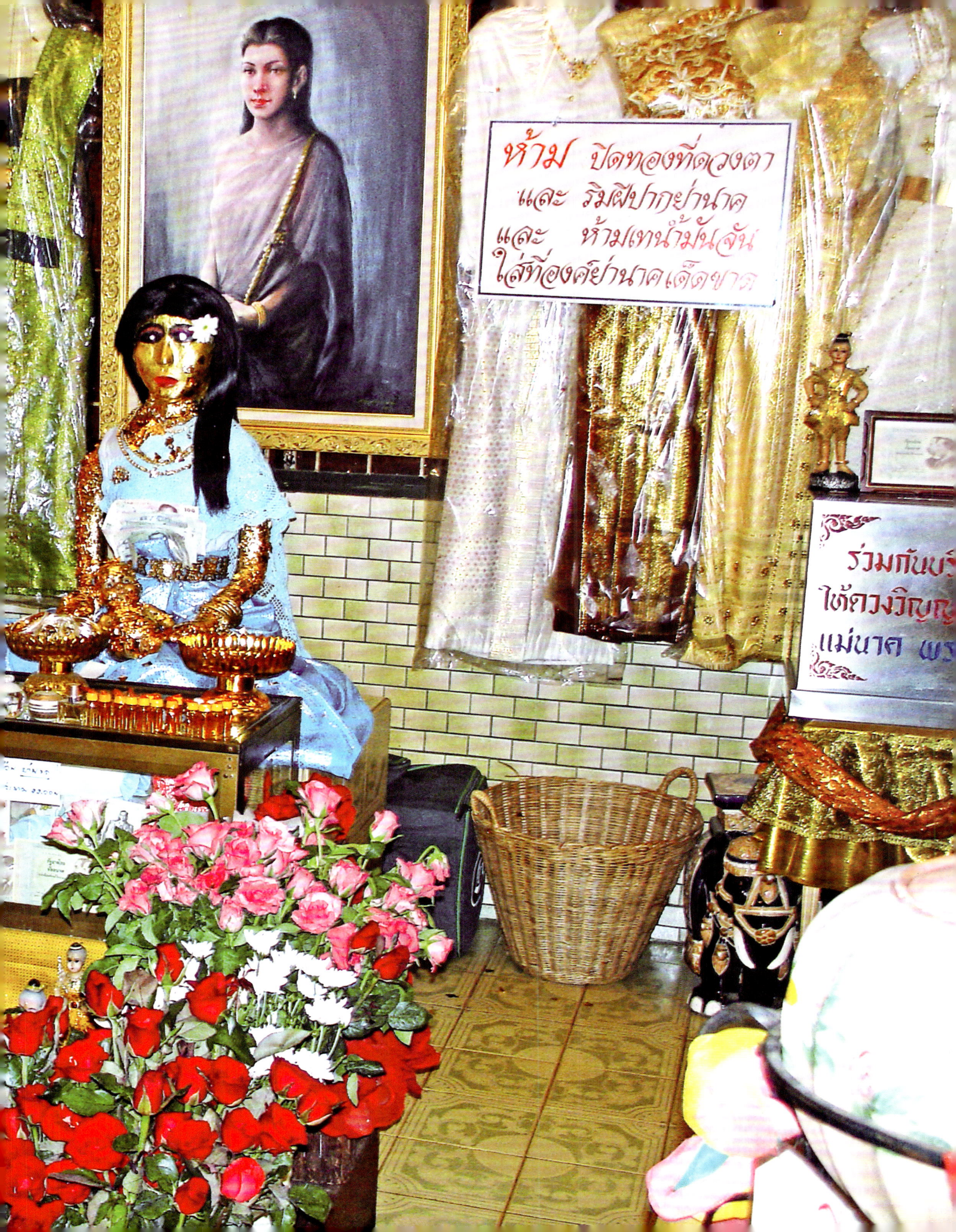
ห้าม ปิดทองที่ดวงตา
และ ริมฝีปากย่านาค
และ ห้ามเทน้ำมันจัน
ใส่ที่องค์ย่านาคเด็ดขาด
ร่วมกัน
แม่นาค

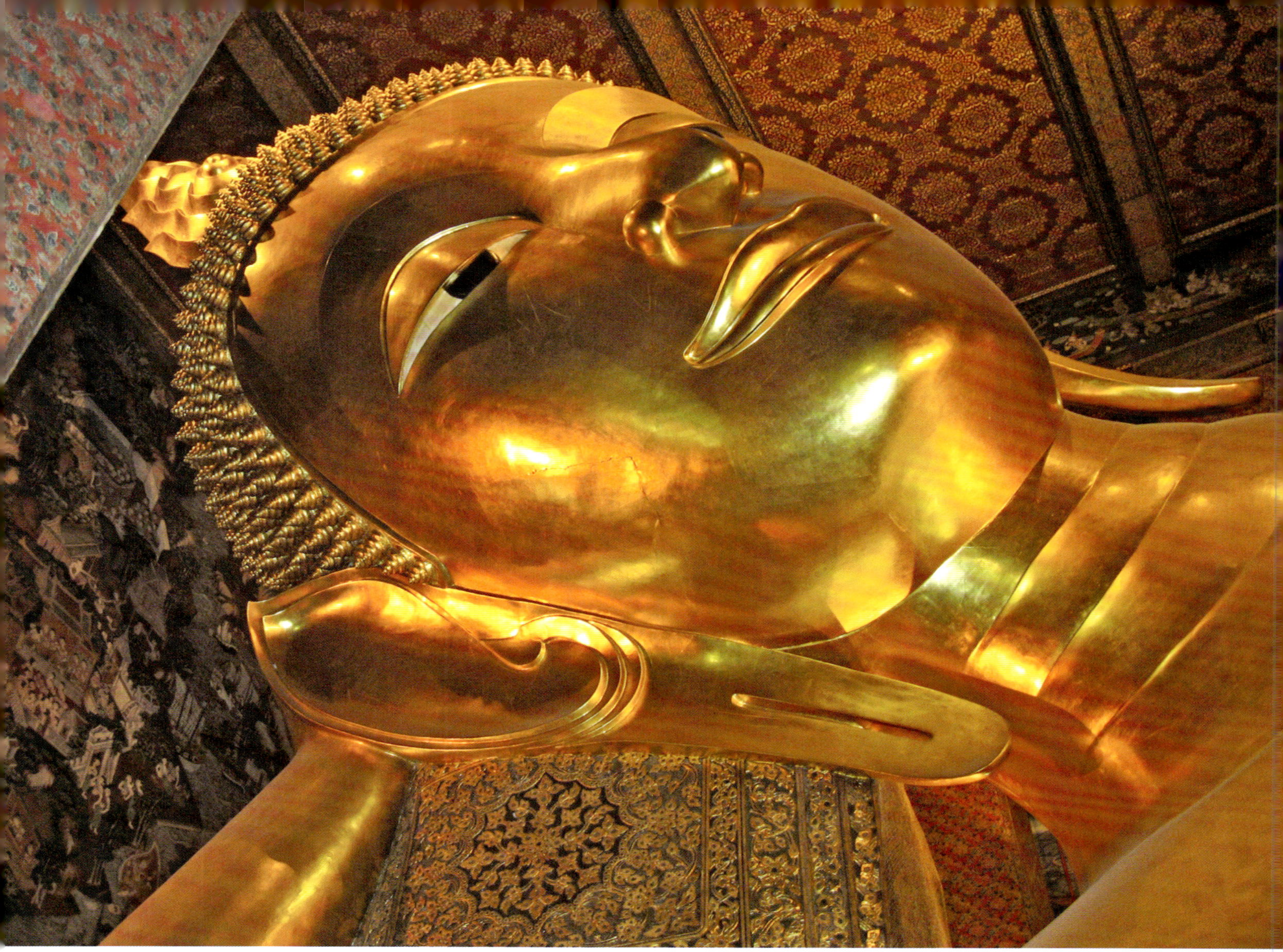

WAT PHO

Wat Pho is the largest monastery complex in Thailand, covering 20 acres of walled land, housing over 1,000 Buddha images. King Rama I ordered restoration on the site of an older temple, Wat Phodharam in 1788; it underwent major renovation under King Rama III, who extended the western assembly hall to house a giant Reclining Buddha, constructed of stucco bricks, molded in plaster, and covered with gold leaf. Measuring 150 feet in length and 49 feet in height, each foot is inlaid with mother-of-pearl detailing the 108 auspicious *laksanas*, characteristics by which one can identify the Buddha. Murals behind the statue illustrate the life stories of the 13 female monks (*bhikkhuni*), and male and female laypersons, as recorded in the ancient Pali texts, the *Tipitaka*. Included is the story of a woman who hired a prostitute to serve her husband, allowing her time to make merit and listen to the Buddha's sermons. Another mural depicts scenes from the *Mahawong*, the transferring of a branch from the *Sri Maha Bod*, the Bodhi tree under which the Buddha gained enlightenment, to Sri Lanka.

A large Buddha image in the posture of concentration sits atop a three-tiered pedestal in the main chapel or *ubosot*, where some of the ashes of King Rama I are interred. Behind the icon is a wall-sized mural depicting the *Mahosadha Jataka*, where the Buddha, in a previous life, was a sage who settles the dispute of two women each claiming to be the mother of a child. Outside the *ubosot*, 152 bas-relief scenes from the *Ramakien* are depicted on marble balustrades. There are 16 pavilions within the monastery, the ceilings decorated with scenes of the *Jakatas*, depicting the 550 previous lives of the Buddha. The scripture hall, *Phra Mondop*, also contains murals from the *Ramakien*, depictions of Songran, the Thai New Year water festival, and Thai proverb verse. Each of the 16 sheltered gates on the grounds features a *Lan Than Nai Tvarapala*, a warrior gate guardian in armor, weapon at the ready. These protectors were sculpted from ballast used in trade ships returning from journeys to China. Enormous rock figures of Chinese monks, nobleman, workers, and ladies of the court grace doorways and yards. A shrub garden is populated with stone lions, monkeys, tricksters, and Chinese figures in European and ceremonial dress.

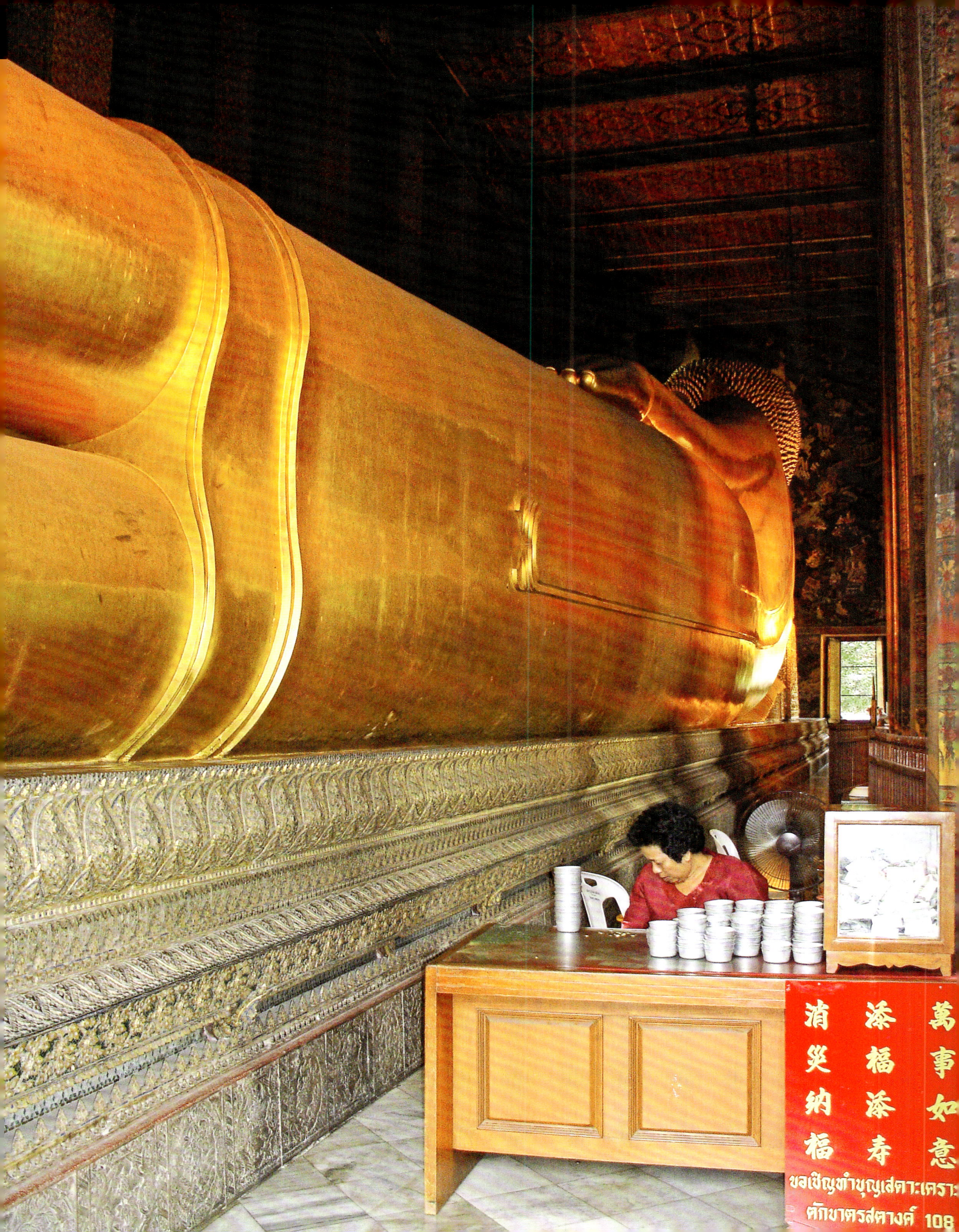
萬事如意
添福添寿
消災納福
ขอเชิญทำบุญเสดาะเคราะ
ตักบาตรสตางค์ 108

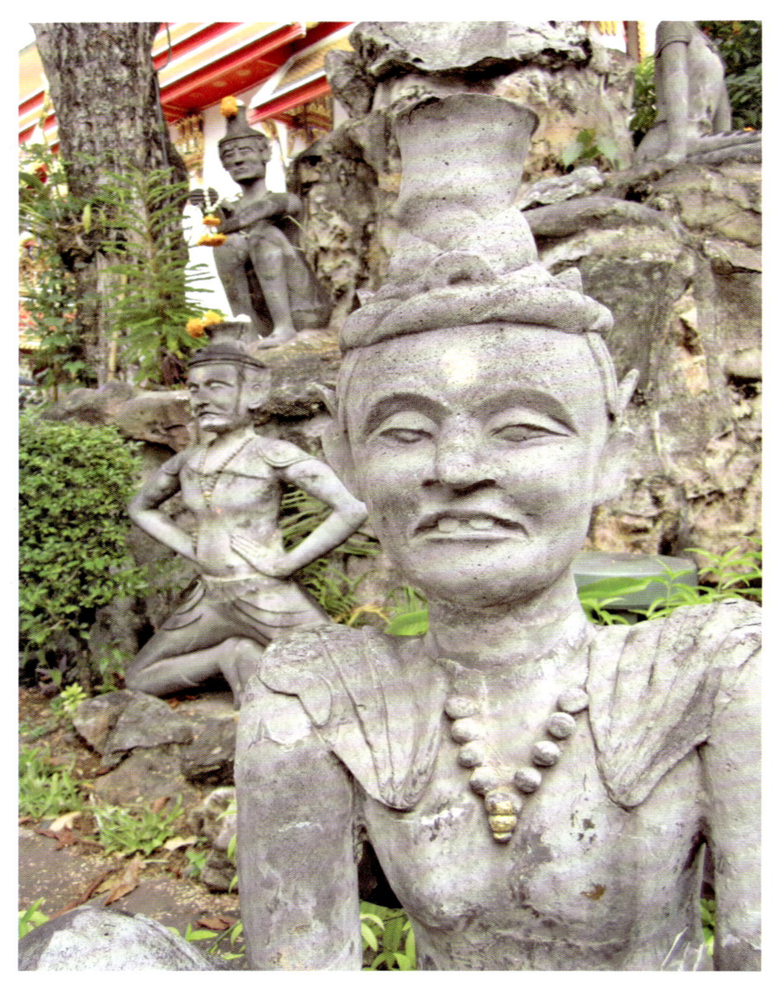

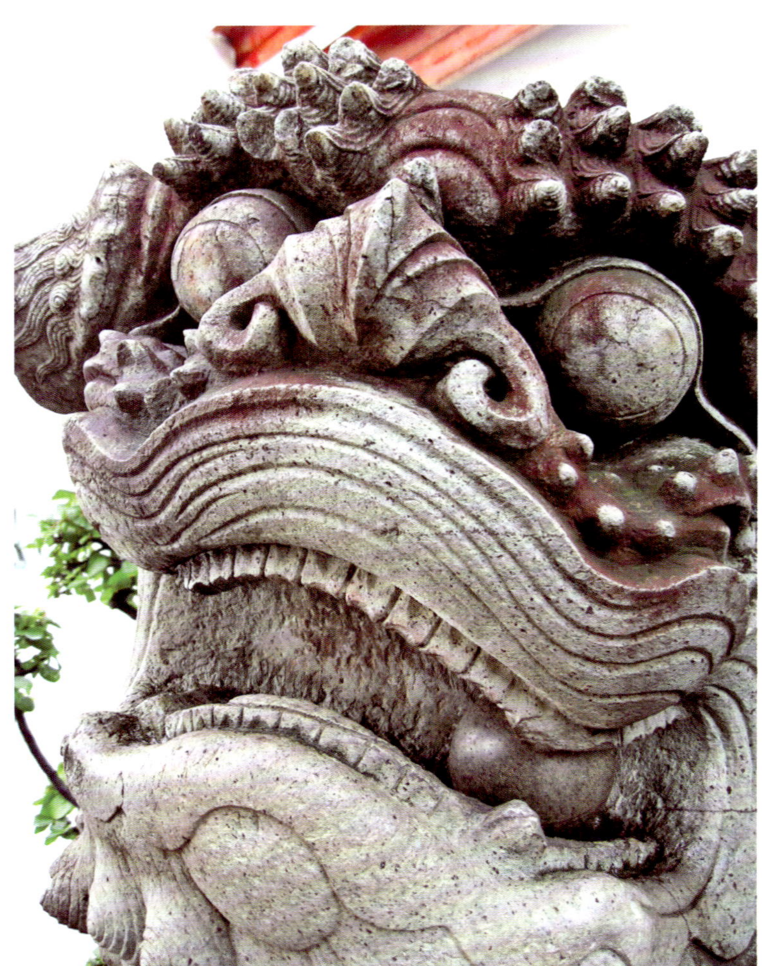

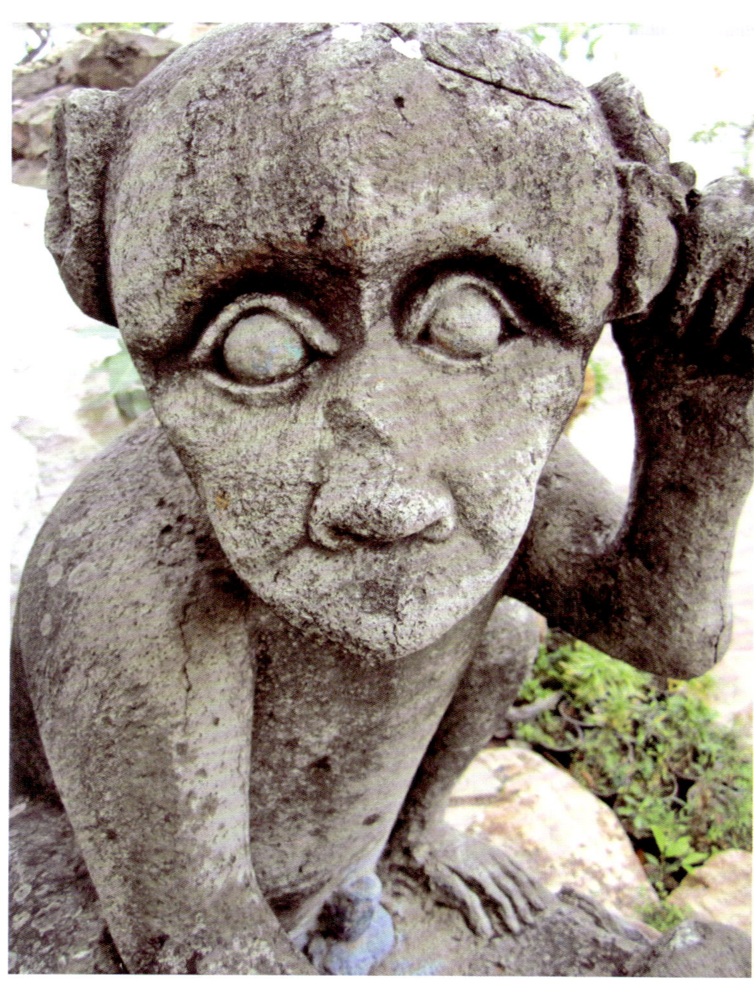

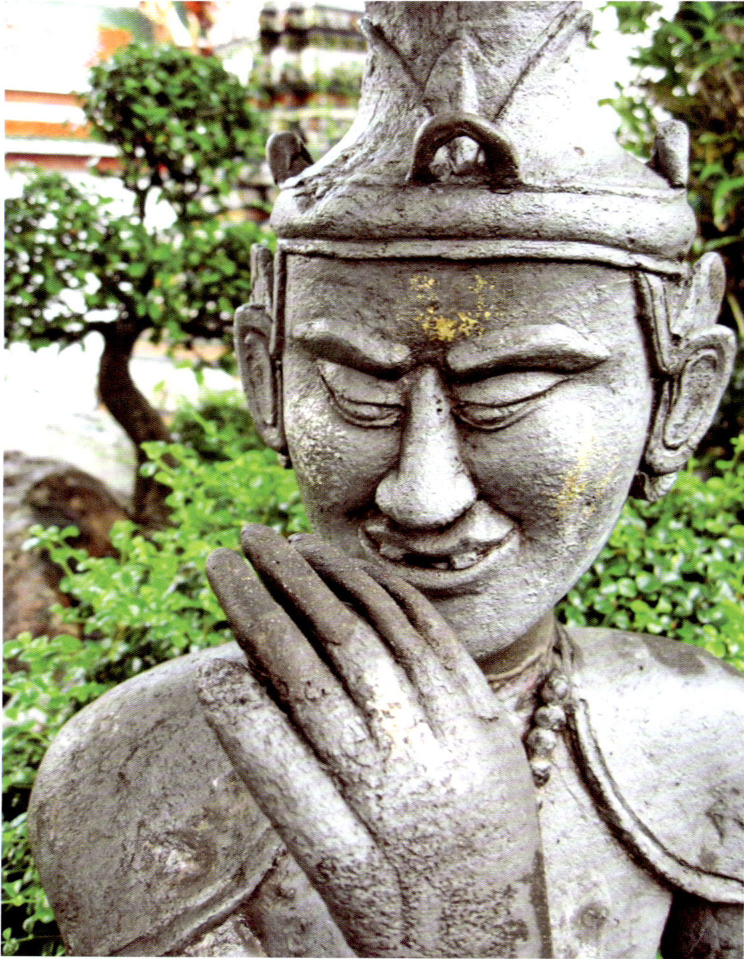

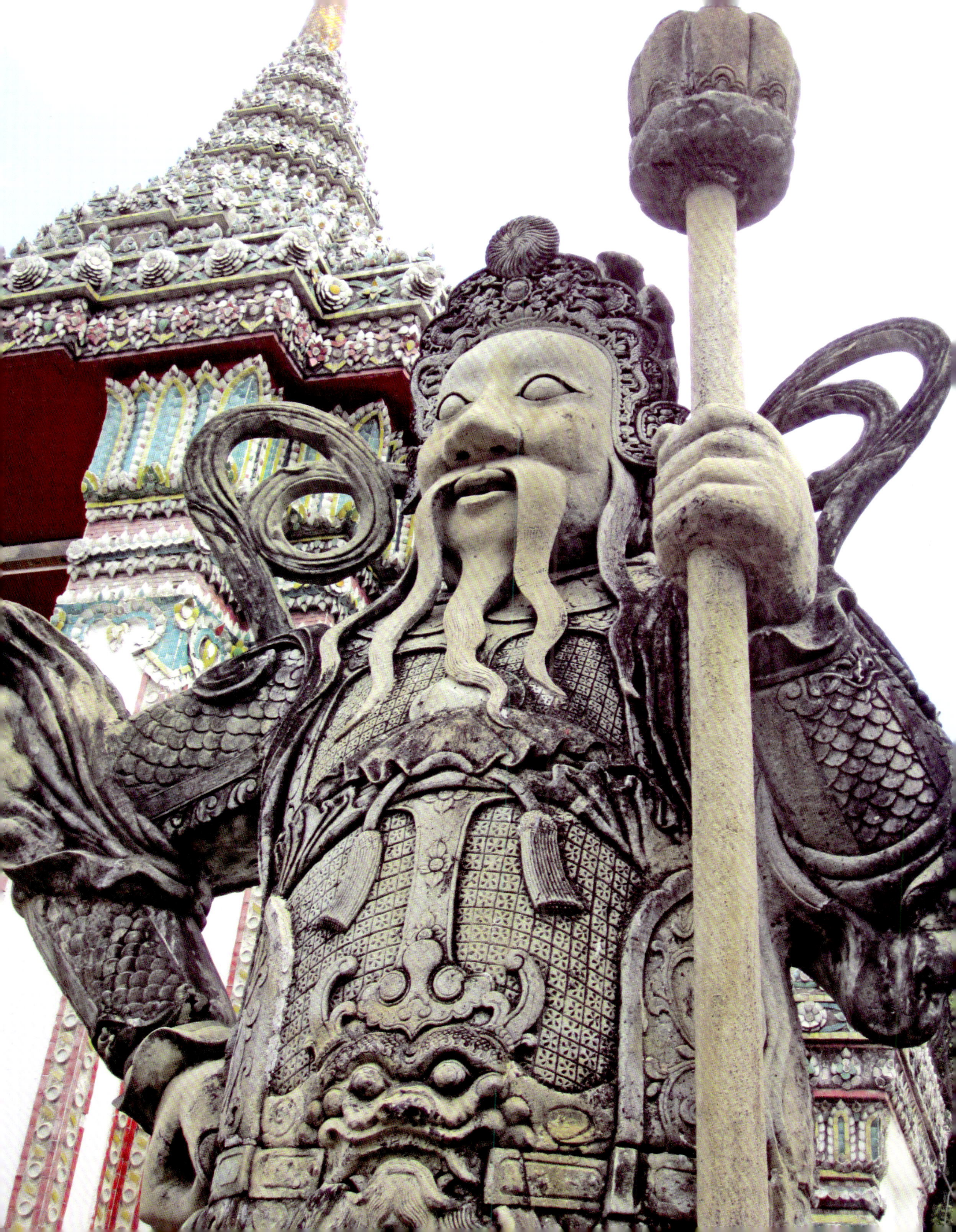

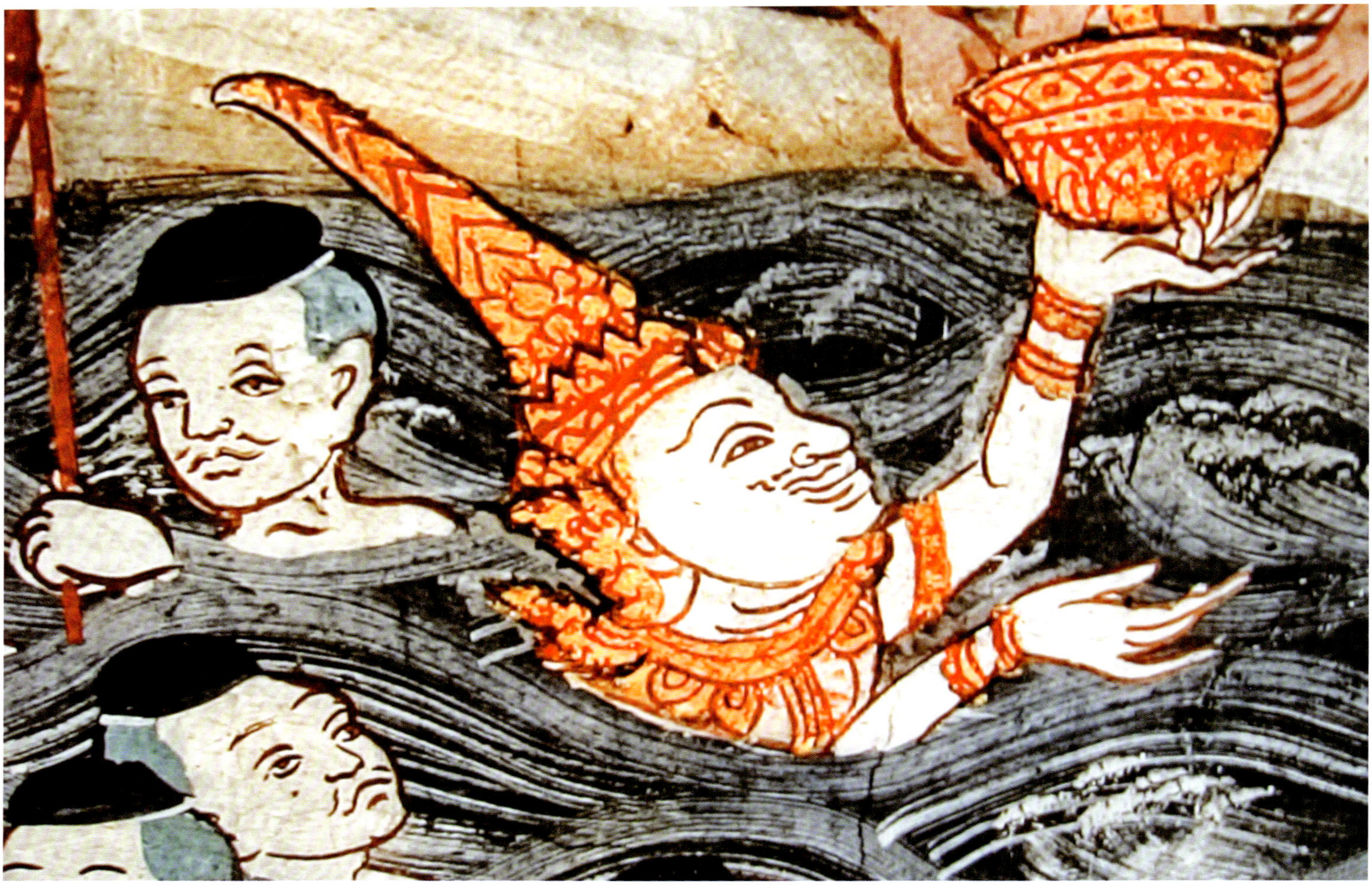

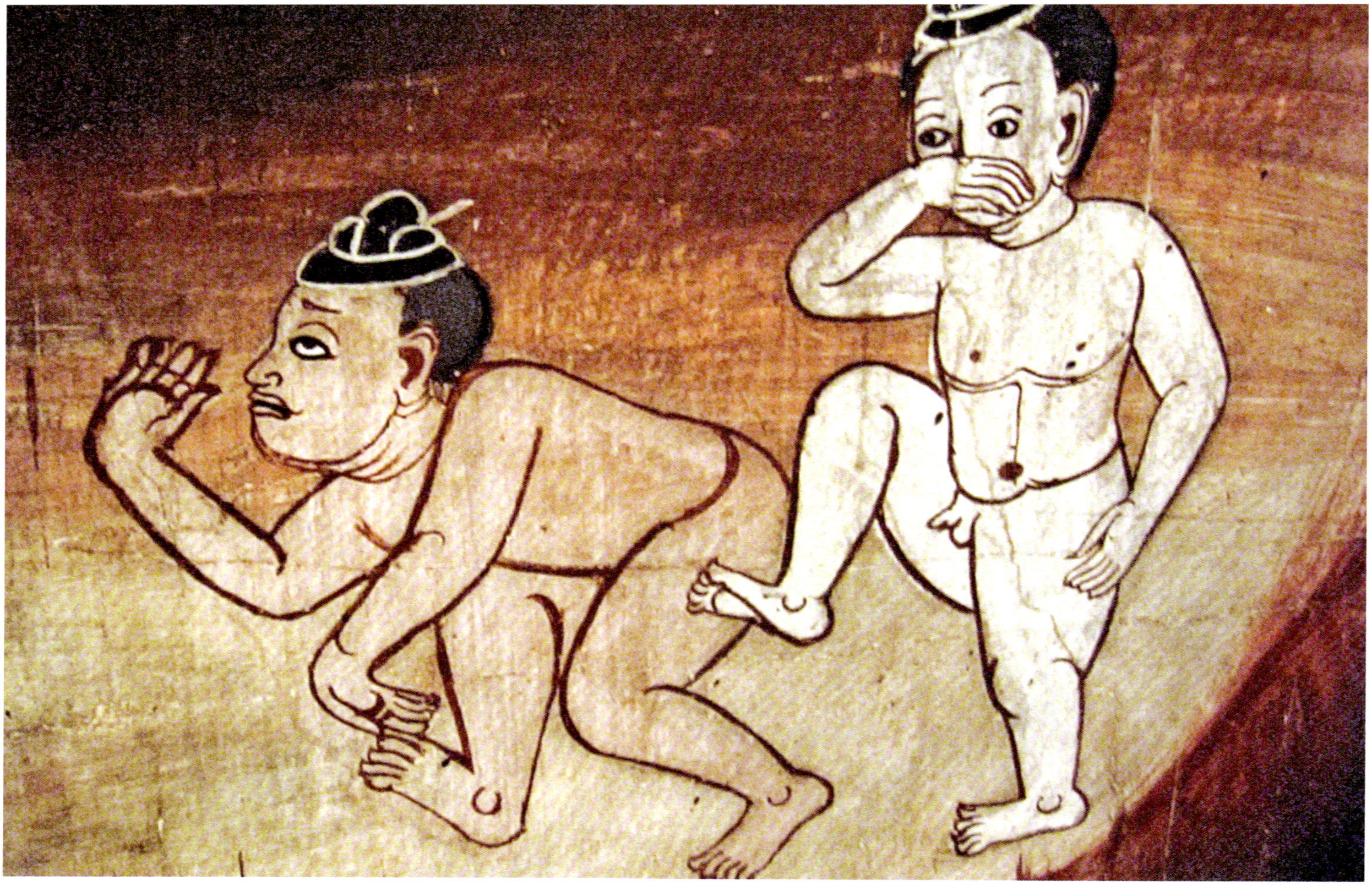

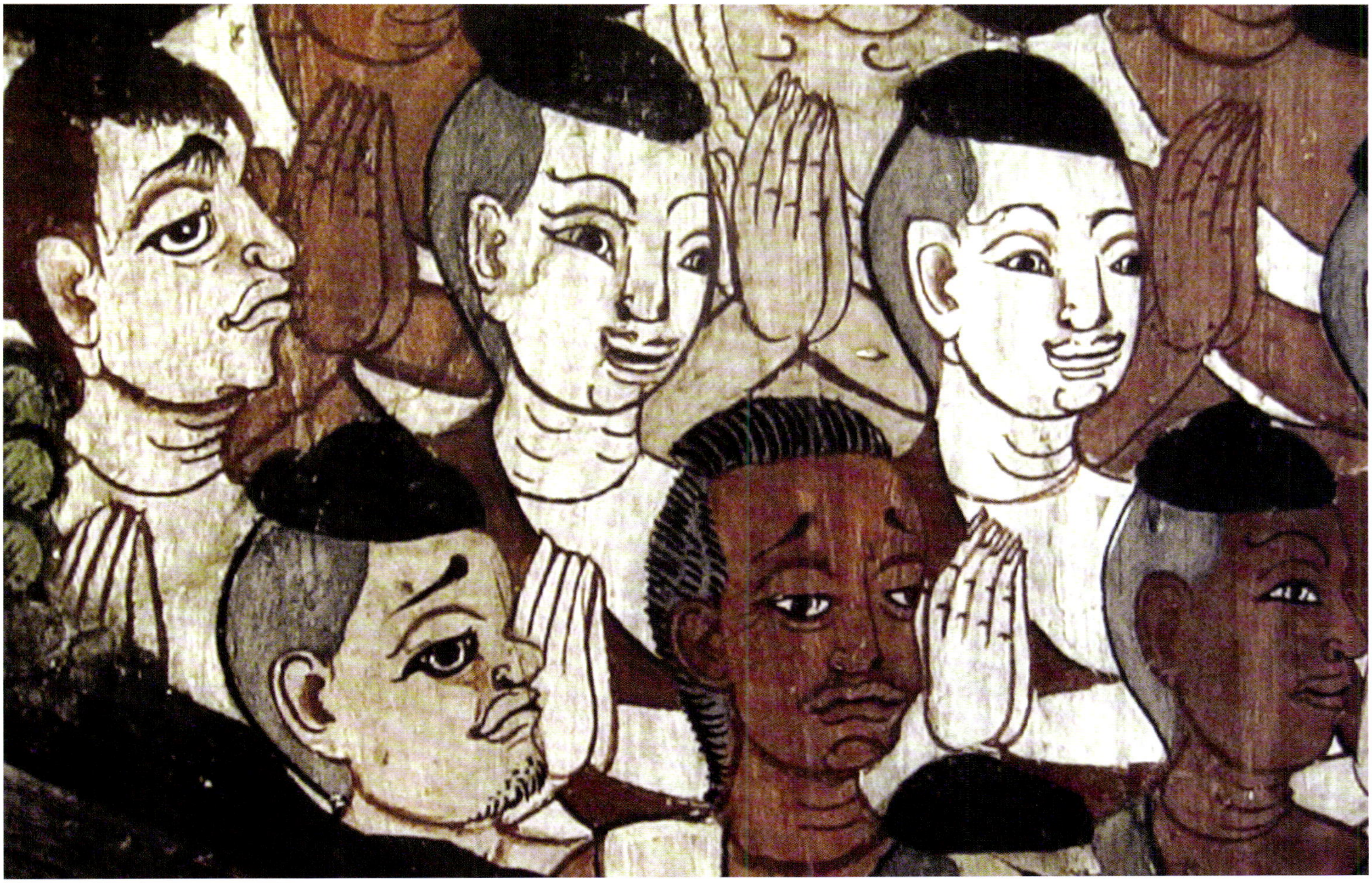

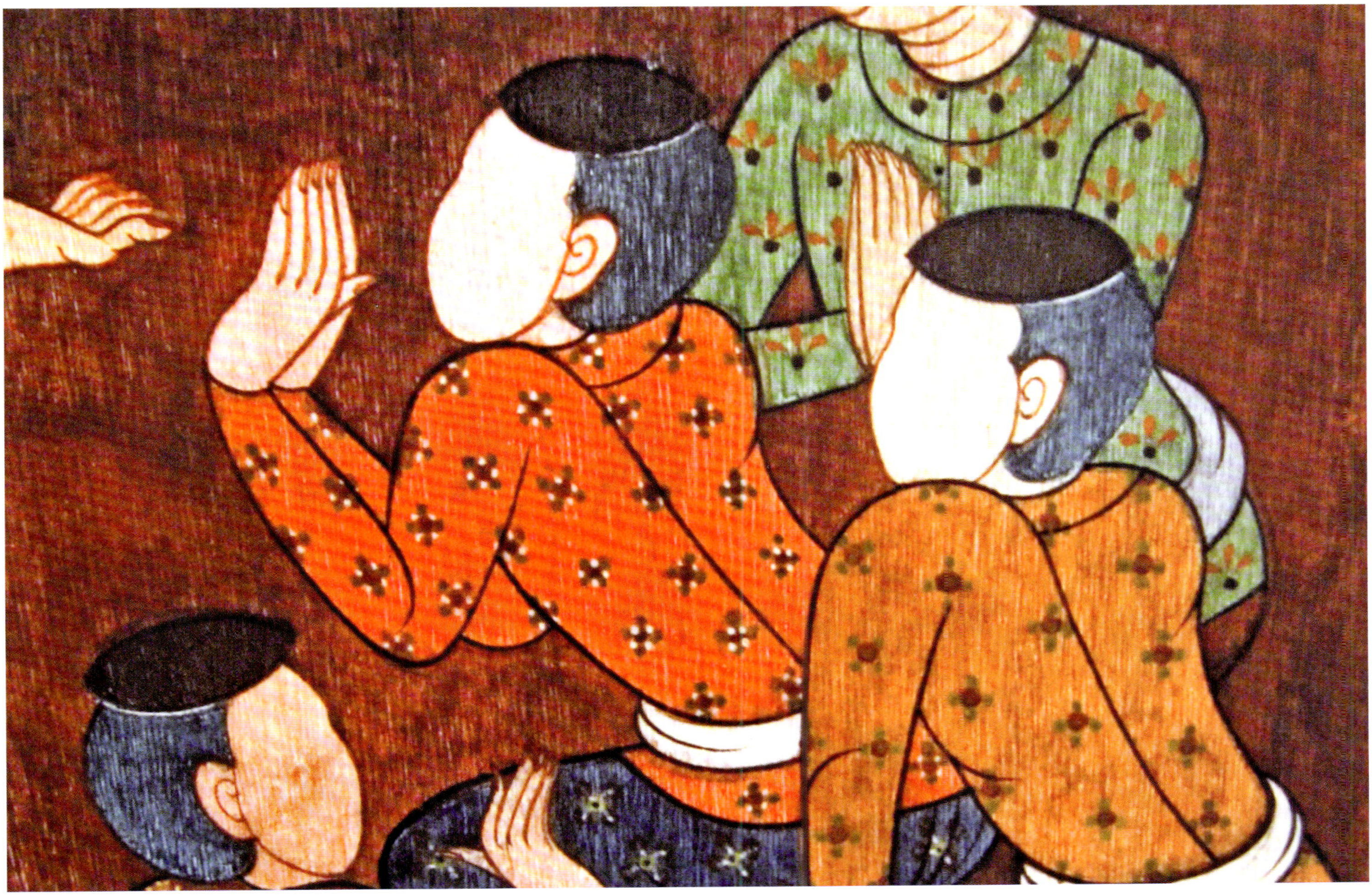

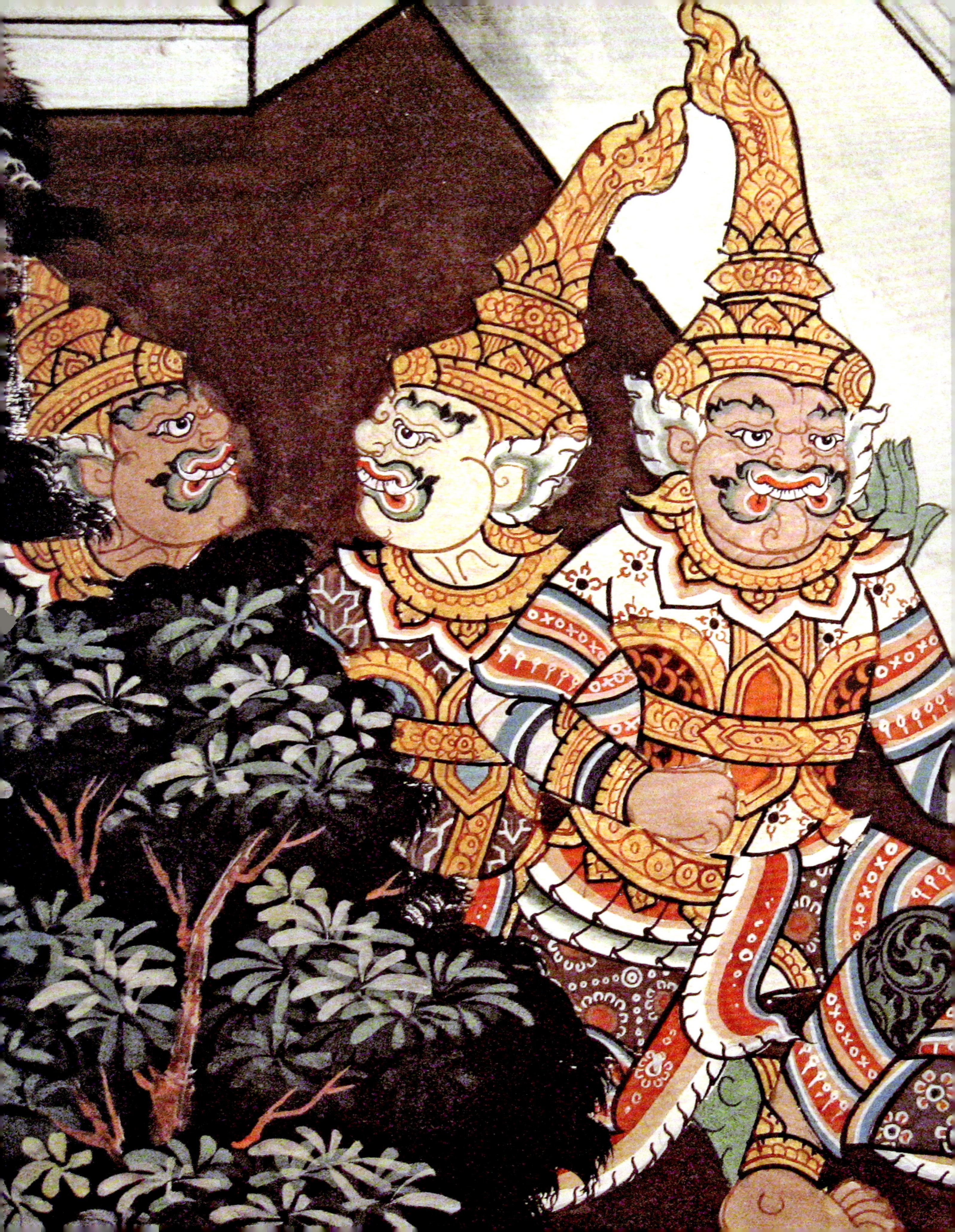

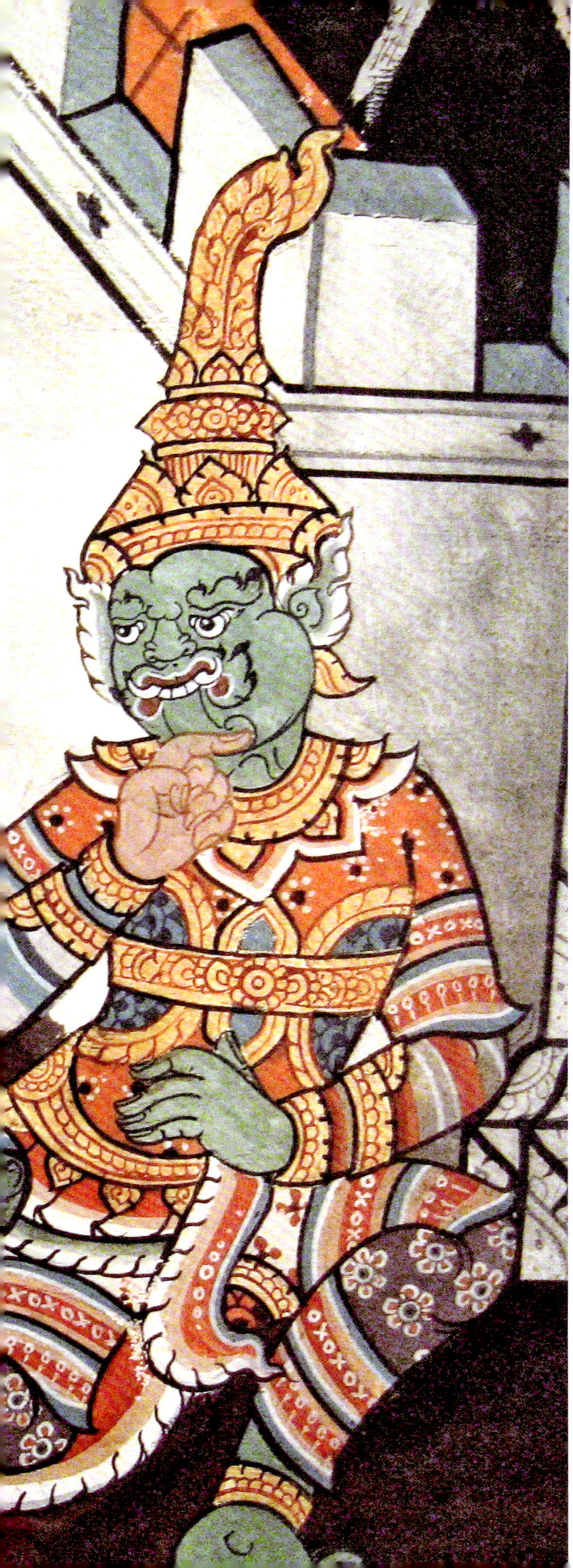

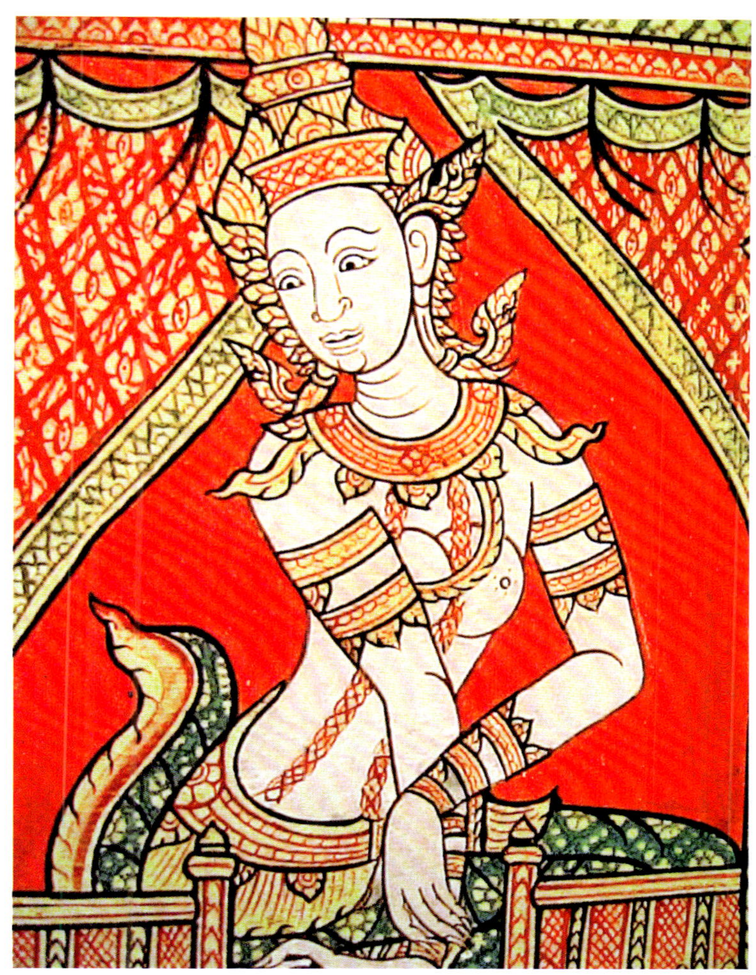

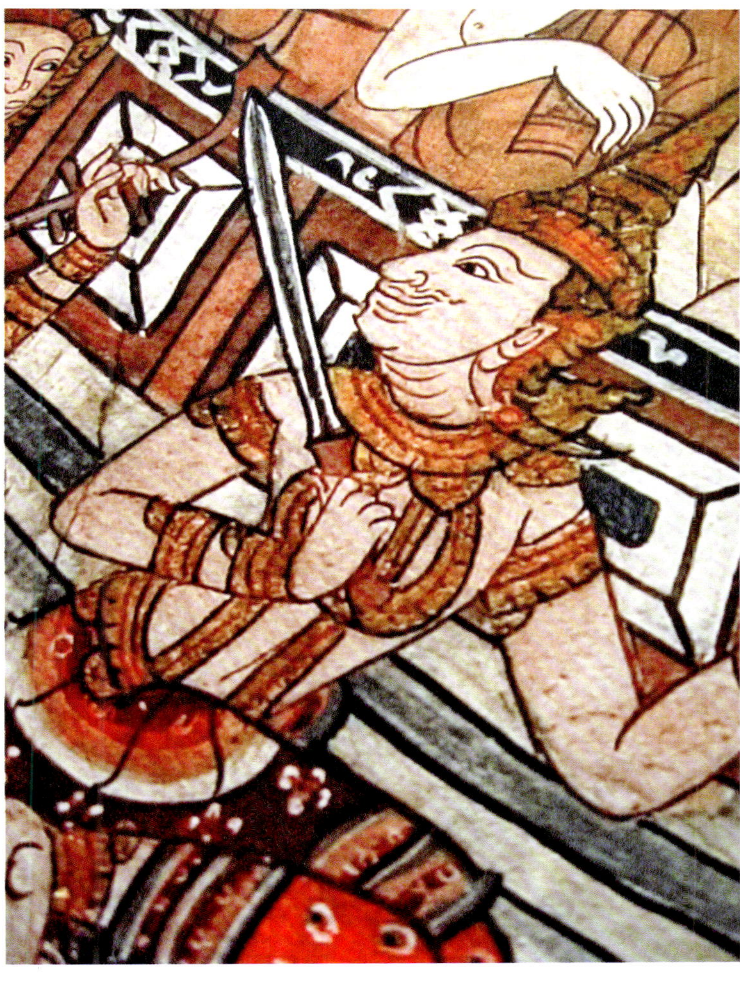

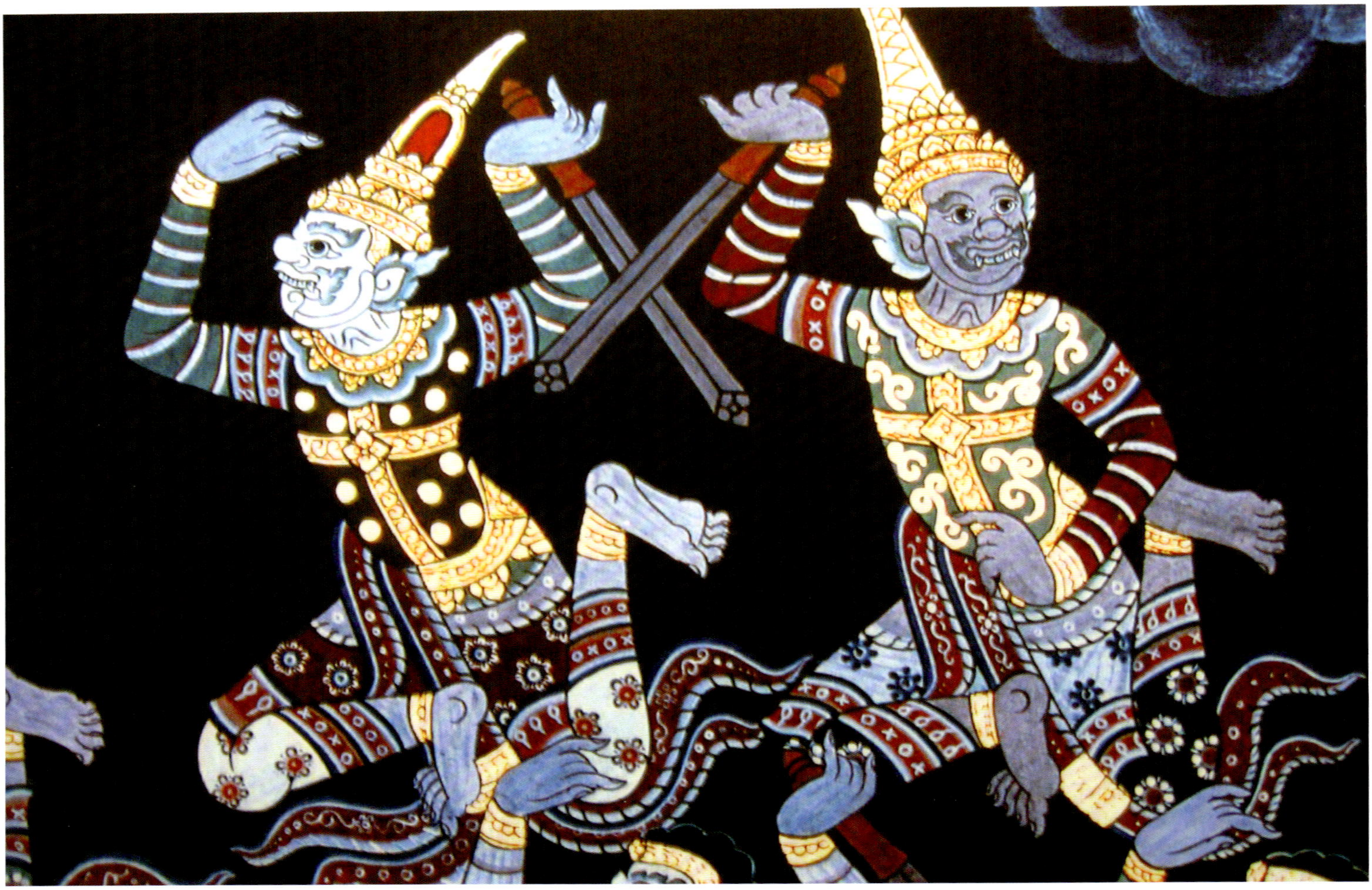

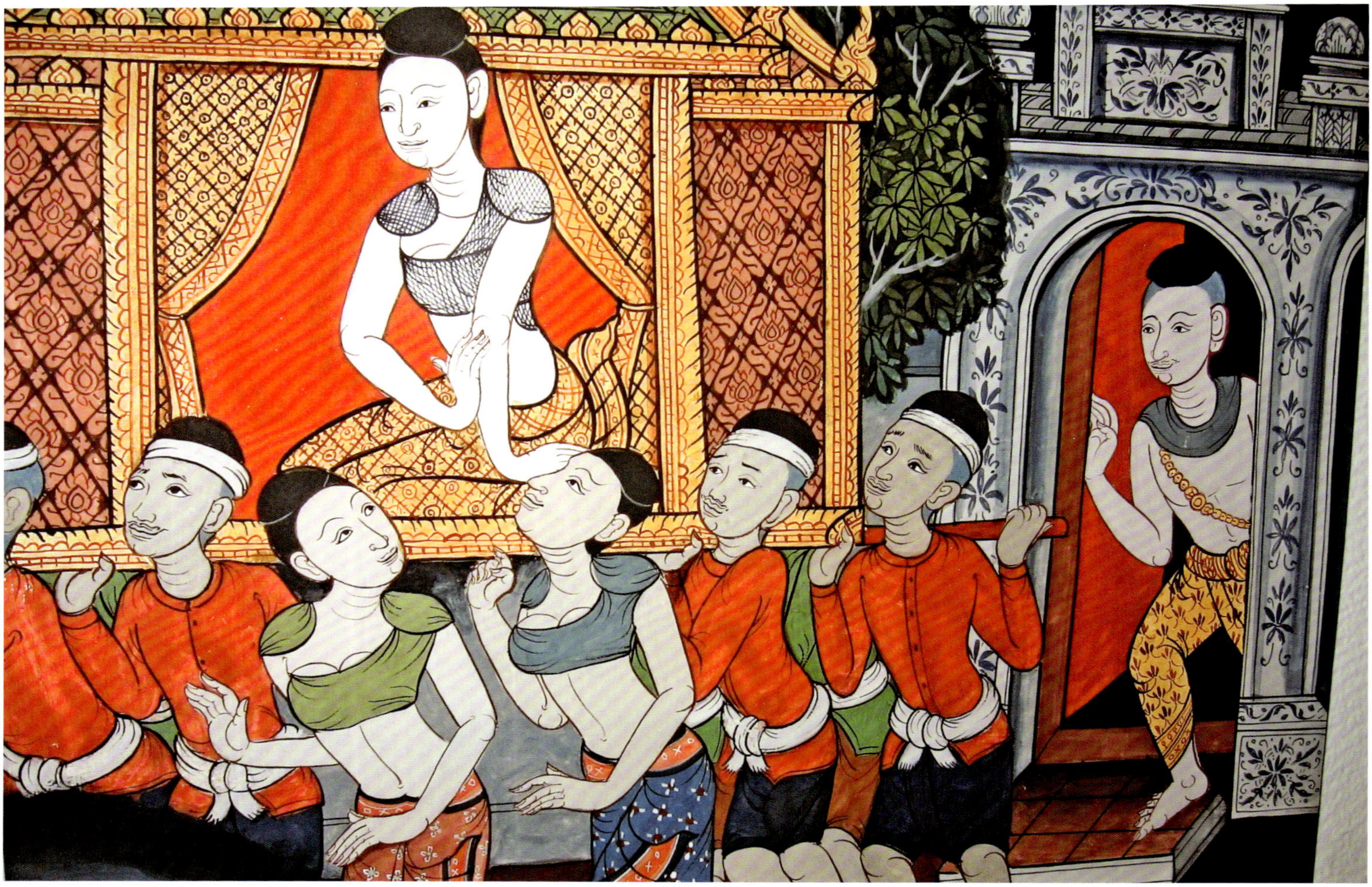

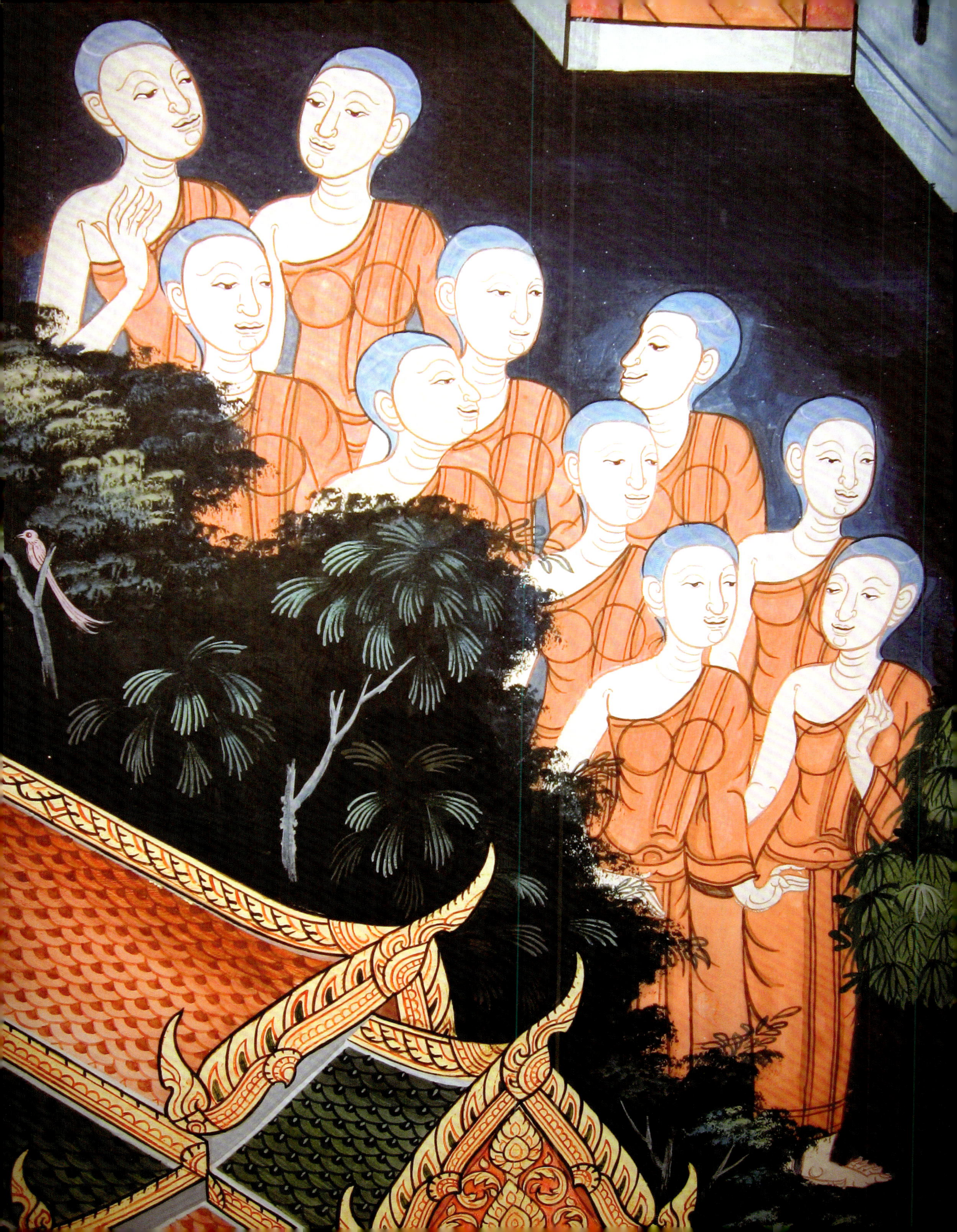

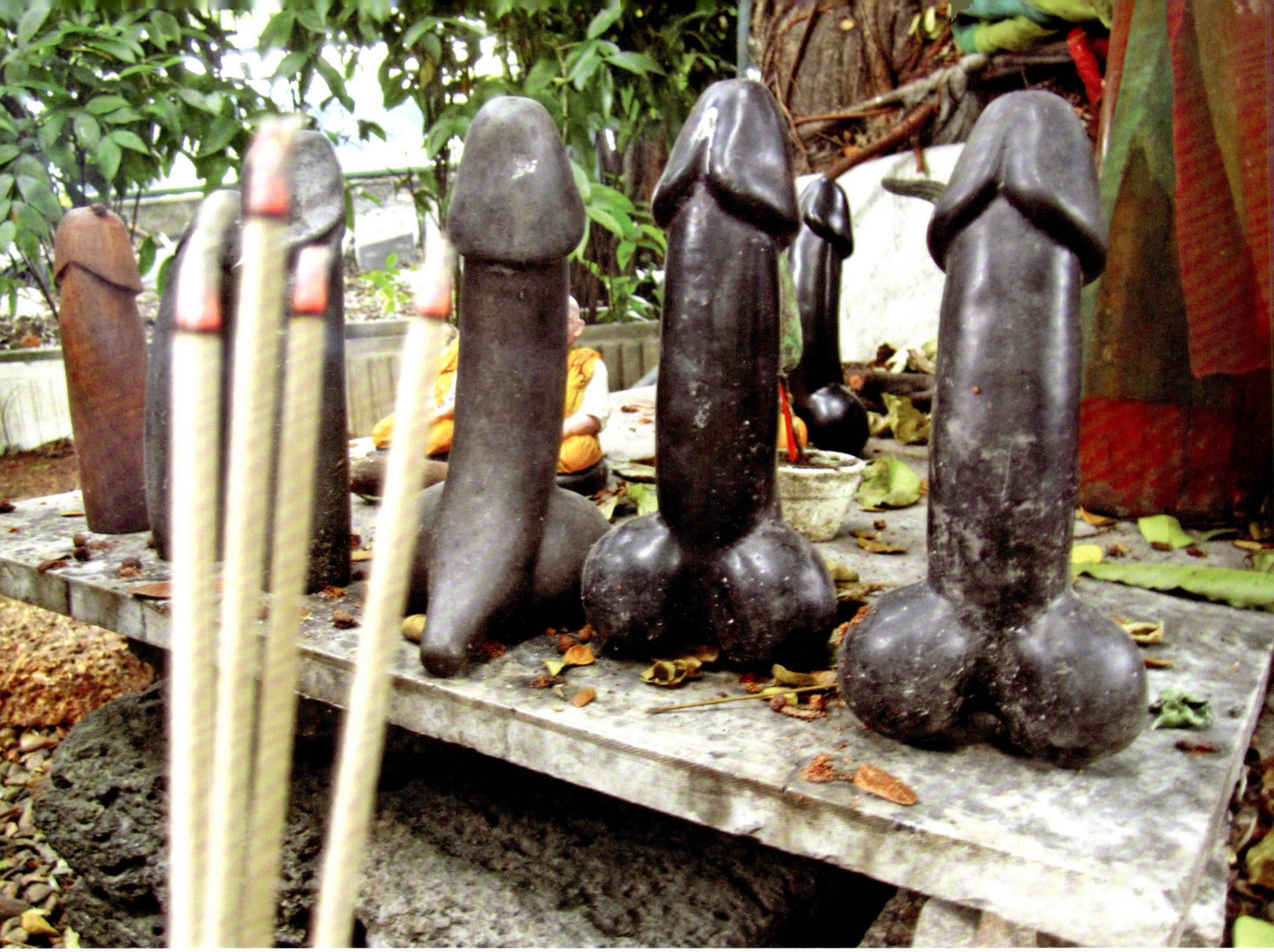

CHAO MAE TUPTIM SHRINE

Past the British Embassy, behind the Nai Lert Hotel, in a corner of a park, is a shrine to Chao Mae Tuptim, a water deity from southern China. Legend states the only thing a fisherman caught every night was the same piece of wood. He came to view it as sacred, so he kept it and paid homage to it. His catches became bountiful, and in thanks he carved the wood into a special totem. This belief spread among the Teachew and Hiananese fisherman, and as they migrated to Thailand, shrines were built by waterways in Chao Mae Tuptim's honor (Warren, 2005 pp. 46 & 49). The original shrine was erected along a busy *klong* or canal, used for transportation and shipping, next to a large overhanging *Sai* or *Ficus* tree. Such trees are believed to be inhabited by female spirits, and are often ribboned with colorful fabrics. When businessman Nai Lert purchased this land in the 1920s, it was uninhabited, far different from today's bustling Chit Lom area. He built a new shrine to Chao Mae Tuptim, and erected a large wooden spirit house with a ladder that stands on a stone platform. Today there is an elephant-protected prayer altar in front, a table of *Khon* dancer attendants behind, and the *Ficus* tree to the left of the small shrine area. Incense is burnt, wreaths of jasmine flowers are offered, requests are made and pledges promised.

One story says a woman prayed for a son, made an offering, and had a baby boy nine months later. She returned and left in thanks a *lingam*, a phallic representation of the Hindu god Shiva. Word spread, others prayed for the same, and brought phalluses as gifts. In Krabi, there is a cave temple dedicated to princess Phra Nang, where phalluses are also left as tokens, offering no apparent connection between a fisherman's protection spirit and a fertility goddess. In Thailand, phallic *palad khik* are amulets of protection and good luck, also used in ceremonies requesting rain for the new rice crop. Young boys wear them while swimming to avoid capture and blood sucking by Phrai Nam, the water ghost (Cornwell-Smith, 2005, p. 156). Regardless of the reason, this shrine is filled with hundreds of wooden, concrete, clay, and metal penises, wrapped in colorful sashes, some with wings, legs, or penises of their own.

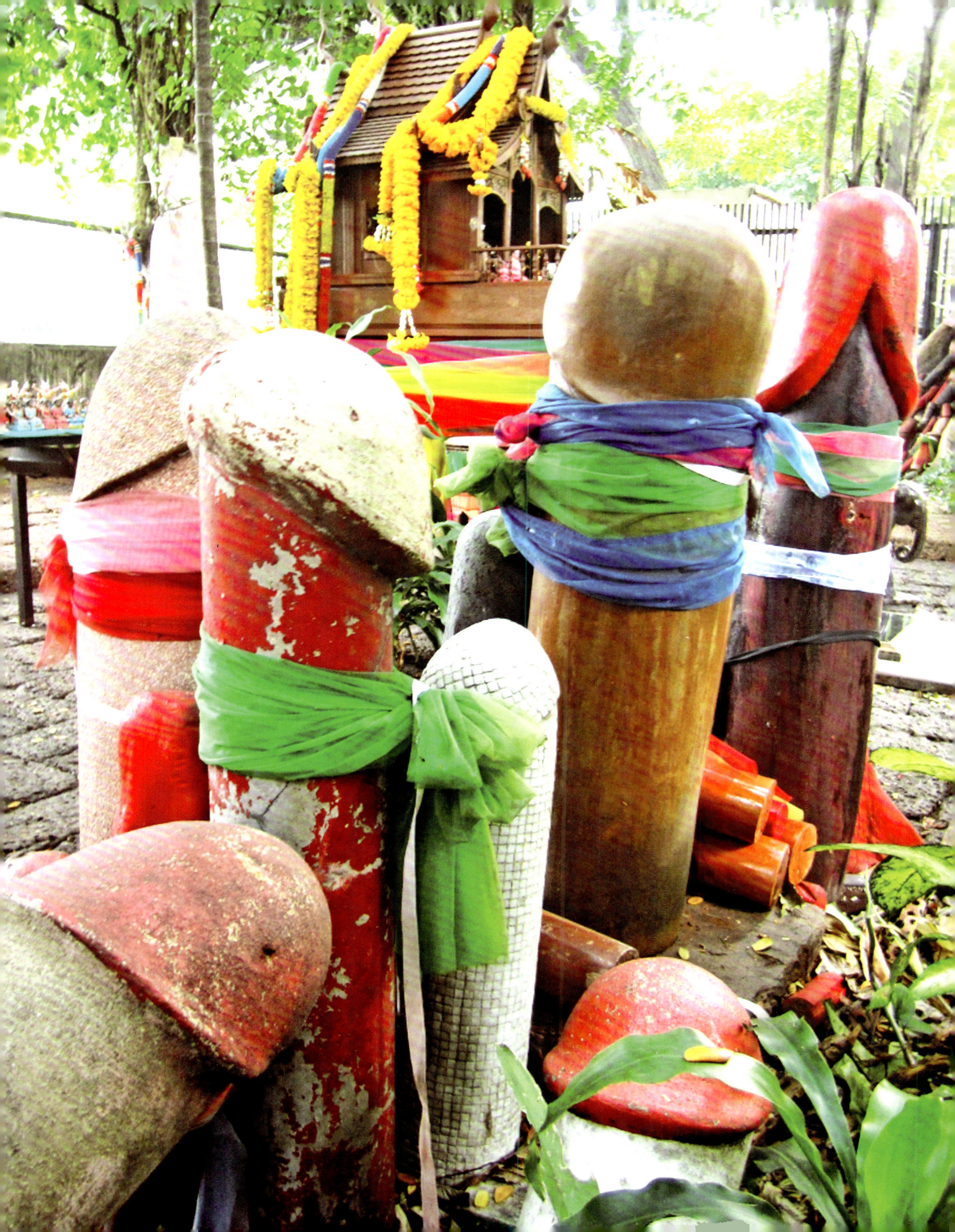

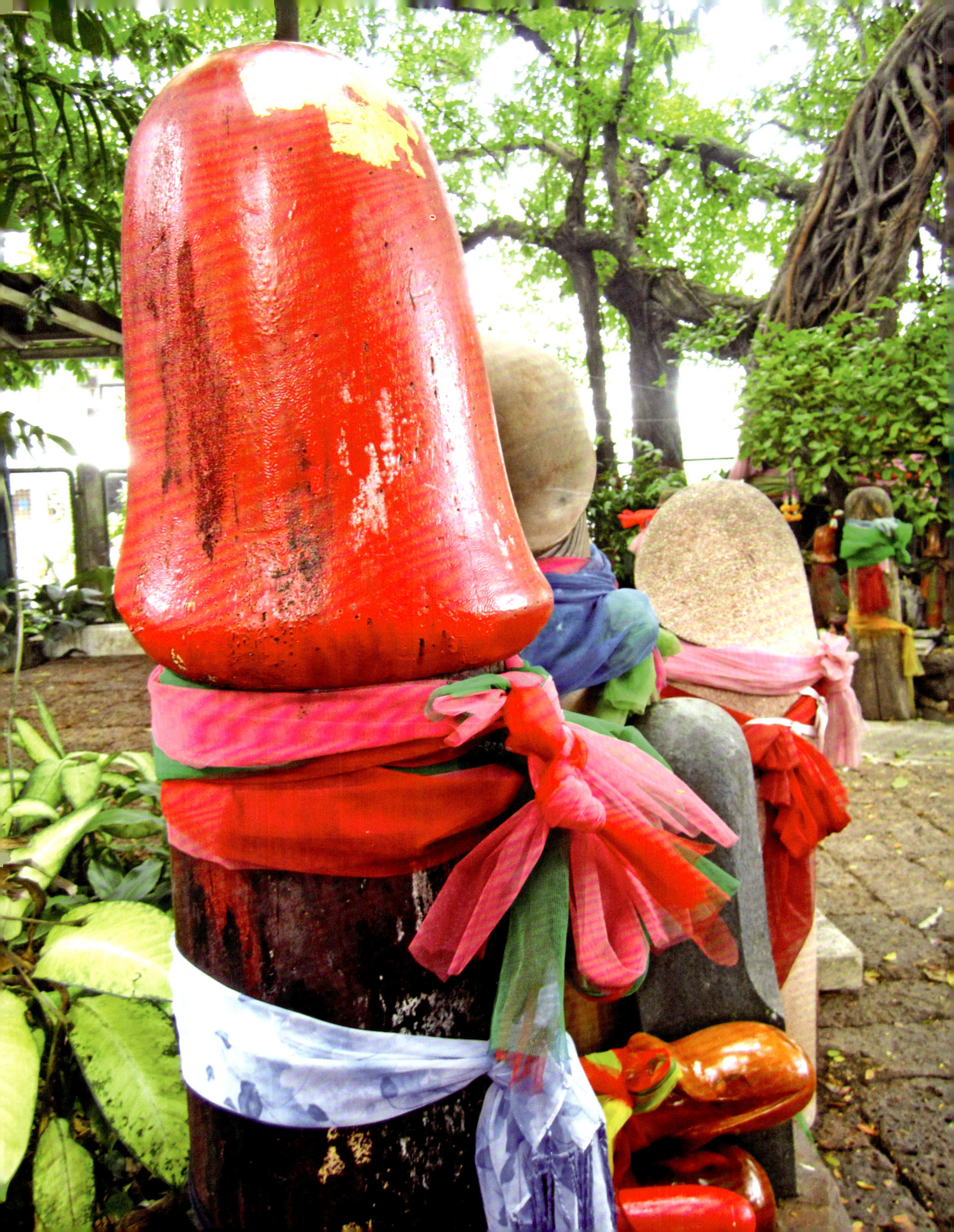

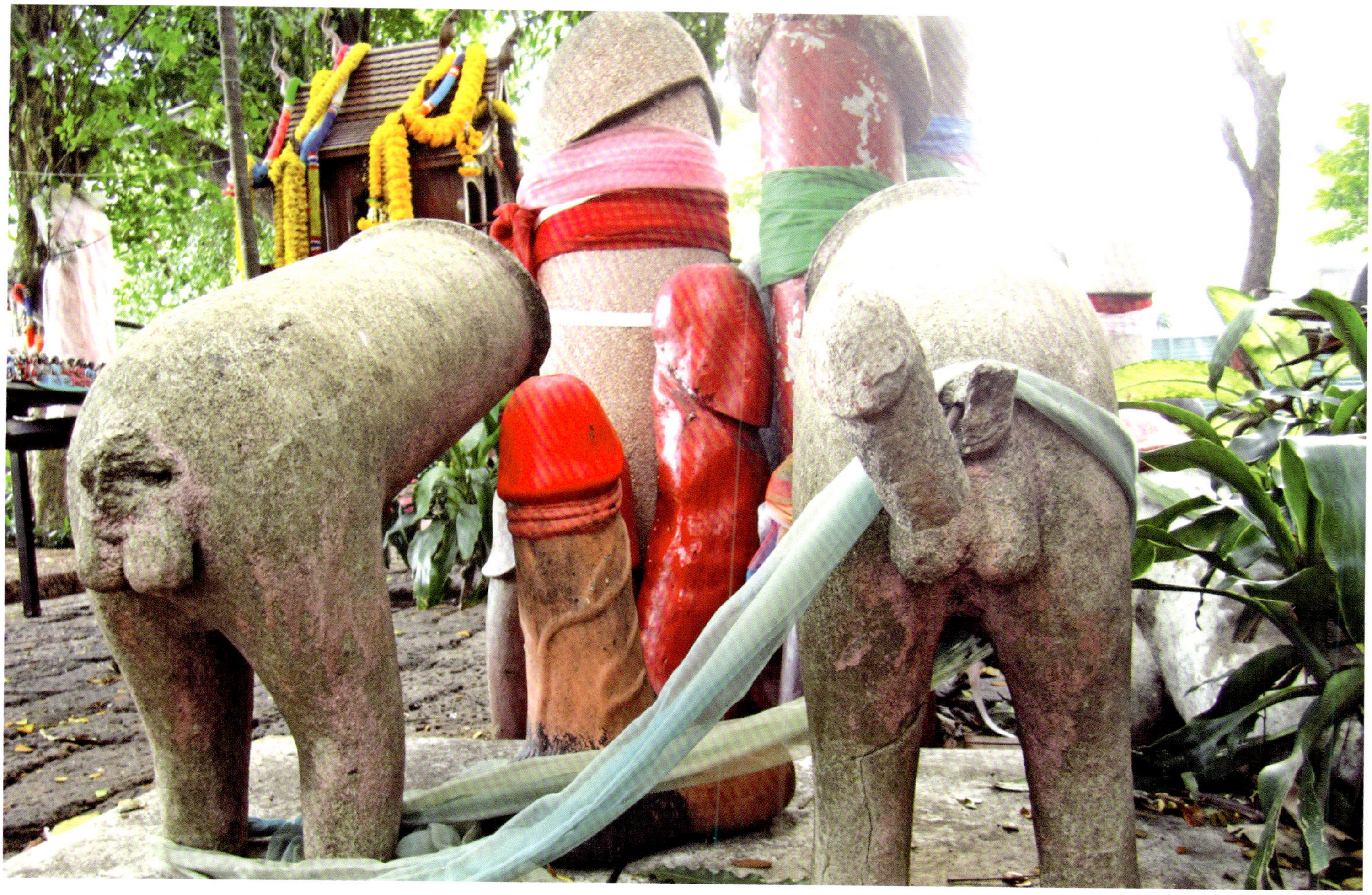

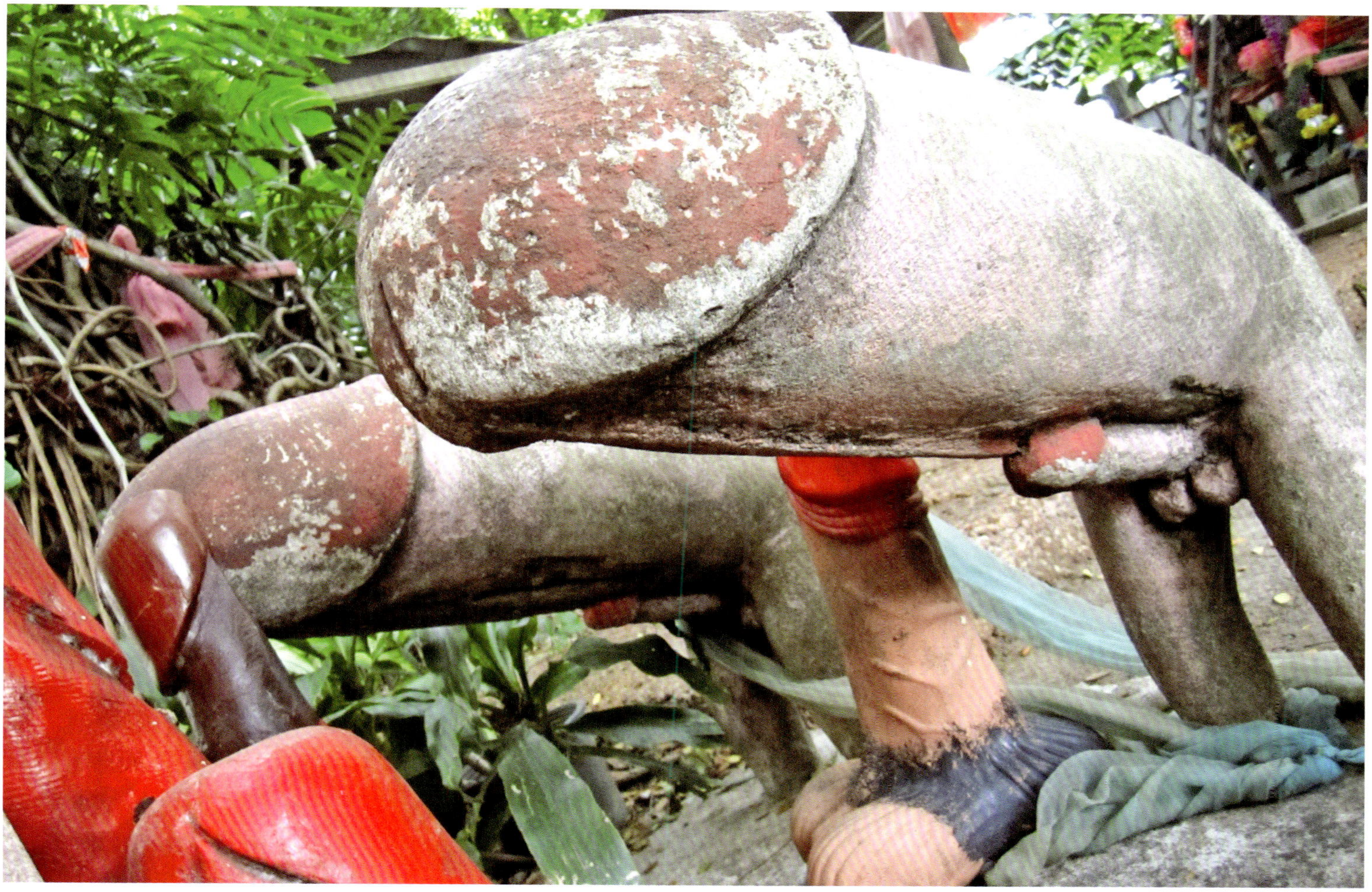

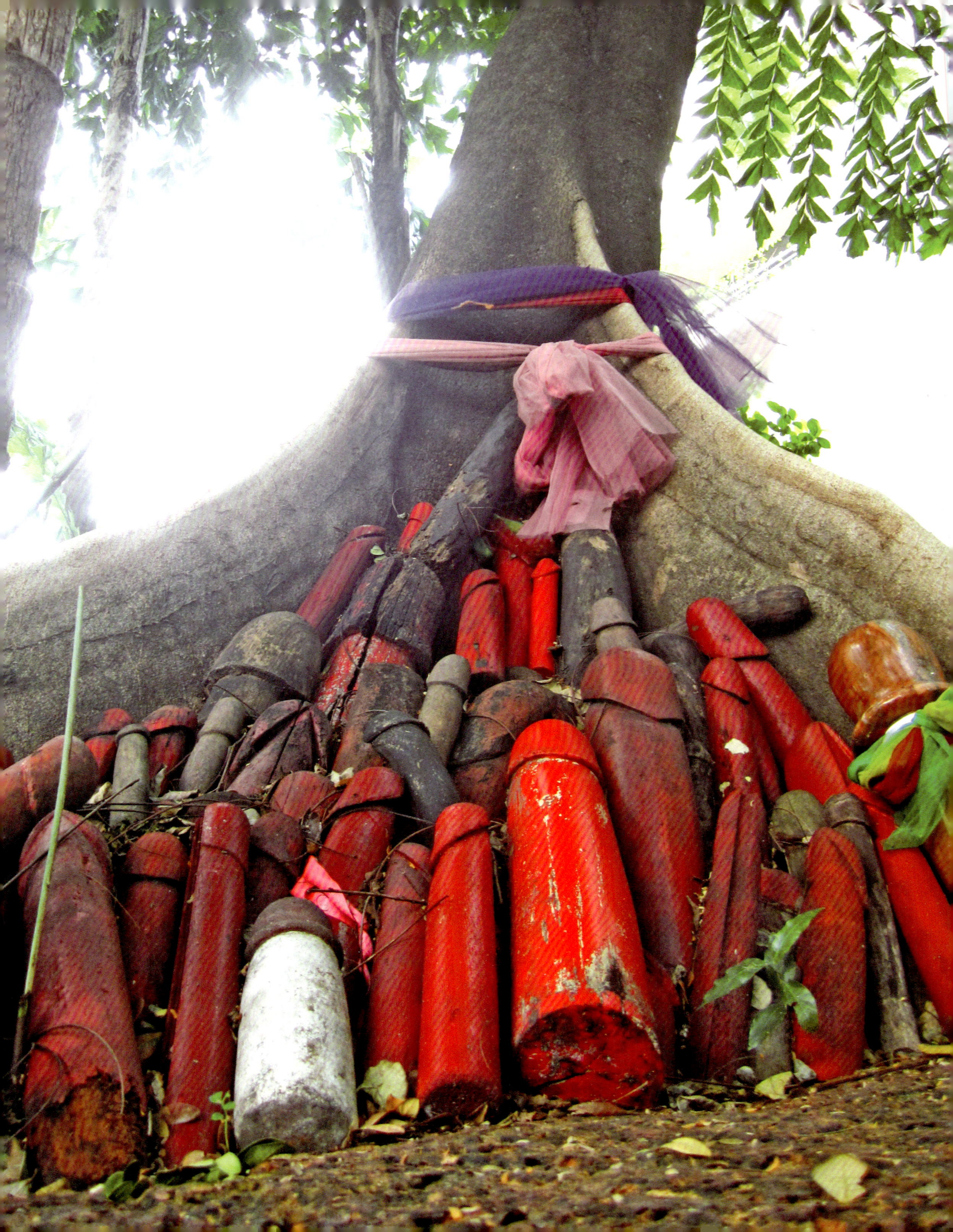

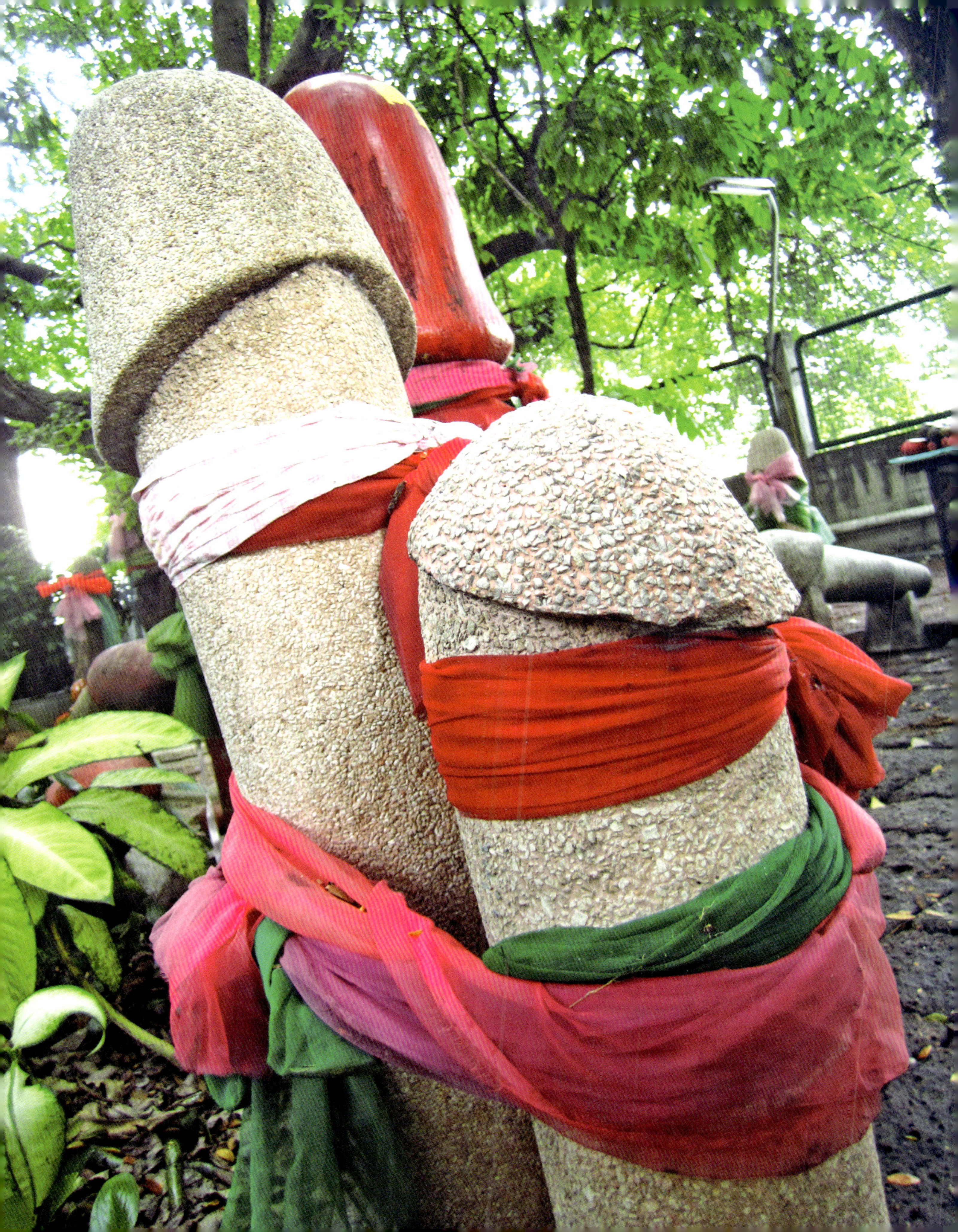

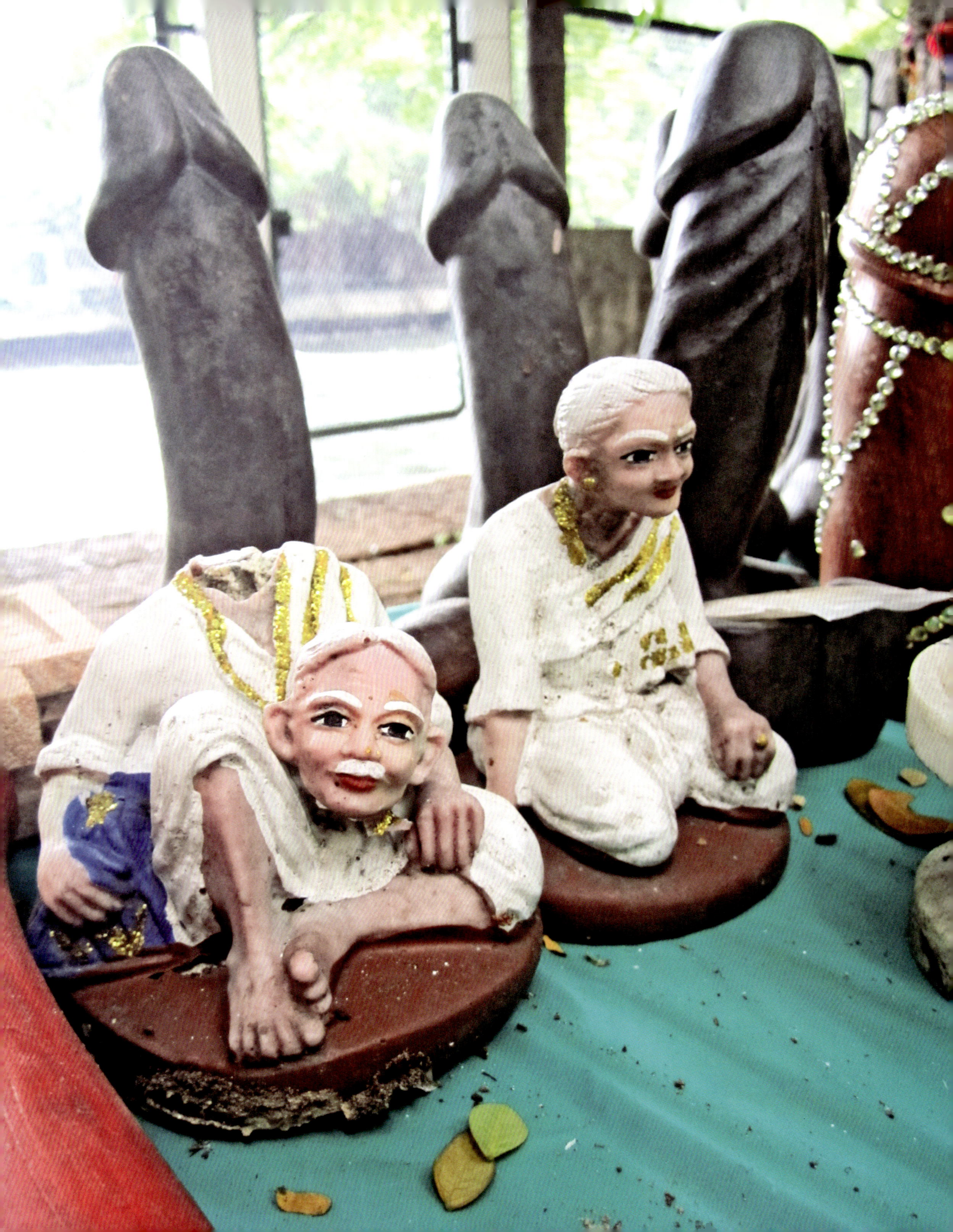

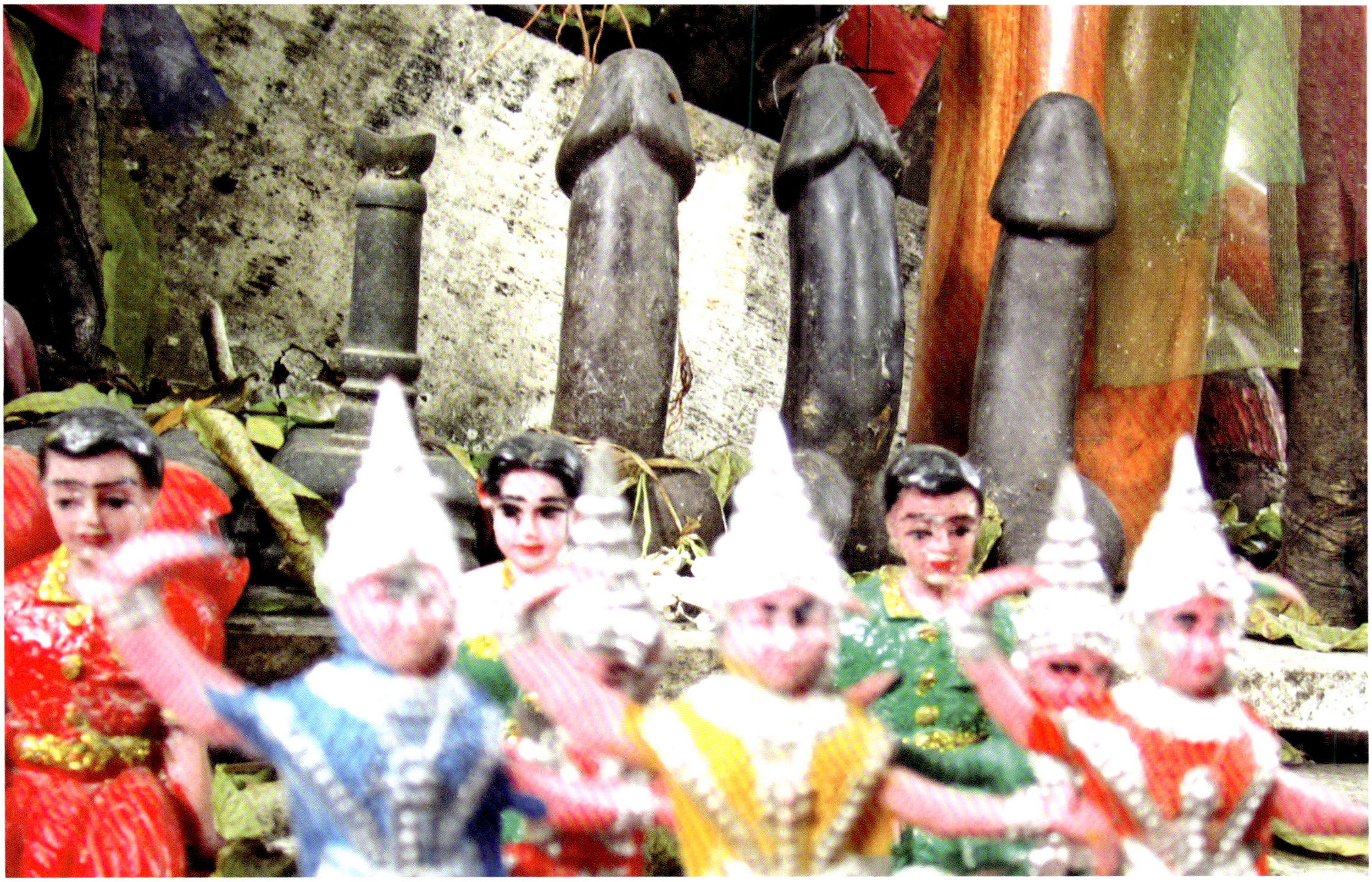

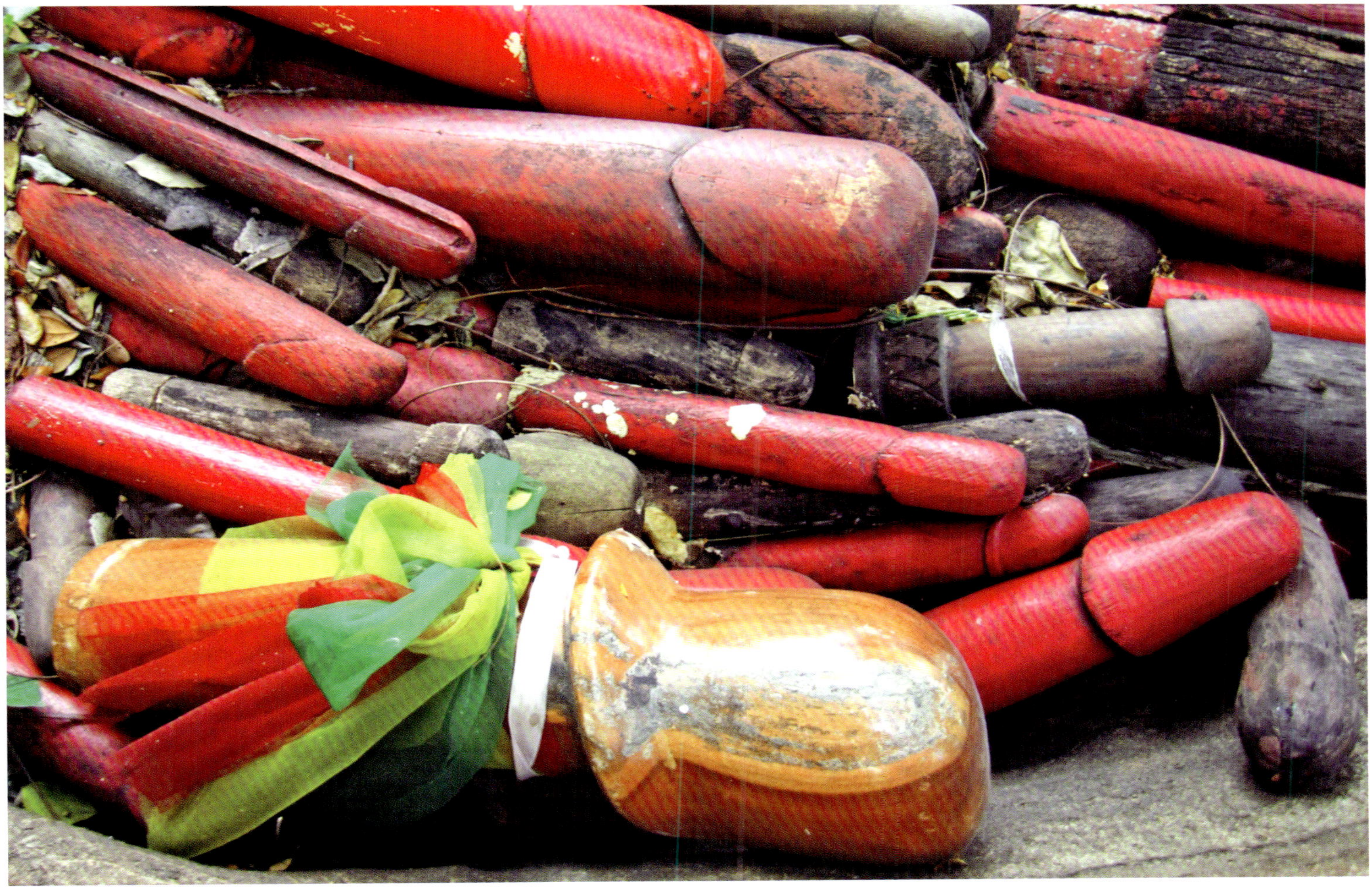

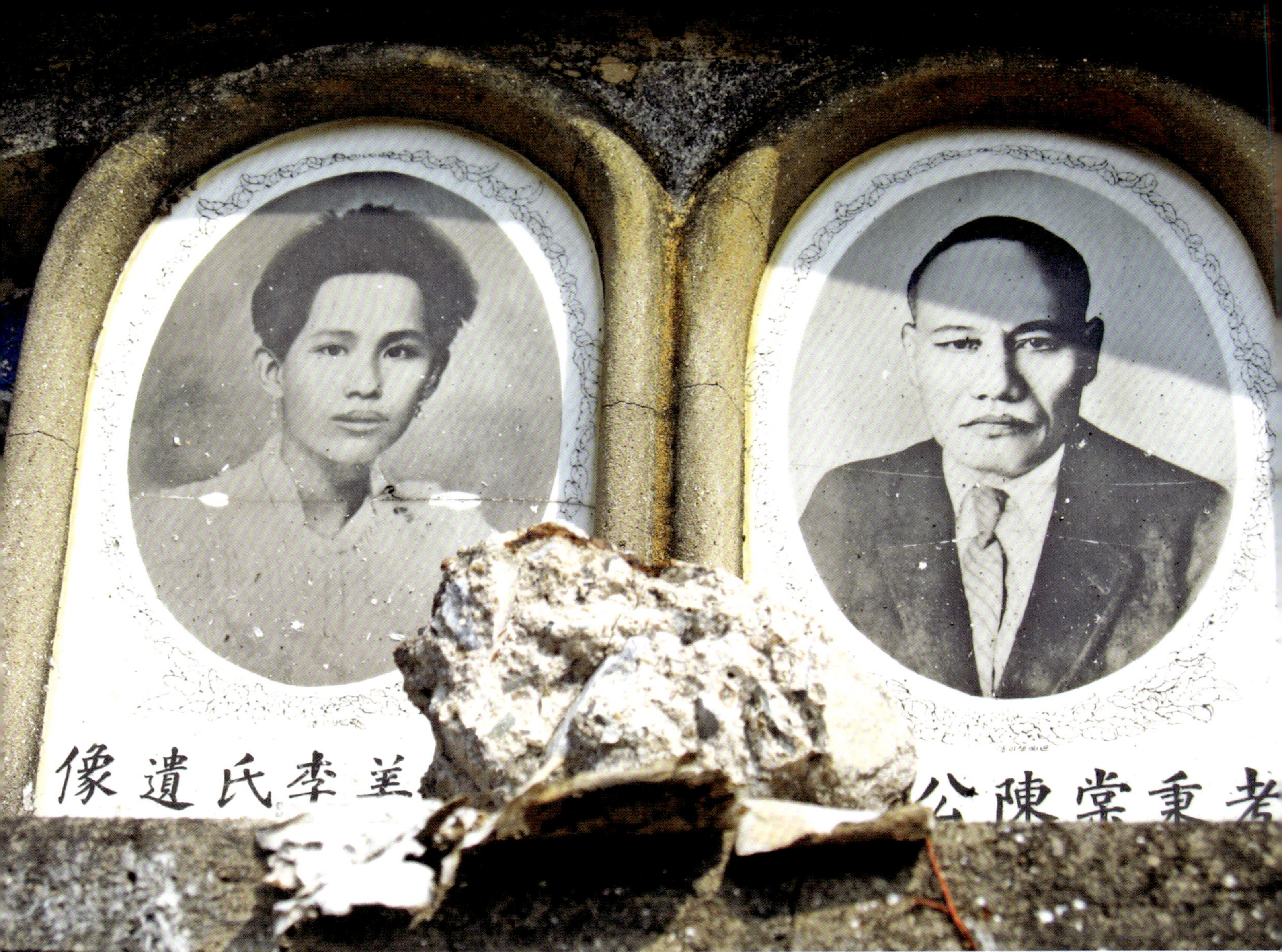

CHINESE CEMETERY

Visible from the BTS Skytrain, just beyond Chong Nonsi, lies a dilapidated cemetery. The entrance off Silom Soi 9 is foreboding: a rusty broken gate, a potholed courtyard used as a makeshift car park, where a pack of mangy *soi* dogs sleep or bark as a slothful potbellied pig suns itself. Chinese cemeteries are usually built into hills to increase the flow of positive *chi*; this one is on flat land. A small broken concrete path separates the graves, difficult to reach between piles of broken branches and debris. Stagnant water puddles on pedestal bases. Stone lions protect the tombs, their features eroded and covered in bird droppings, while dogs fiercely growl and bark, frightening all who approach the decaying crypts. Several graves have lids broken in half, or hang askew, crushing their crumbling brick supports; one hopes the bones have been removed. Several cement mausoleums remain sealed, the portrait of the interred centered in the main panel or above the upper ledge, marked with a stone. Others are smashed open, the ashes removed, vines and roots spread out like capillaries across the once-polished stone. A series of *chedis* with corncob-like *prangs* embossed with Chinese characters tilt on cracked pedestals, a small cement pond in front, filled with black water and trash. Dollhouse-sized cement abodes pitch and scrape into each other, the ground no longer level. A large Bodhi tree is wrapped in colorful scarves, its girth elevating and cracking a concrete slab, a broken spirit house resting on its exposed knotted roots. Beyond the broken plaster wall towers the pristine white Bangkok Bank and a blue-windowed hotel.

The cemetery's neglect is in stark contrast to the level of respect the Chinese hold for their ancestors, as they affect our world and one must provide for them in the afterlife. Considering the *yin-yang* dichotomy, there is a separation between the soul and the grave: the *po* remains at the grave, while the *hun* or soul is linked to the ancestral tablet, a piece of inscribed wood in the family shrine at home. What has happened to the relatives? Did they all move away, or have the dogs scared them from their obligation? The ancestral spirits must have moved on. All that remains are the solemn black and white or sepia-toned images of those that have departed, staring back, formal and unsmiling.

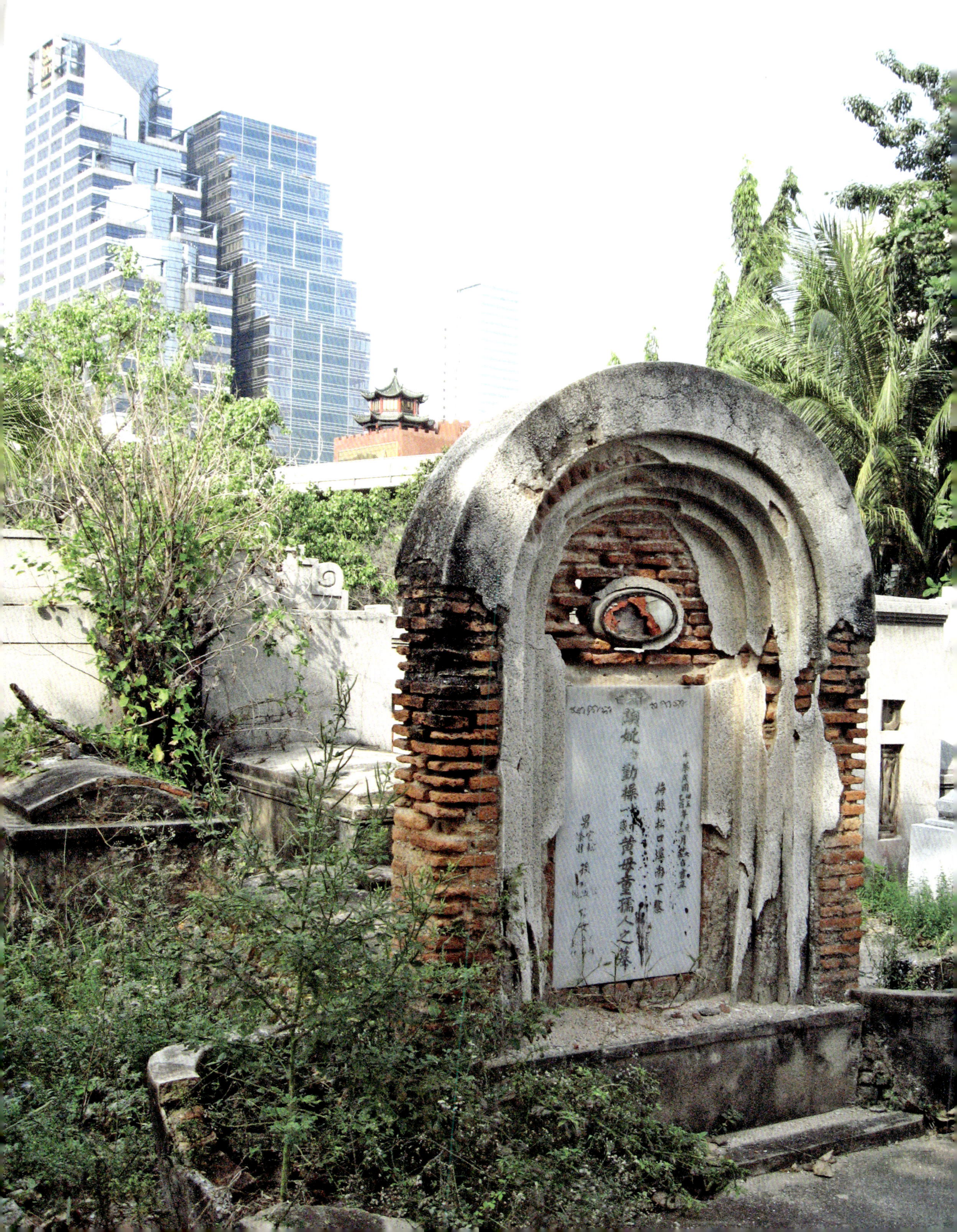
顯妣
勤操
黃母董孺人之墓

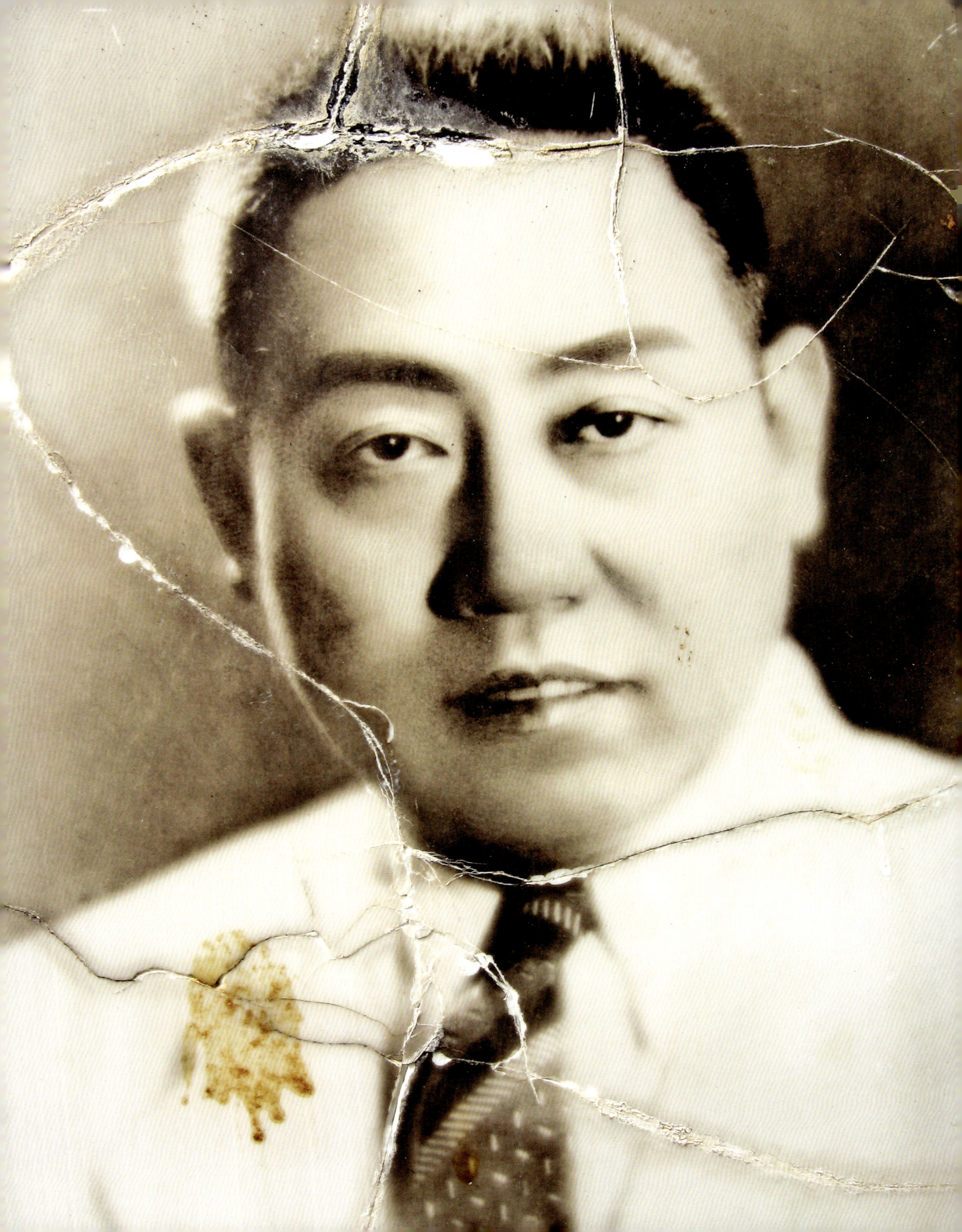

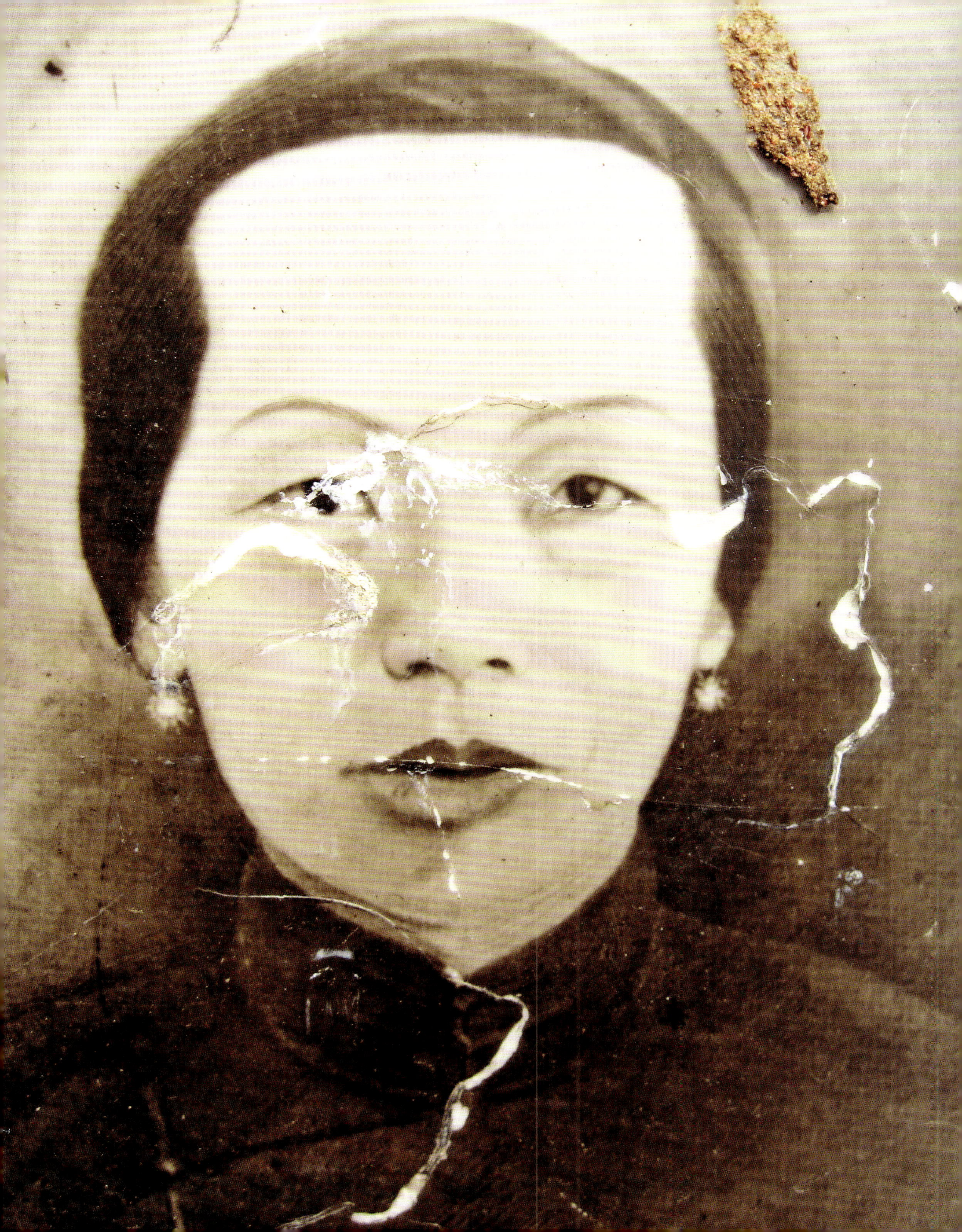

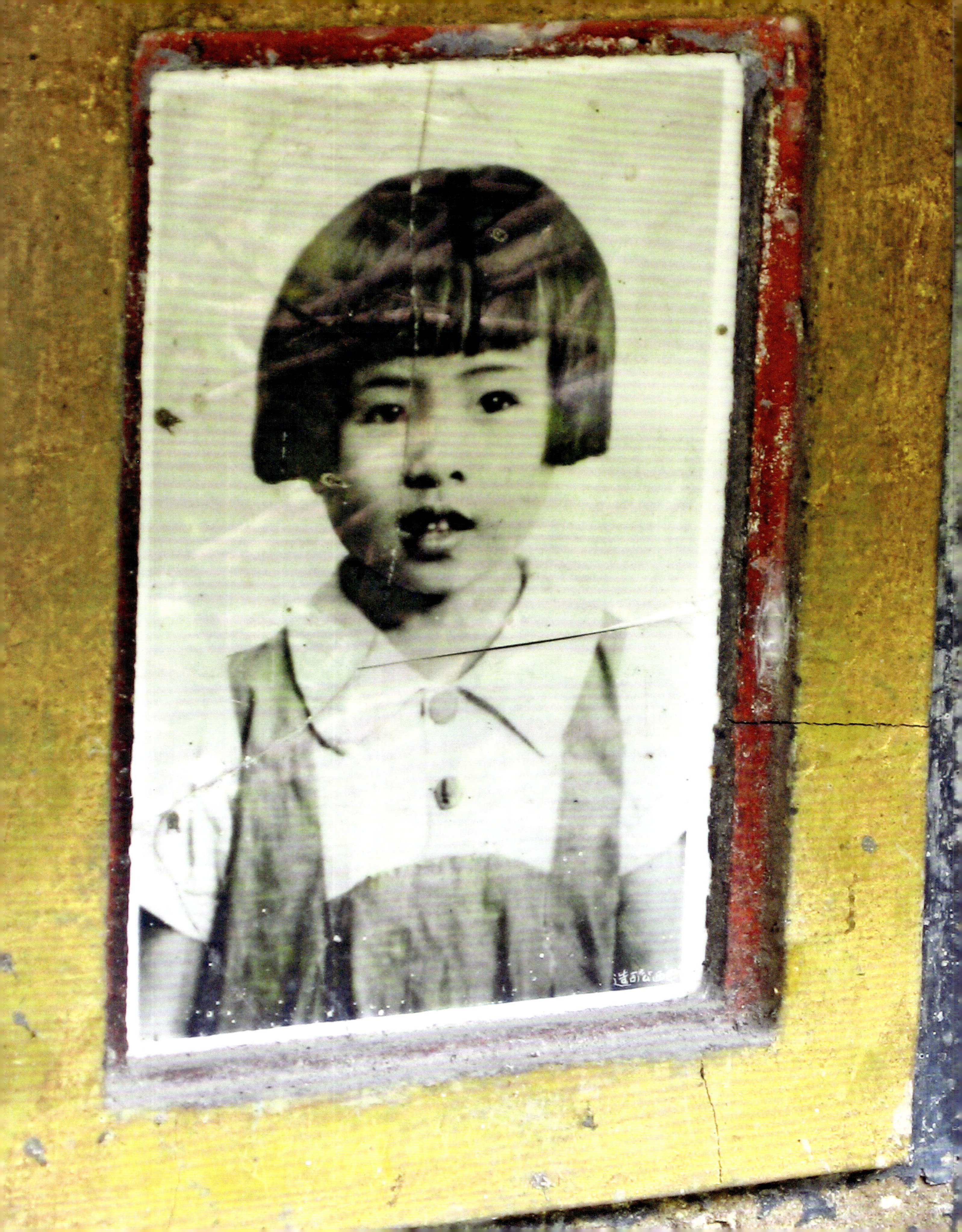

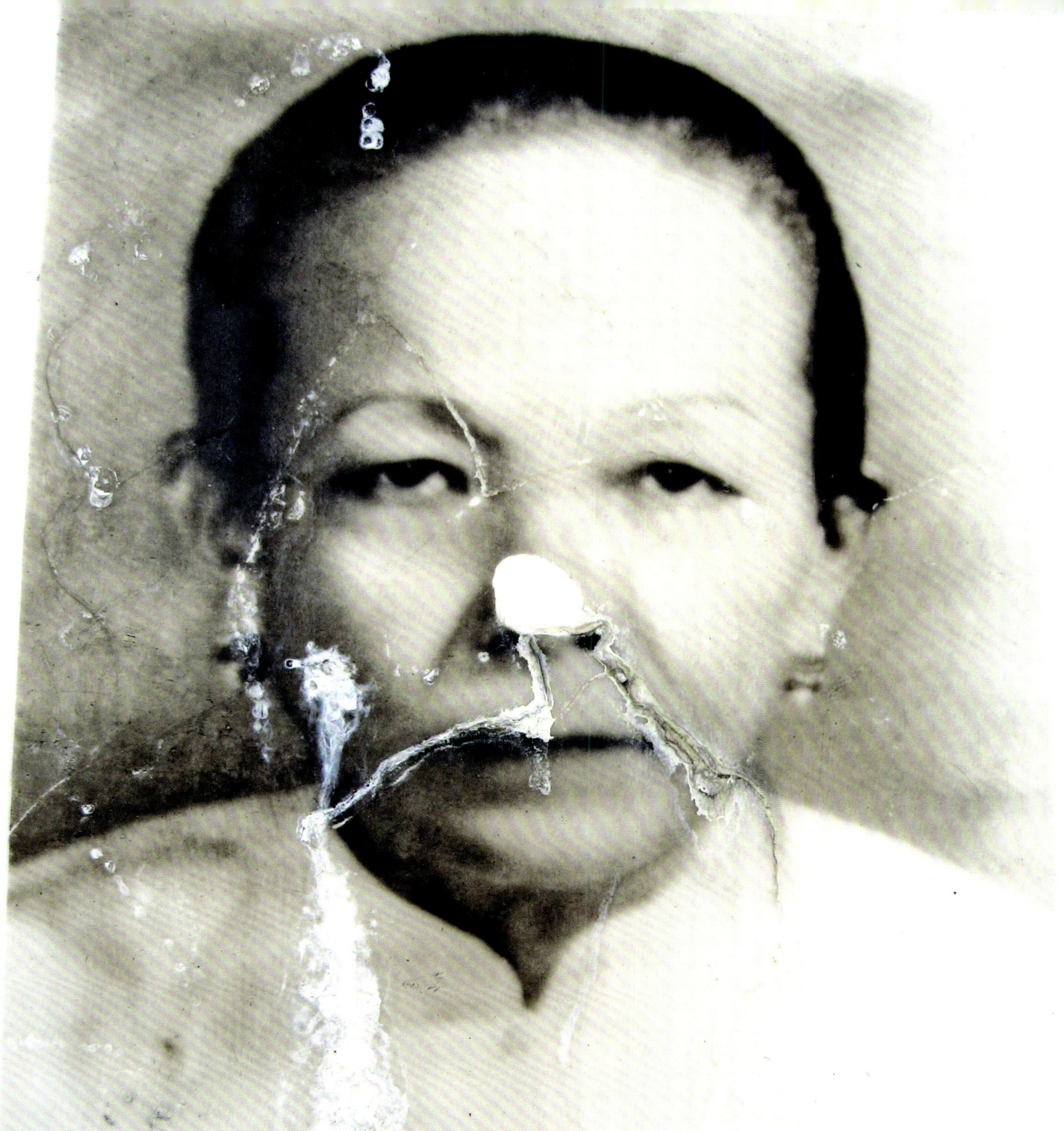

壽終于一九六一年三月二十一日
年丑辛二月初五日

周母鍾太孺人遺像

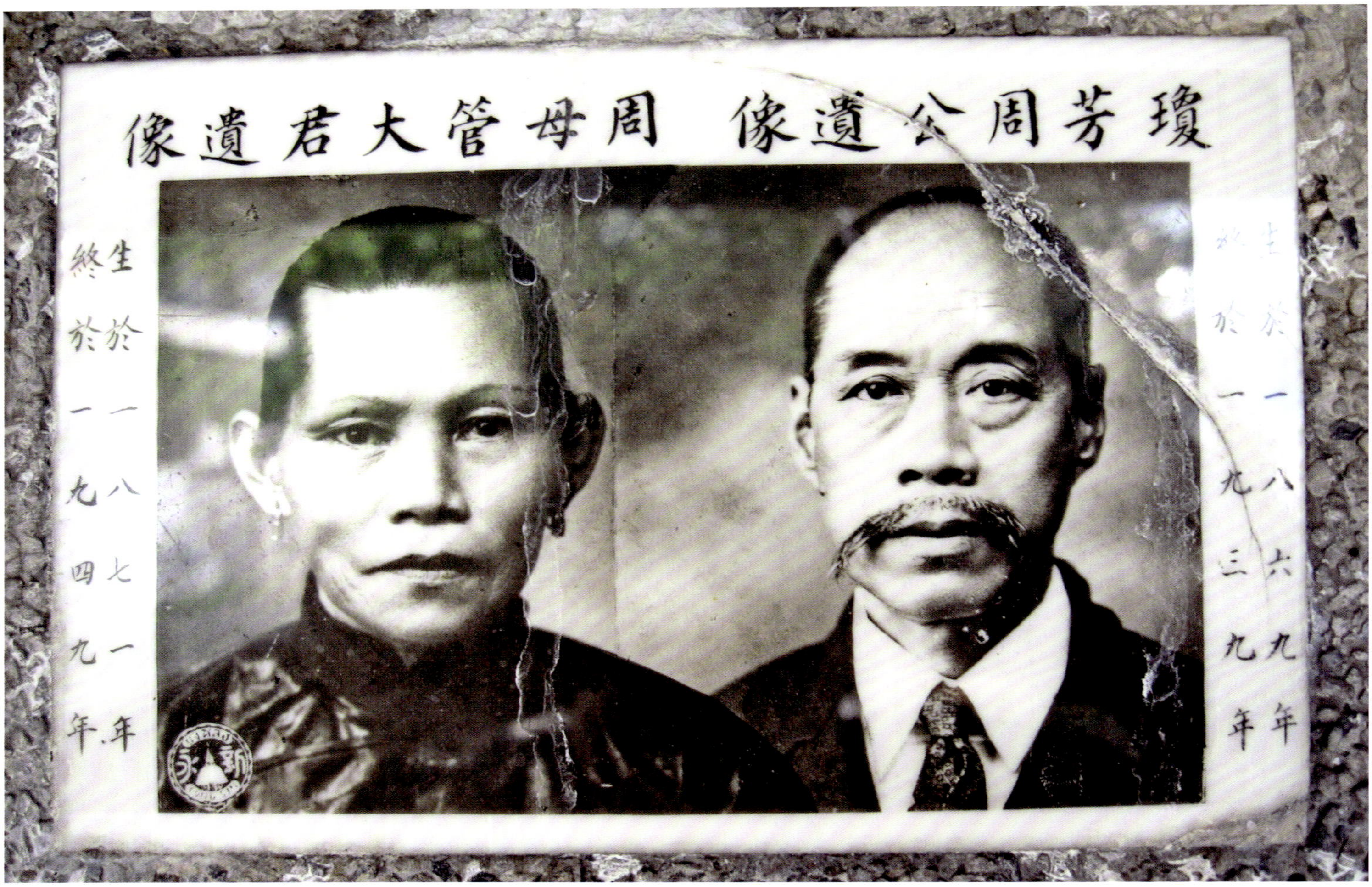

瓊芳周公遺像　周母管大君遺像

生於一八六九年

終於一九三九年

生於一八七一年

終於一九四九年

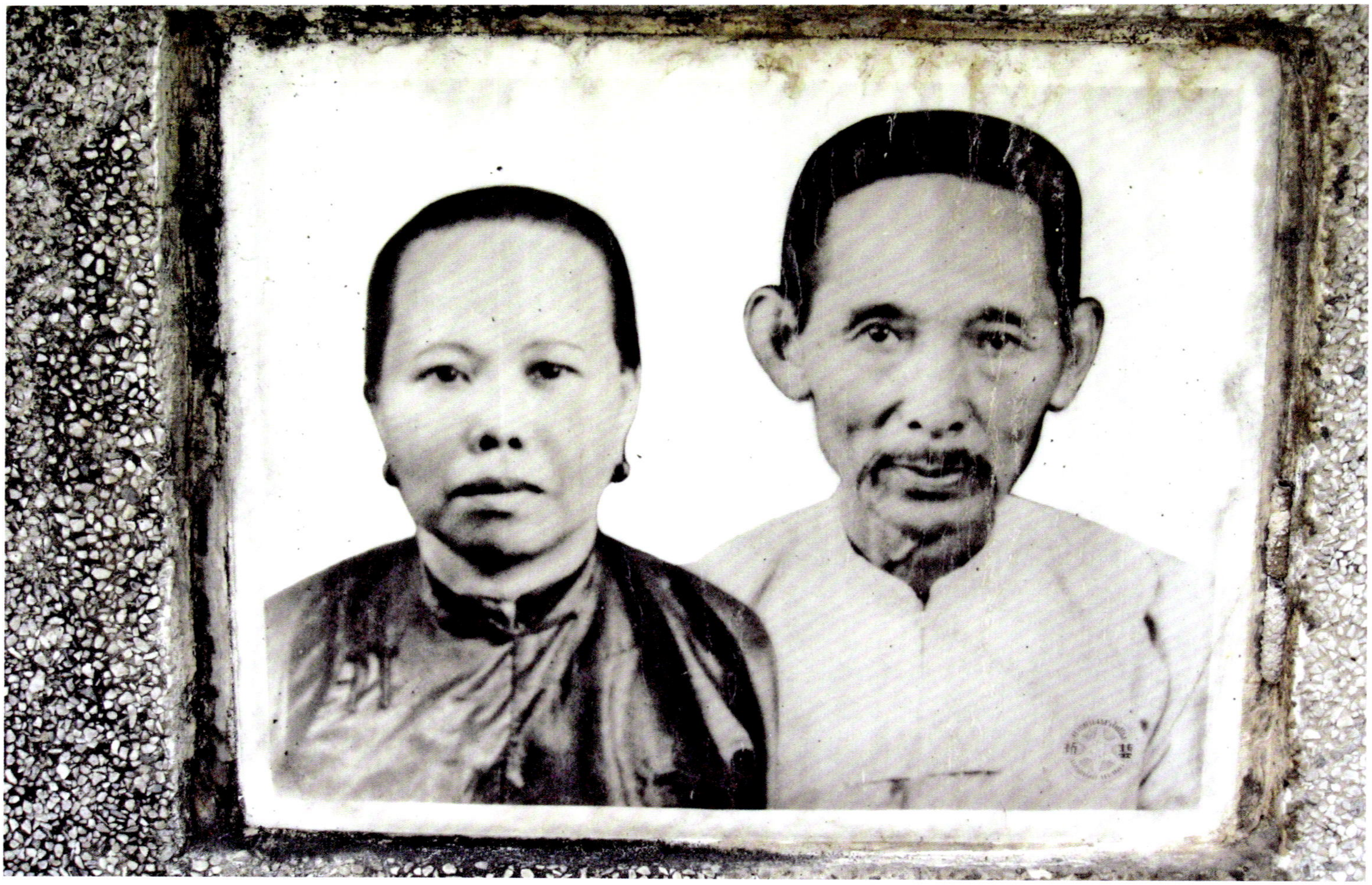

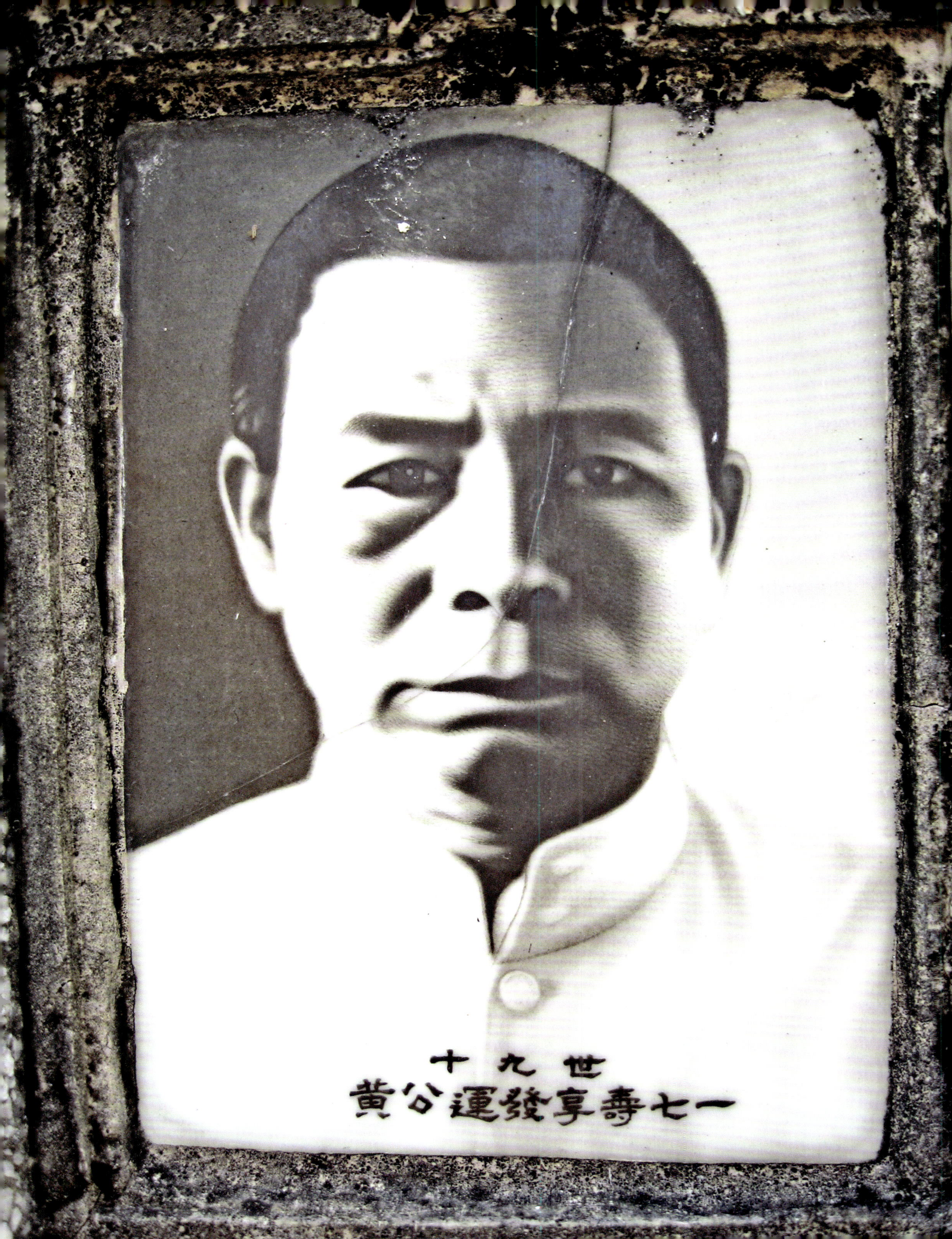

十九世
黃公運發享壽七一

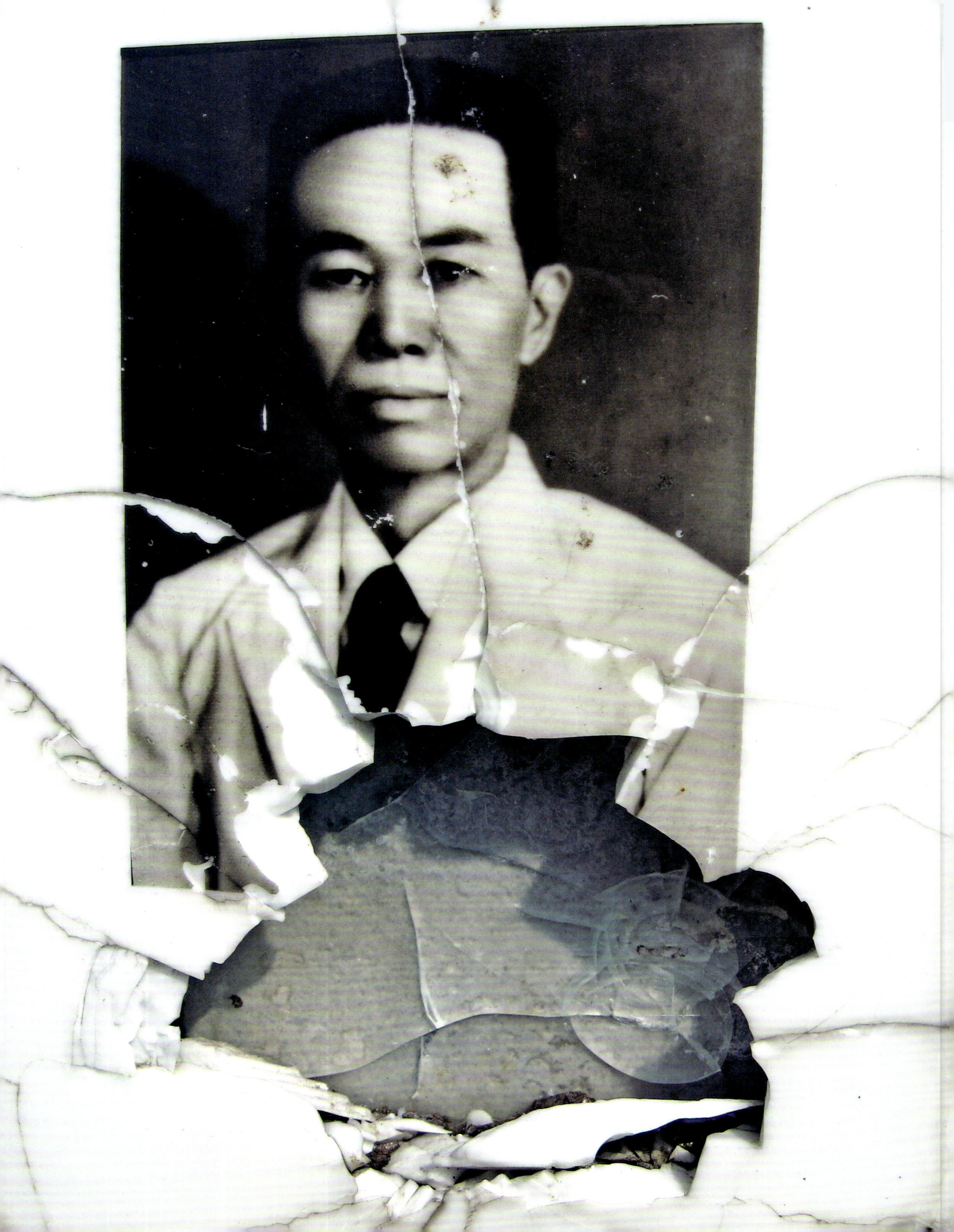

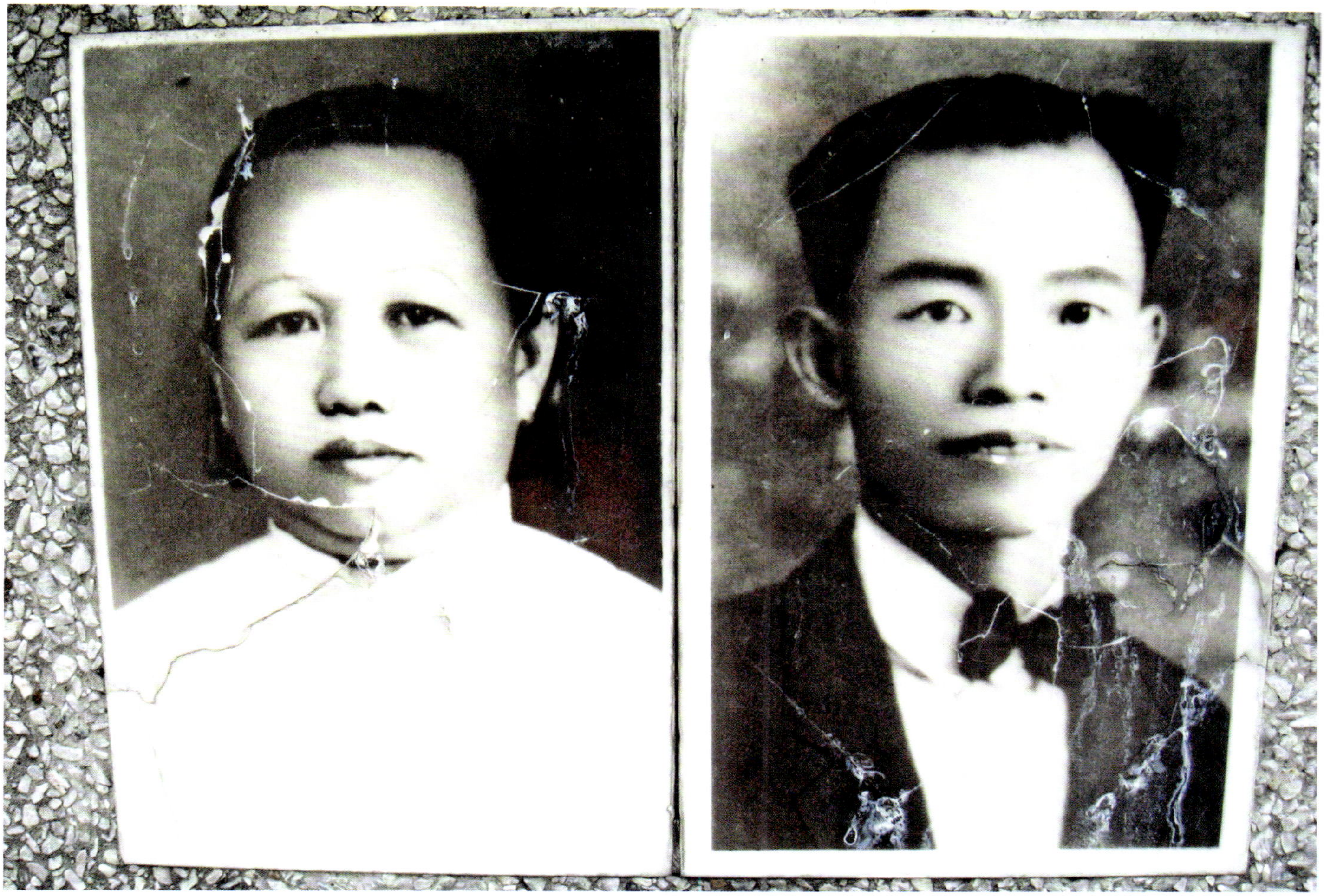

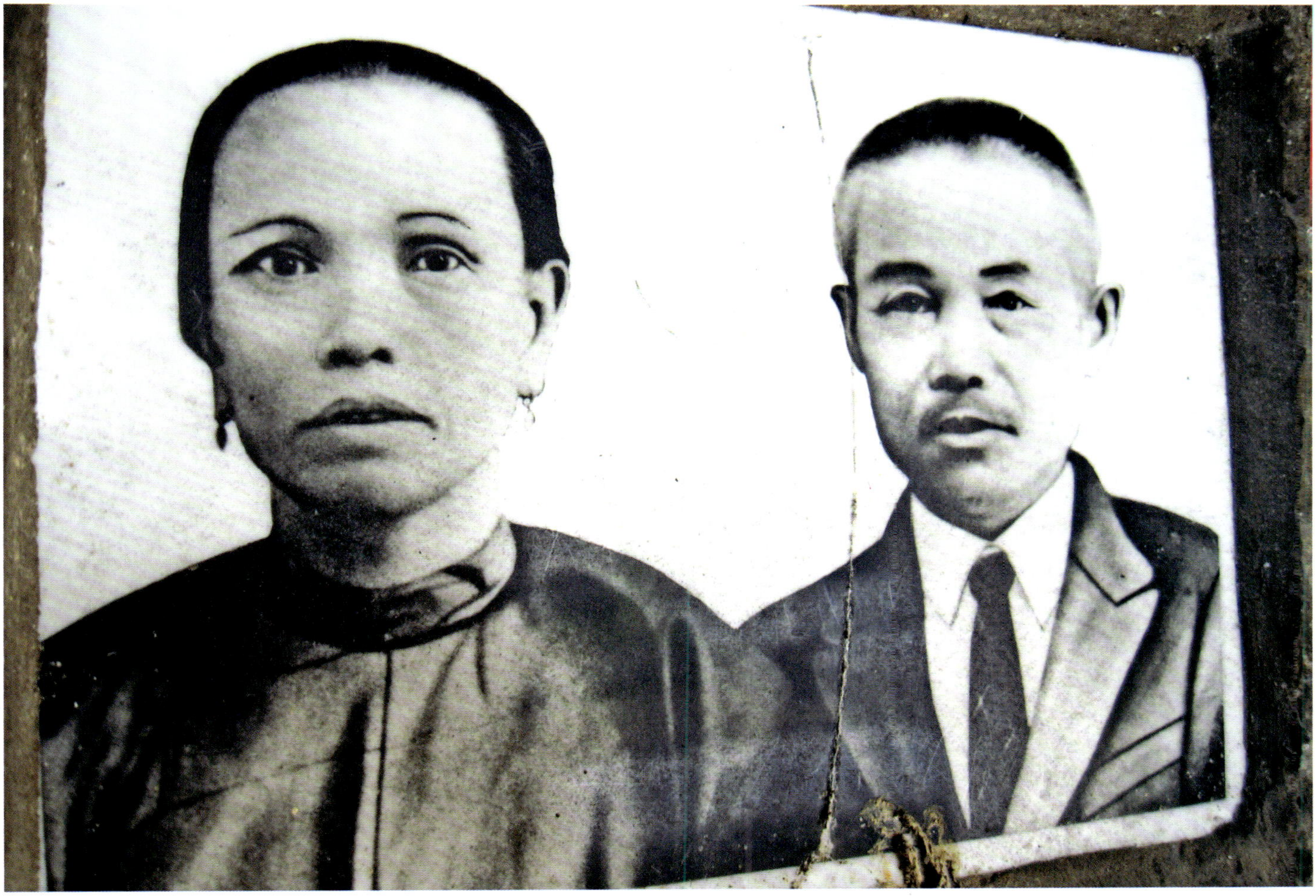

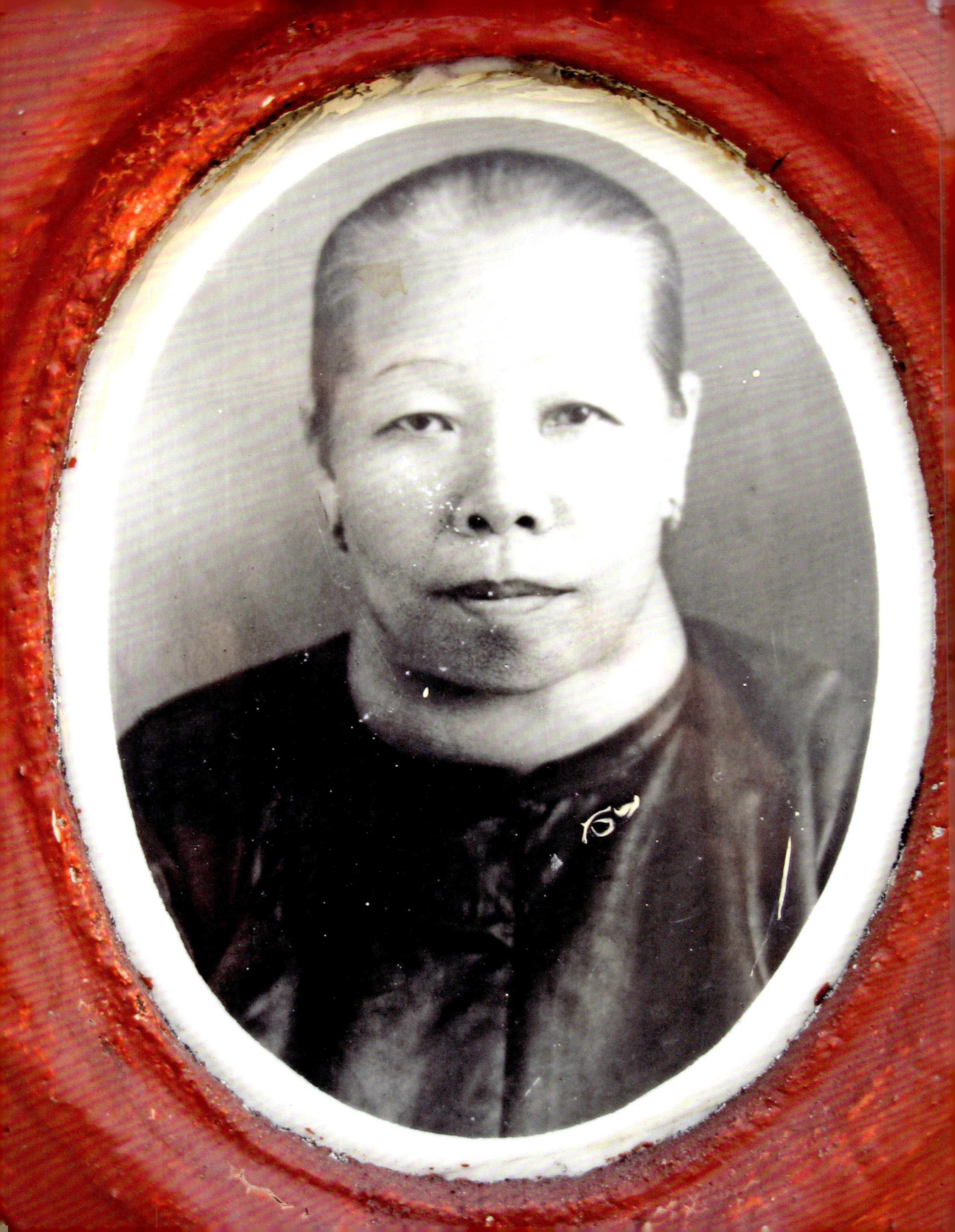

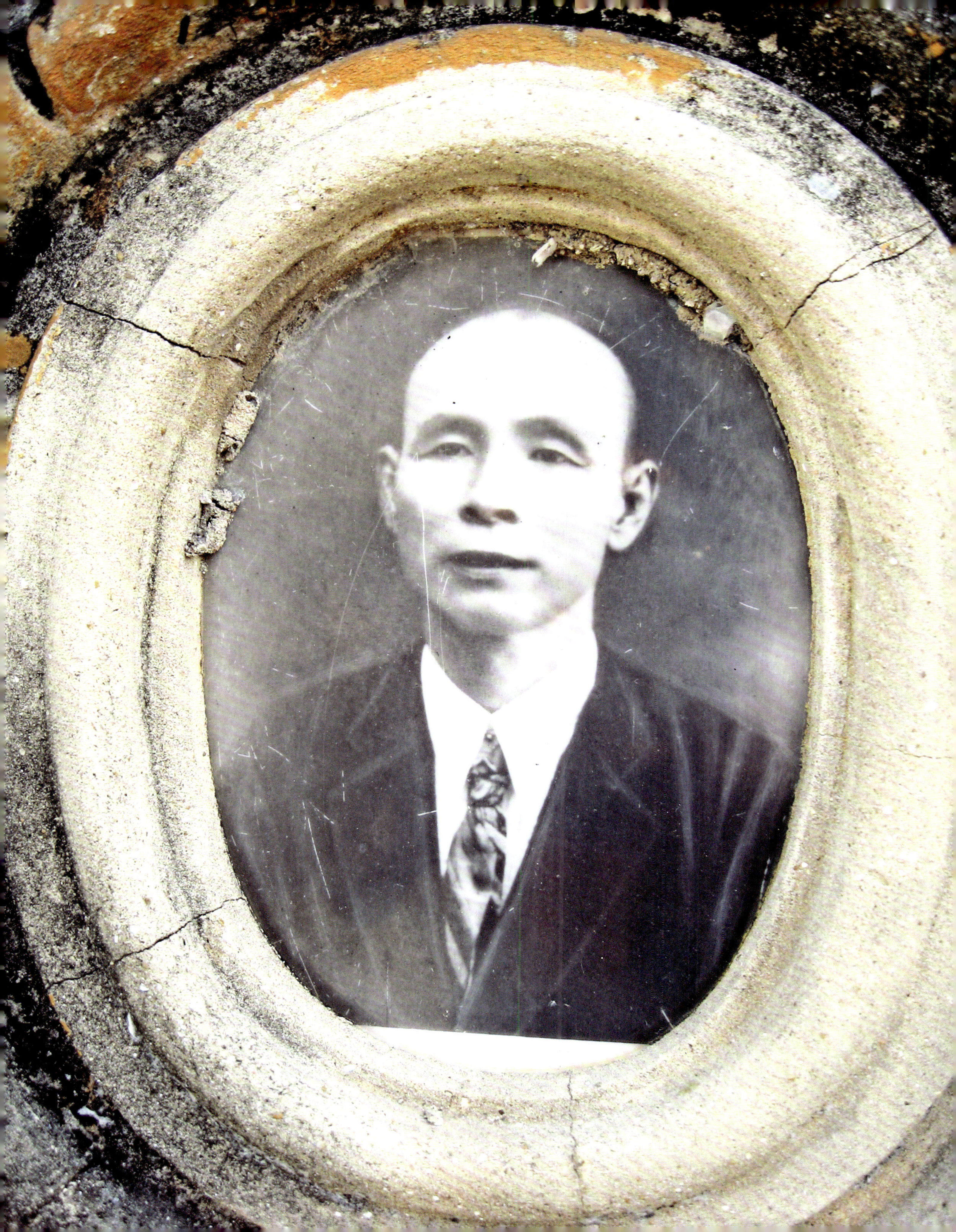

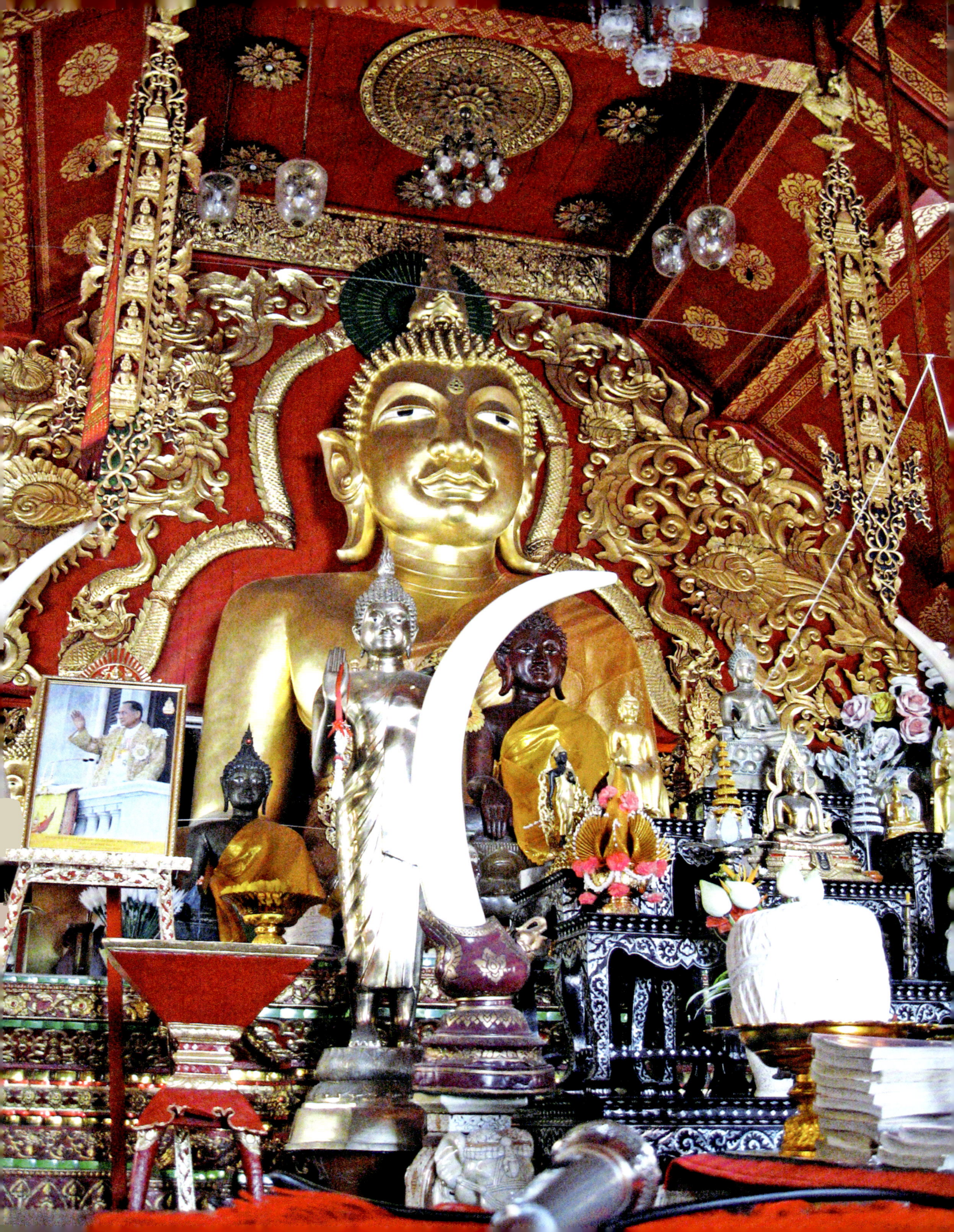

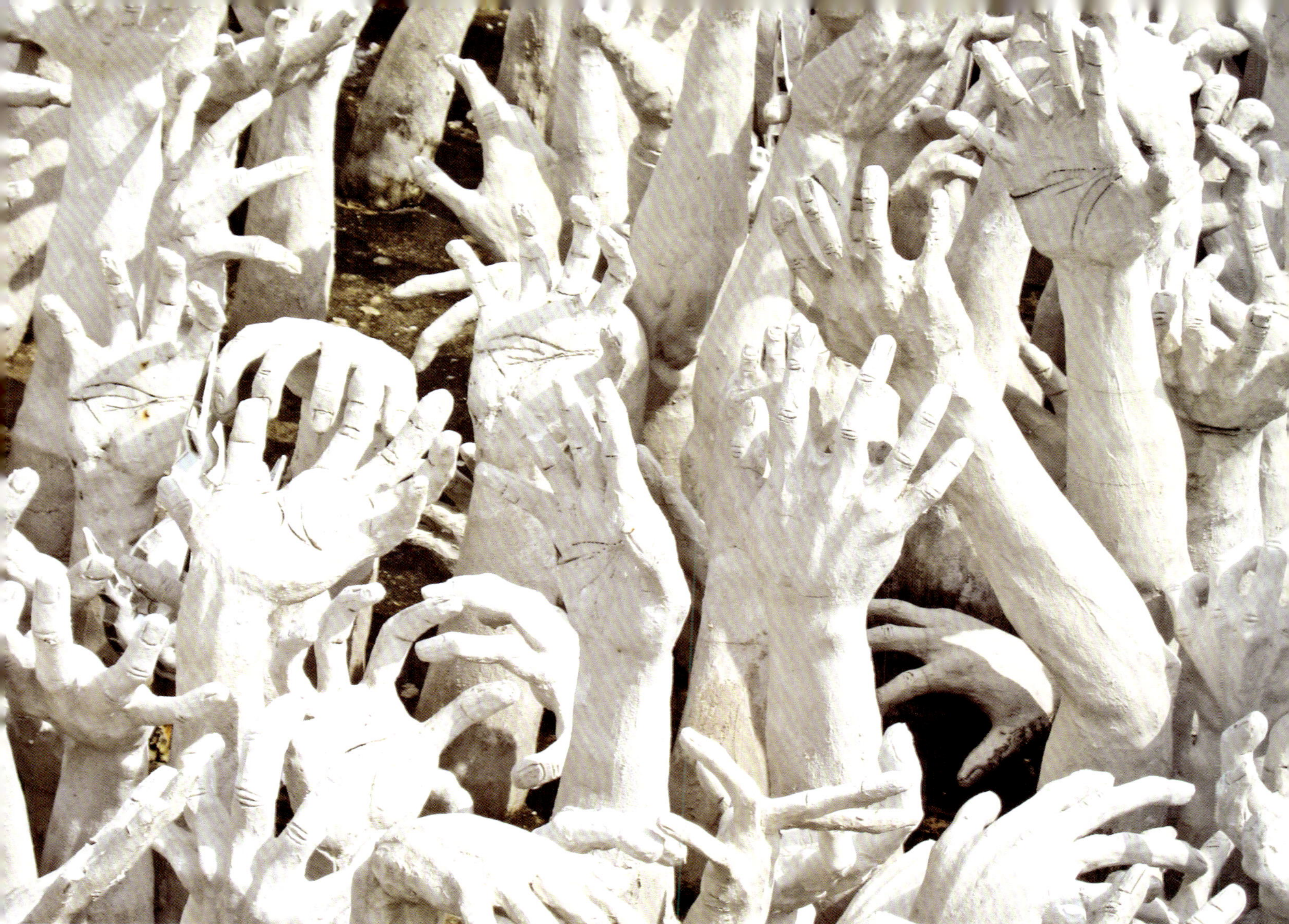

2. TEMPLES AND SHRINES

The Thai word for a Buddhist temple is *wat*, which pertains to the entire complex and not one specific building. Temples always house a Buddha image. The architecture reflects the period of temple construction, or reconstruction, and the ethnicity of devotees. Often residing within a temple, shrines are connected to holy places dedicated to a deity, spirit, or relic. Shrines are also found in homes and shops, dedicated to ancestors or spirits, royalty, or to the Buddha. Statues of monks are often gilded in gold leaf in reverence.

Of most significance is a temple's *ubosoth* or *bot*, the ordination hall or prayer room, usually facing east, where monks take holy vows and religious rituals are performed. Its roof is angled and multi-tiered, extending beyond the building to protect the structure during heavy rains. Containing Buddha images and wall murals, it remains closed to the public. Six or eight sacred boundary stones, or *bai semas*, surround the *bot*, marking consecrated ground; these vary in design, some resembling Bodhi tree leaves, some as four or eight-sided columns. Often similar in design to the *bot*, the *viharn* is a sermon or assembly hall containing large and small Buddha images where followers worship throughout the day. Roof ornaments are often in the shape of *nagas*, or serpents, which descend from the tiers of the roof gables, heads rearing above the bottom eaves. The roof peaks end in *chofahs*, decorative finials in the shape of a bird, swan, elephant or *naga*, or *garuda*, often with small bells at the tip.

Most temples have a *chedi*, a Thai *stupa*. Historically clay burial mounds covering the ashes of Indian holy men, Thai *chedis* house physical relics of the Buddha, revered teachers or ancient texts, within or underneath the dome structure. A pagoda usually refers to a *stupa* that can be entered. The *chedi*'s shape suggests the seated Buddha image: the base his throne, the dome his body, the spire his crown. It can be bell-shaped in the Sri Lankan style, often with a multi-ringed spire atop a pedestal base, or of a Mon pyramid design. Khmer-style temples feature a *prang*, a phallic corncob-like *chedi*. The *sala* is an open-sided pavilion and center for social activity where visitors may spend the night. The highly decorated *ho trai*, or library, houses religious manuscripts, and is usually elevated to protect against flooding and insects.

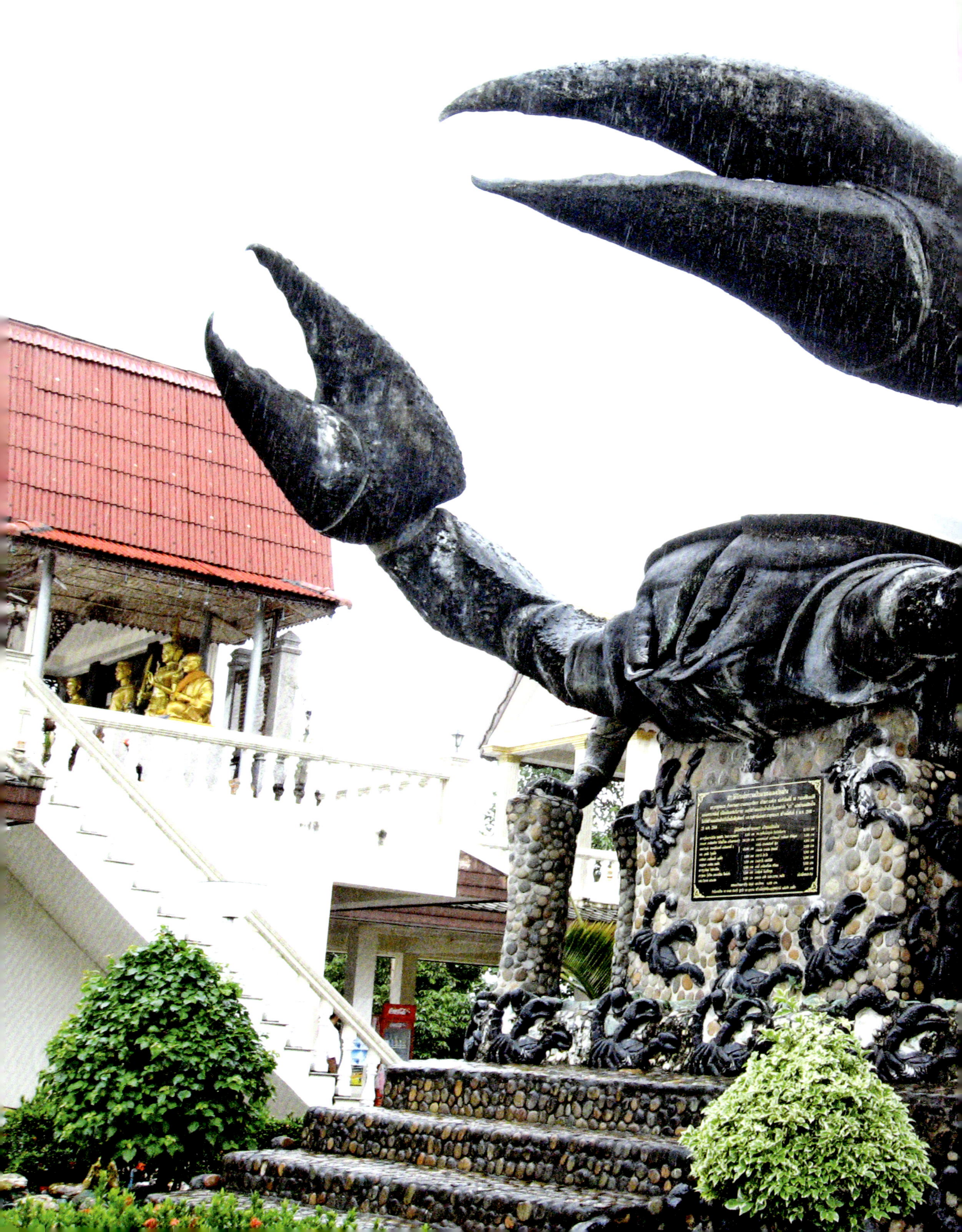

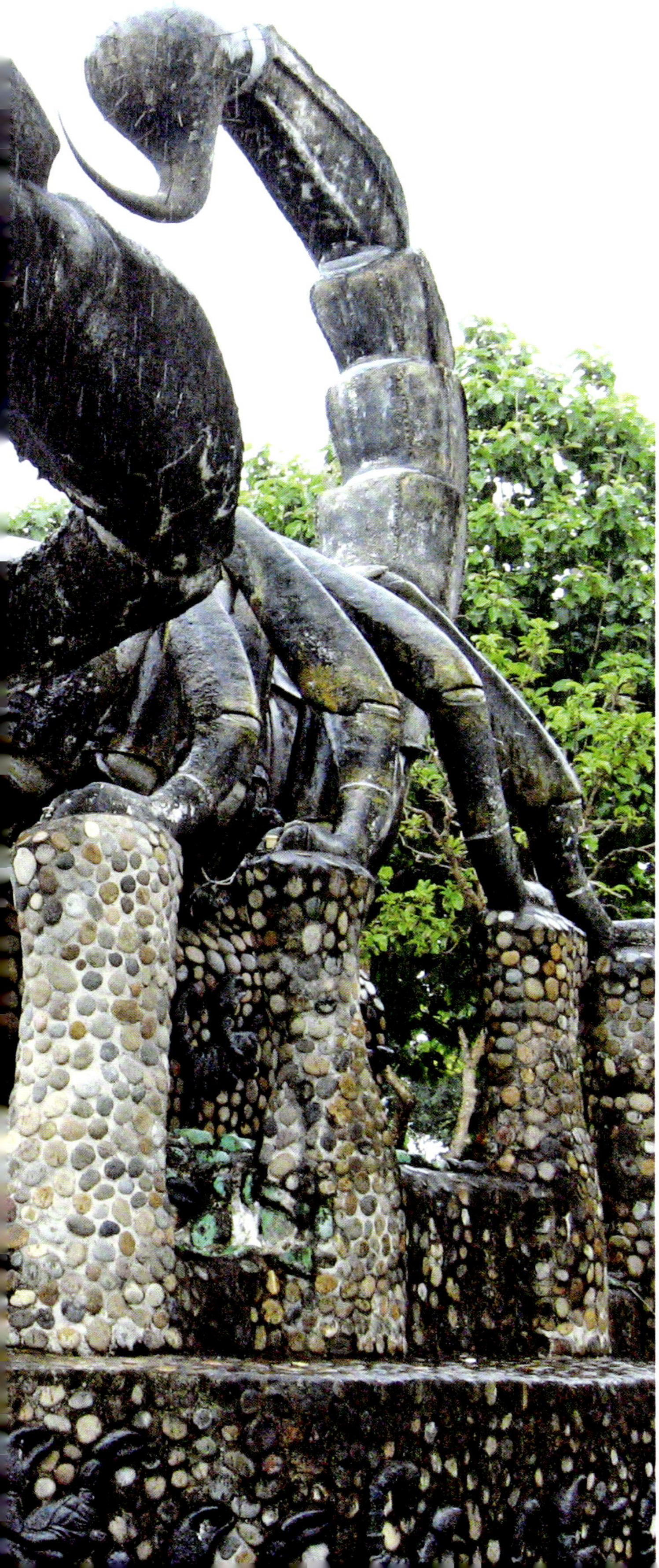

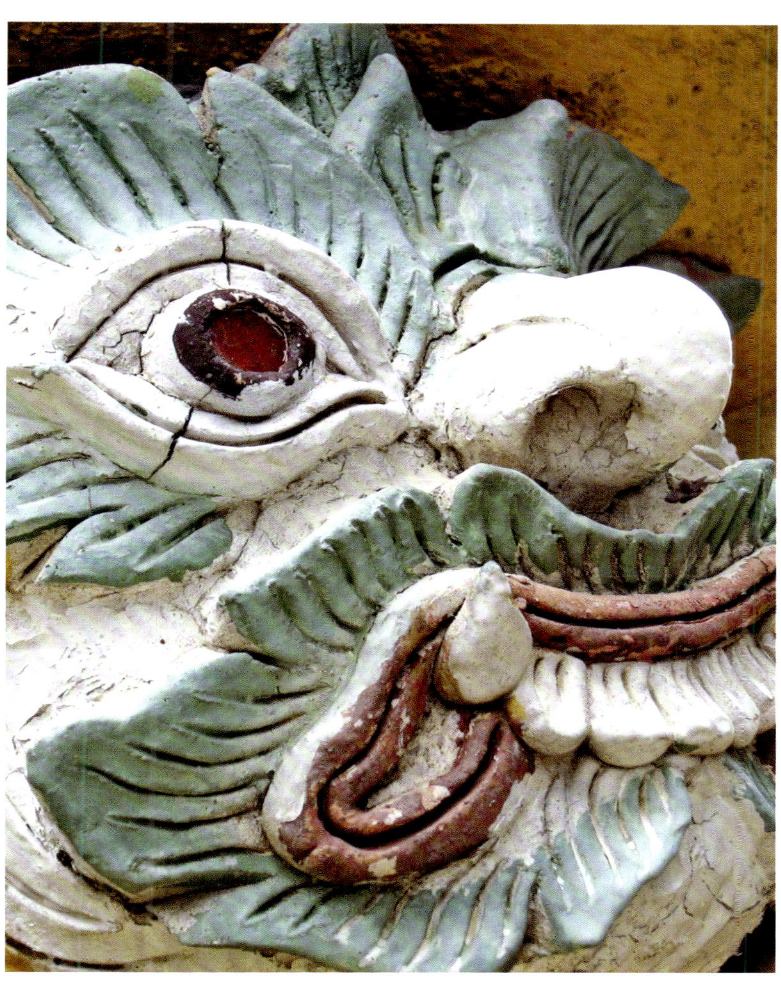

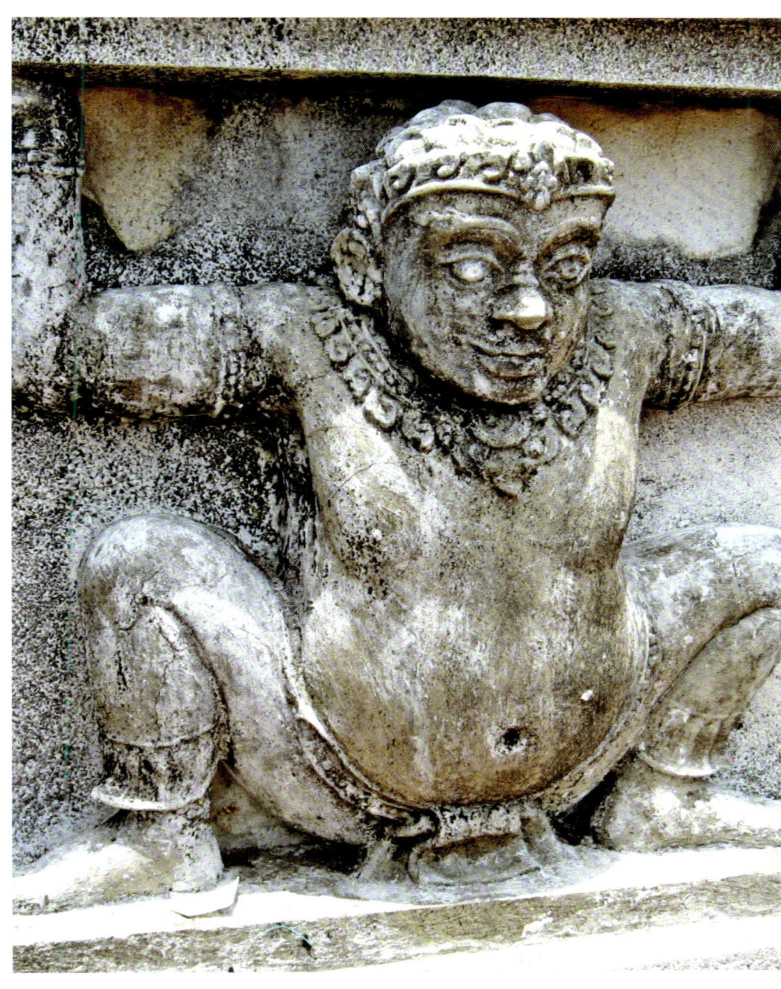

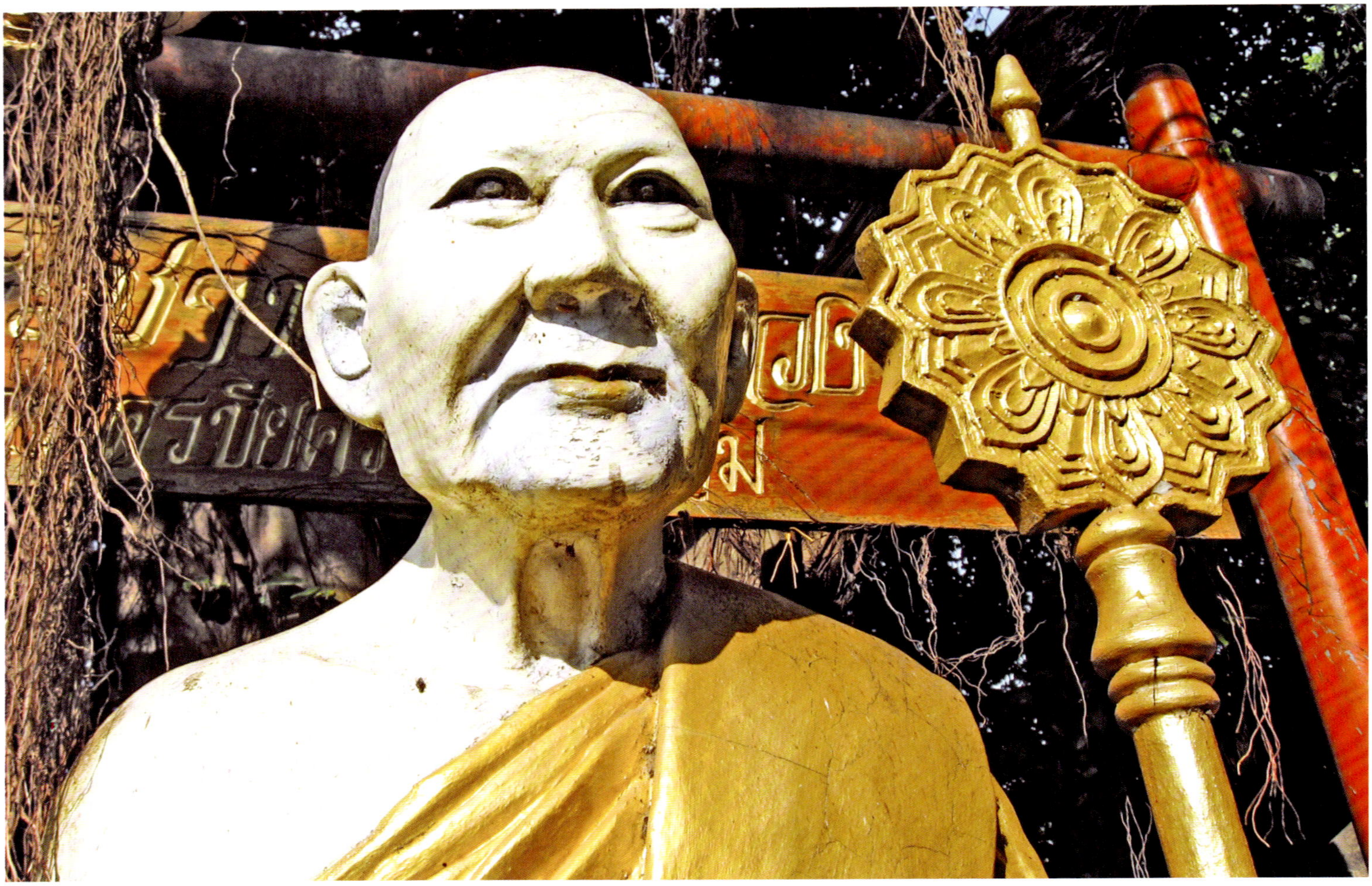

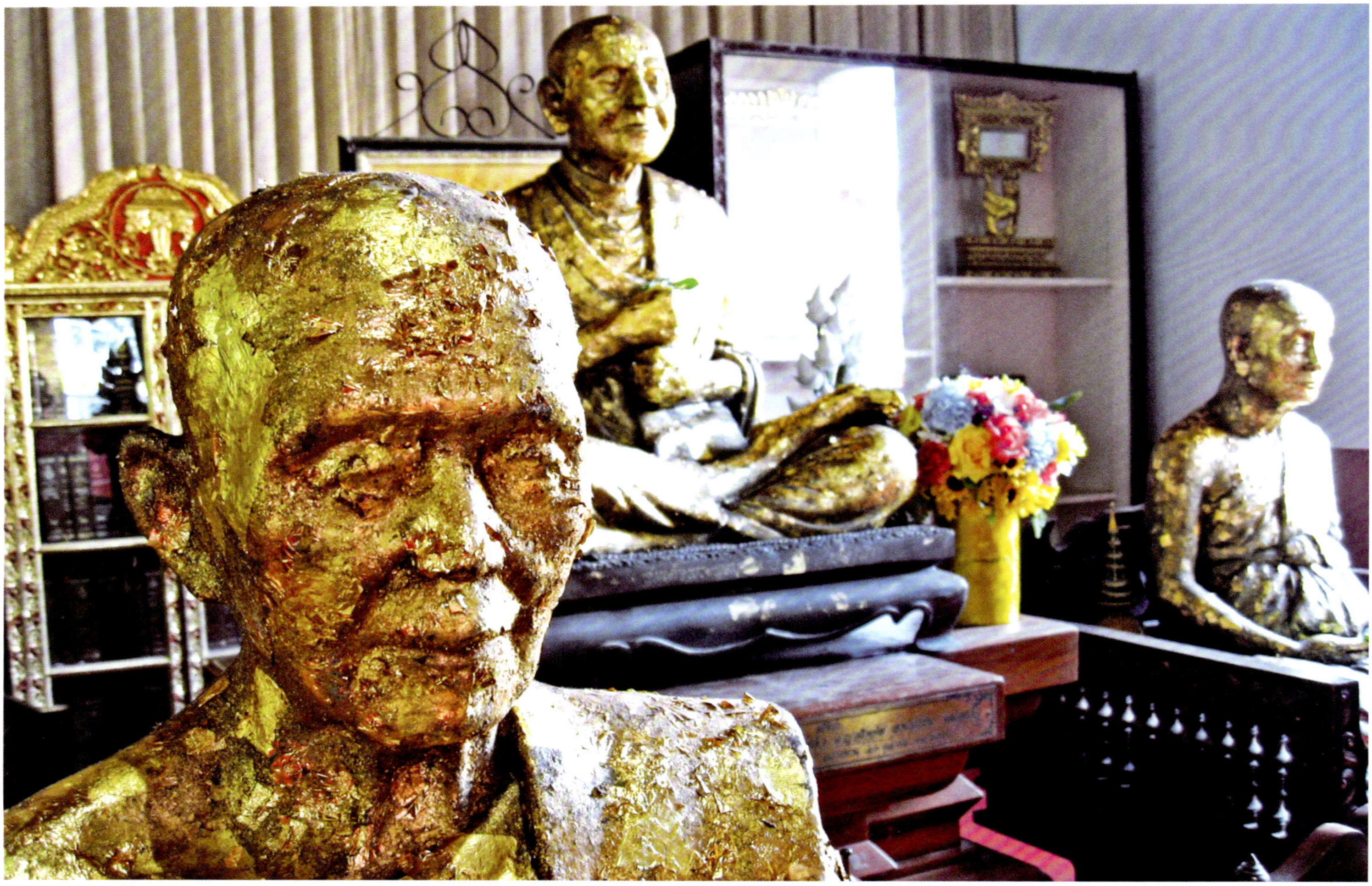

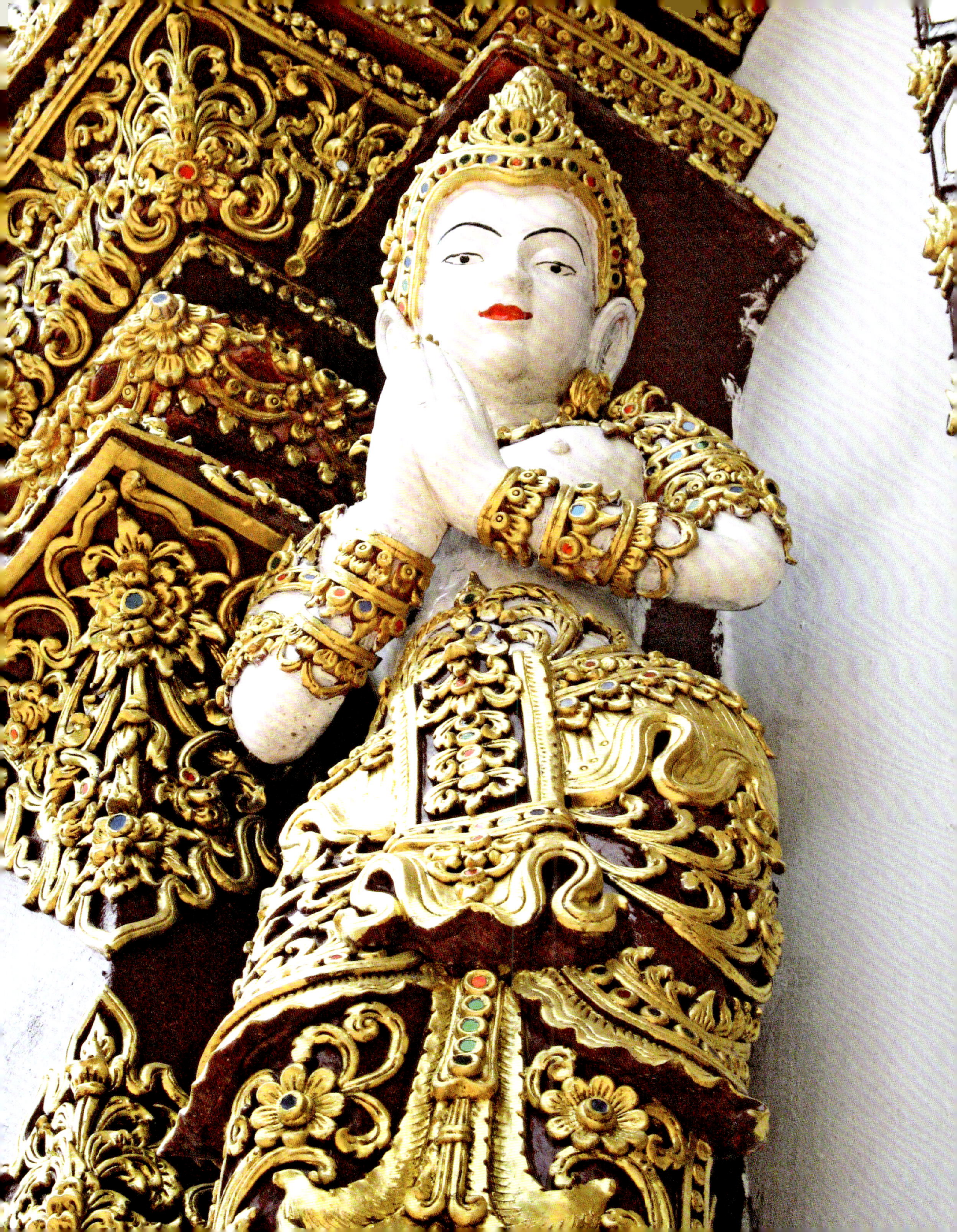

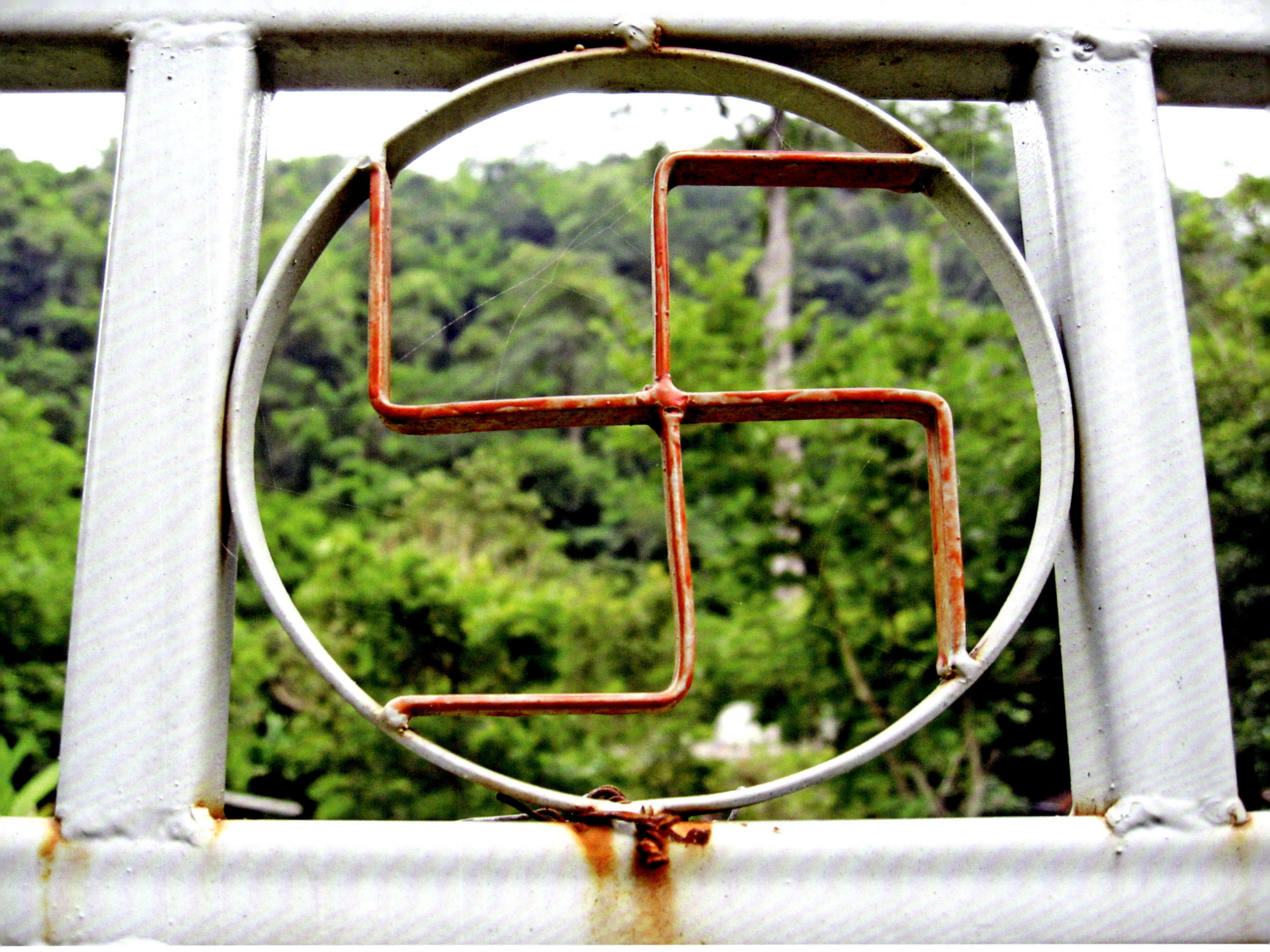

WAT THAM PHA PLONG & THAM CHIANG DAO

Chiang Dao, the City of Stars, is located 52 miles north of Chiang Mai on Doi Chiang Dao, the third highest mountain in Thailand. Well known for its cave (in Thai: *tham*) complex, Tham Chiang Dao is believed to reach between six and eight miles into the mountain. Approximately 100 interconnected caves exist, but only five are open to the public. A guide will point out interesting rock formations in the shape of elephants, chickens and fried eggs among the limestone stalagmites and stalactites. The caves were historically places of worship: Buddha images and shrines line the path, complete with bats, spiders, and pools of water. Legend says a 1000-year old *Reusli*, or hermit, inhabited the caves and convinced the deities to create seven wonders, nestled deep in the cave's bowels. A tile-covered *naga* and two comical figures in hats man the entrance to one cave. Outside, beyond a small market selling herbs, roots and plants, stand several ancient moss-covered *chedis* and a large Burmese-style temple protected by a five-headed *naga*. The temple's spire is decorated with a *chat*, or ceremonial umbrella, multi-tiered and adorned with bells.

Further up the mountain is Wat Tham Pla Plong, a cave temple surrounded by forest. Two large *nagas* drape and protect the first 16 steps of the 510-step staircase to the temple. The climb is punctuated with sayings in Thai and English: "There's a chance to get refreshed, once you are tired. But there's no chance to re-live your life, once you are dead," or "Do not grumble when you suffer. Just persevere." Another informs, "You've passed 201 toughest steps, with 309 easy steps left to reach the *chedi* and the Venerable Phra Ajarn Sim's cremated remains." The temple was built by Phra Luang Pu Sim Buddhacero in 1969; he spent over a decade teaching there. Clips of his hair, his razors, pens, flashlight and false teeth are on display inside the cave. A bronze image of the monk wears his former glasses. A series of full-sized gold Buddha figures line a *naga* staircase to a cave assembly hall where photographs of monks adorn the limestone walls and Buddha icons decorate the altar. Views from the temple grounds are extraordinary any time of day. A 3AM trip to the temple, with your own illumination, is otherworldly as a large bell rings, thus beginning the monk's morning incantations and meditations.

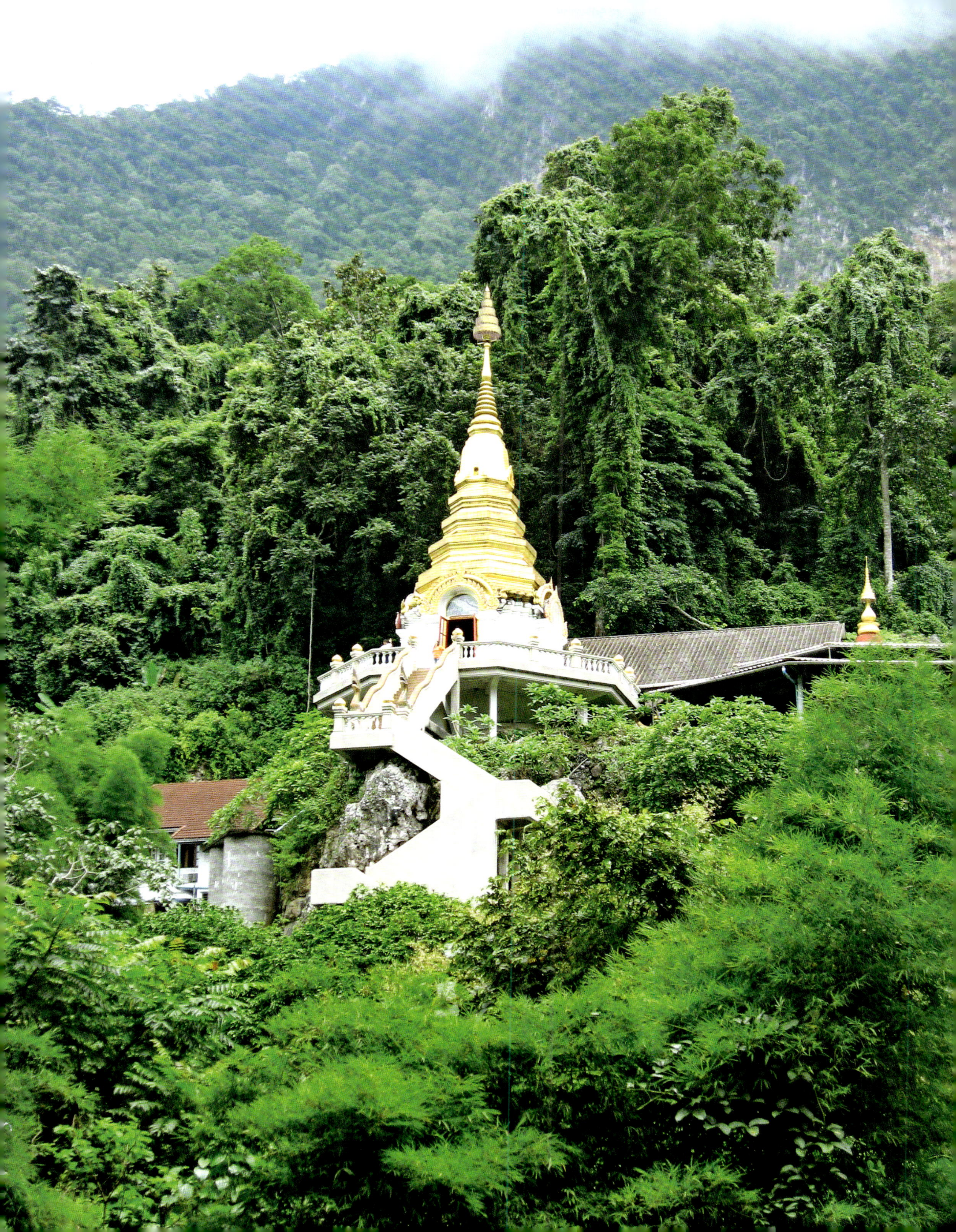

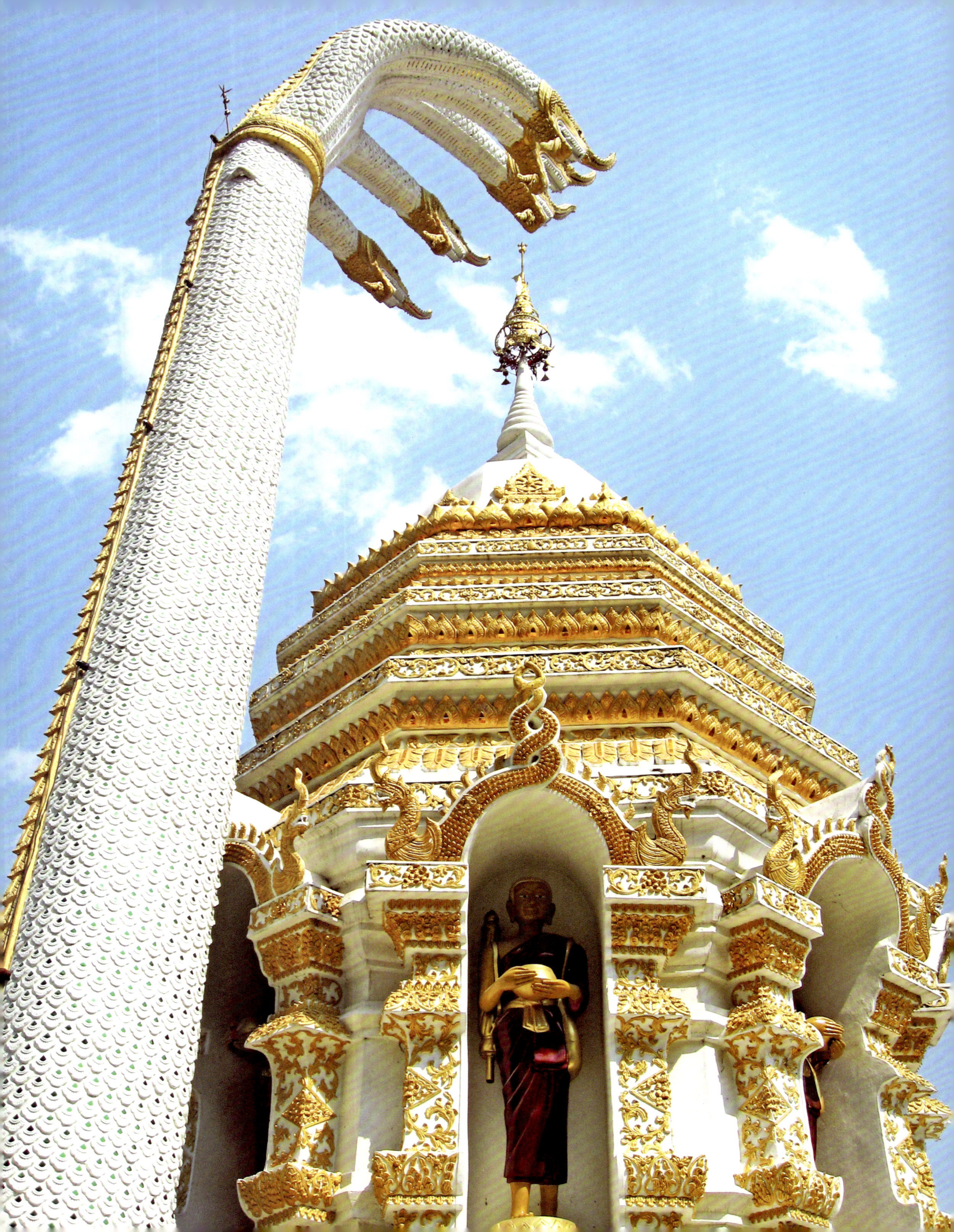

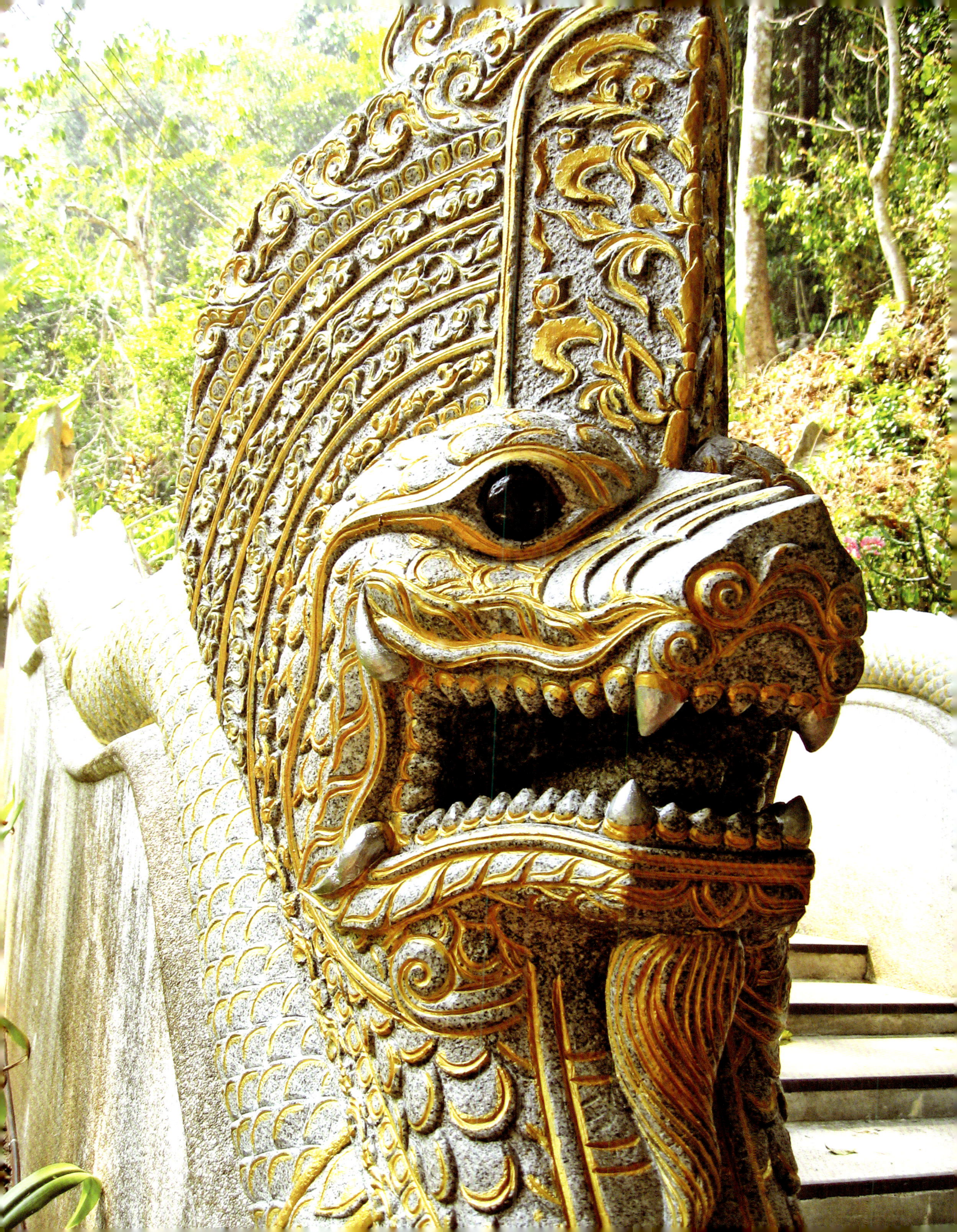

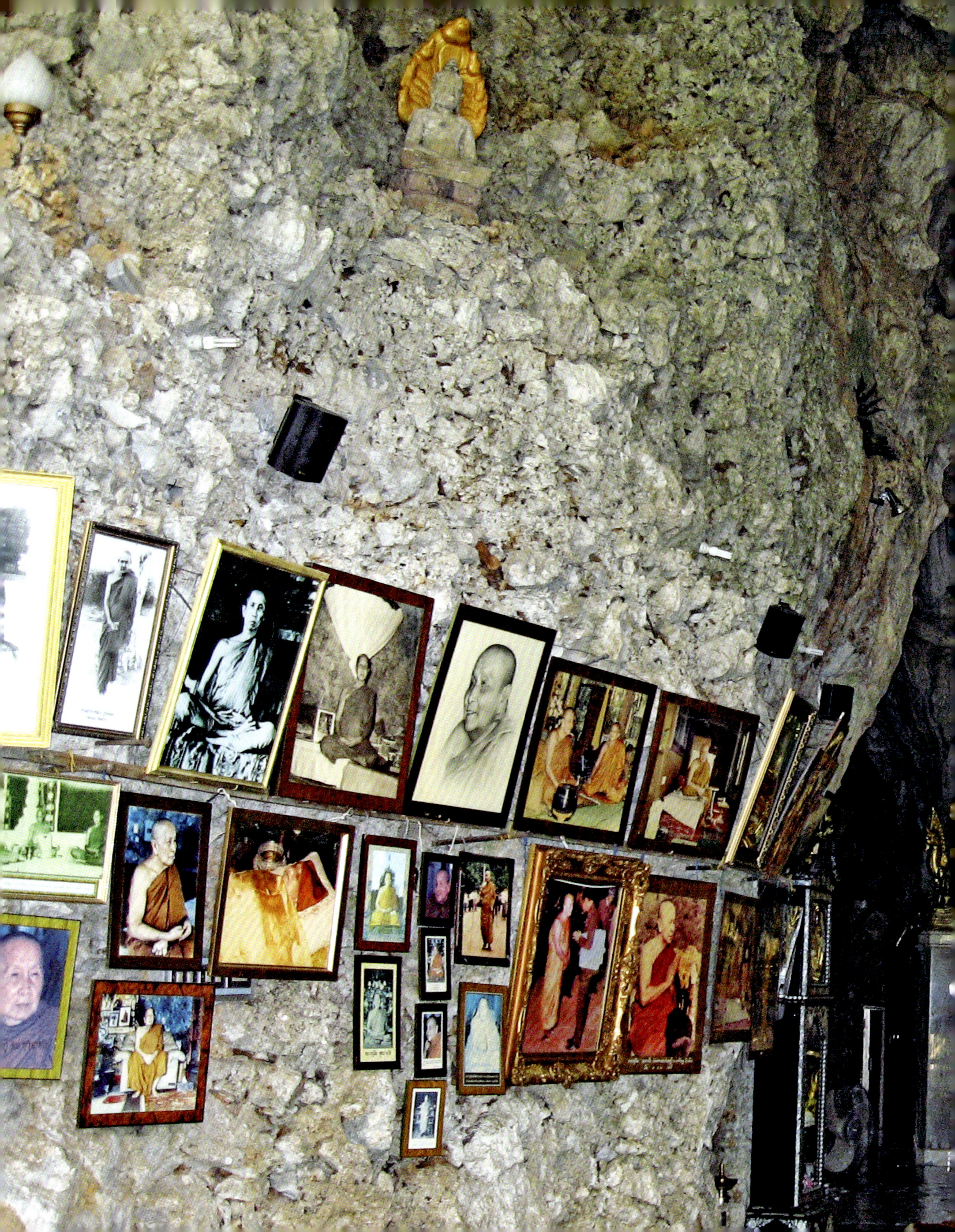

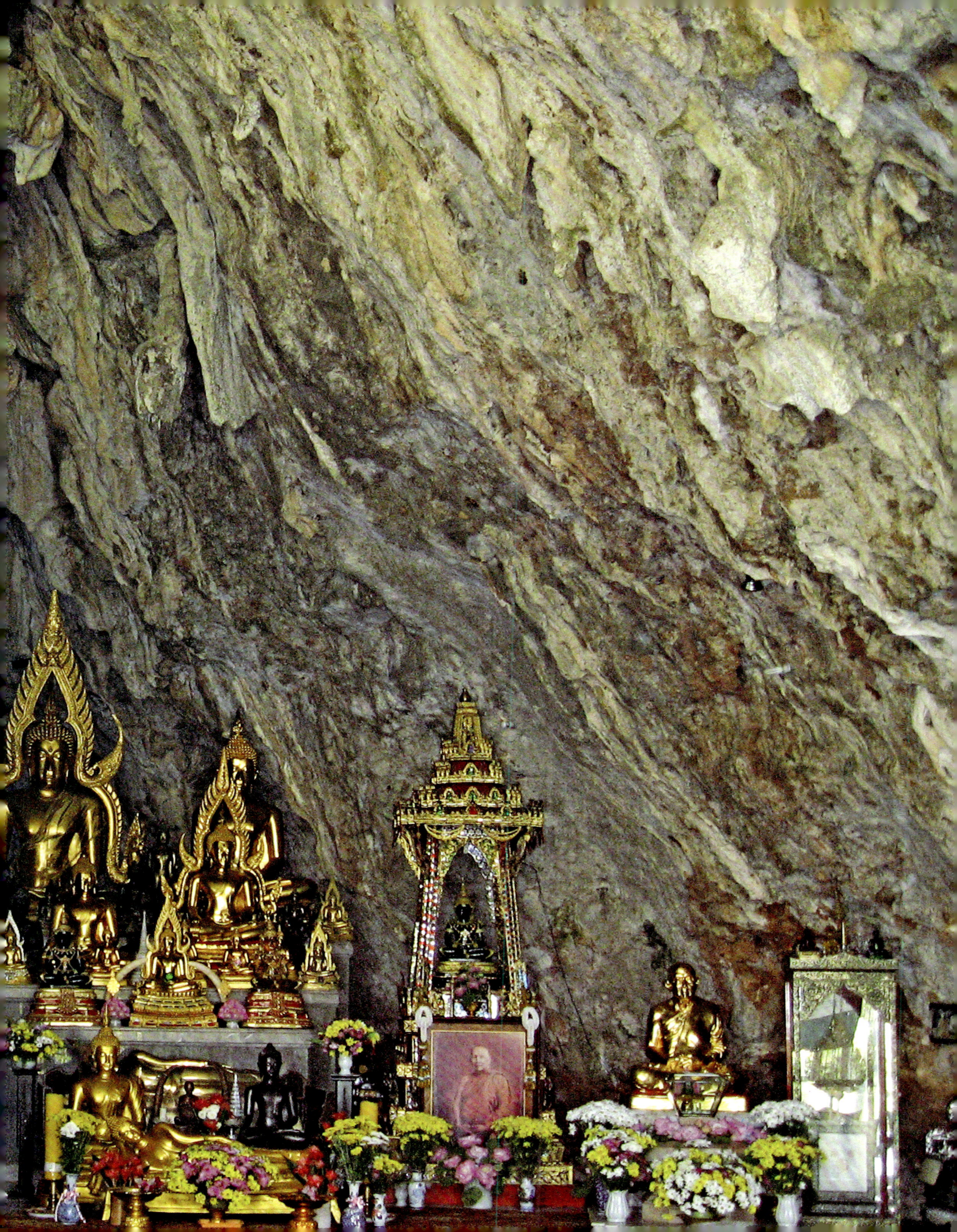

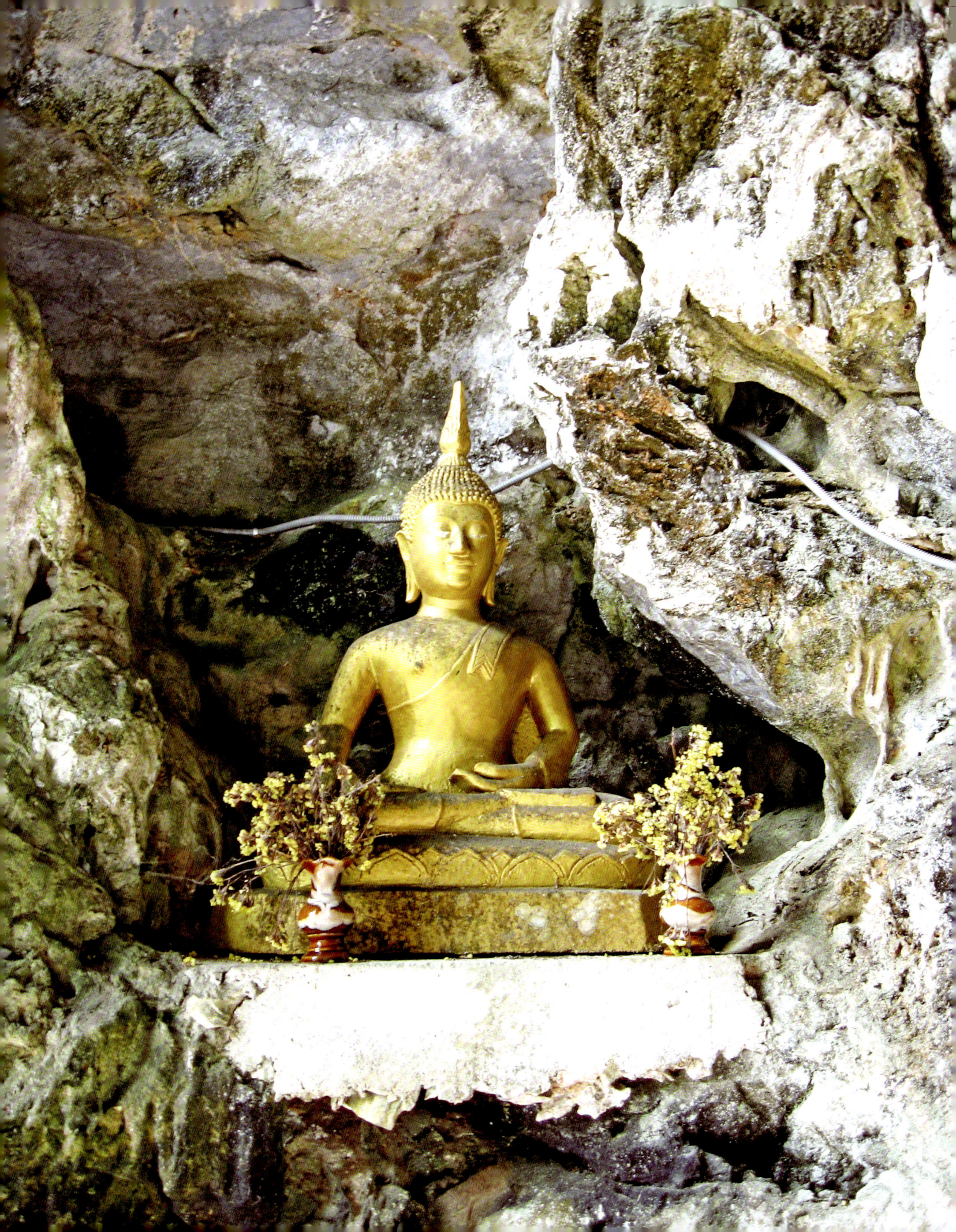

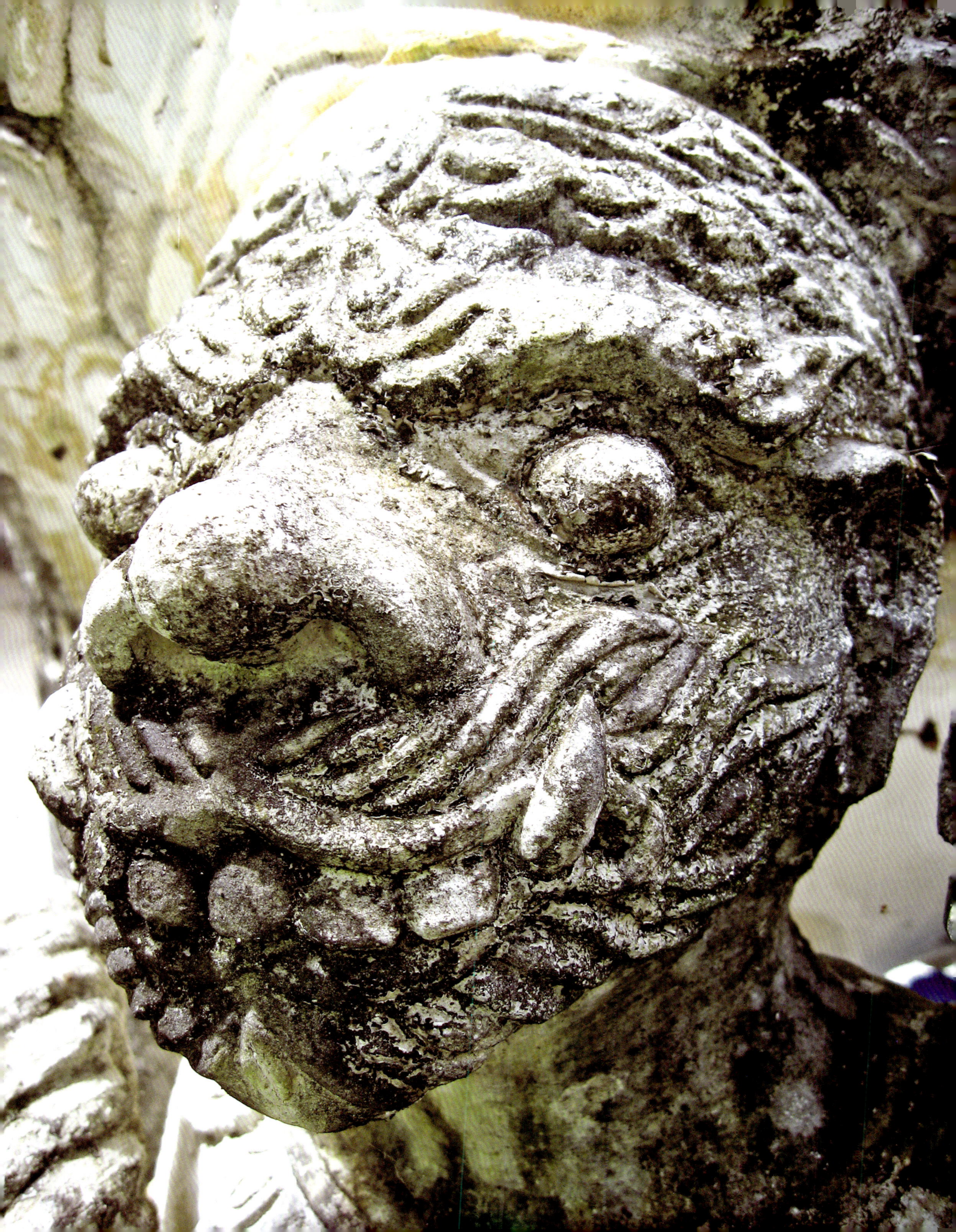

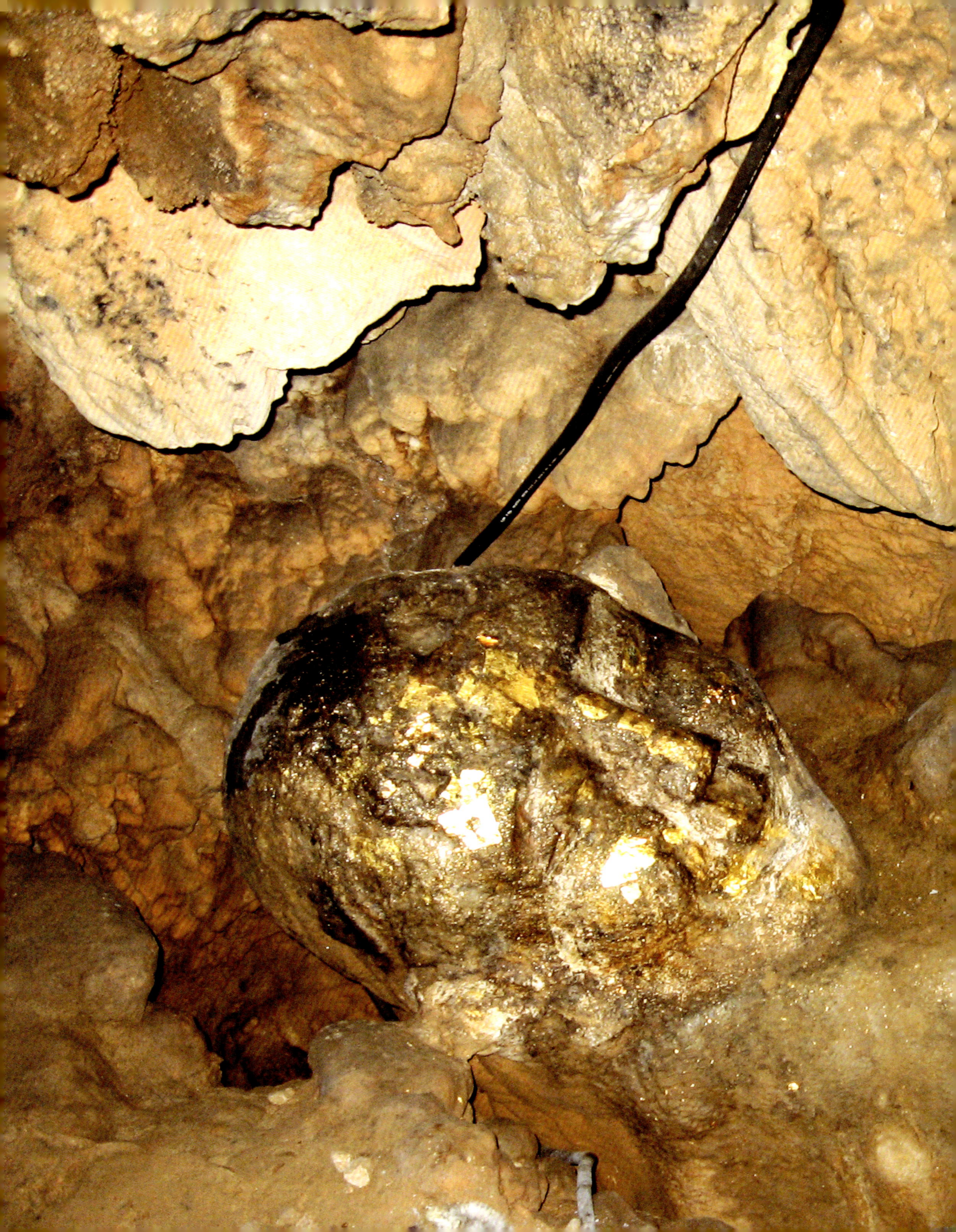

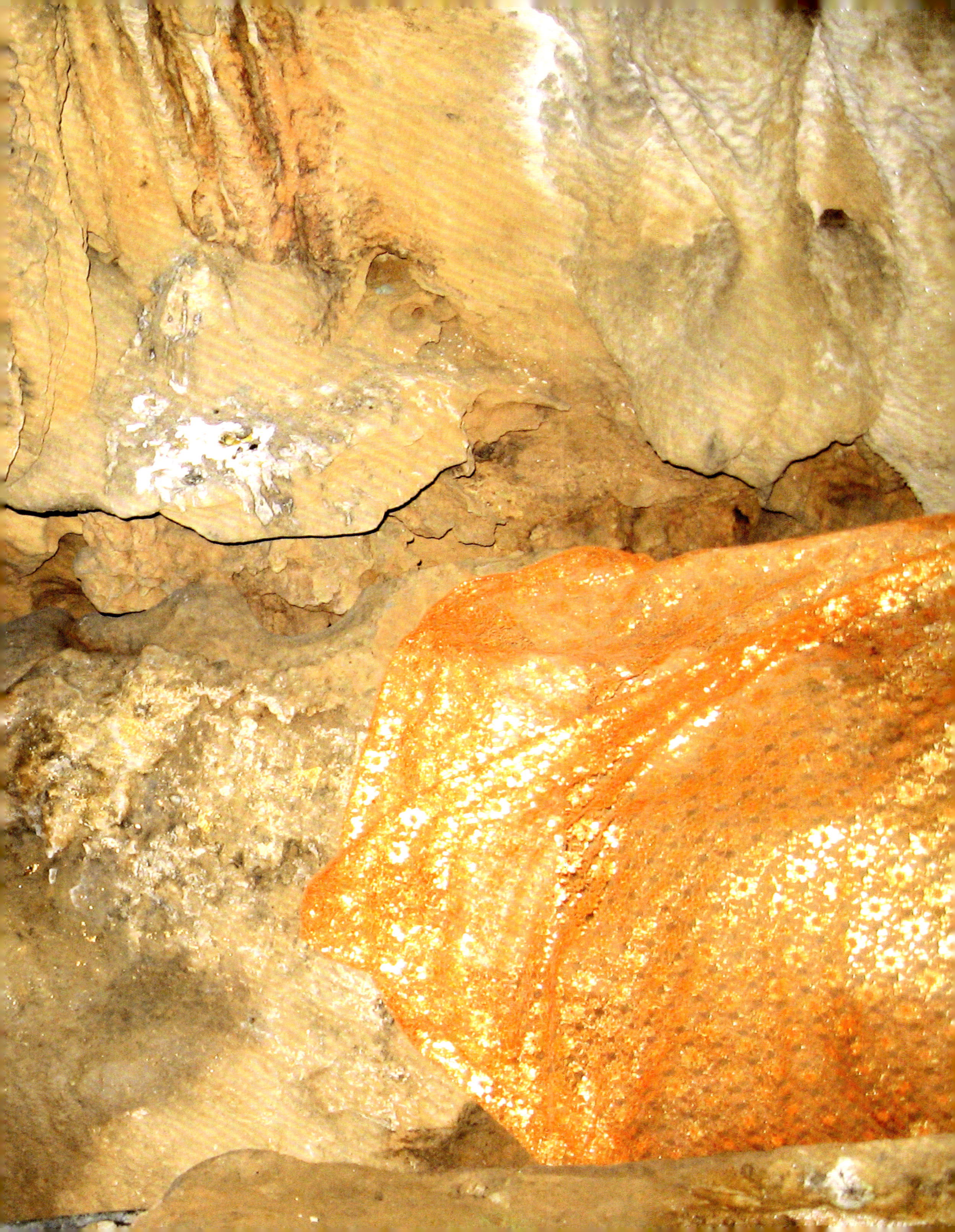

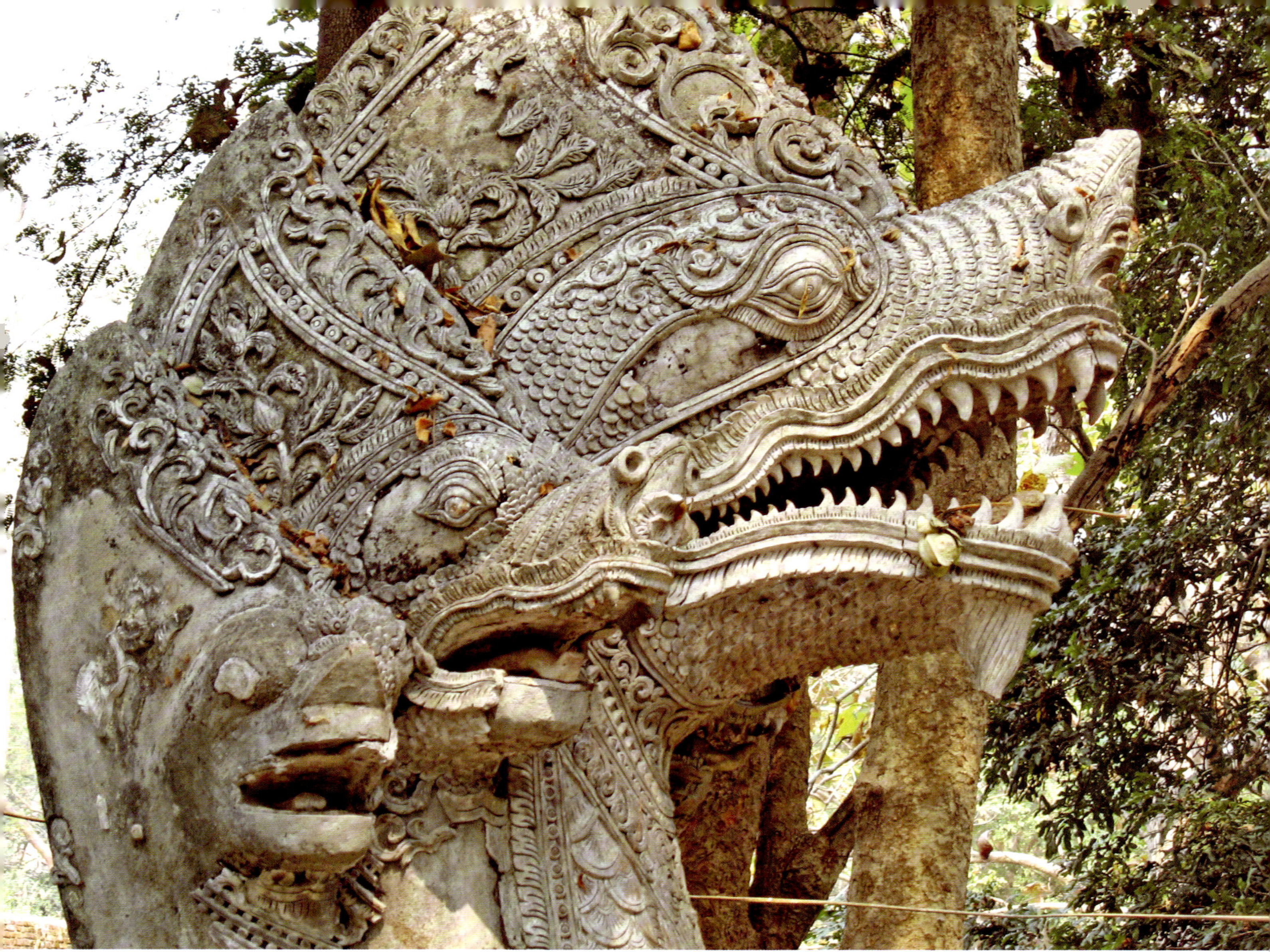

WAT UMONG

King Mangrai, born in 1239, founded the northern Thai city of Chiang Mai in 1296 and later assembled the smaller cities of the region to form the Lanna Thai Kingdom (Land of a Million Rice Fields). Now known as Wat Umong, he built Wat Werukattatharam in 1927, the Temple of the Eleven Clumps of Bamboo. This 15-acre *aranyavasi* forest temple lies west of Chiang Mai at the base of the mountains leading to Doi Suthep and offered a sanctuary for meditation to those already educated in the ways of Buddhism. A brick tunnel (in Thai: *umong*) was constructed at the command of King Kuena (1355 to 1385) to house a discerning seer-monk, Phra Thera Jan; it then became known as Wat Umong or Umong Thera Jan. A giant bell-shaped pagoda or *chedi* resides on a mound above the tunnel, constructed over an earlier *stupa*. The Burmese Mungrai Dynasty conquered Chiang Mai in 1518, and the temple was abandoned for over two centuries. In 1948, Thai prince Jao Chun Sirorot began reconstructing the temple; in the late 1960s he began collecting broken Buddha images sculpted between 1400 to 1550 A.D. from deserted monasteries in the Phayao provinces. Nearby residents bring small broken headless Buddha figures or plastic figurines to the temple, as it would be bad luck to destroy such icons. Along the outer wall of the monastery, people have created a spirit house graveyard near a Bodhi tree (see **Spirit House** chapter). A black Fasting Buddha sculpture also adorns the grounds. A gallery of paintings by former monks is surrounded by a series of reproductions of ancient Indian Buddhist sculpture (see **Temple Art** chapter). A series of proverbs attached to trees written in Thai and English line a path to a small lake where one can feed fish, birds and turtles, offering words of wisdom such as "The thing that is liked or disliked just appears, exists for a moment, then expires," and "Nothing is permanent. Things come in and go out." Stranger yet are a series of sayings painted on sheets of metal below posters of dogs shown smoking and gambling, driving motorcycles, or betting on cock fights, stating "A moral life in poverty is more noble than an immoral one in affluence," or "Tomorrow I shall do good! – This is a fool's word. Even today is a bit too late. A wise man did good yesterday."

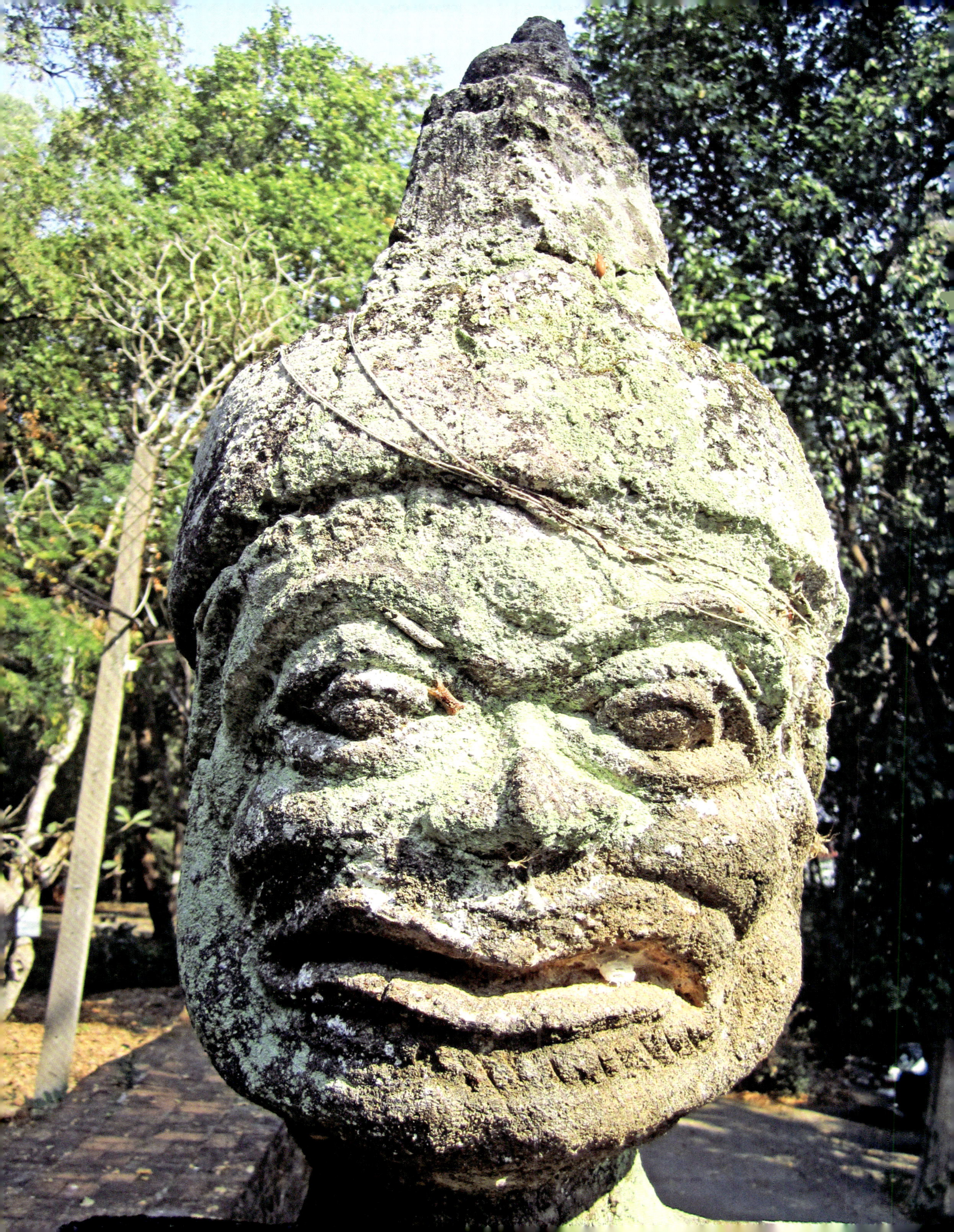

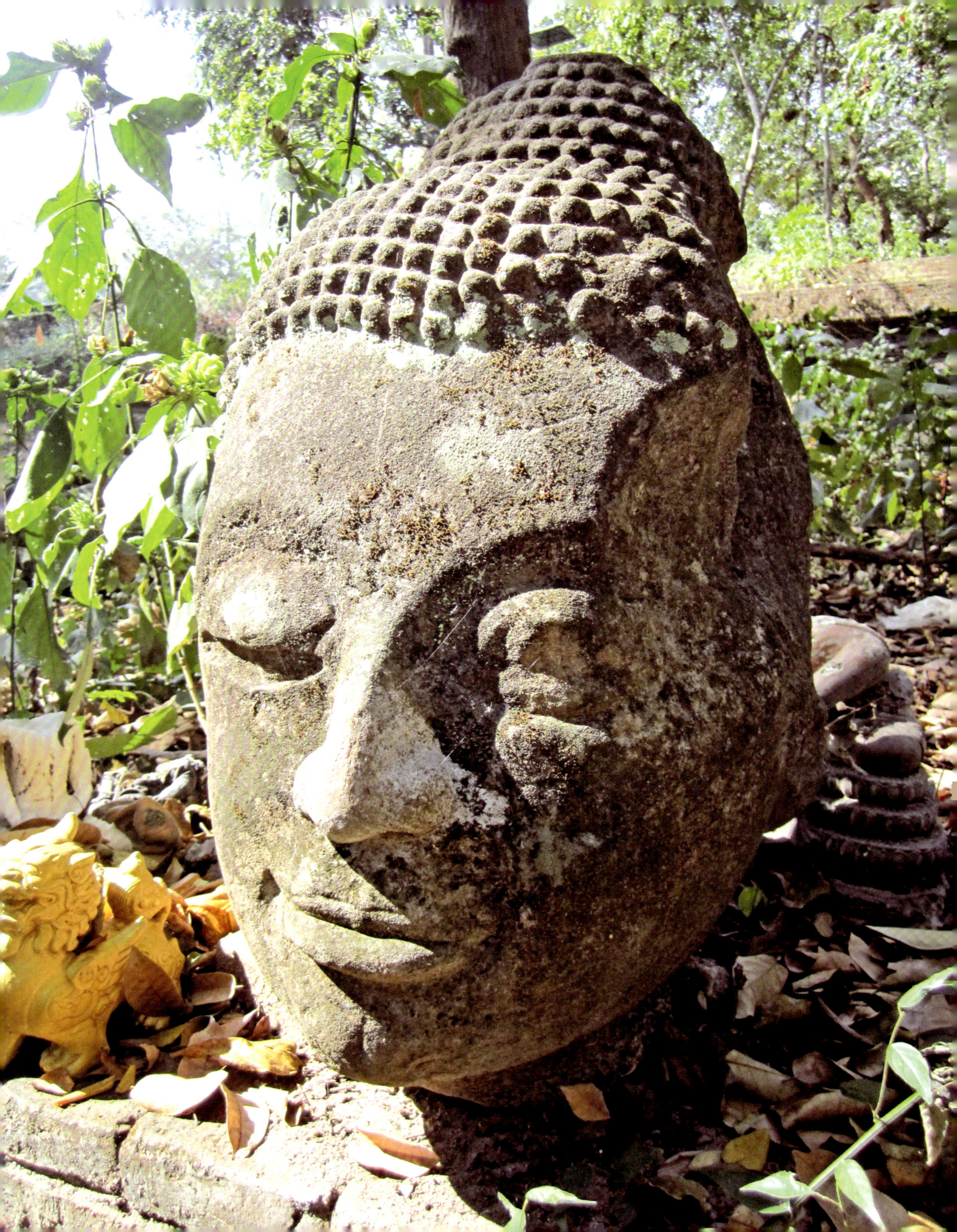

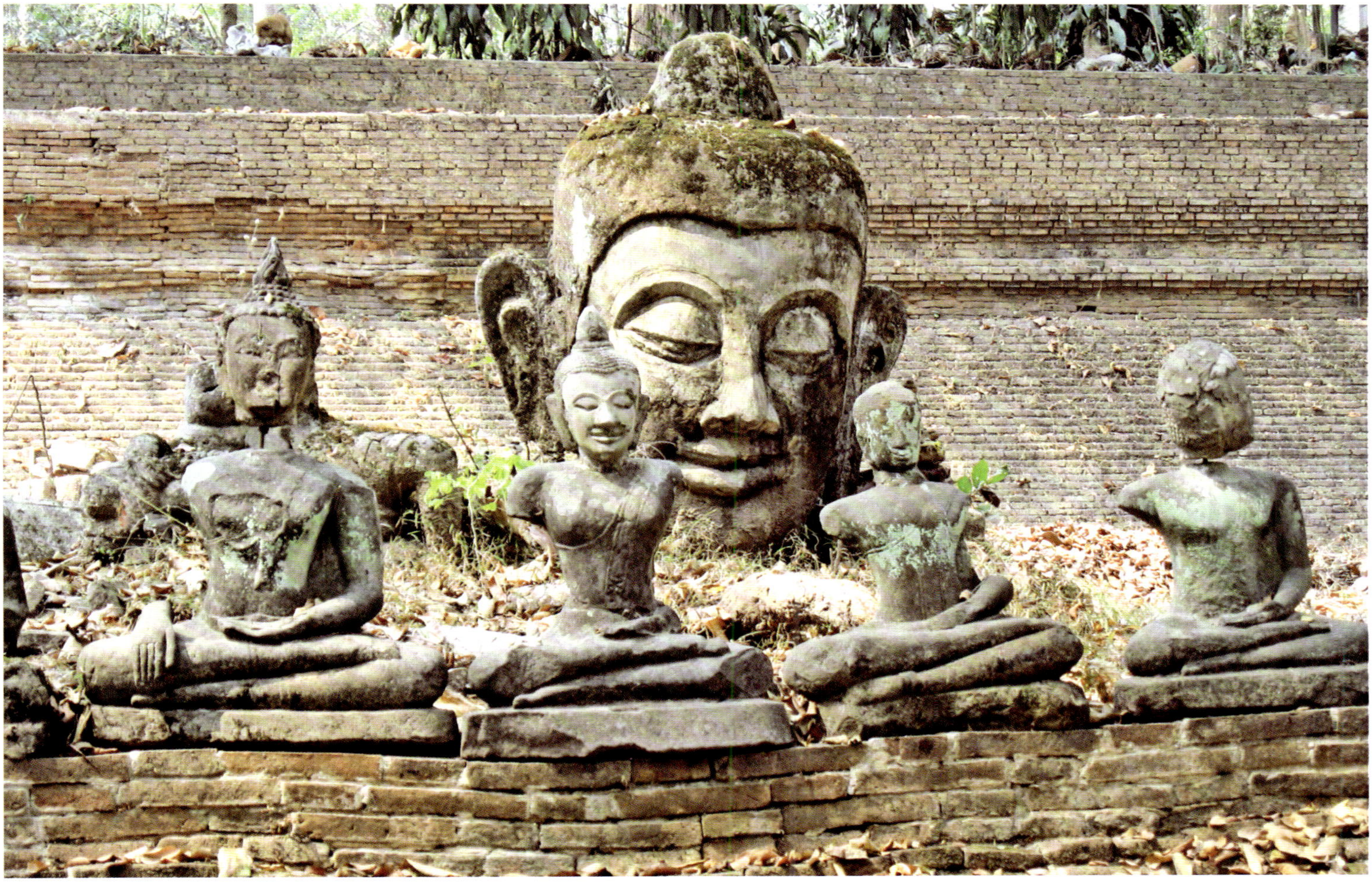

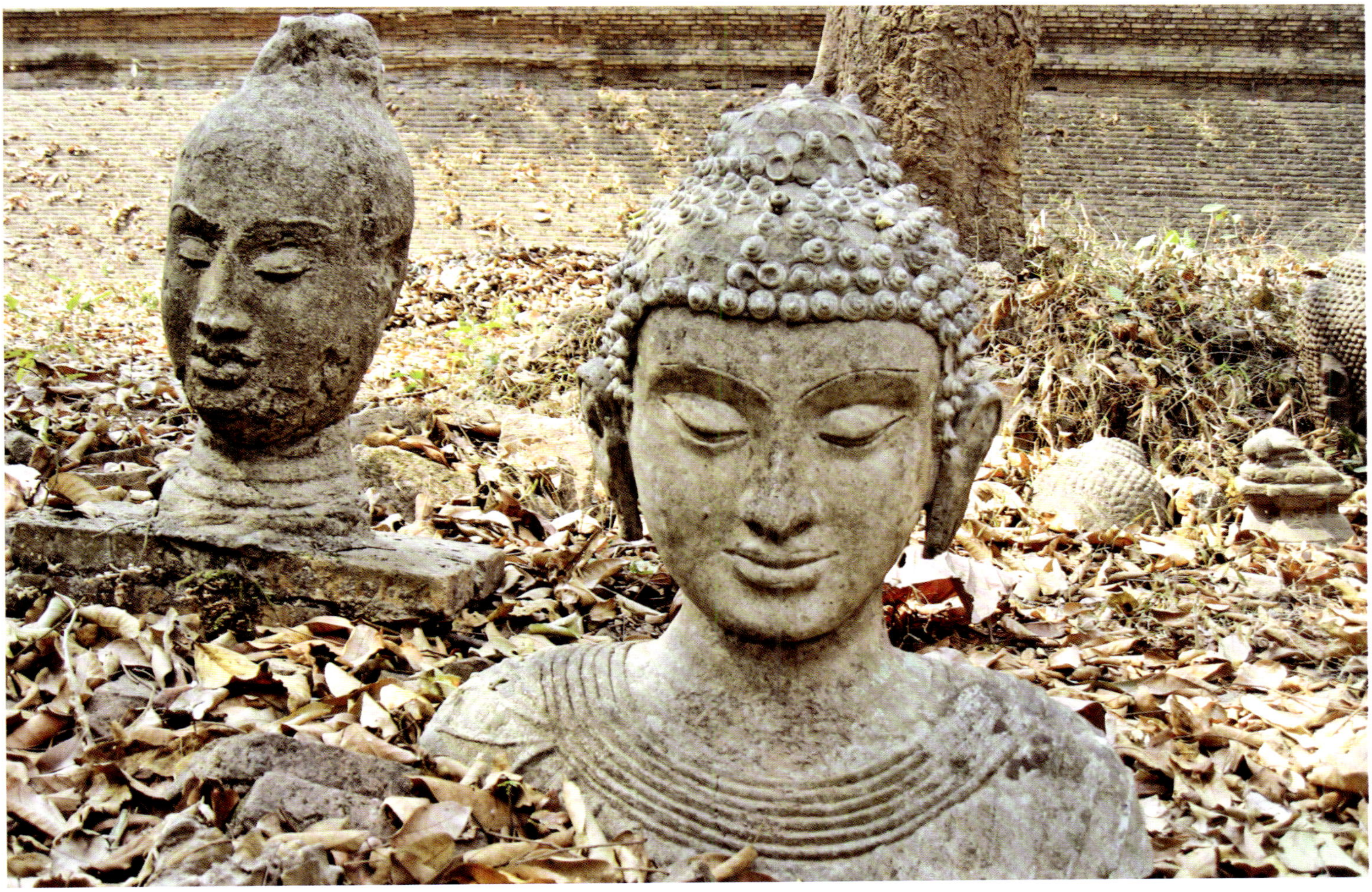

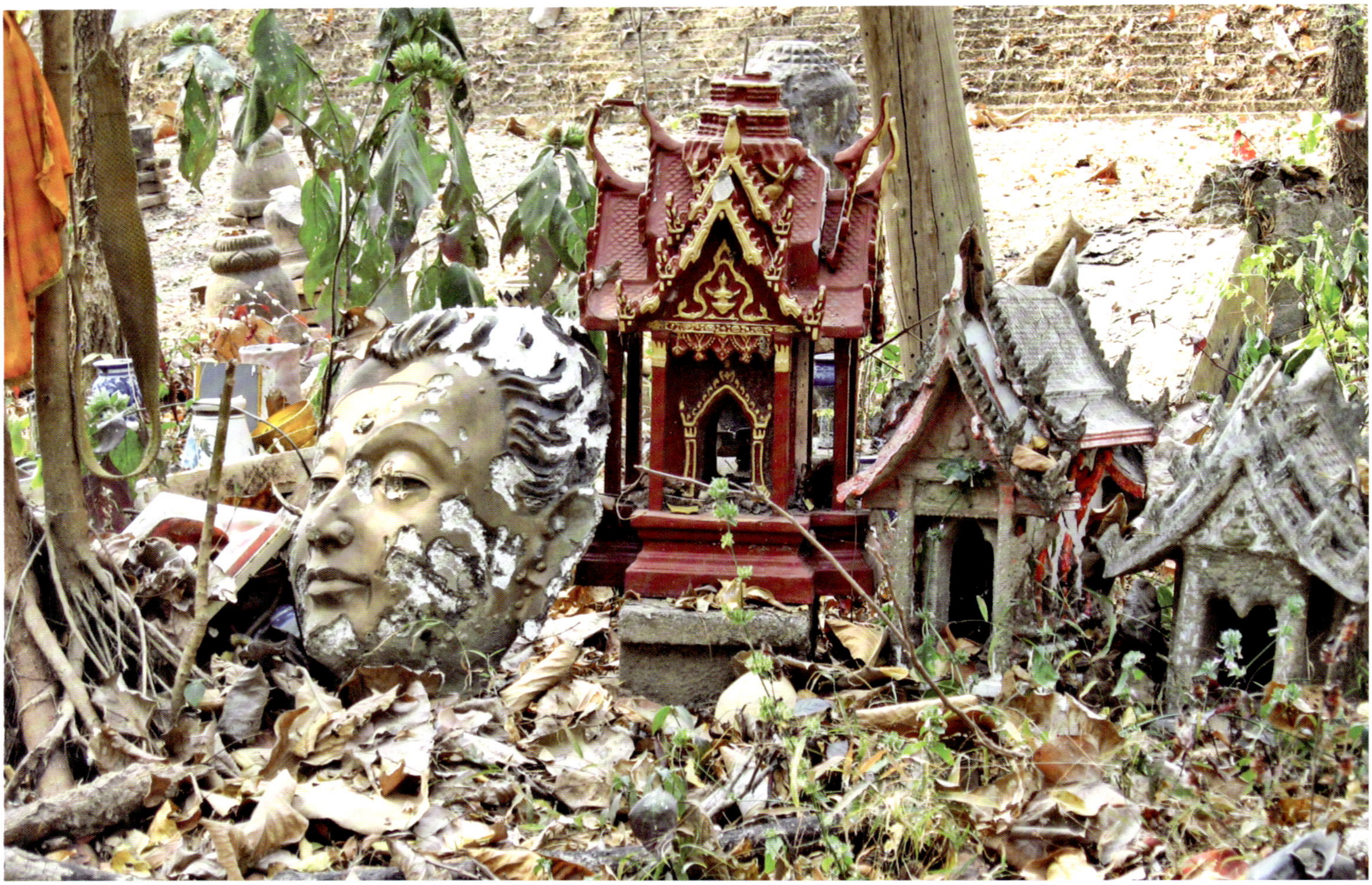

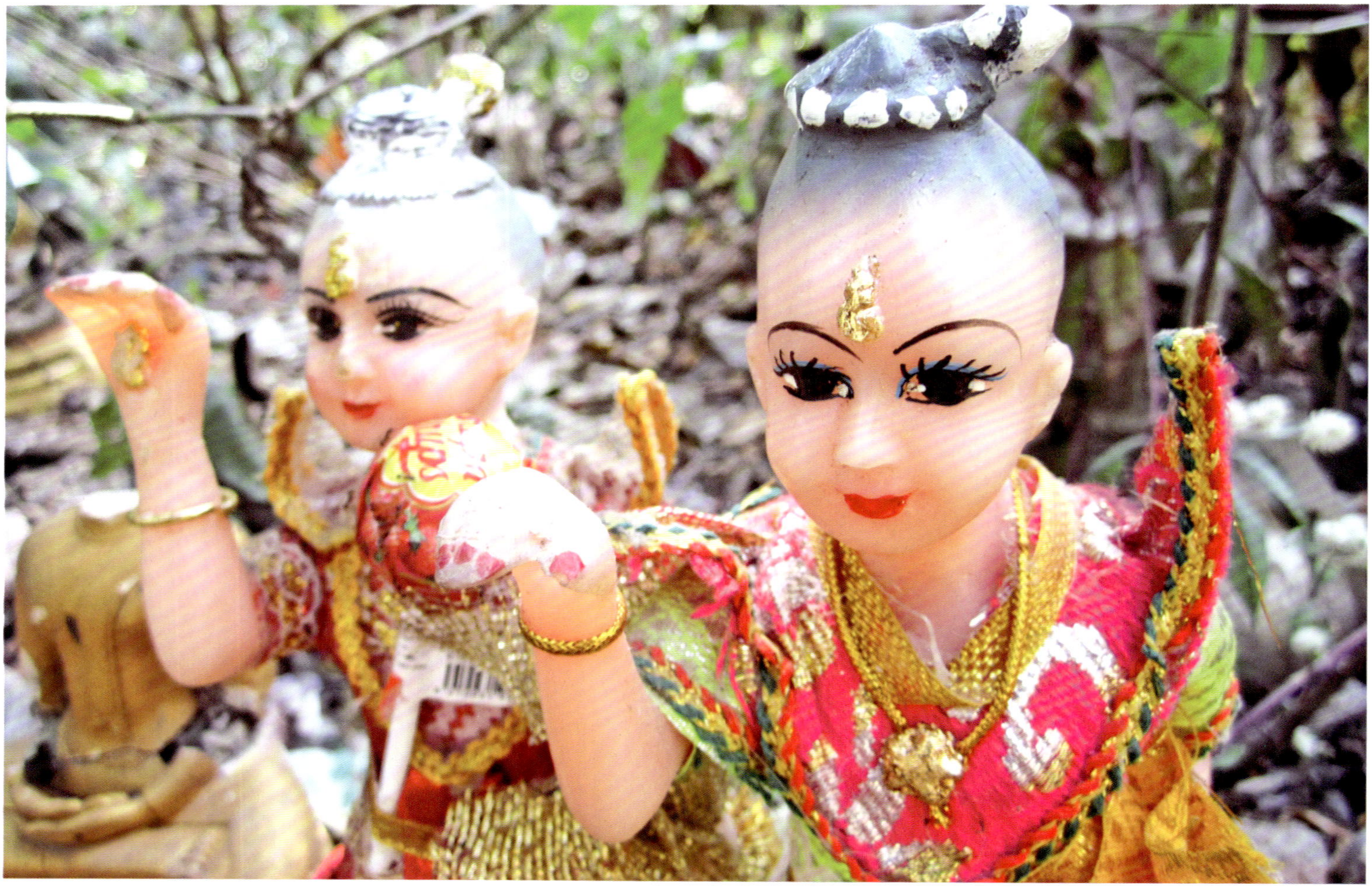

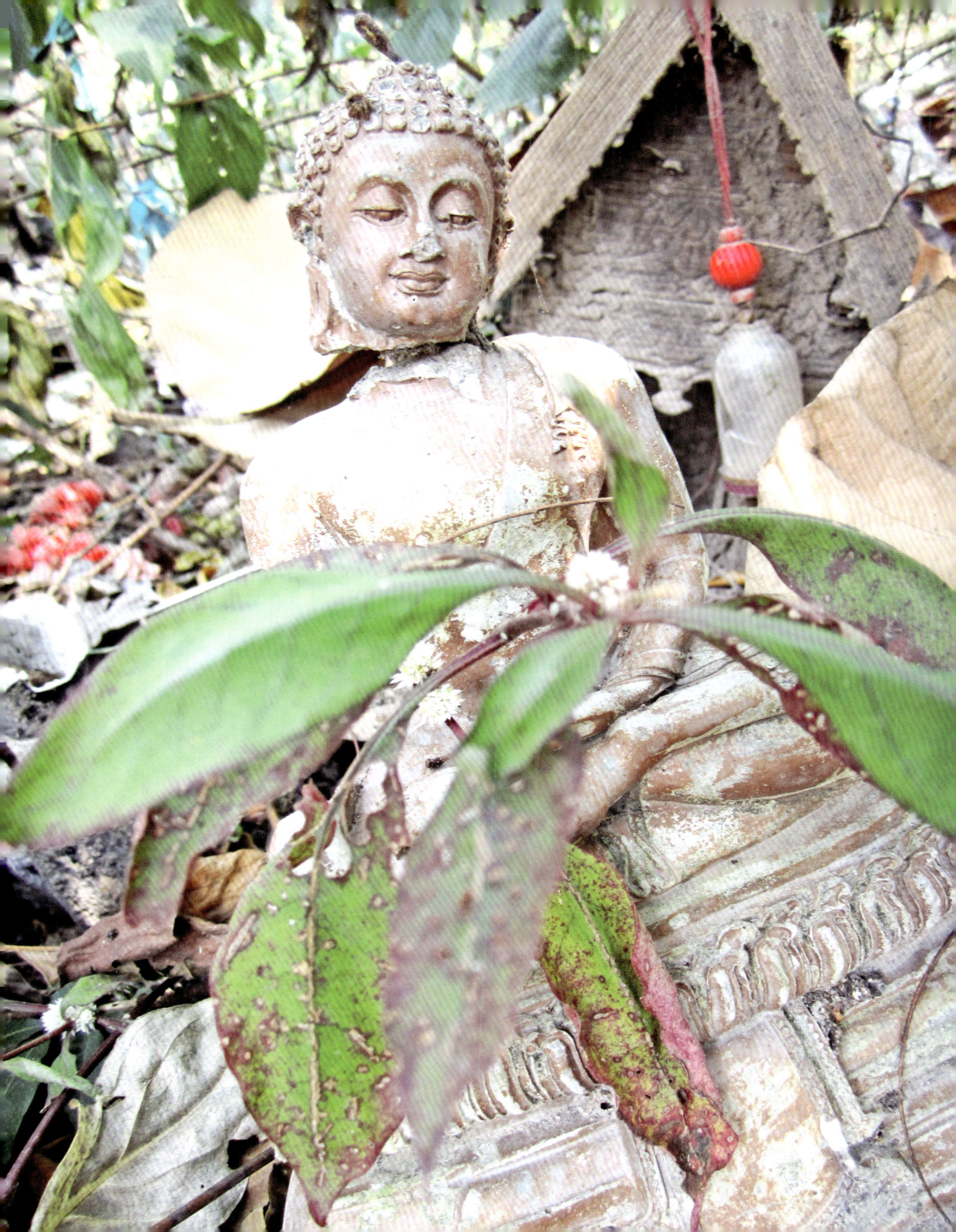

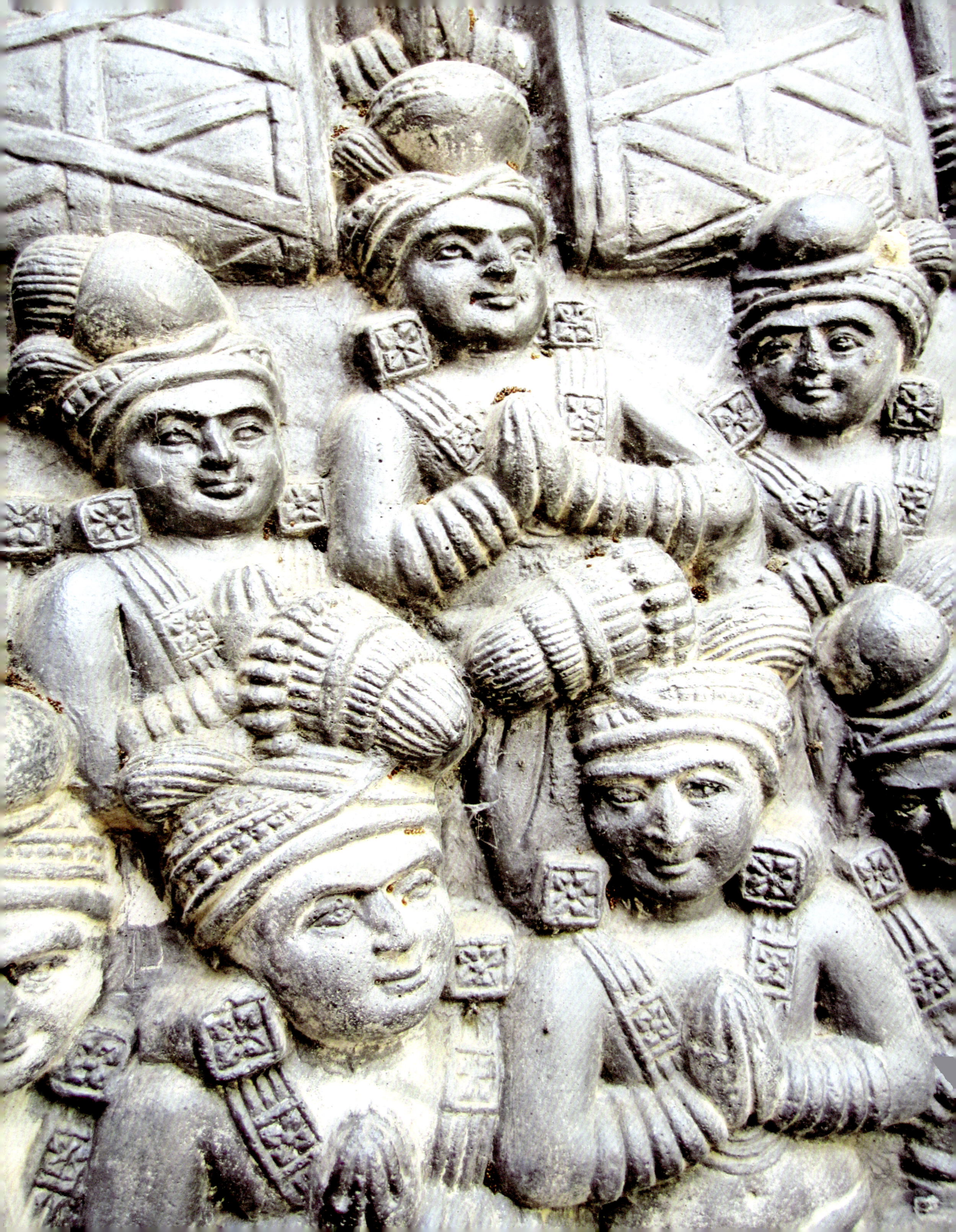

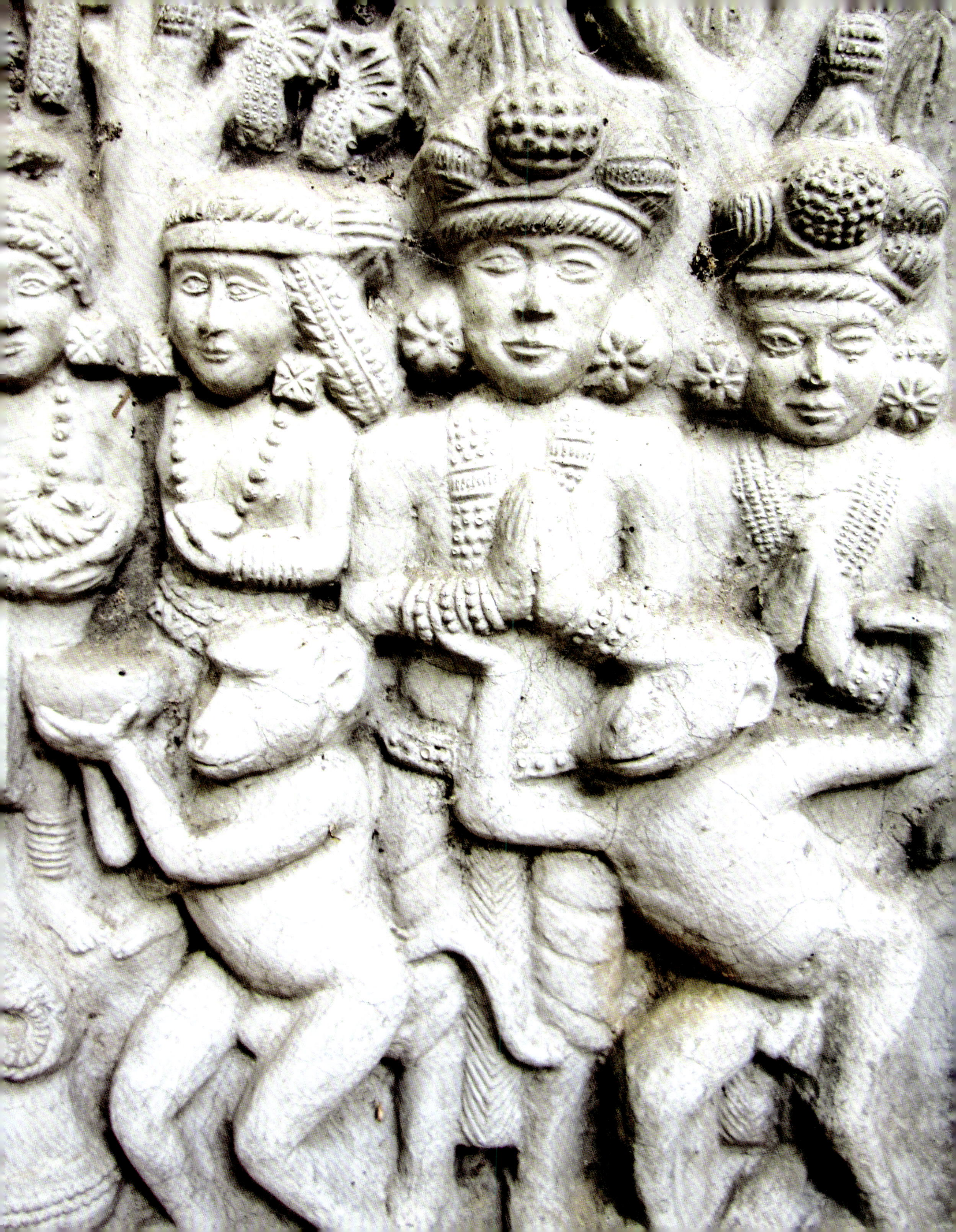

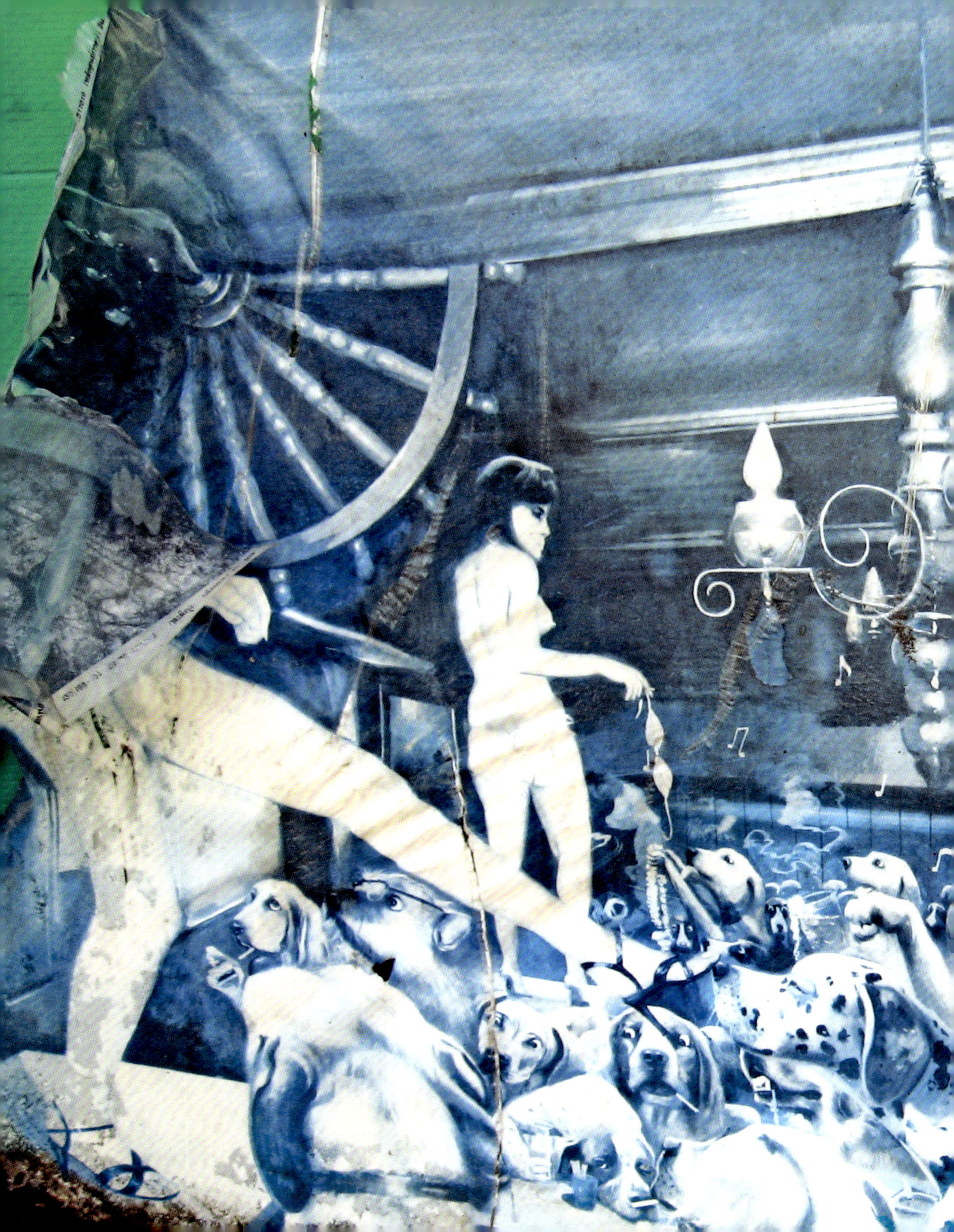

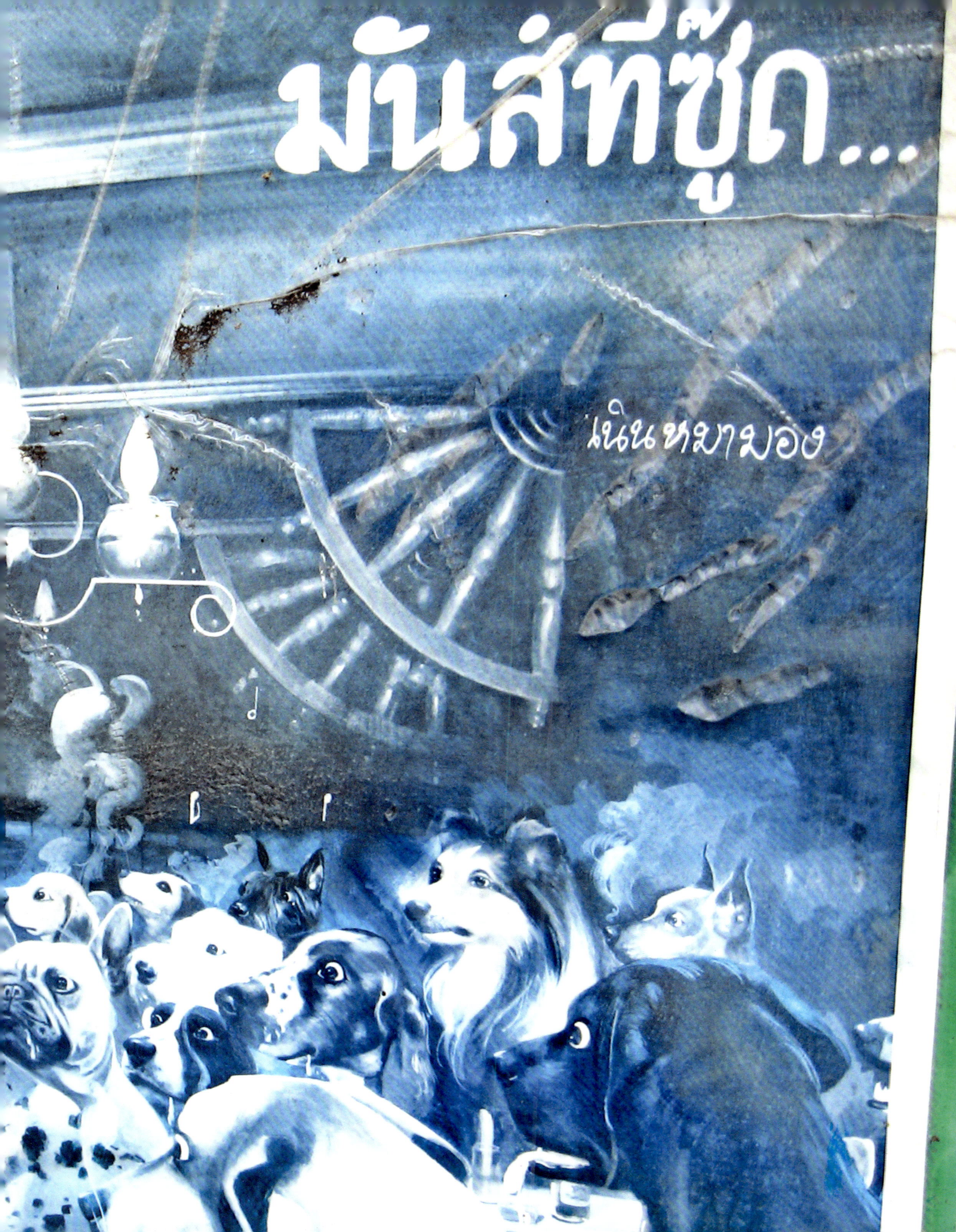
มันส์ที่ซู๊ด...
เนินหมามอง

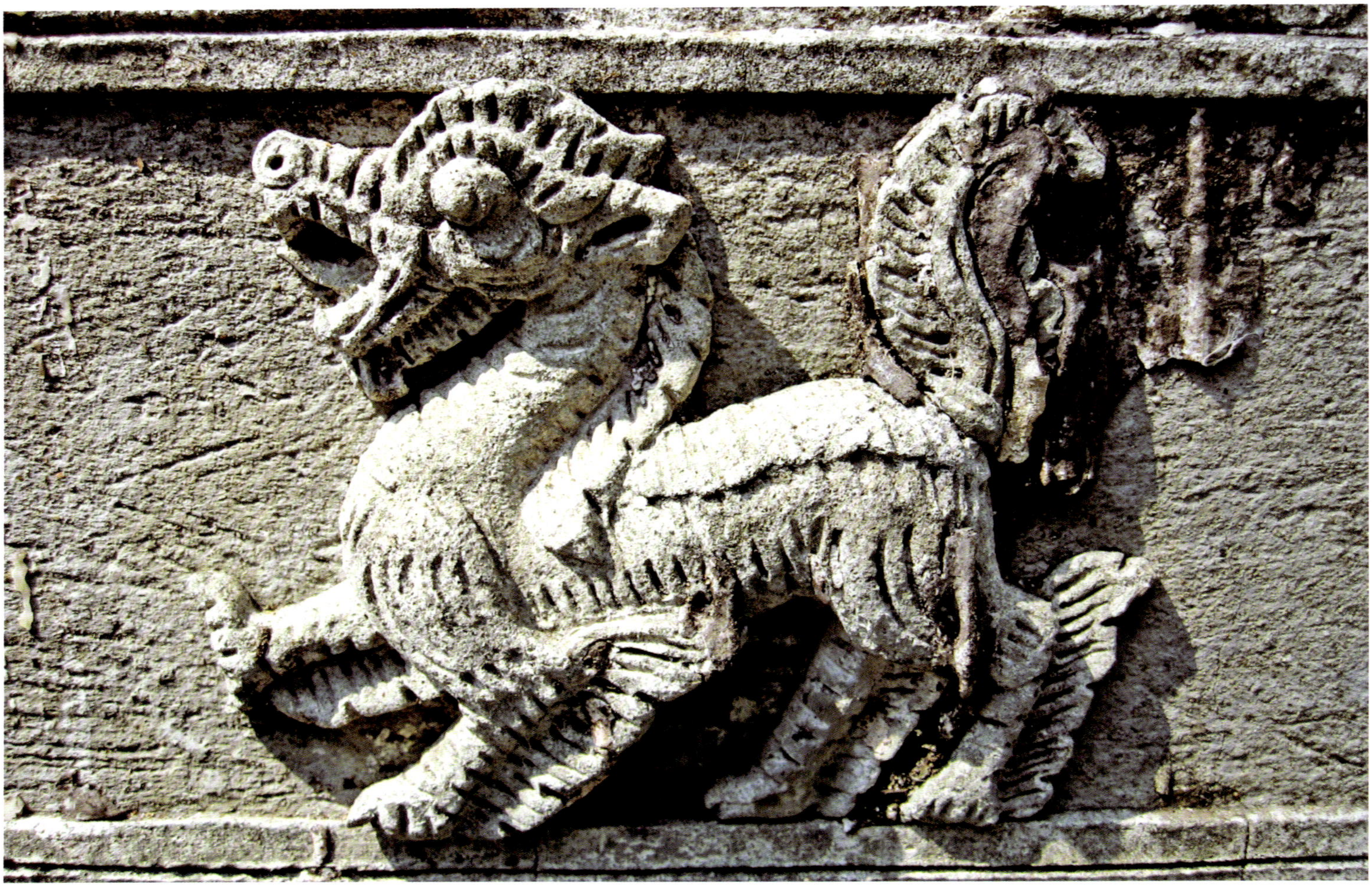

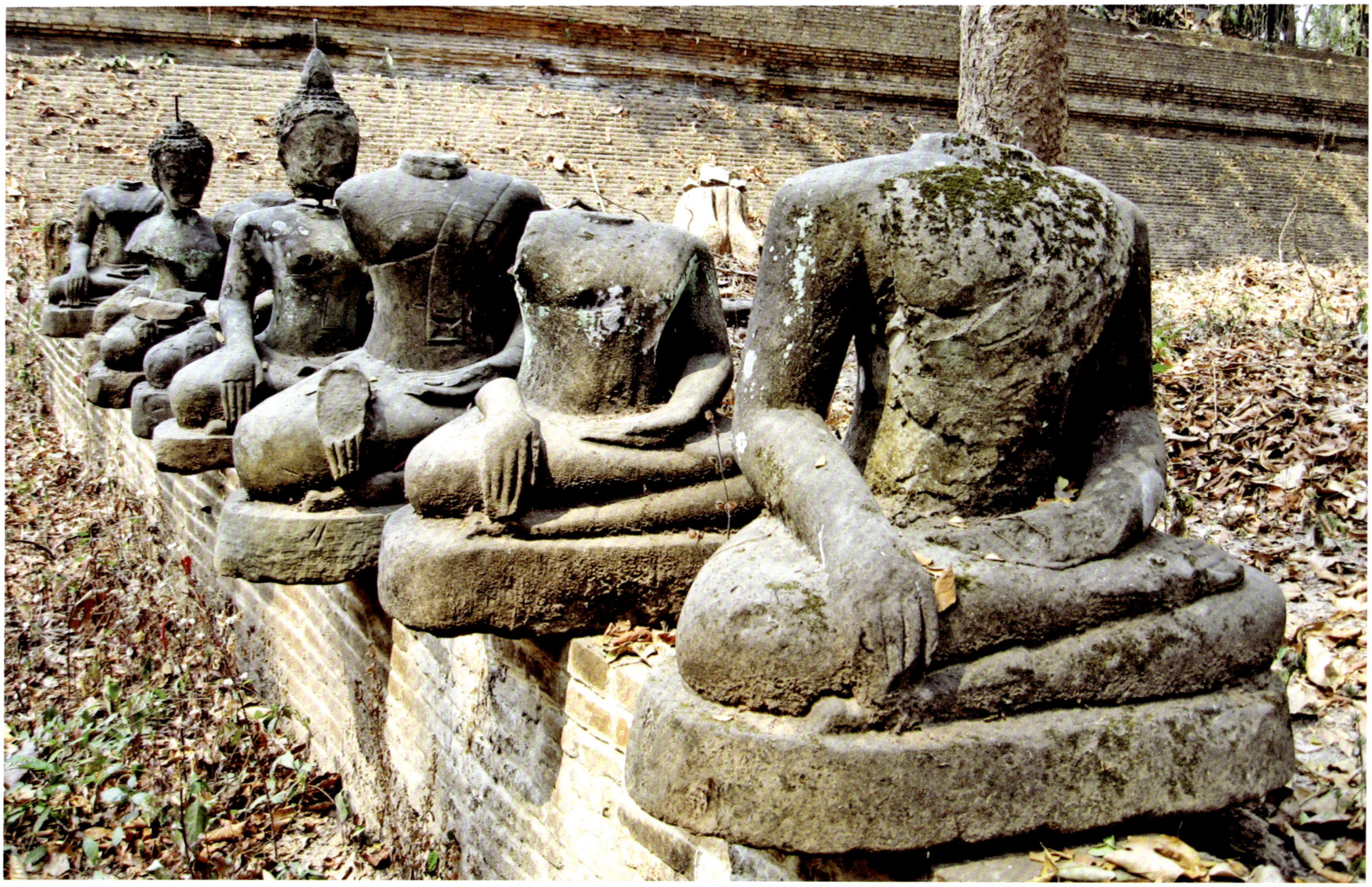

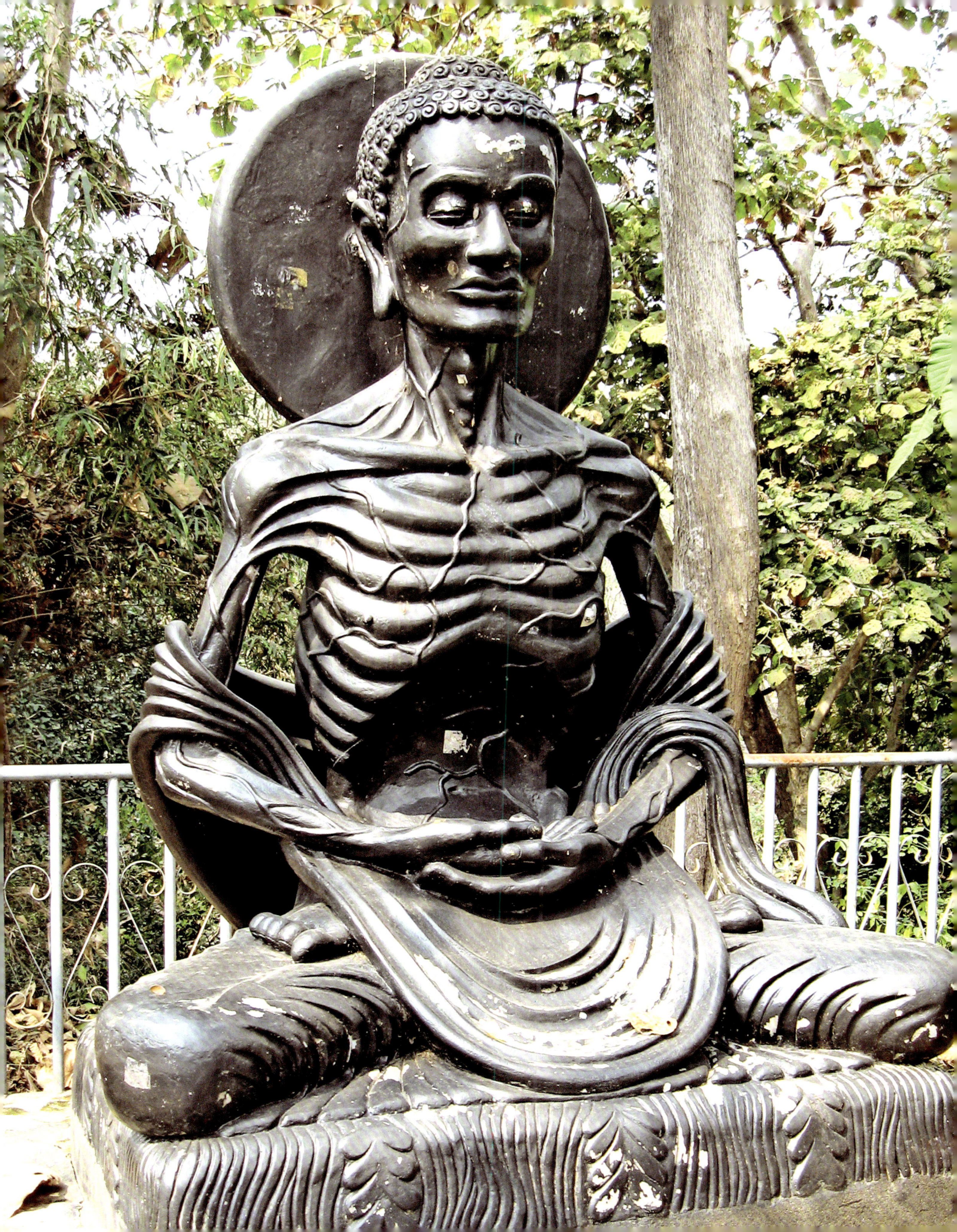

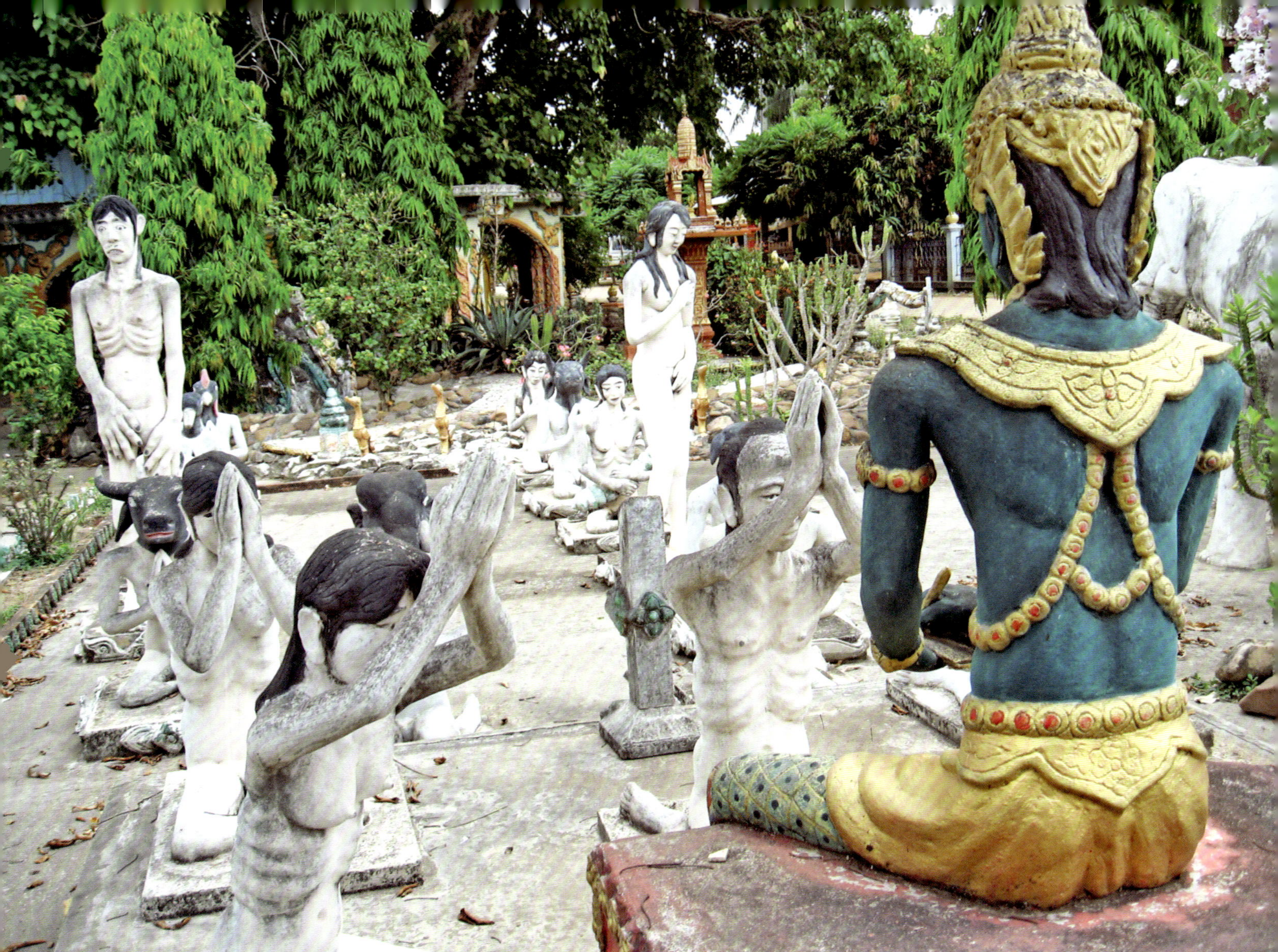

WAT THAWET

In Sukothai lies Wat Thawet, a temple with a Buddhist Hell Garden. Abbot Phra Sumroeng Thamanantho took over a rundown monastery in 1976 and began constructing what he called a Buddhist Learning Garden, based on visions from his dreams. Later, he built his own tomb on the temple grounds where his ashes were placed in 1995. His son, also a monk, runs the temple and supports his father's dream (Wild, 2012, para 4).

Four *naga*-protected staircases lead to a three-tiered pagoda decorated with hundreds of Buddha images. Beyond the pagoda, life-sized cement dioramas detail scenes from the *Jatakas*: Buddha attended by a monkey and elephant, the defeat of Mara depicted as two four-armed demons on elephants, the cutting of the Buddha's hair. In a scene from the *Ramakien*, the four-faced Brahma, Indra and Rama, kneel in front of a gold figure. Next, one encounters the torso of a man with ancient script tattooed on his chest. Nearby is a praying figure of Anguimala, wearing a dark finger garland necklace collected from 999 victims. He intended to make the Buddha his 1,000th victim but the Buddha forgave him, despite his evil deeds, and taught him how to foreswear violence on all living things. A green-skinned Yama, the wrathful god of *Narok* (hell), presides over emaciated sinners, pleading hands in a *wai* above their head, awaiting judgment for transgressions against the five precepts of Buddhism. Rebirth continues until enlightenment is reached; Yama determines where a being goes next. Hell has eight pits, each with 16 subsections, totaling 136 levels of karmic retribution, the lowest a dark frozen hell for those who disrespect or murder their parents or monks.

Buddhist hell is similar to Christian purgatory, as residency is not permanent but lasts until the negative effects of one's actions are exhausted, however long that may be. Kneeling figures of reincarnated sinners with animal heads as punishment abound: a pig for the corrupt, a bird for rice thieves, bulls and a rooster. Alcoholics are force-fed boiling liquids. South of Bangkok, Wat Wang Saen Suk is a larger, more gory version of the hell temple as folk art morality tale, but Wat Thawet is the effort of one man's vision. Actions have consequences that must be atoned for, and one can alleviate suffering tomorrow by making merit today.

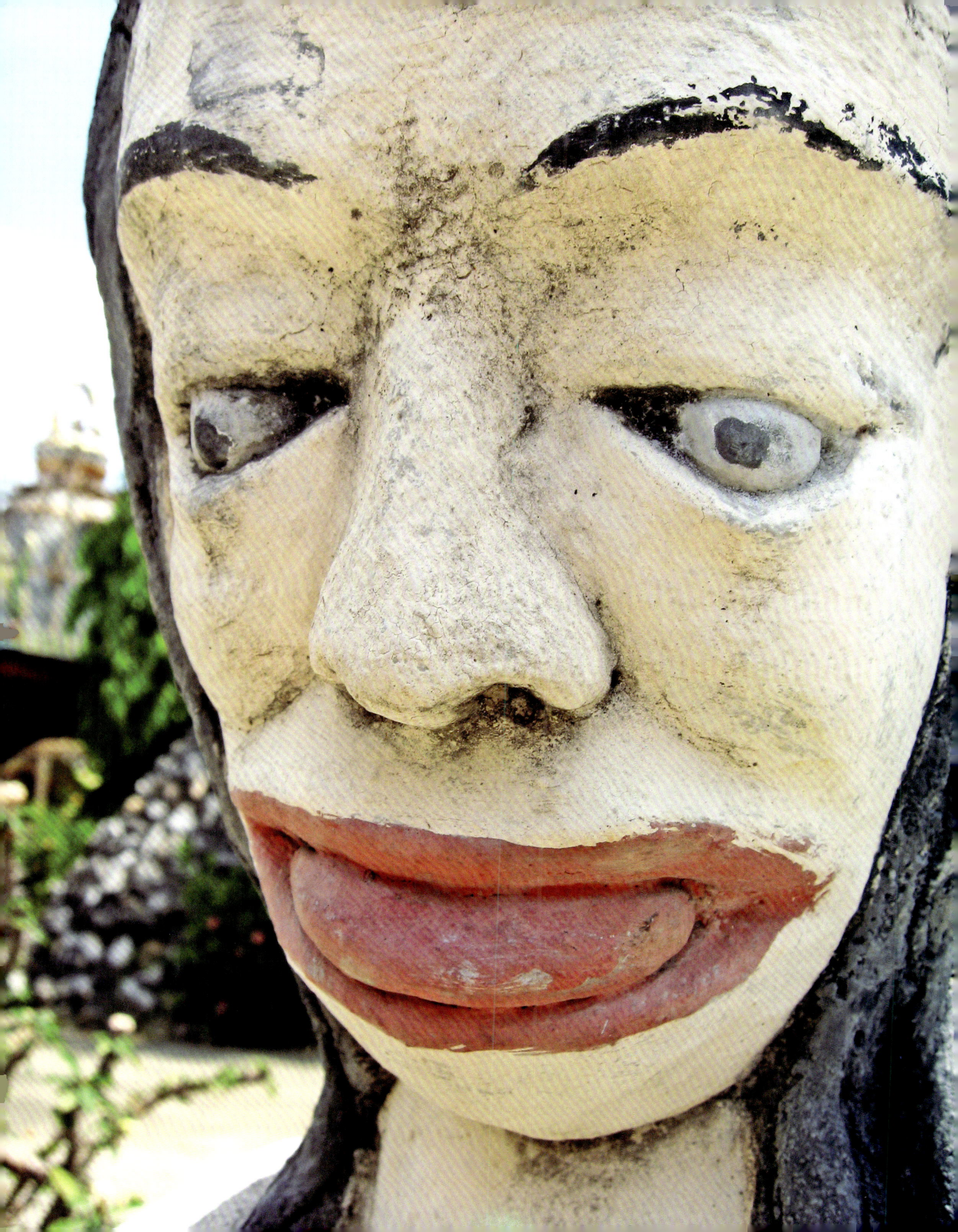

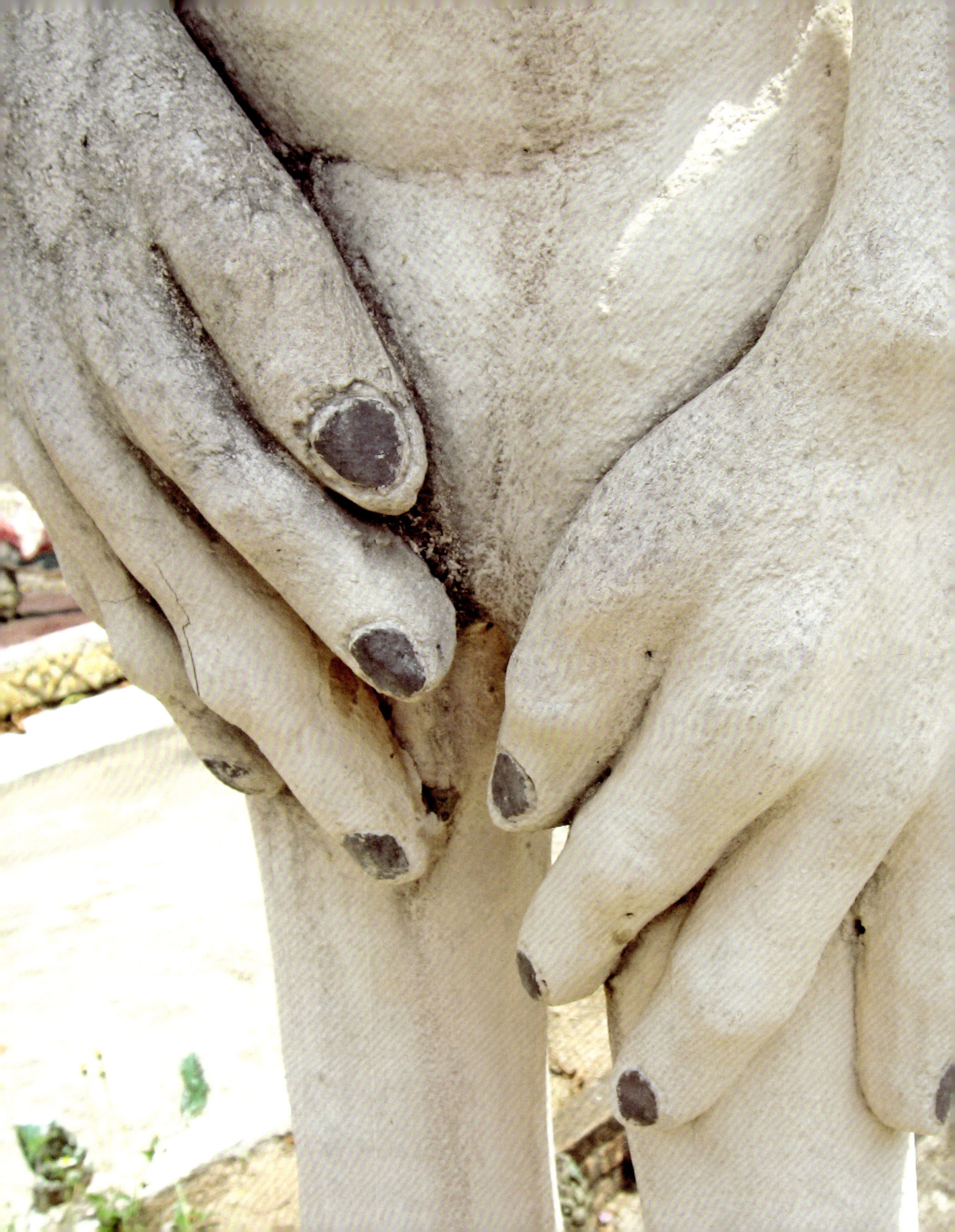

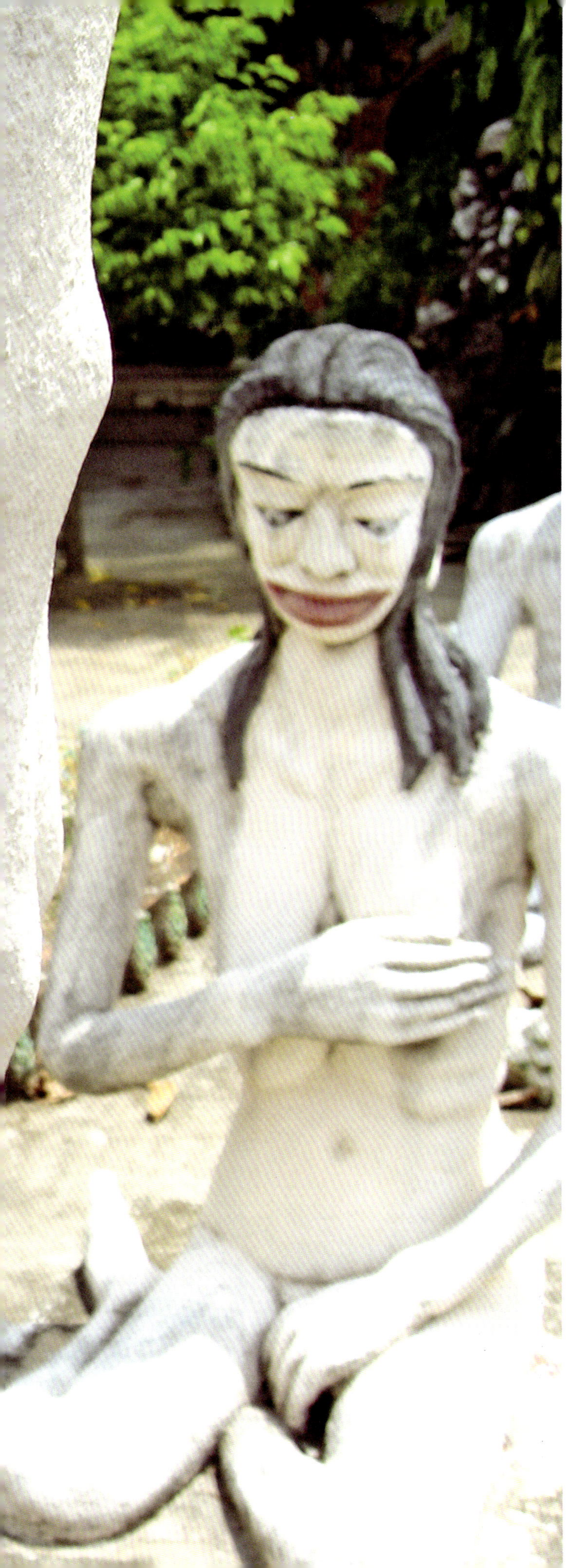

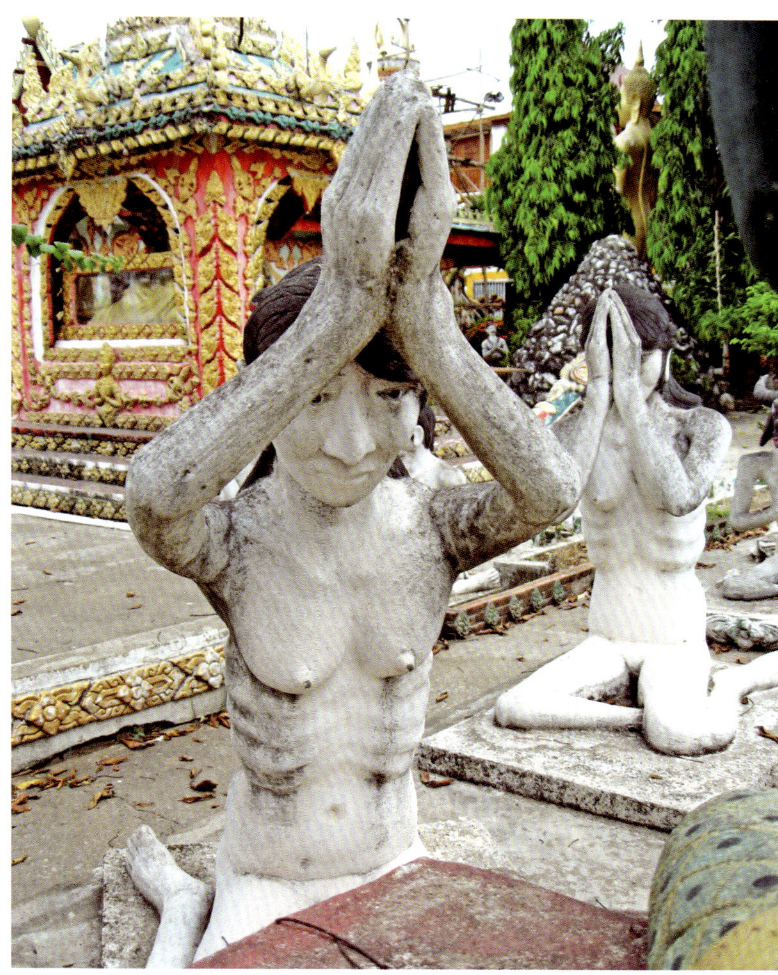

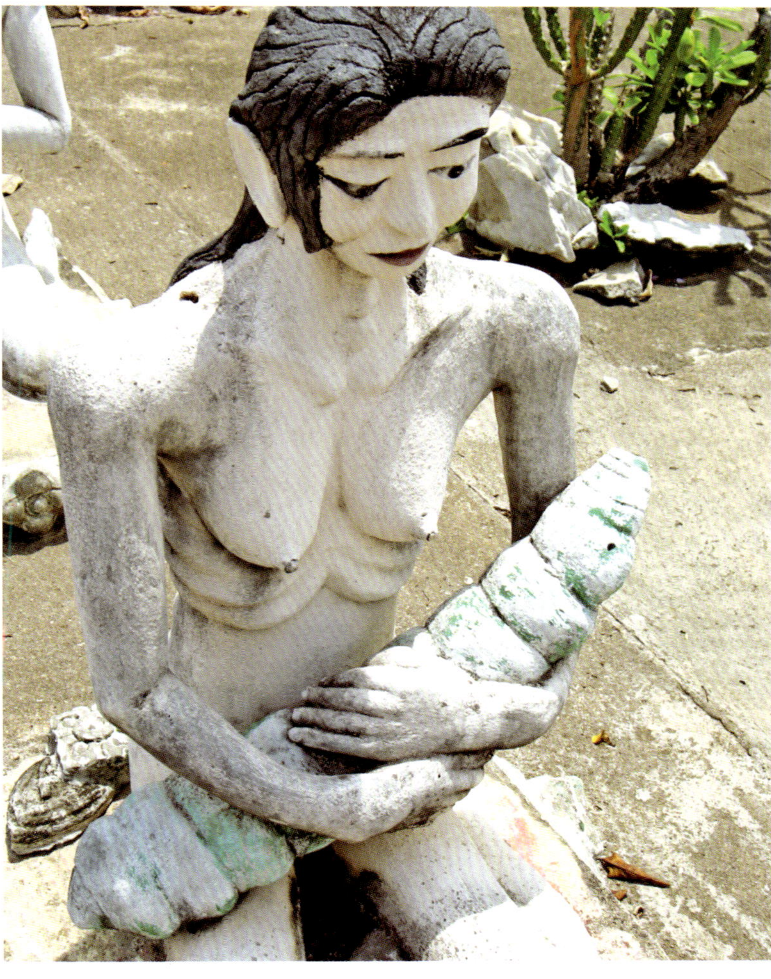

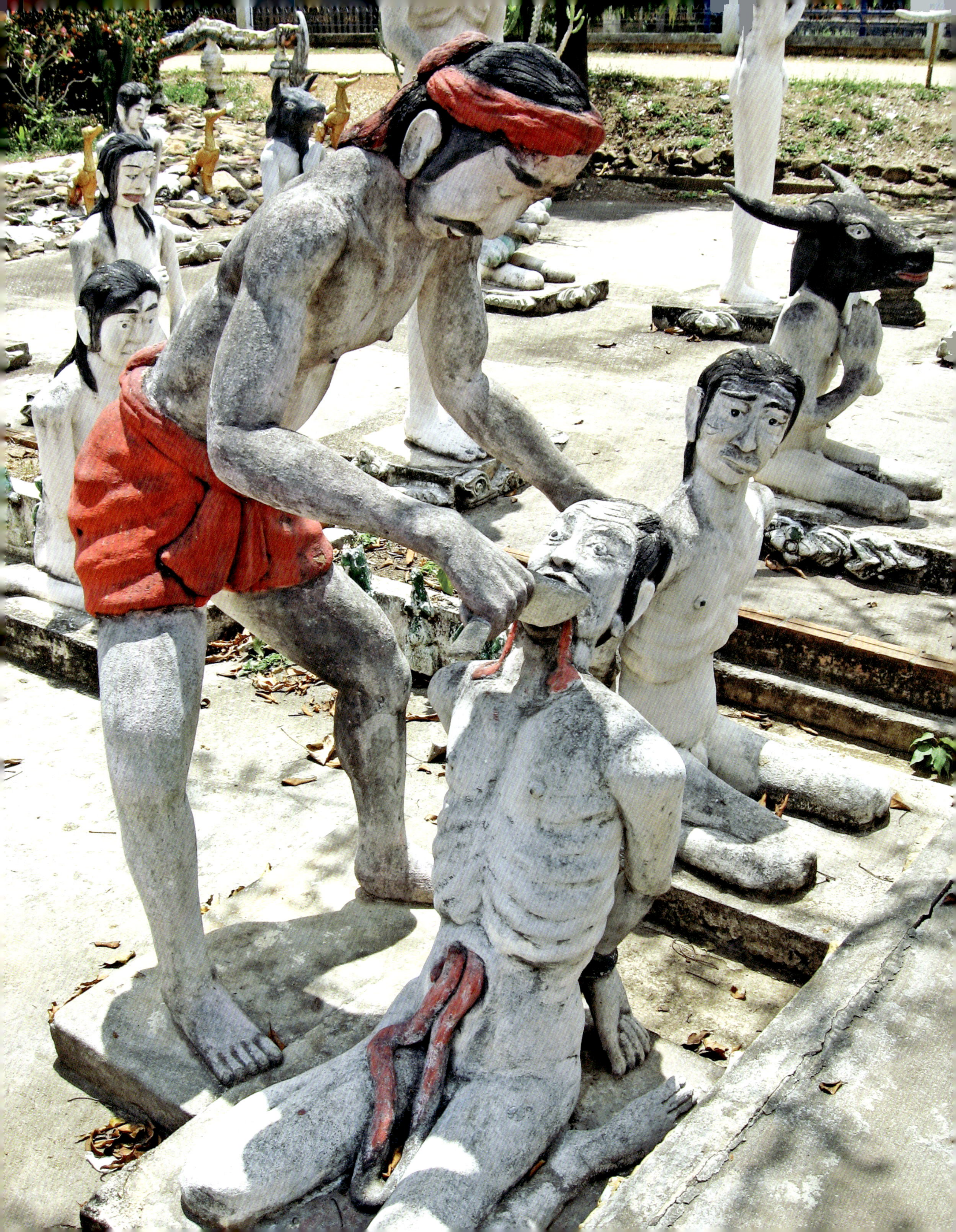

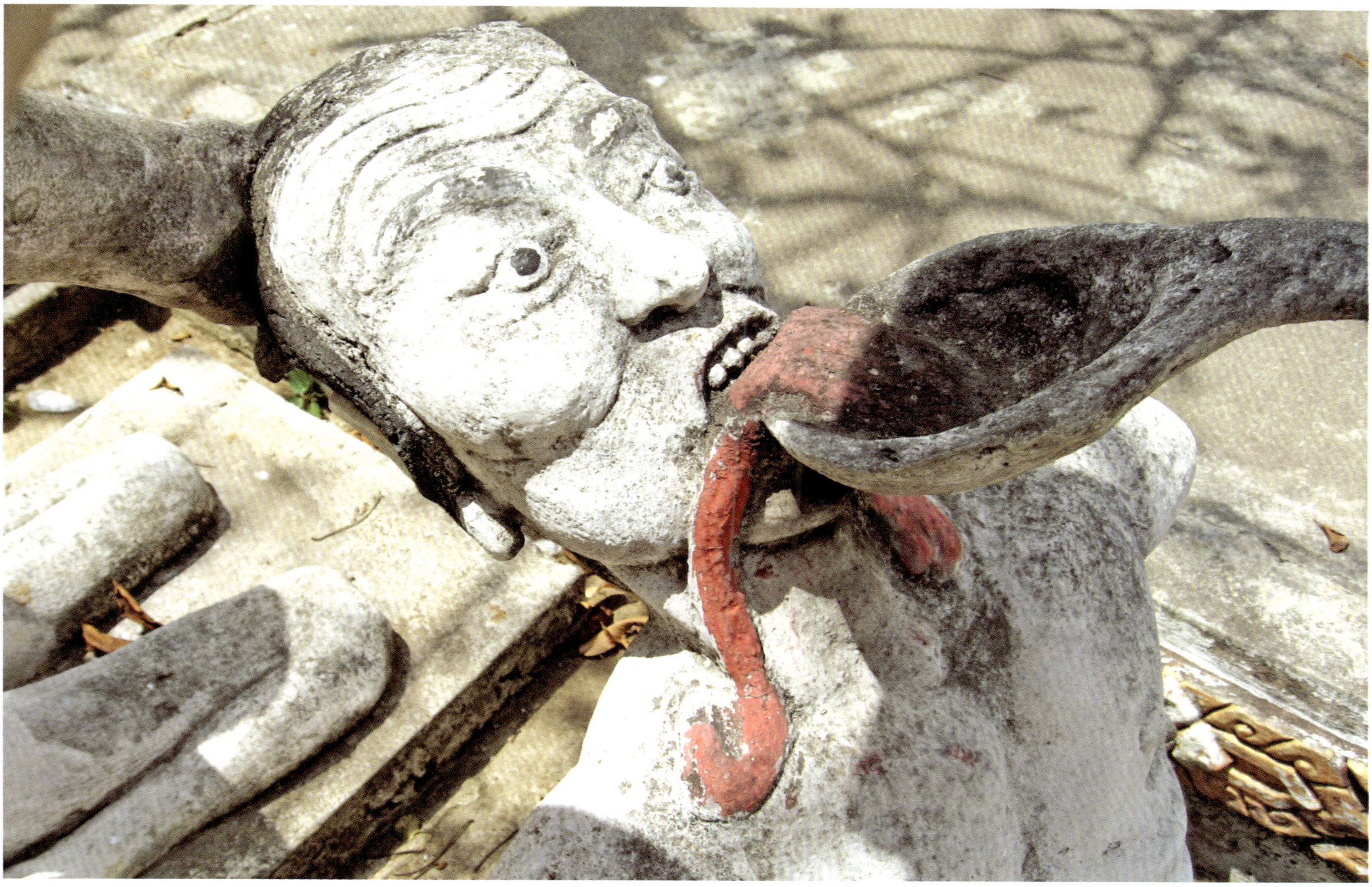

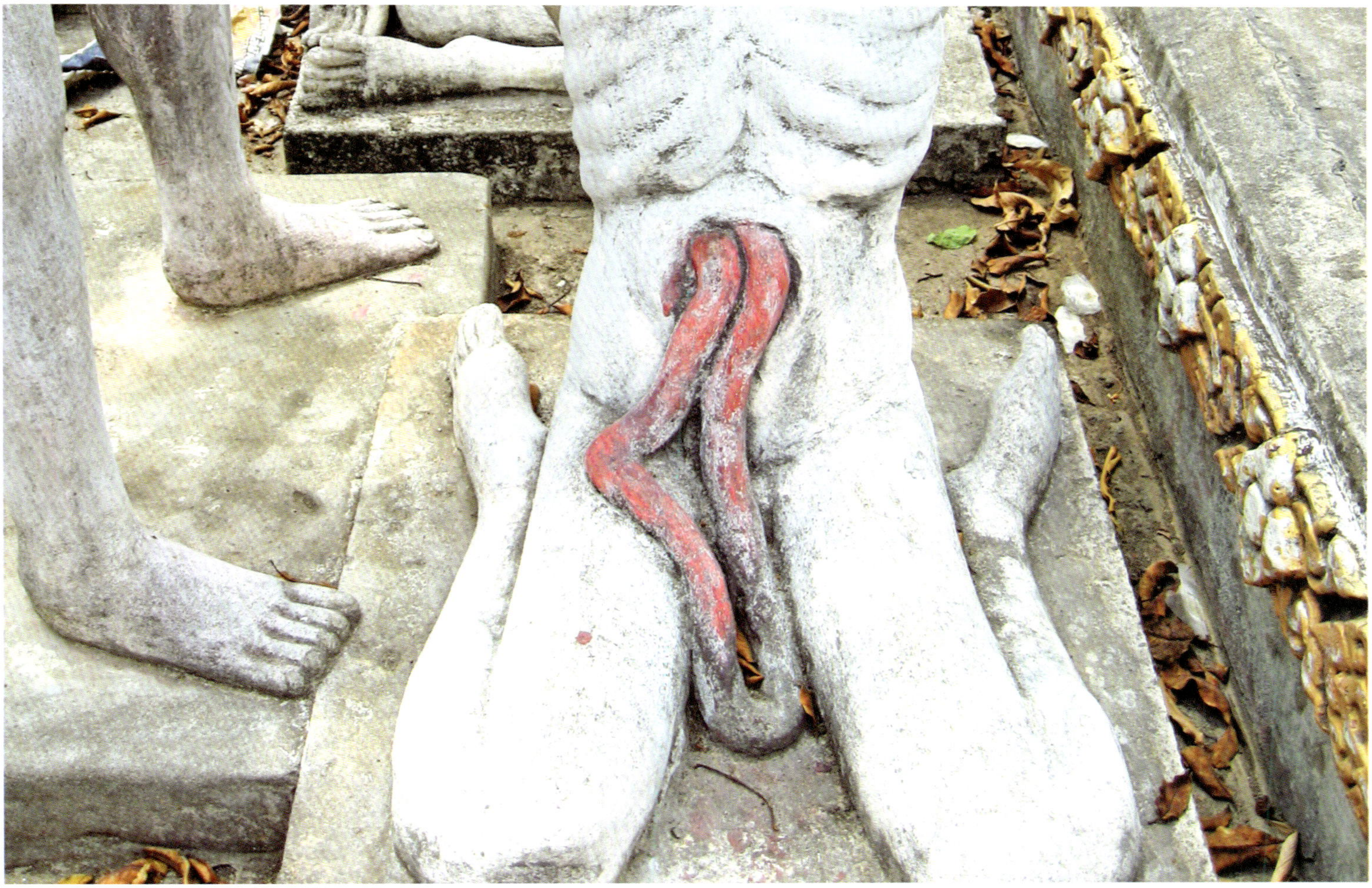

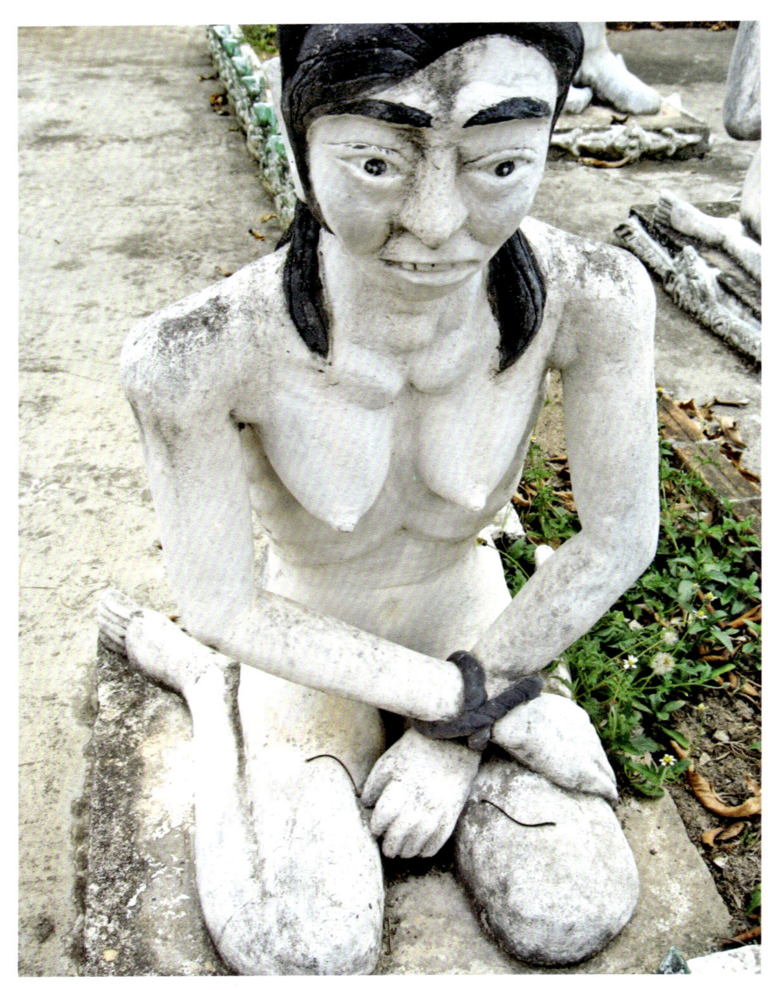
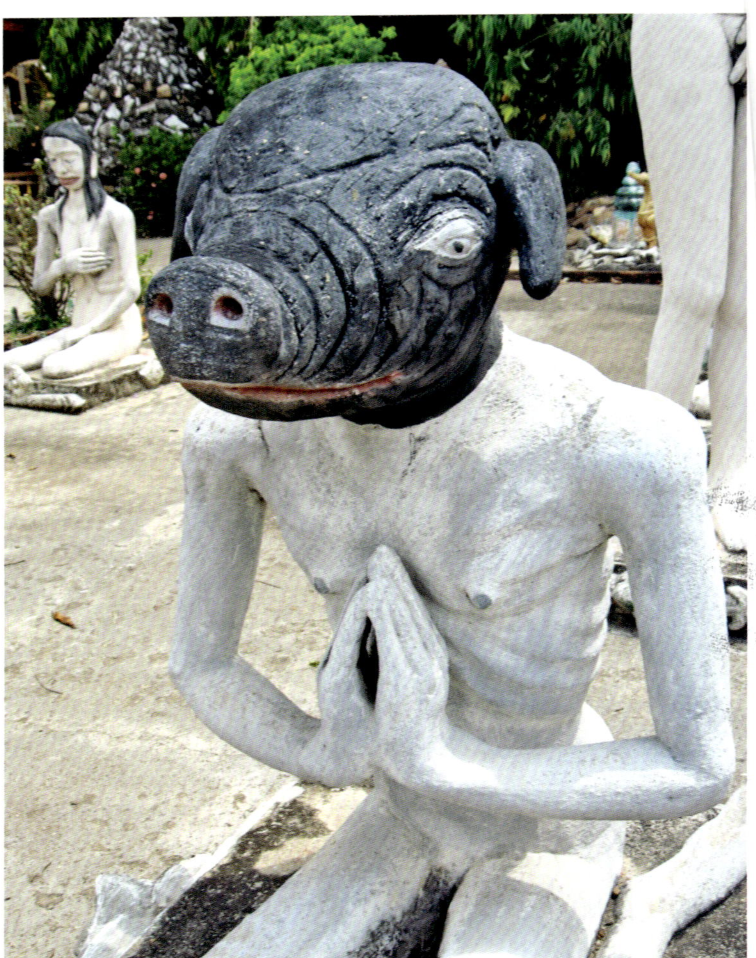
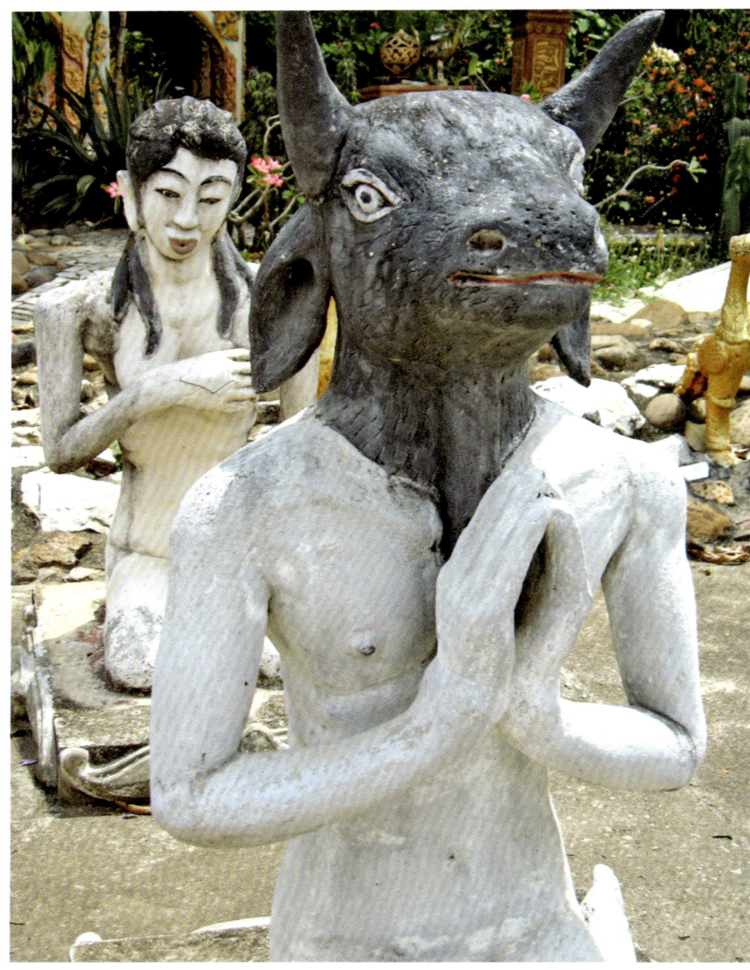
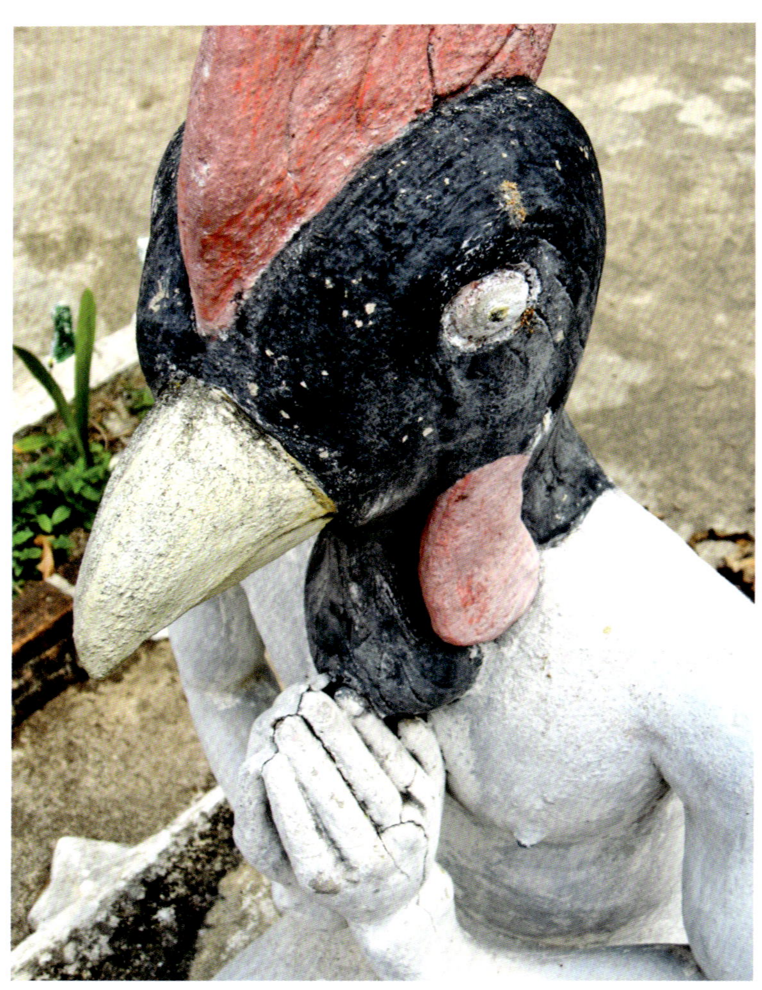

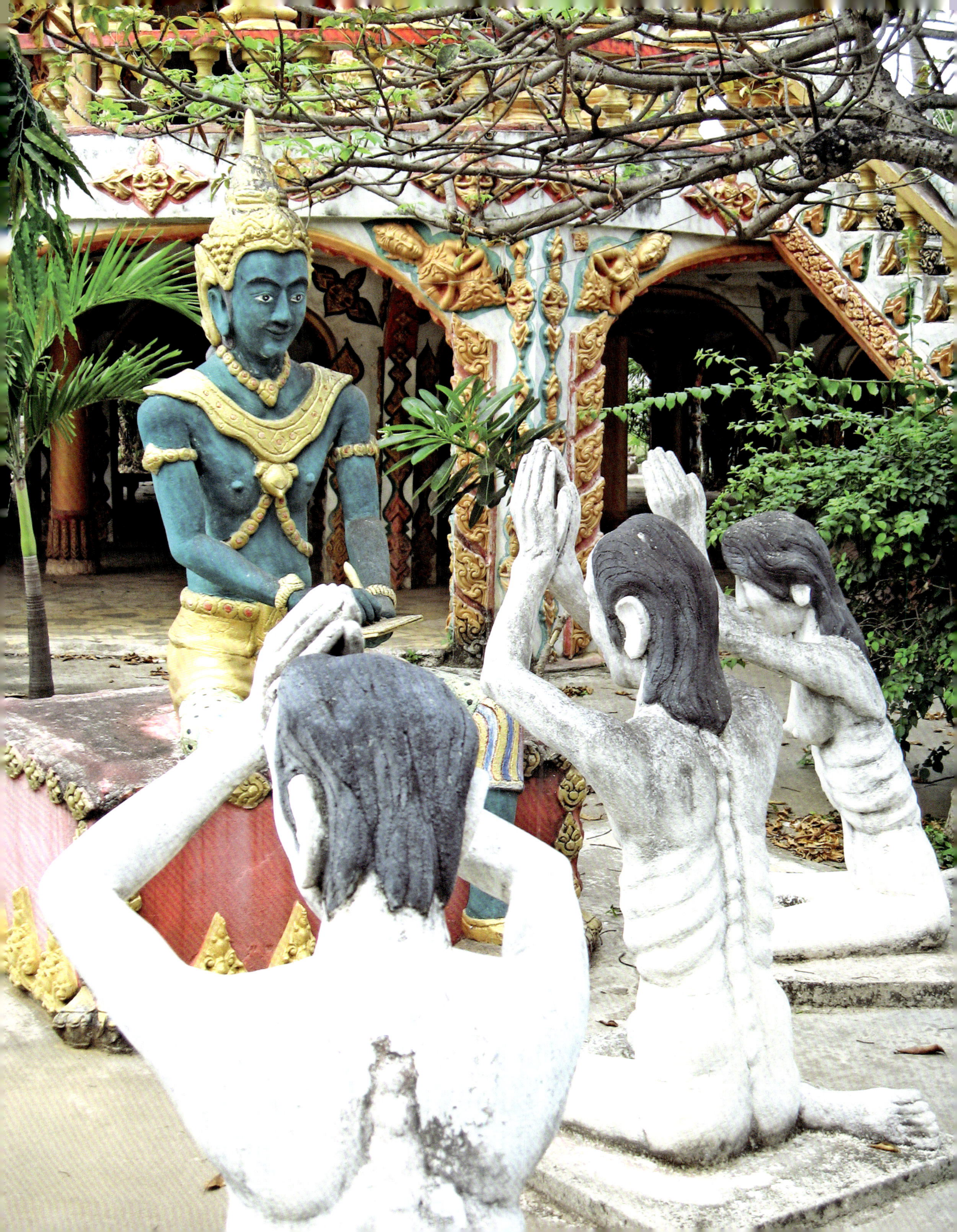

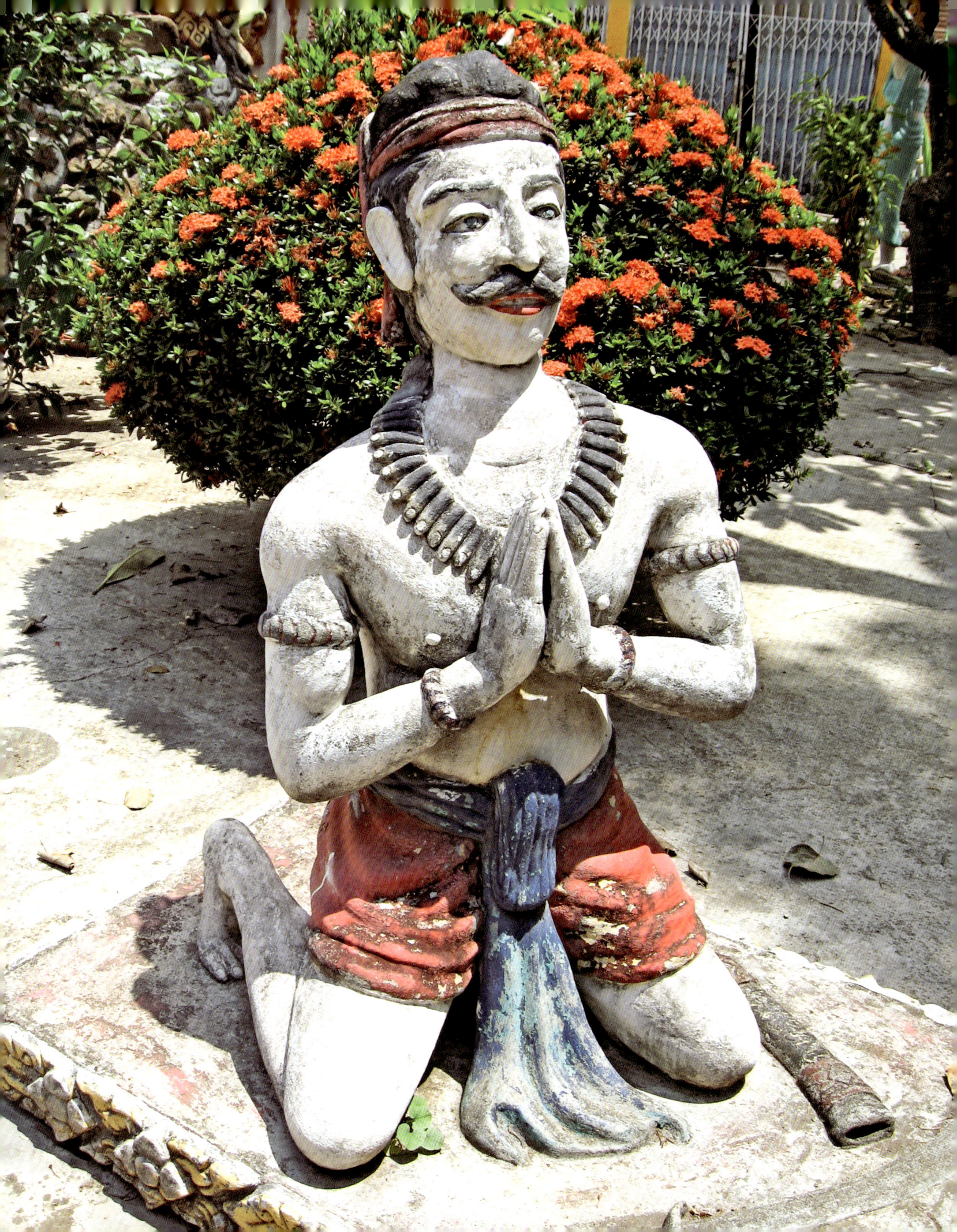

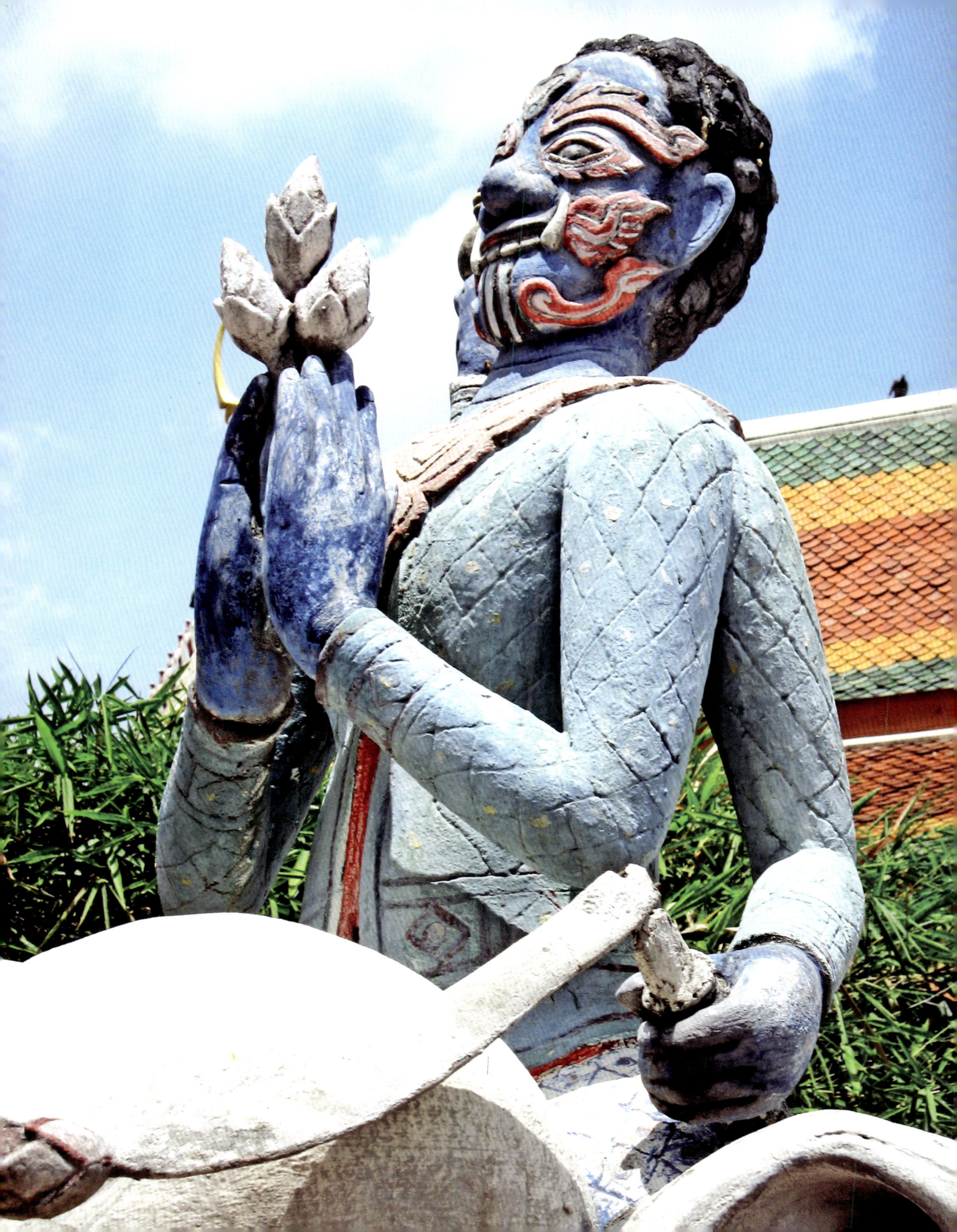

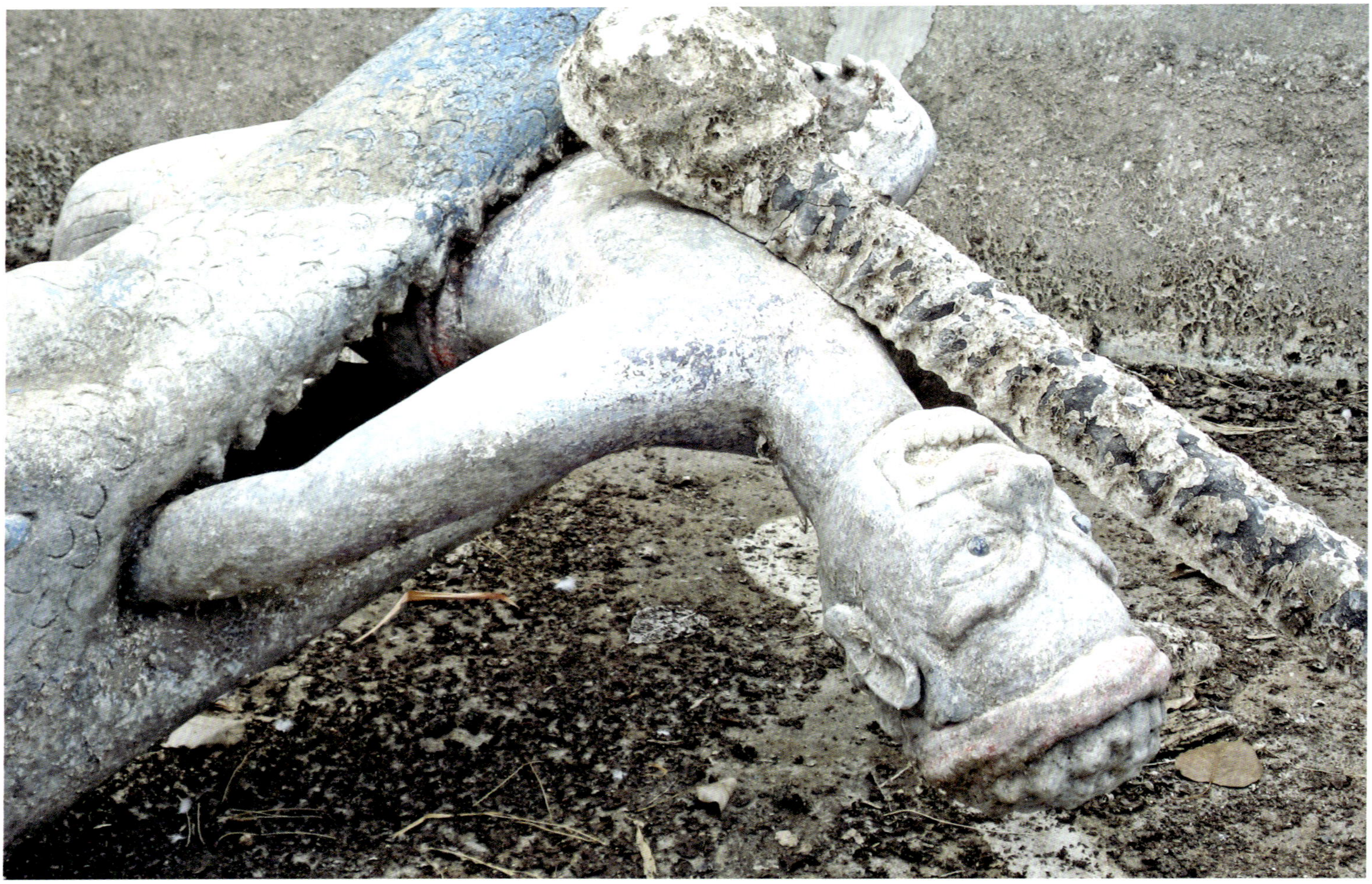

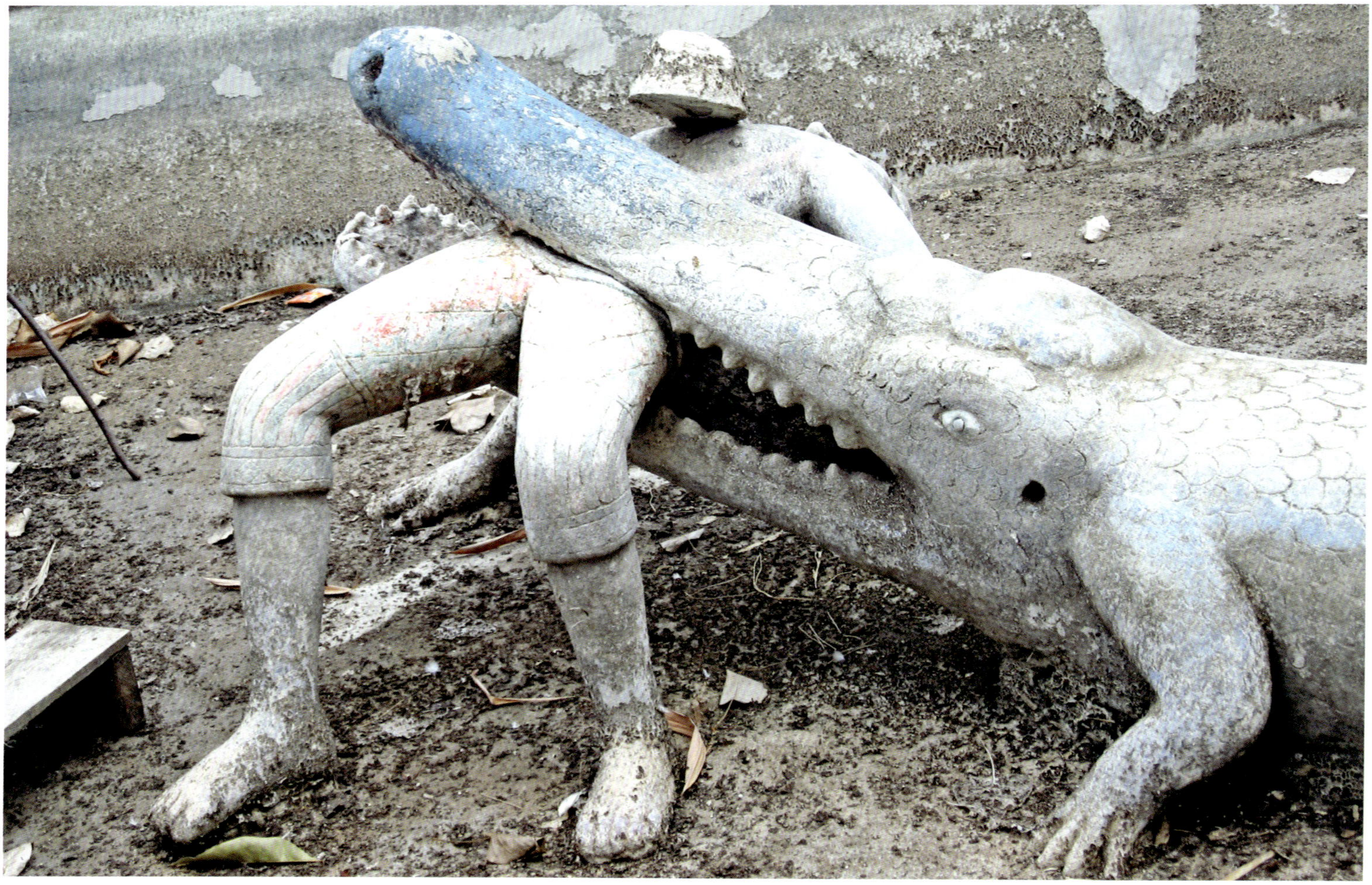

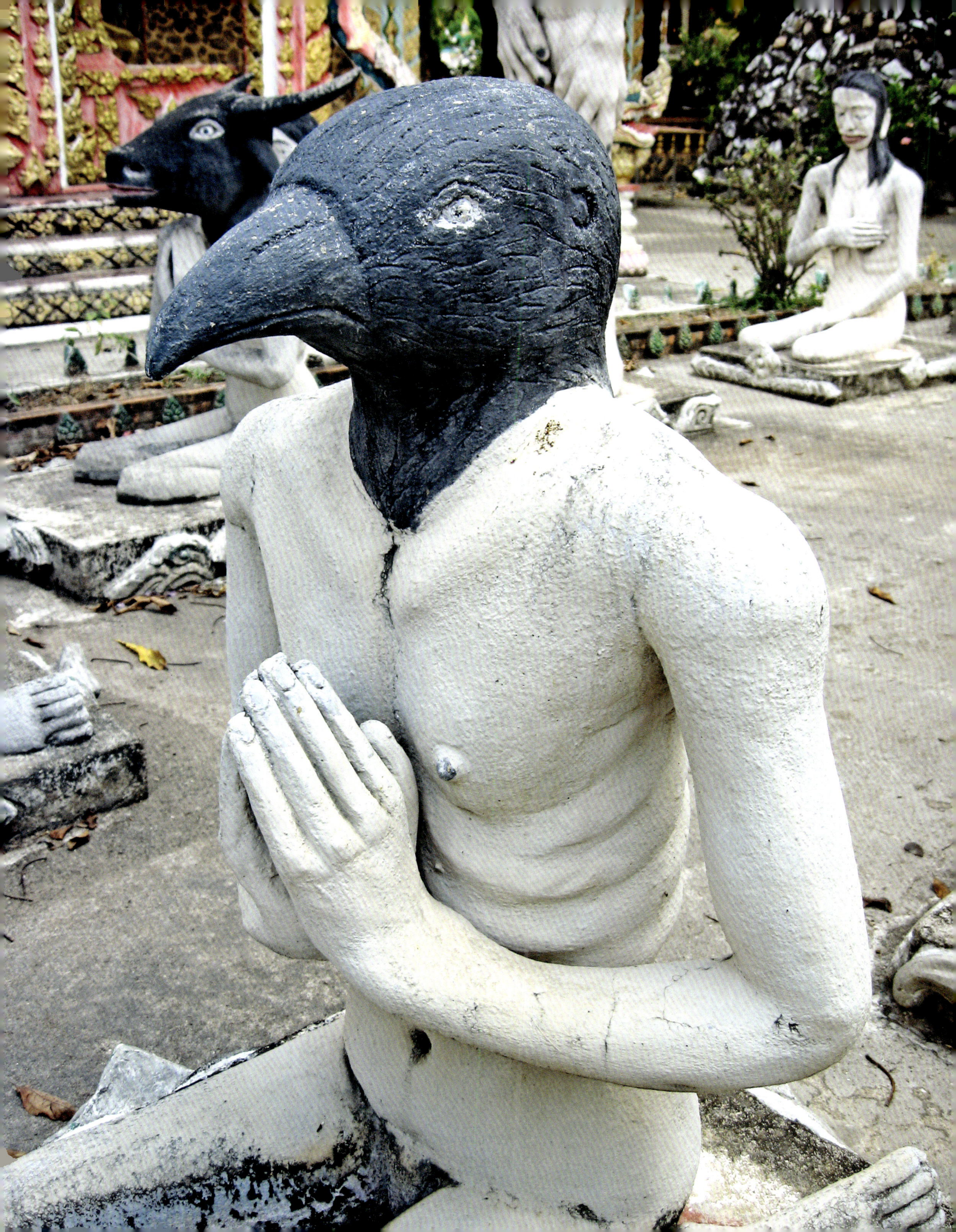

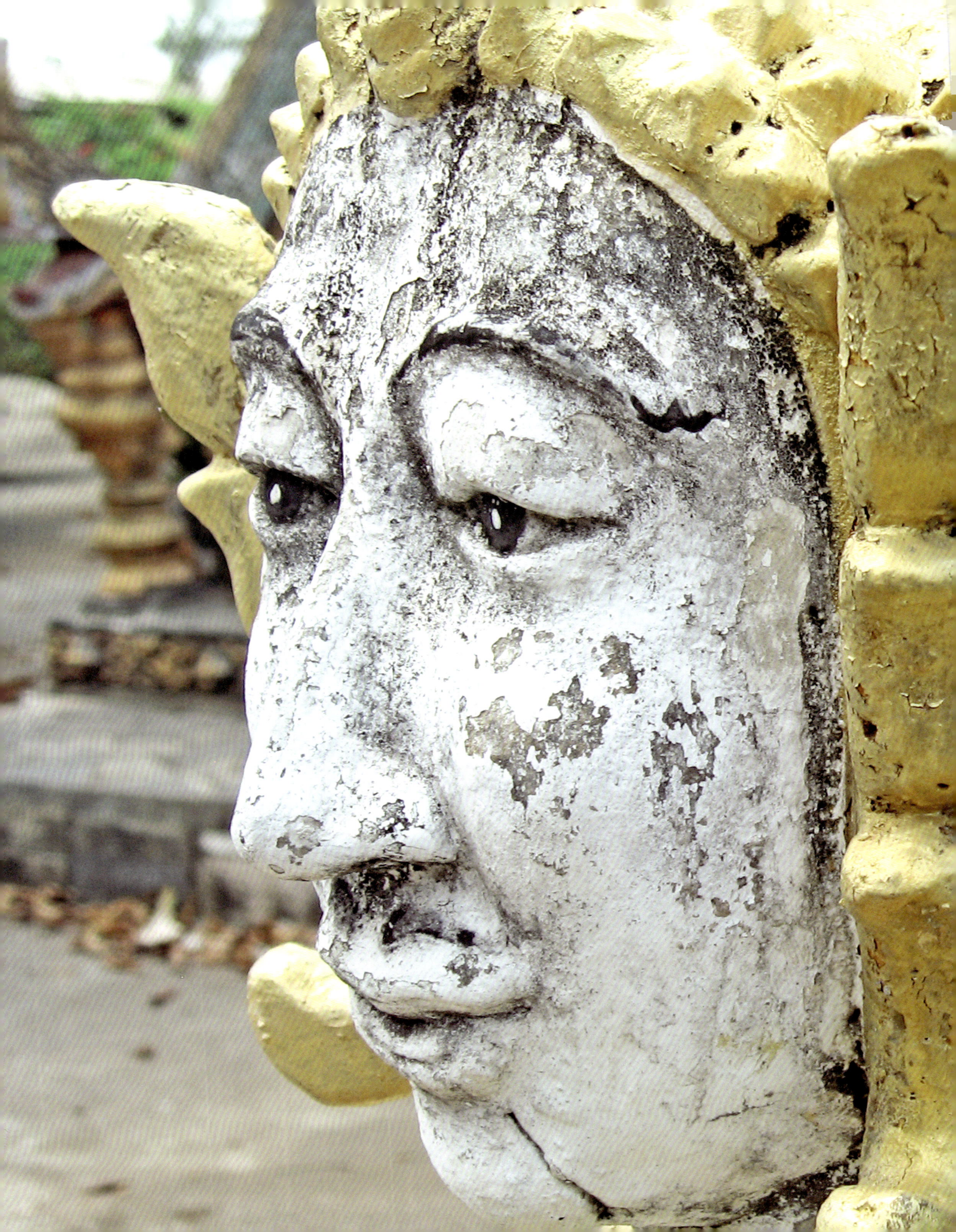

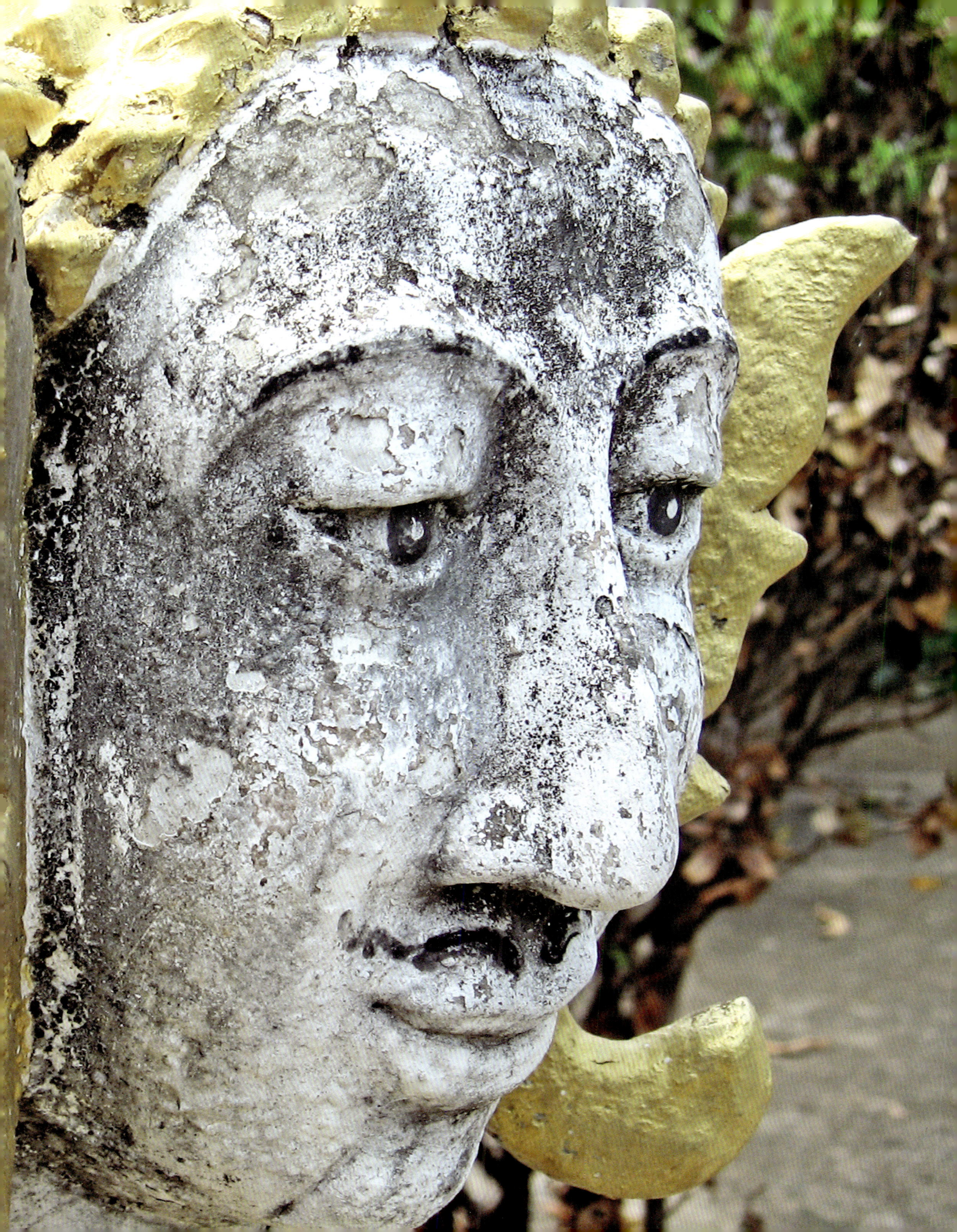

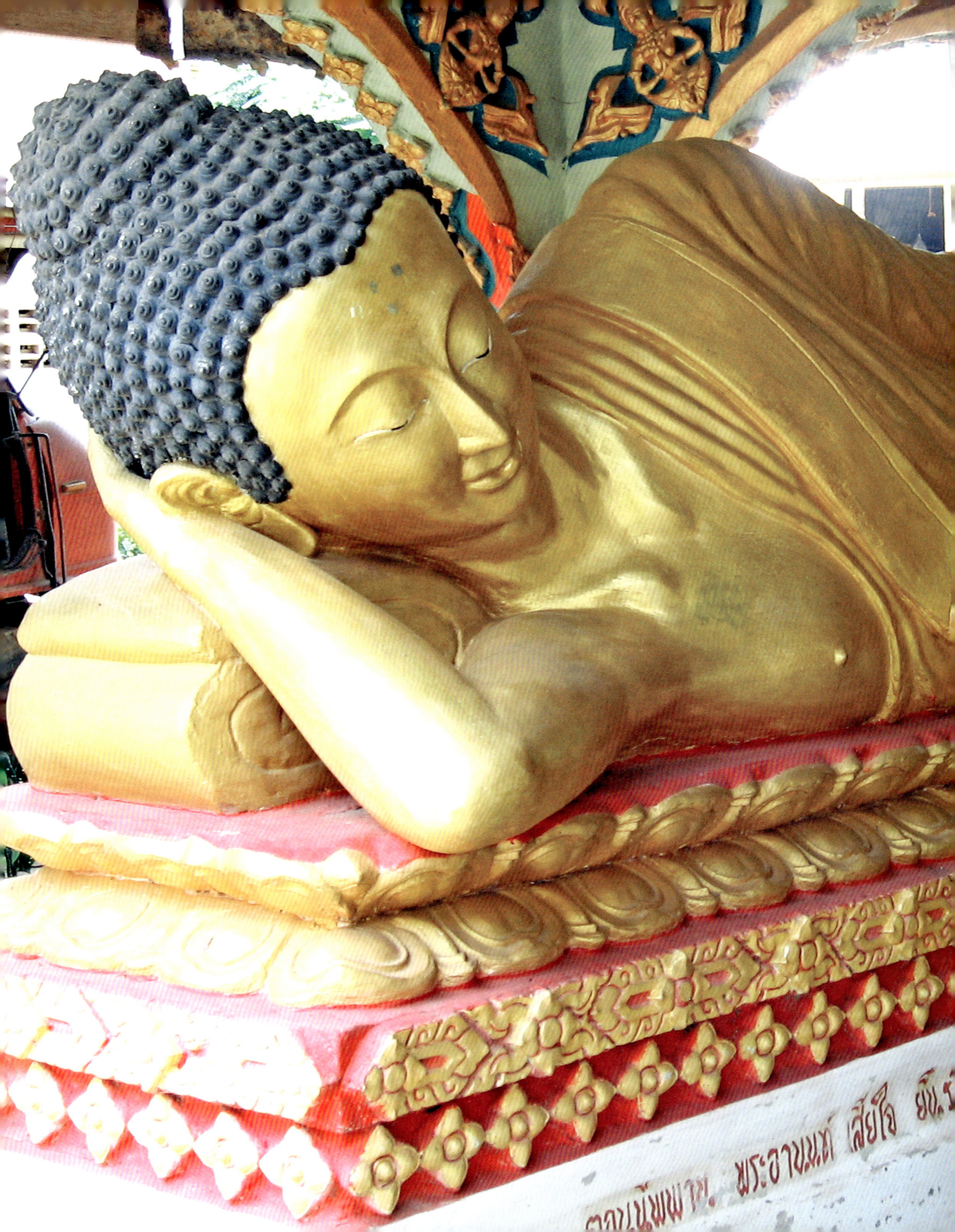
พระอานนท์ เสียใจ

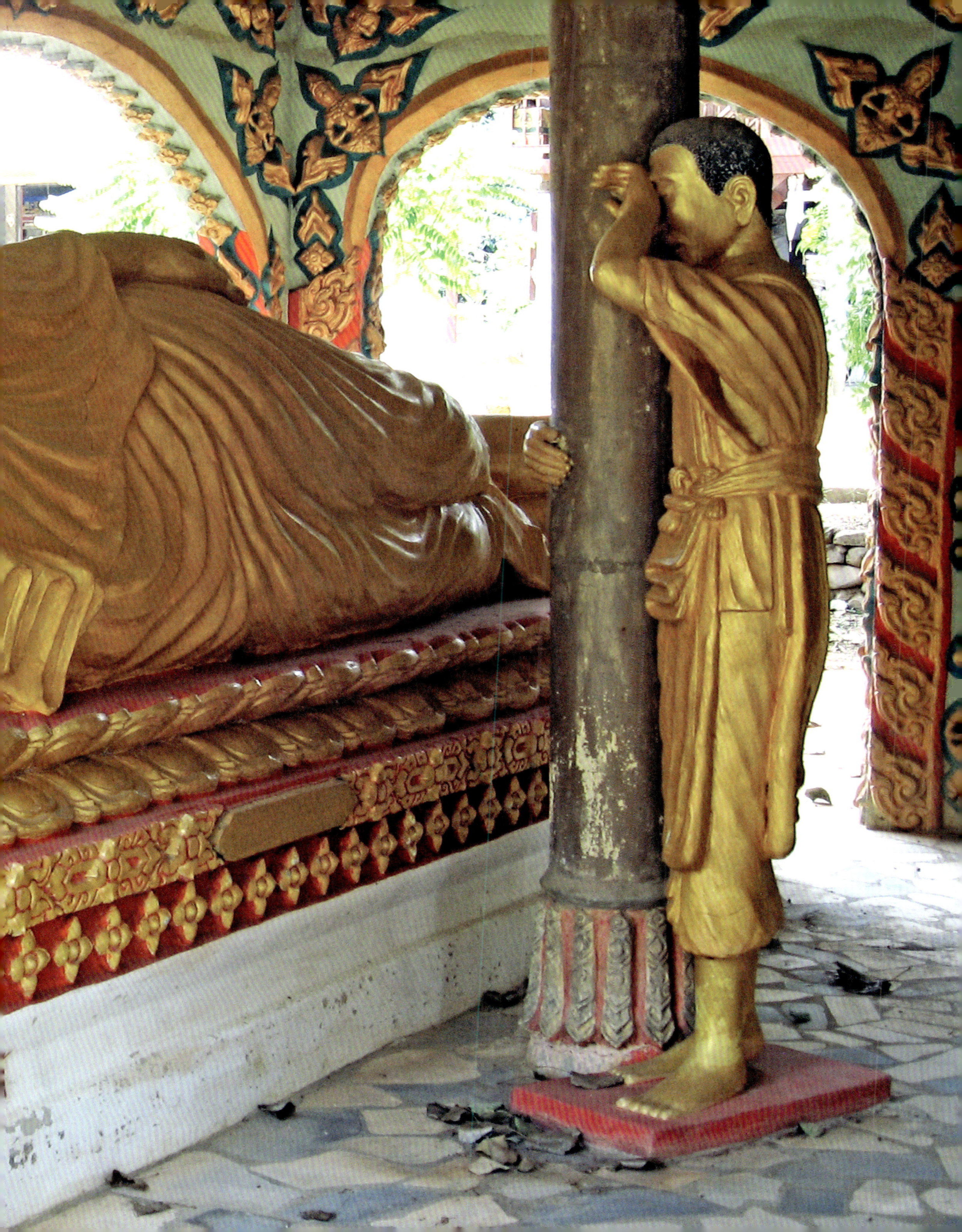

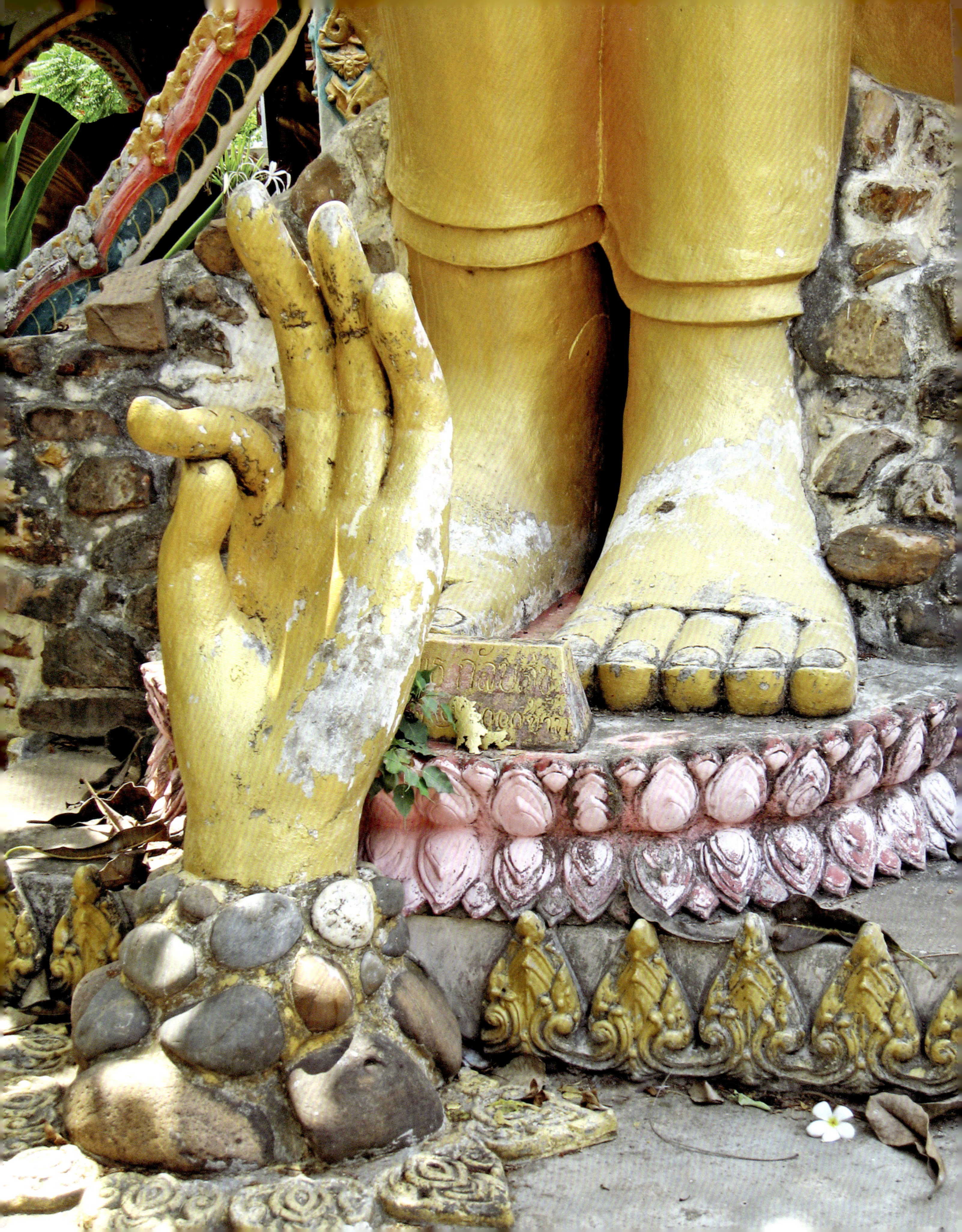

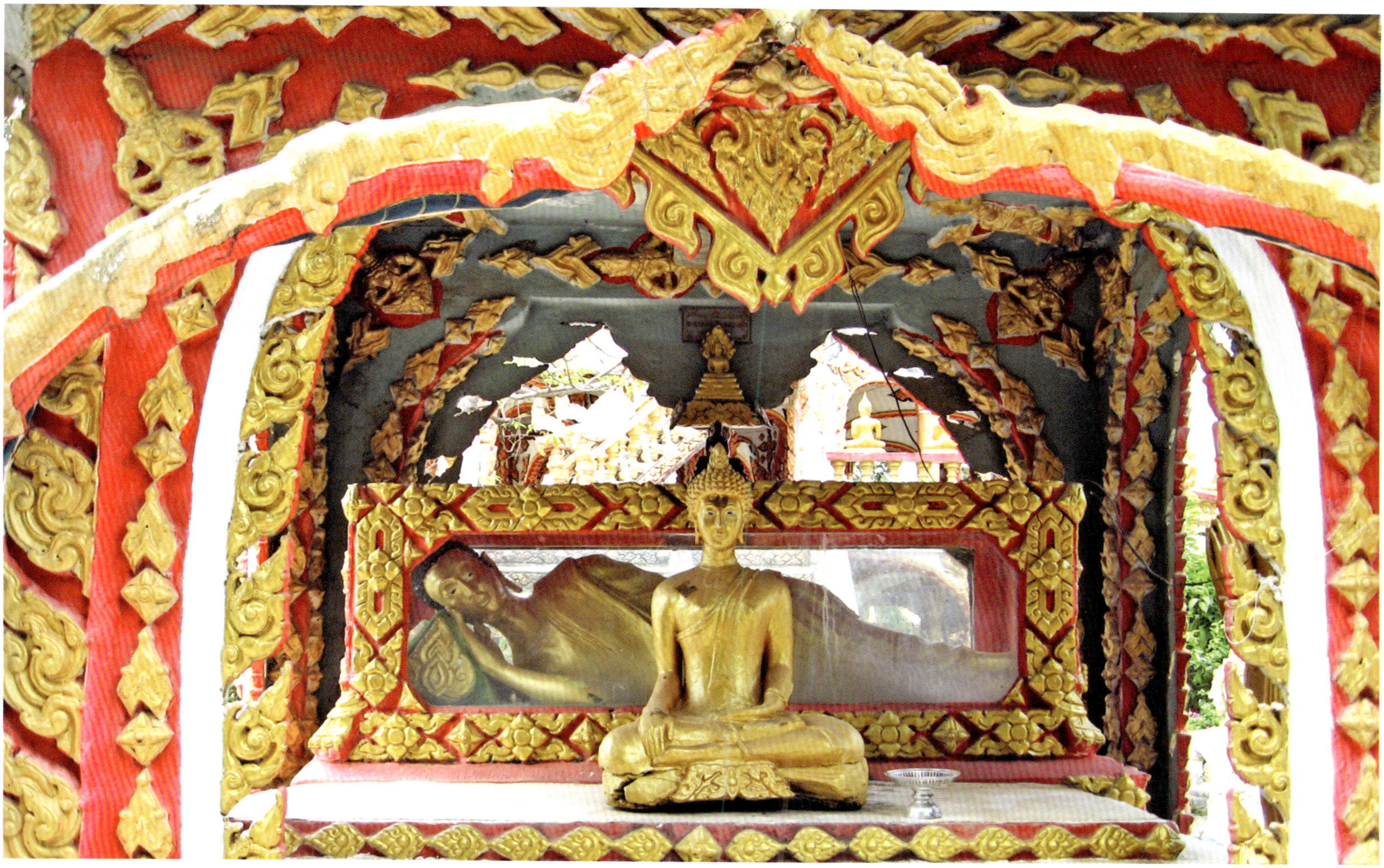

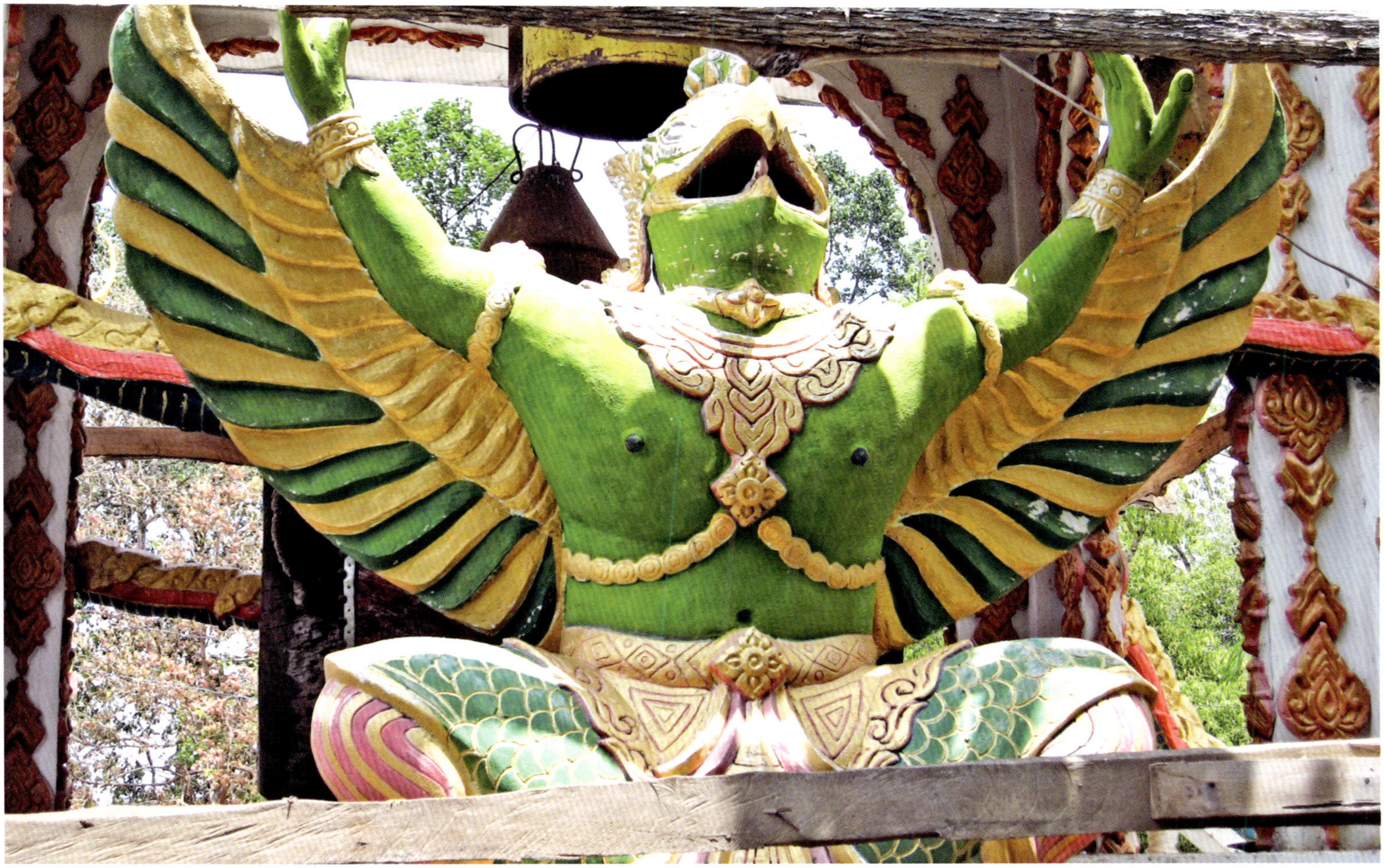

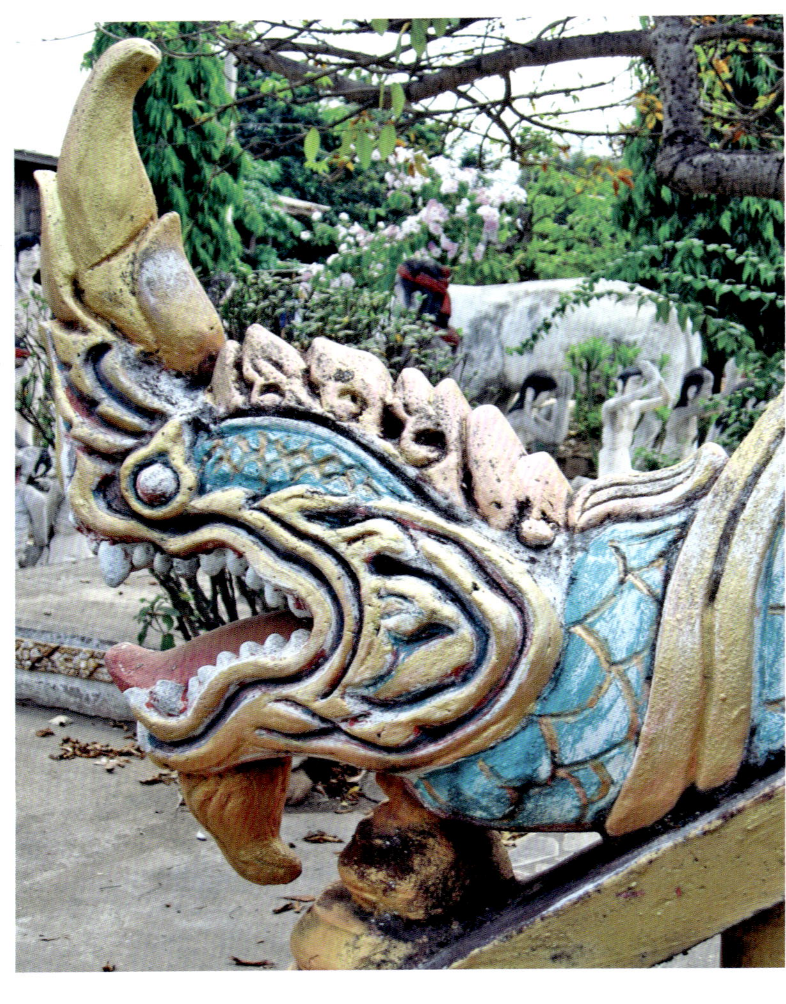

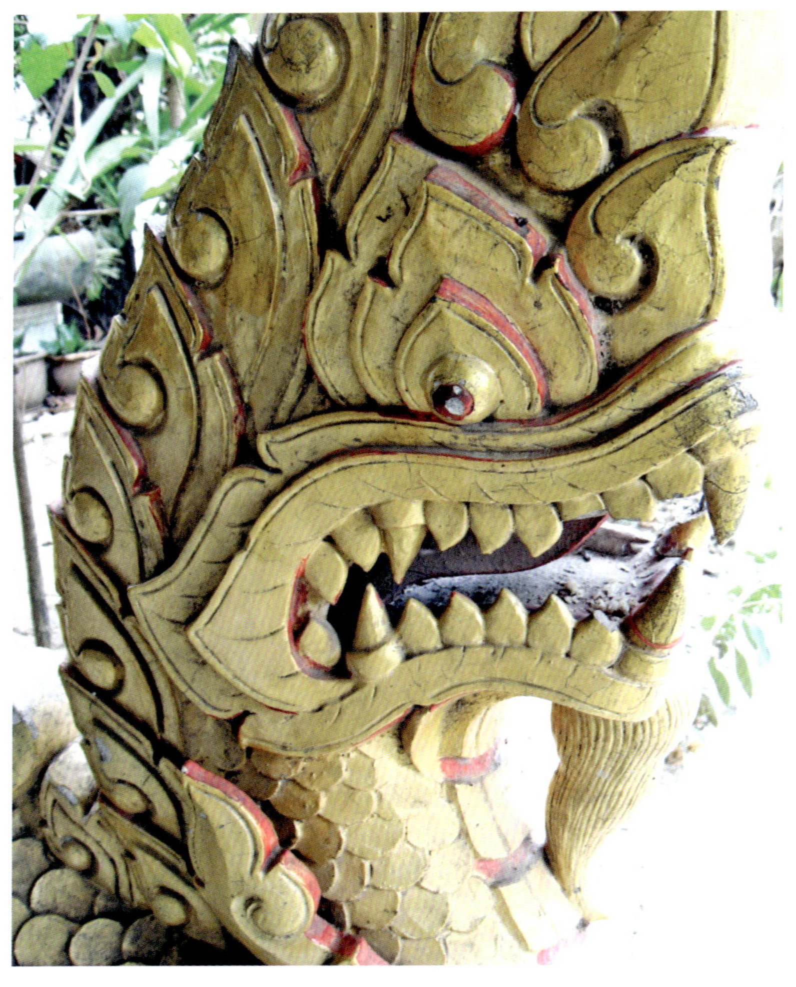

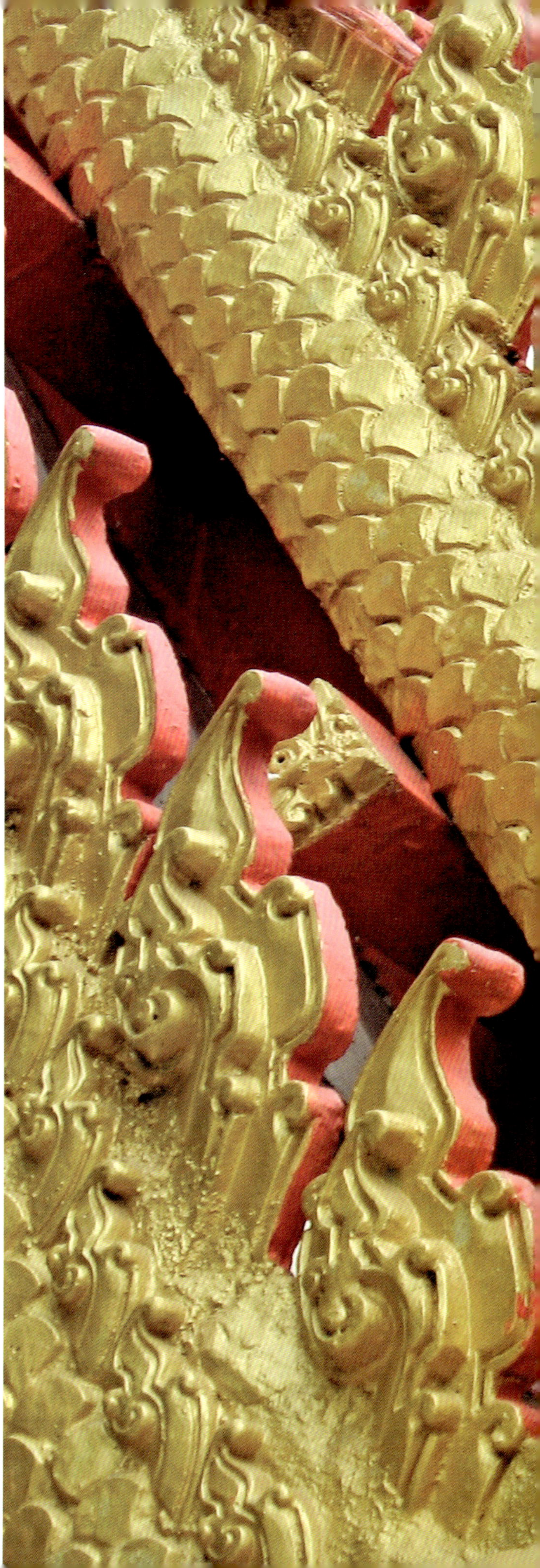

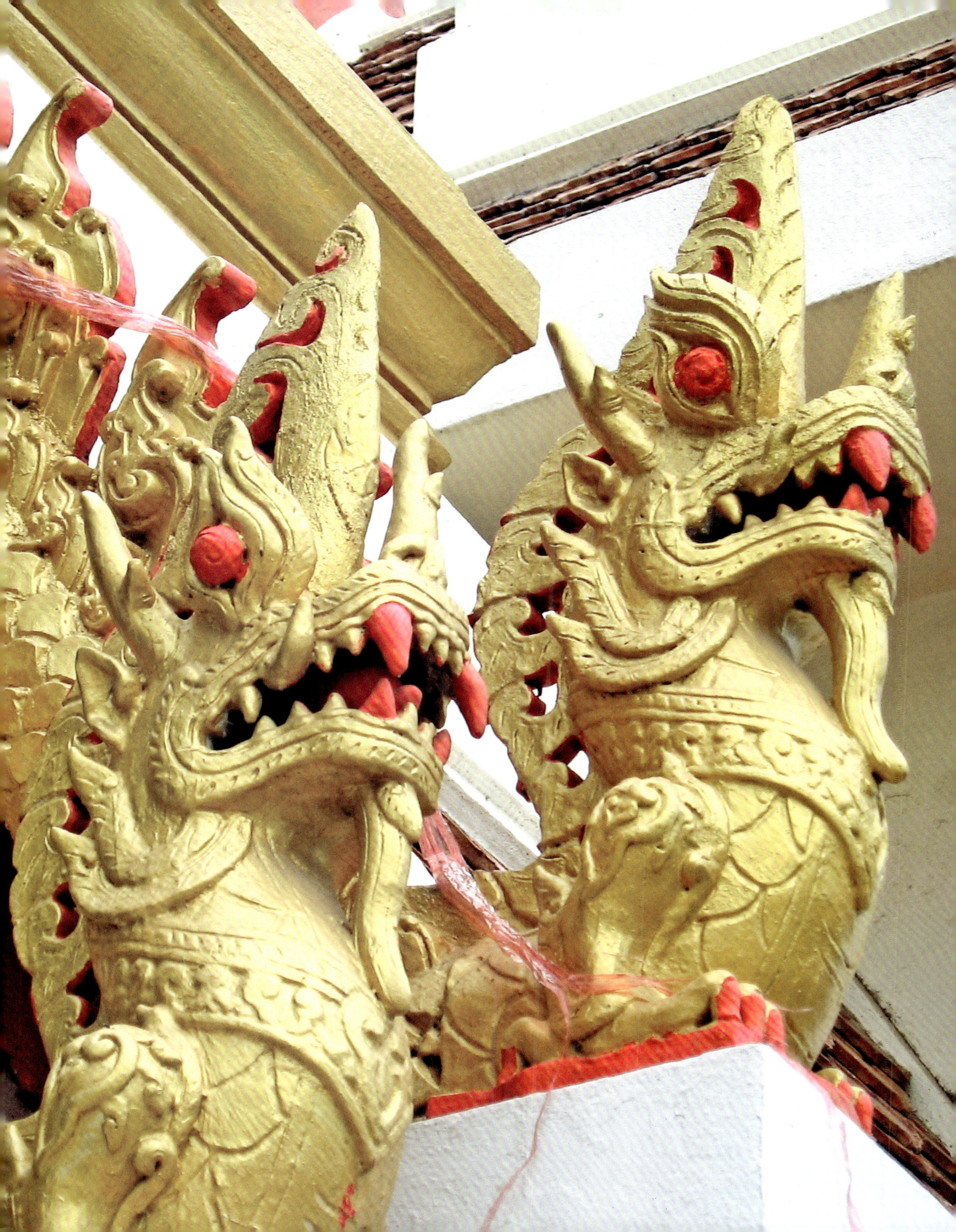

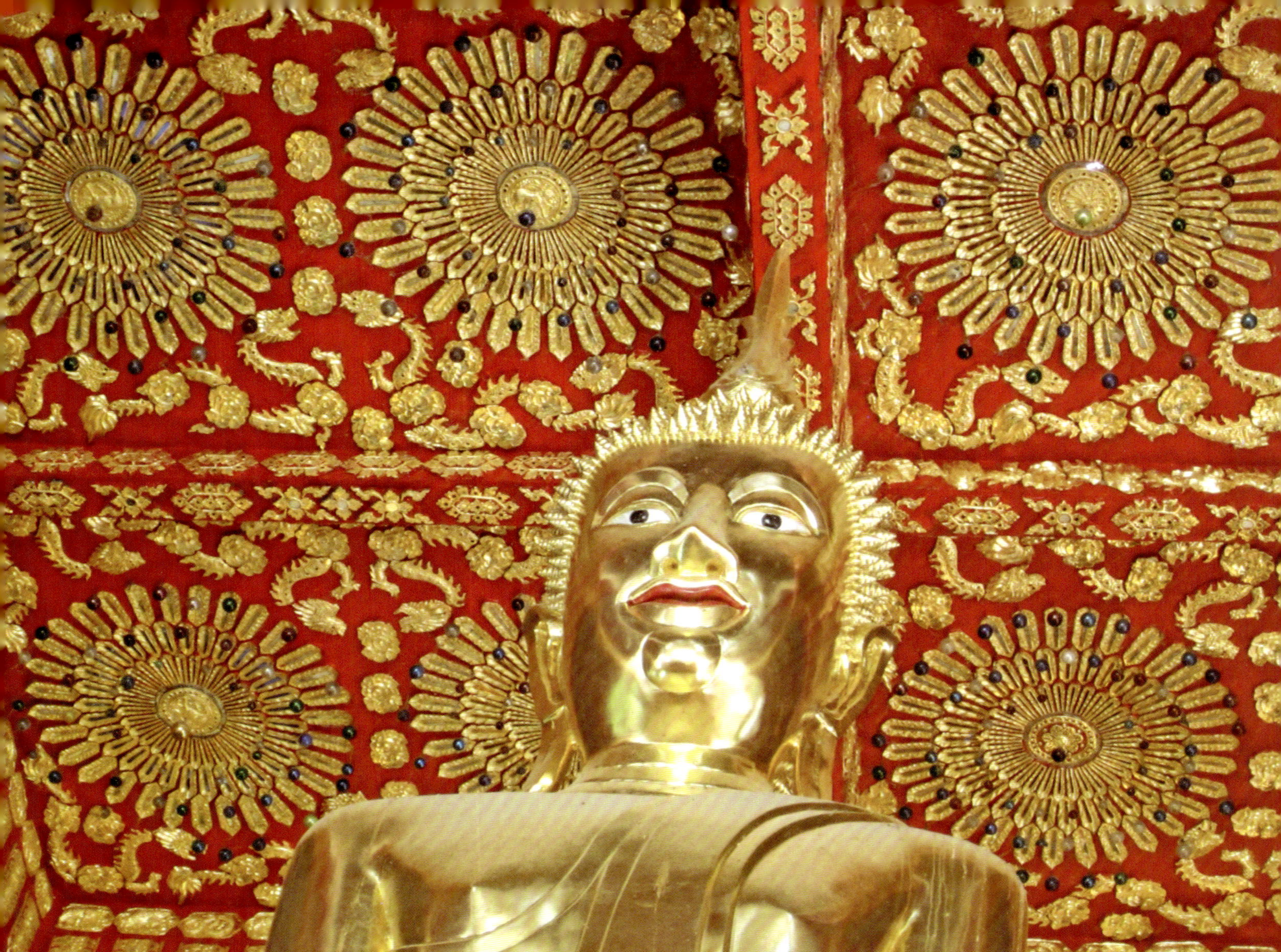

WAT SUAN DOK

Located two miles west of the walled-city of Chiang Mai and a mile east of Wat Umong, construction on Wat Suan Dok began in 1371 and was completed in 1373. Lanna King Kuena invited Phra Sumana Thera, a pious monk from Sukothai, to bring Sri Lankan Buddhism to this region and offered him a royal flower garden (in Thai: *suan dok*) as a site. Legend says while living in Sukothai, Phra Sumana Thera had a vision showing him where to find a buried holy relic of the Buddha in Pang Cha. In Sumana Thera's possession, the relic proved miraculous and was brought to Chiang Mai to be housed at Wat Suan Dok. Before it could be enshrined at the newly constructed temple, the relic split into two pieces. Following Phra Sumana's instructions, the self-replicating second relic was placed on the back of the king's white elephant that was allowed to travel until it found a location for a second temple. The elephant climbed up Doi (mountain) Suthep (named after a 1300 year-old hermit), chose a specific spot, trumpeted three times, and died. Wat Phrathat Doi Suthep was built on this spot in 1383, nine and a half miles west of Chiang Mai.

Wat Suan Dok's large *viharn* preaching hall was rebuilt in the 1930s. This *sala* pavilion is open on all four sides and protected by a series of crafted metal gates, many depicting *apsaras*, or angels. A large standing Buddha, with straw in his right hand, faces west towards the main *chedi*, while a seated meditating Buddha faces east, towards the hall entrance. Ornate Buddha images, many in the Lanna style, surround the larger icons. The 157-foot golden Sri Lankan-style *chedi*, which houses the relic, has newly-renovated stairs guarded on all four sides by white *nagas* (see **Mythical Beasts** chapter). Bells around the *chedi* alert the gods when one is making merit. To the northwest, a collection of *stupas* house the cremated remains of Lanna royal family members, relocated from other resting sites in 1909. A smaller *ubosot*, or ordination room, to the south of the main *chedi* contains a seated Buddha image, the walls decorated with murals depicting the previous lives of the Buddha; it is generally open only to monks. The temple compound also contains the campus of Maha Chulalongkorn's Buddhist University, and the weekly monk chats offer a chance for discourse with novices from many countries. A vegetarian restaurant, Pun Pun, is yet another reason for a visit.

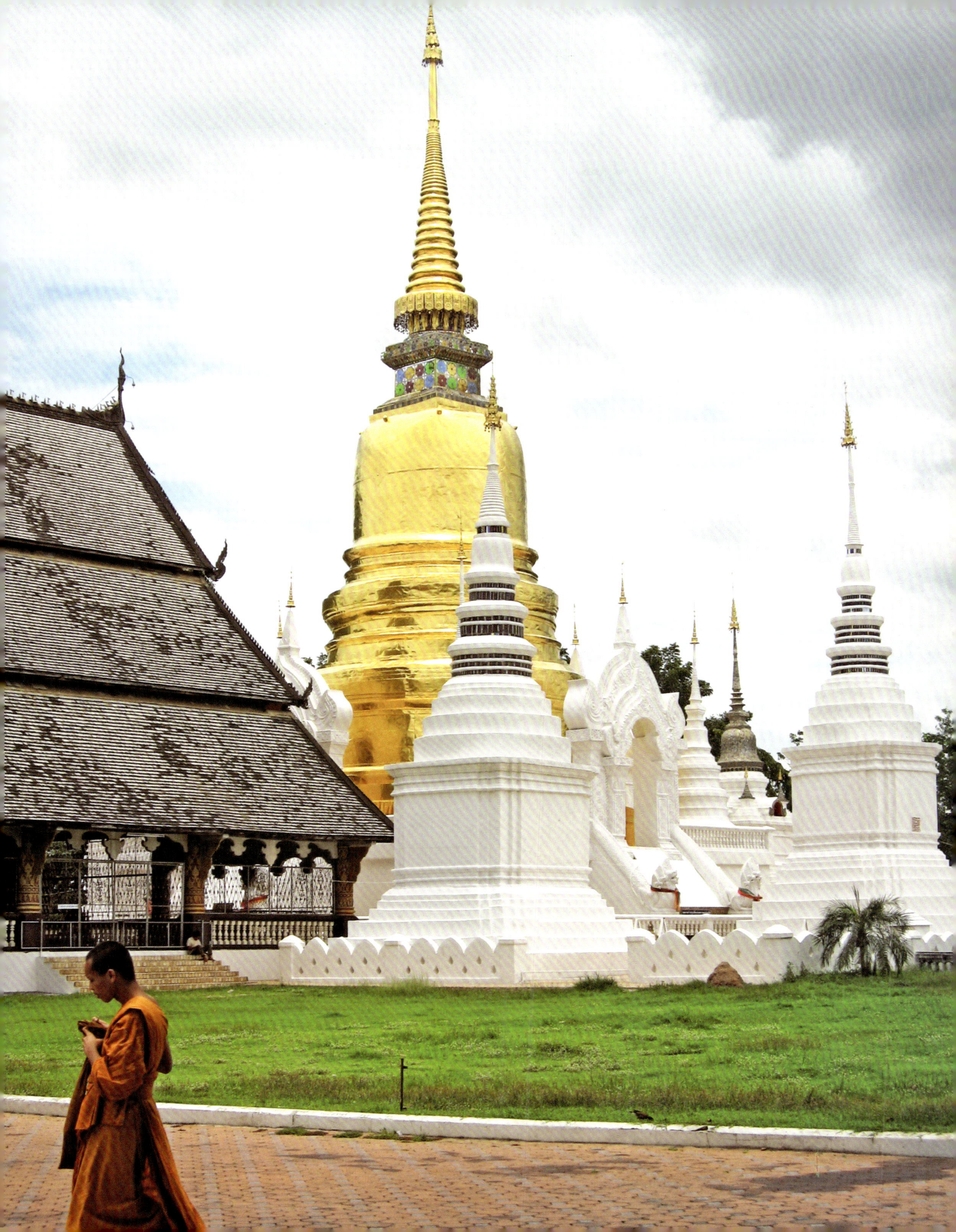

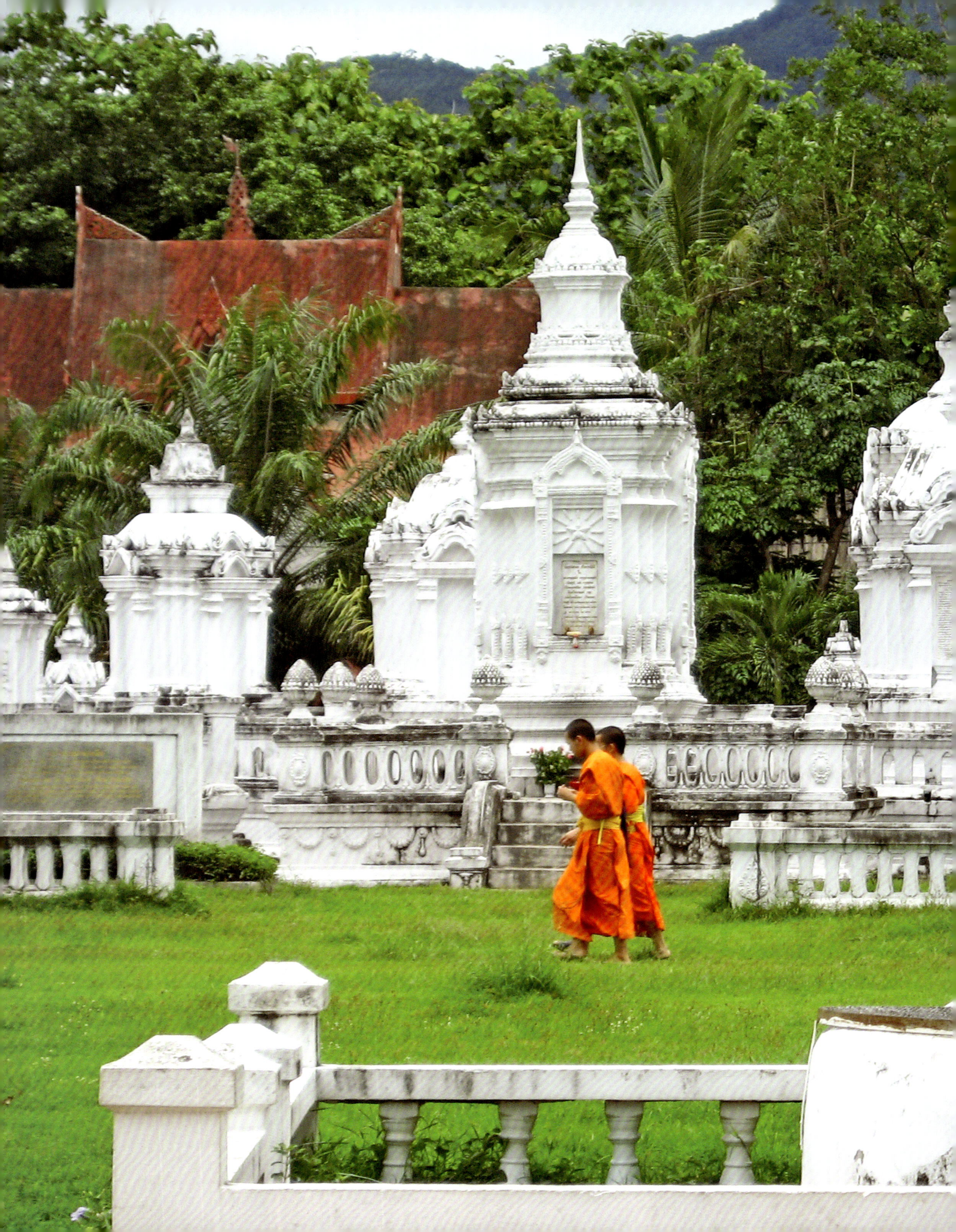

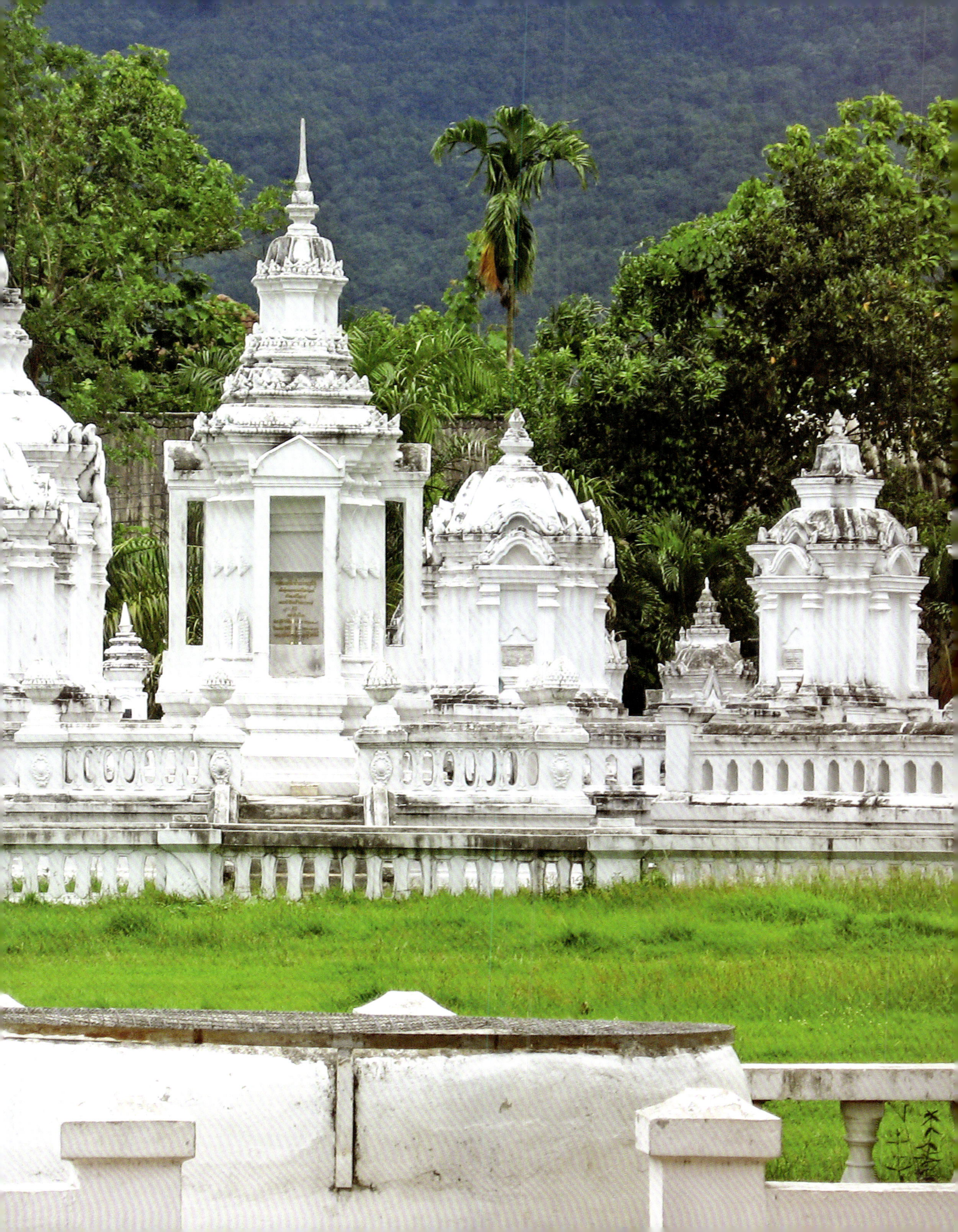

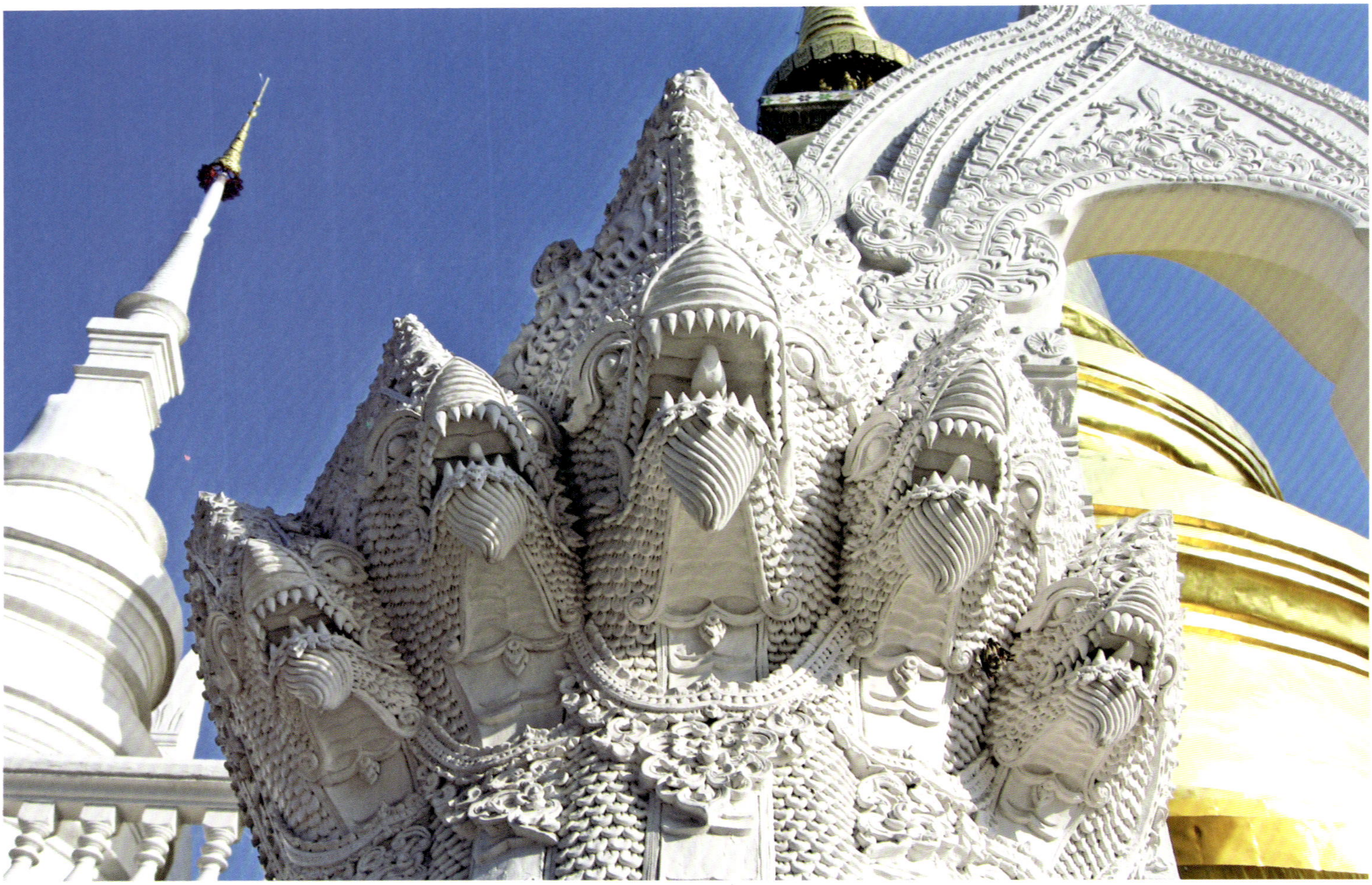

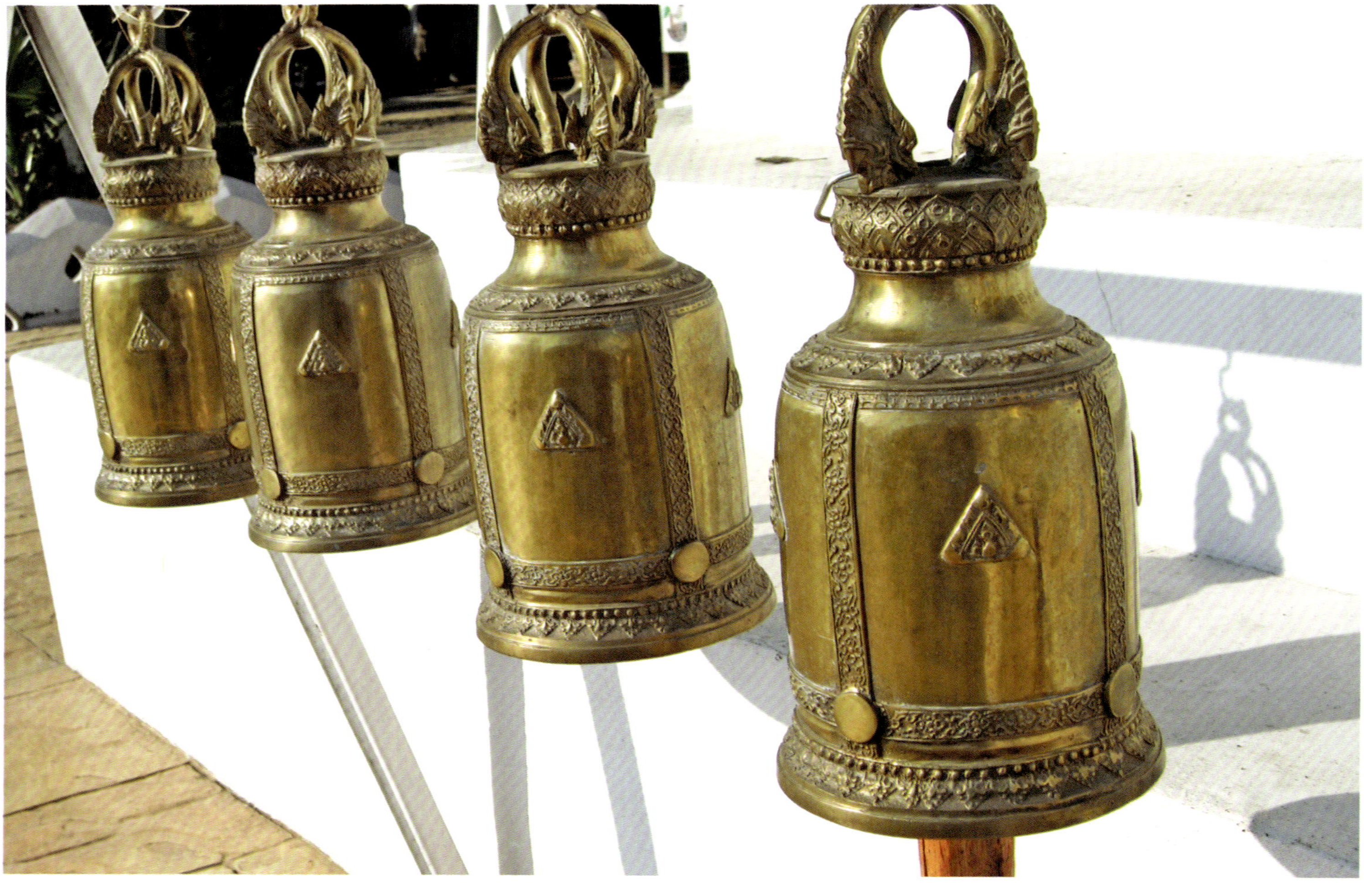

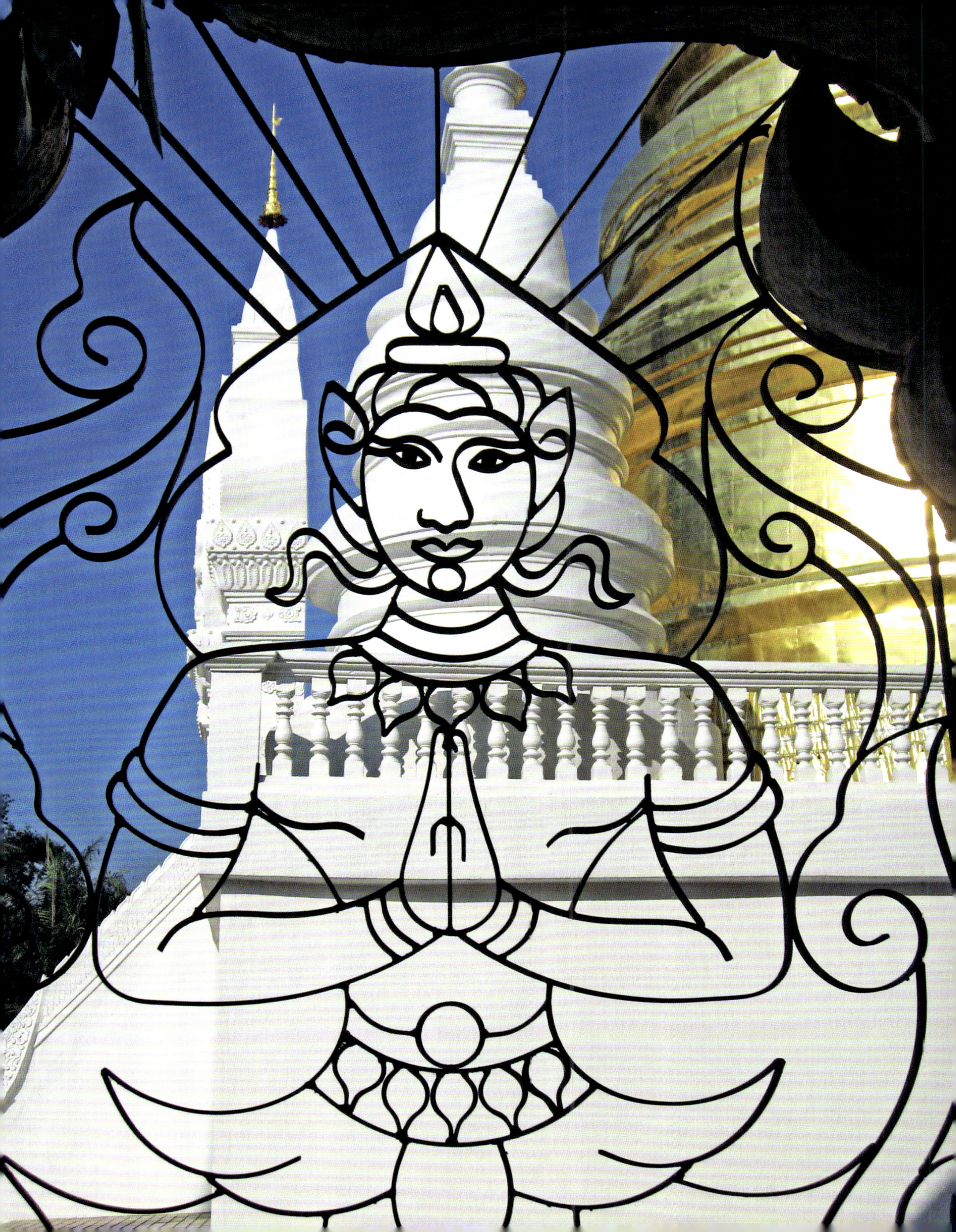

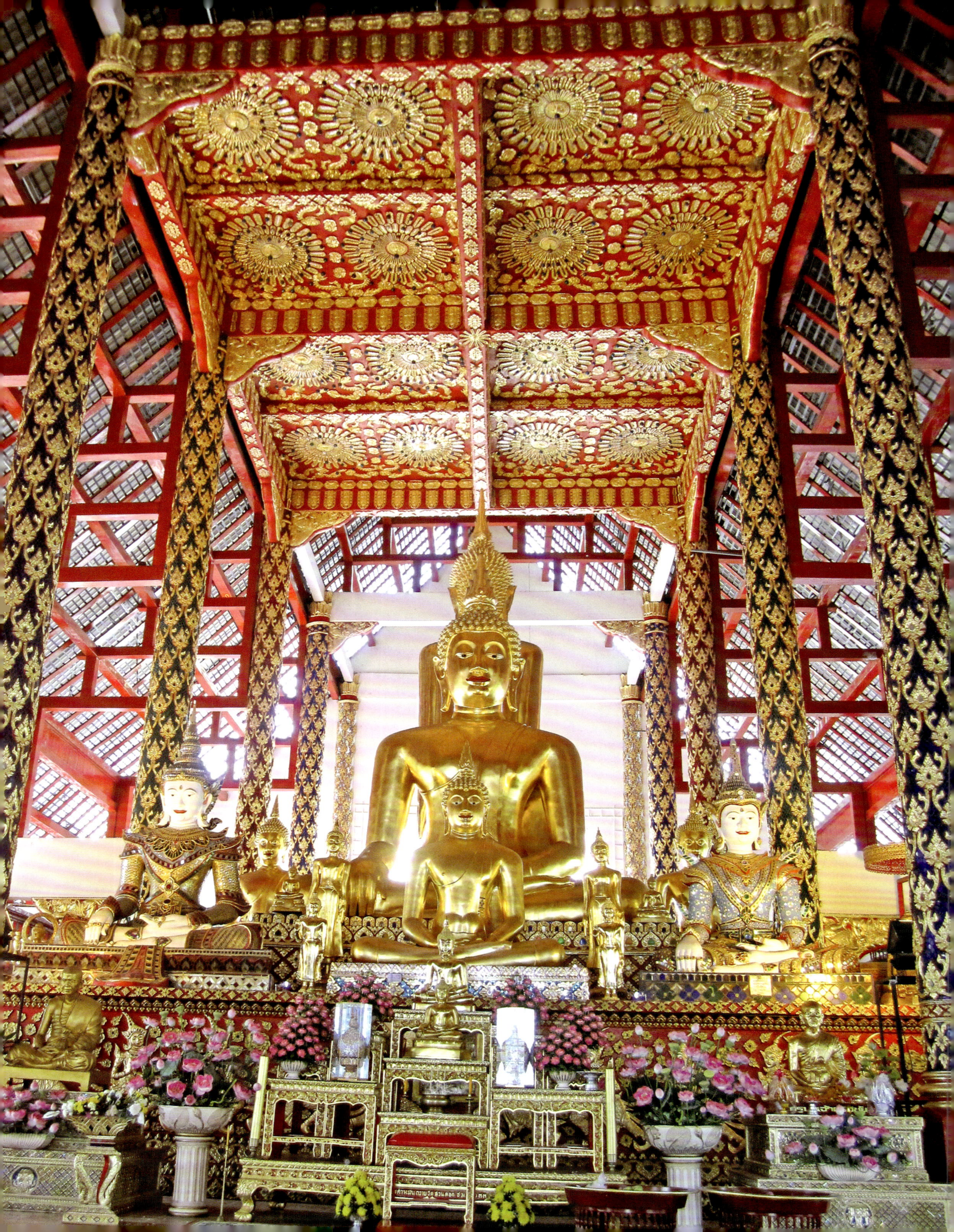

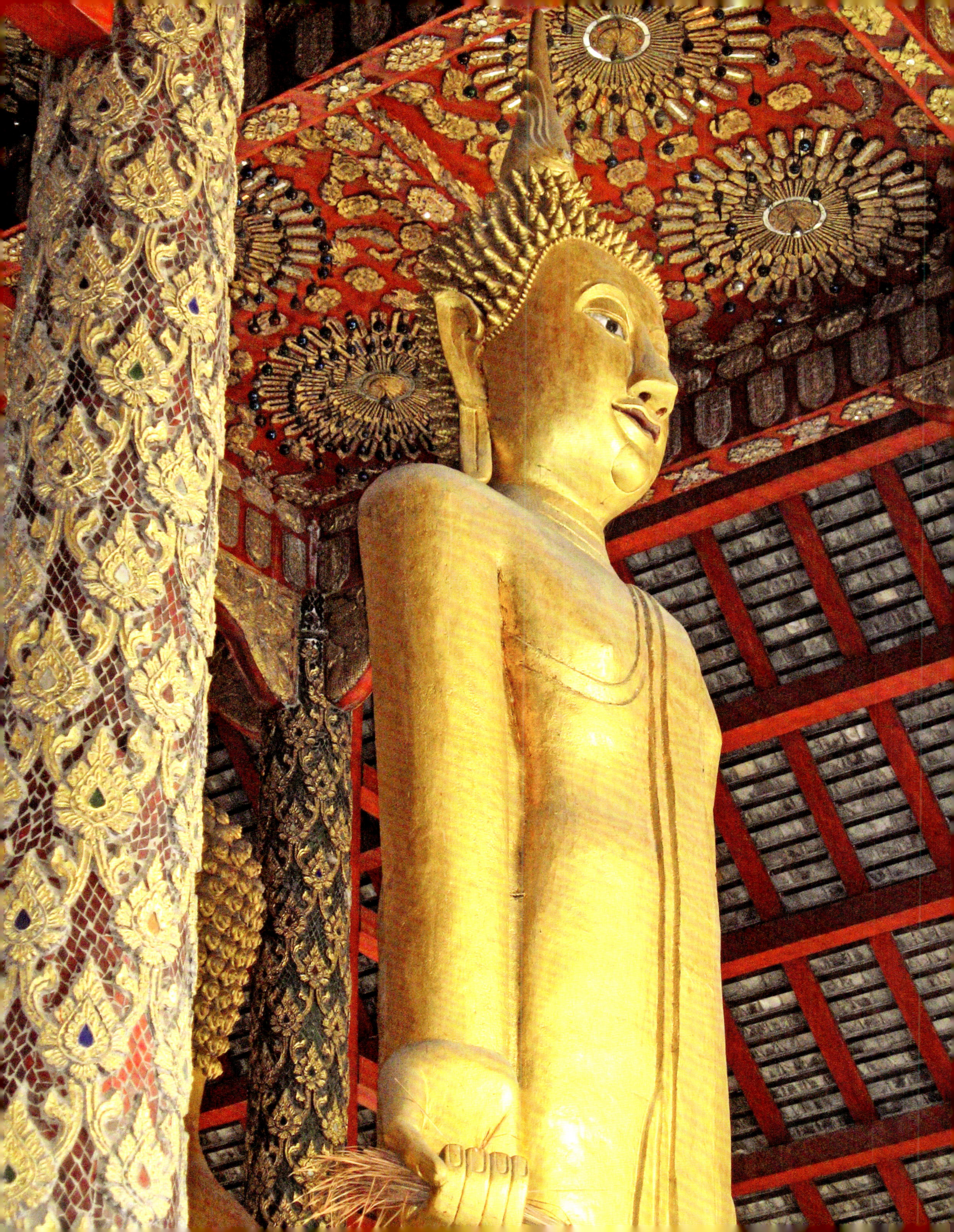

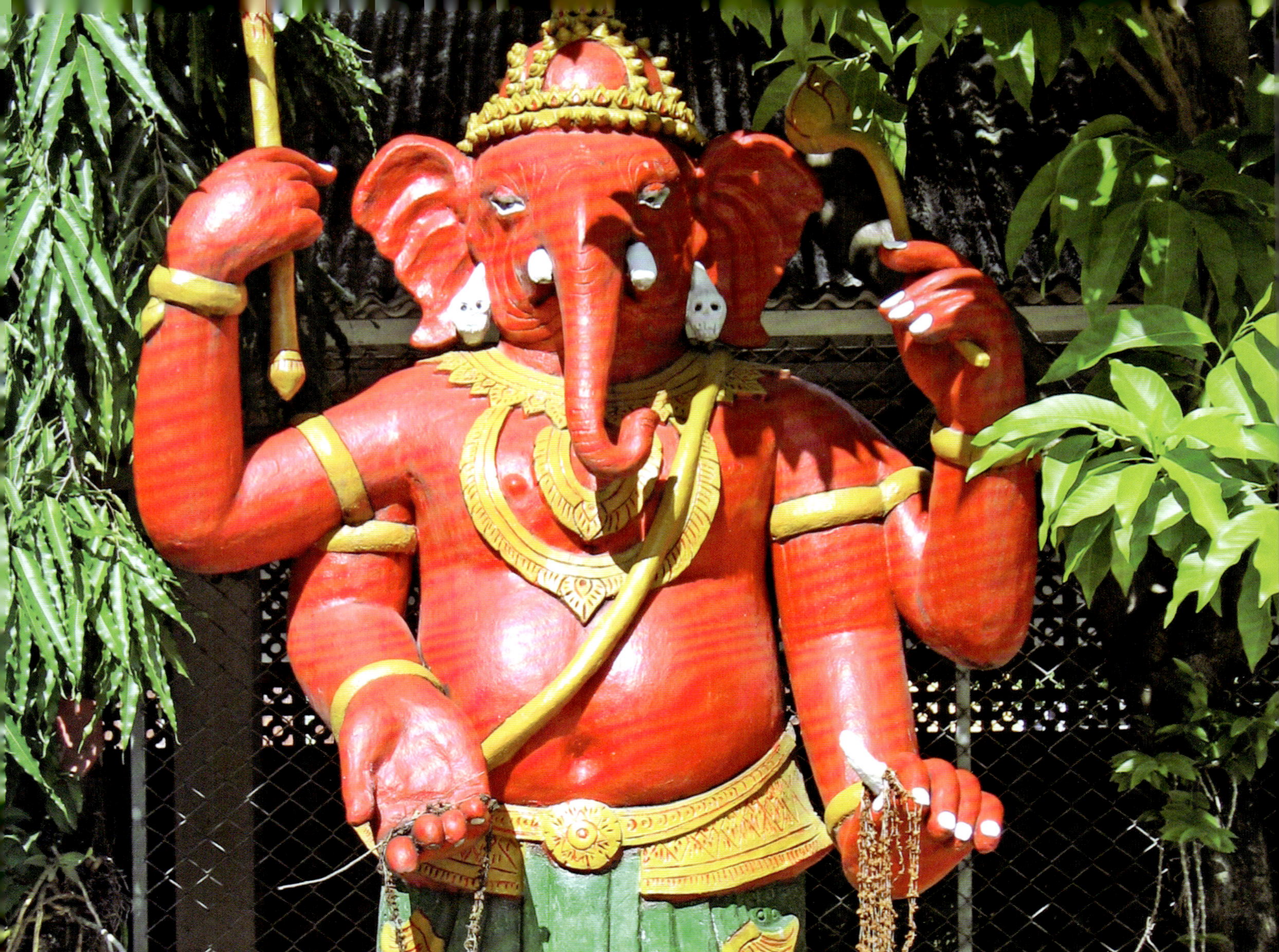

HINDU SHRINES

Despite Hindus accounting for less than 0.1% of today's population, the effects and importance of Hinduism in Thailand are significant. The use of holy strings and the pouring of water from conchs are Brahmin (orthodox Hindu) rituals incorporated, along with Hindu deities, into Buddhist traditions. Three aspects of God exist in Hinduism: Brahma the Creator, Vishnu the Preserver, and Shiva the Destroyer. In front of the Intercontinental Hotel in Bangkok, stands a large statue of Vishnu atop his steed Garuda, king of the birds. Across the street under the Chitlom Skytrain walkway is the Erawan Shrine (officially Thao Maha Brahma), with a statue of the four-faced four-armed Brahma, Phra Phrom, in a mirror-tiled Khmer-style open-air canopy. It was built in 1956 to appease angry spirits that reputedly took the lives of workers and caused accidents during the building of the Erawan Hotel, as the laying of the foundation began on an inauspicious date. This statue of Brahma was blessed during numerous ceremonies at sacred spots by both Buddhist monks and Hindu Brahmins. Once consecrated, all injuries stopped. In 2006, a mentally unbalanced Thai man attacked the shrine with a hammer and was beaten to death by worshippers; a new statue was quickly erected. Devotees believe Brahma can answer one's prayers and bring good fortune.

Diagonally located from the Erawan Shrine is the shopping center Central World Plaza, with a large shrine dedicated to Lord Ganesh, the remover of all obstacles and grantor of success. The four-armed god Ganesh was born of fertility goddess Parvati's sweat, created to guard her while bathing. Shiva, her husband, returned home and Ganesh blocked his entrance. Shiva was so enraged he cut off Ganesh's head. When Parvati explained, Shiva repented and put a baby elephant's head on Ganesh's body. Nearby is the Trimurti Shrine, a gold two-headed four-armed statue representing the three aspects of god, combined to form the god of love. The largest Hindu artifact in Bangkok is at the Erawan Museum, where resides a 150-ton statue of the triple-headed elephant Airavata (in Thai: *Erawan*), the mount of Indra, king of all deities and the god of thunder and war. These are just a few examples of the incorporation of Hindu deities into the Thai belief system.

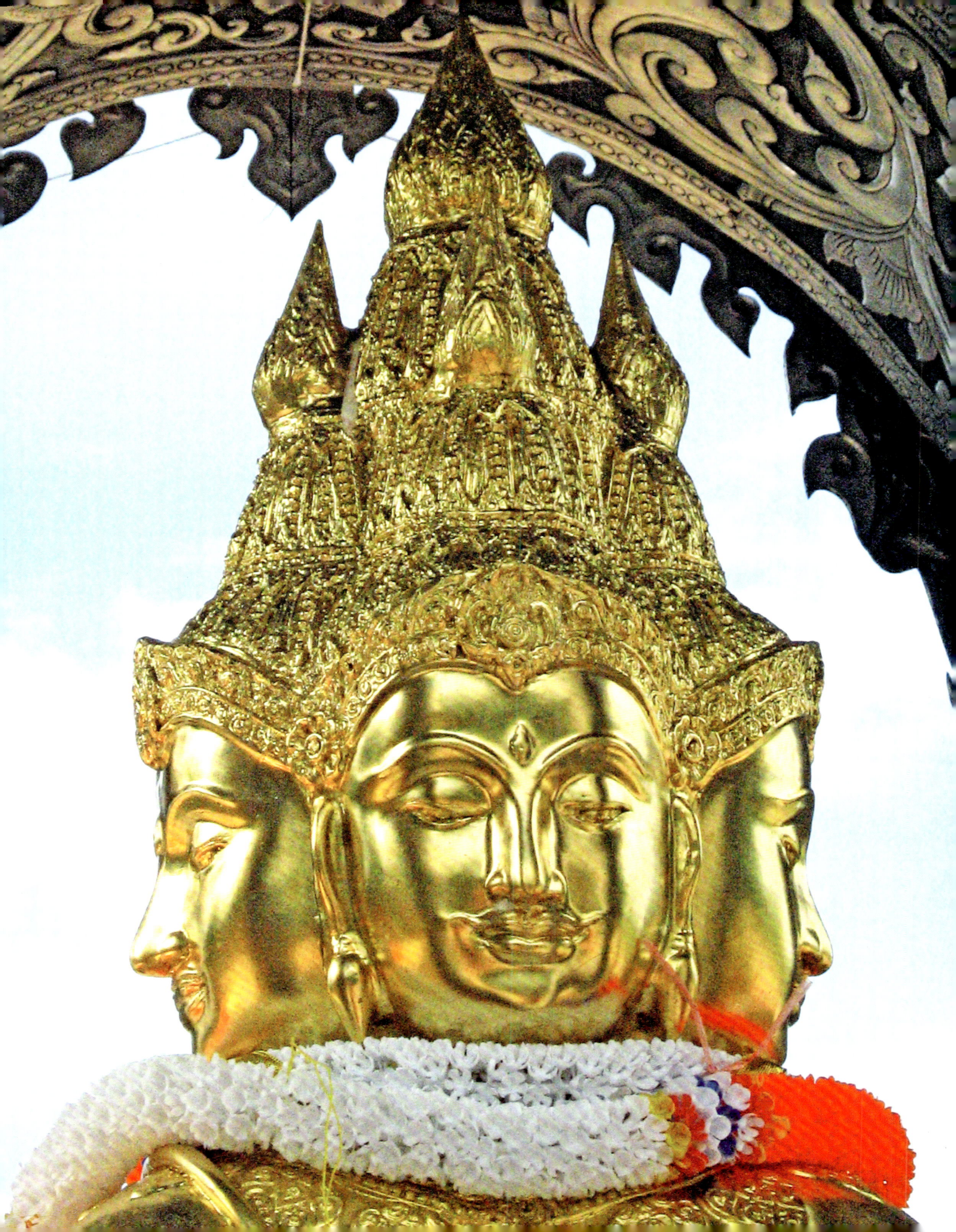

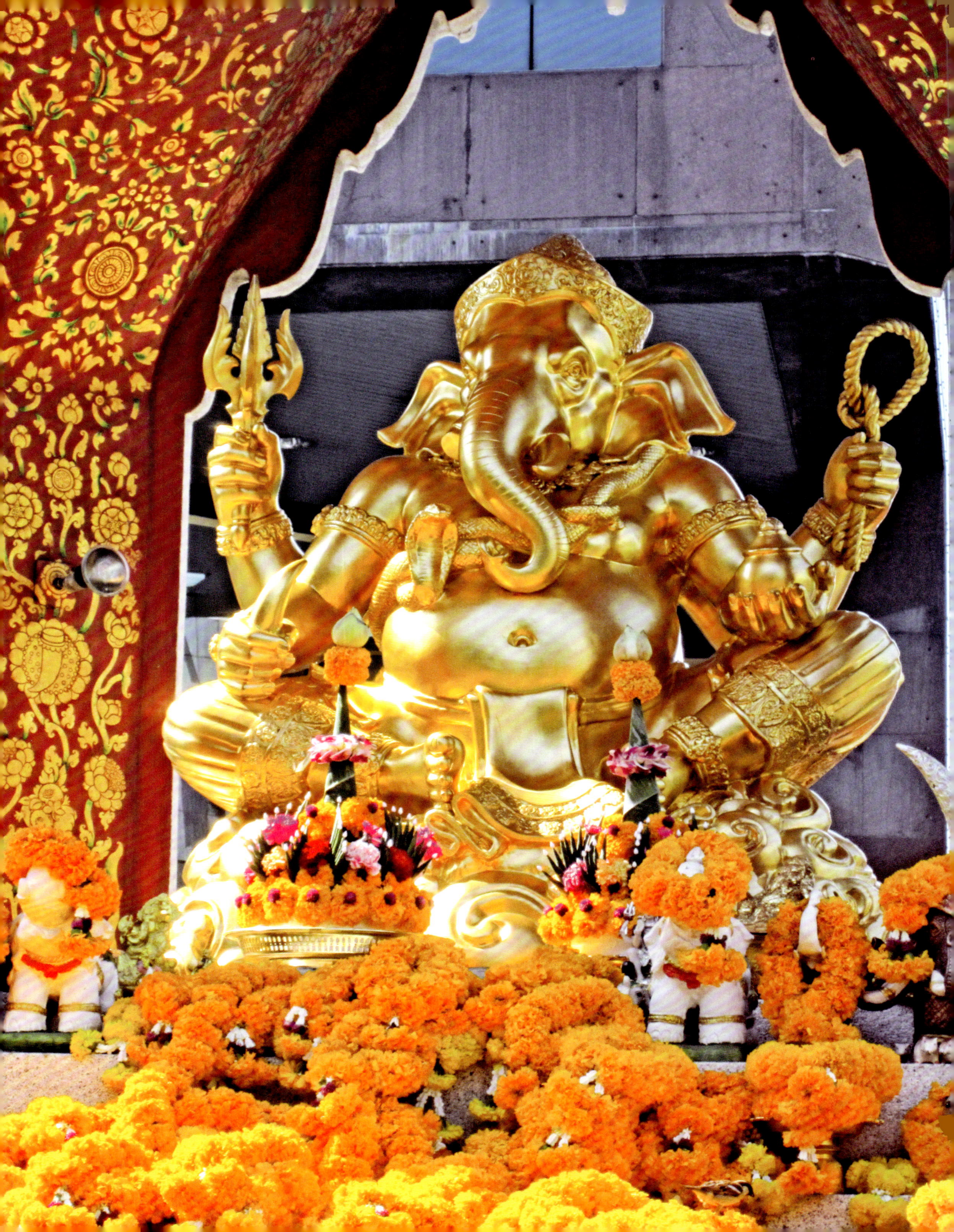

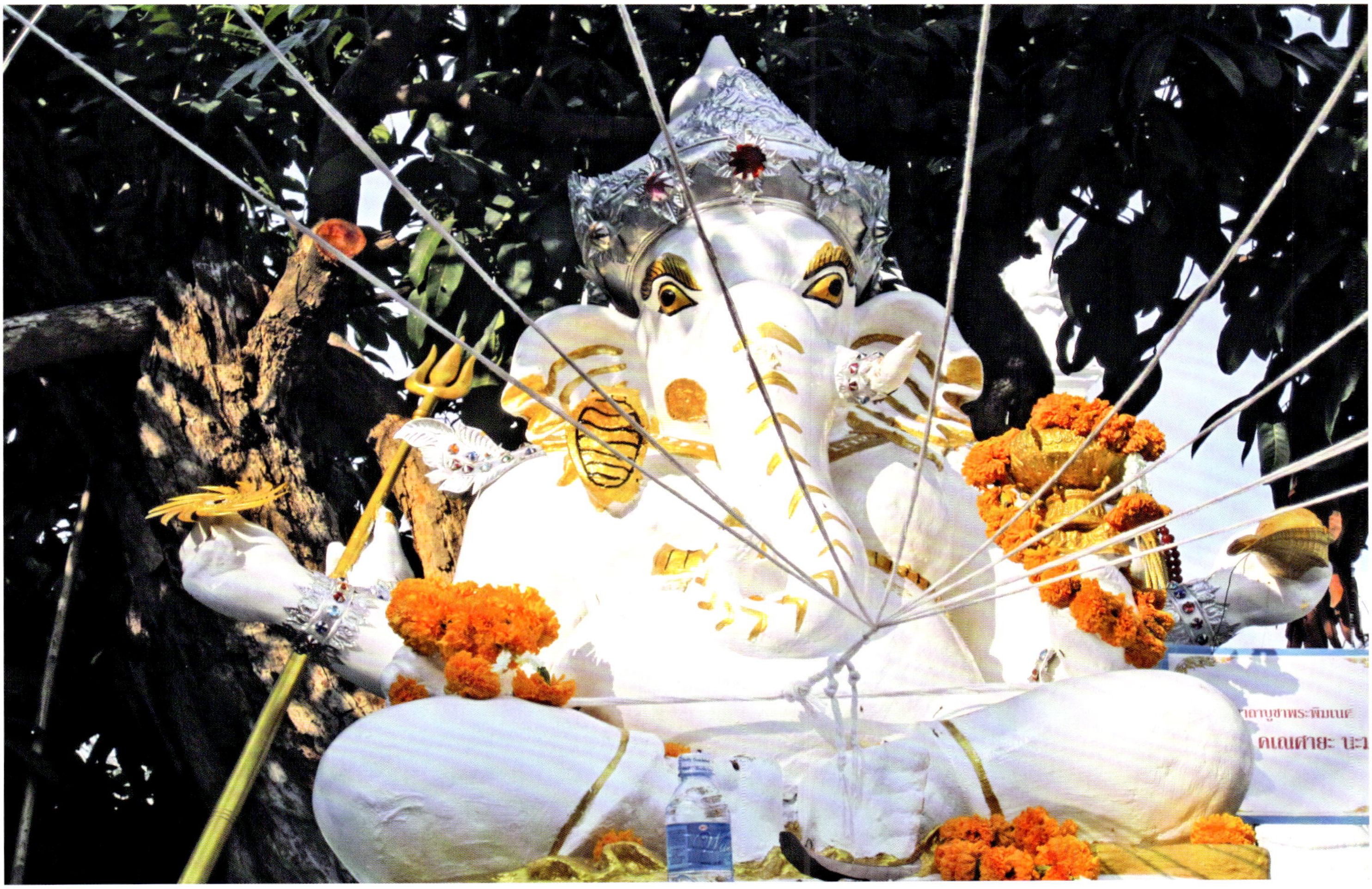

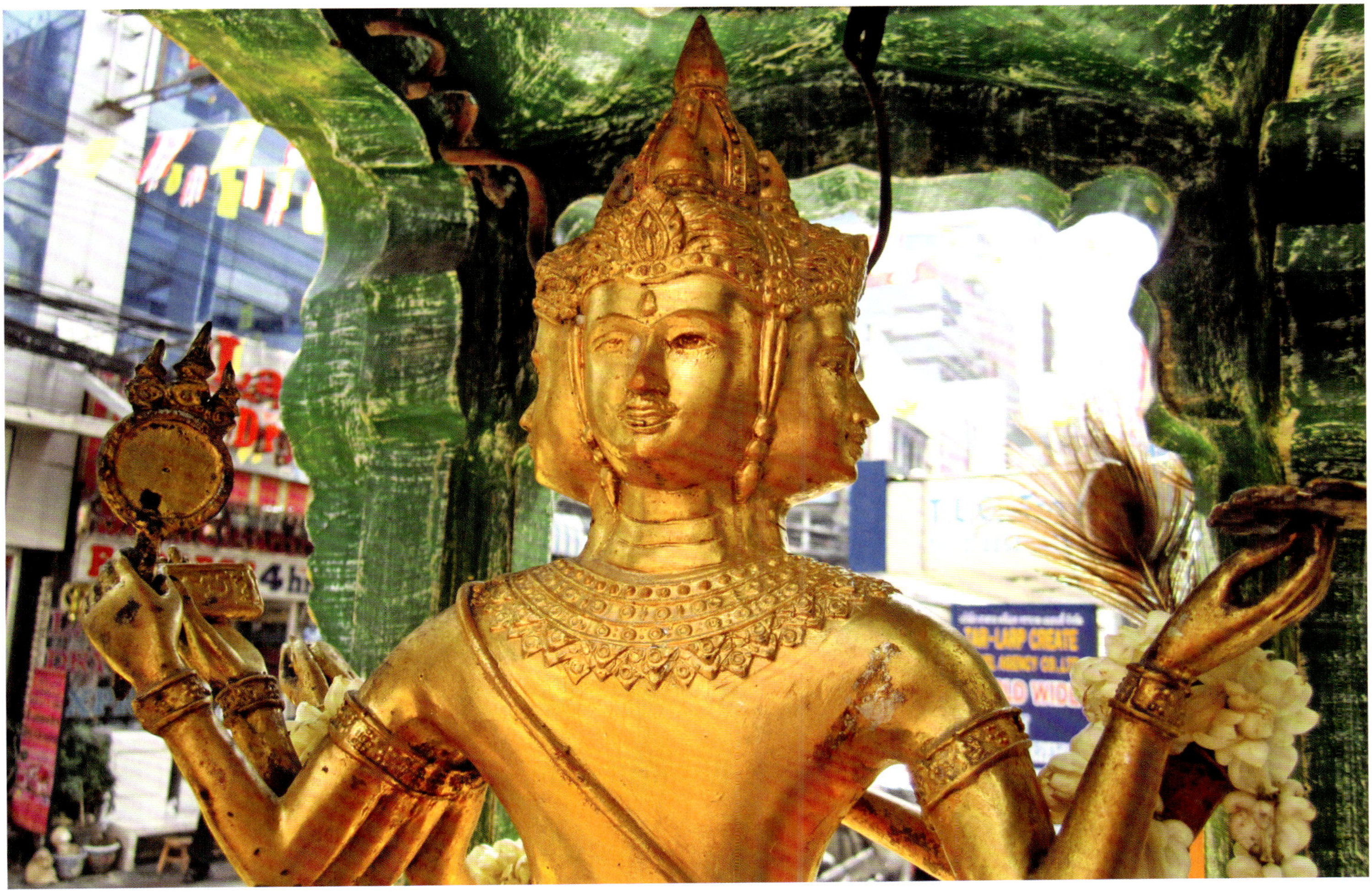

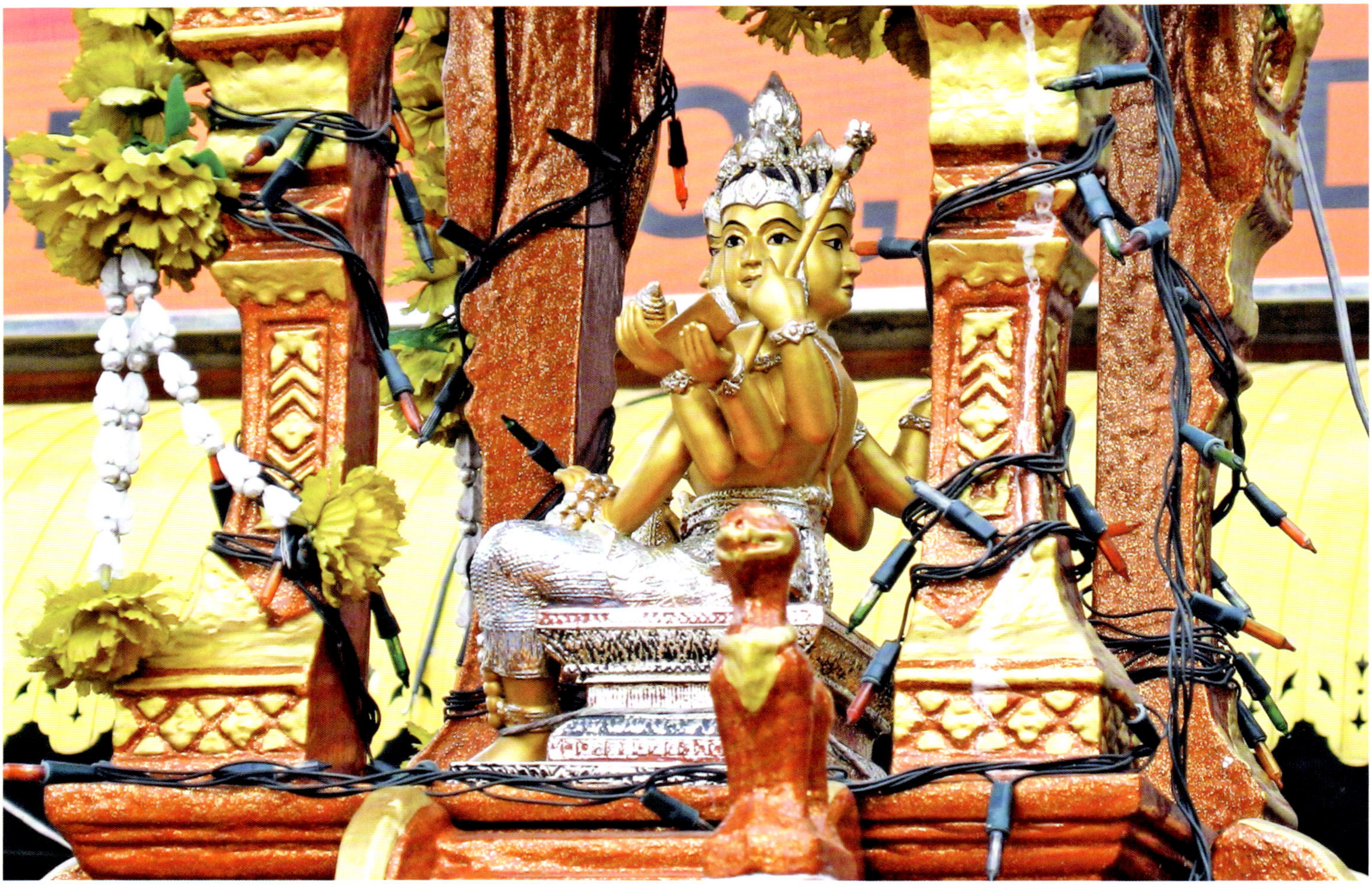

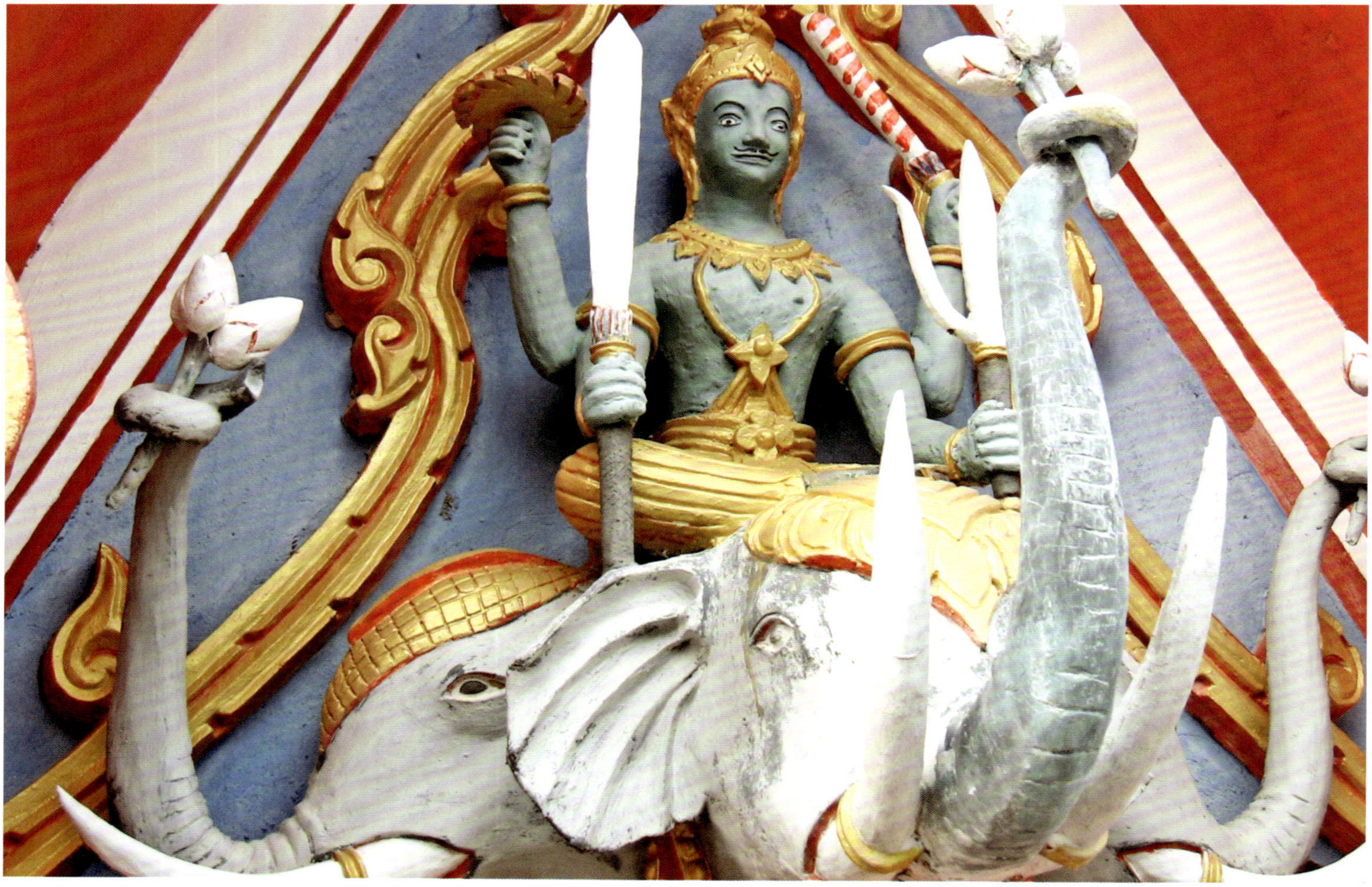

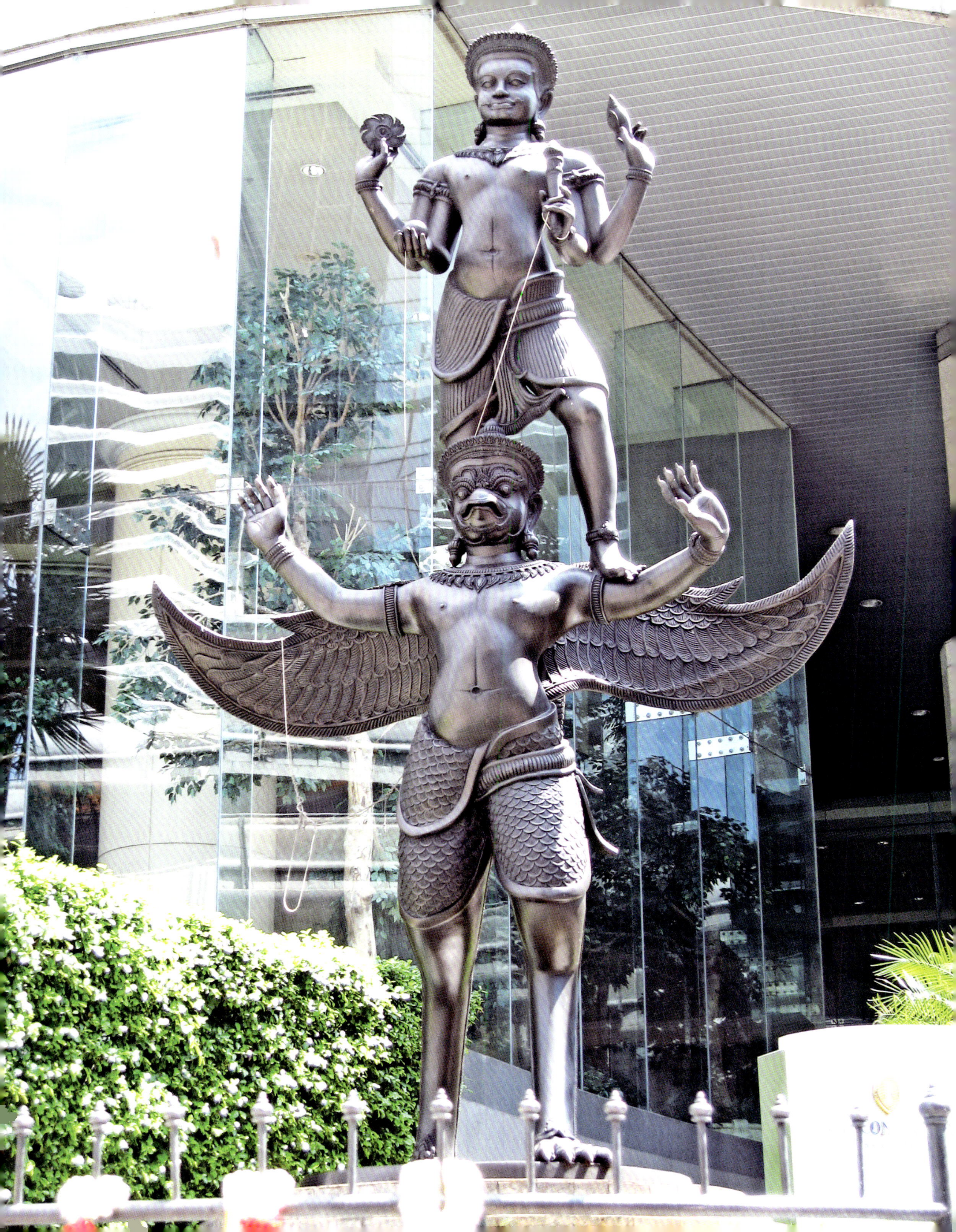

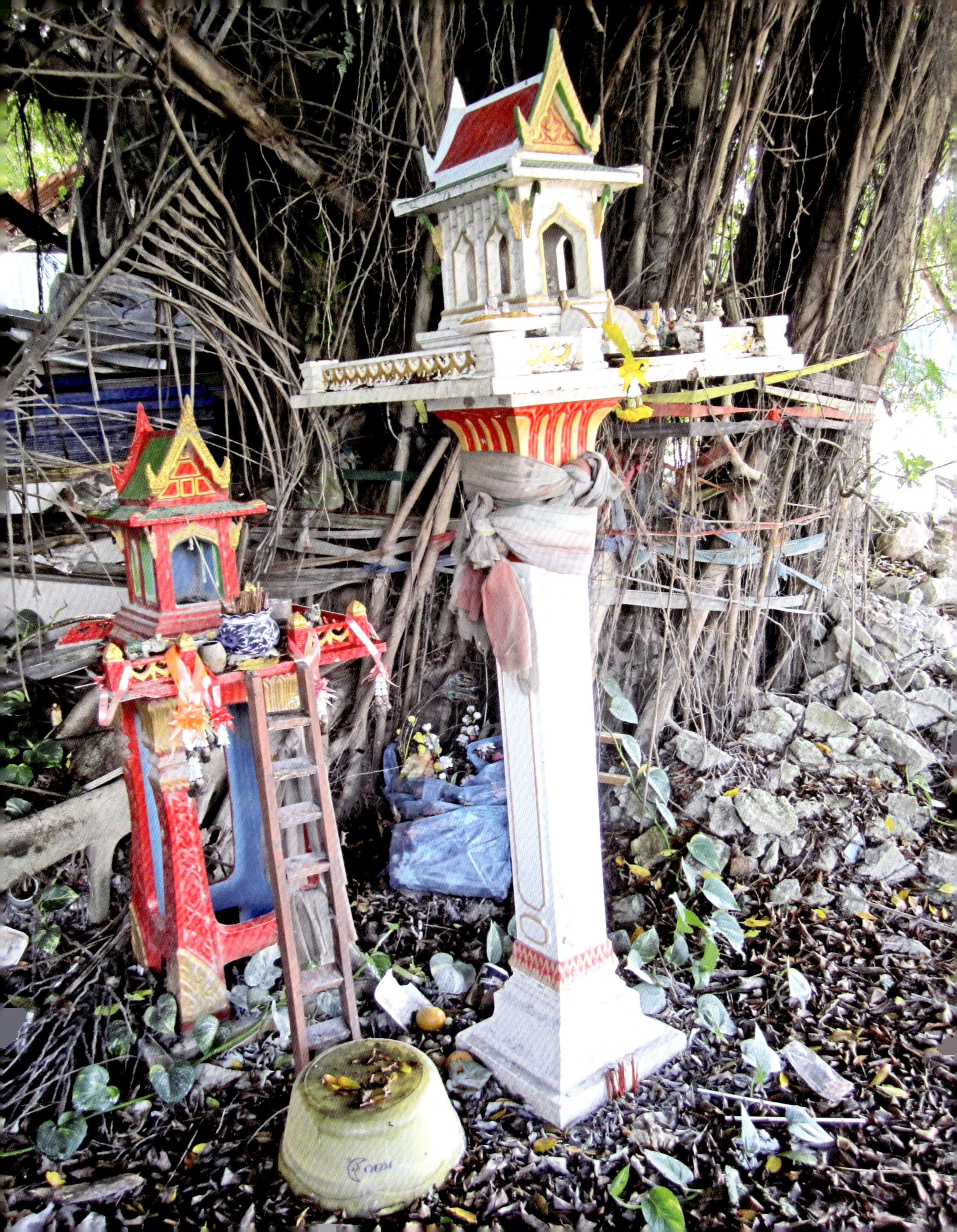

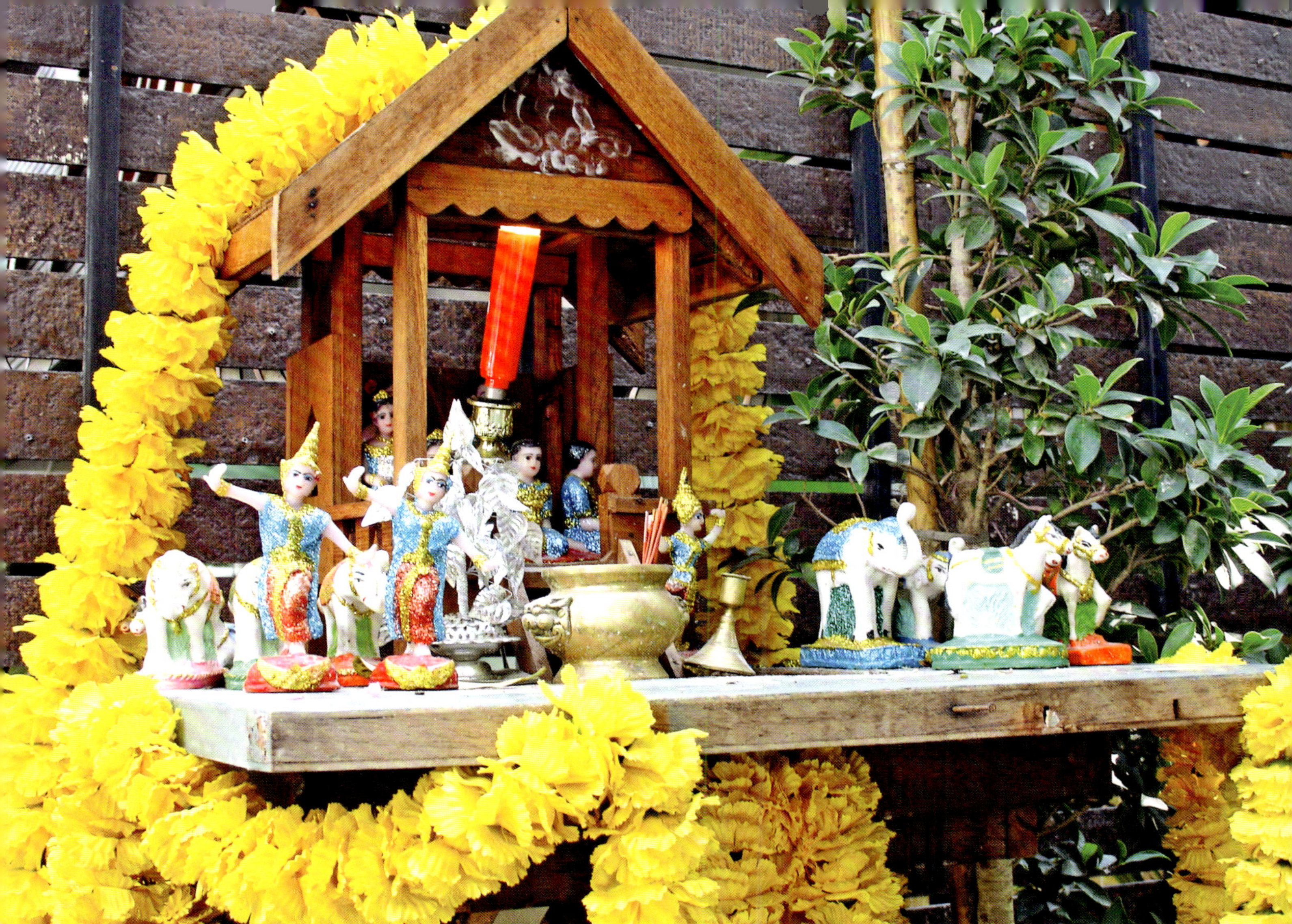

3. SPIRIT HOUSES

Spirits, or *phiis*, are everywhere in the Thai pantheon, and virtually anything good or bad in a person's life can be attributed to the effects of these forces. *Phra phums* are the spirits of the land, and when building a house on their territory, they must be placated with another residence to avoid disharmony and disruption in one's life and home. A *san phra phum* or spirit house can vary in design and expense appropriate to the splendor of the human abode, but must contain a room for the spirit to live in and a veranda to leave daily offerings of food, drink, incense, flowers and garlands. Figurines of animals, servants and dancers are presented to assist *phra phum*, represented as a drawn or pressed figure on stone or plastic, or a figurine, sword in his left hand, a bag of money in his right. The spirit house should face north or east but must not be placed in the shadow of the main residence. A Brahmin priest performs a ceremony on an auspicious date and time and invites the spirit to take up residency (Reichart & Khongkhunthian, 2007, pp. 1-3, 20). Often there are two spirit houses, one on four posts with a ladder close to the ground, and a taller more elaborate house on a single post. There may be a separate shrine for one's ancestors or grandparents. Spirit houses are found in caves, built onto Bodhi trees and in most temples, as Buddhism embraces these animist and Hindu traditions into its modern-day belief system.

Traveling on mountain highways in Thailand, one finds a gathering of spirit houses near a bad curve, erected as housing to pacify the souls of those who have died in motorbike and car accidents, who are now feared to have turned into violent *phii tai hong* spirits. Passing motorists sound their horns in respect (Broman, 2005, p.65). An old spirit house cannot be dismantled or discarded as trash: it must be placed near a Bodhi tree or in a corner of a *wat* and allowed to disintegrate over time. A ceremony must be held to transfer the spirit from the old to the new spirit house. Broken spirit houses and figurines are often left in roadside graveyards near banyan trees to return to the elements or set further back beyond the houses left for the spirits of motorists (Reichart & Khongkhunthian, 2007, pp. 40-41).

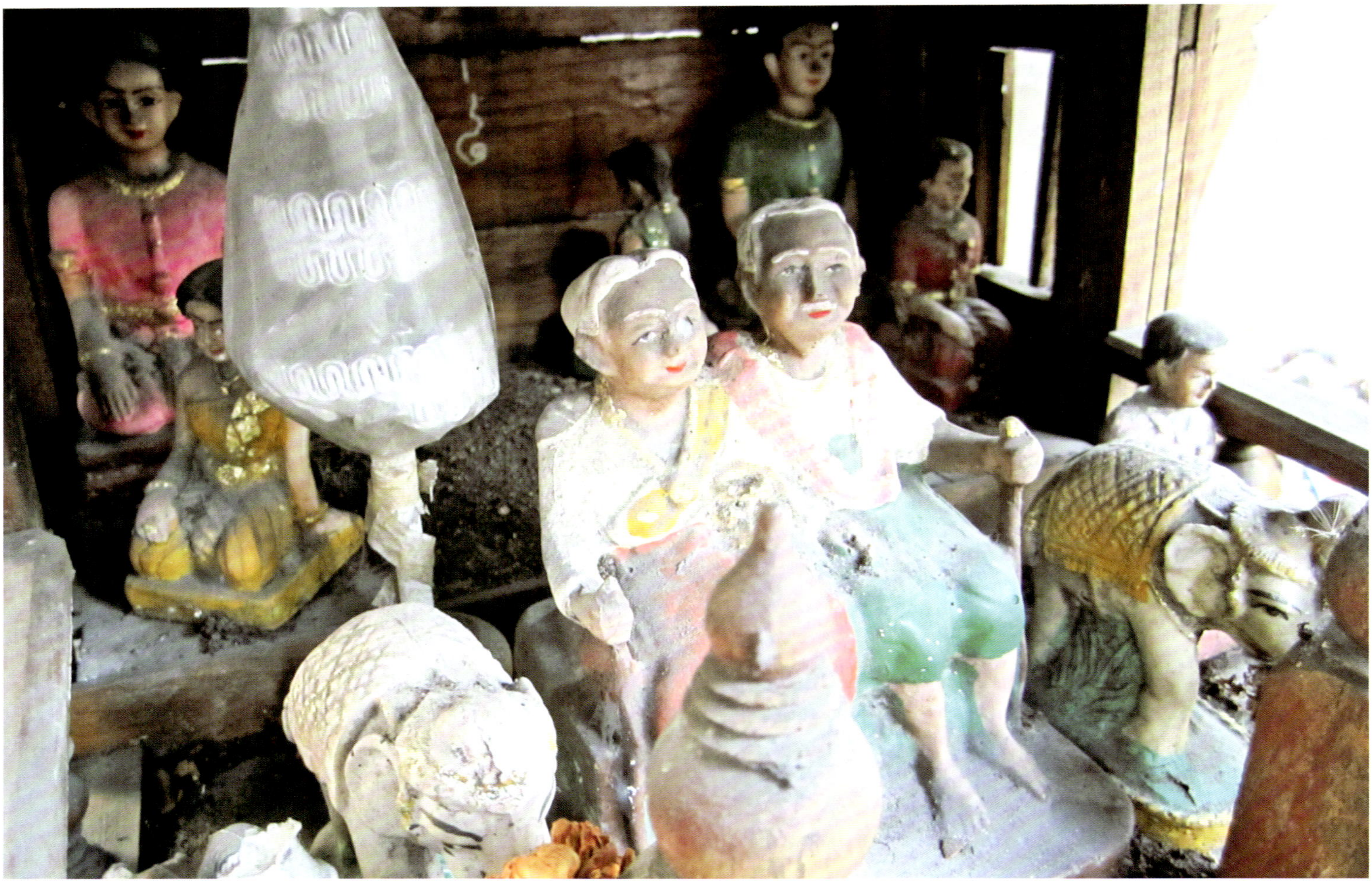

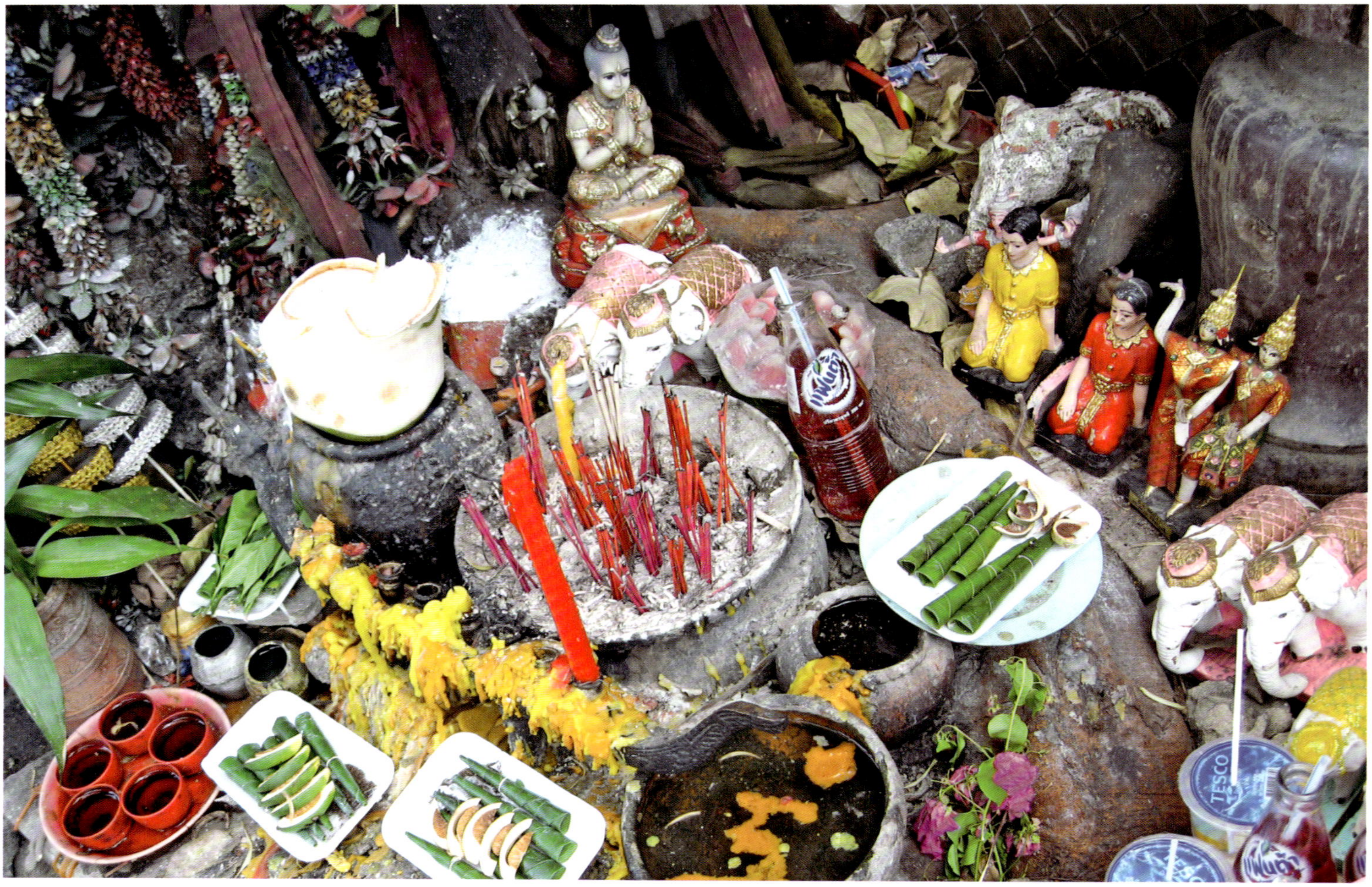

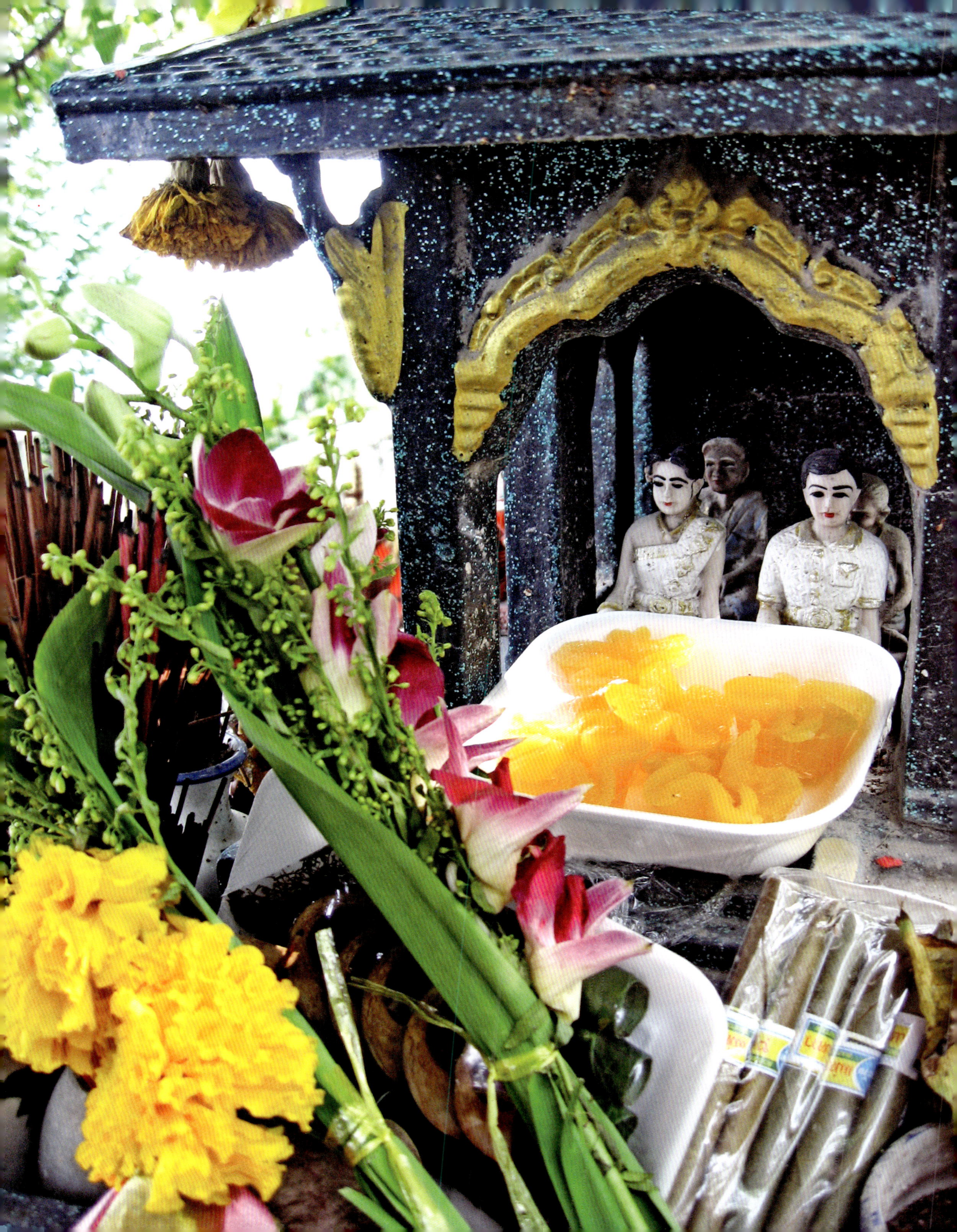

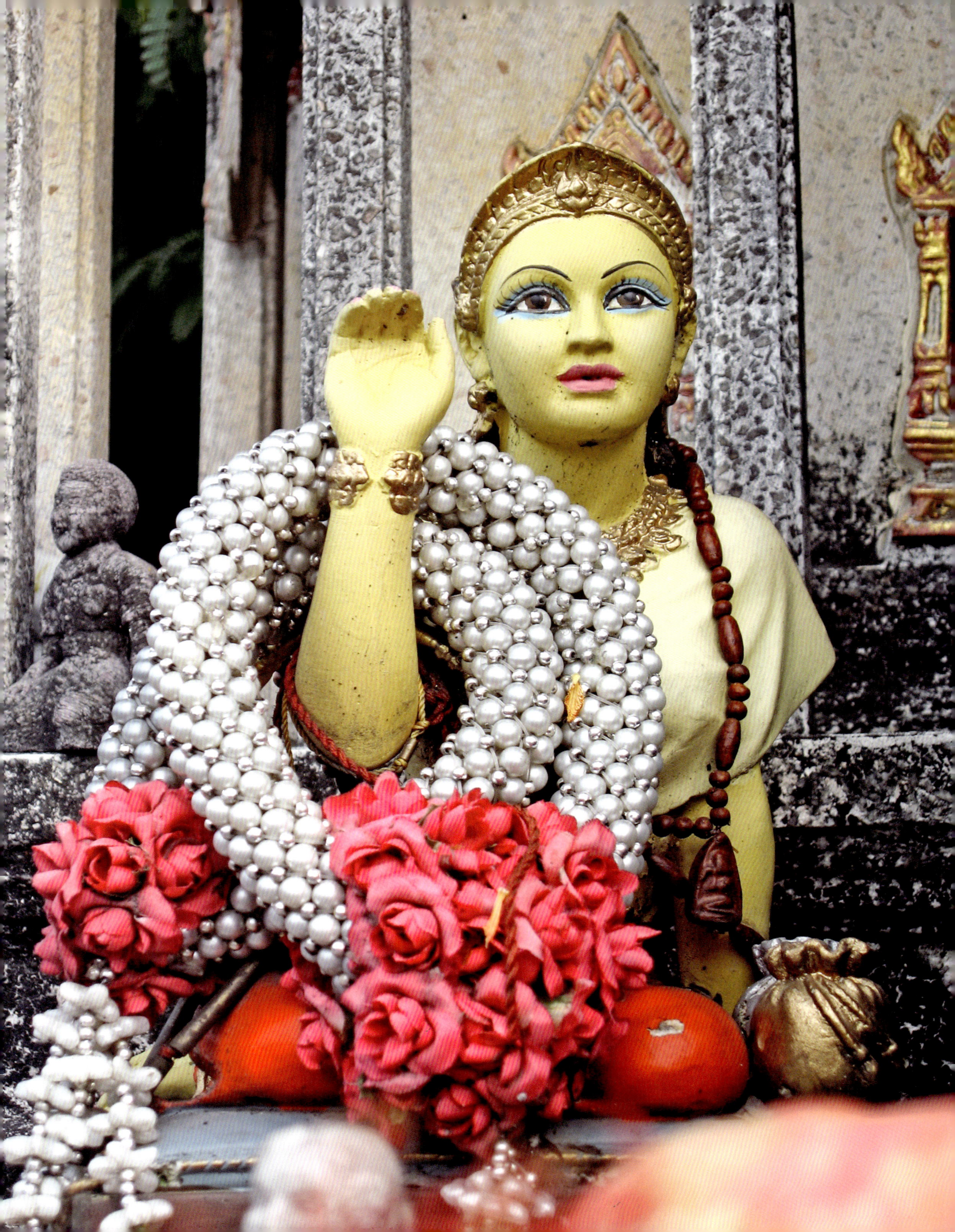

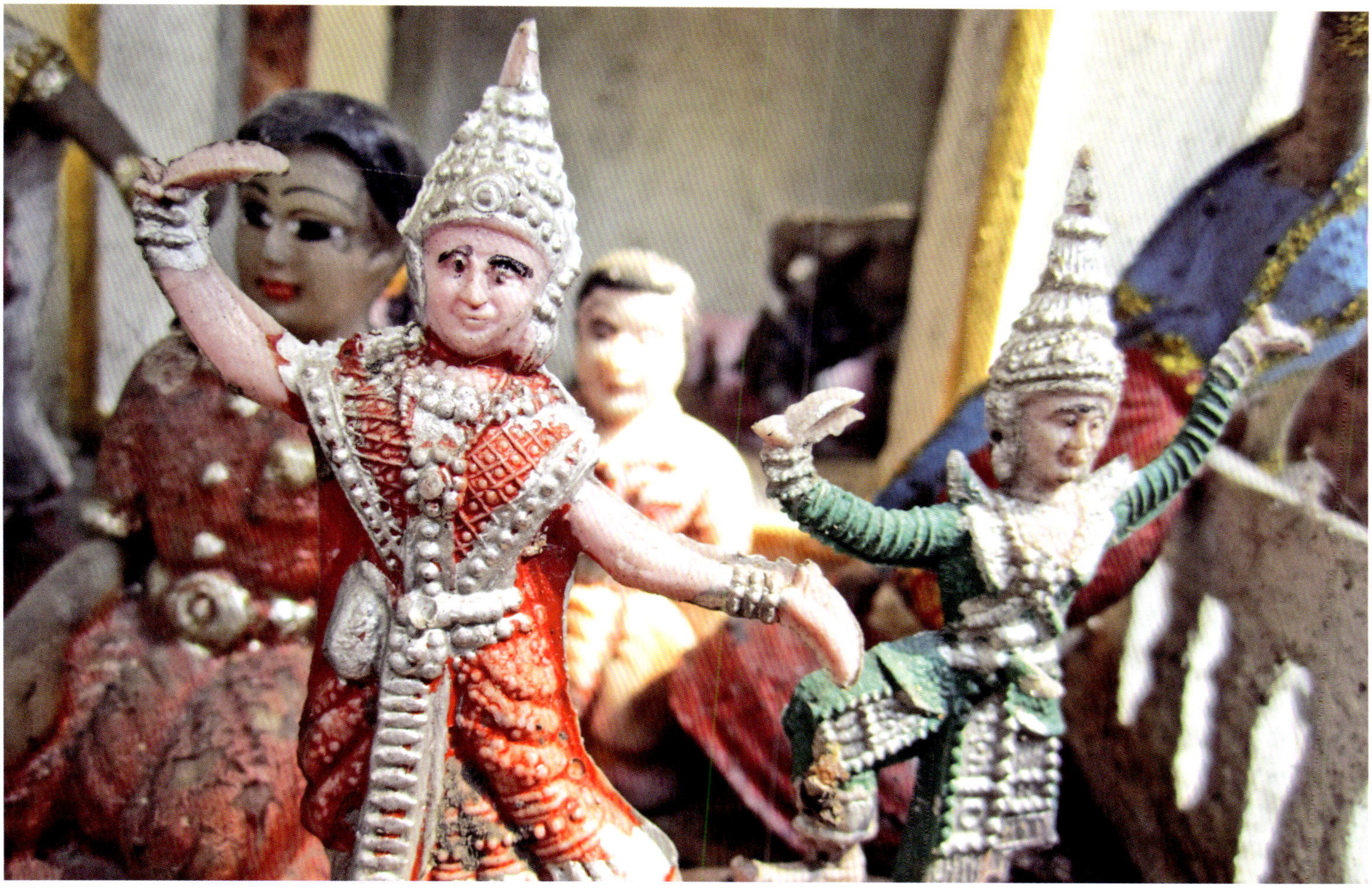

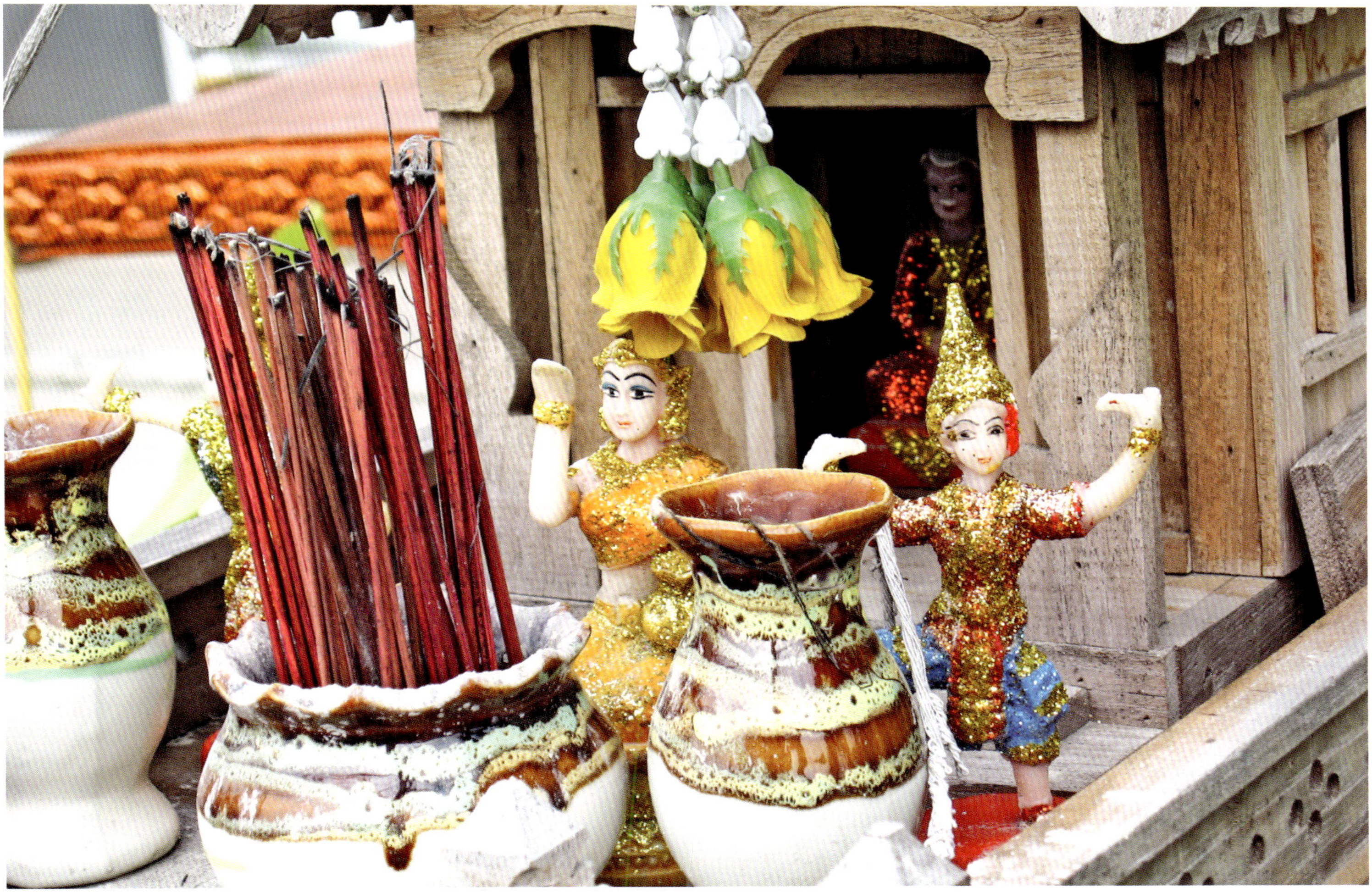

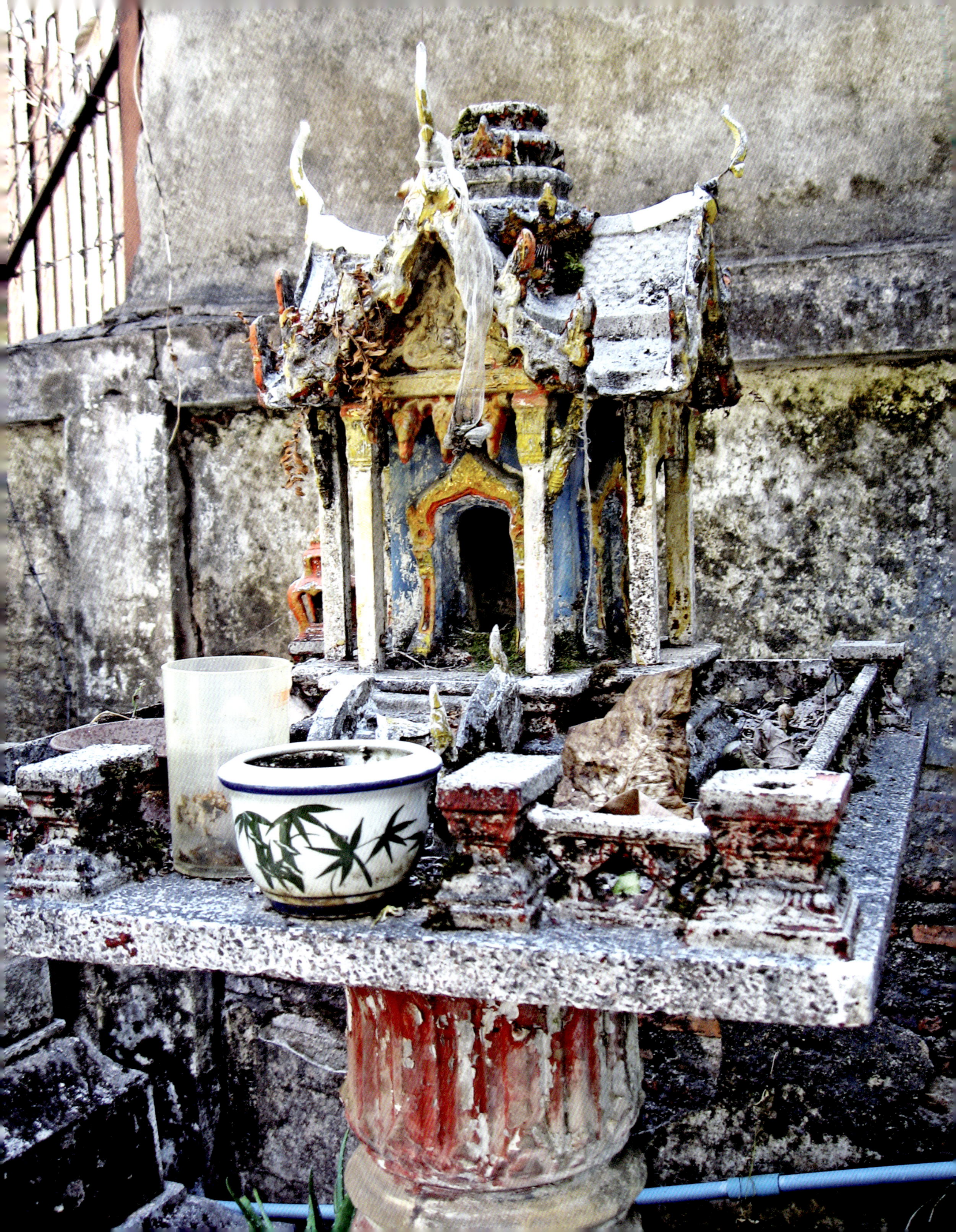

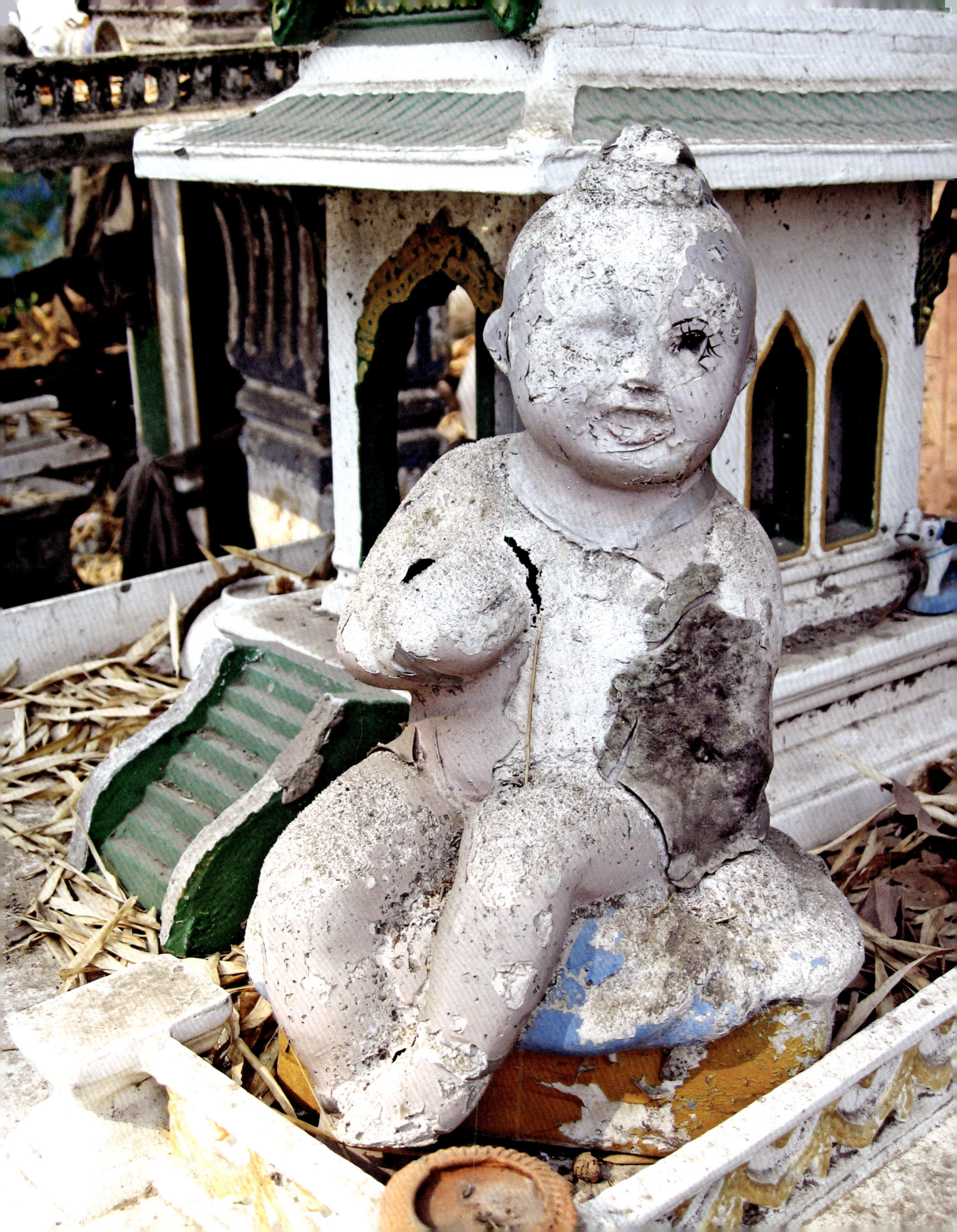

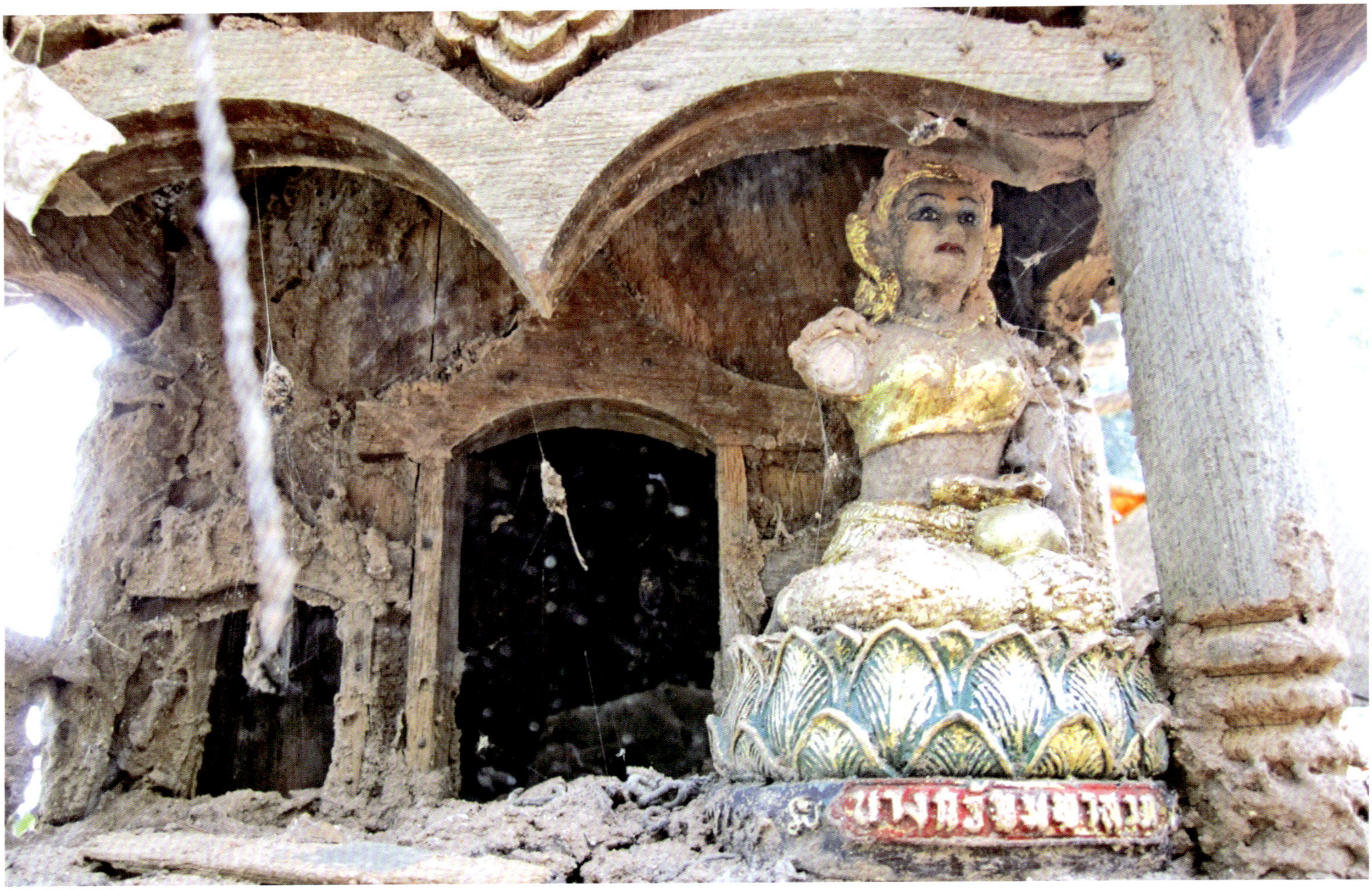

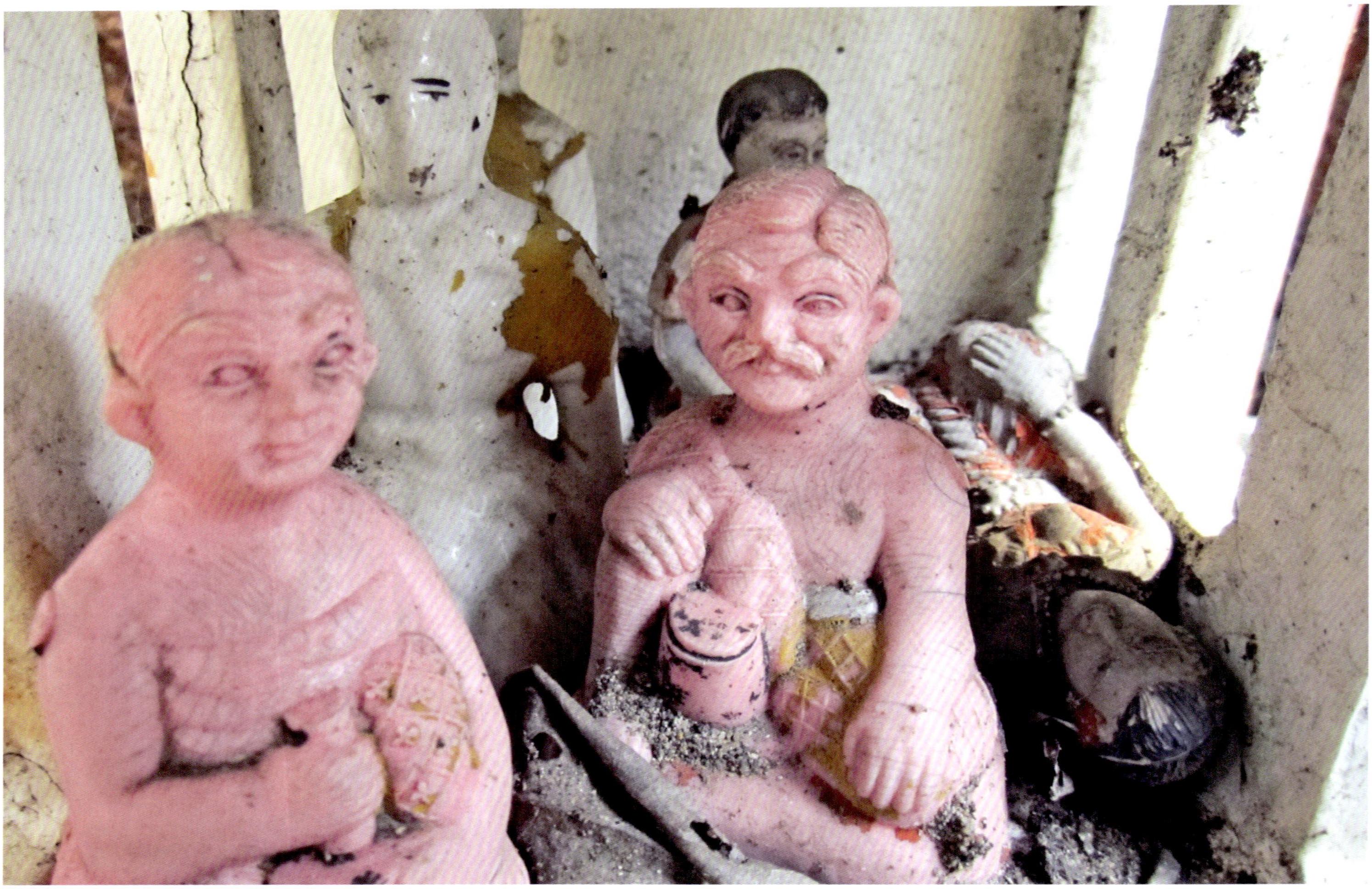

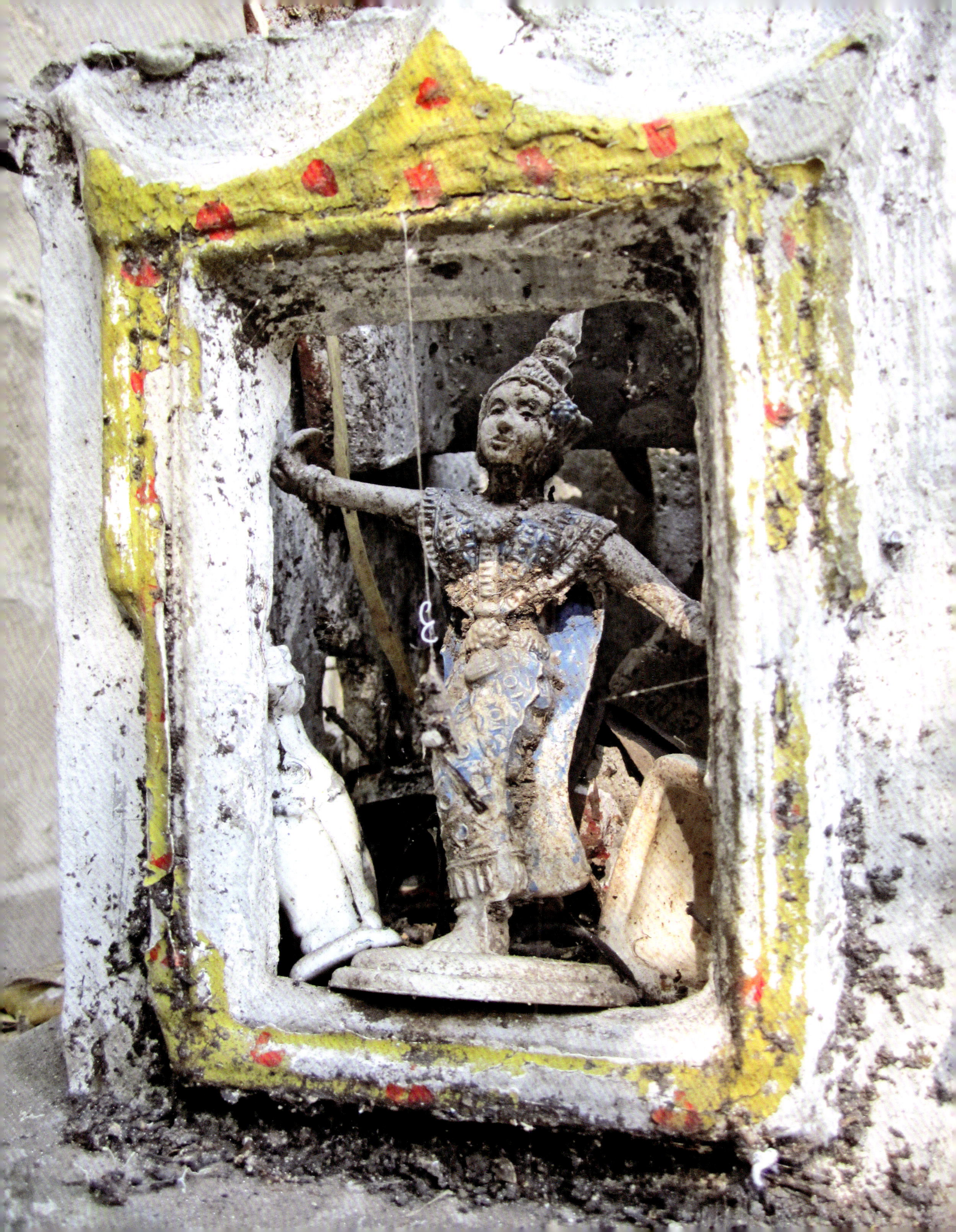

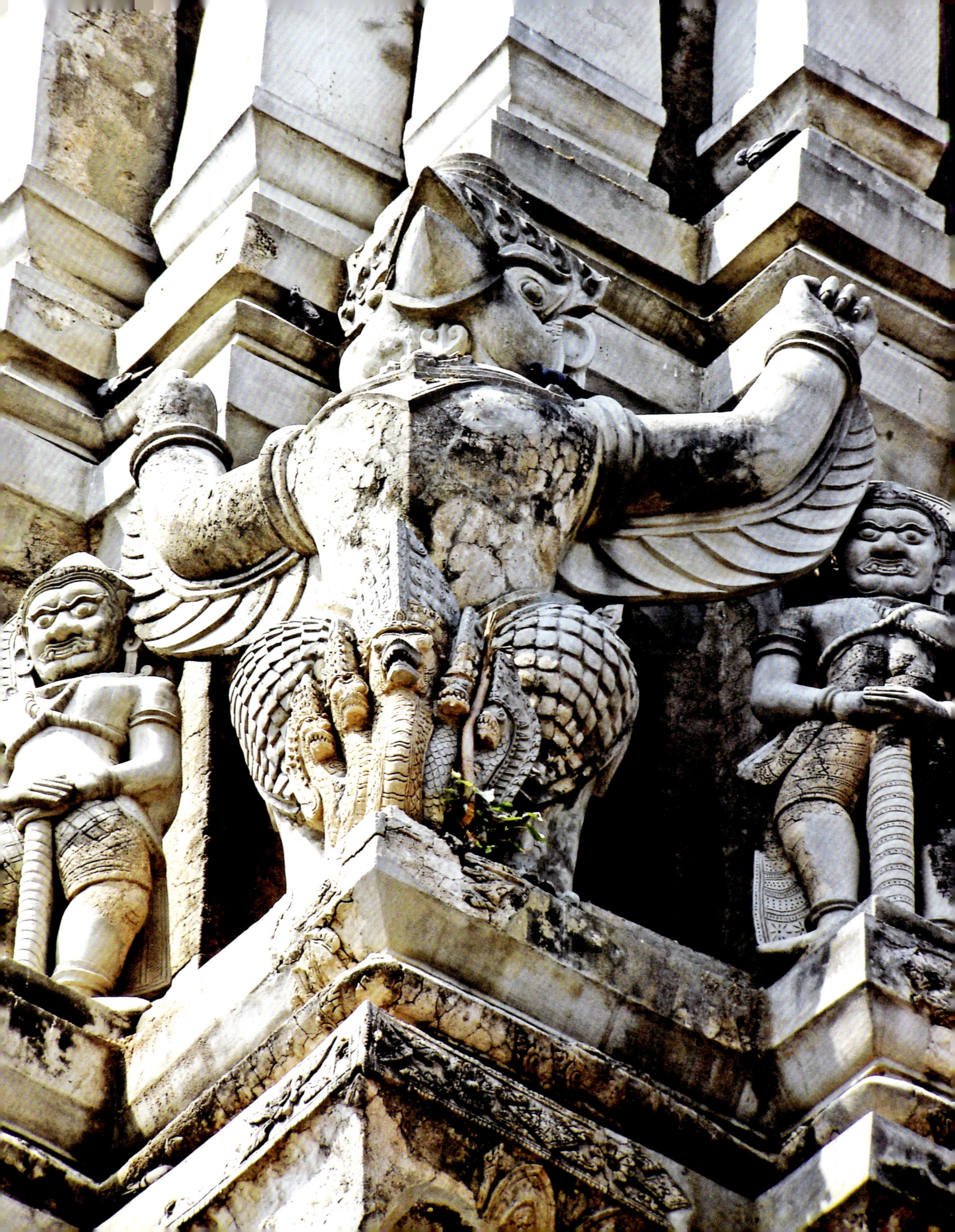

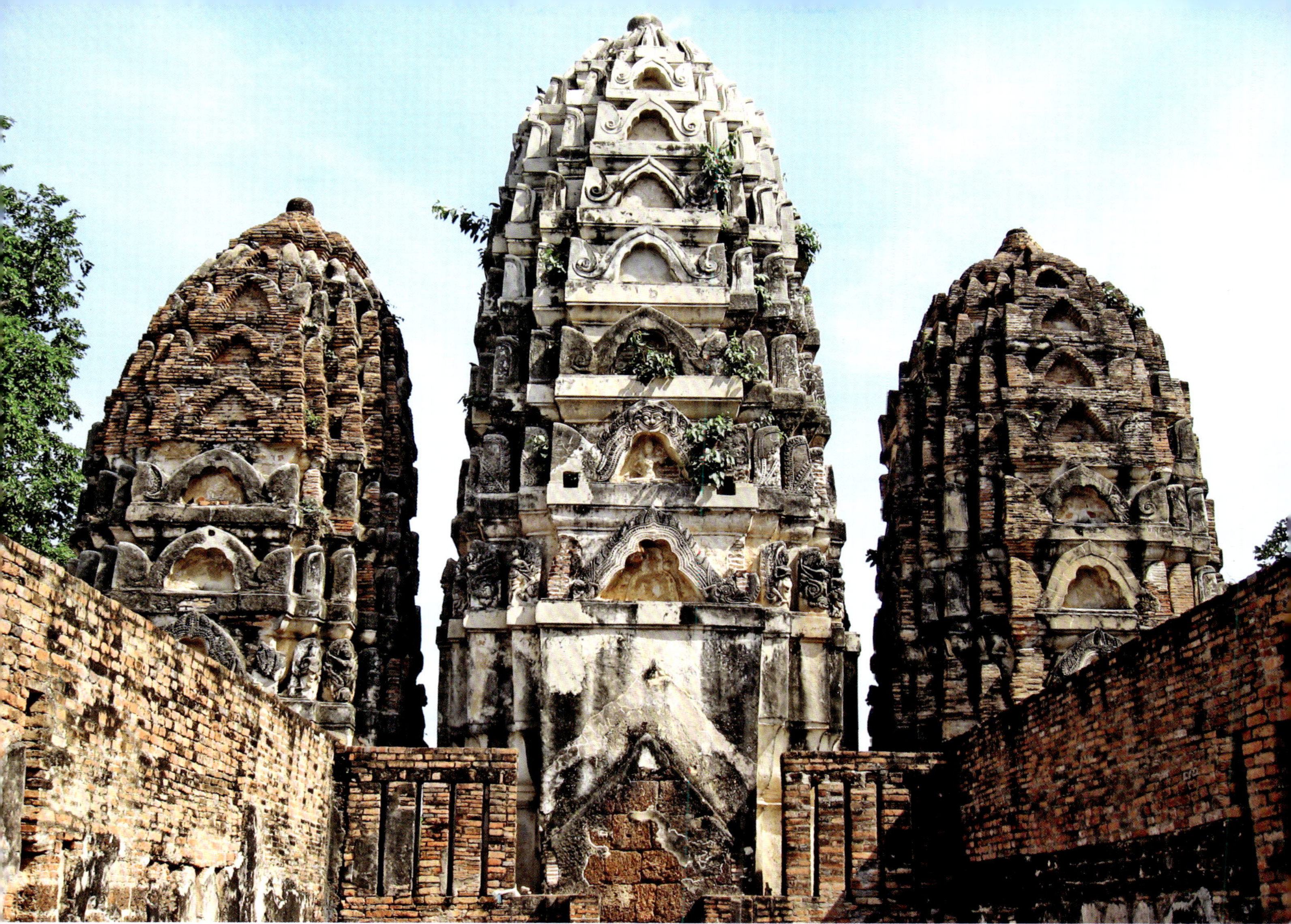

4. KHMER TEMPLES

When examining Khmer-style temples in Thailand, consider the Thai and Cambodian border as a nineteenth century concept, which has fluctuated over time. By the end of the eleventh century, Tai-speaking people of Yunnan Chinese origin settled in present day Thailand. They developed communities, built towns and intermarried with the ruling classes, the Khmers and the Mons. They became known as the Siamese, as Sukothai was called Siam by the Chinese. Sukothai, the first Thai kingdom and center of art, began in approximately 1238 when it separated from the Khmer trade center of Lop Buri. Sukothai became Siam's first capital in 1270, under the leadership of King Ram Khamhaeng, moving the focus from a Hindu-based ideology to a Theravadin Buddhist foundation. Ayutthaya, on the Chao Phraya River in the north central region, became the second capital city in 1350, incorporating Sukothai into its kingdom in 1438, remaining in power until sacked by the Burmese in 1767. Early Ayutthaya kings were greatly impressed with Angkor Wat when they invaded in 1352, and copied much of its style. They were particularly attracted to the notion of the king as divine entity. The *prang*, or reliquary tower, with its bullet-like or corncob profile, was a direct derivation of Khmer architectural style. Wat Ratchaburana, built in 1424, with its towering *prang* prominently featuring a *naga*-treading *garuda* flanked by *yakshas*, is a testament to Khmer influence (Roveda, 2005 pp. 458-9). The *prang* eventually gave way to the Singhalese-based bell-shaped *chedi*, but its design is still present in spirit house production today.

The classic Sukothai Buddha image features a seated Buddha in an earth-touching pose, the head crowned with a flame-like finial or *ratsami*. His robe is barely suggested, a line across the right chest and a stole-like fold over the left shoulder to the navel. The second image is a standing Buddha, one foot forward, right hand raised to the middle of the chest (Rawson, 1967 p. 146). Some temples were of Hindu origin and were converted into Buddhist temples, such as Wat Si Sawai with its three magnificent *prang* towers. Prasat Pueai Noi in Khon Kaen was also as a Hindu sanctuary, built in the tenth to eleventh century. The compound has three east-facing buildings, constructed of rectangular laterite blocks. The ruins feature intricate lintels depicting Kala with garlands or demons coming from his mouth (Pg. 137-8).

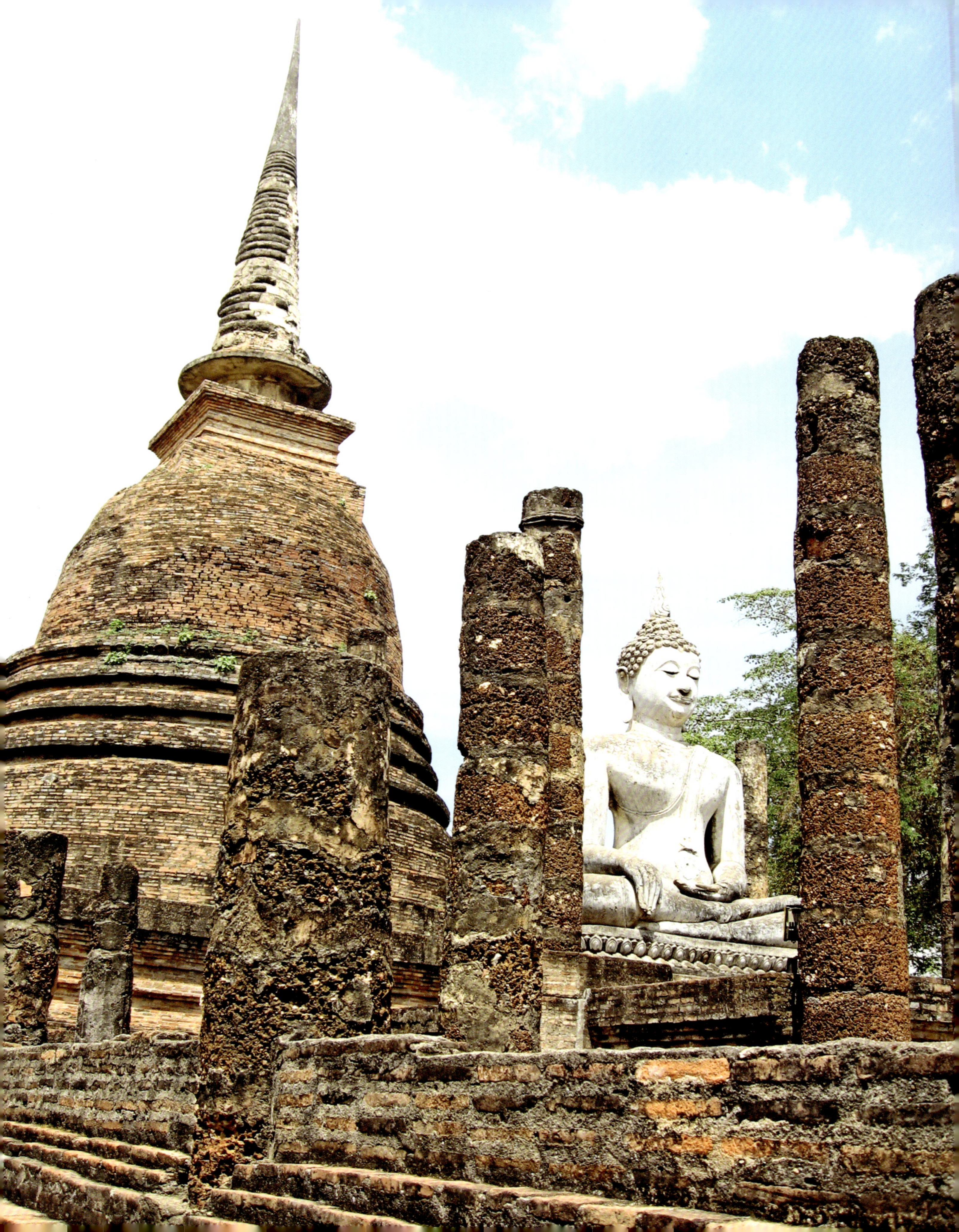

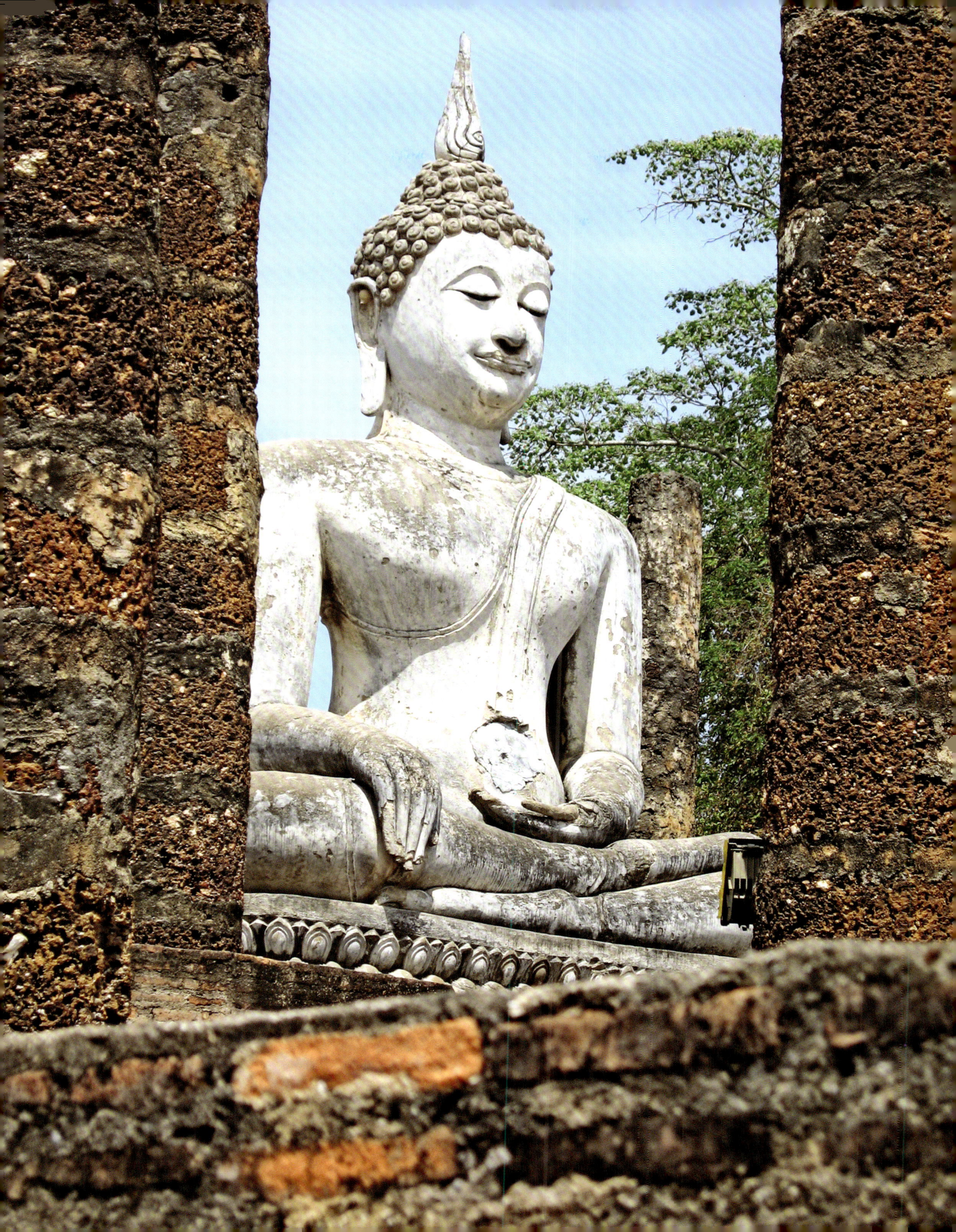

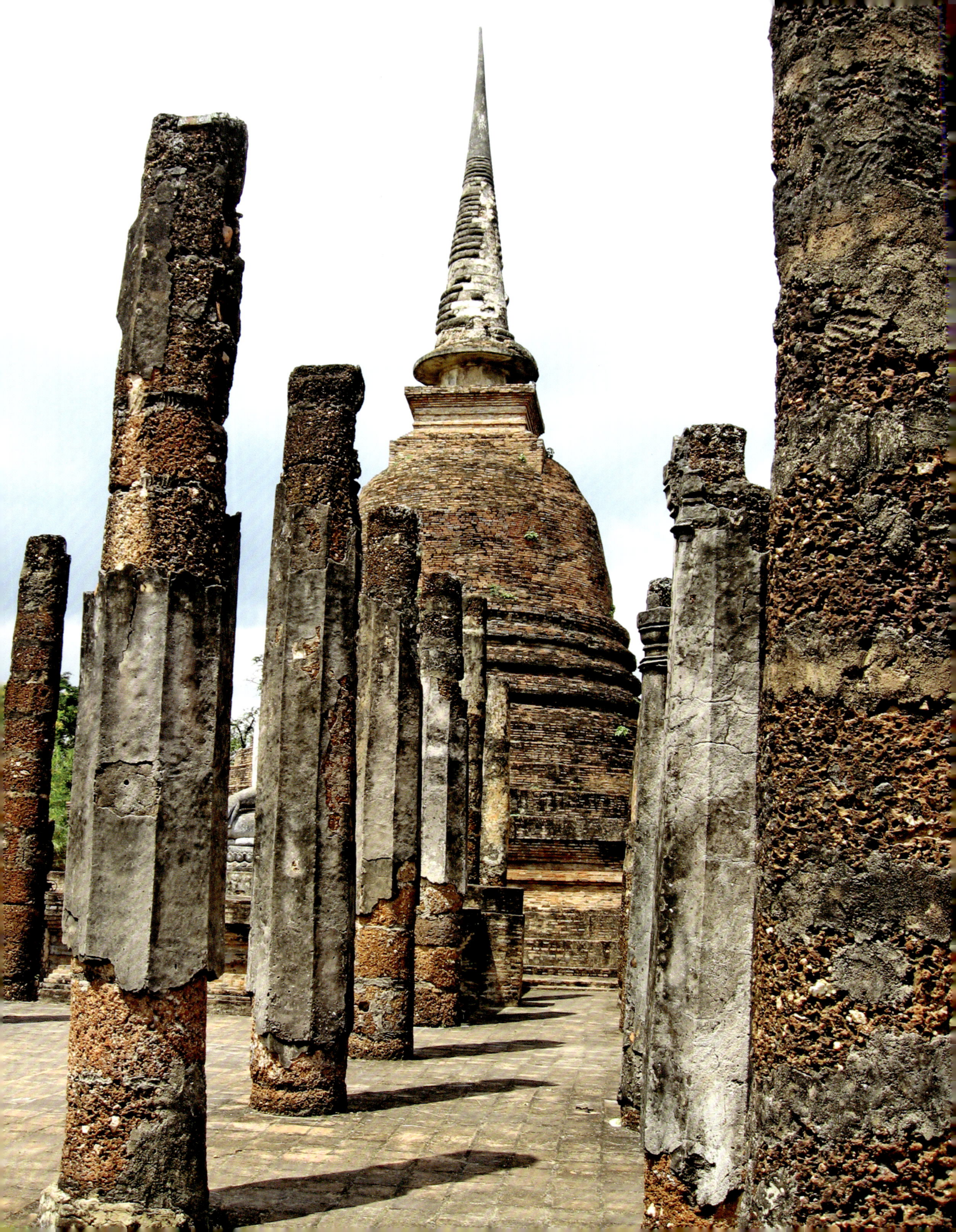

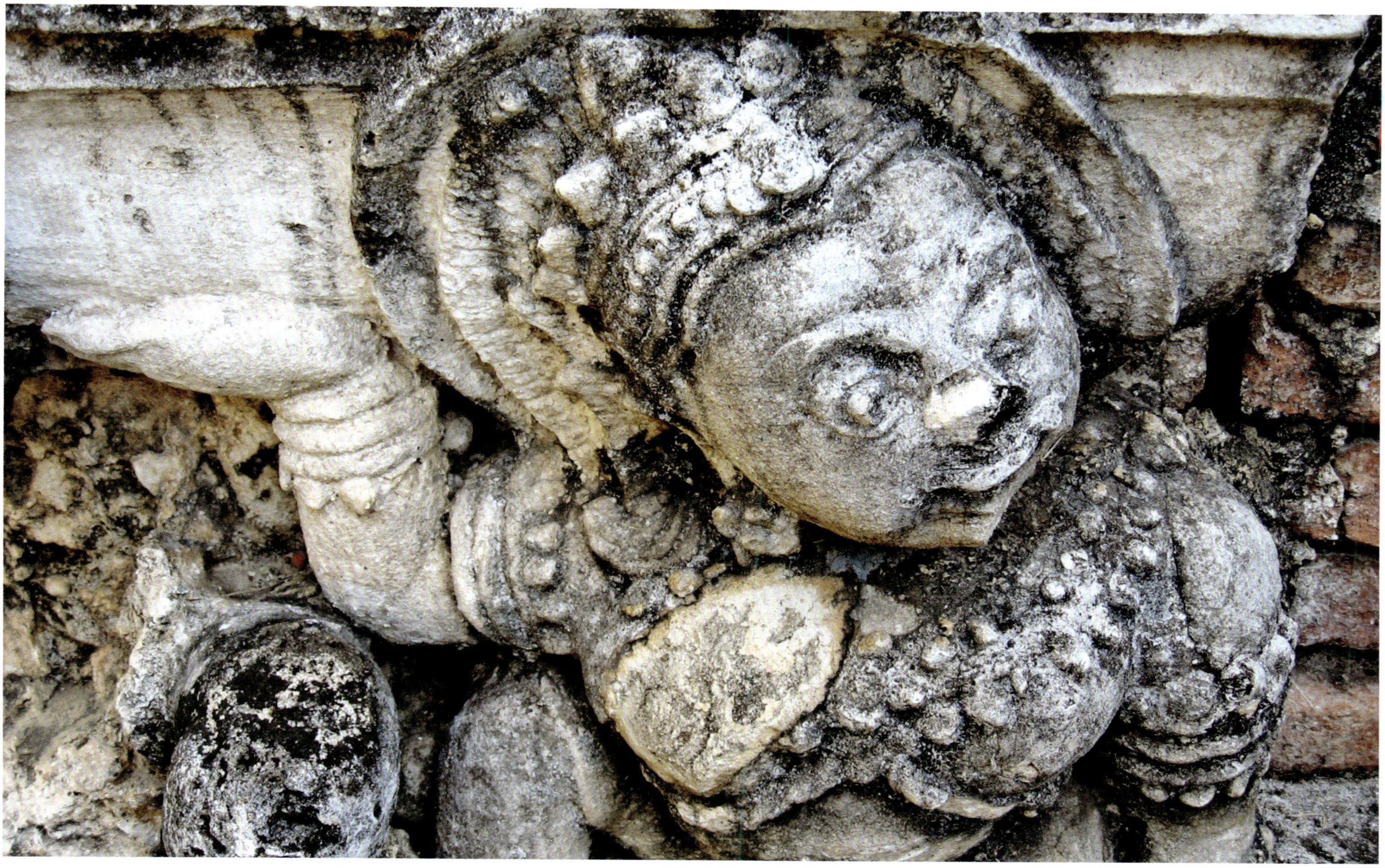

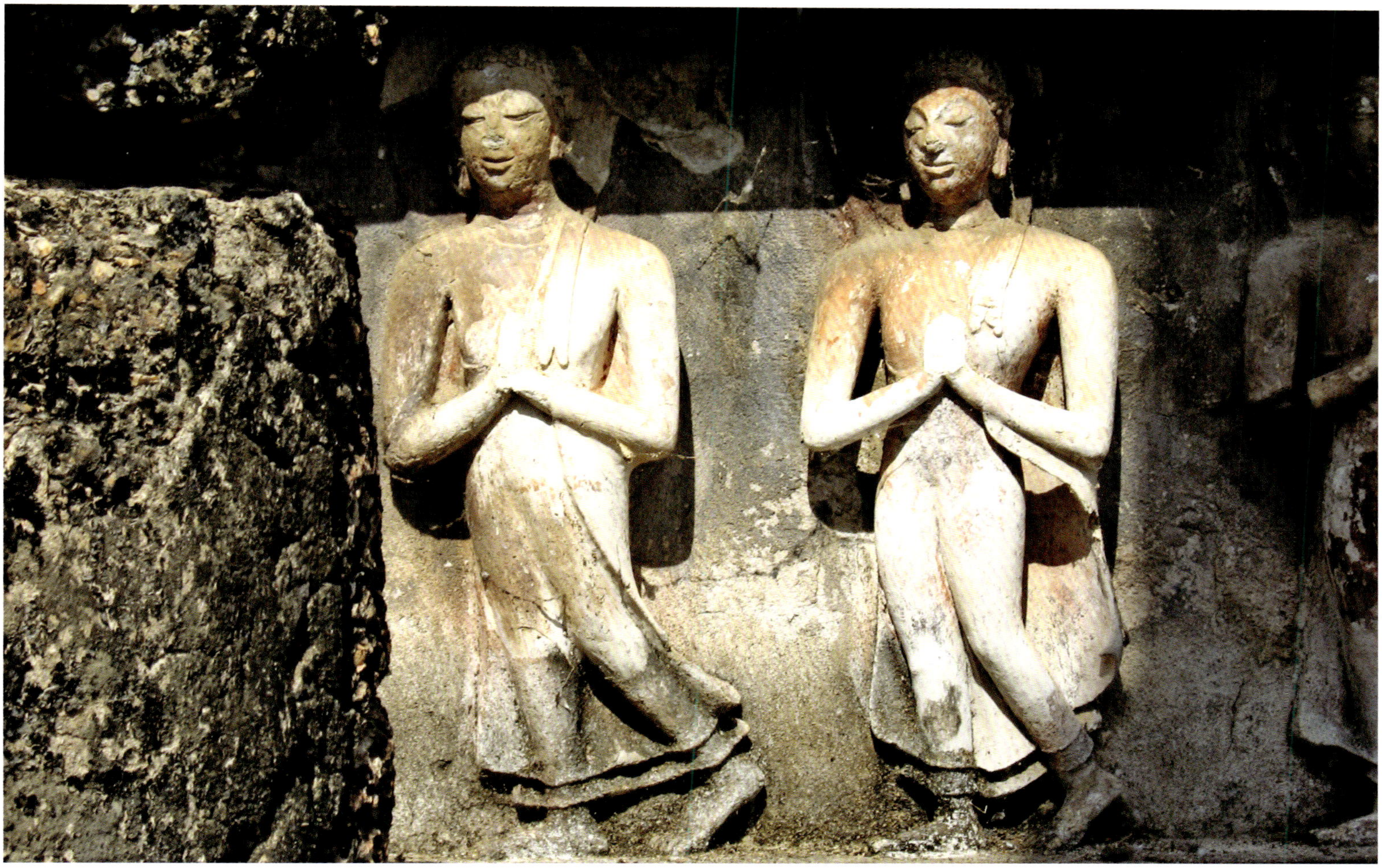

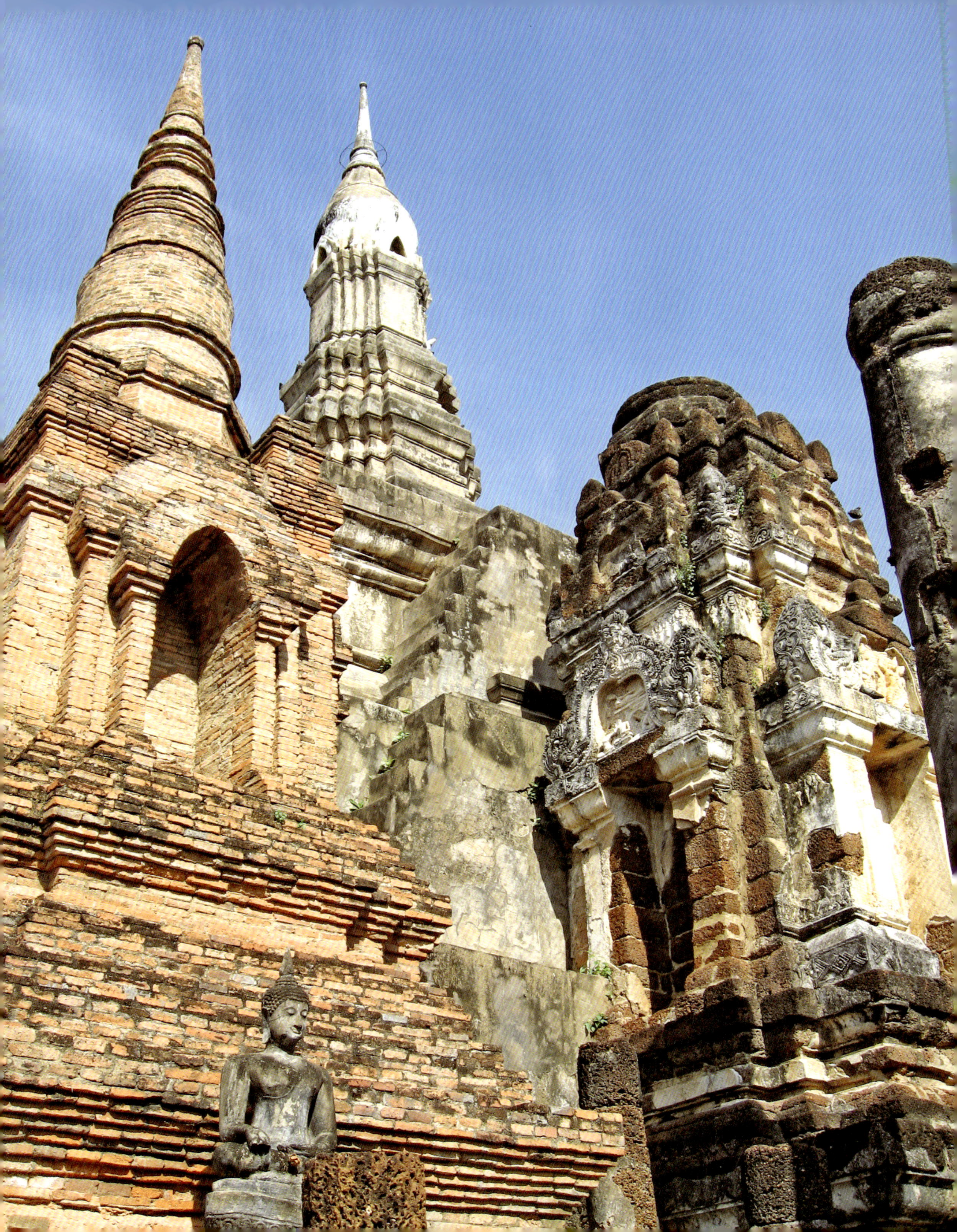

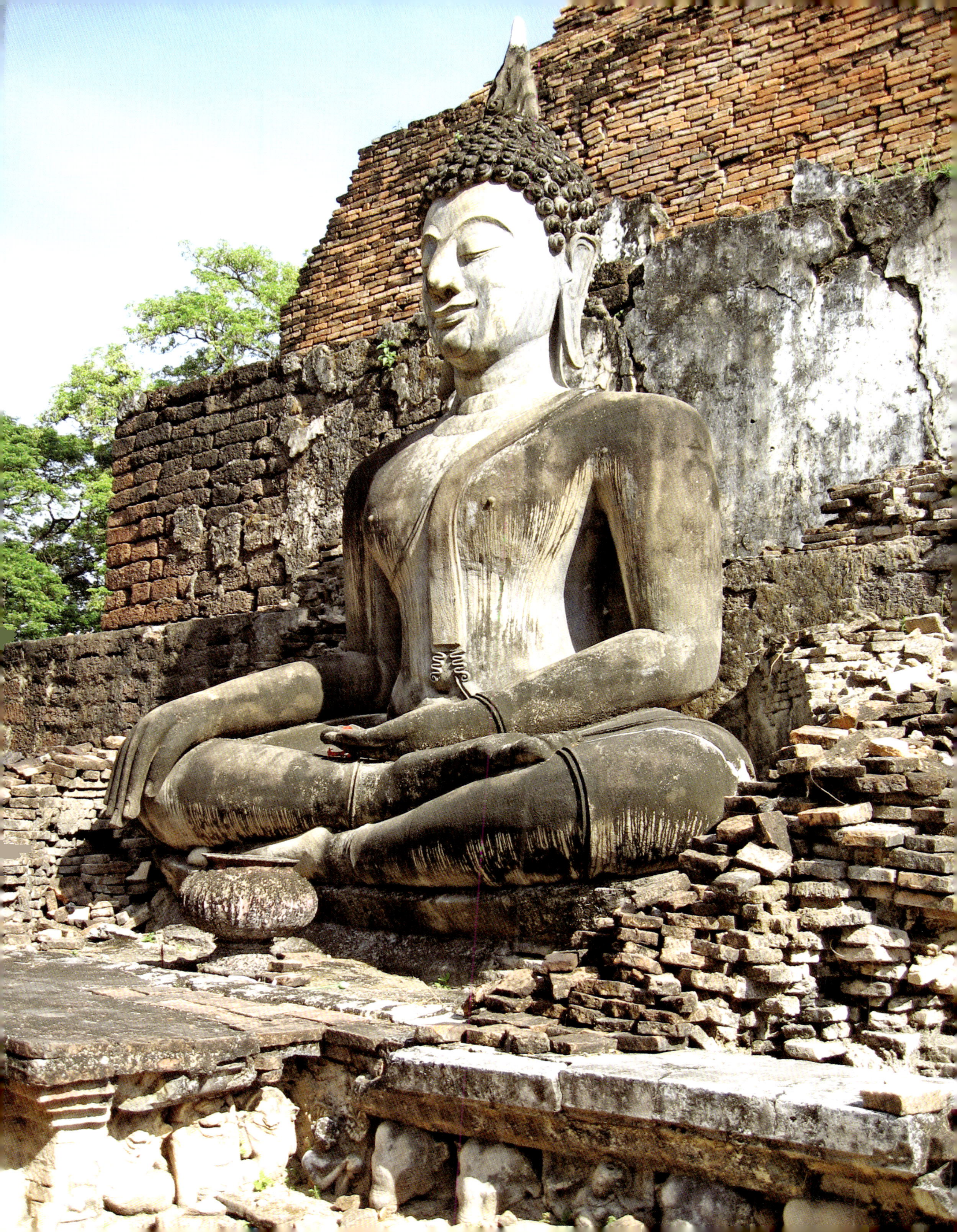

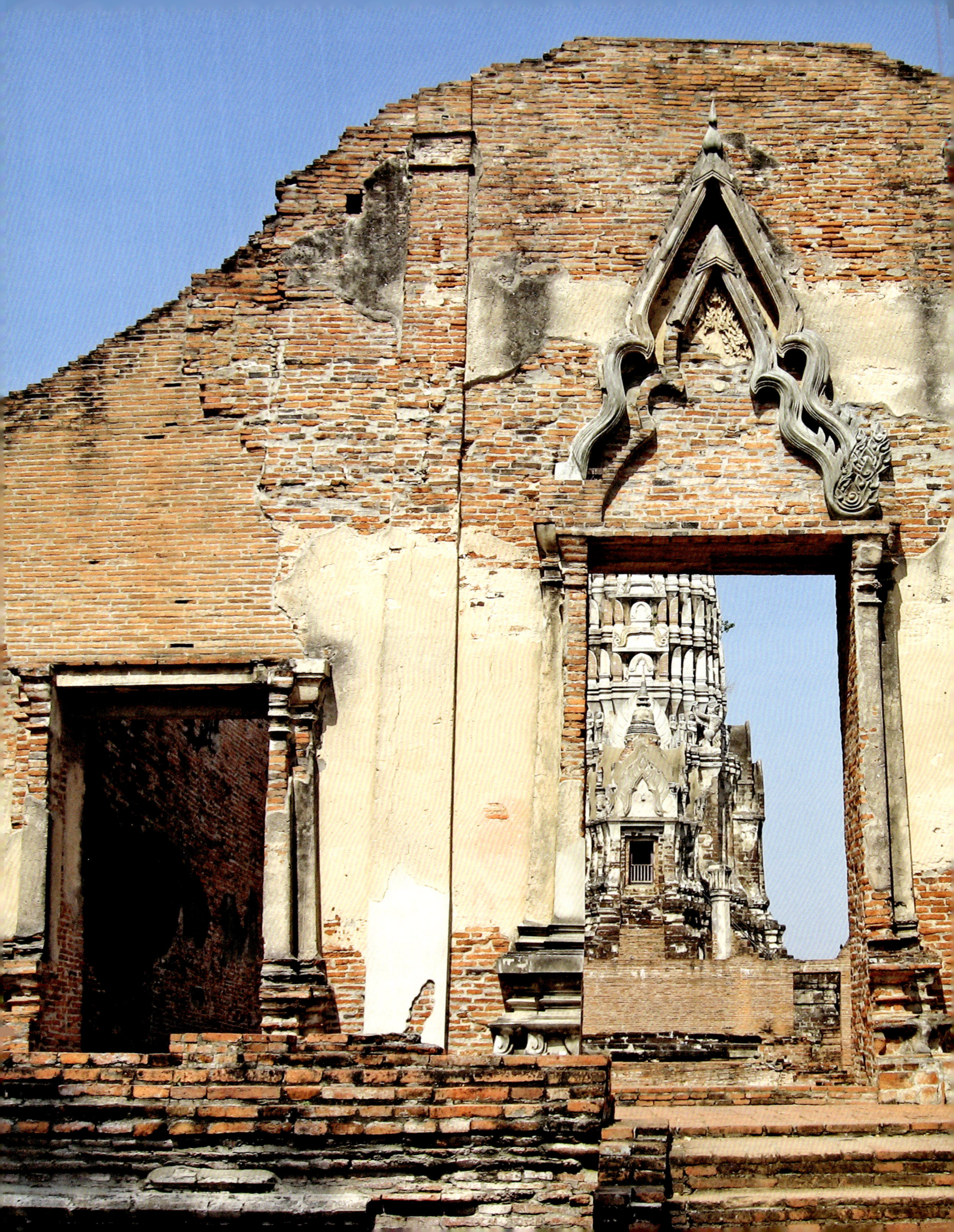

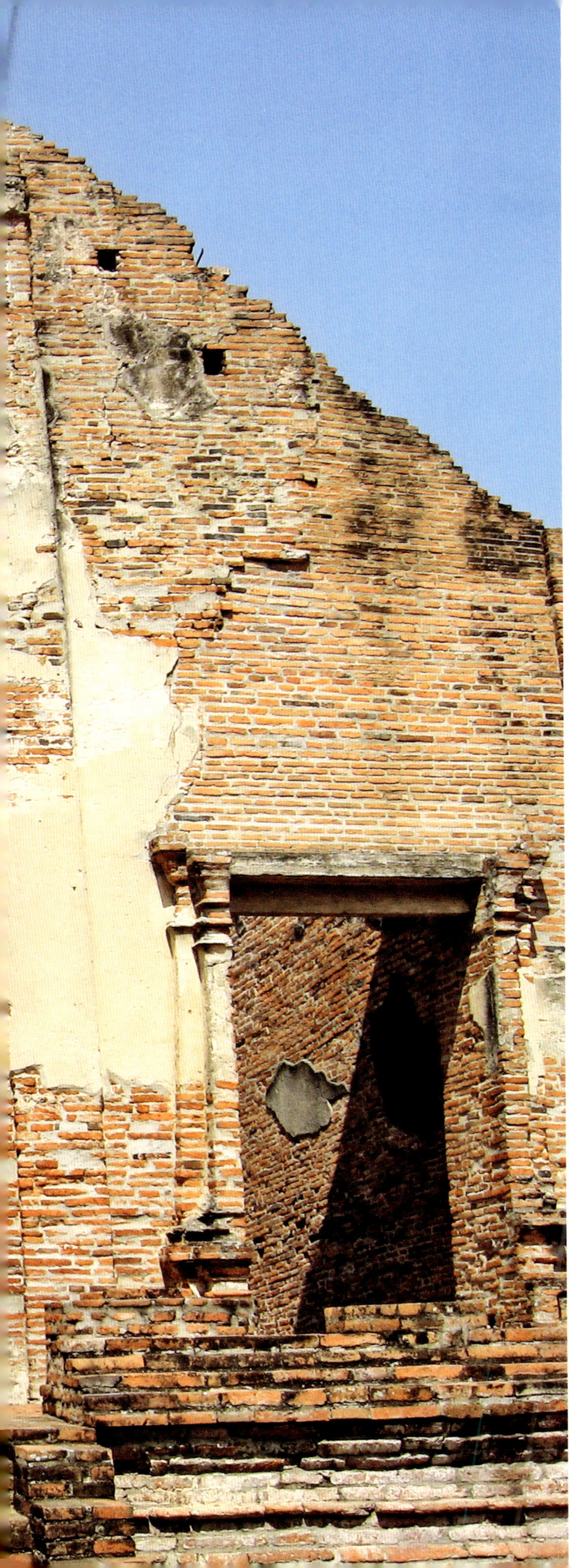

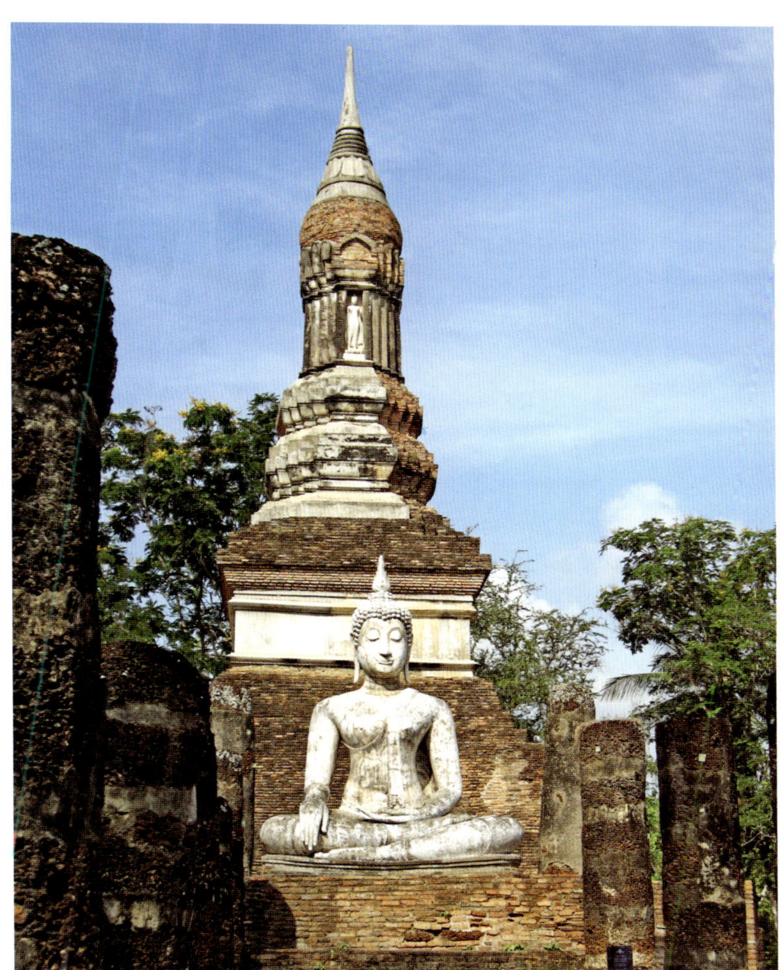

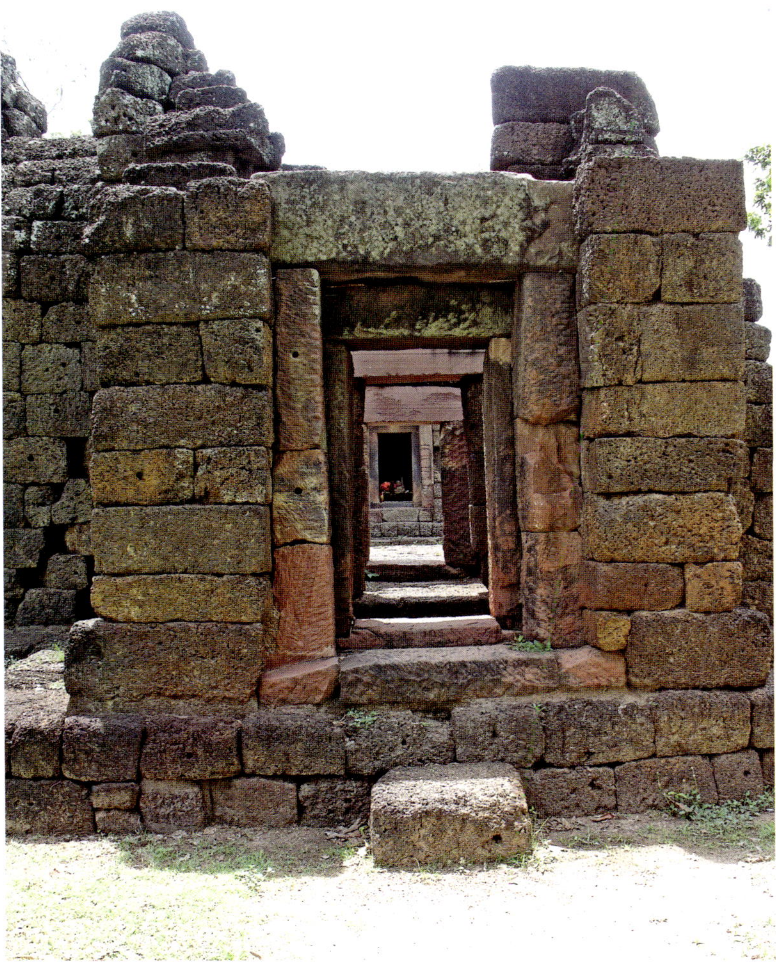

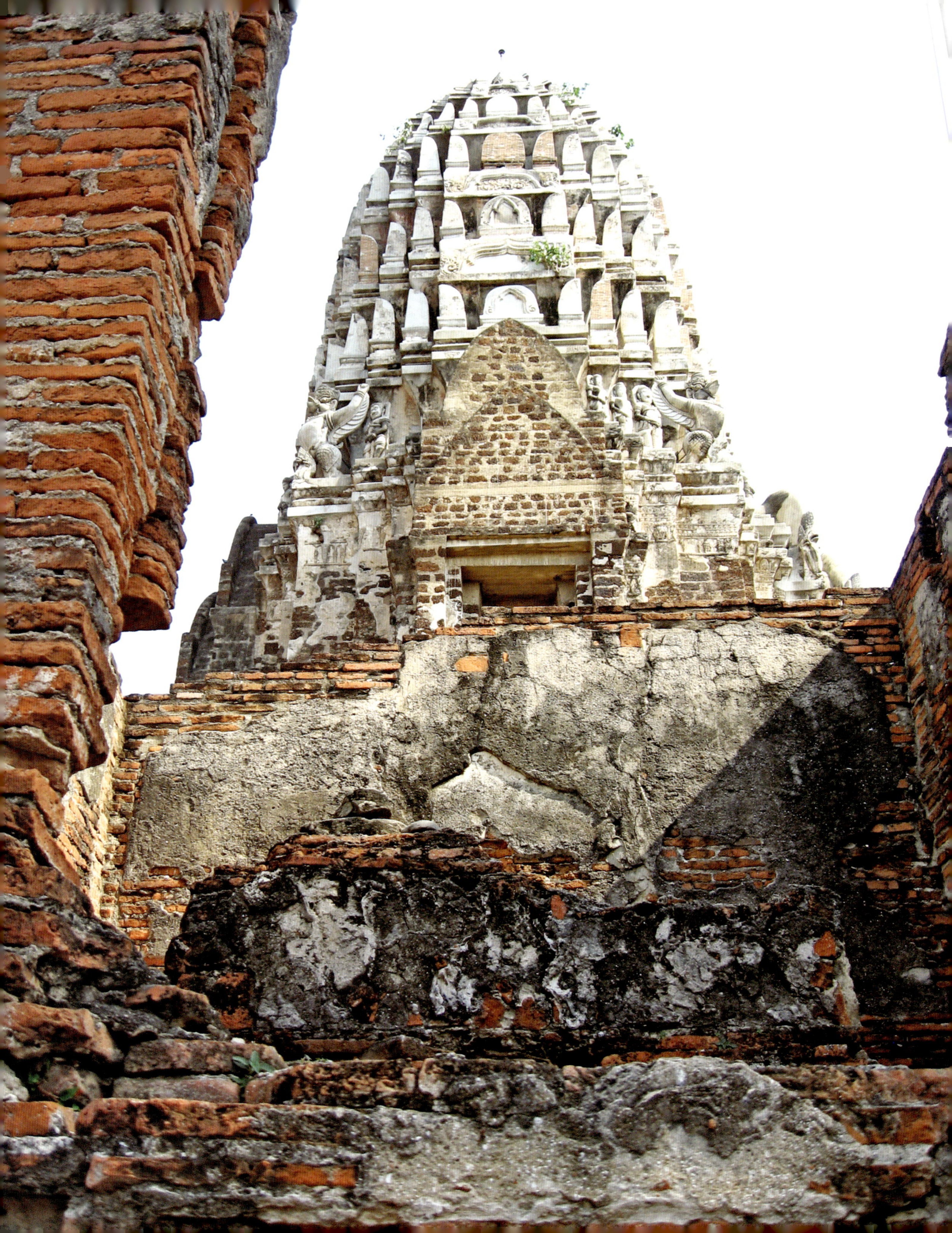

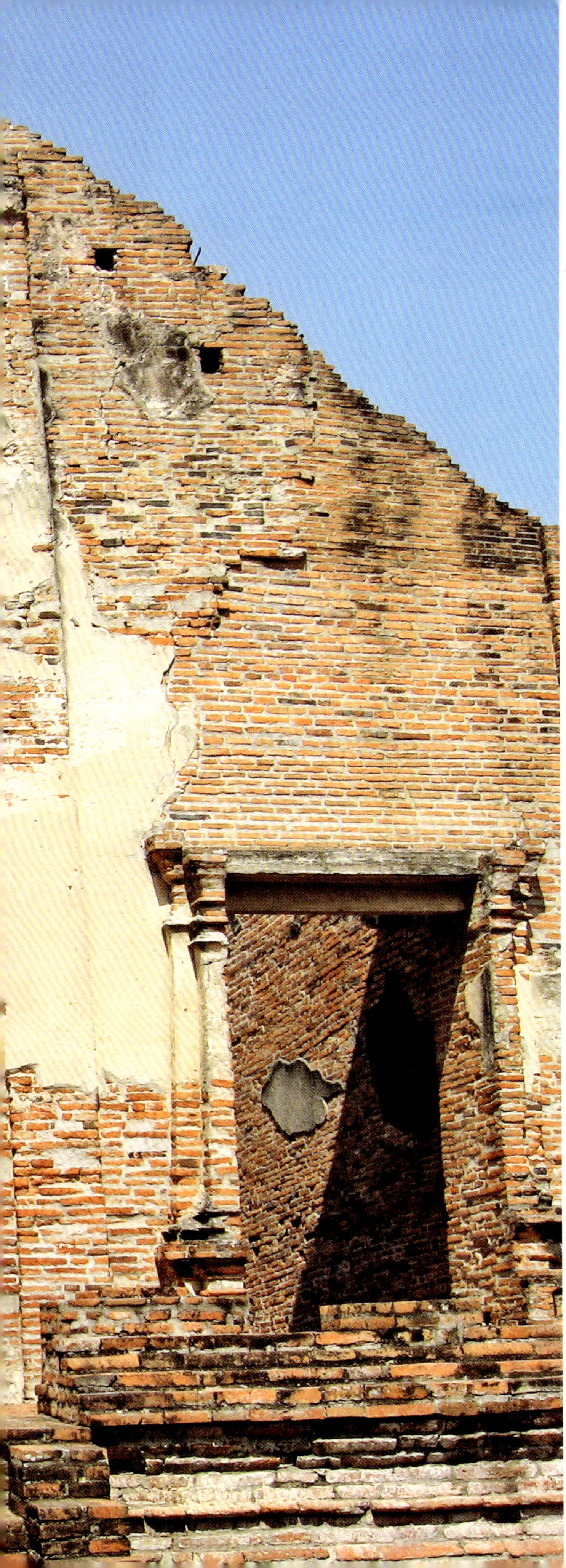

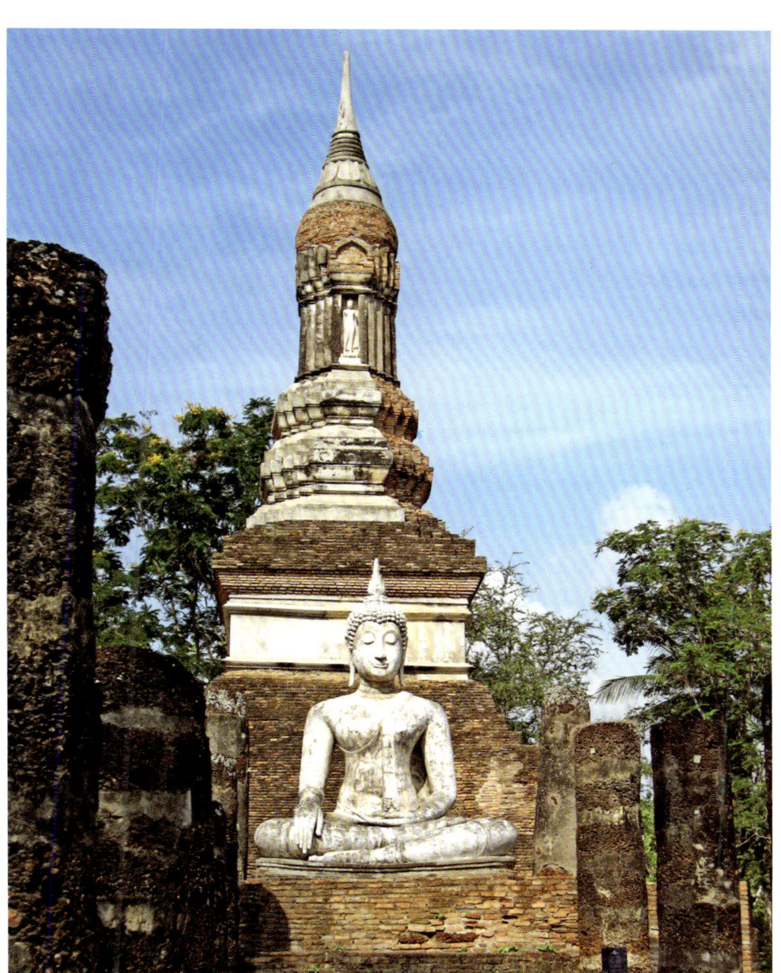

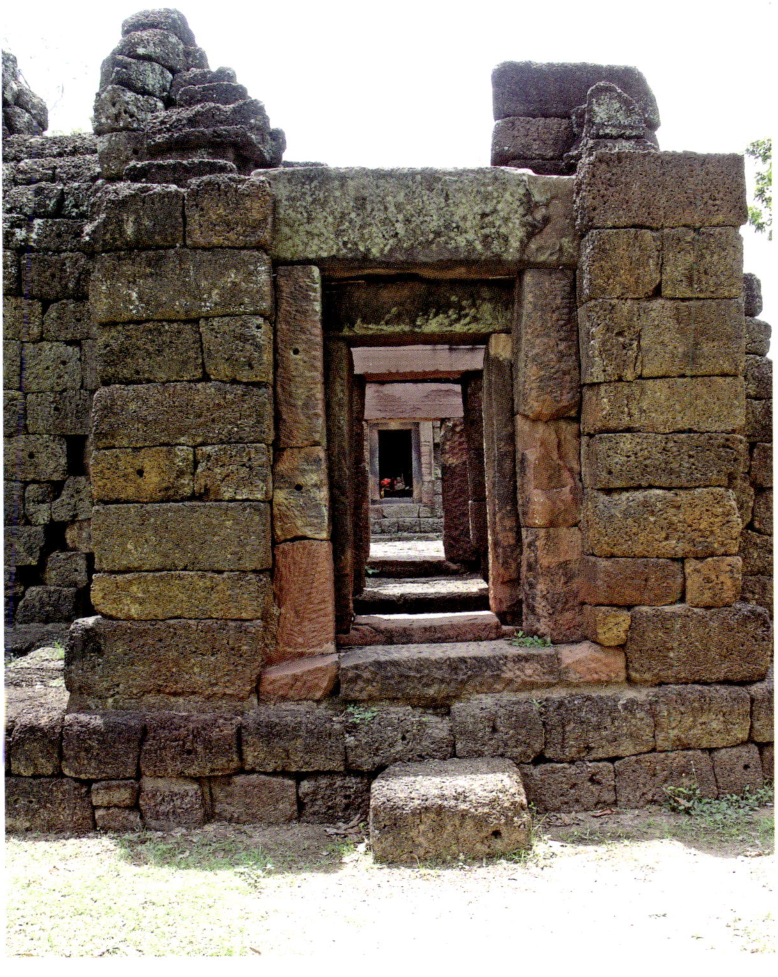

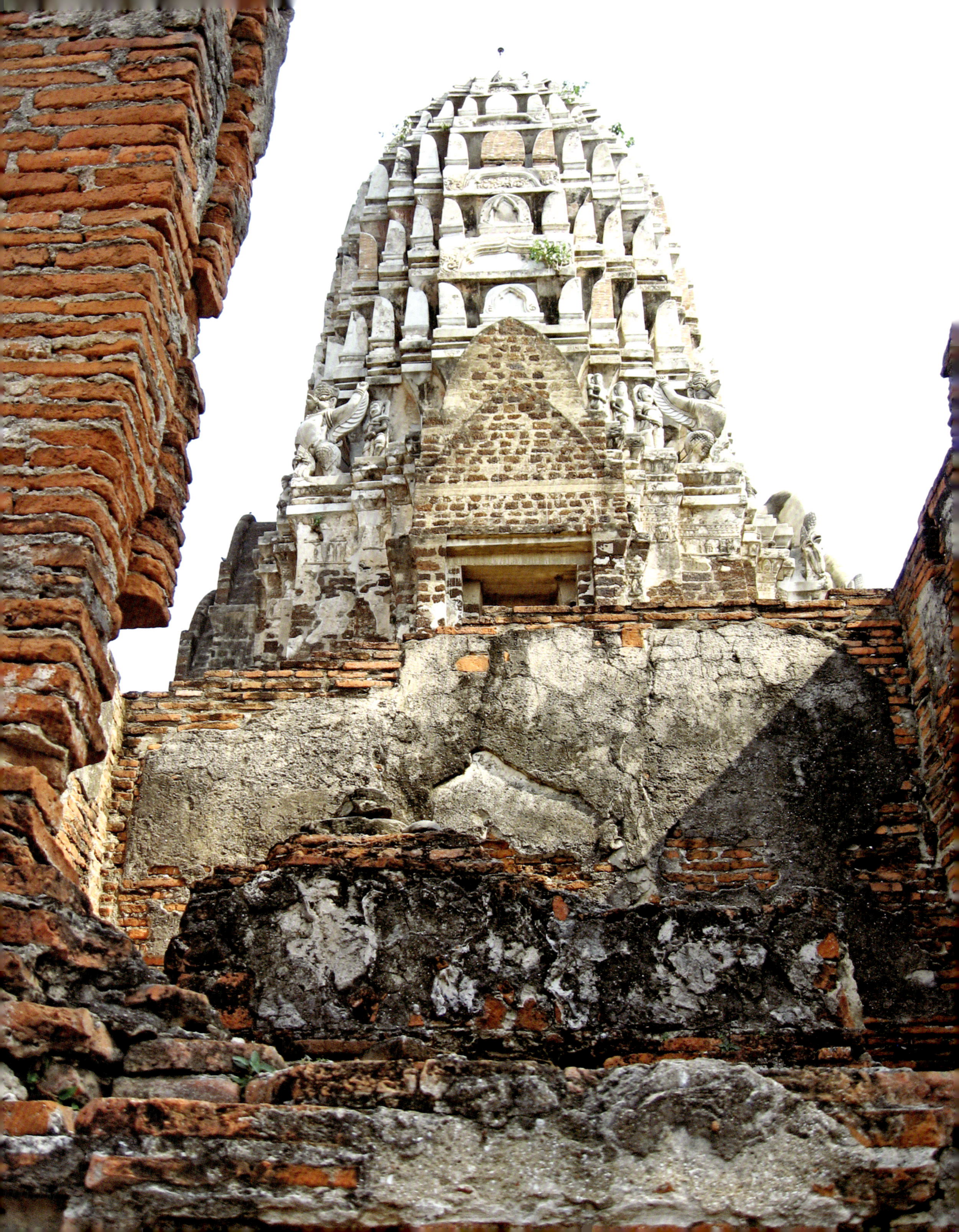

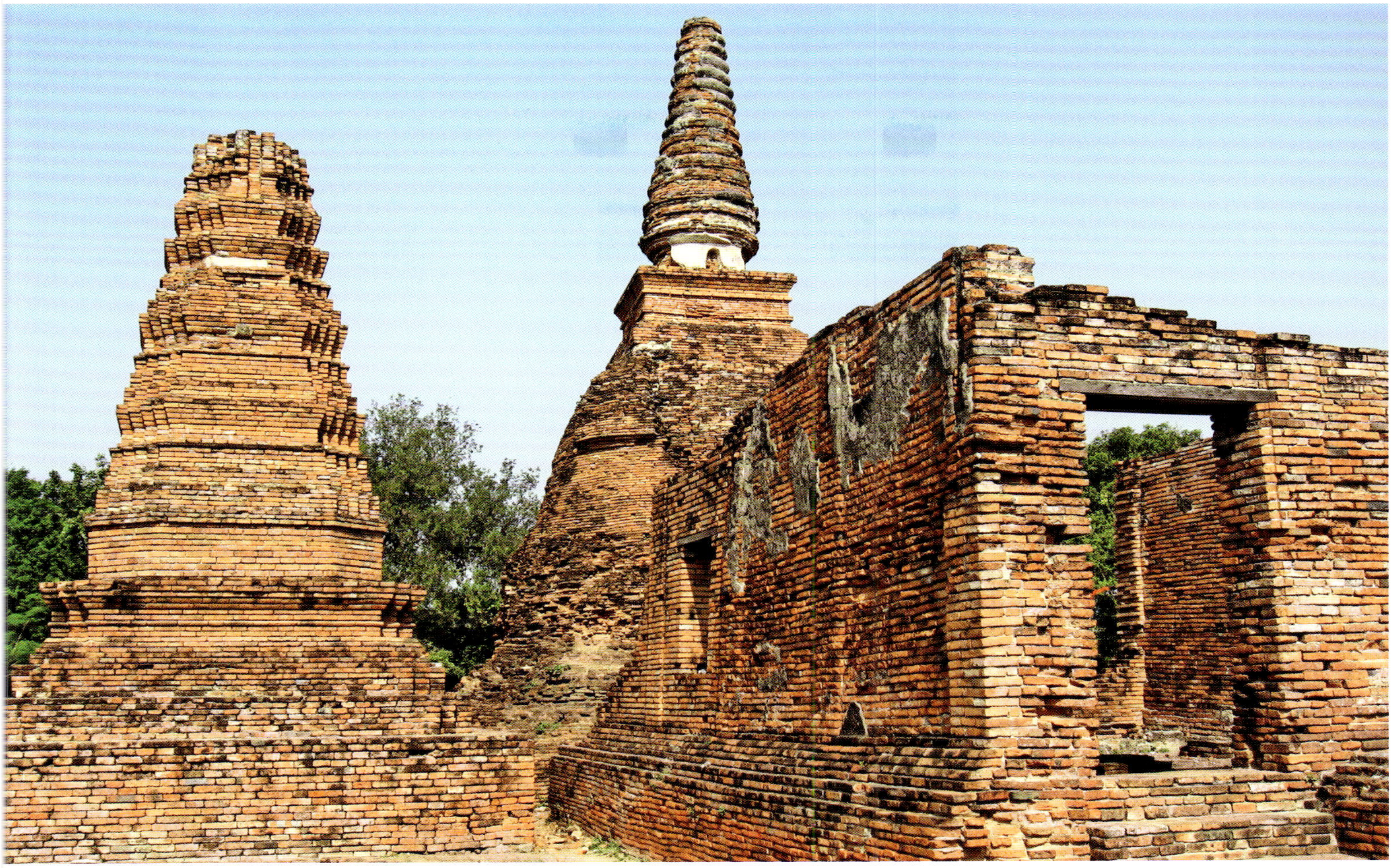

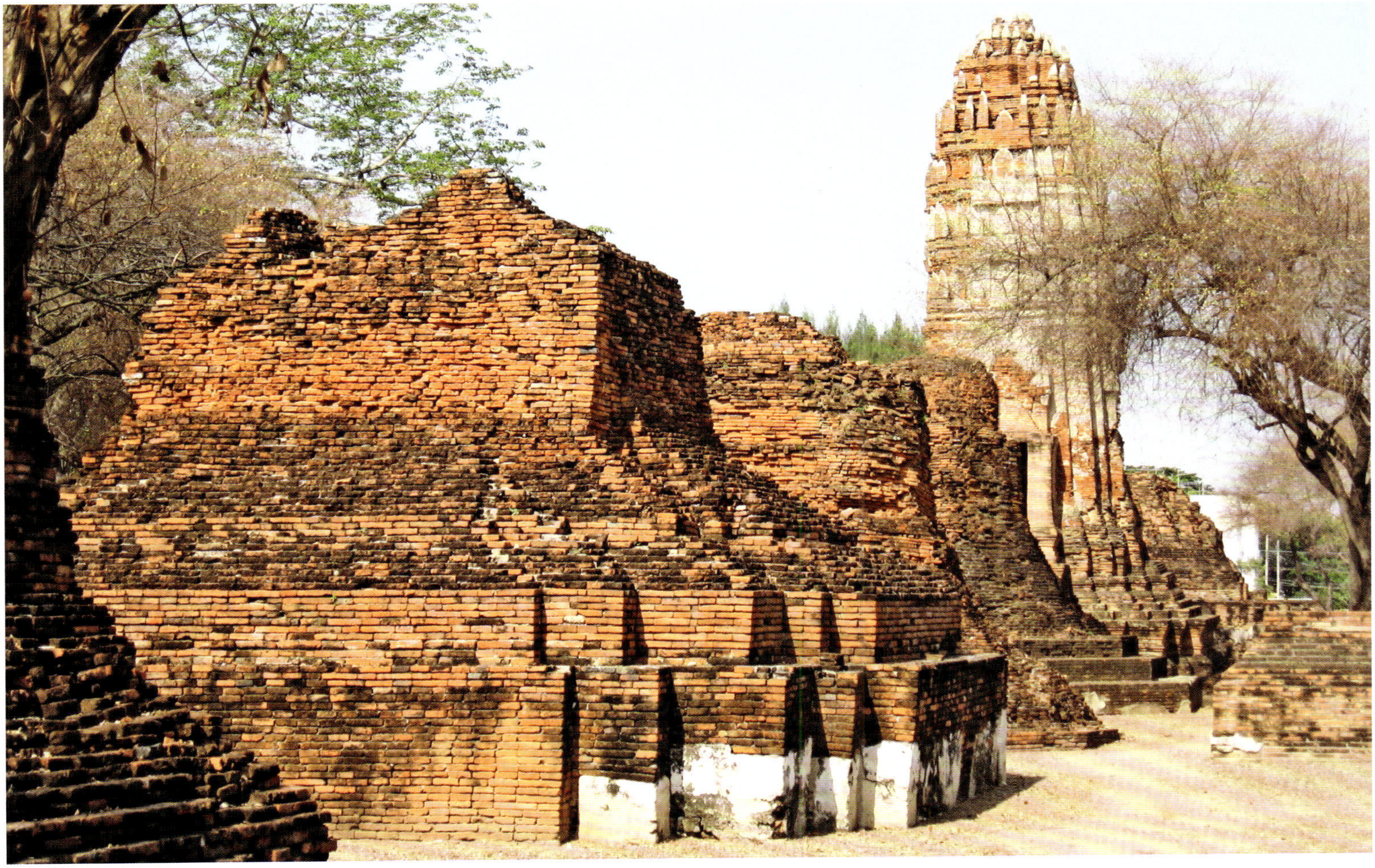

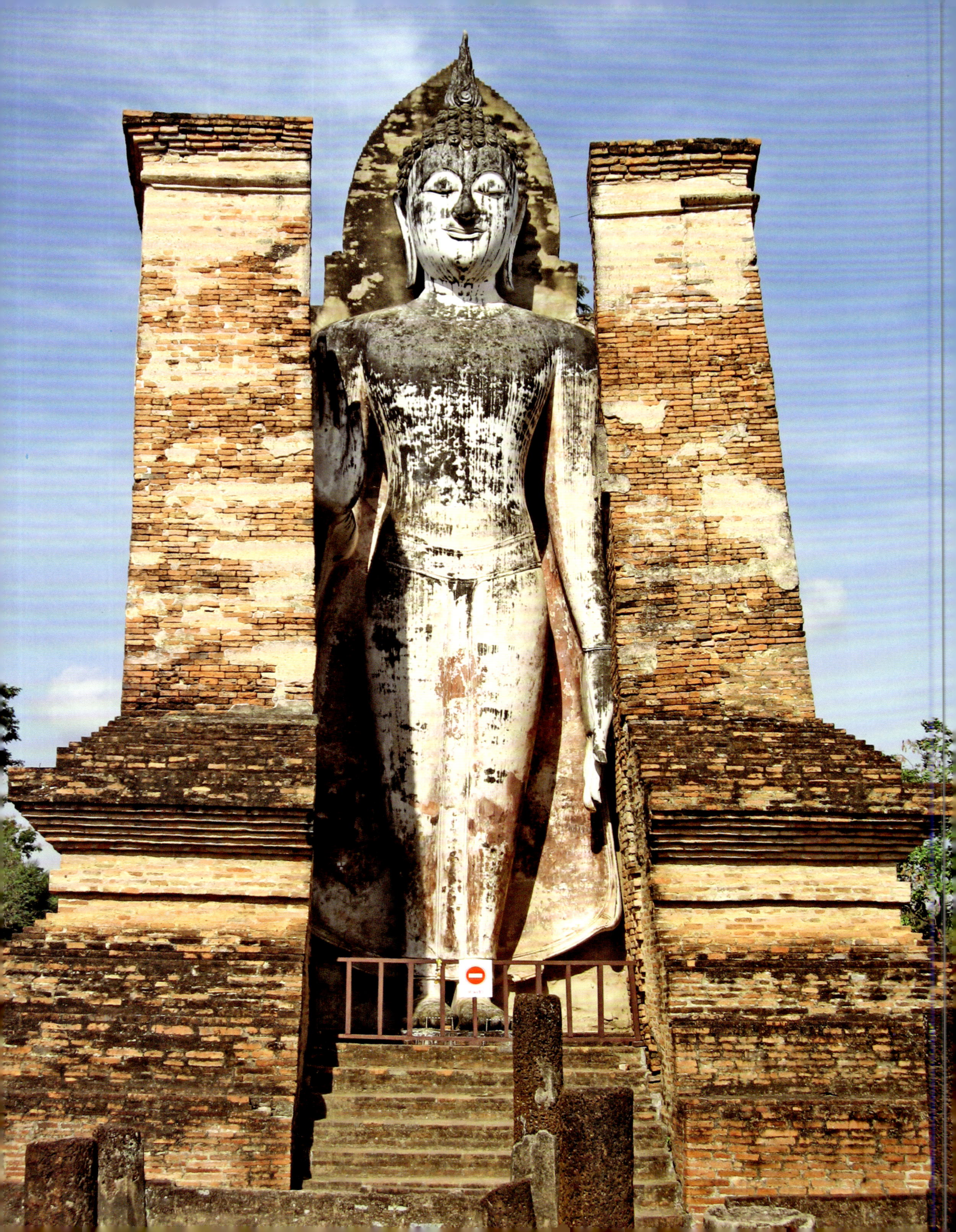

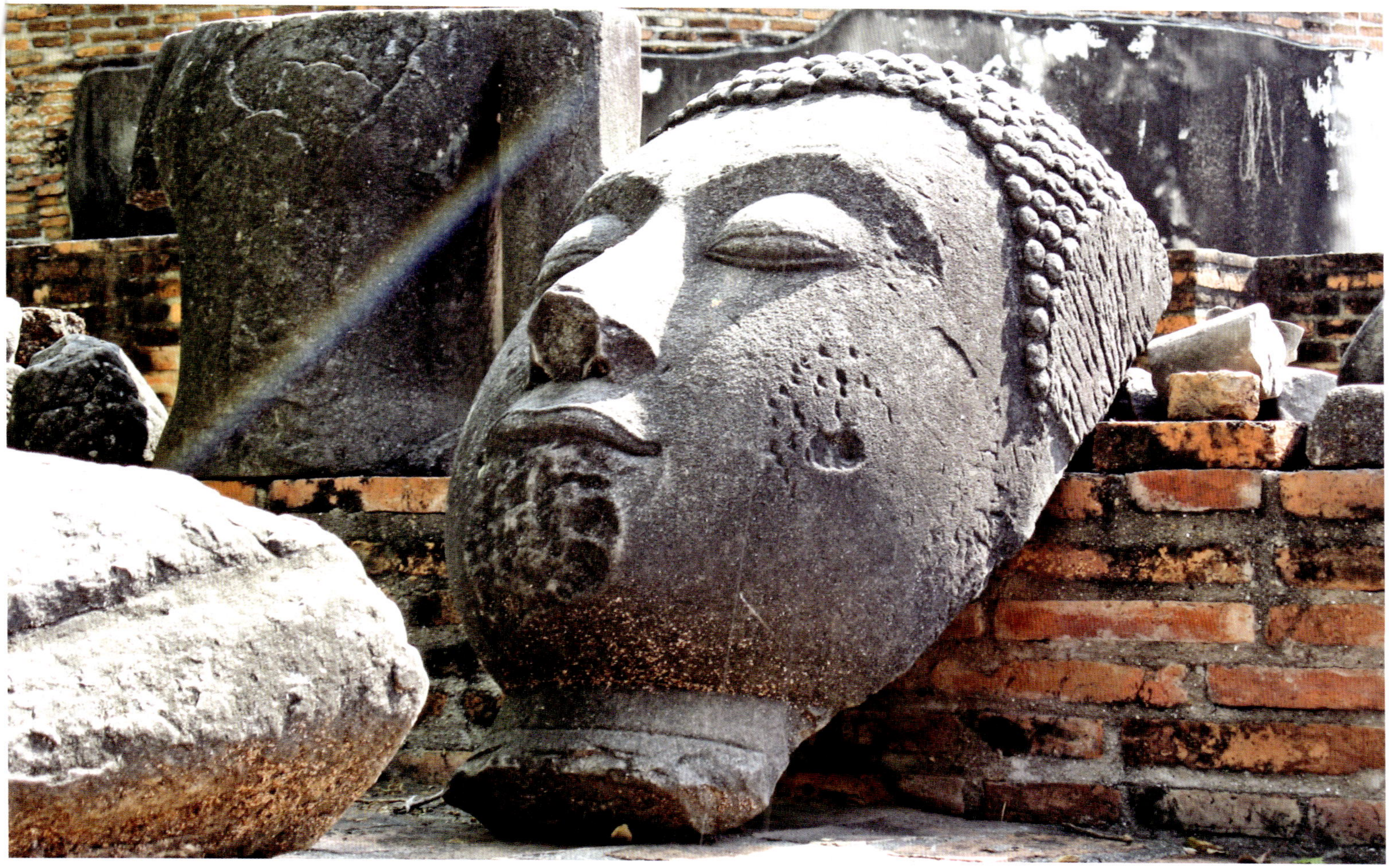

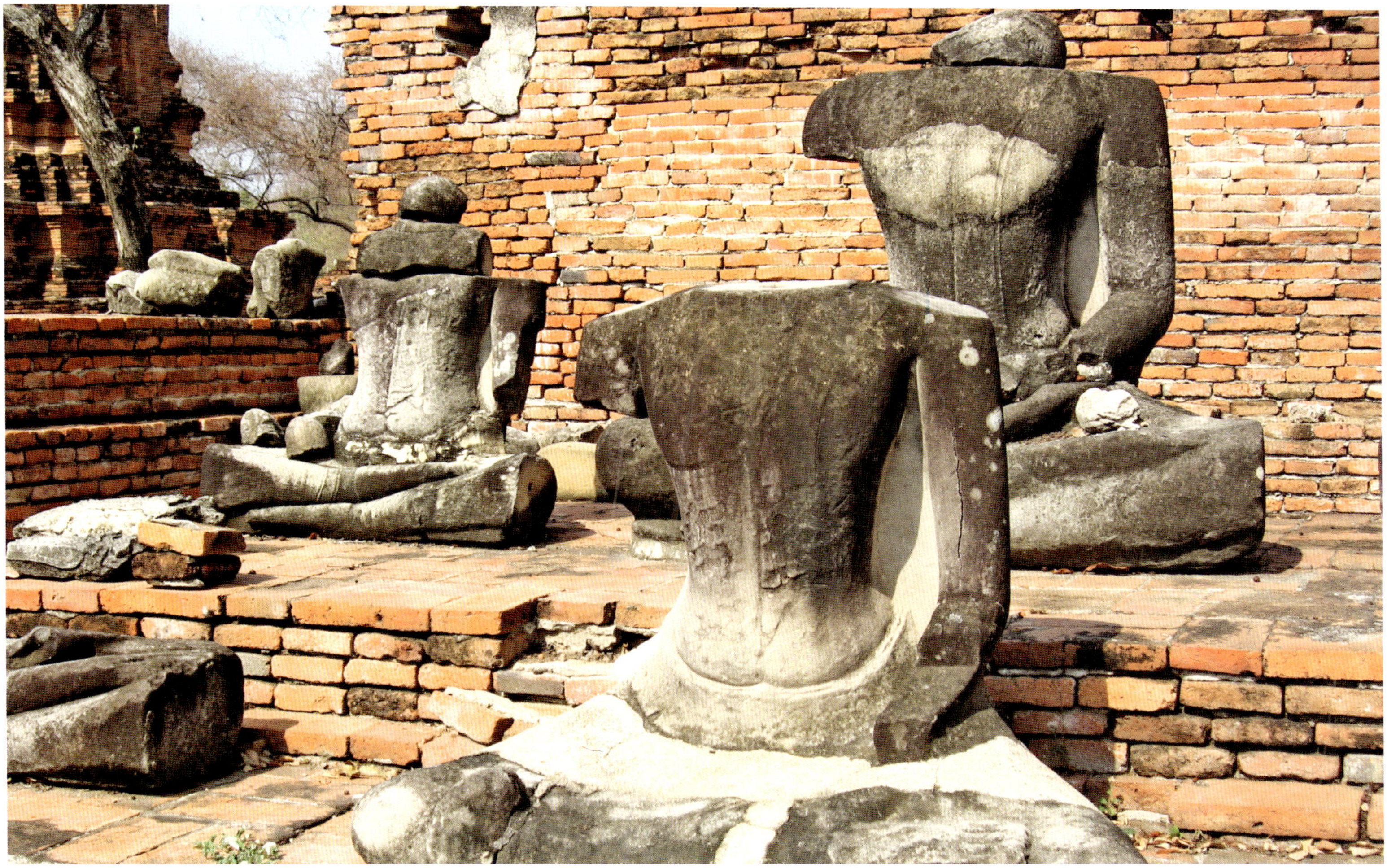

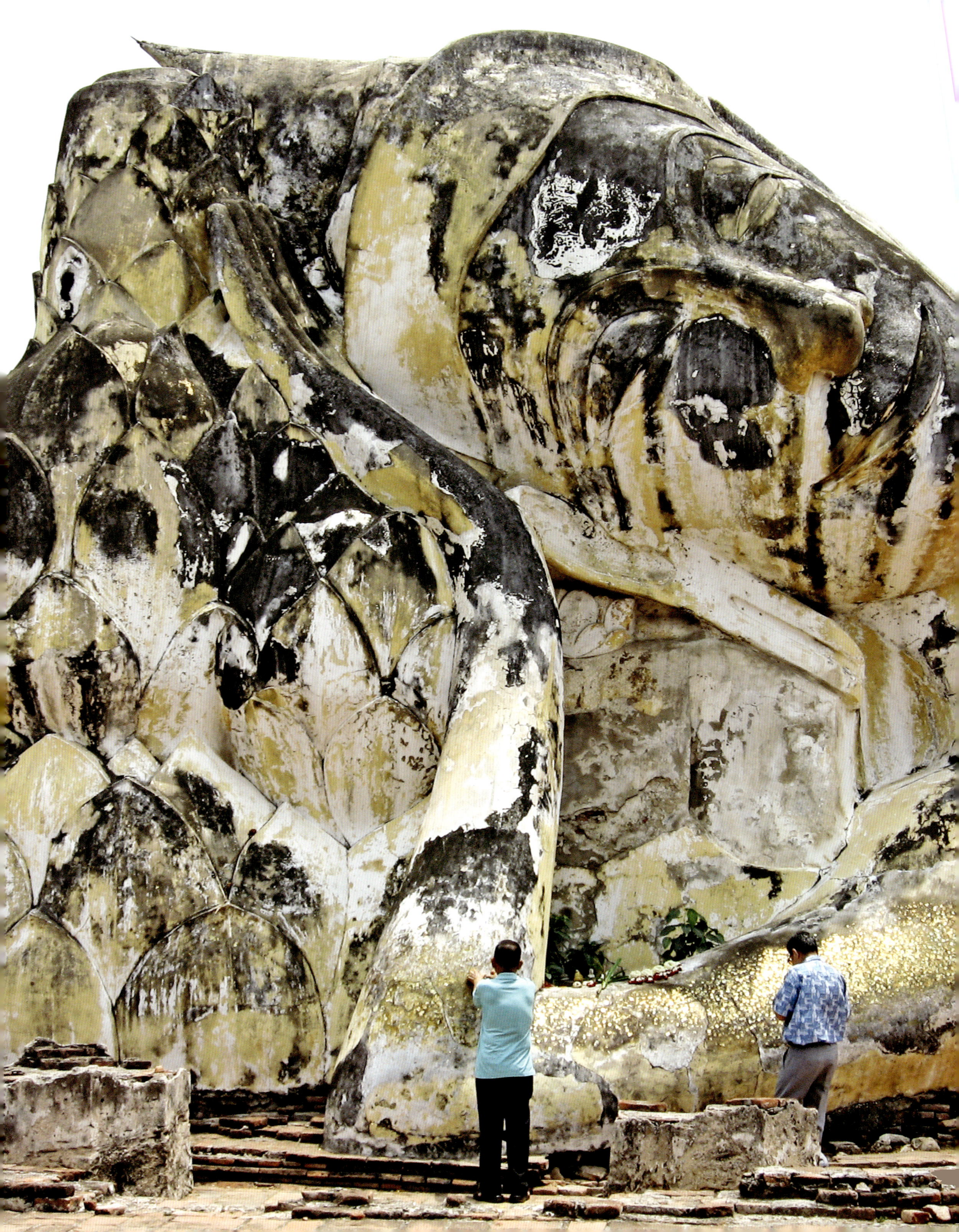

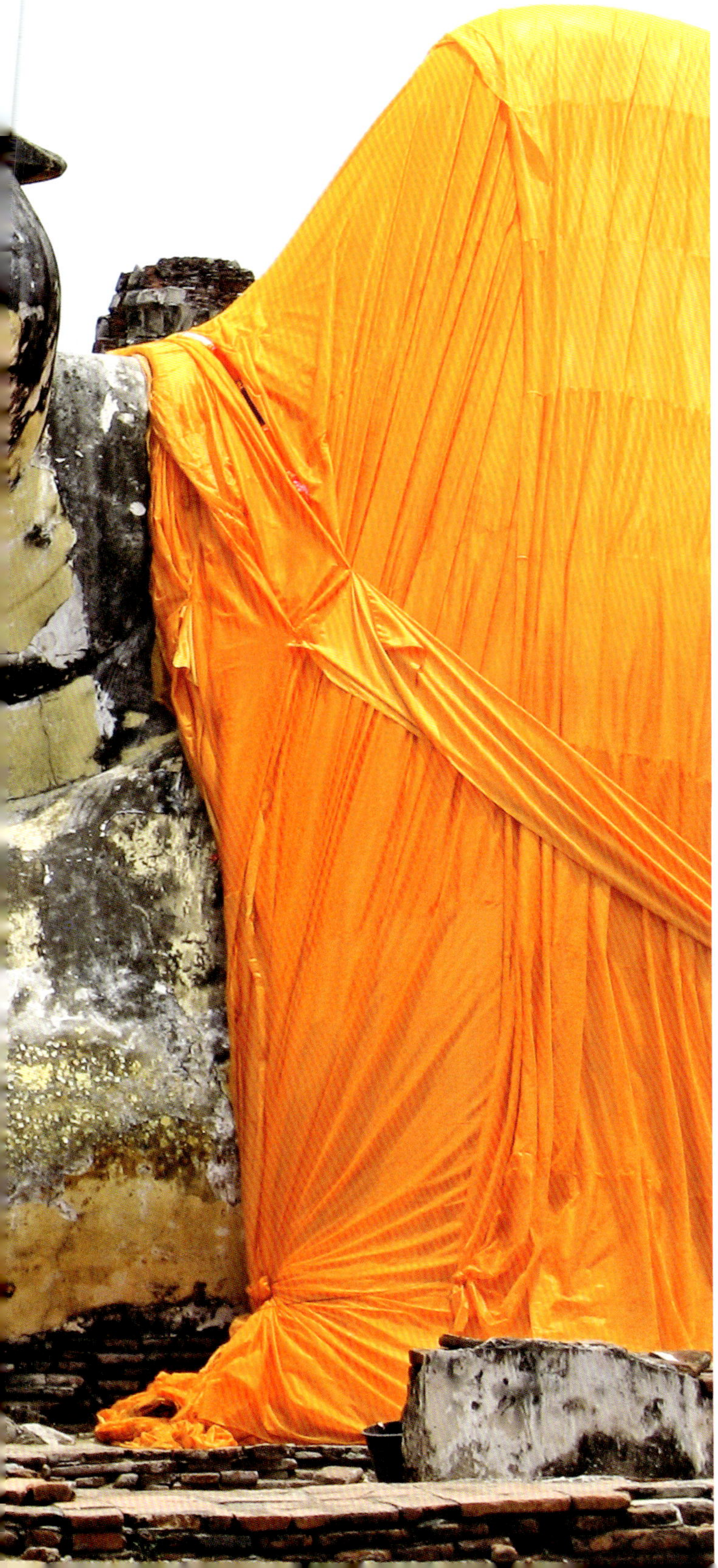

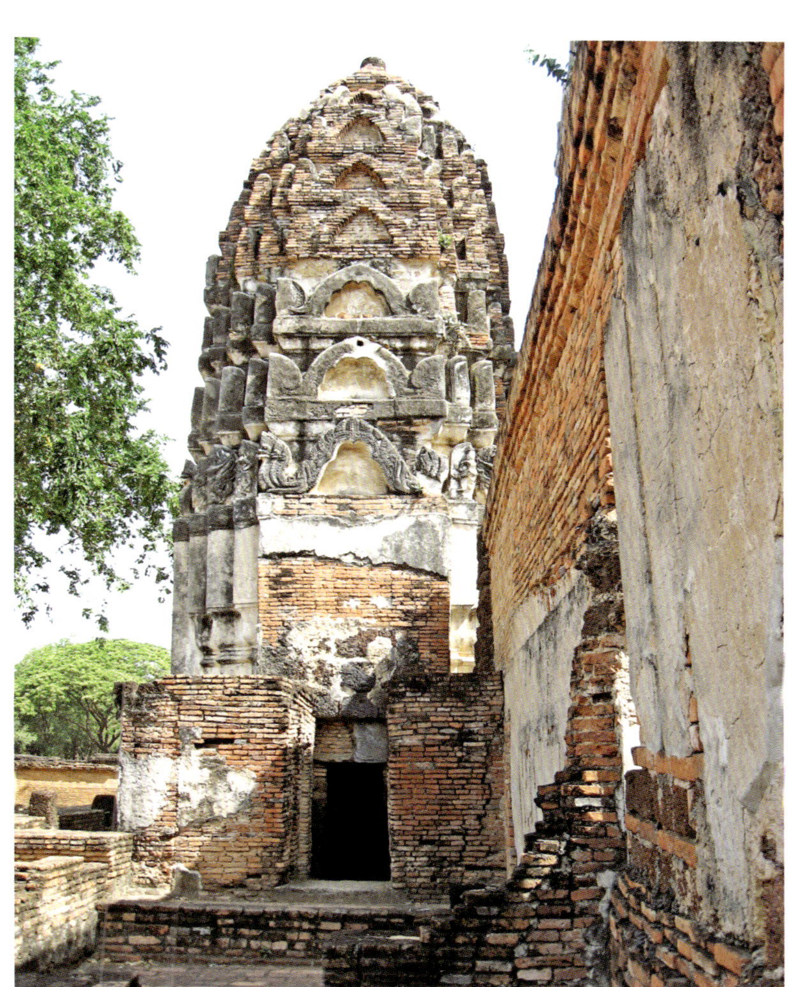

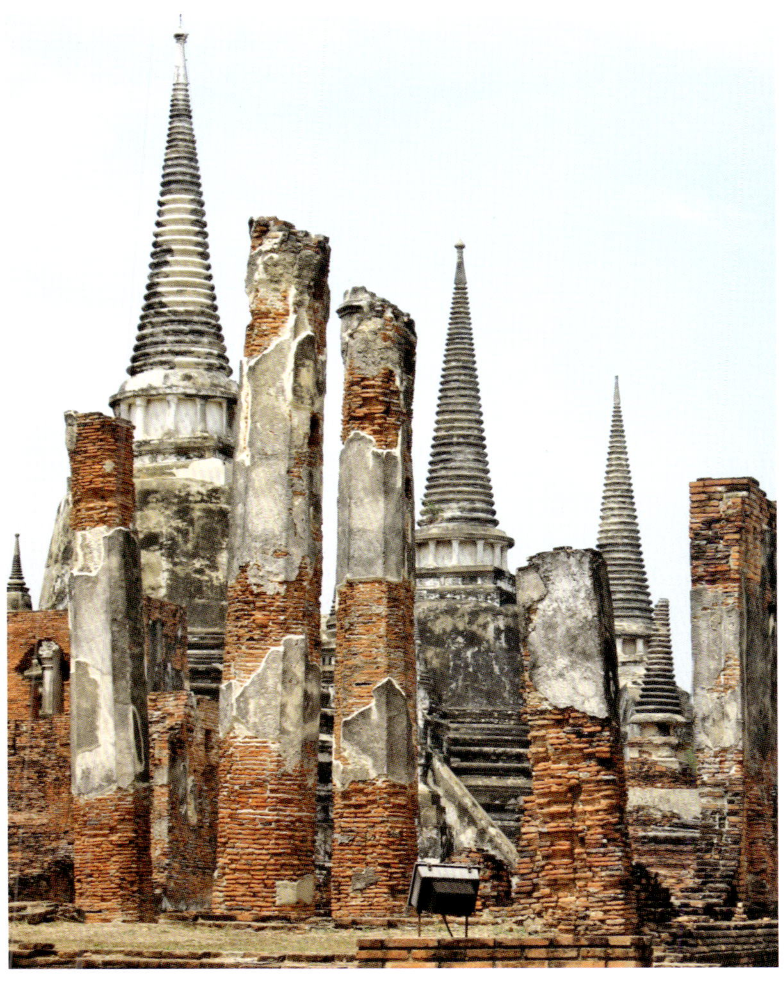

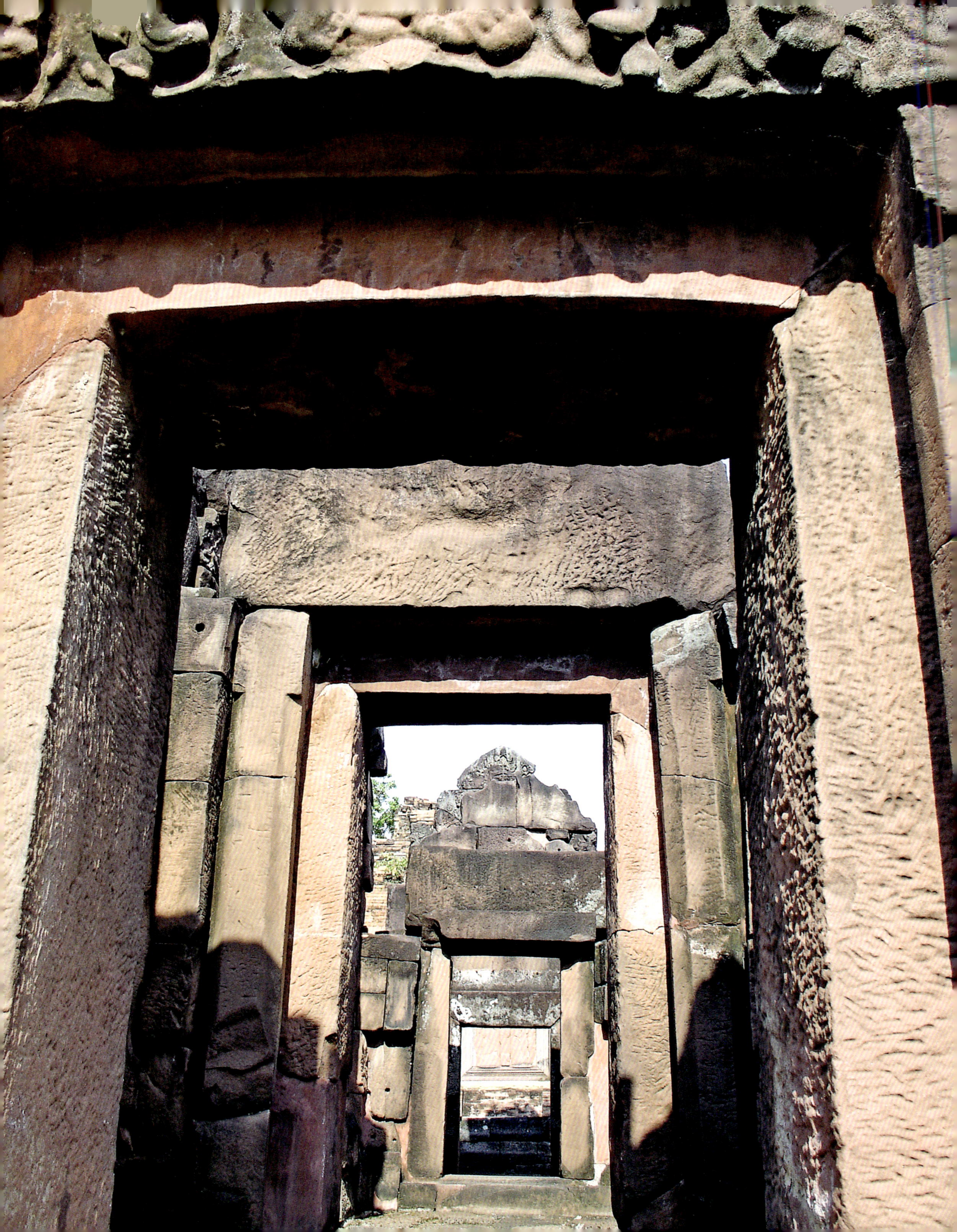

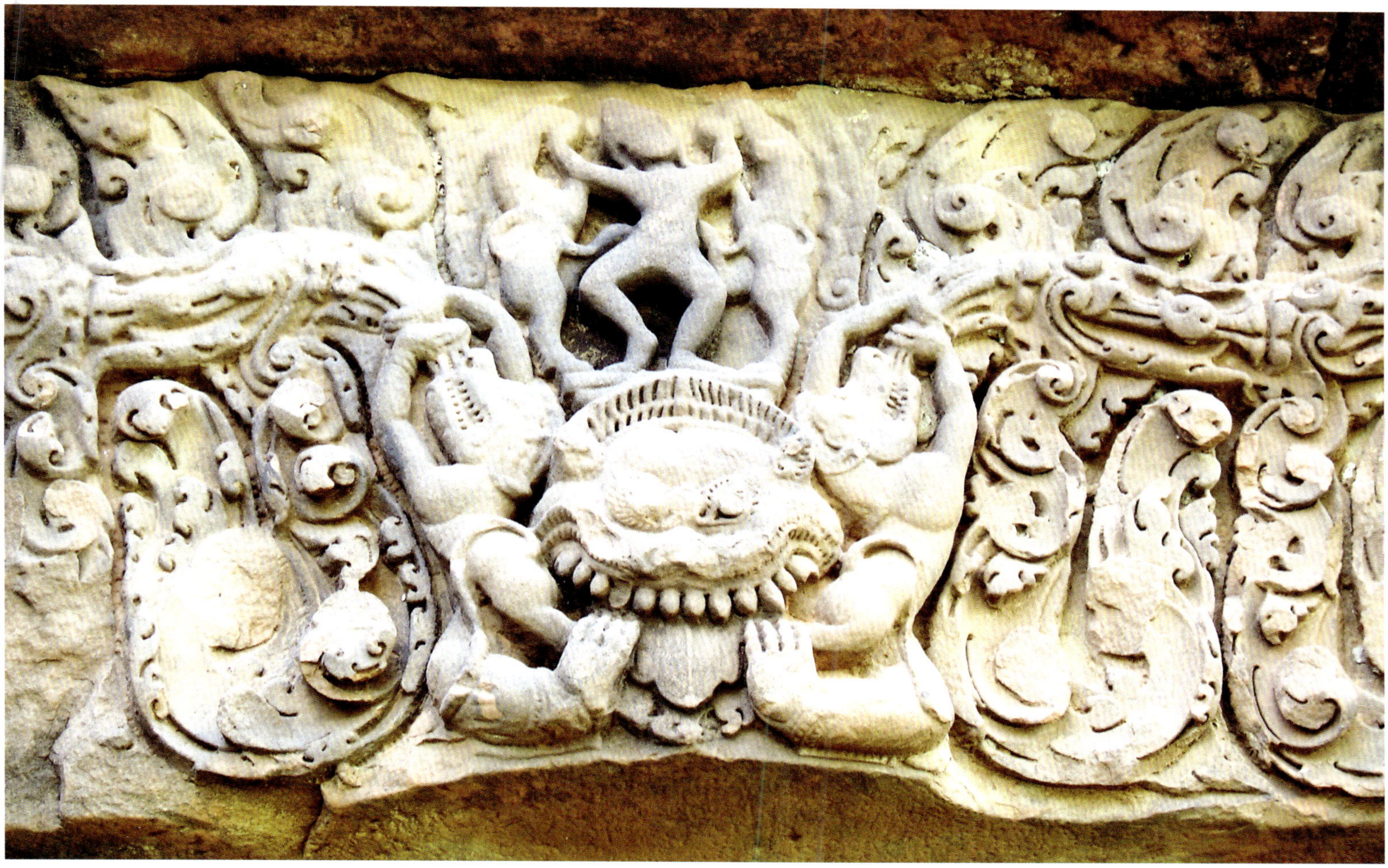

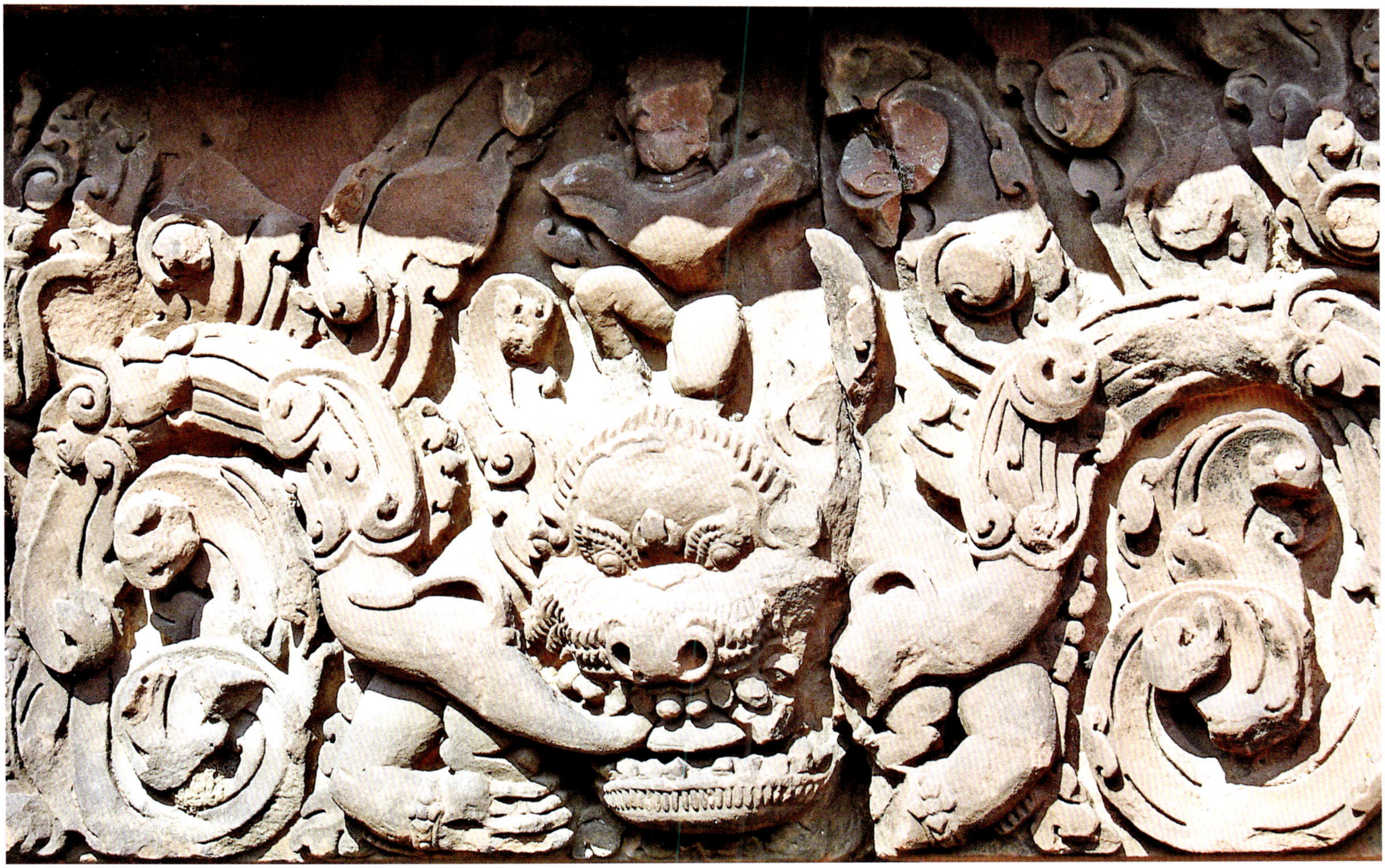

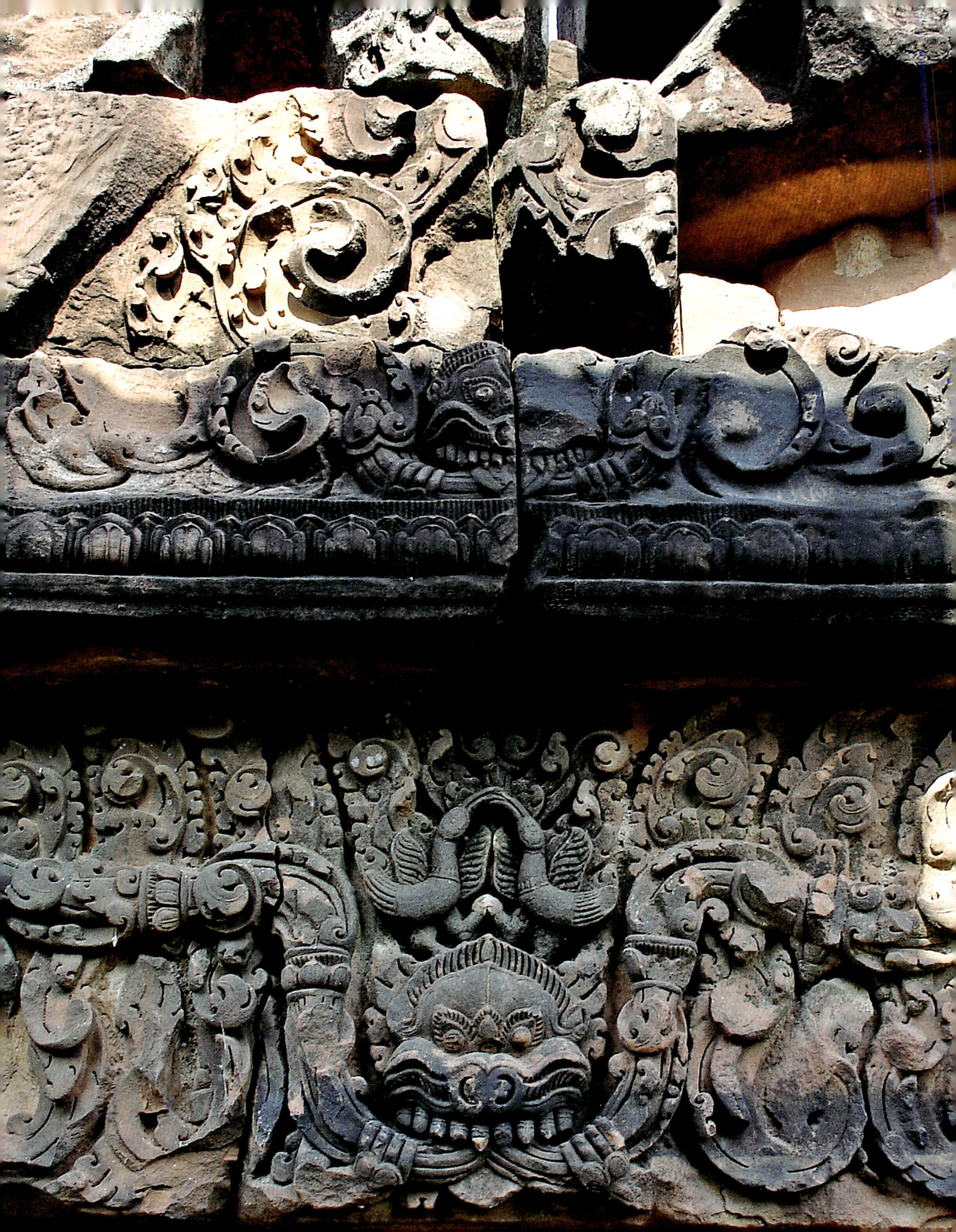

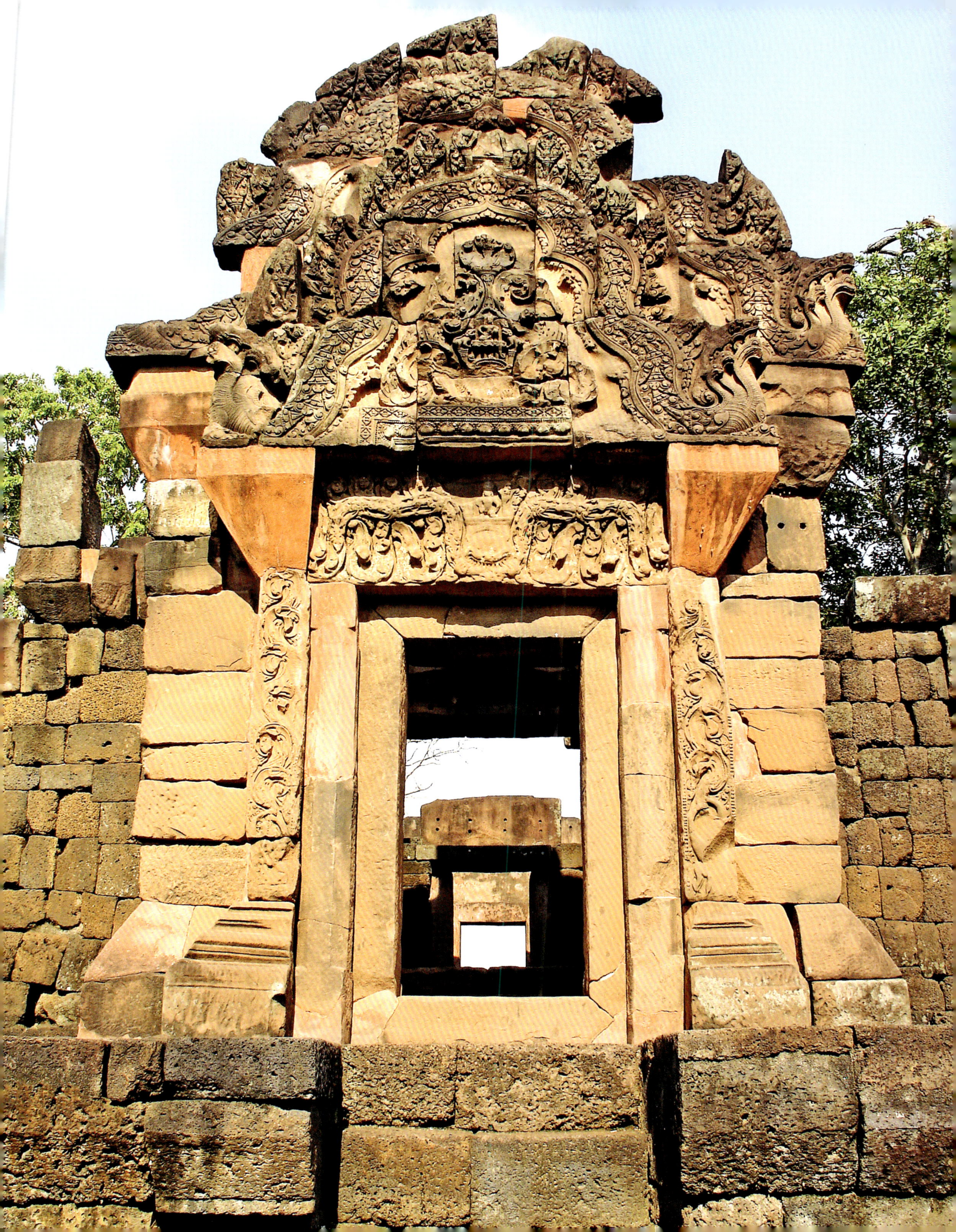

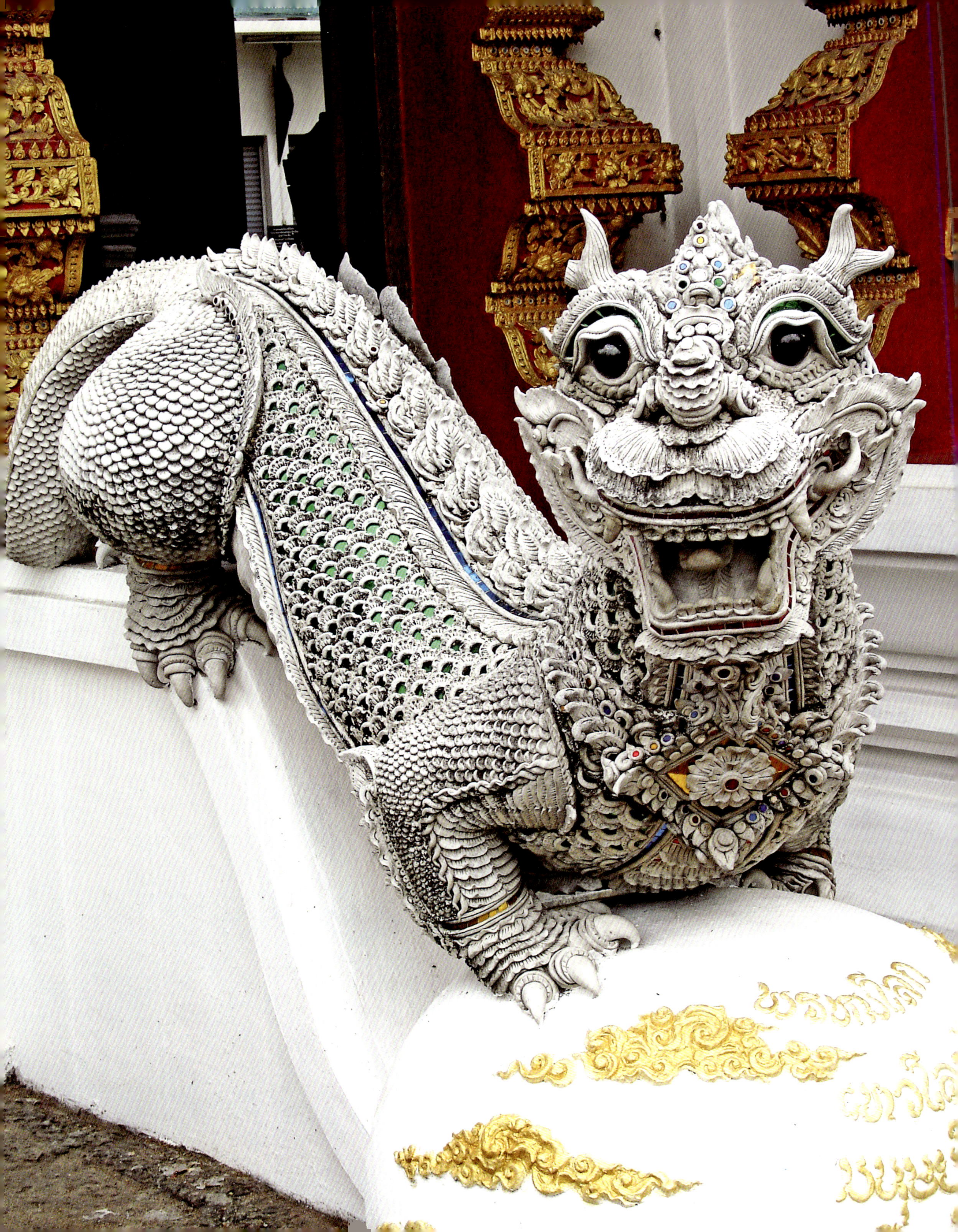

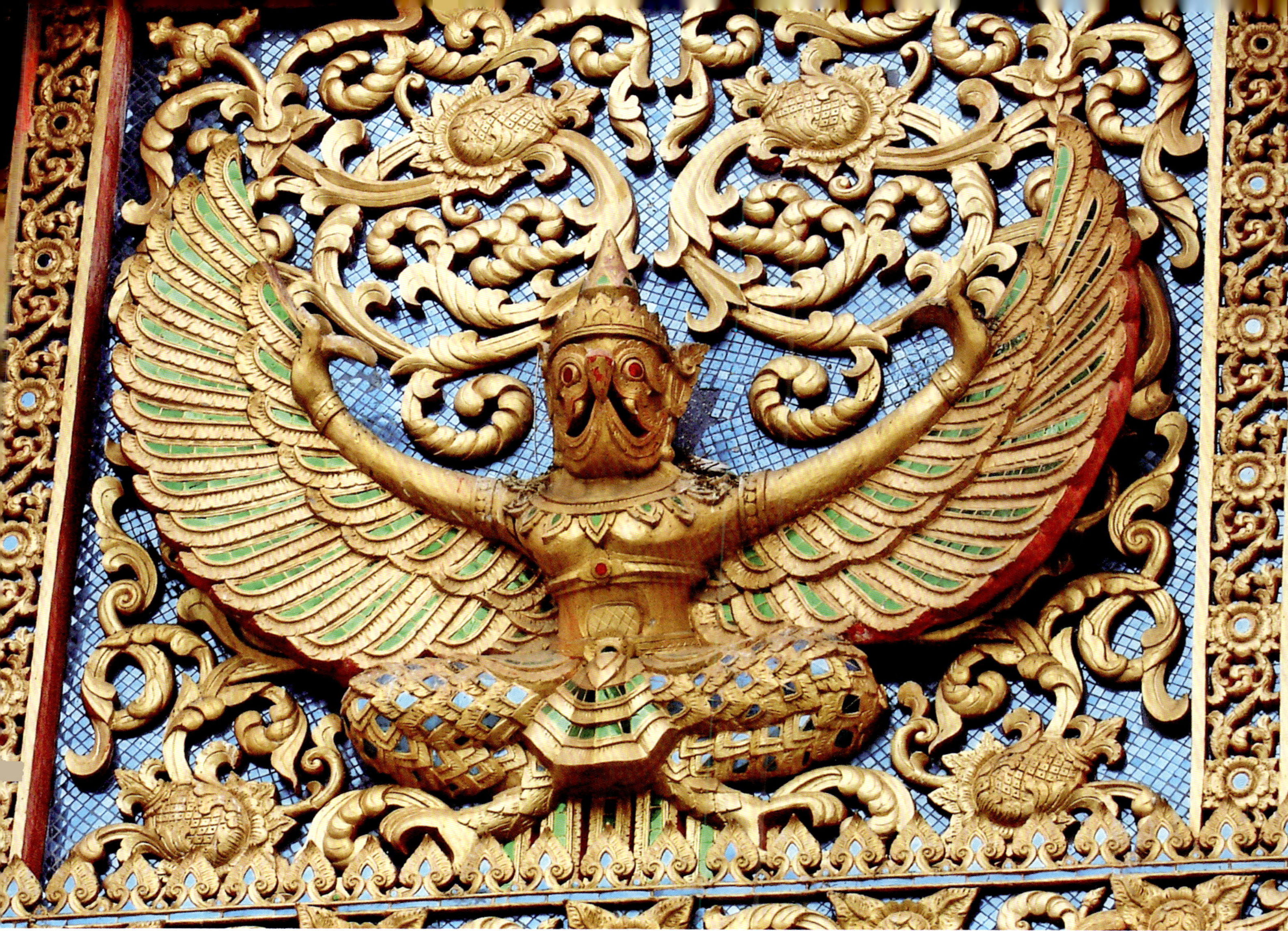

5. MYTHICAL CREATURES

The religions and folklore of Thailand are filled with mythical creatures, some righteous, some following their own path. Once converted to the doctrine of the Buddha, all became powerful protectors of the Buddhist sacred sites, their purpose to frighten evil spirits away from temples (Stratton, 2004, p. 326, 339). The most prevalent defenders are the *yaksha*, the *singh* and the *naga*, detailed in this chapter; however, the most powerful mythical creature is Garuda, in Thai Phra Krut or Suparna, half-eagle, half-man, the trusted steed of Vishnu (Pg. 142). In the *Mahabaruta*, Garuda was of exceptional power straight from the egg, a flap of his wings enough to create a hurricane. Garuda's enemies are his cousins, the serpent race of *nagas* who held his mother for ransom in exchange for the elixir of immortality, *amrita*. Garuda made a bargain with Indra, king of the *devas*, tricked the *nagas*, and reclaimed his mother. In retaliation, all *garudas* swoop down and prey on *nagas*. Every Thai bank has a *garuda* for an official emblem, perched above the entrance signifying undefeatable strength. It is the symbol on the Royal Seal, the post office, and stamped on Thailand's tourist visas.

The *kinnaree* is a mythical bird-woman, female from the waist up, swan from the waist down, with wings for transport between the mystical and human realms. Renowned for entrancing dance, poetry and celestial music, their images grace temple walls and doorways. The most famous is Manohara, subject of classical Thai dance based on the *Sudhana Jakata*. A hunter captures a beautiful *kinnaree* swimming at a lake and presents her to the prince, who undergoes many otherworldly challenges to prove his devotion. In the *Ramakien*, Supanna Matcha is a golden mermaid who attempts to trick the monkey god Hanuman but becomes his lover instead. Her image is displayed as a good luck charm (Pg. 25). Other mythical creatures include the *hongse*, a golden swan-like creature and the mount of Brahma, seen on ornamental gates and eave supports of temples, and the *hatsadiling*, an elephant-fowl, symbolizing passage from one life to another. *Moms* are four-legged dragon guardians similar to the *makara*, often standing on a globe (Pg. 140,143). One Lanna temple offers a variation of Ganesh, with two arms rather than four, carrying his father's trident, with much less girth than other depictions (Pg. 142).

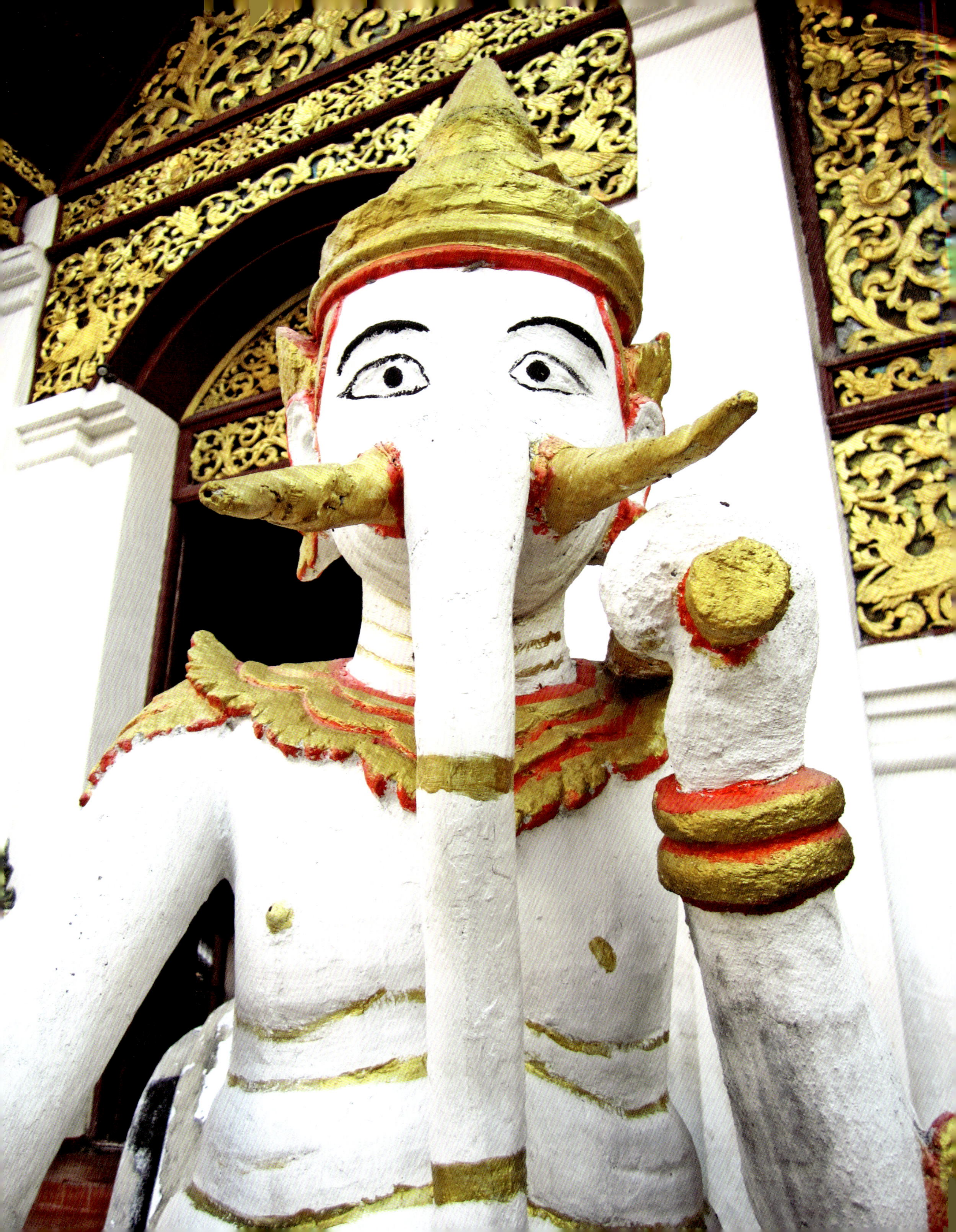

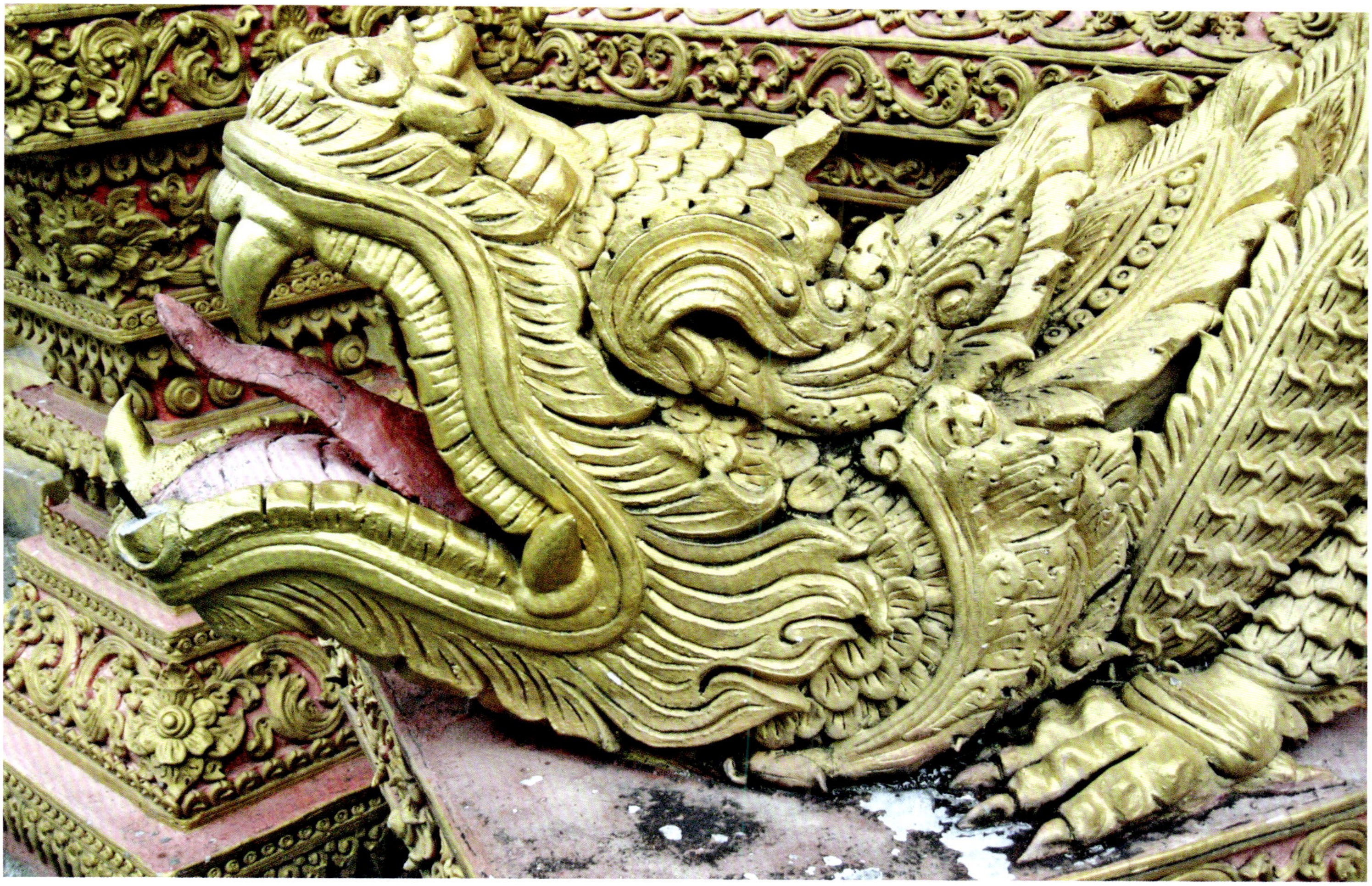

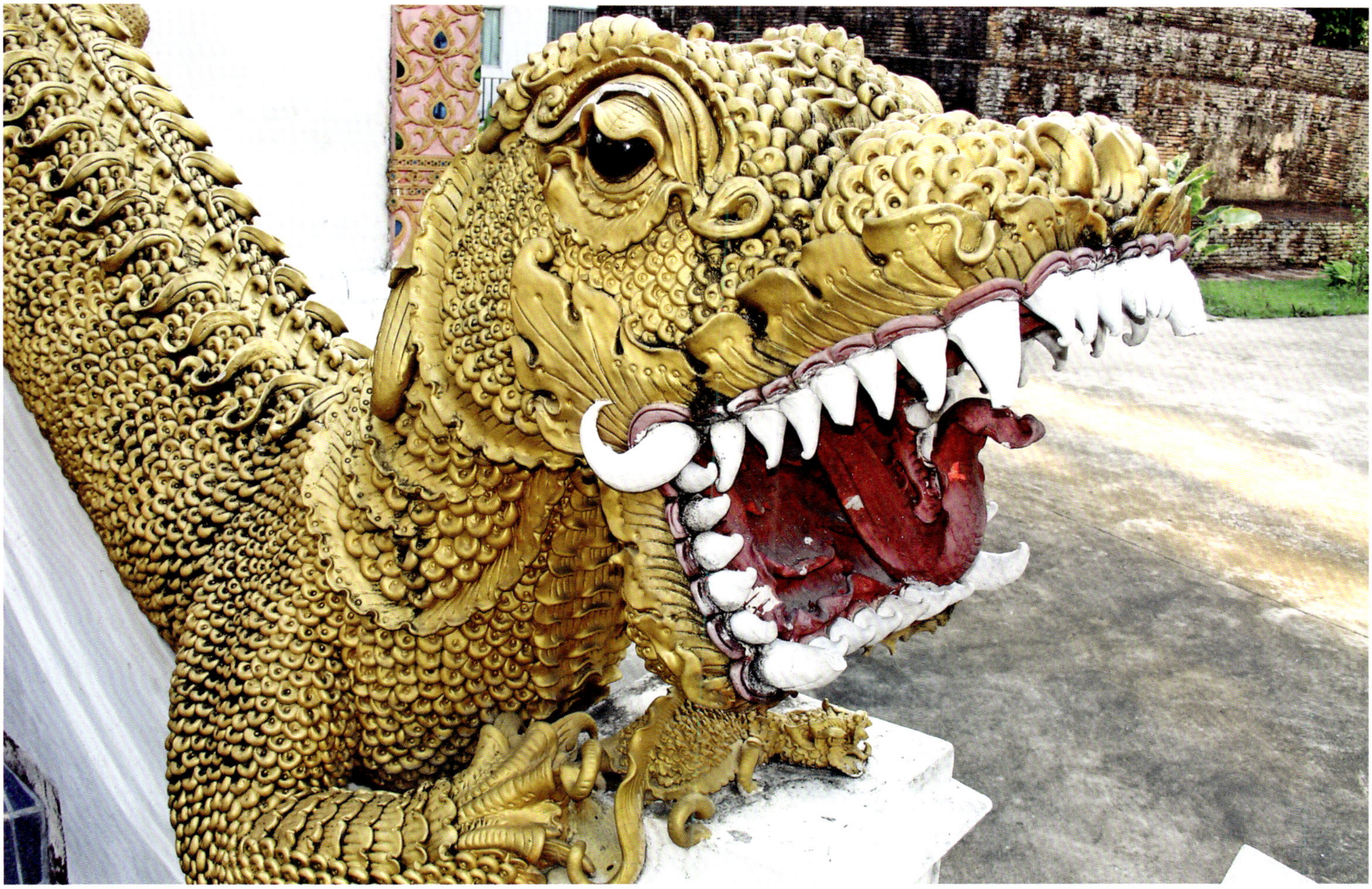

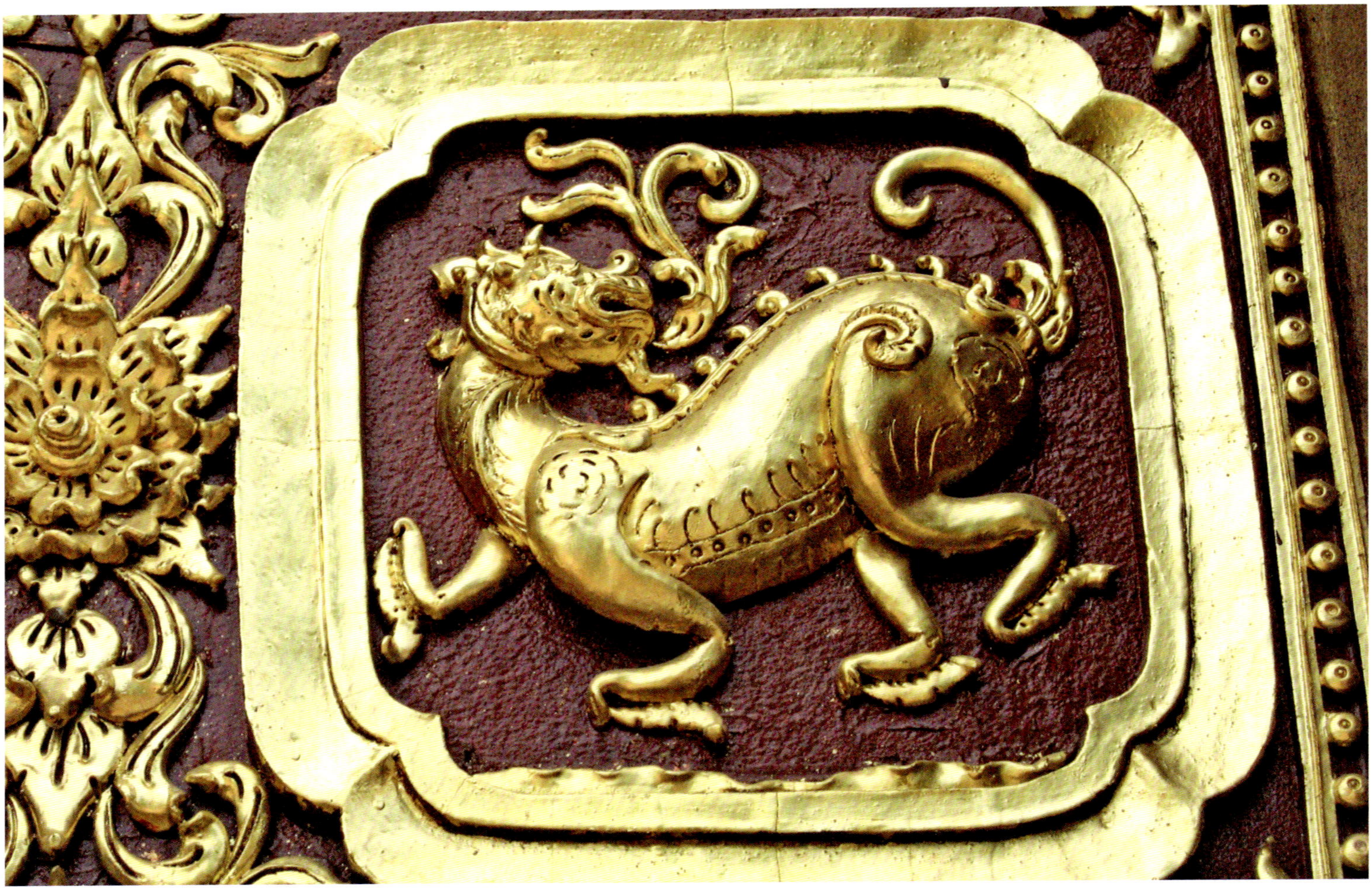

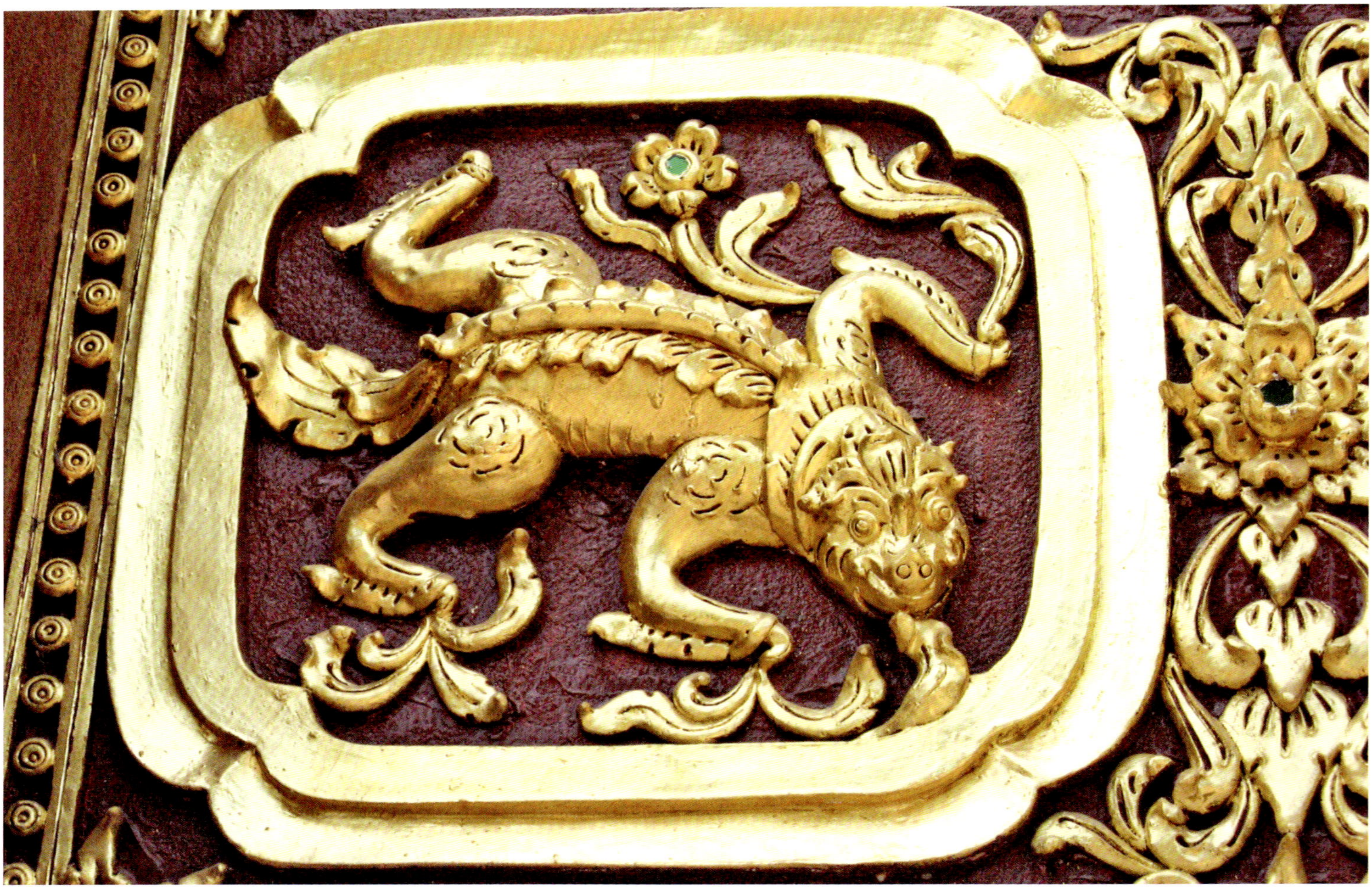

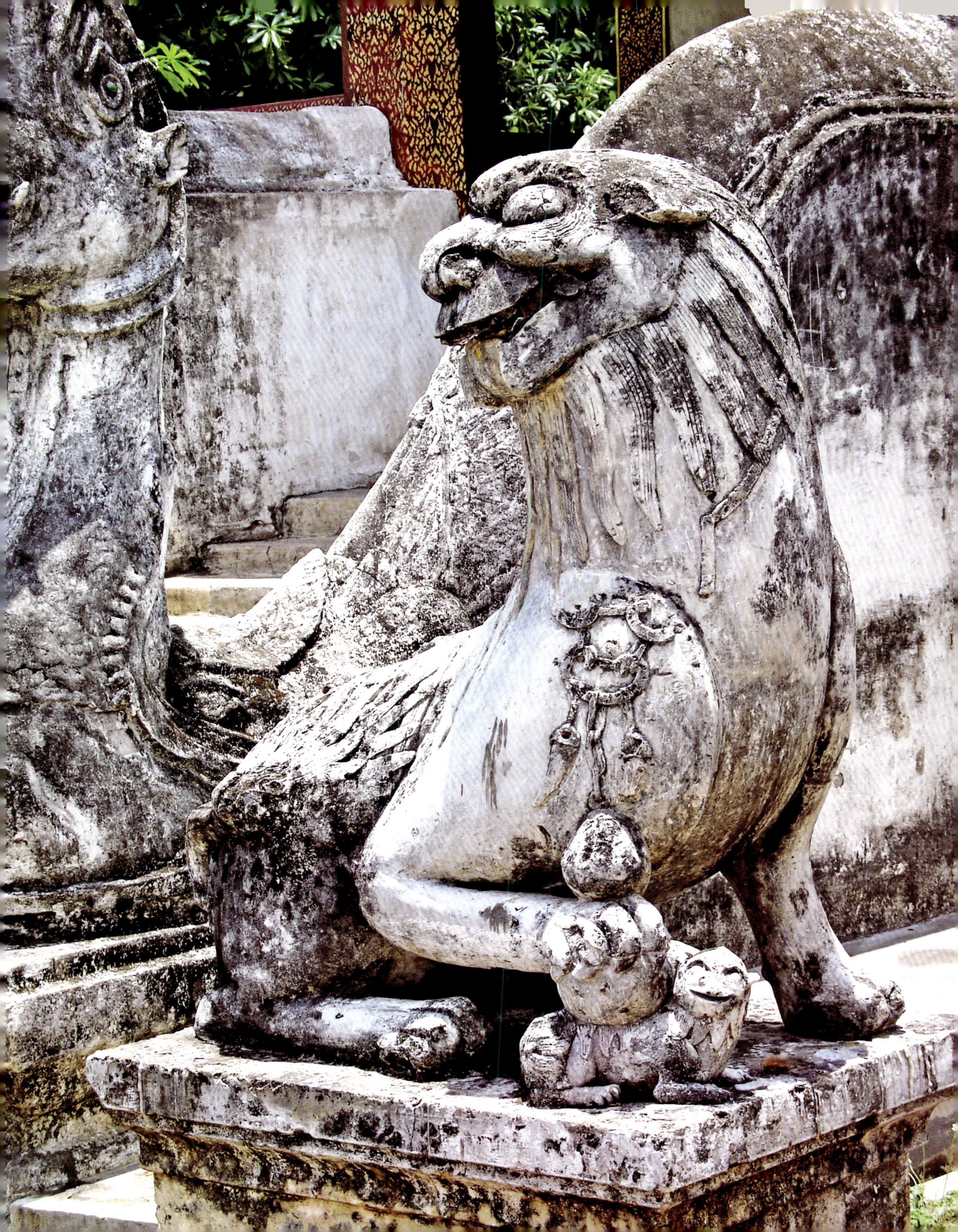

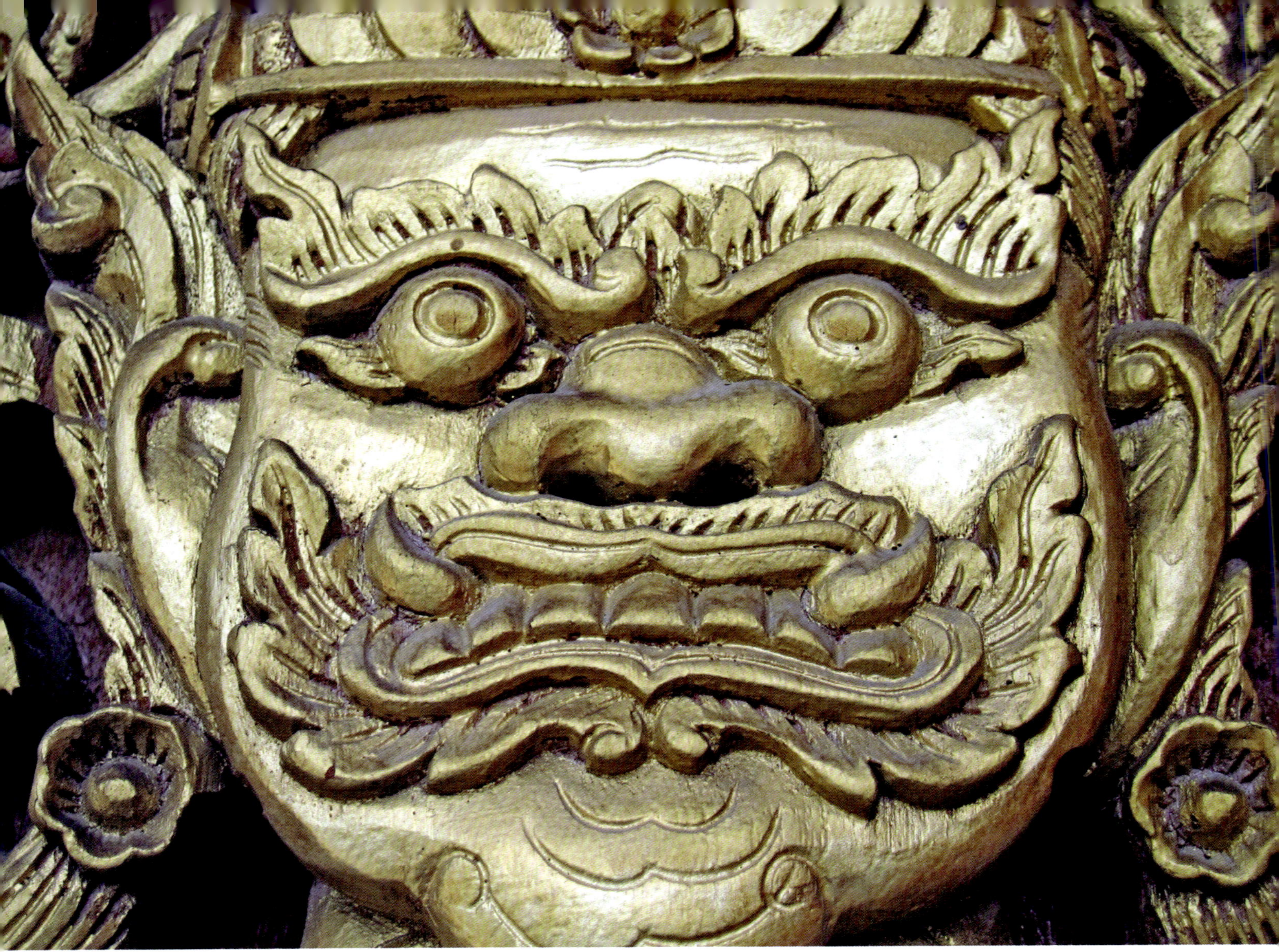

GUARDIANS

In Thailand, temples and palaces are guarded by ferocious giants called *yakshas*. Worship of these creatures as fertility gods and goddesses associated with the soil and trees began with the Dravidians of southern India and northern Sri Lanka. These Animist beliefs later became incorporated into Jain, Hindu and Buddhist mythologies. Described as both harmful and helpful in tendency, depictions vary over time from fairy-like forest sprites to fanged ogres. Portrayed in both the *Ramakien* and in the *Mahabharata*, the second epic of ancient India, they are semi-divine shape-shifters with supernatural powers yet remain mortal, caught in the cycle of life and rebirth. *Yakshas* are governed by the deity Vessavana, sometimes called Kubera, his Brahmin name from a previous life when still a man. He is the god of wealth, the head of the Four Heavenly Kings, and guardian of the north gate. The *yakshas* are his attendants and protectors of the earth's minerals and resources. In the *Ramakien*, he is Thao Wessuwan, the elder stepbrother of Ravana, the ten-headed multi-armed king of the *asuras*, or demons, cousins to the *yakshas*. Ravana, or Thotsakan in Thai, abducts Nang Sida, the hero Phra Ram's wife, which triggers the epic war between man and demon as overseen by the gods.

Usually depicted with green or red skin, two large tusks, and blazing red or amber eyes, *yakshas* wear a suit of armor and elaborate helmets, often with an ornate protective sash covering the genitals. Some have arms raised overhead with jewel-encrusted batons in each hand, fingers often displaying rings or spikes. Most hold a spear or thick stake planted firmly on the ground, knees slightly bent, giving a three-legged appearance: Kubera, or Kuwen in Thai, meaning deformed, is described as a one-eyed giant with three legs in ancient texts. An emblem of Kala often adorns the center of their chest armor. Kala, a guardian in its own right, comes from Hindu mythology: Kala demanded a sacrifice of Shiva, who became enraged and commanded the demon to eat itself. The face of Kala hangs above the doorways of many temple entrances (Pg. 148 bottom), and on the lintels of Khmer temples (Pg. 137,138), having no lower jaw but many sharp teeth, sometimes with hands present. Some *yakshas* are portrayed as stout and dwarfish, often crowned, usually seated and asleep, holding a club.

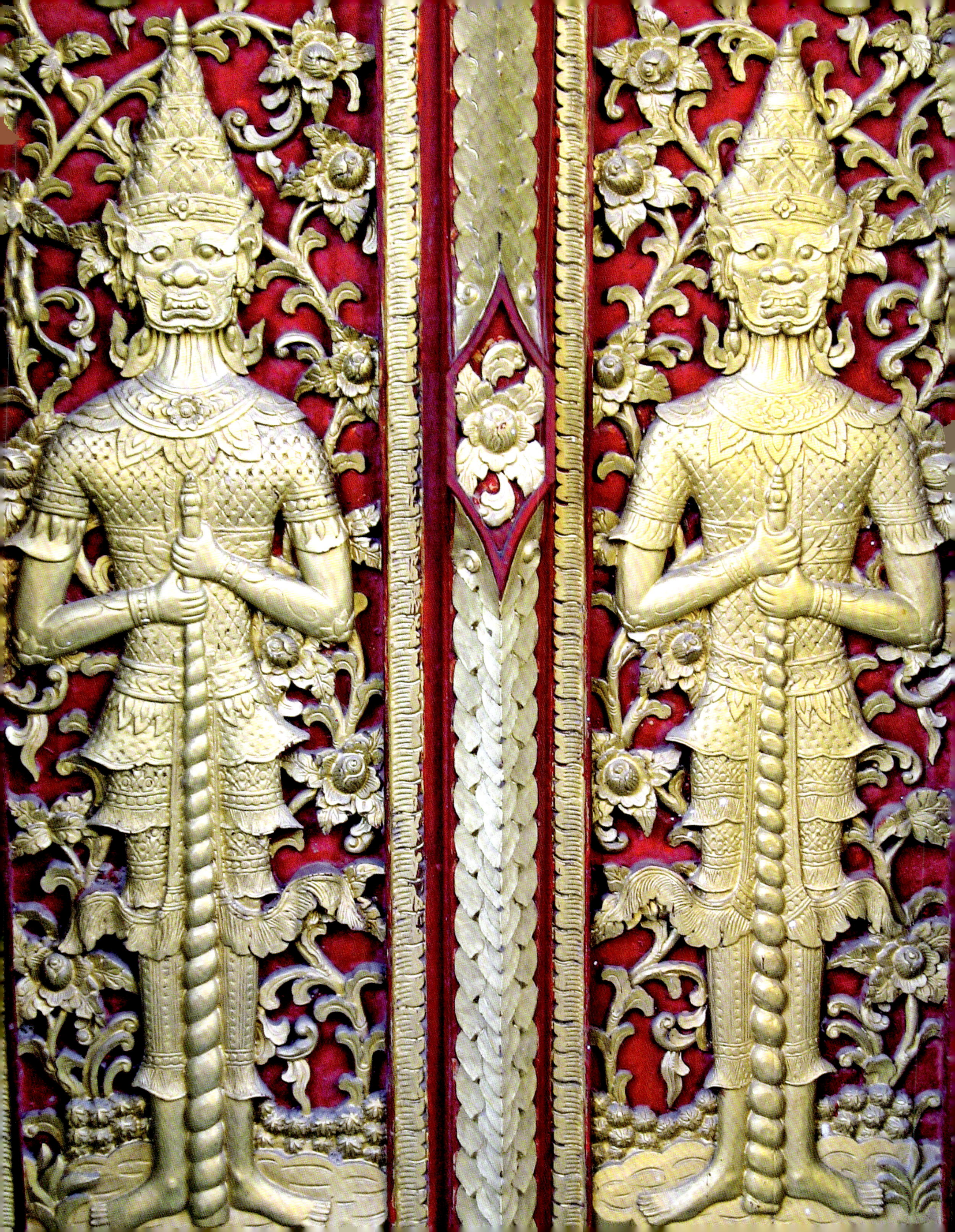

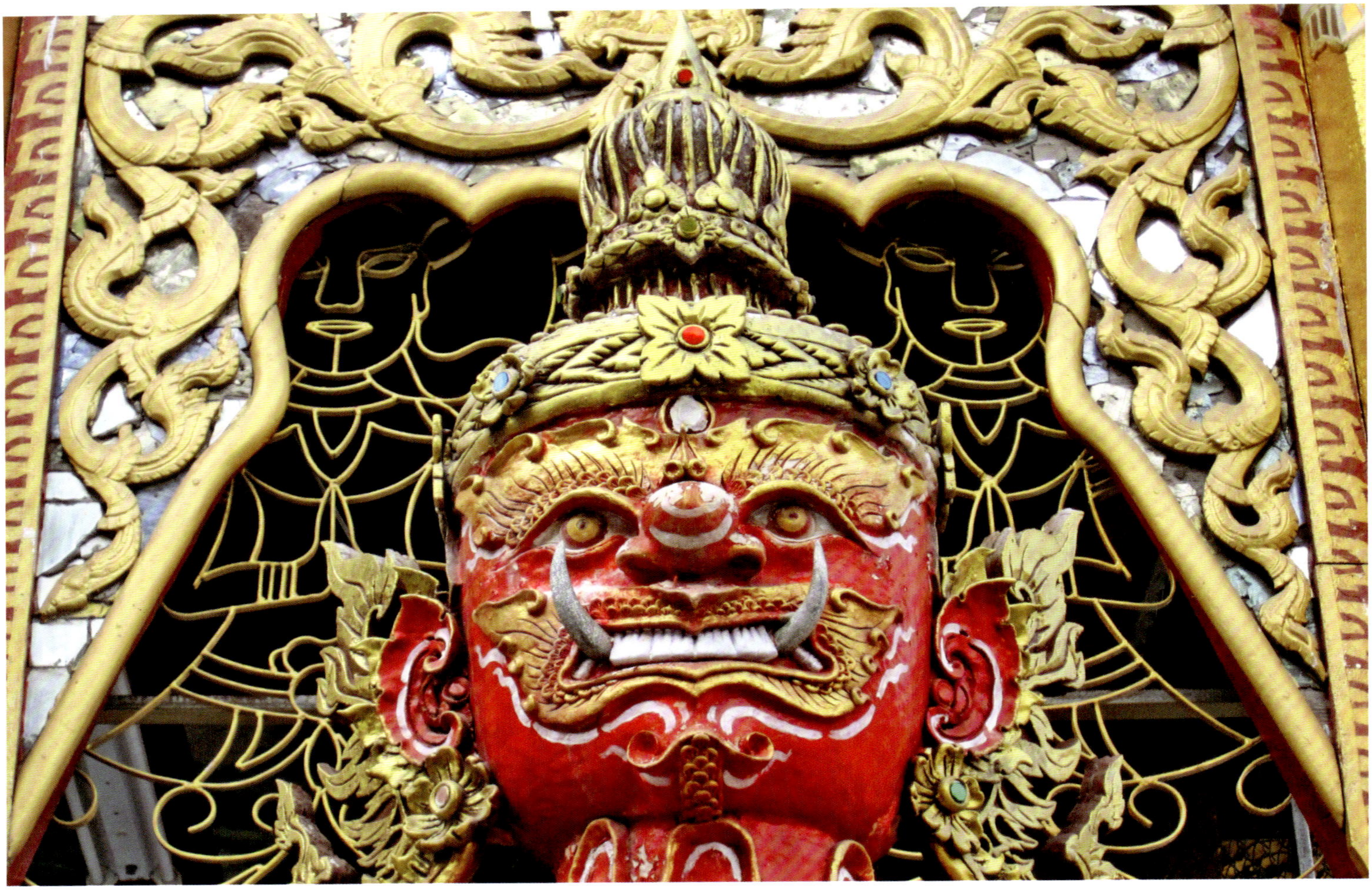

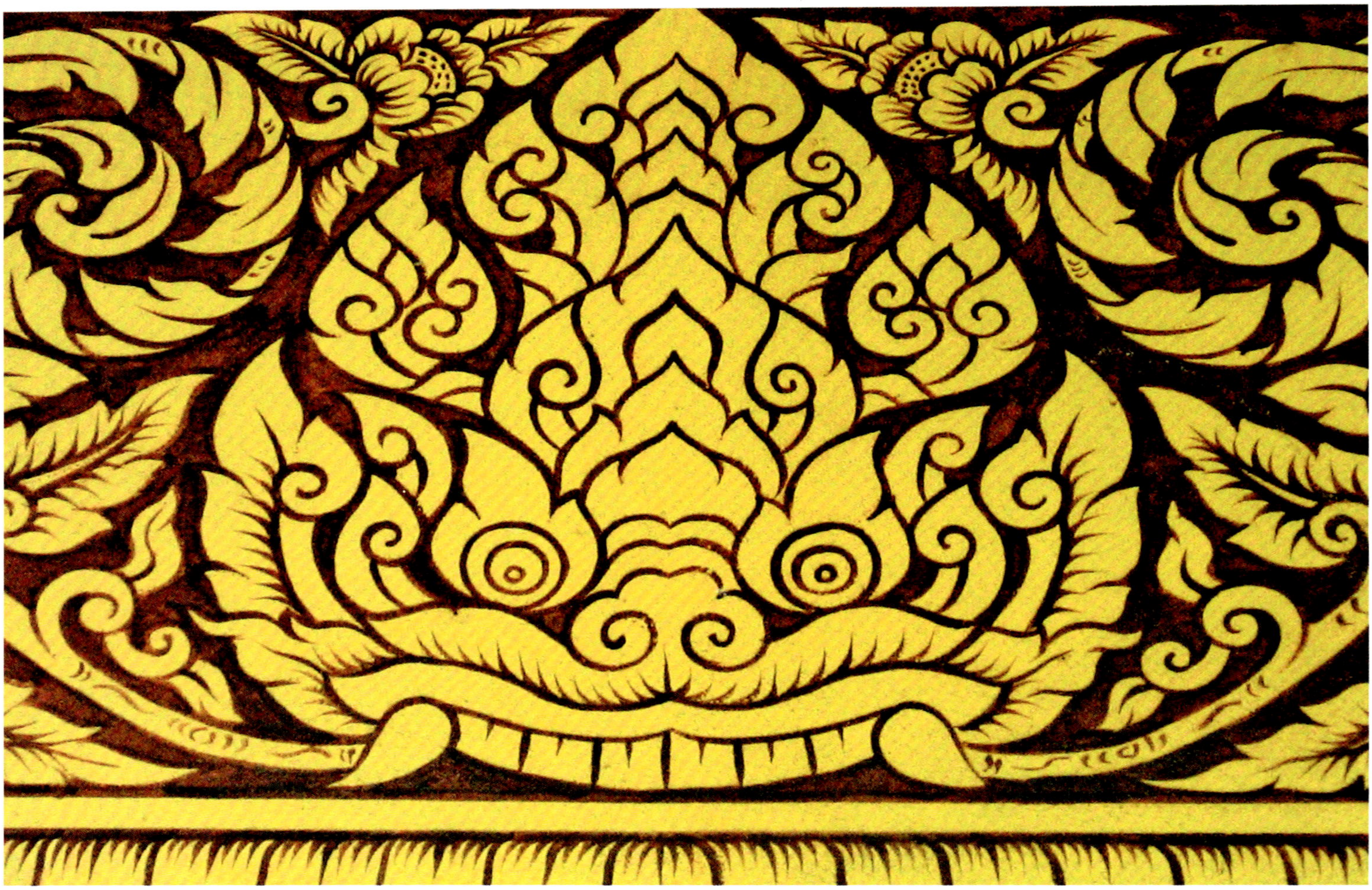

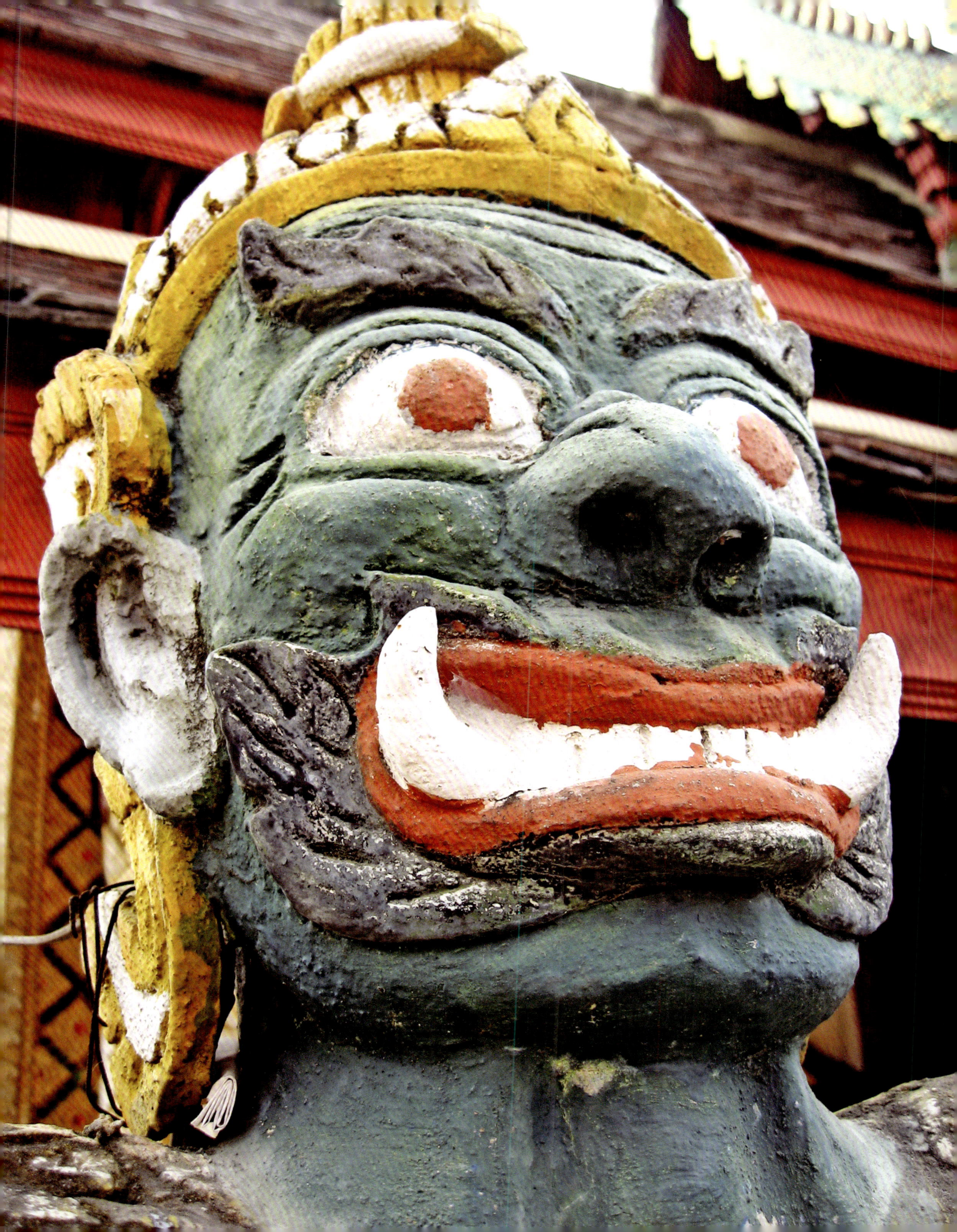

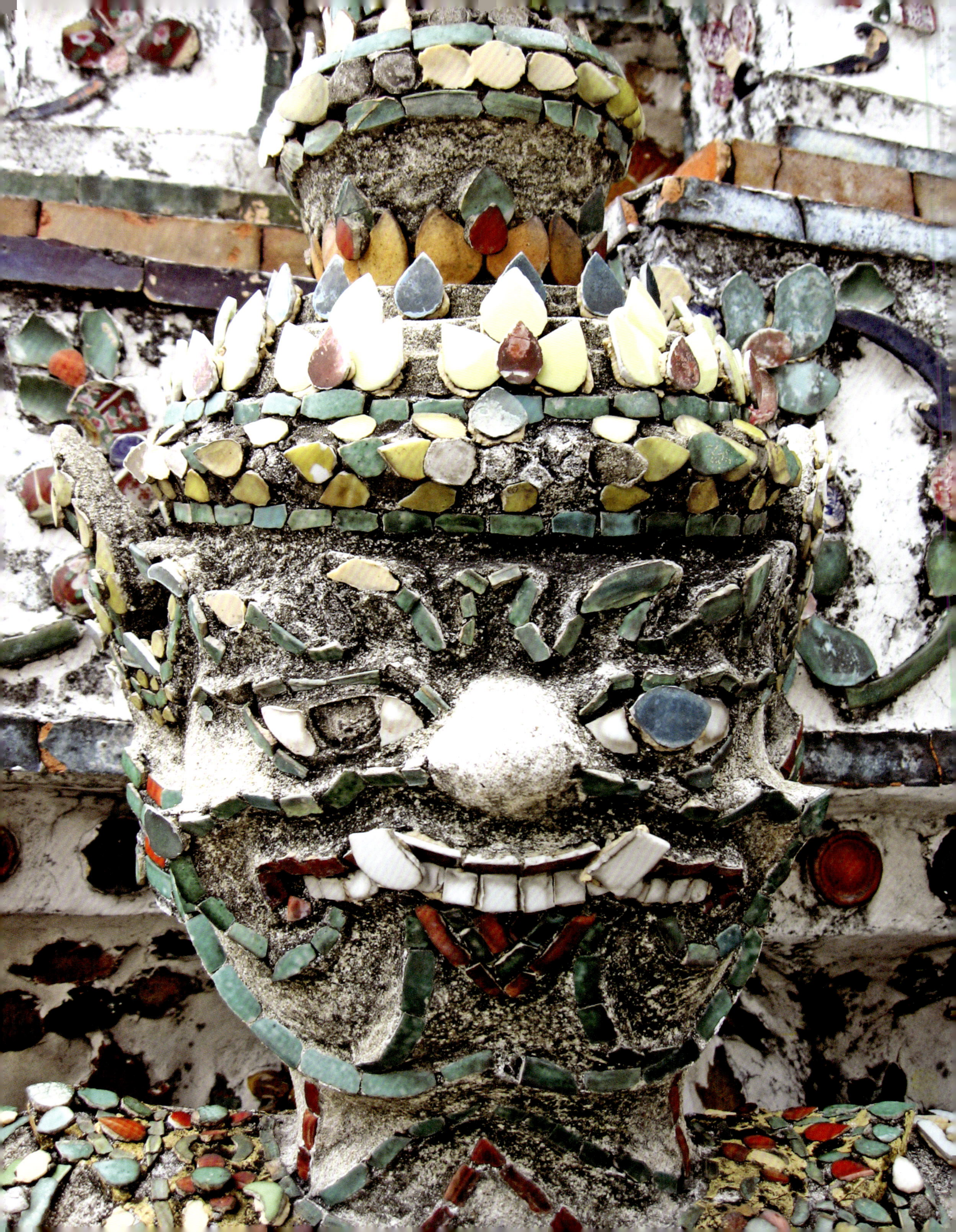

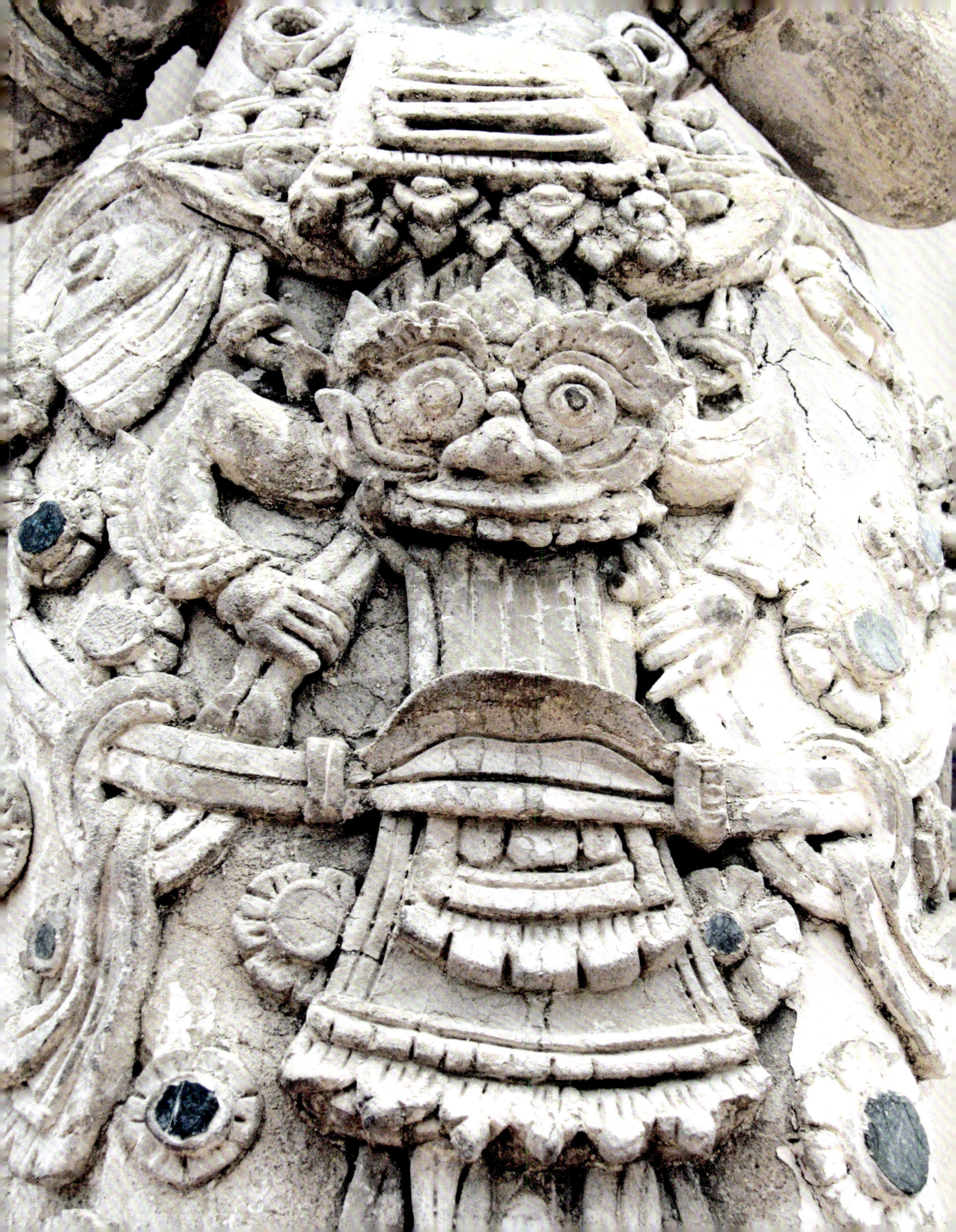

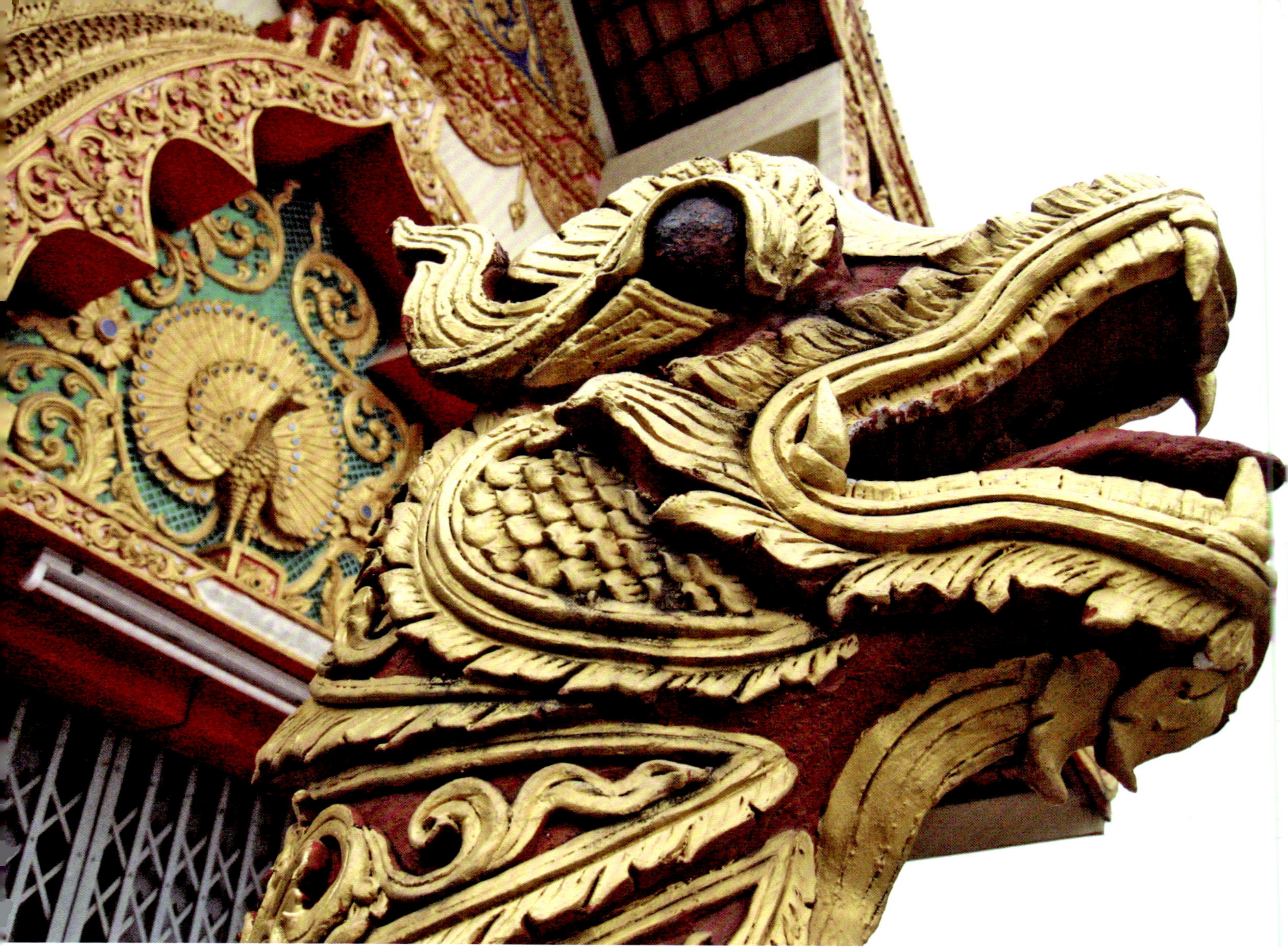

SINGH

The *singh* is a mythical lion and temple guardian, the name first used in an ancient Indian *veda* more than 2000 years ago, signifying grace and power, loyalty and protection. It has also been the symbol of Thailand's Boon Rawd's Singha Beer since 1933. Early images of the lion protecting sacred sites of Thailand date from the mid-seventh century. Vairocana, one of the Five Jina Buddhas from the seventh century Vajrayana school of Buddhism, is depicted riding a lion. Cabalistic cloth, hung by truck drivers and in taxis as protection against adversity, portray the *singh* on all fours, with the right paw lifted. The Chinese also believe the lion protects against evil spirits and demons: two lion statues guard most temple entrances. As the lion is not indigenous to Southeast Asia, the depictions of strength, nobility and fearlessness were influenced by early Indian Buddhist culture. The *naga* and *singh* protect all Khmer-style temples, which are dedicated to the Hindu god Vishnu, the ultimate creator and the symbol of light. The *naga* is the lunar guardian and the *singh* the solar guardian, representing Vishnu's harmonization of the world. Khmer-style *singhs* found in Thailand are cast in bronze or stone, on all fours, tail upwards if present, wearing a crown, displaying square mouths full of pointed teeth, with rounded pug noses. Far from naturalistic depictions, they truly represent the mythical.

In the Burmese-Lanna style, the *singh* sits on a plinth, facing front or in profile, on its hind legs. The tail is drawn back along the spine, exposing an anus. The lips are exaggerated and pulled back in a snarl, the mouth is square, with a pointed incisor at each corner and two more pointing up from the back corner of the lower jaw. The teeth are often rounded or squared, rather than sharp and triangular. Some *singhs* are crowned; most sport a two or three-layered collar-like mane, and feature a prominent crest or emblem on the chest (Stratton, 2005 pp. 350-351). *Singhs* are often paired with a crowned, bearded, heavy eye-browed guardian figure, dressed in ceremonial attire rather than armor, carrying a scepter instead of a weapon, holding onto one of the lion's paws (Pg. 154). Other times they are pictured with a *Ruesi*, forest hermits or sages with magical animistic abilities, the most famous being Phra Lersi. Occasionally, they are pictured with a lion cub, holding onto one of its paws or wrapped around a leg.

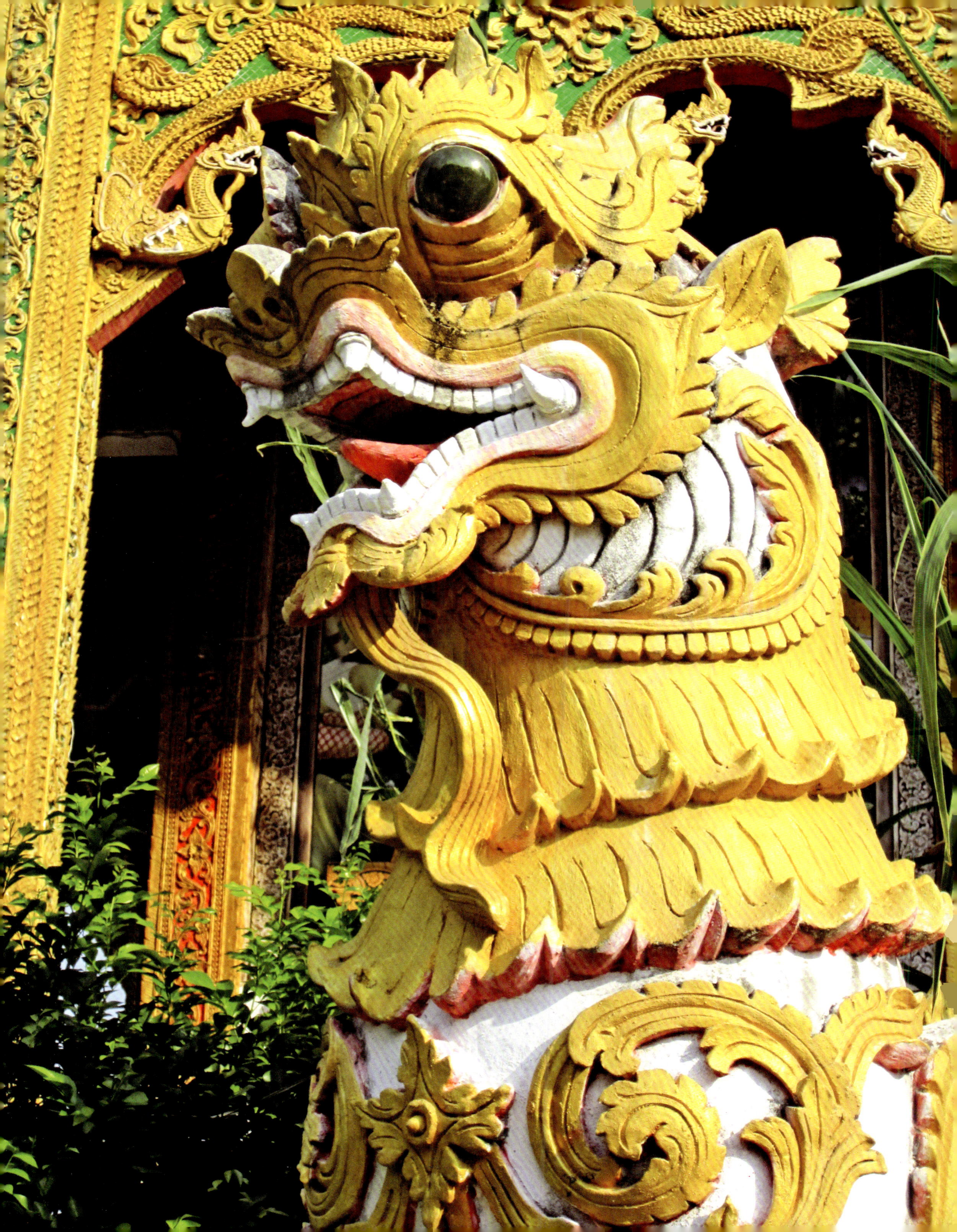

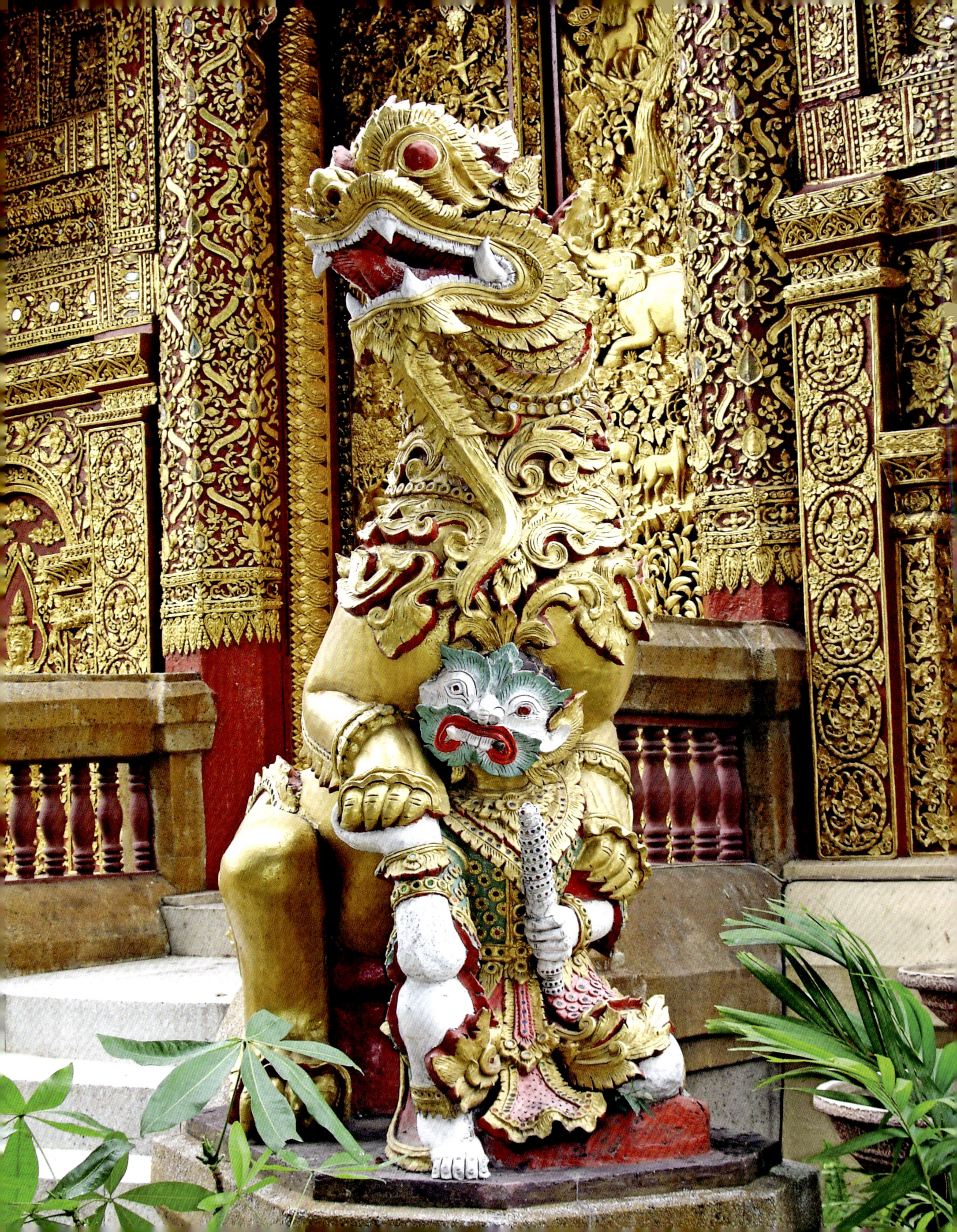

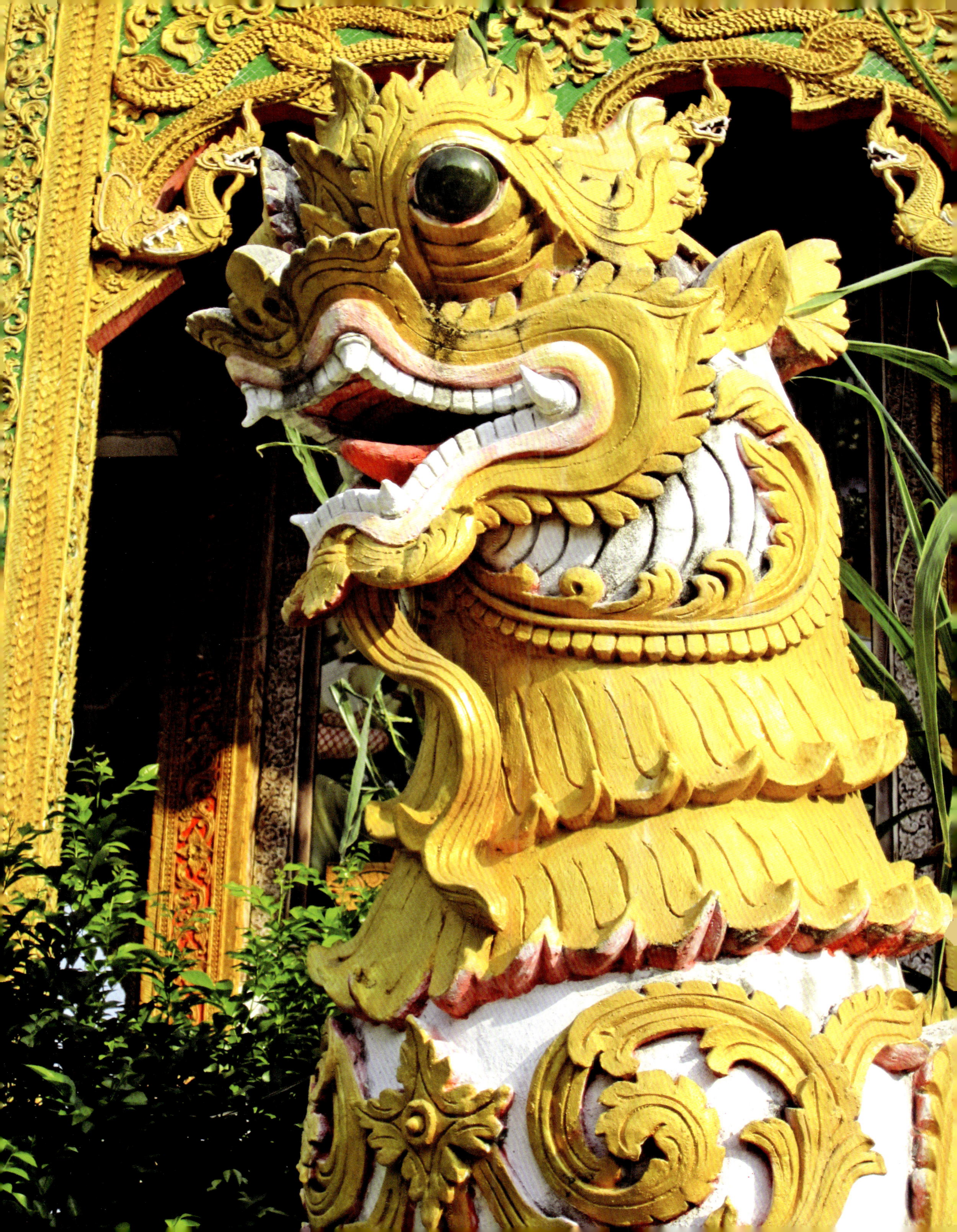

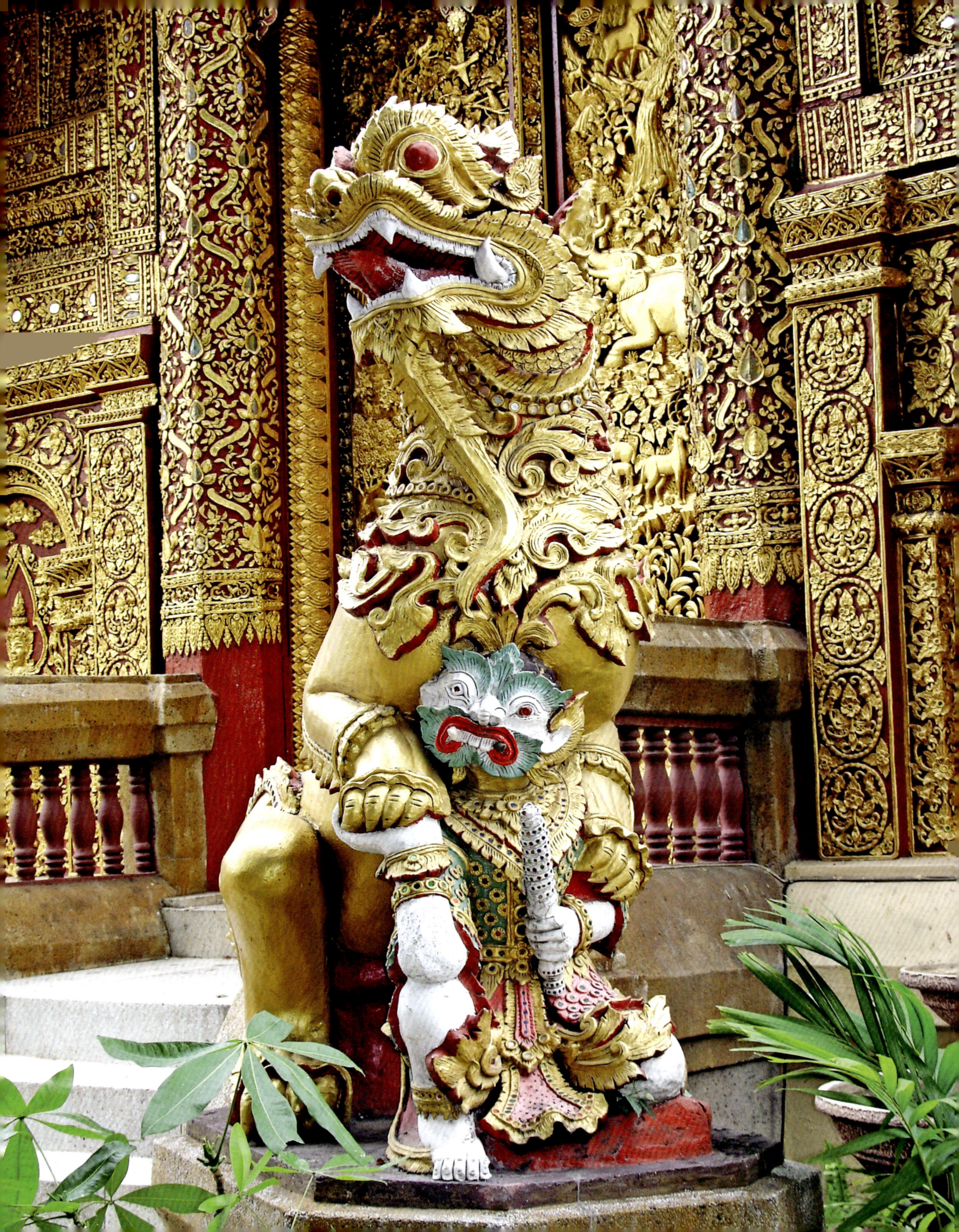

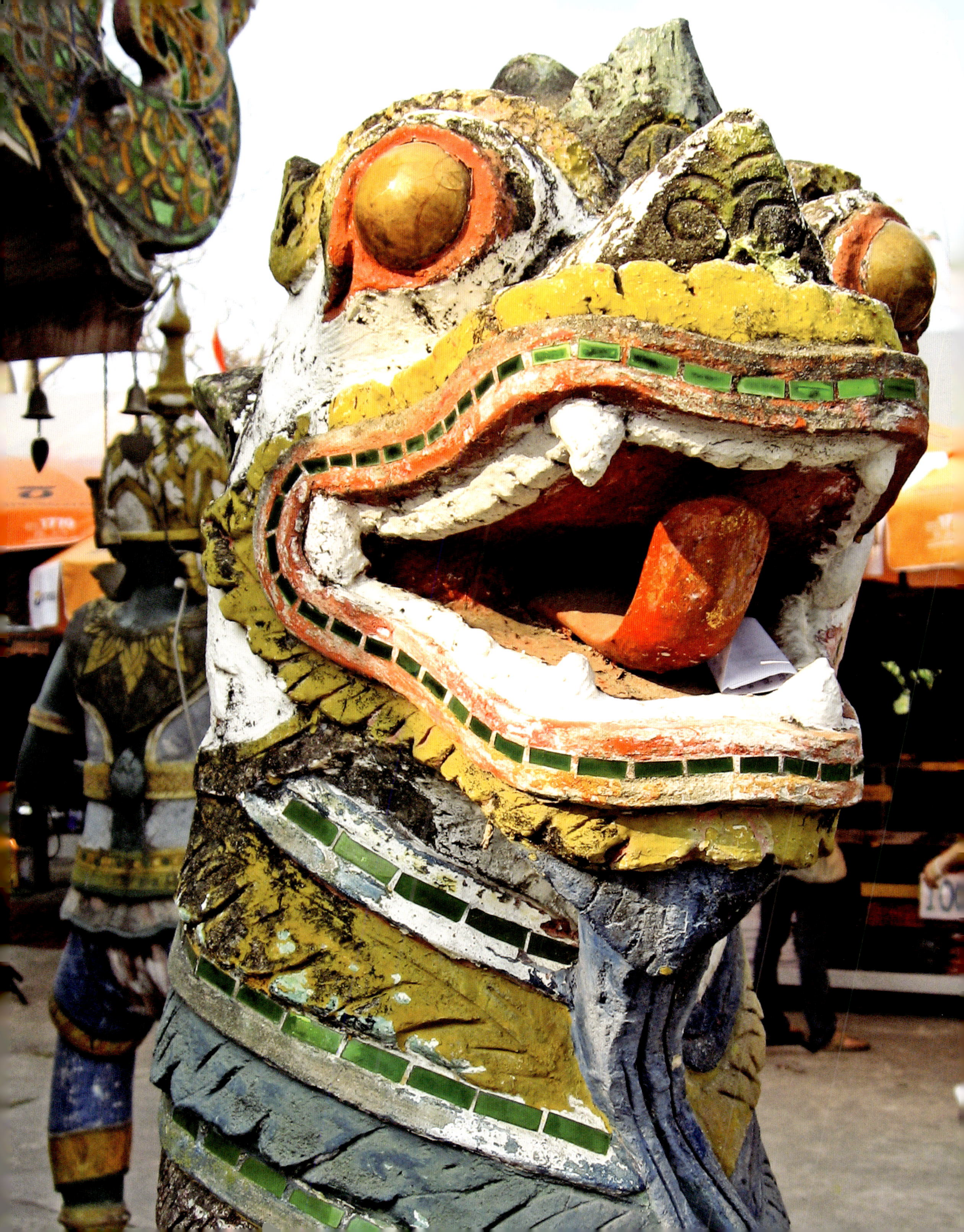

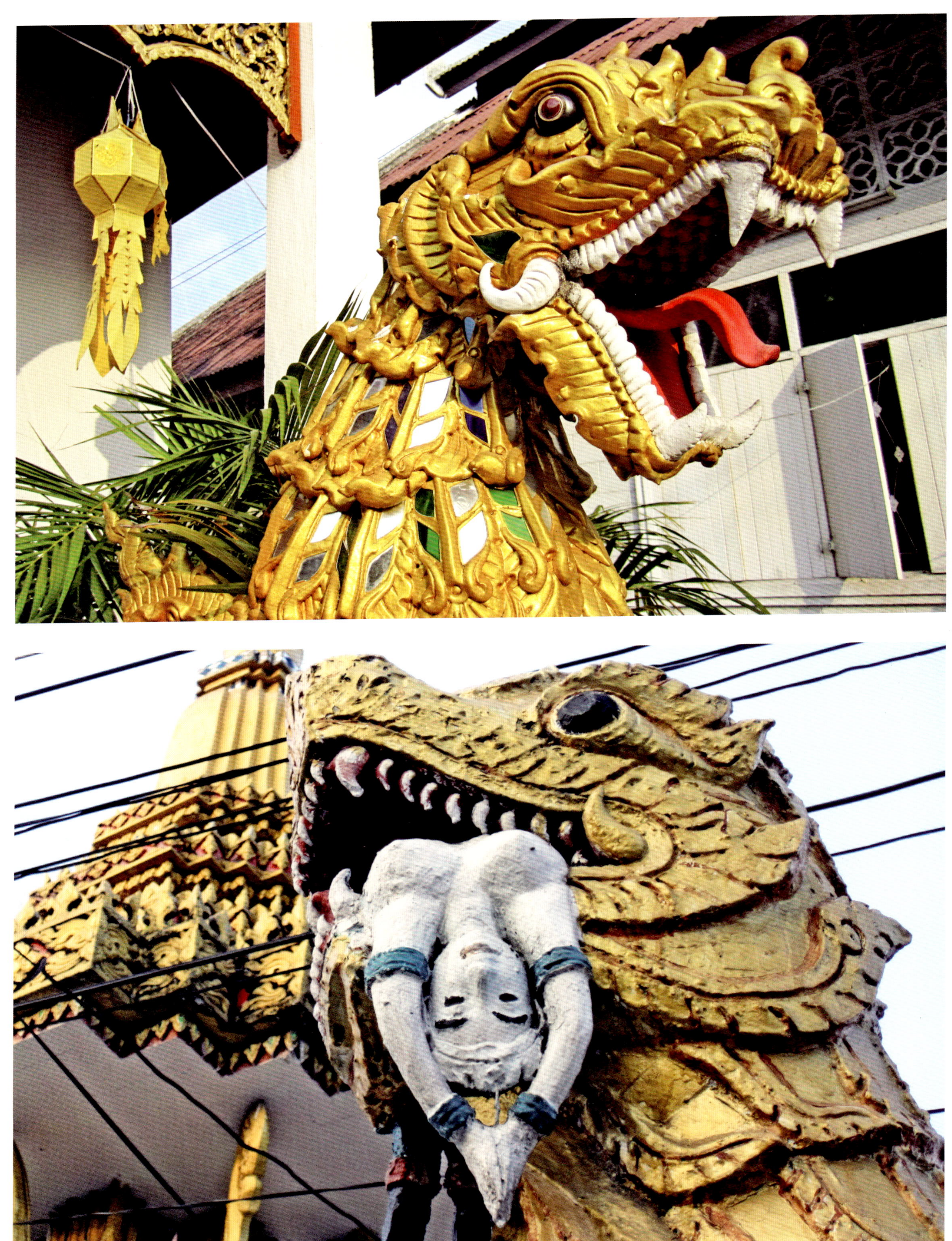

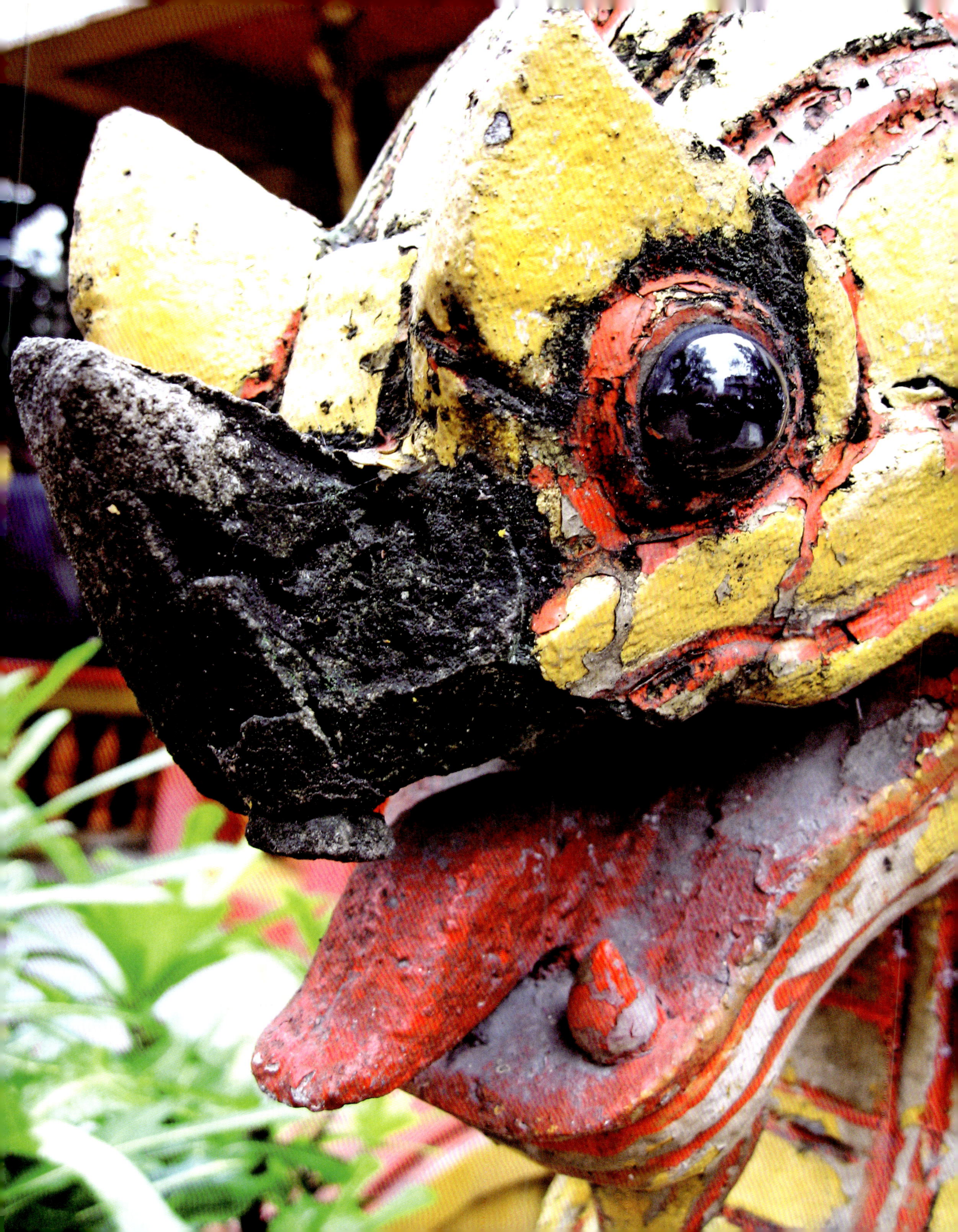

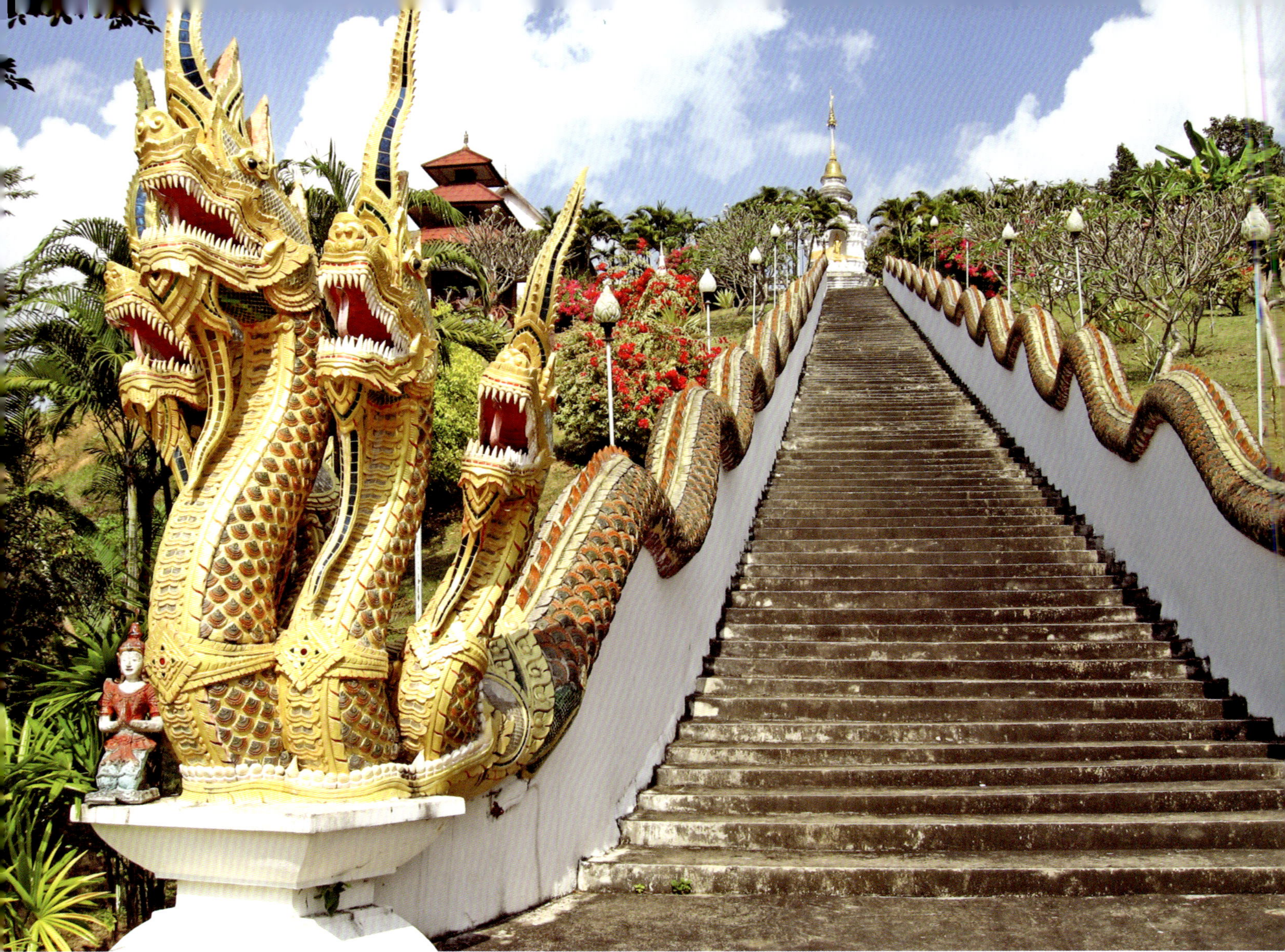

NAGA

Naga (in Thai: *nak*) is the Sanskrit word for cobra. *Nagas* figure prominently in both Hindu and Buddhist canons, as a semi-divine race residing in netherworld palaces. They can fly, control the weather, and shift between serpent, half-serpent, or human form. They suffer the effects of man's disrespect to the environment, and retaliate through droughts, floods, or skin diseases, or reward with bountiful crops. They serve as custodians of the *sutras*, or religious texts, bring fertility and protect waterways. In the Hindu creation myth The Churning of the Milk Ocean, Vishnu convinces all to churn the primeval milk sea to release the nectar of immortality. The demi-gods and the demons use Vasuki, the *naga* king, as a churning rope and Mount Meru, home of the gods, as a pivot rod in a thousand year tug-of-war. A few drops fall to earth, a *naga* slides past, gaining the ability to shed its skin. Bangkok's Suvarnabhumi Airport has a large diorama of this tale.

In Buddhism, the serpent is protector rather than devil, as portrayed in Christianity. The Buddha was meditating under the Bodhi tree, when in the sixth week a fierce rain pummeled the earth. Mulcinda, king of the serpents, came from the underworld, coiled himself around the Buddha, and used his hood as protection from the elements. Buddha images correspond with days of the week, and Saturday's image depicts the Buddha, seated on a lotus flower, on top of a serpent's coils, protected by a seven-headed *naga*. The number of *naga* heads is always odd. A *naga* in human form was ordained a monk, but when asleep, returned to his snake identity. The Buddha explained he must leave the *Sangha*, but to console him, promised that all novices would be called a *nak* once they shaved their head until ordination. In northern Thailand, *nagas* protect temples. Always in pairs, they wrap around balustrades and staircases, or coil under eaves, displaying a tongue and rows of sharp teeth, often crowned. Many are constructed of mirrors or reflective tiles, believed to repel evil spirits who see their reflection and flee (Stratton, 2004, pp. 340 & 342). *Nagas* are often seen emerging from the fierce jaws of the hybrid sea-creature *makara*, with crocodile-like legs and a tail (Pg. 162). Today, a *naga* is said to live in the Mekong River; he sends fireballs into the sky to greet the Buddha following the rainy season.

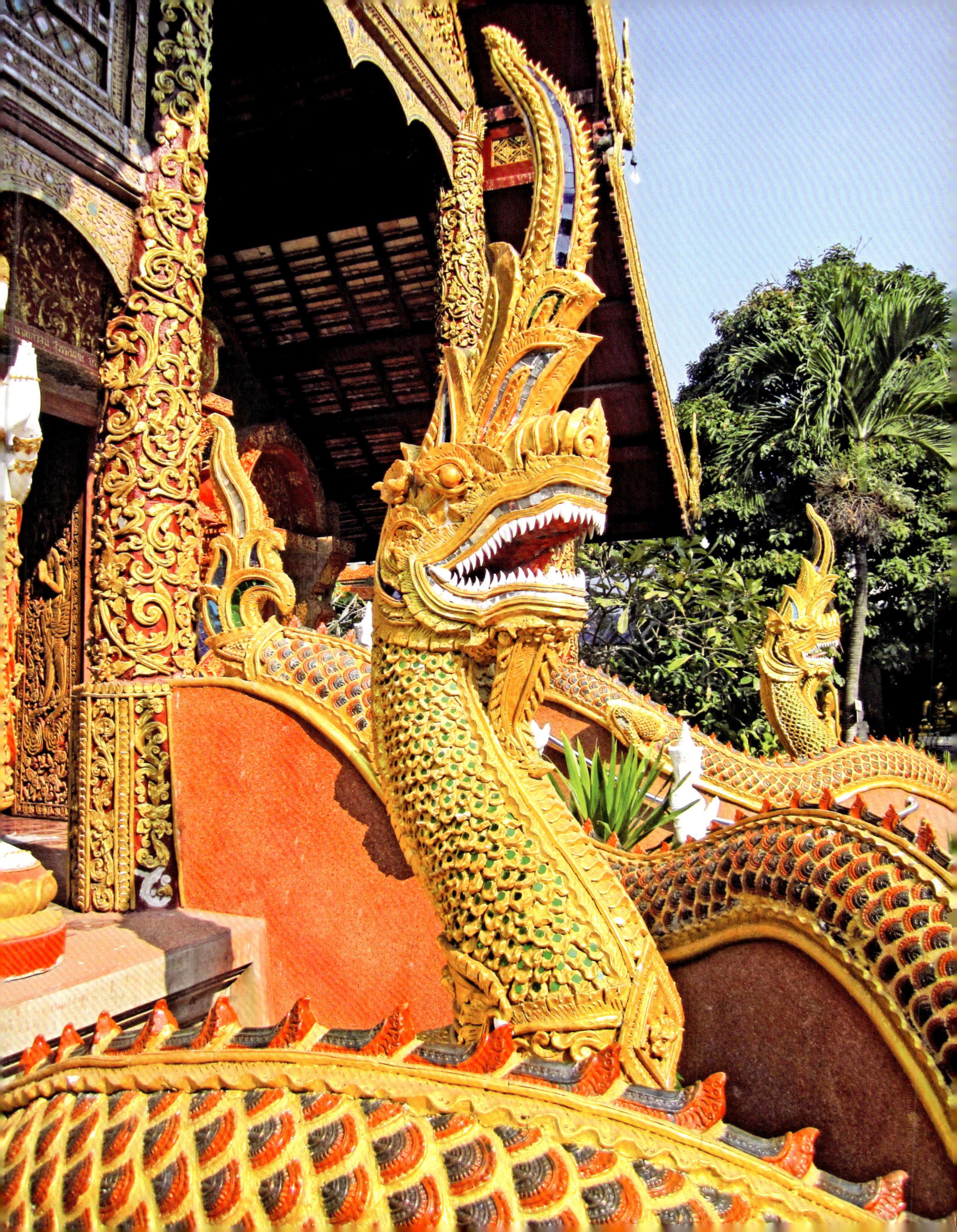

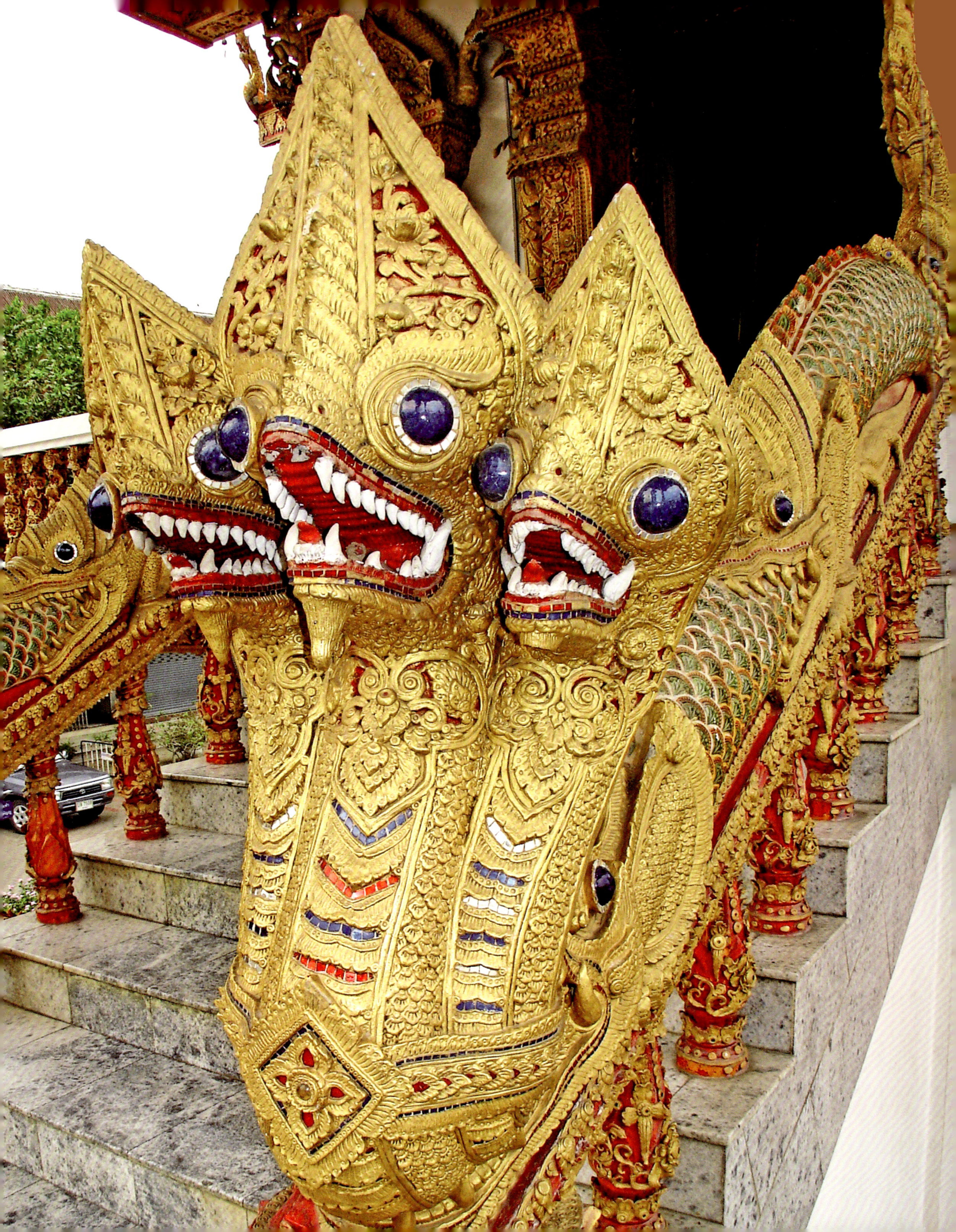

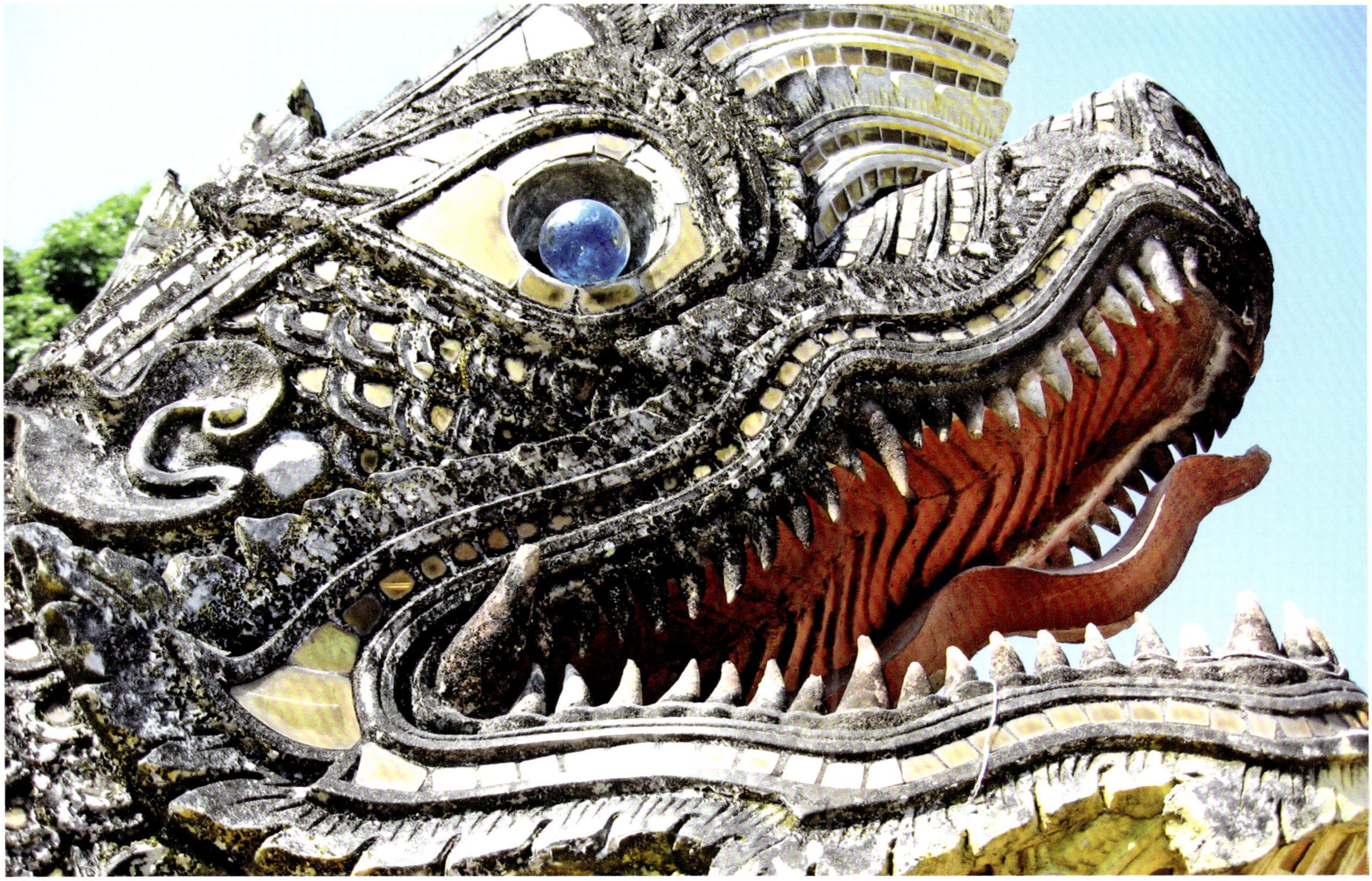

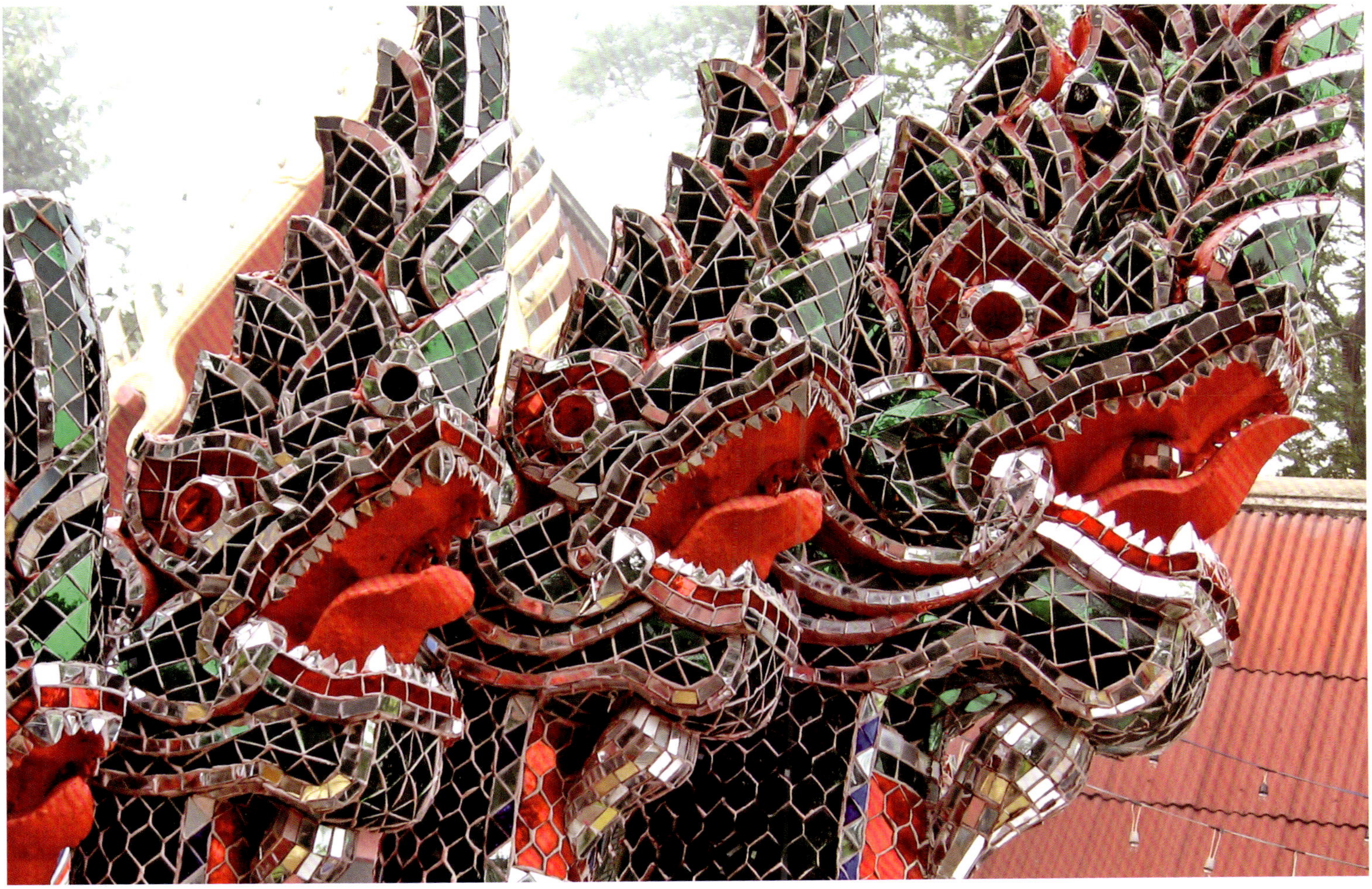

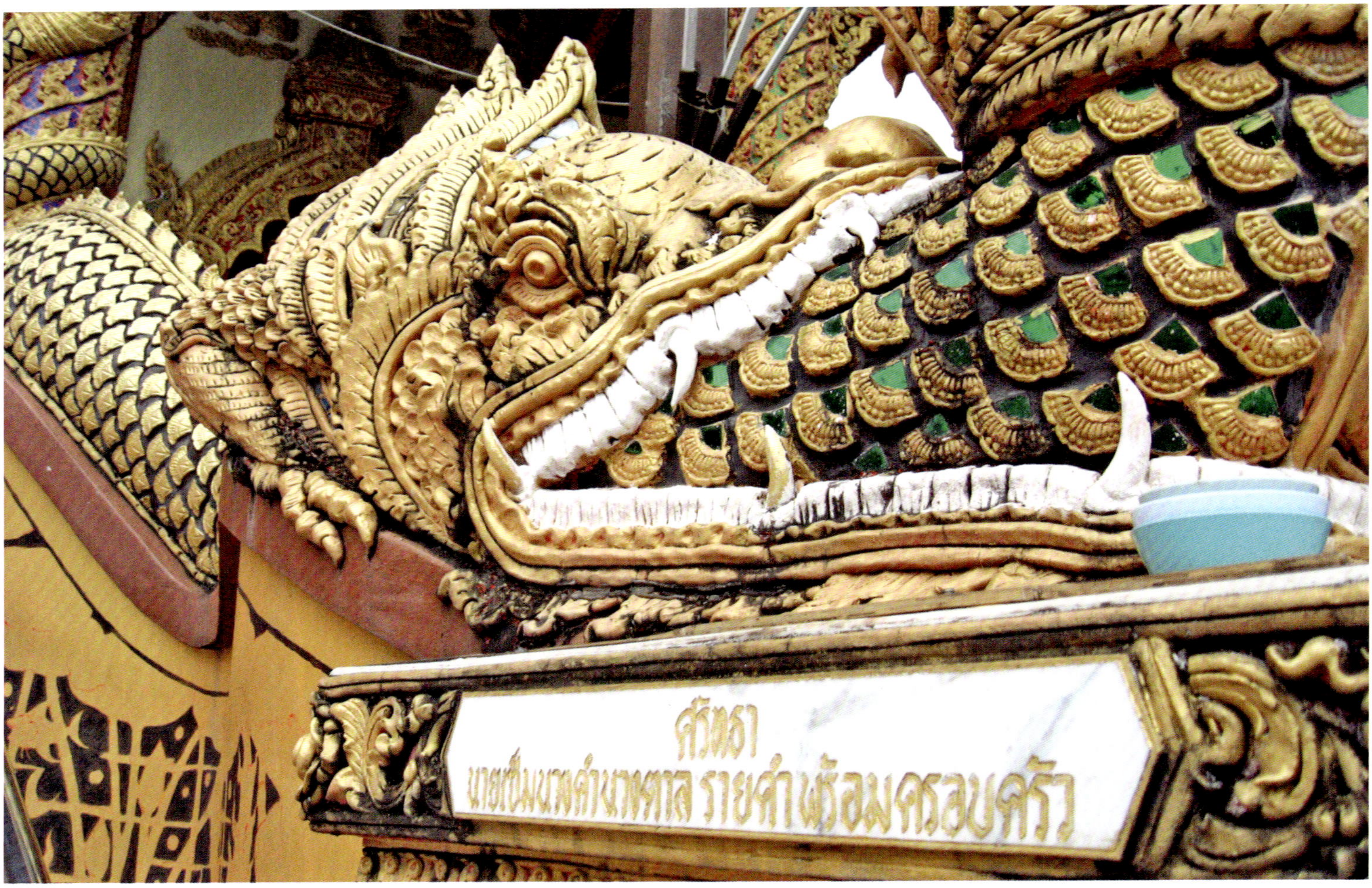

ศรัทธา
รายคำ พร้อมครอบครัว

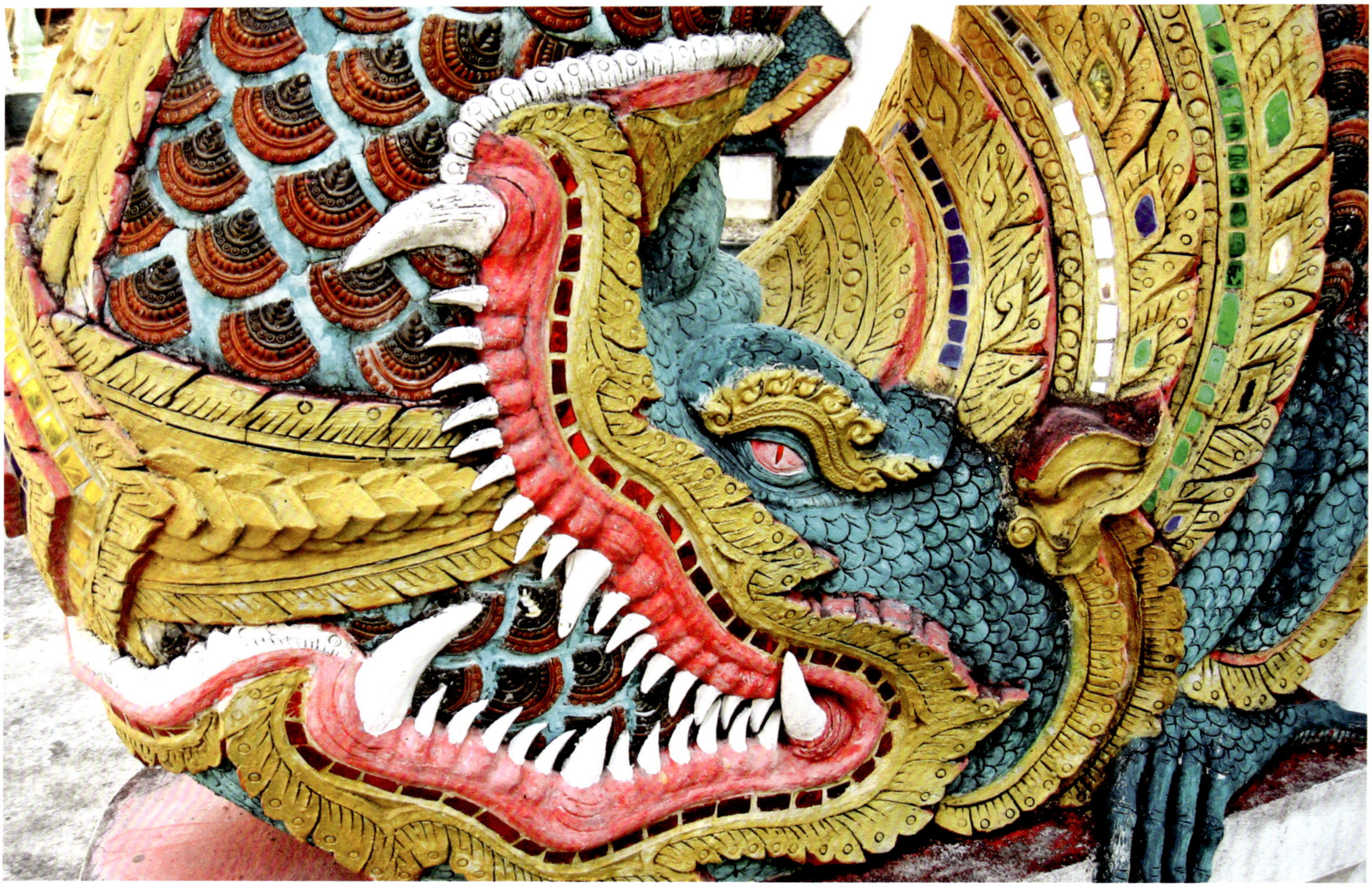

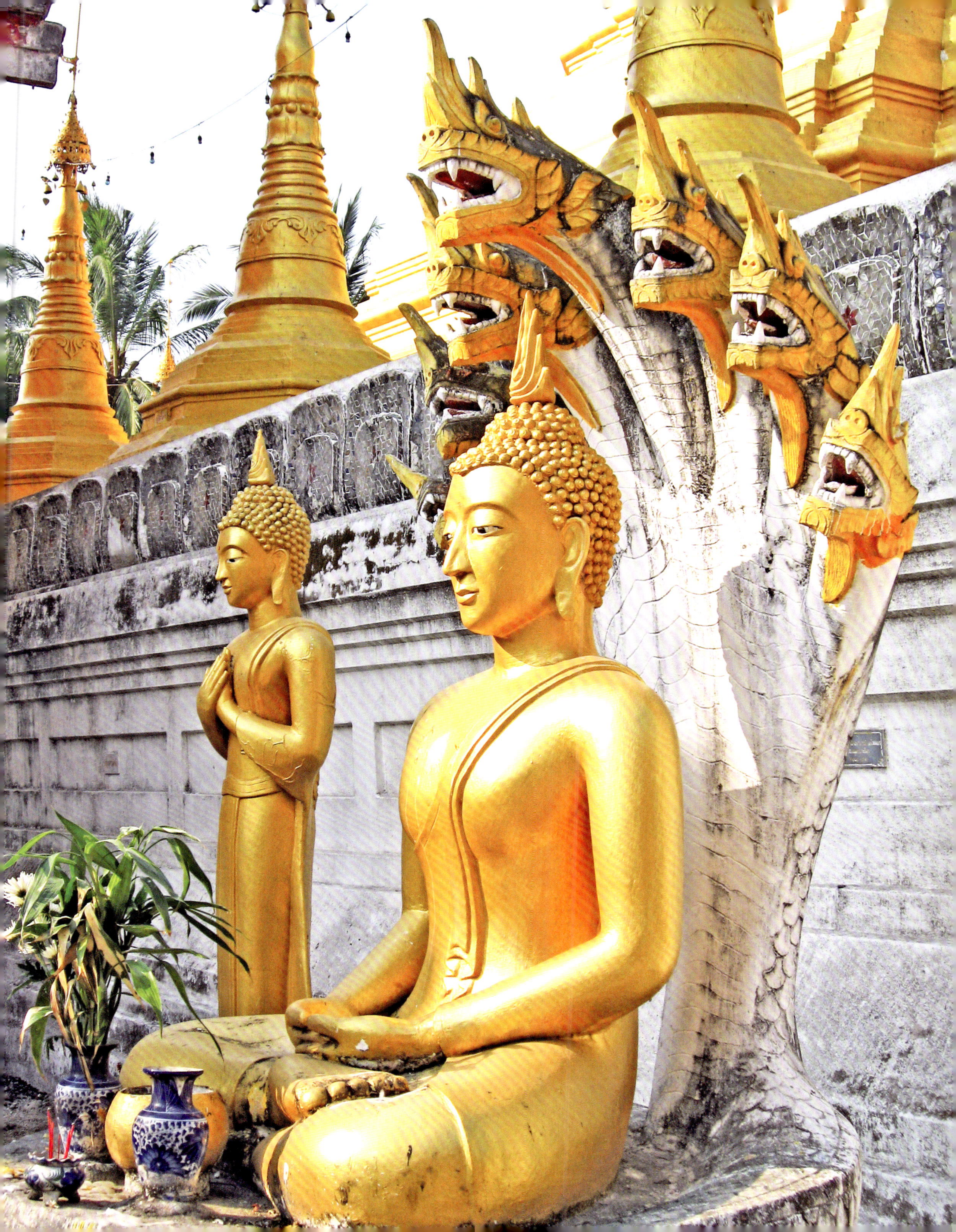

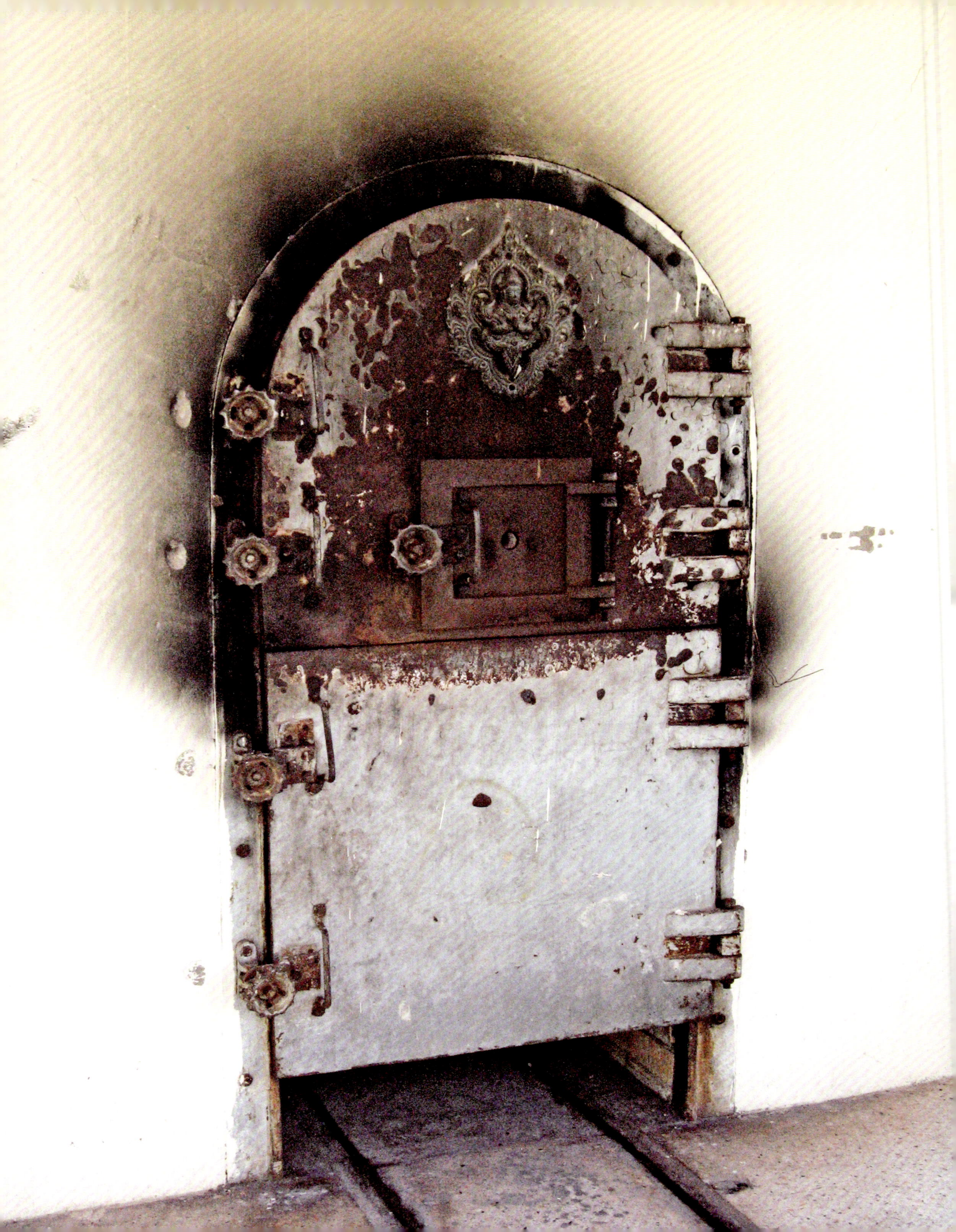

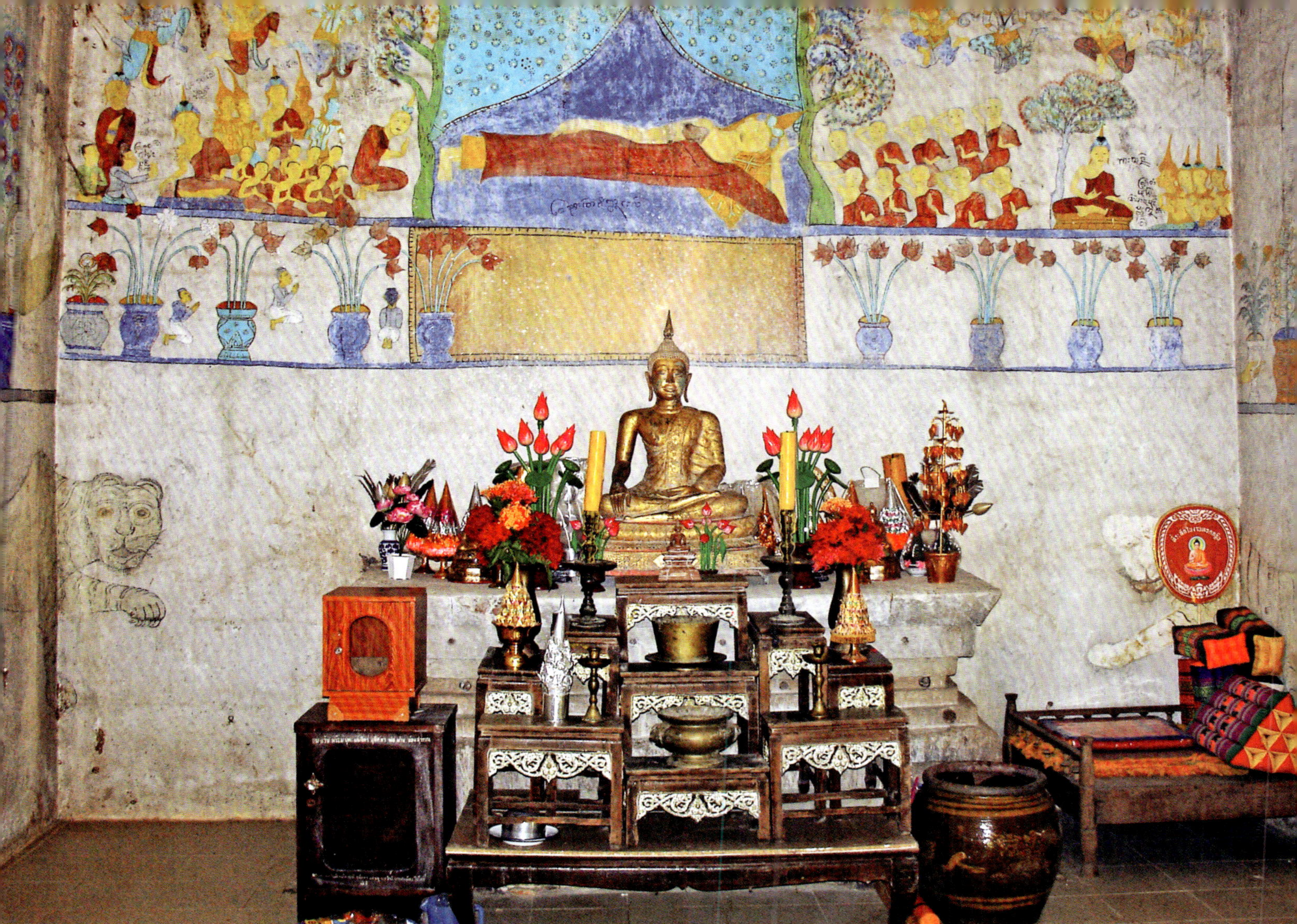

6. ISAAN TEMPLES

Isaan refers to a region in northeastern Thailand, heavily influenced by Laotian culture, famous for its spicy food, *mor lam* and *luk thung* music. The rural temple is the center of the community. In Isaan, the ordination hall is called the *sim* rather than the *ubosot*. It is often the compound's smallest building, previously used only by monks and novices for religious ceremonies. While murals exist on the inside, the primary art is on the outer walls, well-protected by a roof that extends well beyond the brick and mortar structure, accessible by the entire congregation. No longer used for ordination, many old *sims* have fallen into disrepair or have been torn down to make room for shiny new replacements (Brereton & Yenchuey, 2010, pp. 1 & 9). Creating these murals was a merit-making donation by the often uncredited artists or laypersons involved, serving as a daily reminder and illustration of important religious and moral ideals. Today, preservation of these murals is largely ignored as new and modern works of art are favored and funded. As these photos were taken in April 2008, the murals' condition today is unknown.

The storyline of the murals is often hard for a Westerner to decipher. Firstly, human and animal figures lack depth and are drawn much larger than their backgrounds. Palaces resemble puppet marquees or carriages, and a monkey may appear larger than a man or tree. Important female figures tend to address the viewer directly, while heroes are shown in profile. The torsos of each lay flat on the wall with the knees and feet pointing straight ahead, arms free to move in any direction, resembling a puppet (Brereton & Yenchuey, 2010, pp. 17, 19 & 45). Secondly, locale is more important than a linear chronological sequencing of the story. For example, if the location is a palace, all the scenes from the palace are painted together, regardless of differences in time. One mural panel at Wat Ban Lan depicts the prince's forest retreat: the prince is shown in three different windows enacting three different scenes. This is not confusing if the audience knows the story and the art need only remind them of the narrative. The art inspires the viewer to consider the images and apply their importance to everyday life, not provide a realistic or sequential portrayal (Roveda & Yem, 2009, pp. 45-47).

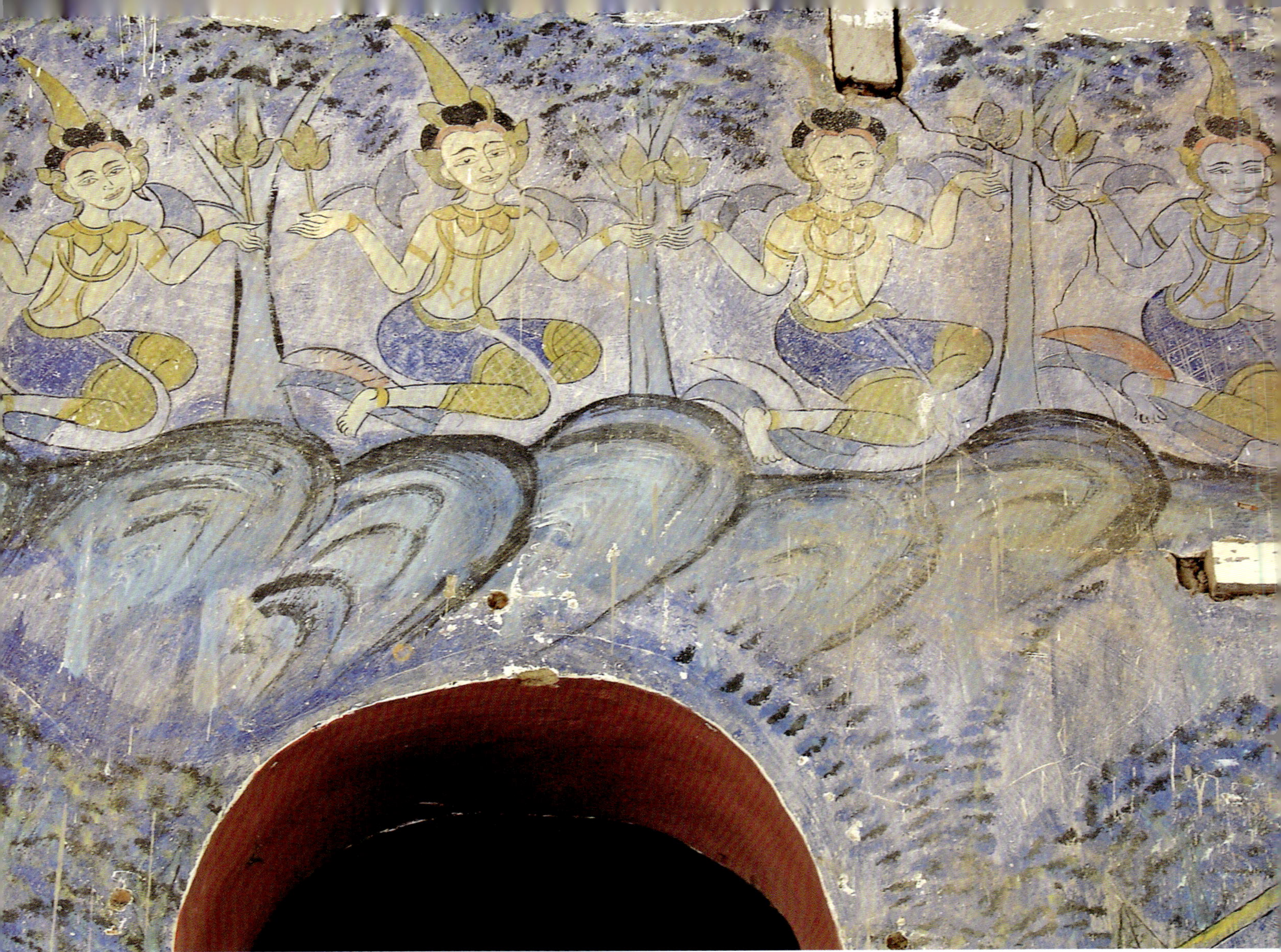

WAT BAN LAN

This mural depicts the *Vessantara Jataka*, the 13-chapter story of Prince Wetsandon and his charity. Historically, the 1000-stanza tale was read once a year during a three-day festival in Isaan. The generous prince, named Pha Wet, has a white elephant believed to bring rain. When a neighboring kingdom requests the elephant, he selflessly gives it to them. The angry townspeople force the king to exile the prince, his wife Matsi and their two children (Pg. 175). They settle in a remote valley living as ascetics, dressed in tiger skins. Elsewhere, Chuchok, an ugly gray-skinned Brahmin beggar, knowing of Pha Wet's generosity, decides to ask for Pha Wet's children as servants. When Chuchok makes the request, Pha Wet realizes his previous charity never involved something dear to his heart, so he agrees. Pior to Chuchok's arrival, Matsi dreams of her heart being ripped out by an intruder. Pha Wet understands this is an omen and sends her off to gather fruit so she will not be present when Chuchok takes the children. Three deities become beasts and prevent her return (Pg. 174).

Sakka, king of the gods, comes to earth disguised as a Brahmin and asks Pha Wet for Matsi as a companion (Pg. 177-8). After receiving Matsi, Sakka reveals his true nature, and informs the prince that due to his merit he will be reborn as the Buddha. Meanwhile, Chuchok beats the children, ties them up and goes to sleep in a tree hammock. Each night two *devas* feed and comfort the children disguised as their parents (Pg. 175). The king sees Chuchok treating his grandchildren as slaves and pays a ransom for their return. Chuchok throws a feast and eats himself to death. The king, queen, and a royal procession collect the prince and Matsi, riding the white elephant, and return to the kingdom where all ends well.

This mural is painted on a blue background, rather than the standard whitewashed wall. Many of the important figures' faces have been scratched off, as have the large genitals on some of the male Brahmin figures. Pha Wet's binding of Matsi's hands is not normally depicted (Pg. 177). The royal procession fills two panels, and includes the Brahmins with the white elephant and three bent old Isaan women, moving from left to right in the top register and right to left below (Pg. 166-171).

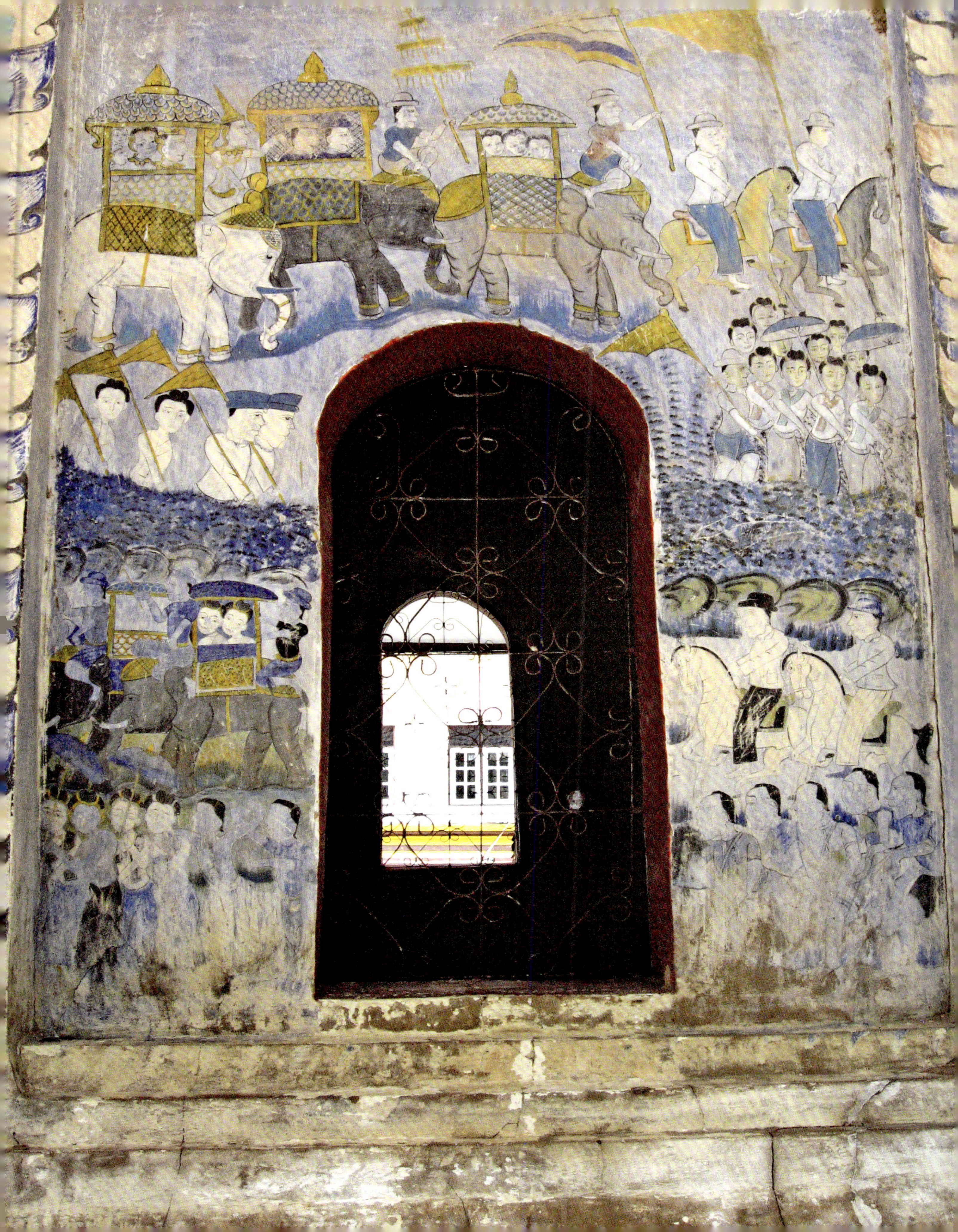

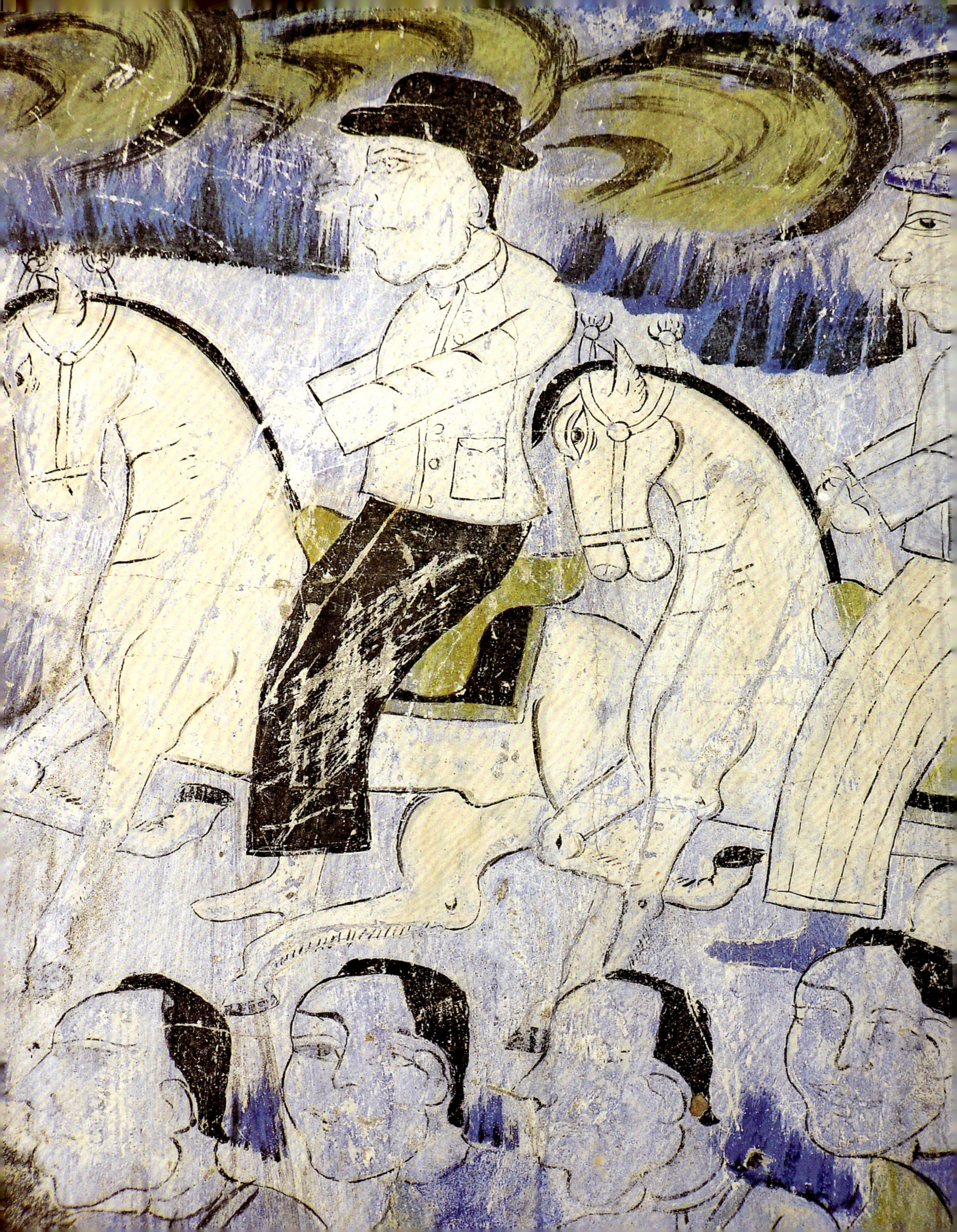

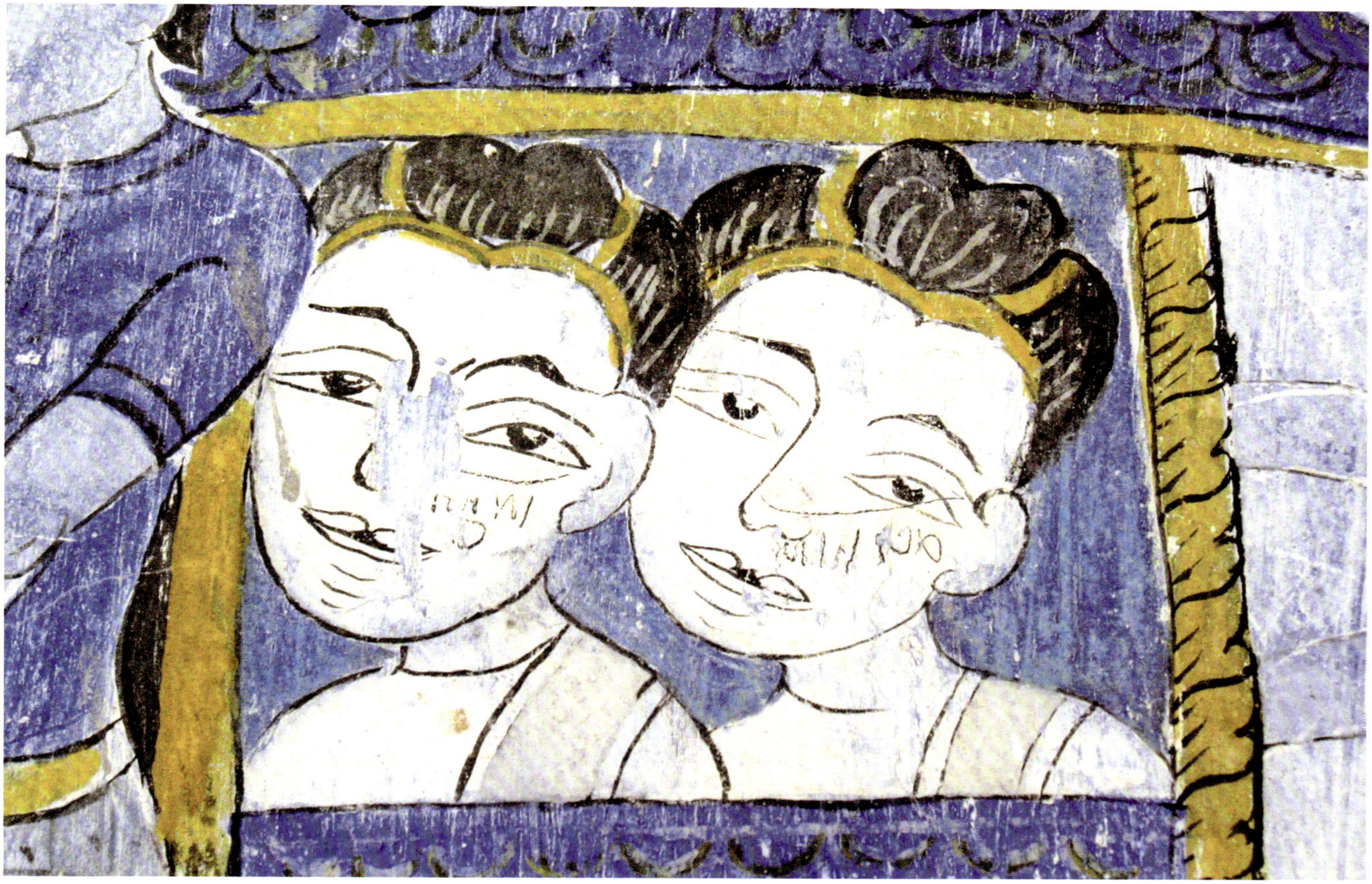

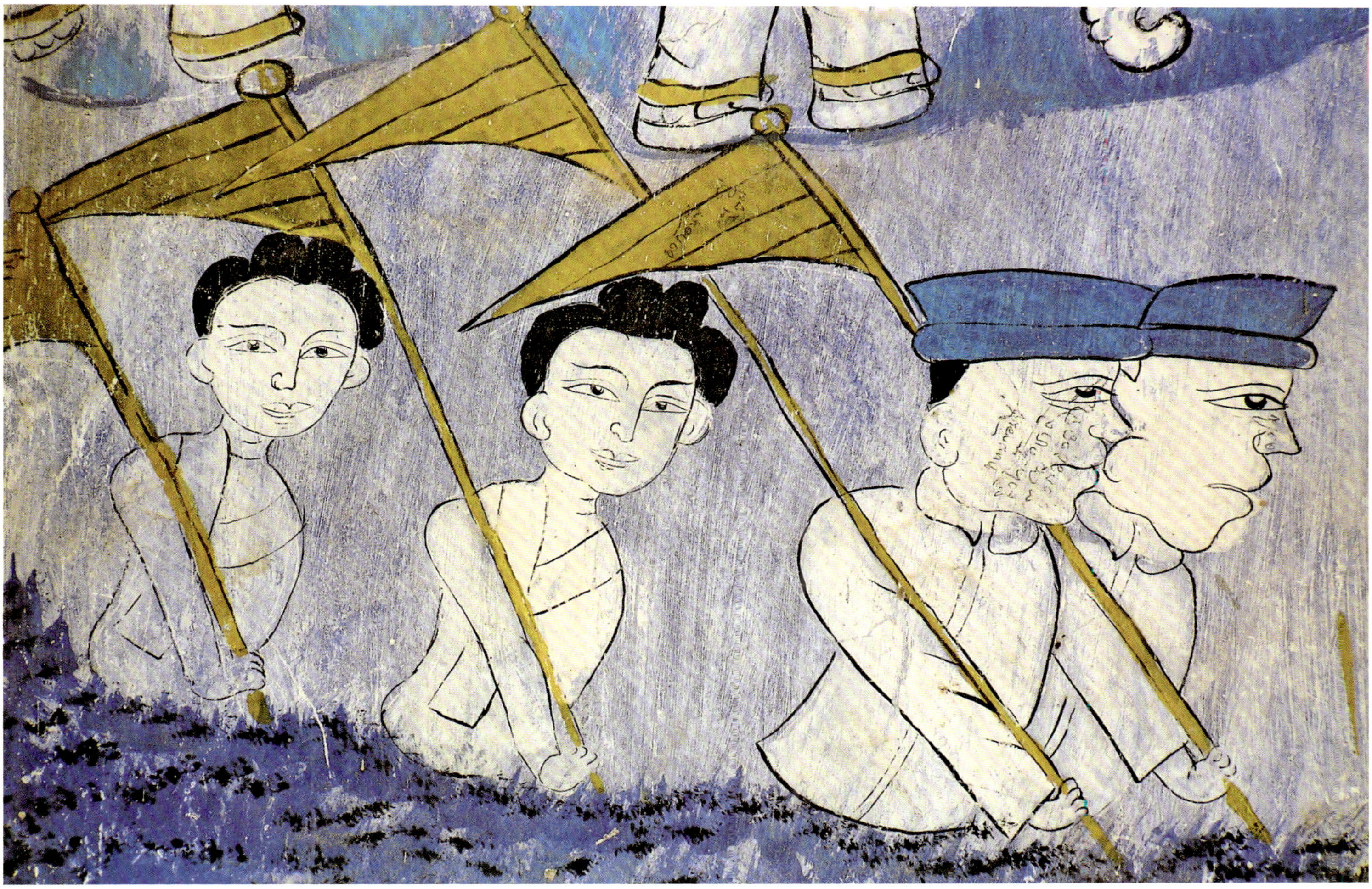

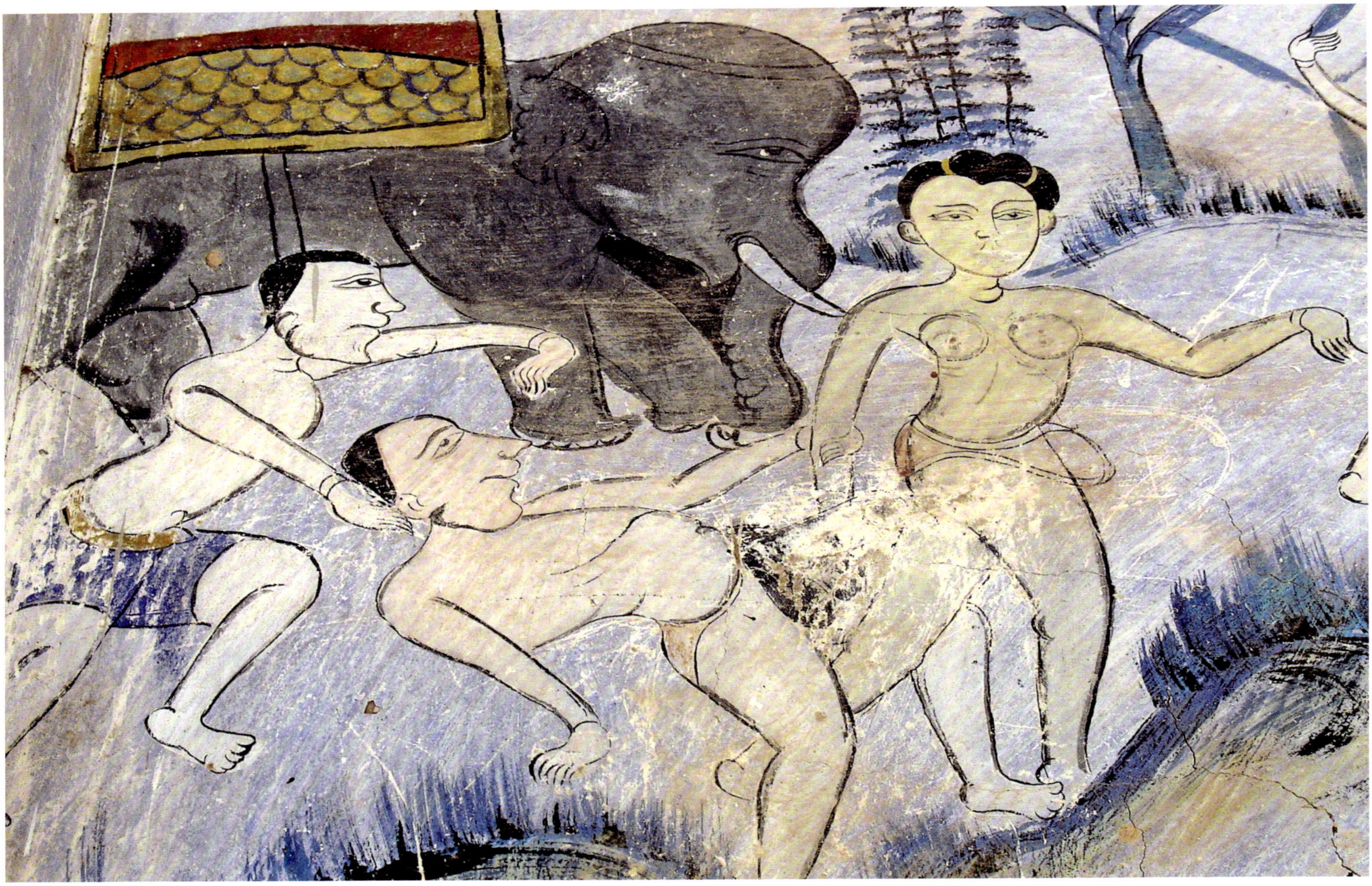

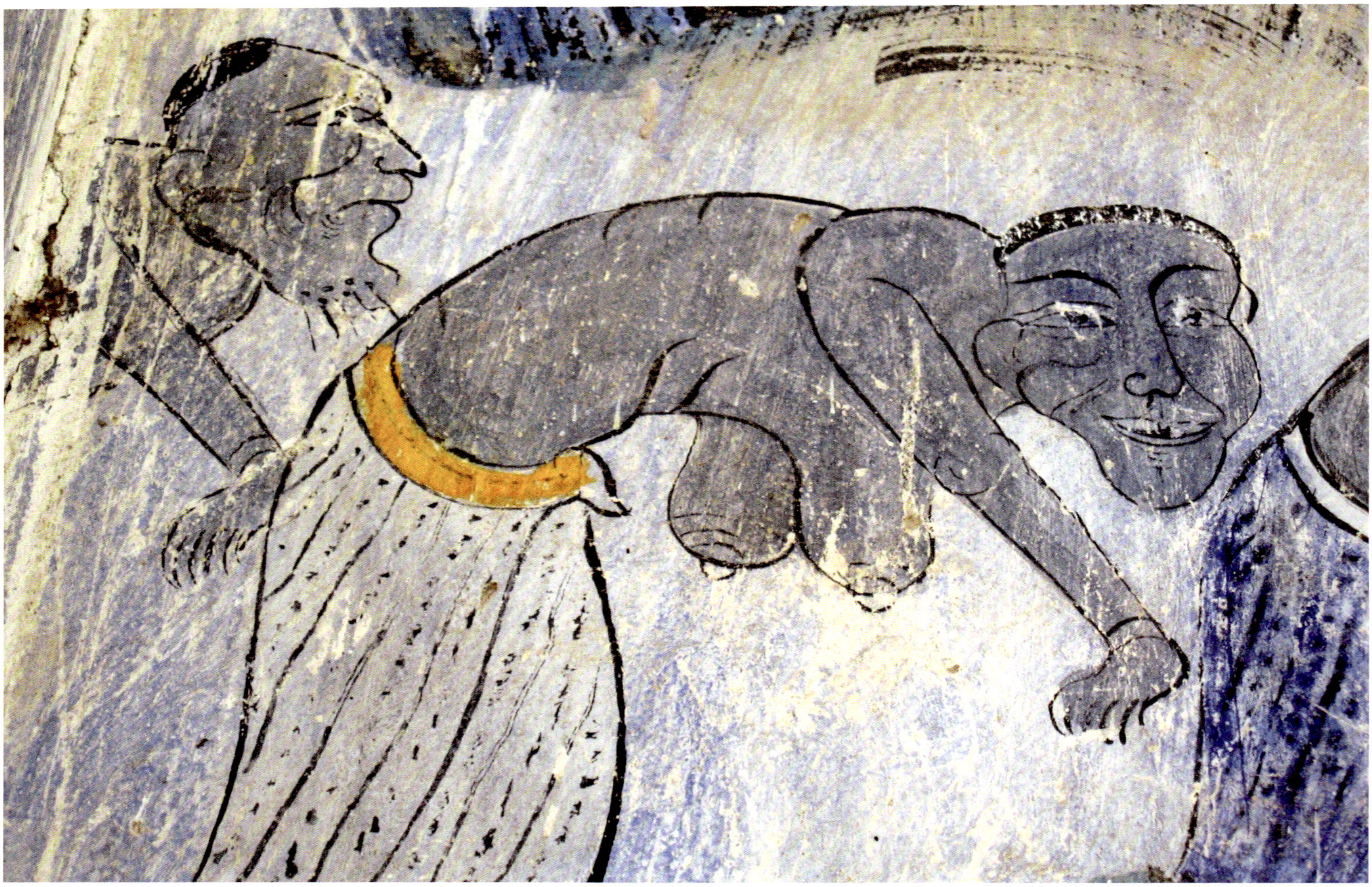

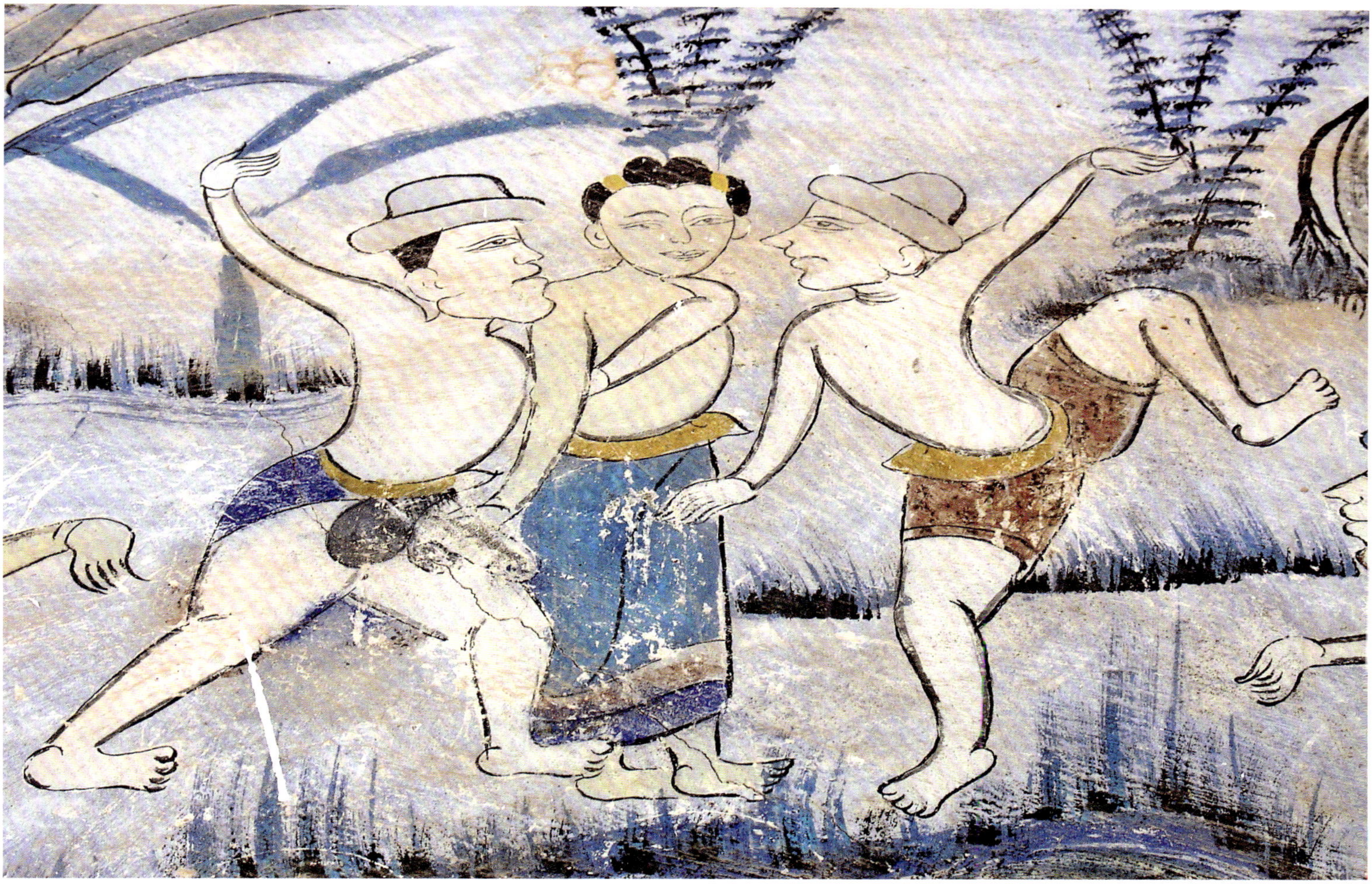

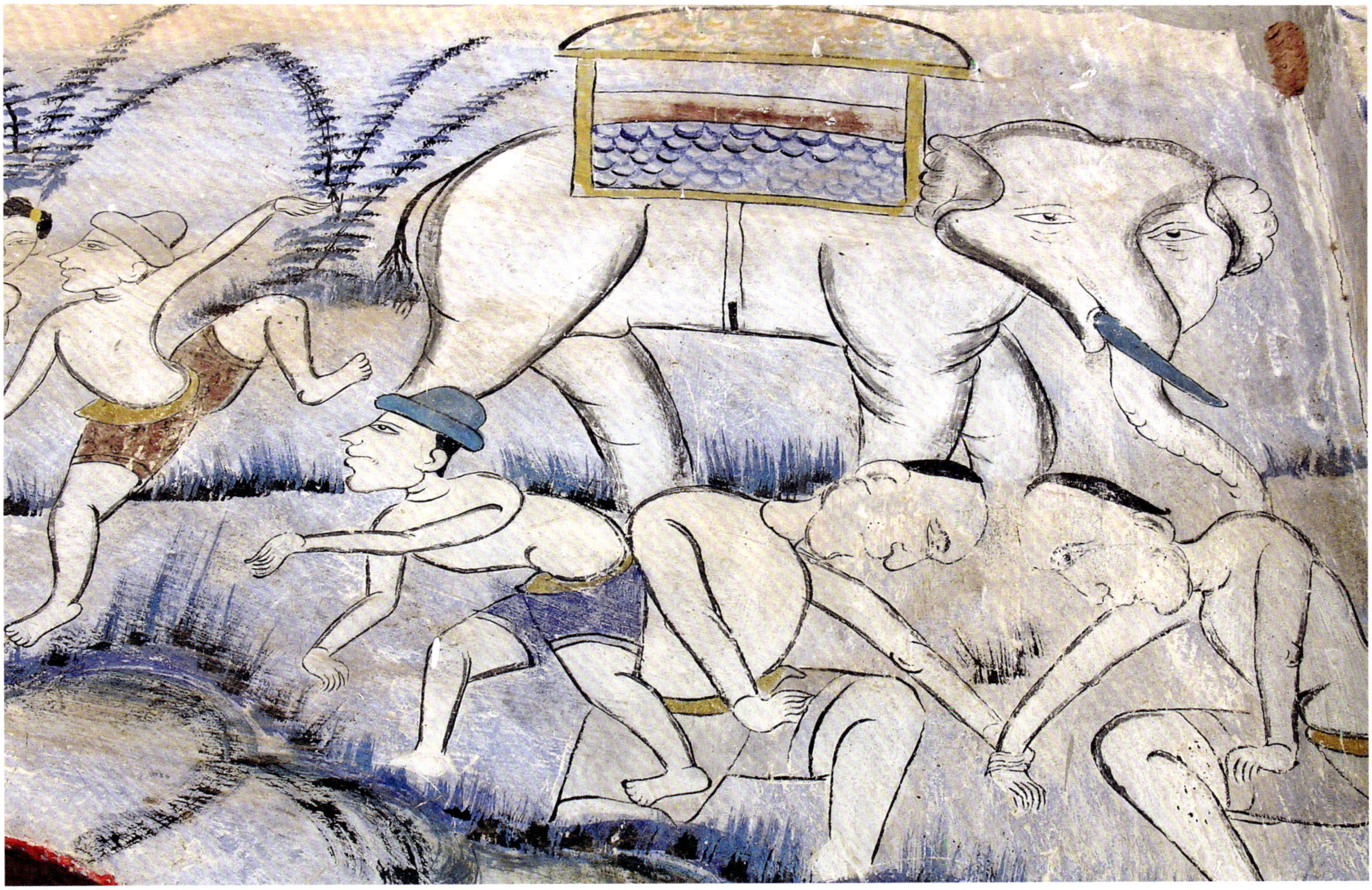

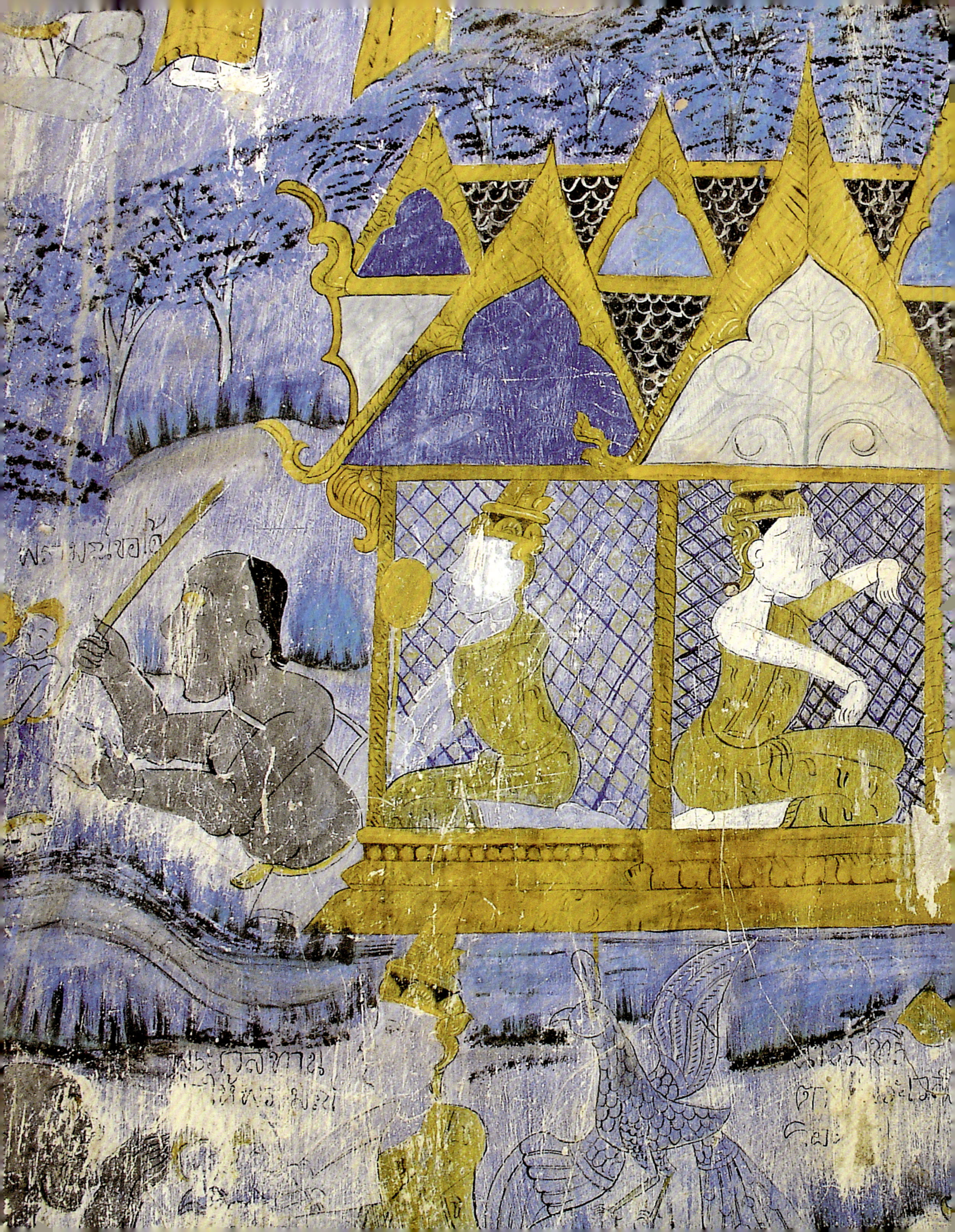

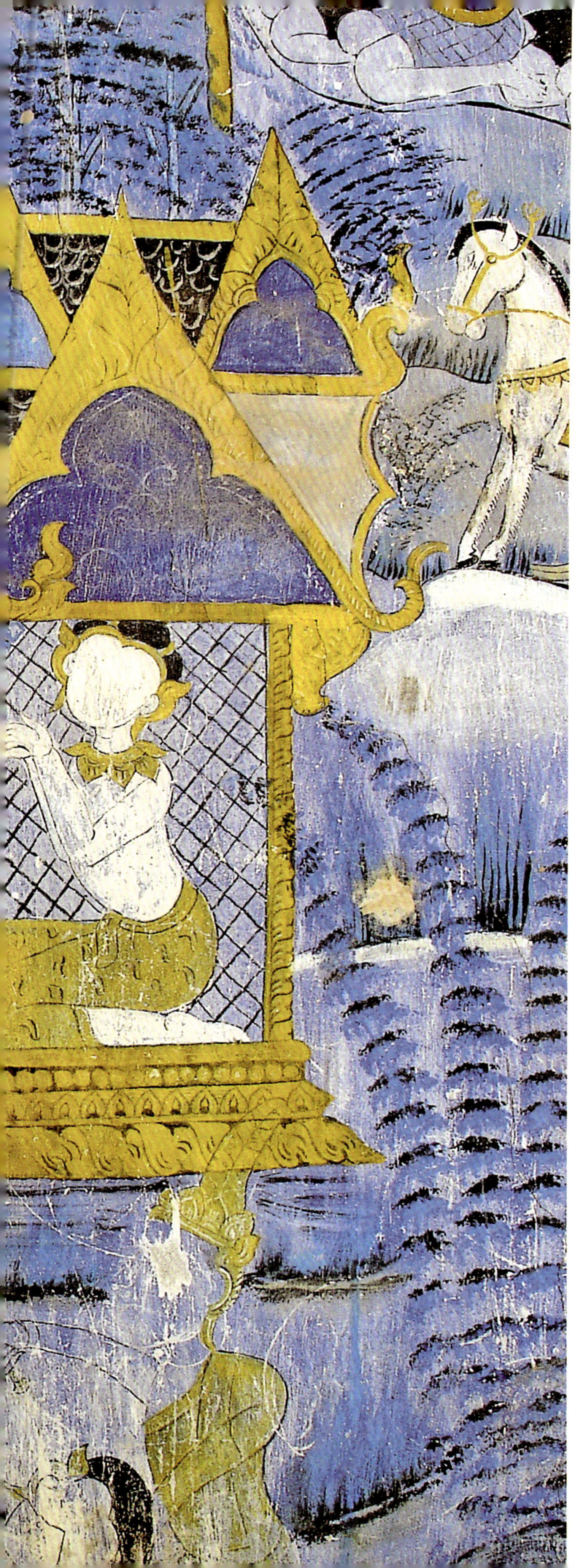

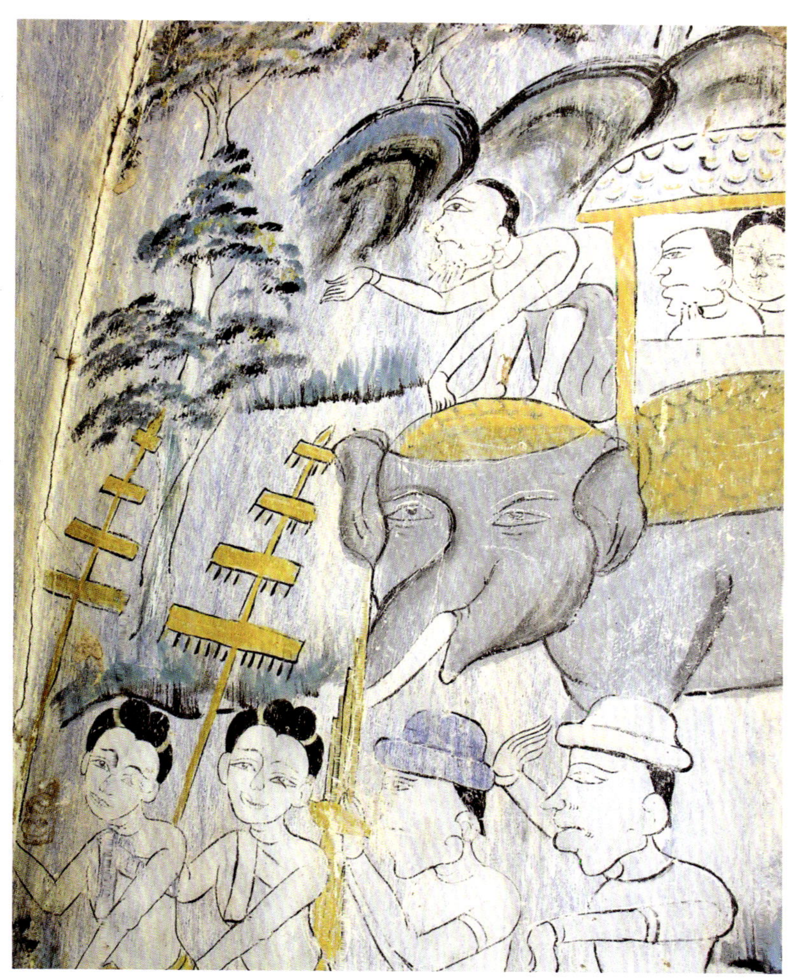

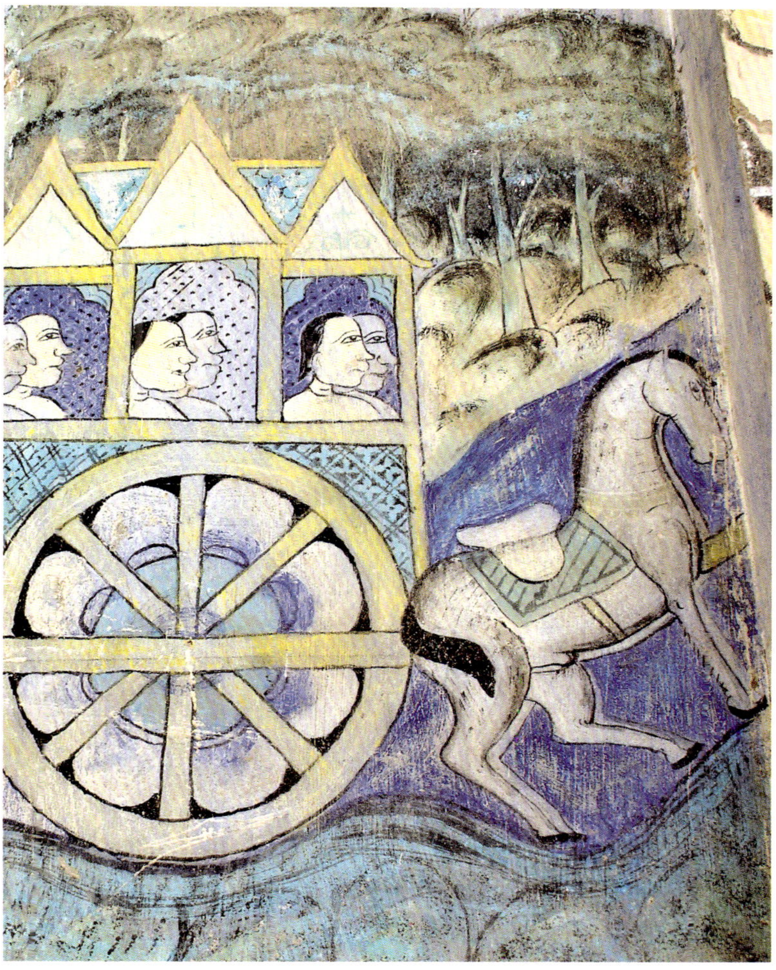

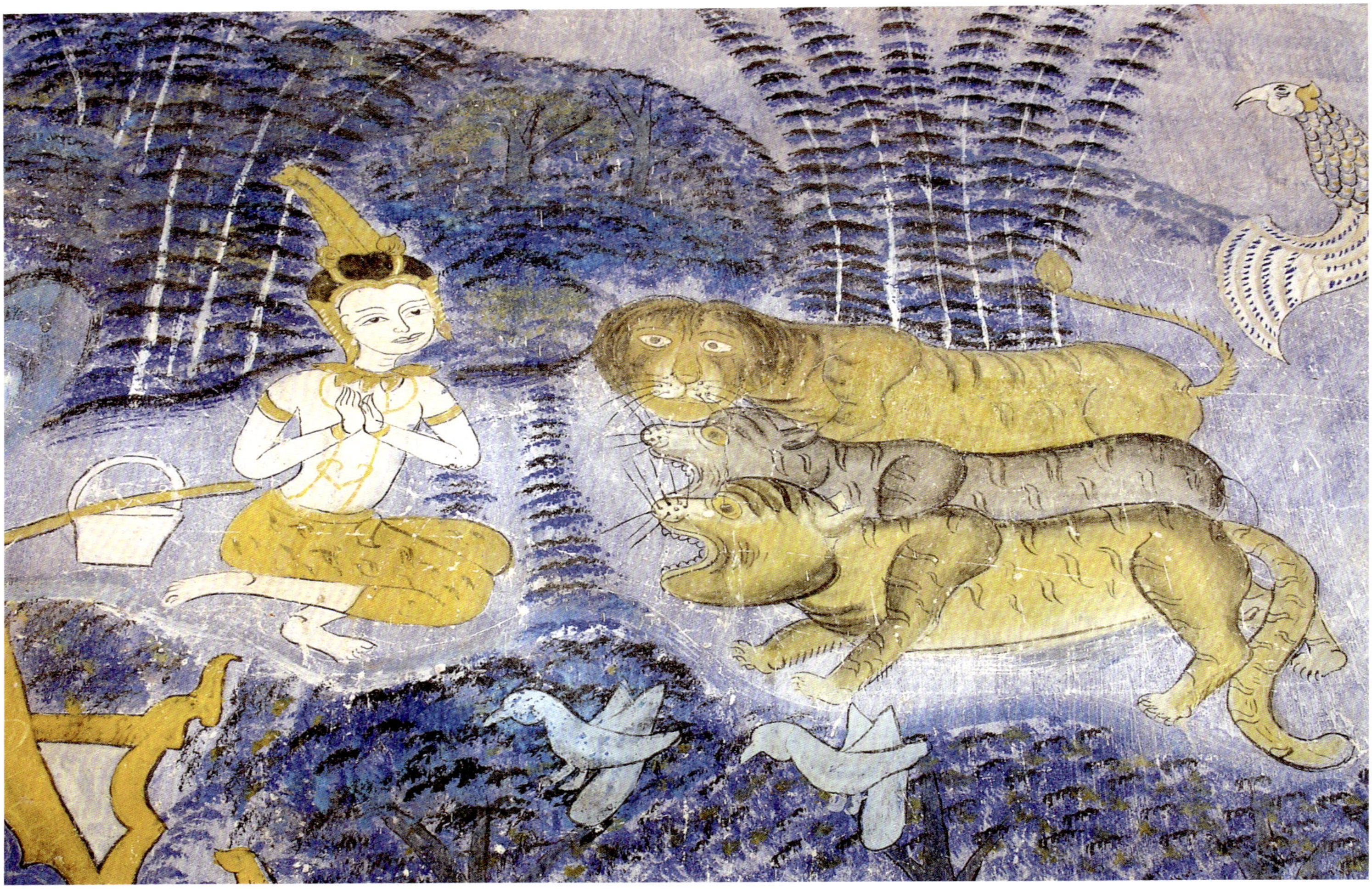

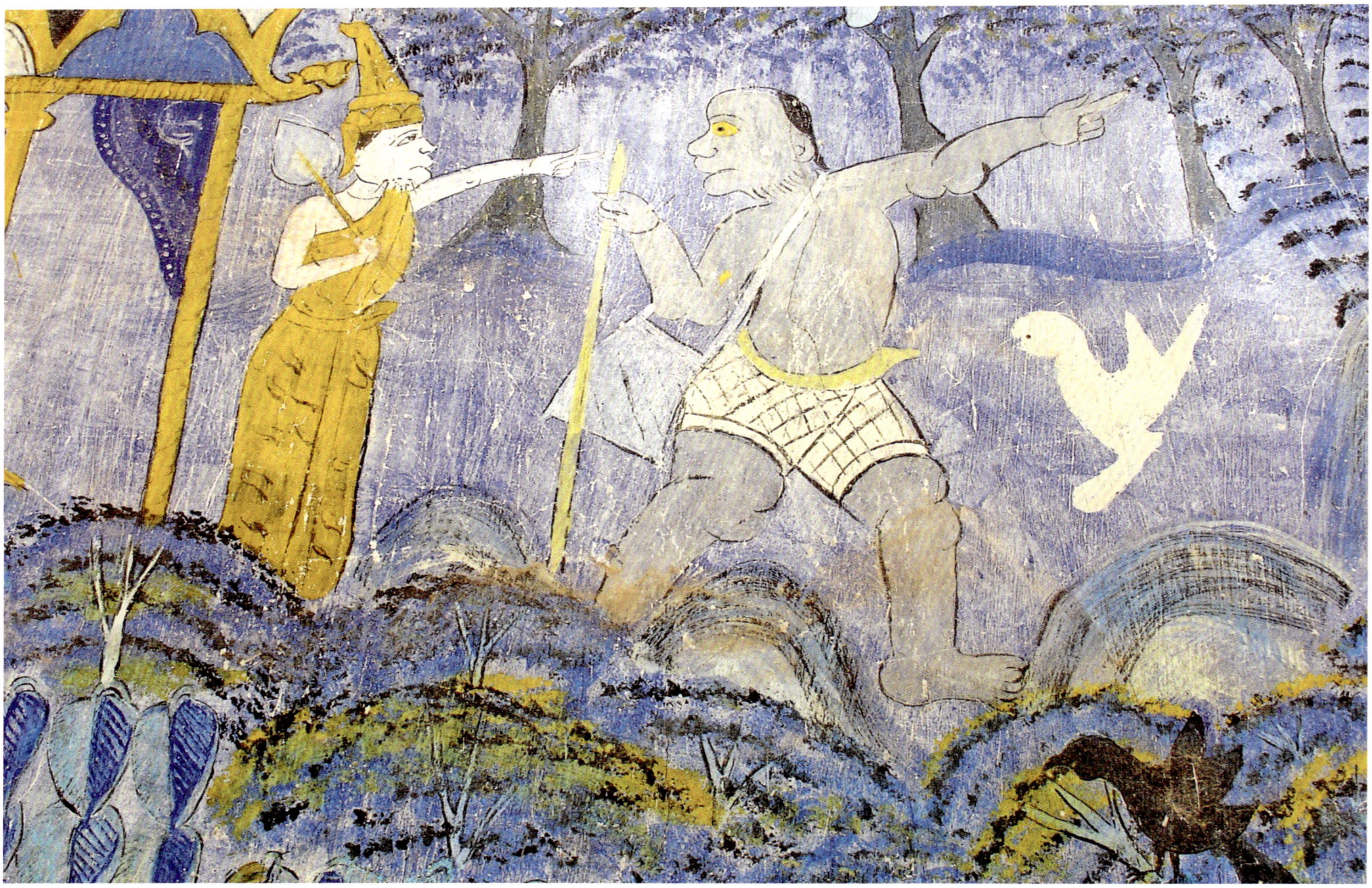

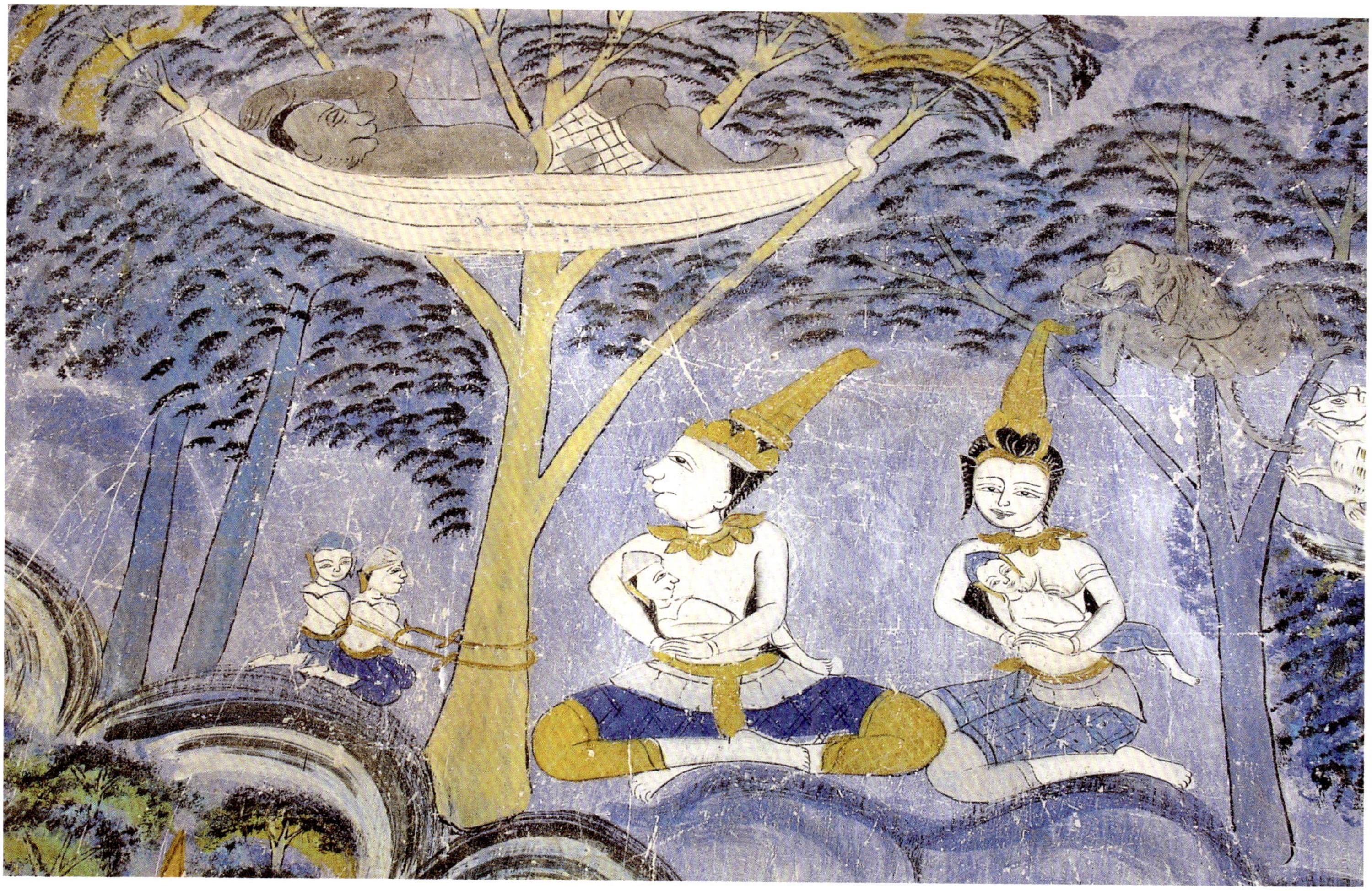

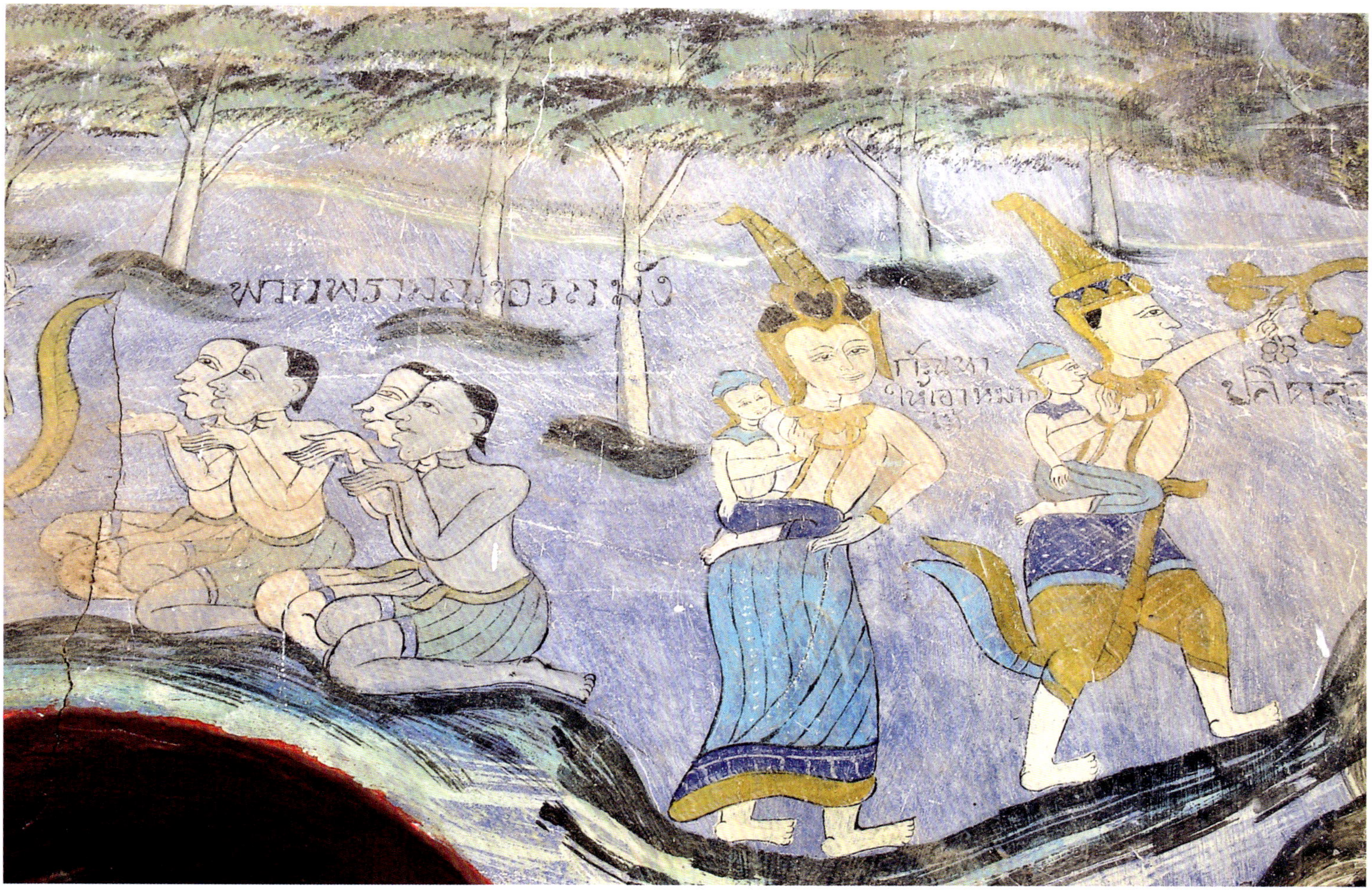

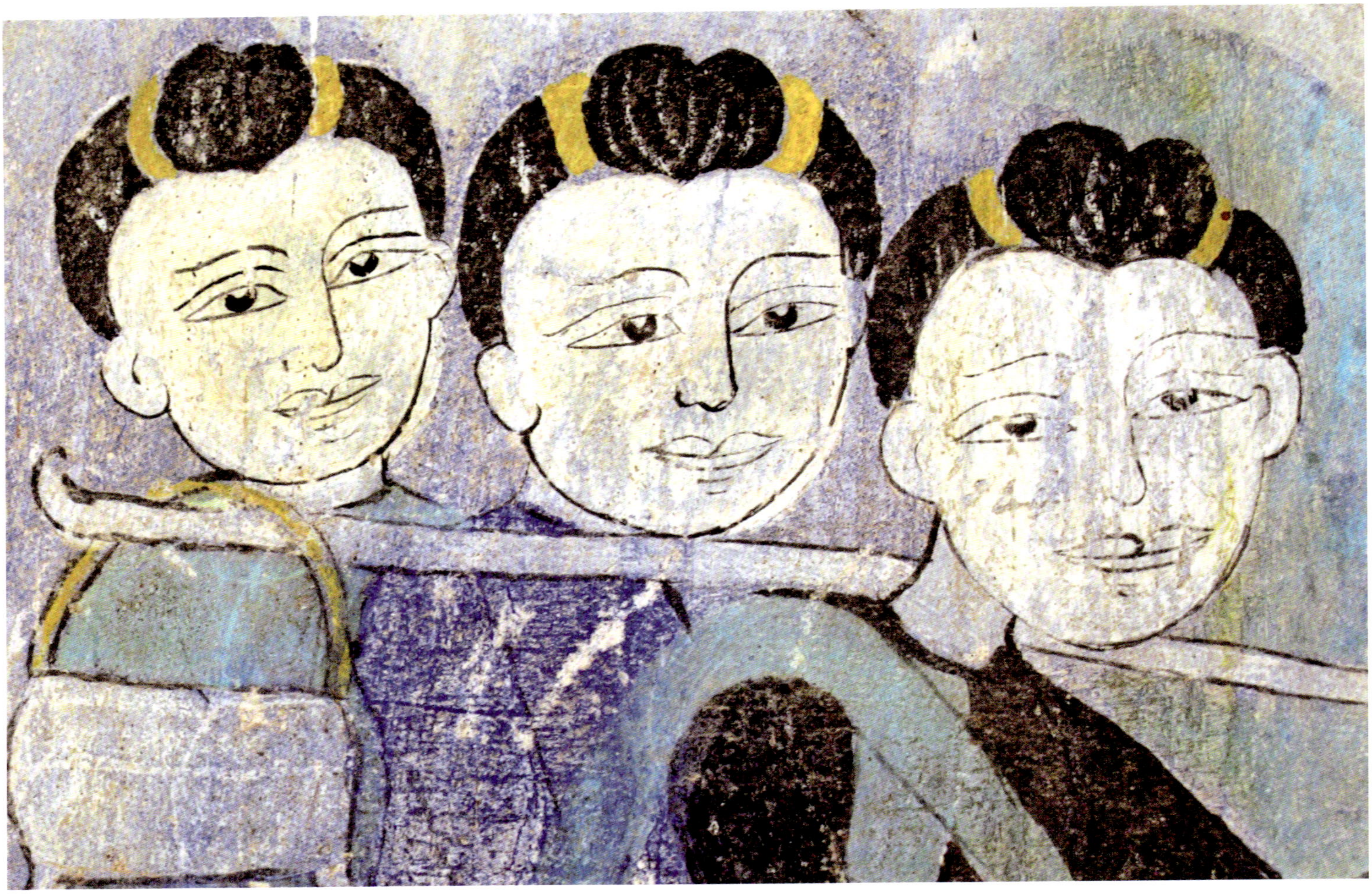

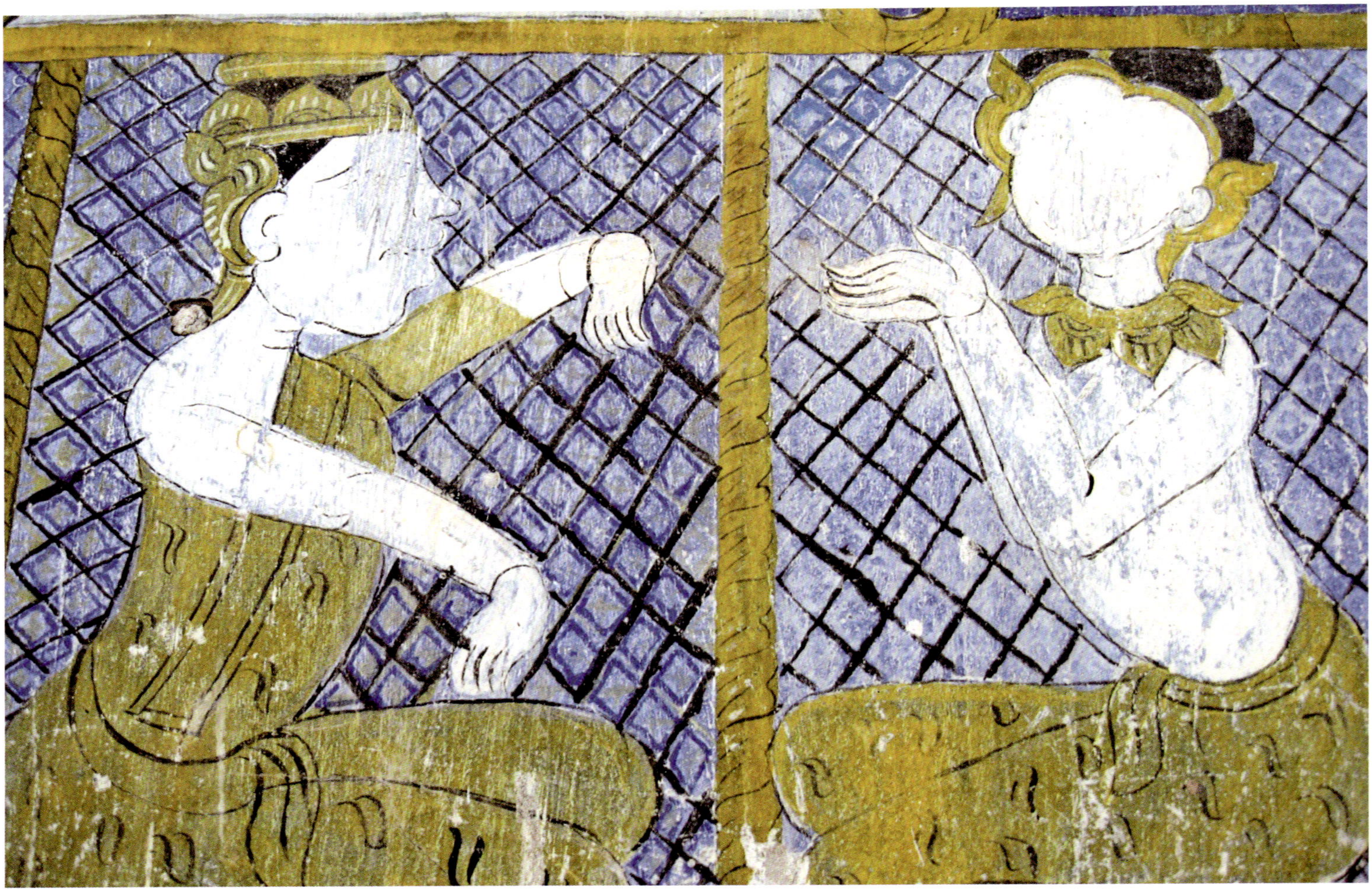

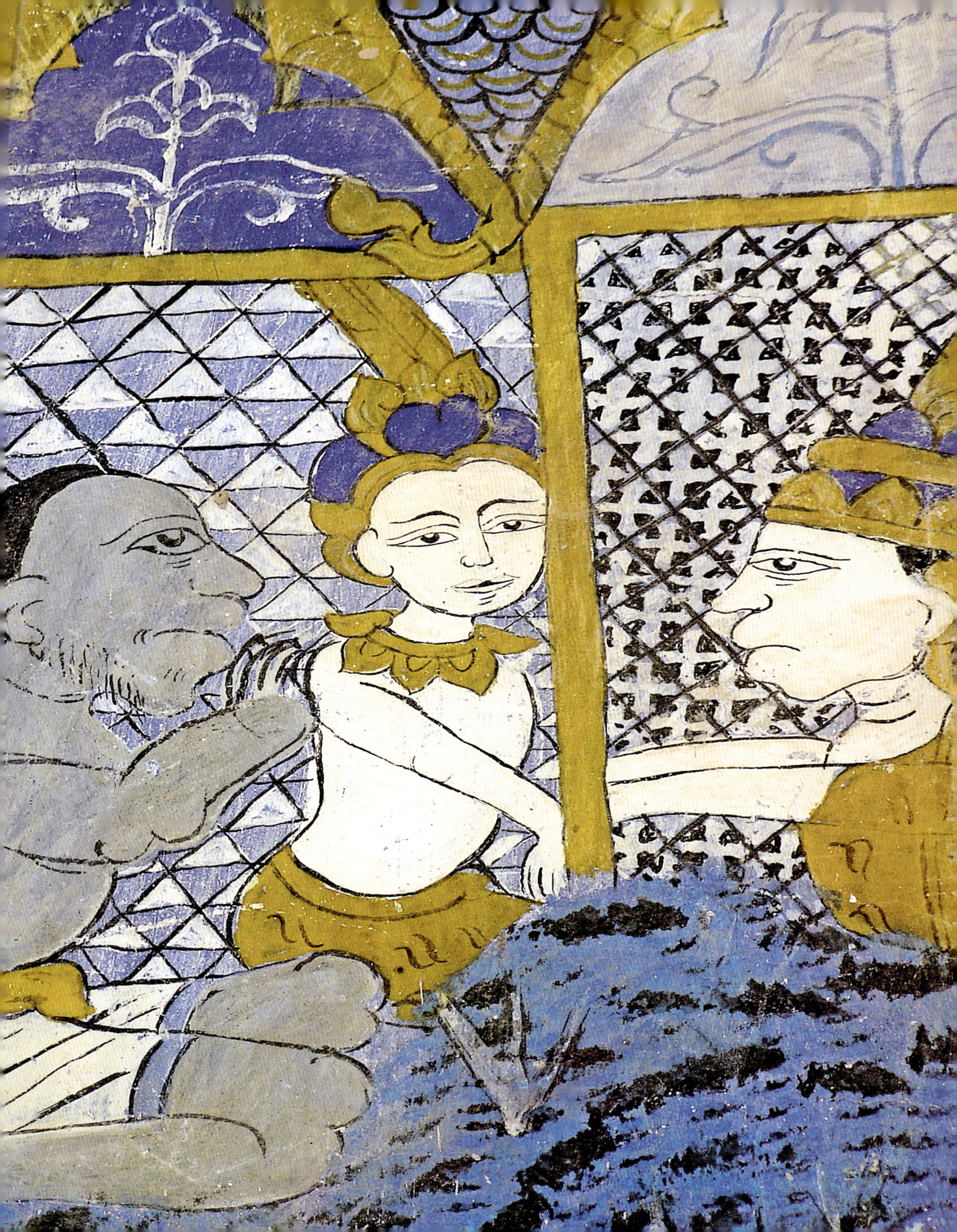

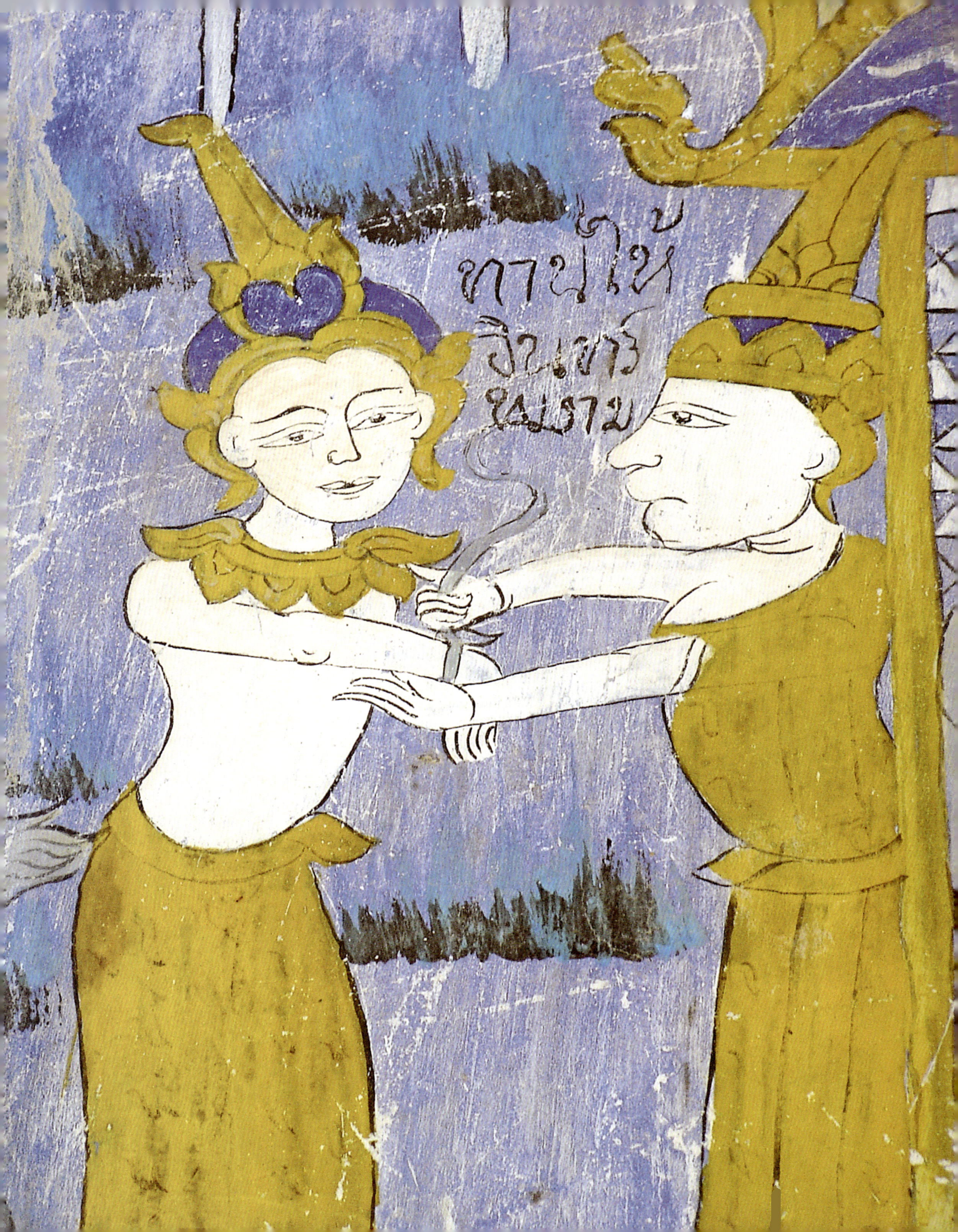
ทานให้

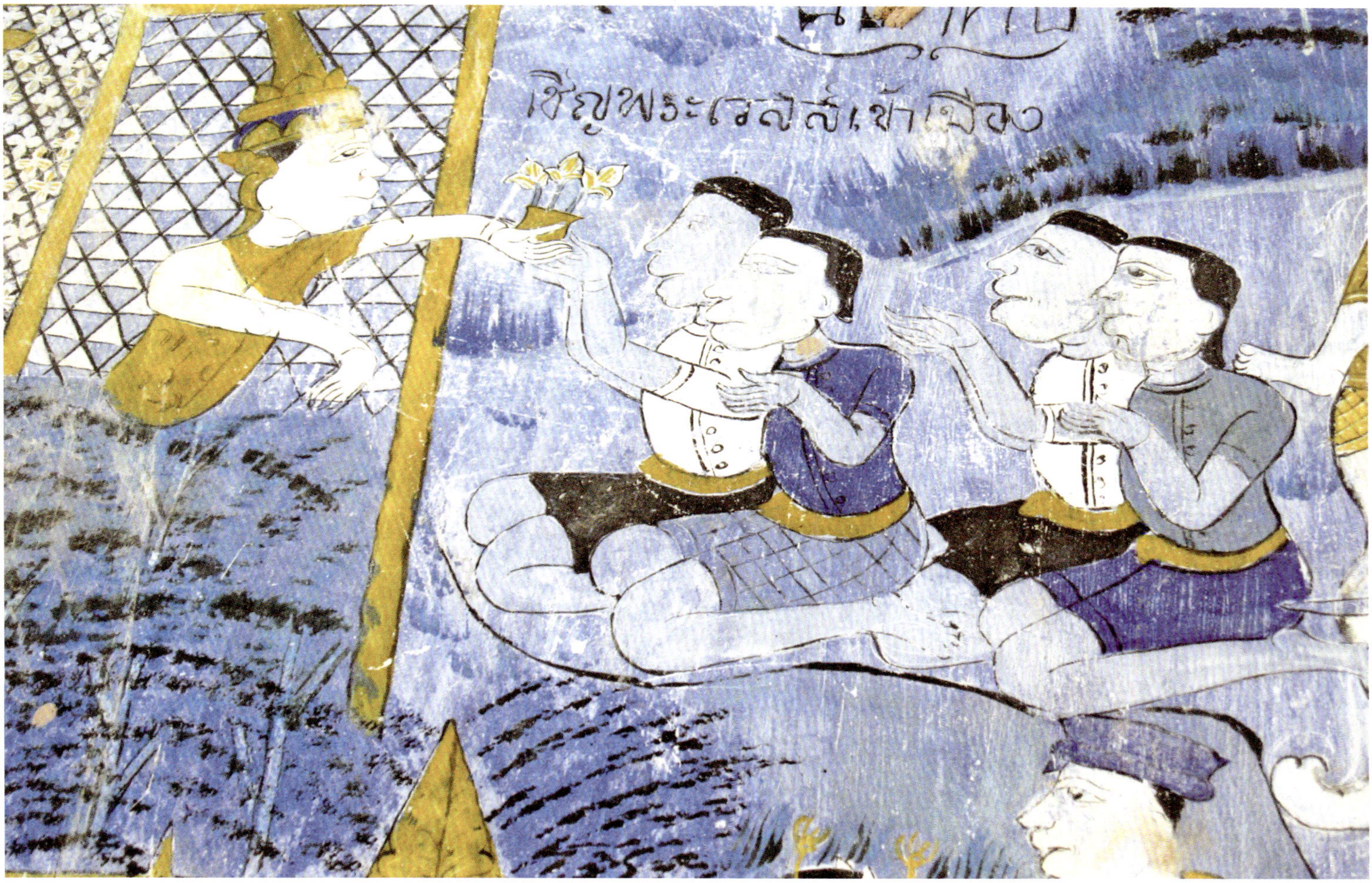

เชิญพระเวสส์เข้าเมือง

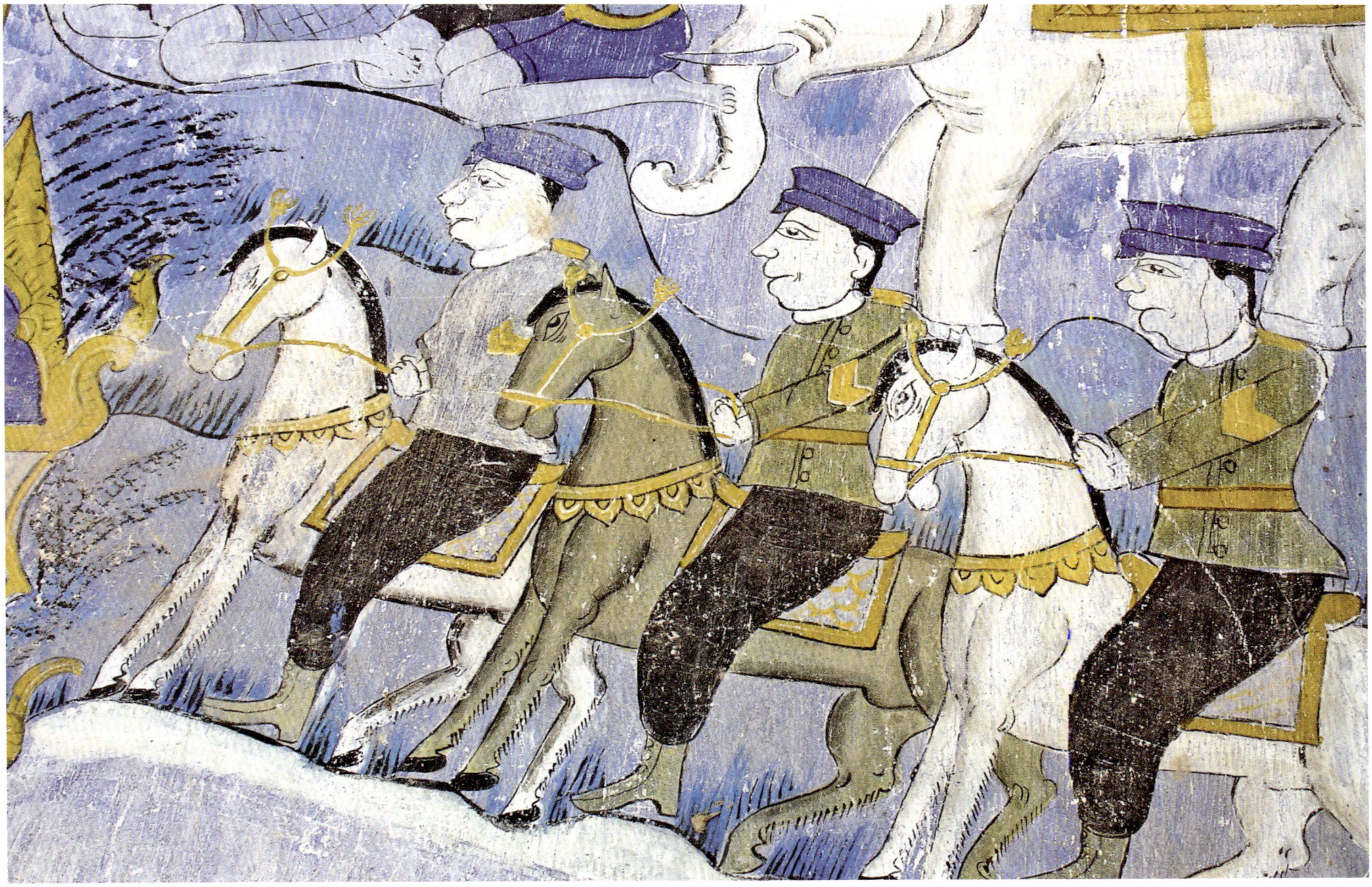

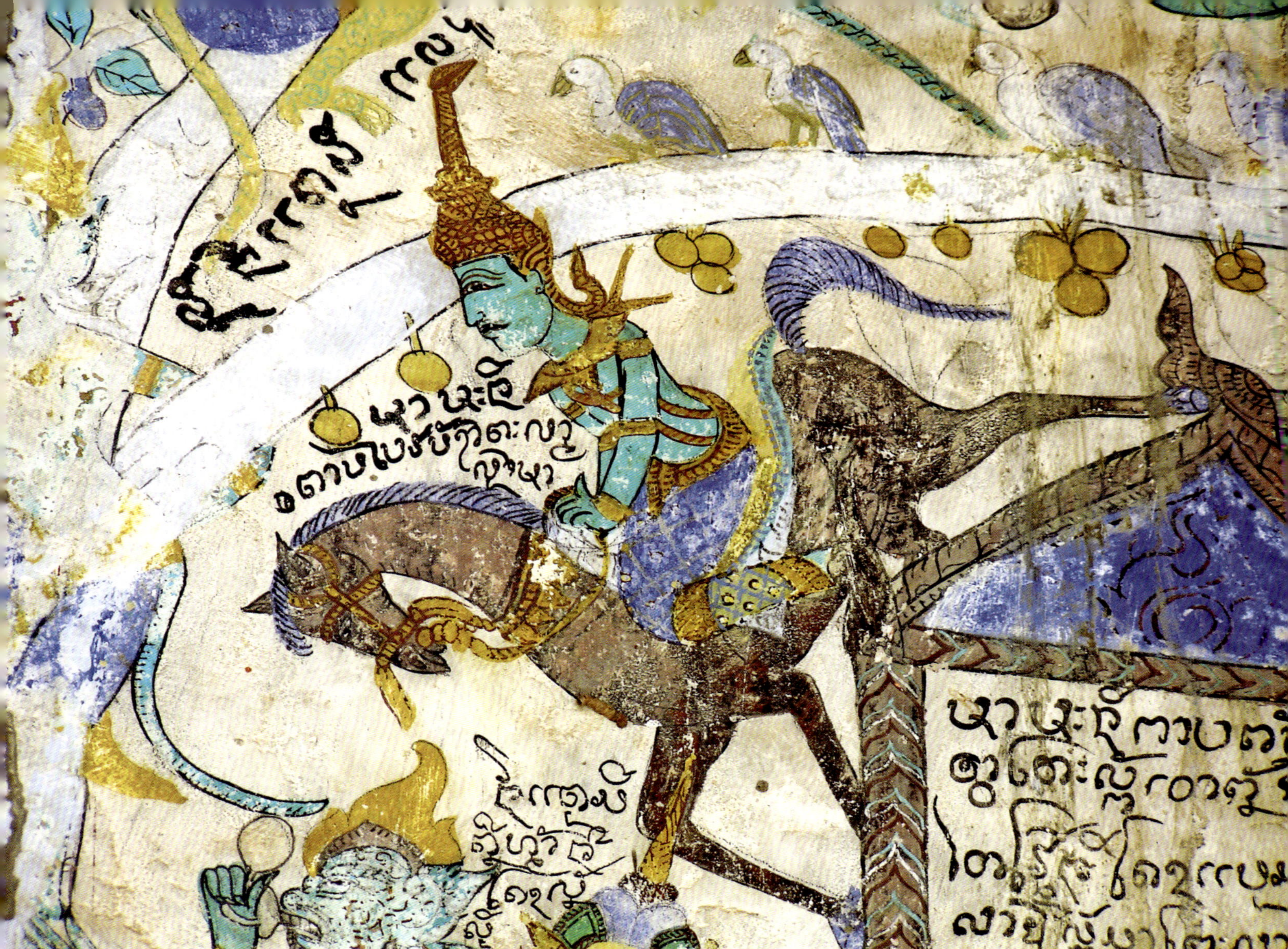

WAT SA BUA KAEO

The entrance to the *sim* is guarded by two seated crowned *singhs* with small human figures on steps in front. Above the eastern entrance sits the *asura* Rahu, with the sun in his mouth, causing an eclipse (Pg. 184). The functional door is flanked with painted panels of flower and vine mosaics, hiding monkeys, bats and birds. The outer walls are divided into figure-packed panels, each separated by a patterned pillar. The action details rural Isaan life: people cook, farmers and water buffalos till the fields, men in boats fish with nets, people dance and make music using traditional instruments. Many are incorporated directly into the *Ramakien* narrative: village folk wearing celebratory garments and carrying parasols move in processions with *devas* and demons while demi-gods travel in *naga* carriages. Nature is active in the murals, with scenes staged in the branches of trees. Water cascades over the top of a wooden window frame, delineating separate scenarios on all three sides. Animals abound in each frame: monkeys, stags and elephants stampede, tigers attack boars, winged elephants fly overhead of Phra Ram and his brother Phra Lak, a *naga* battles a *khochasi*, part-lion part-elephant. Bats and birds flit just above a sword battle between the giants, demi-gods and decapitated men. Strange huge birds stare from trees, *garudas* attack, and soldiers march. The whitewashed walls have yellowed with age, and many of the images closest to the ground appear washed or rubbed out, including a Buddhist hell scene.

The interior of the *sim* has a stone altar and a seated Buddha icon against the western wall, with images from the Buddha's life behind him (Pg. 165). Scenes depicted include the preaching of his sermons to men and *devas*, and the *Mahaparinirvana*, depicting his death among the mourning monks. Three *nats* hop among lotus flowers in vases. On the eastern wall above the door is the Buddha's Victory Over Mara. The six-armed gray-skinned Mara, protected by a demon's parasol, sits atop a trident-wielding elephant (Pg. 190), avoiding the floodwaters created by mother earth Mae Thorani wringing her hair, while his army drowns or is attacked by crocodiles (Pg.191). Buddha wears ochre-colored robes rather than traditional saffron orange, and is pictured among elephants, deer and monkeys, while Prince Siddhartha Gautama meditates under the Bodhi tree (Pg. 186-7).

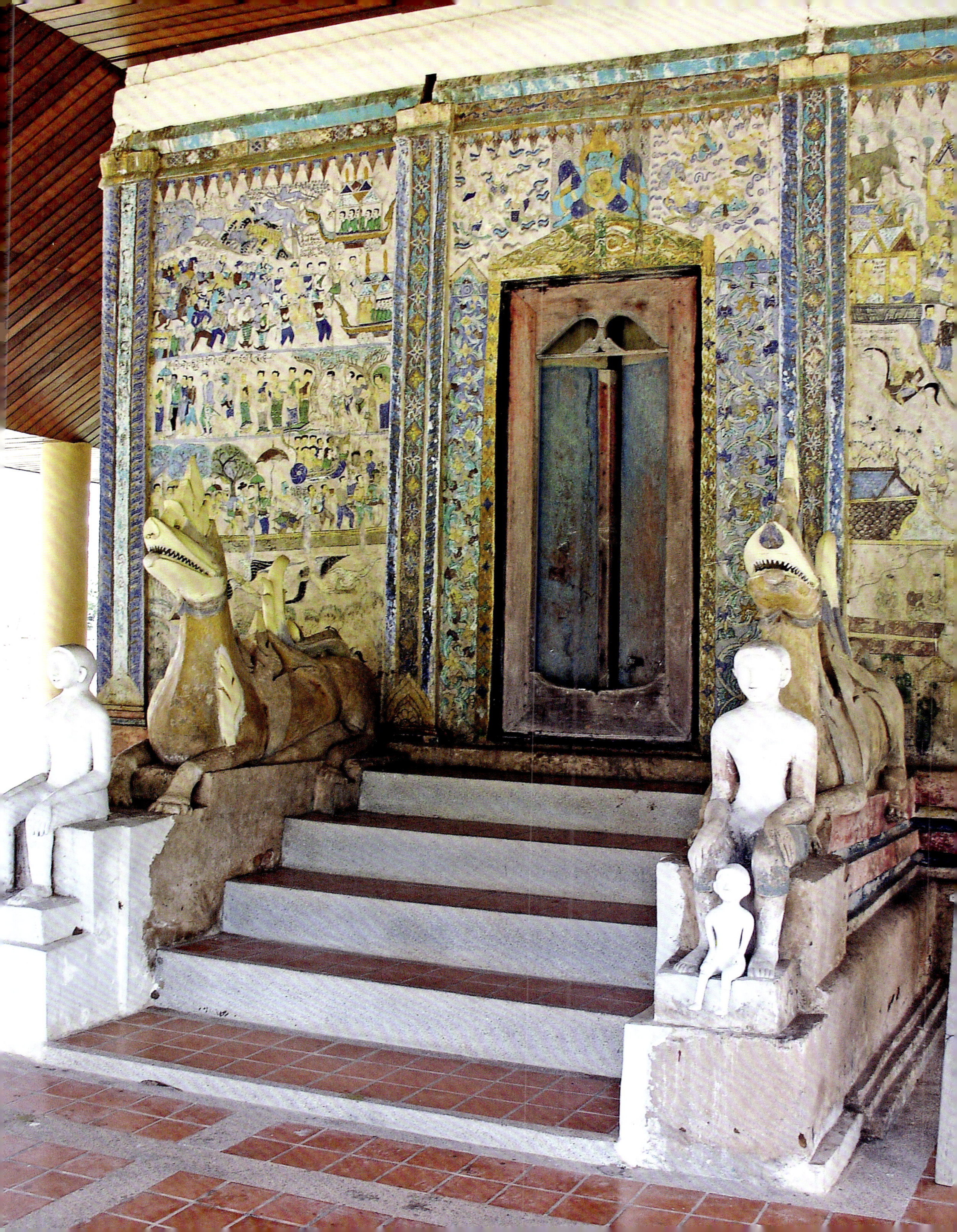

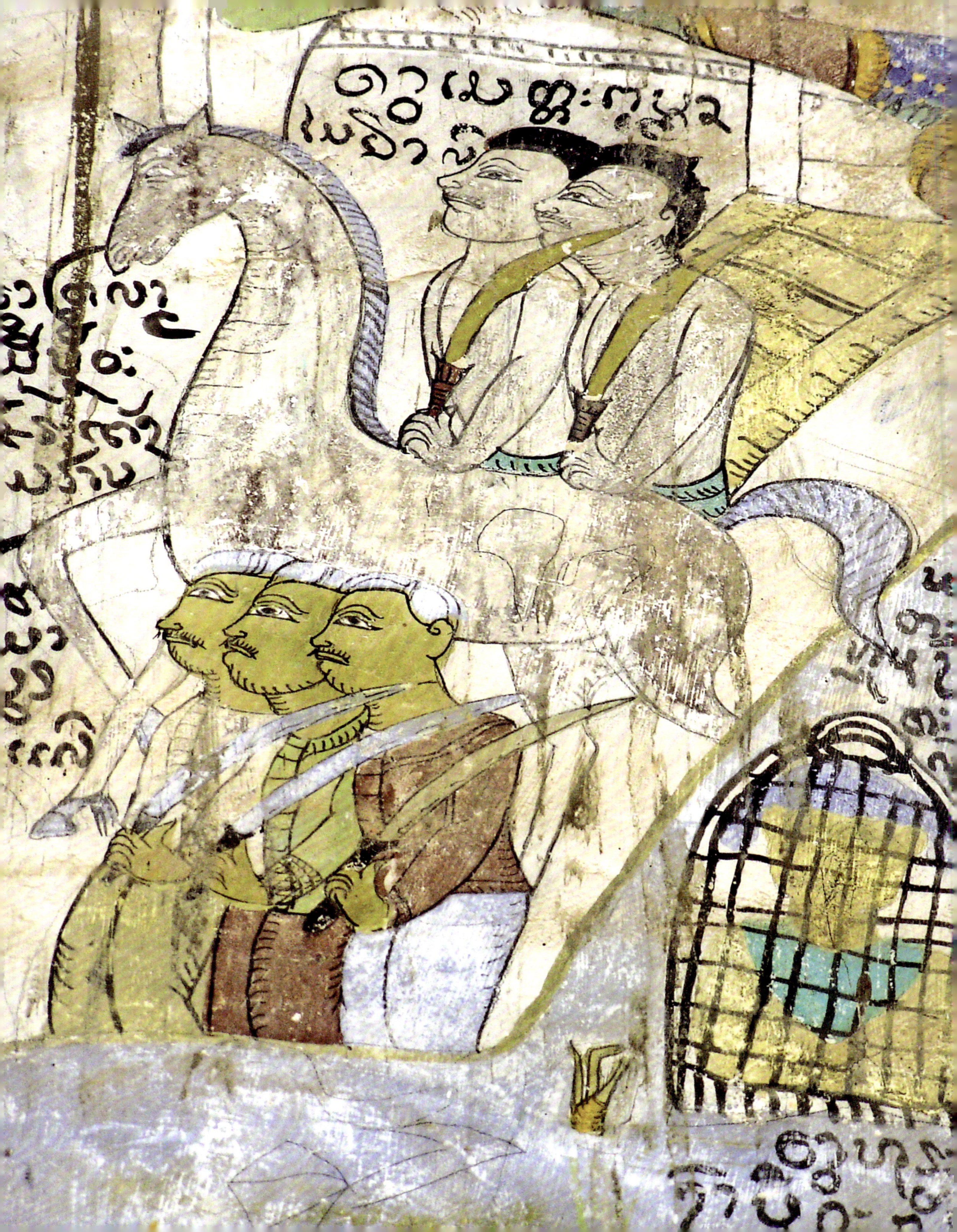

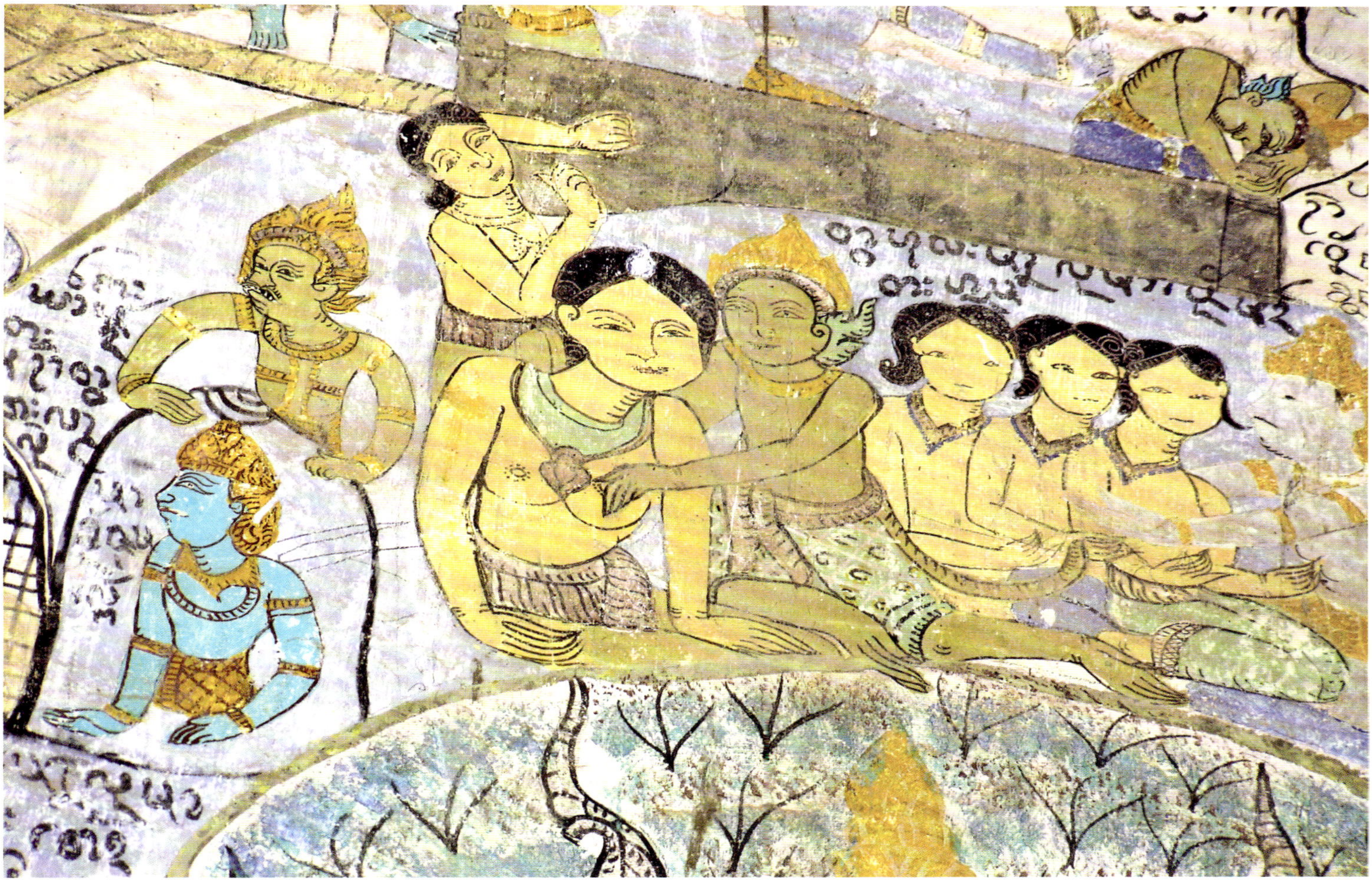

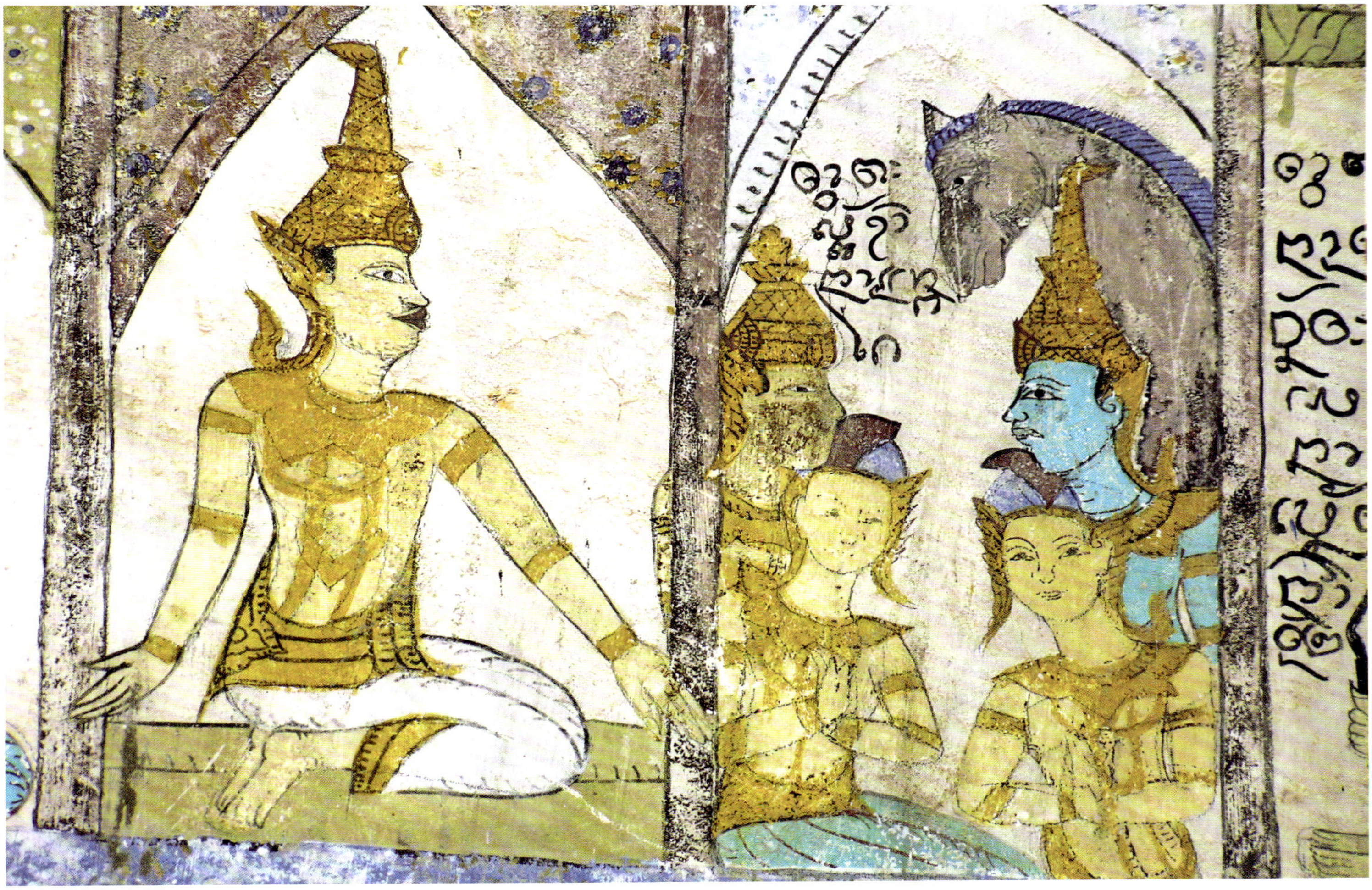

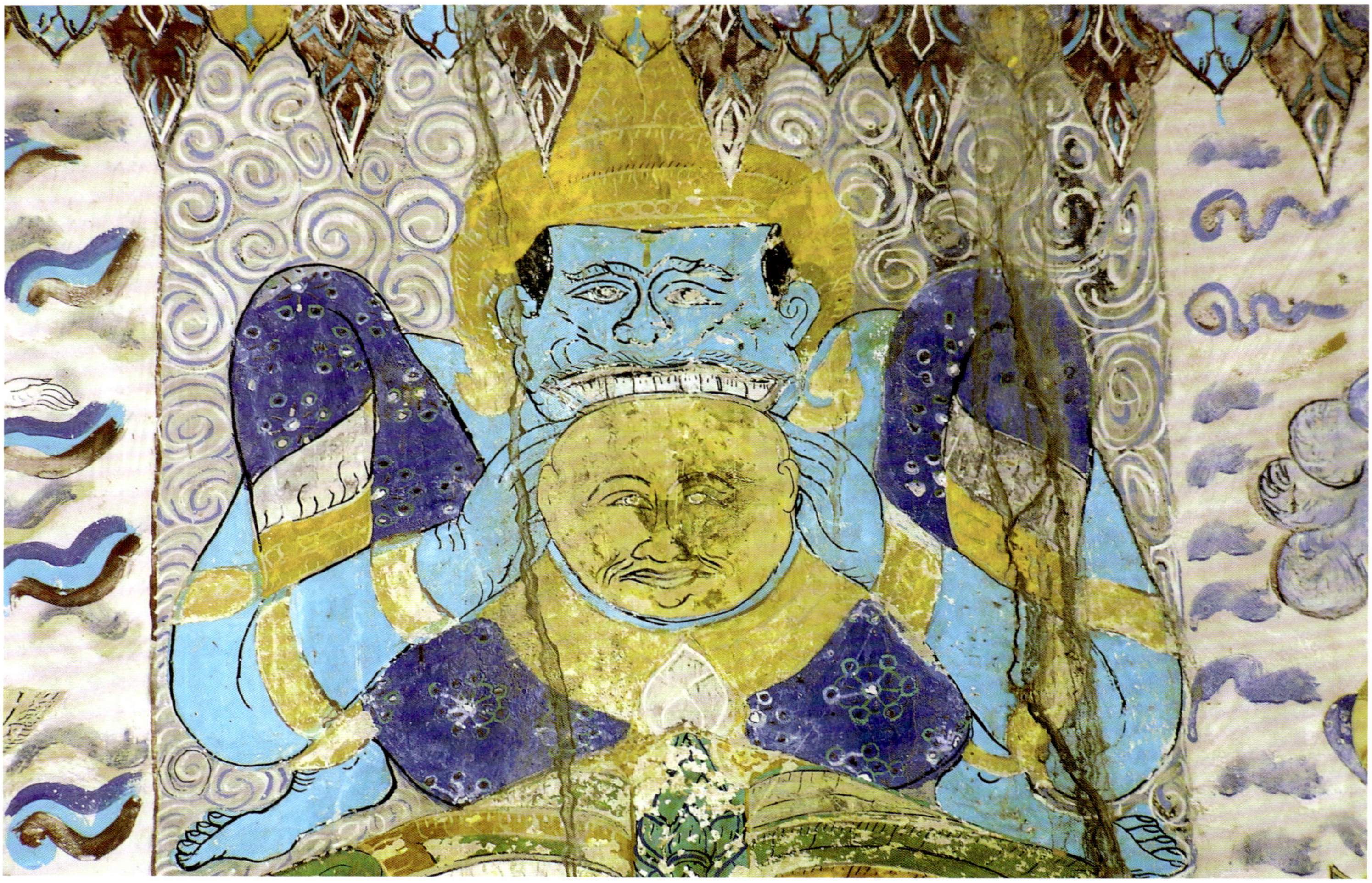

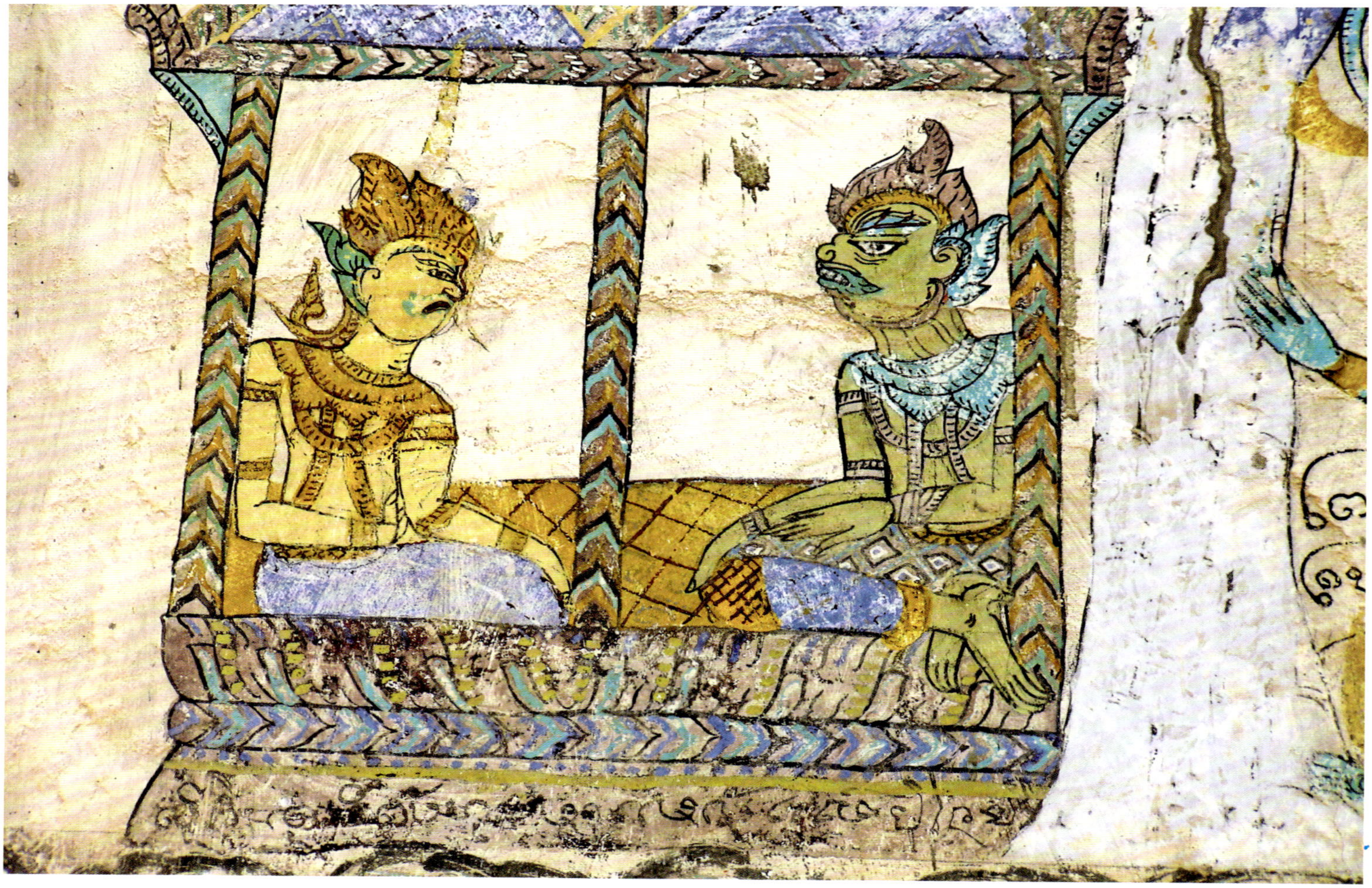

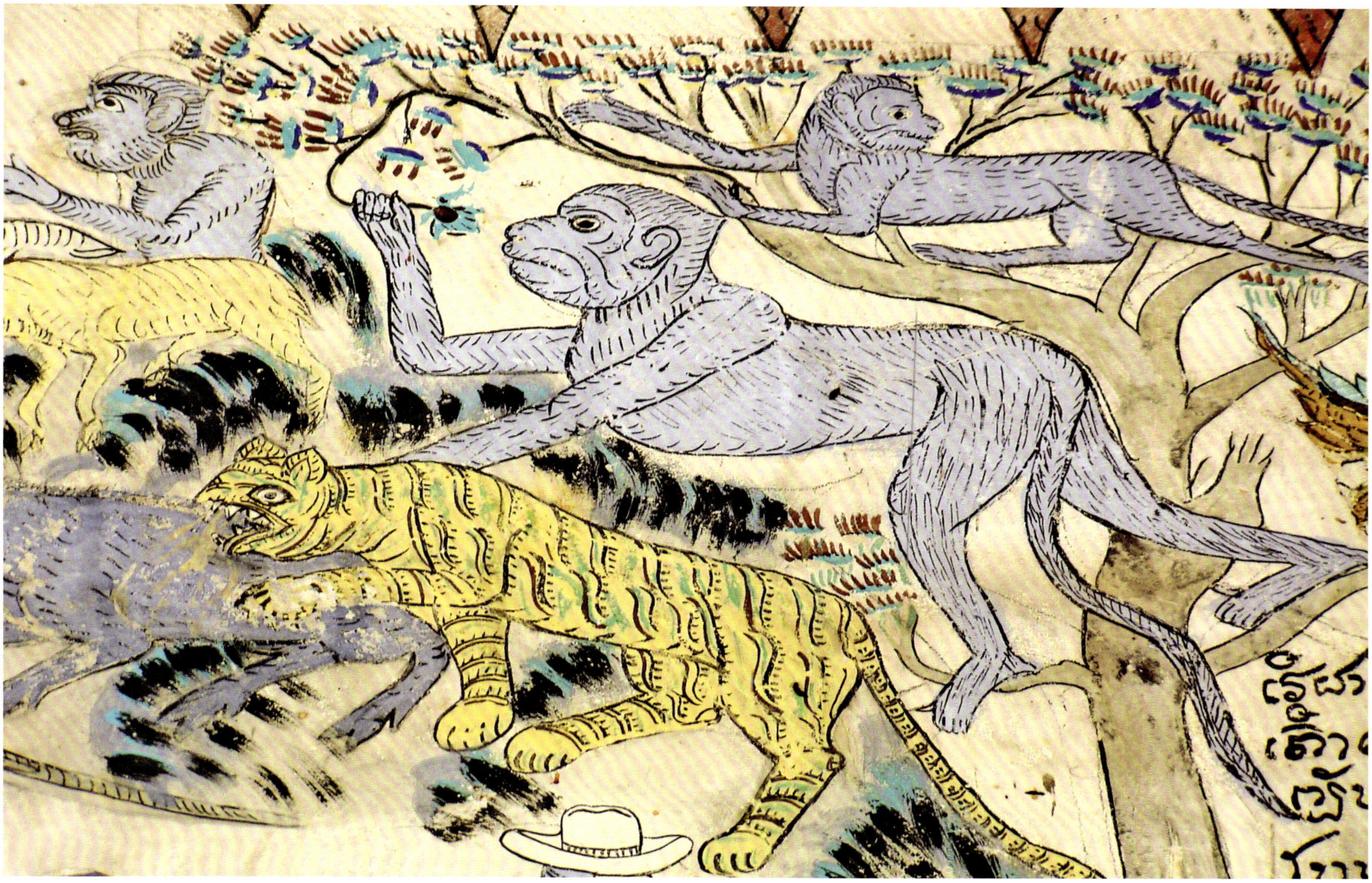

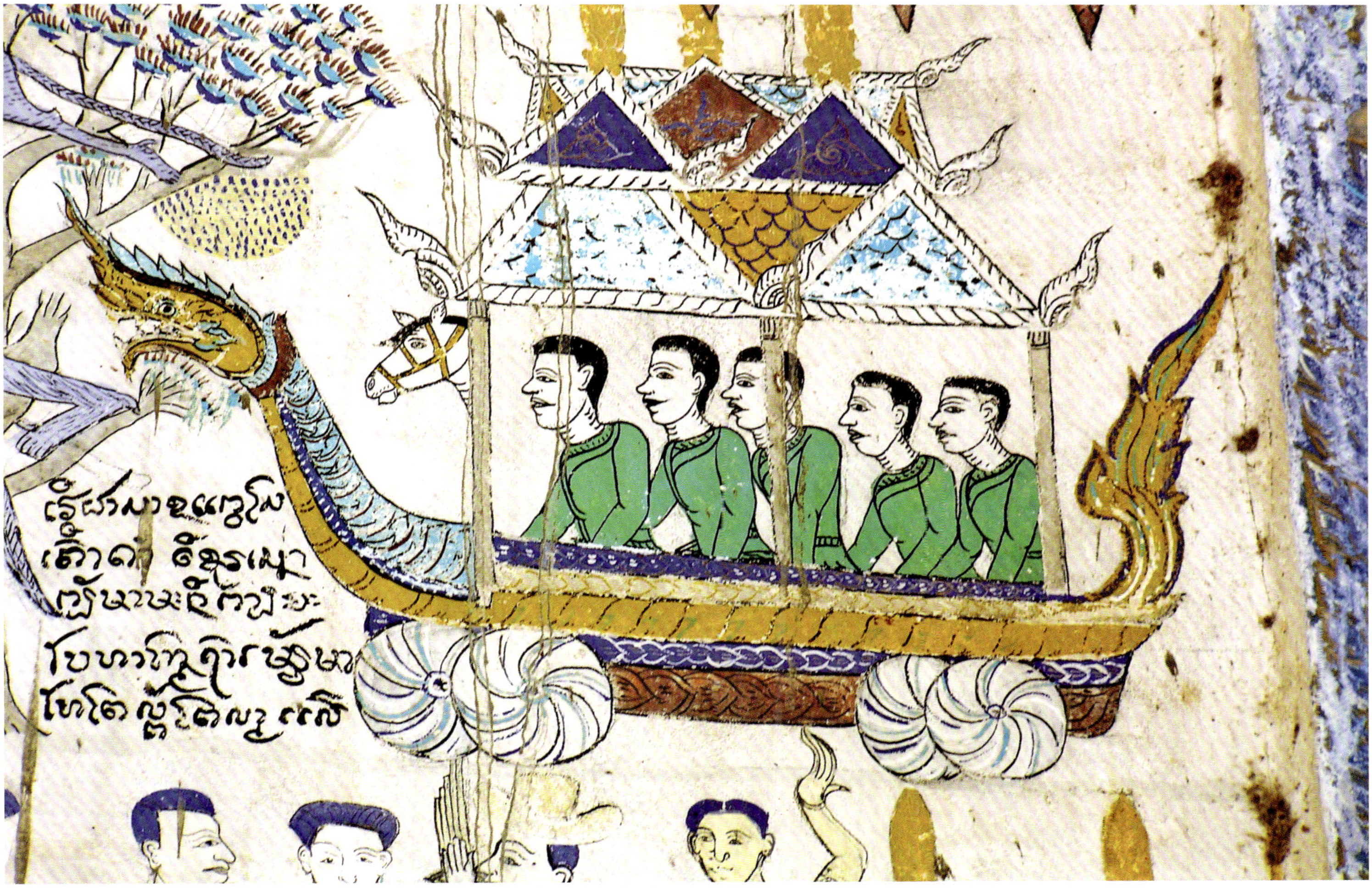

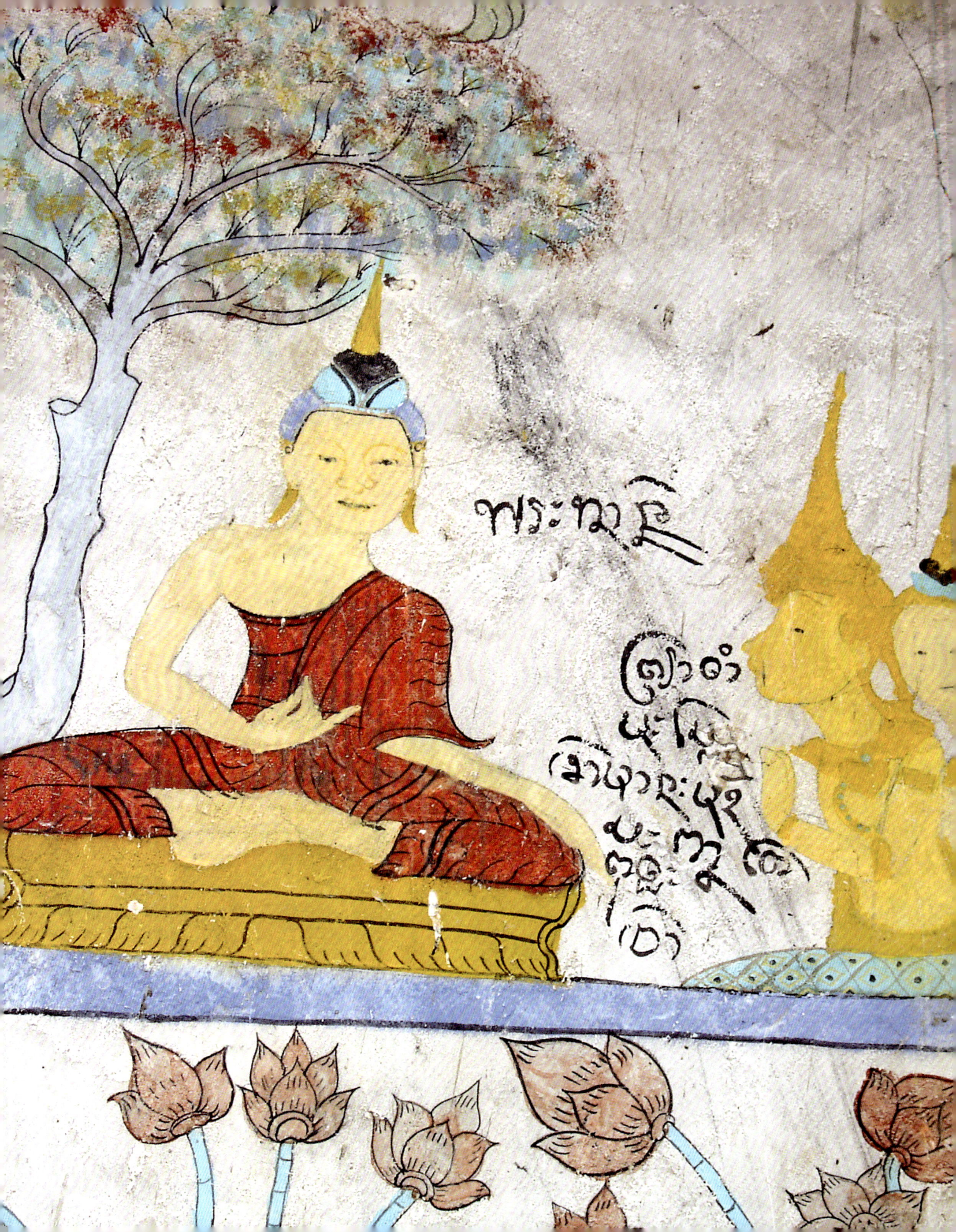

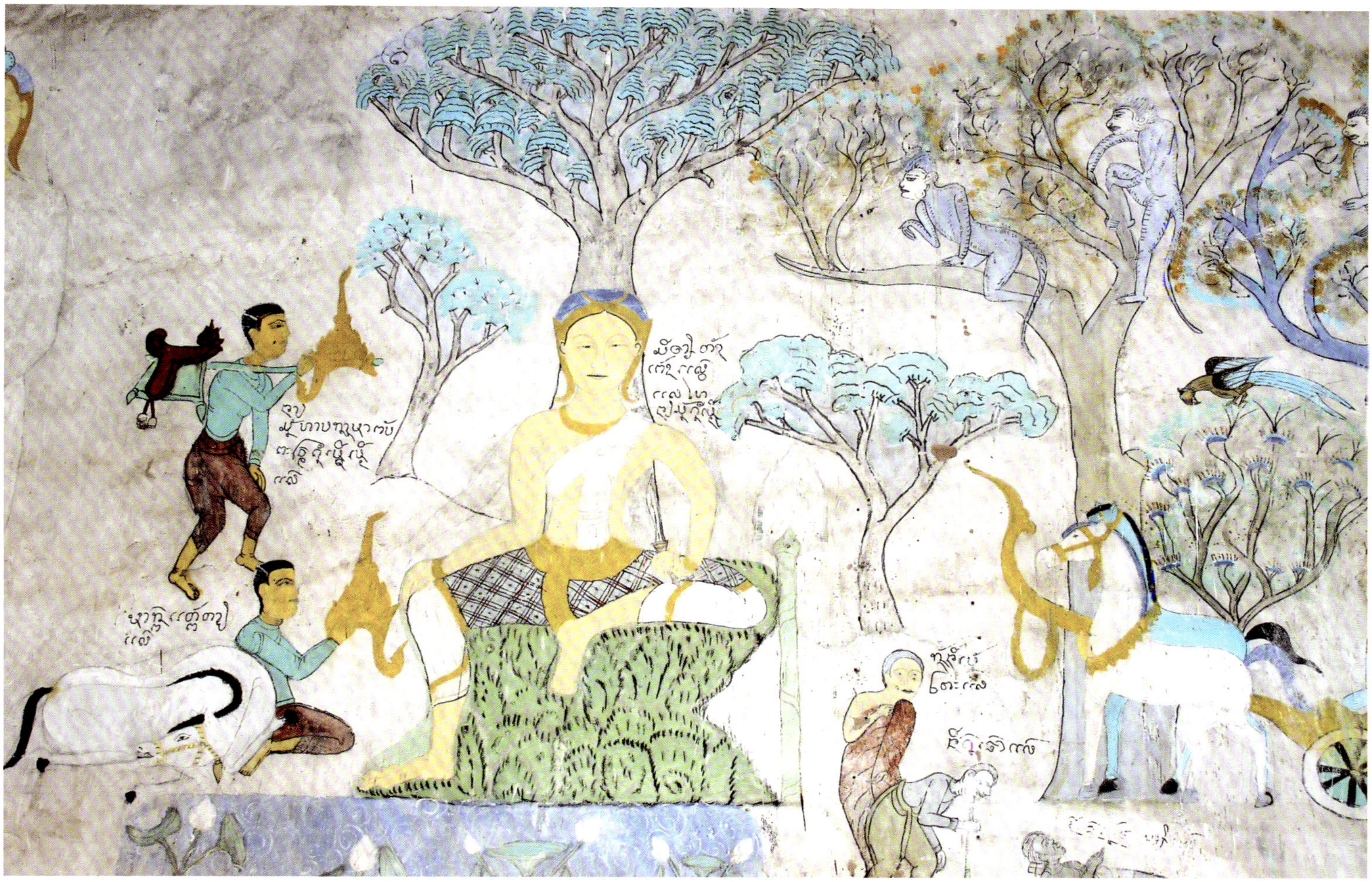

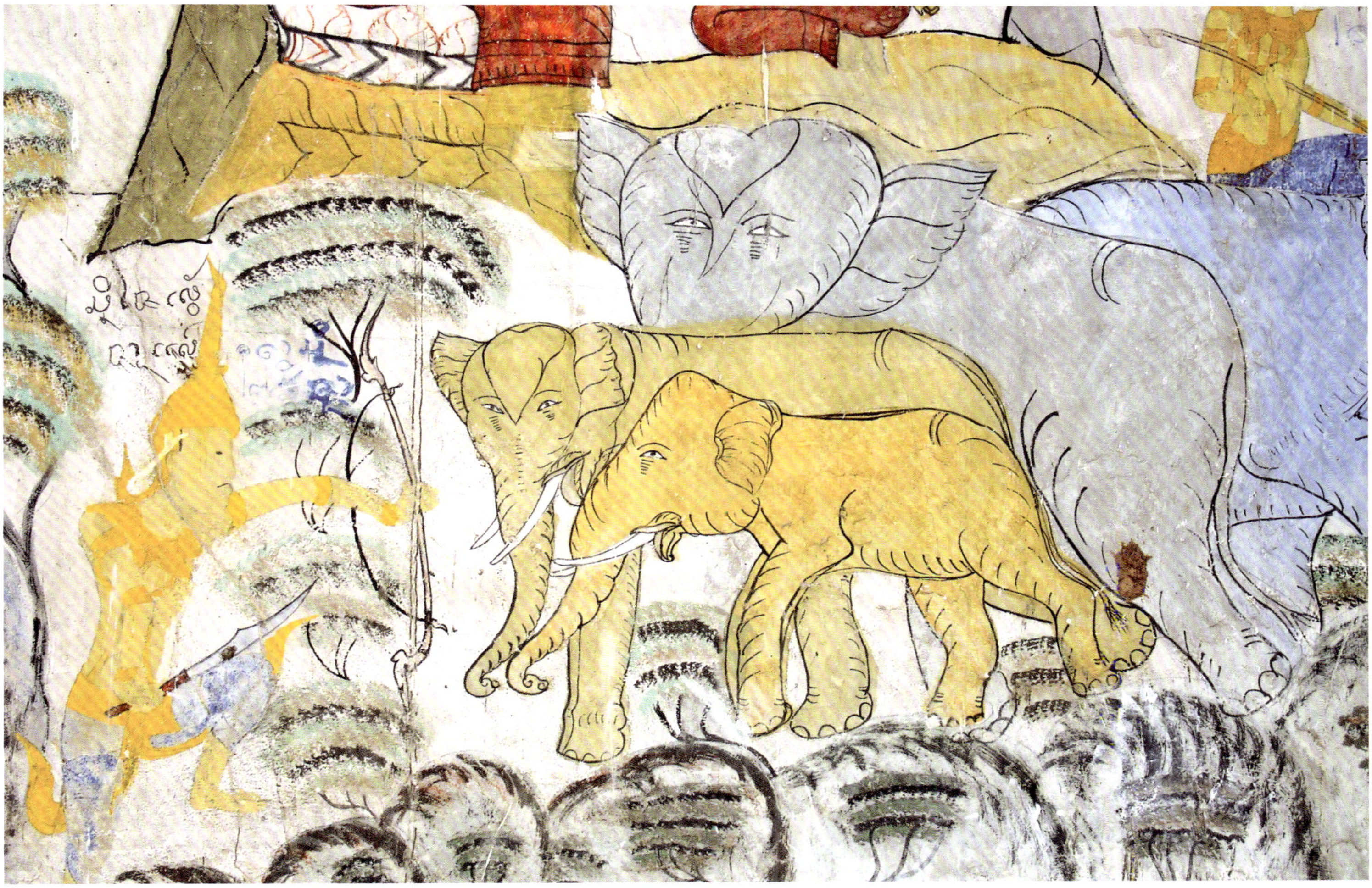

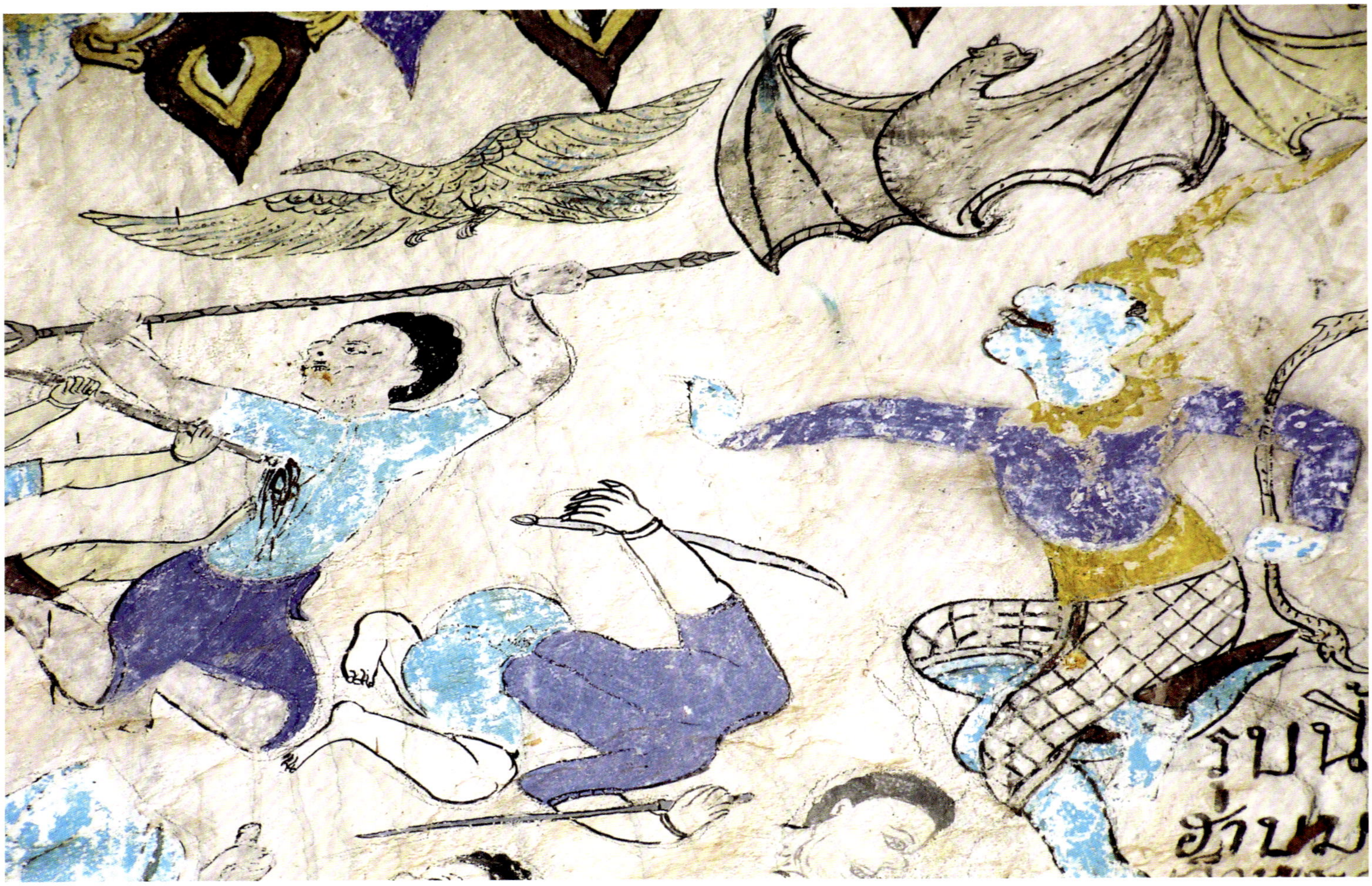

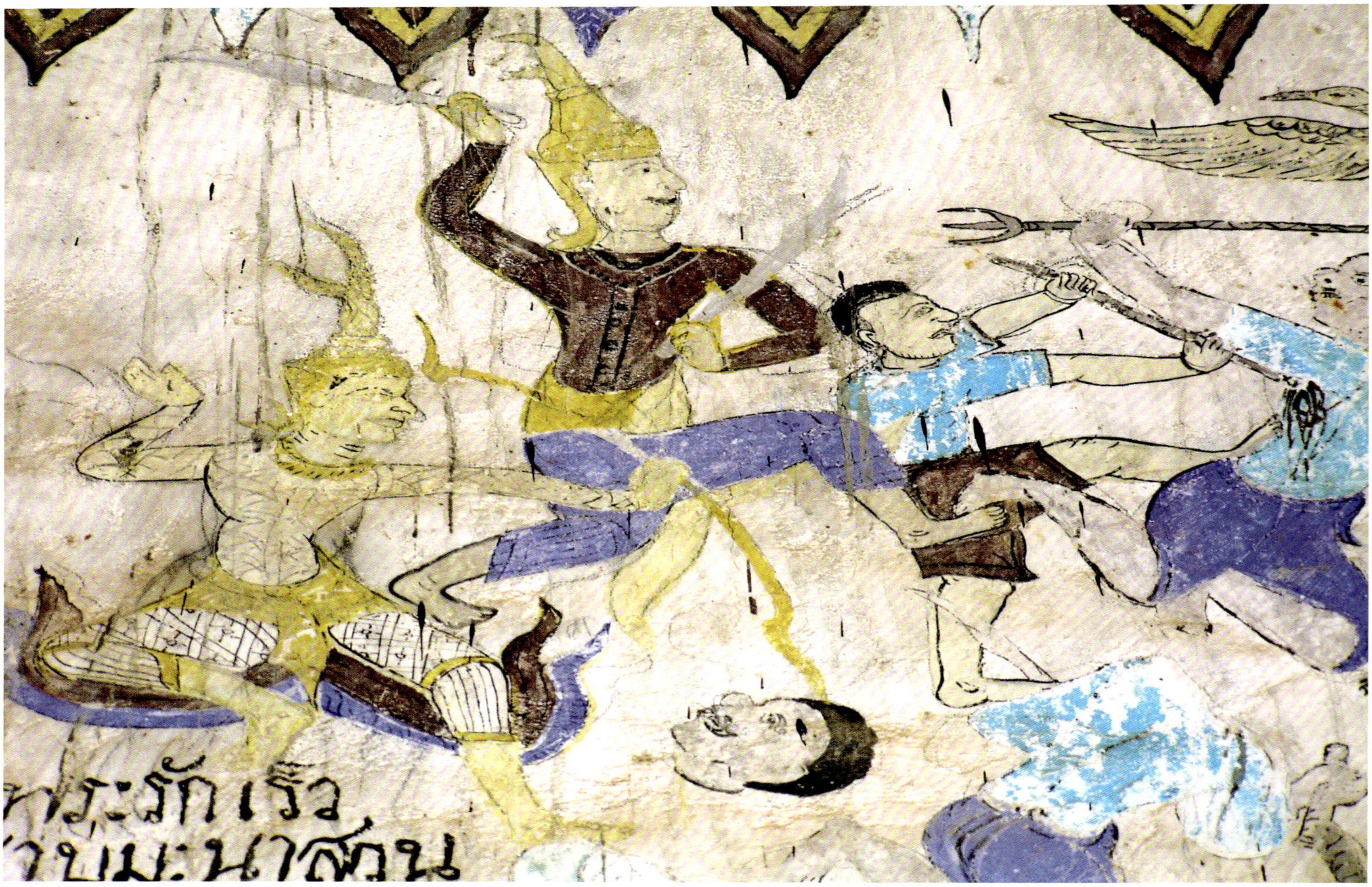

รบนั้
ฮ่าบม
ระะรักเร็ว
บมะนาสอน

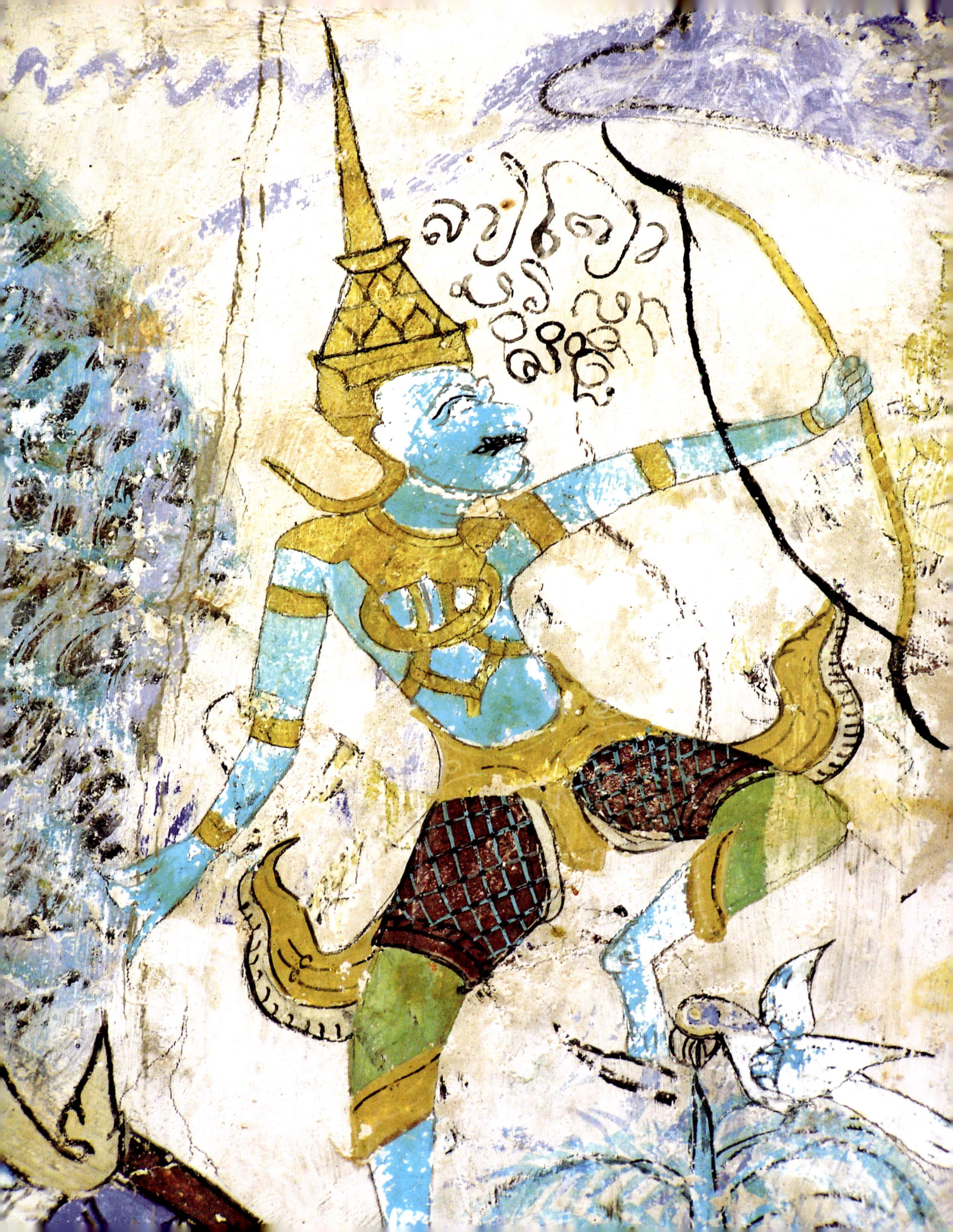

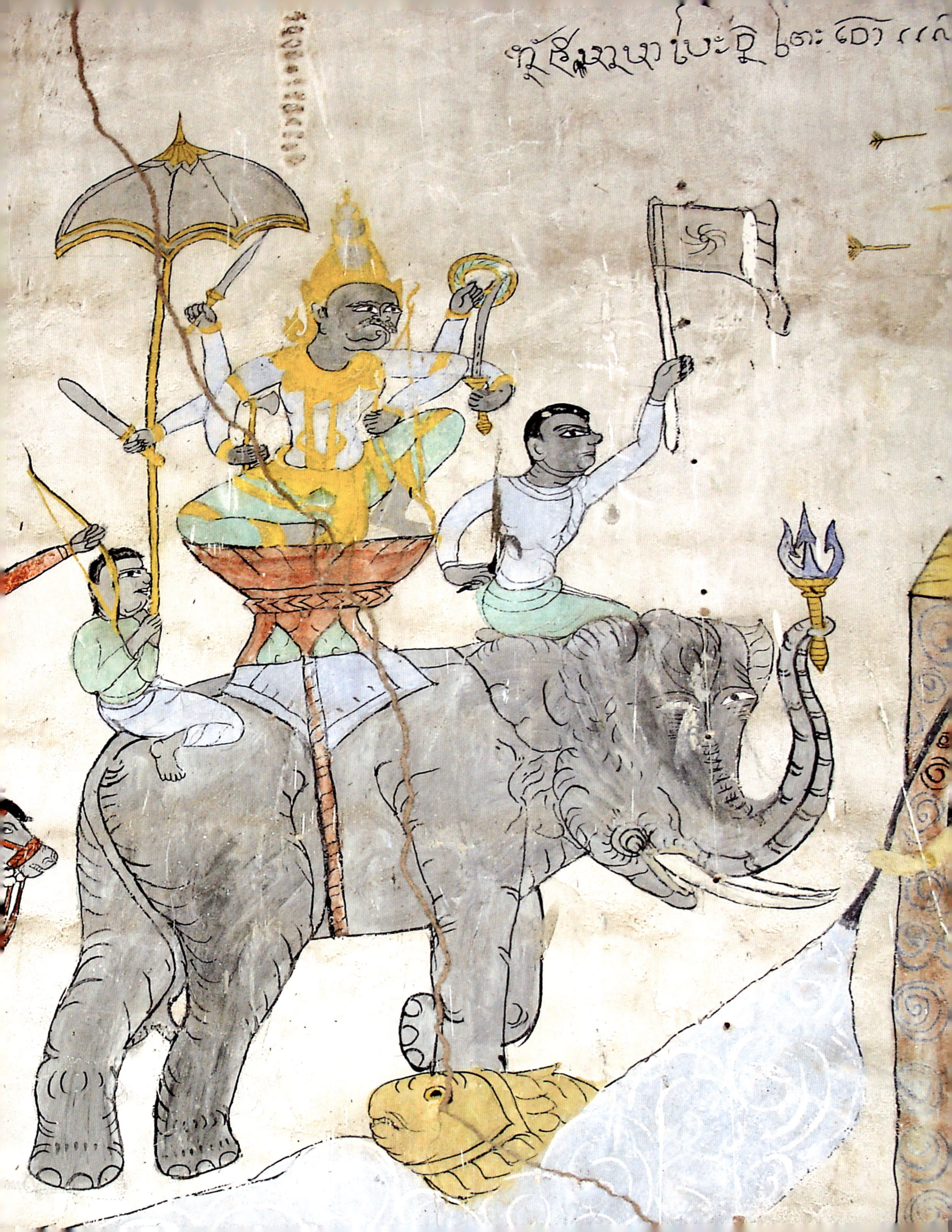

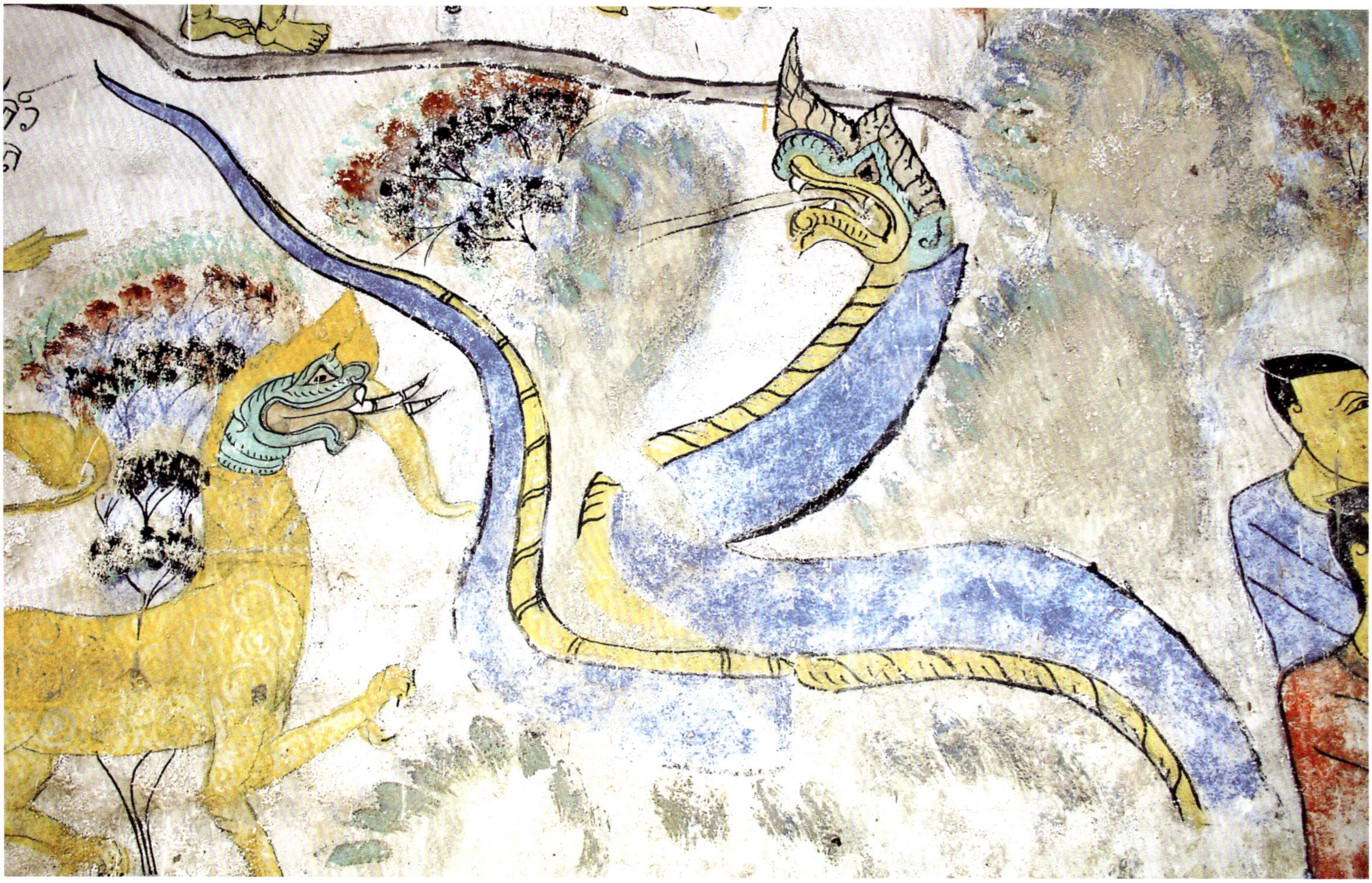

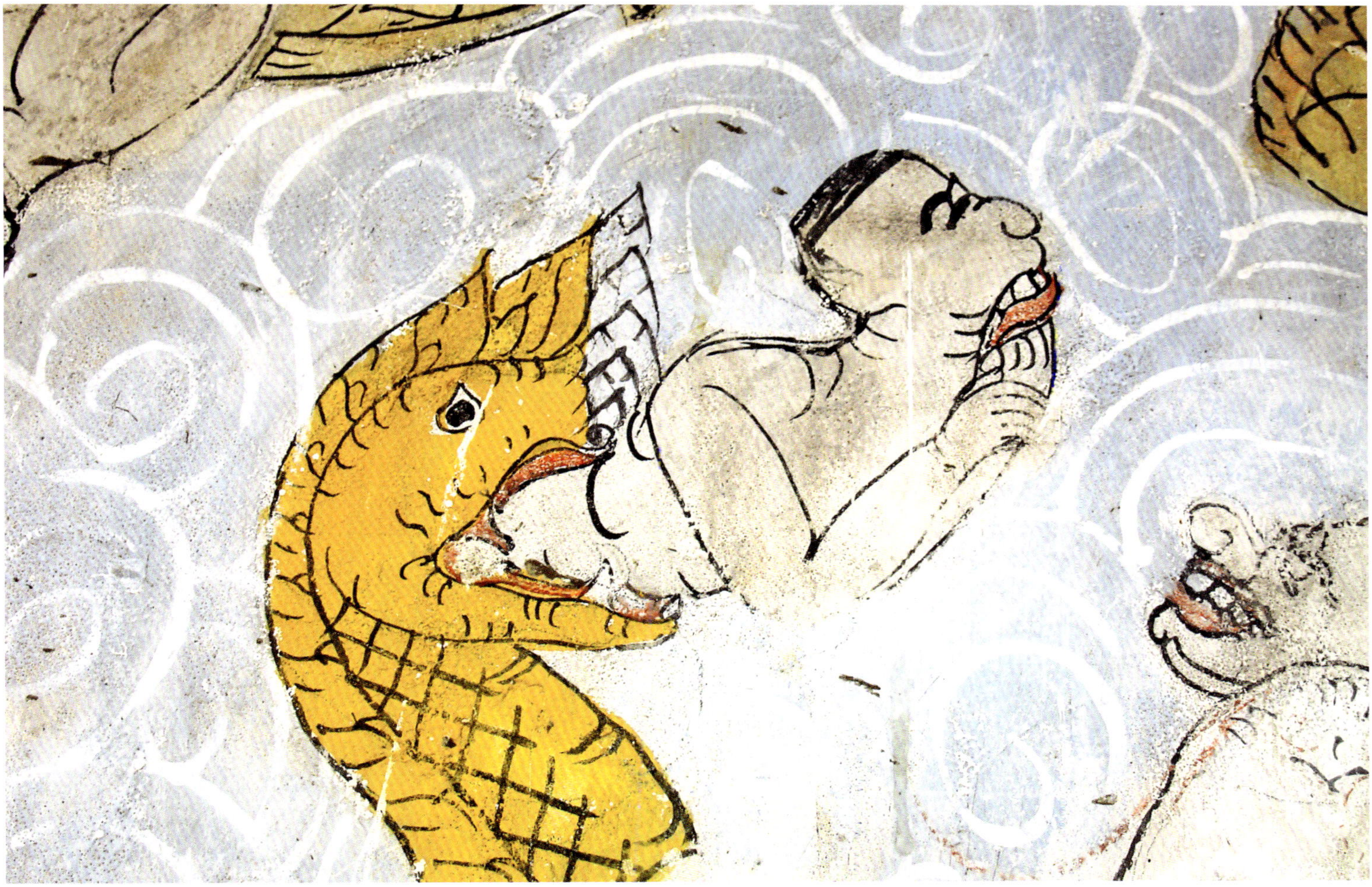

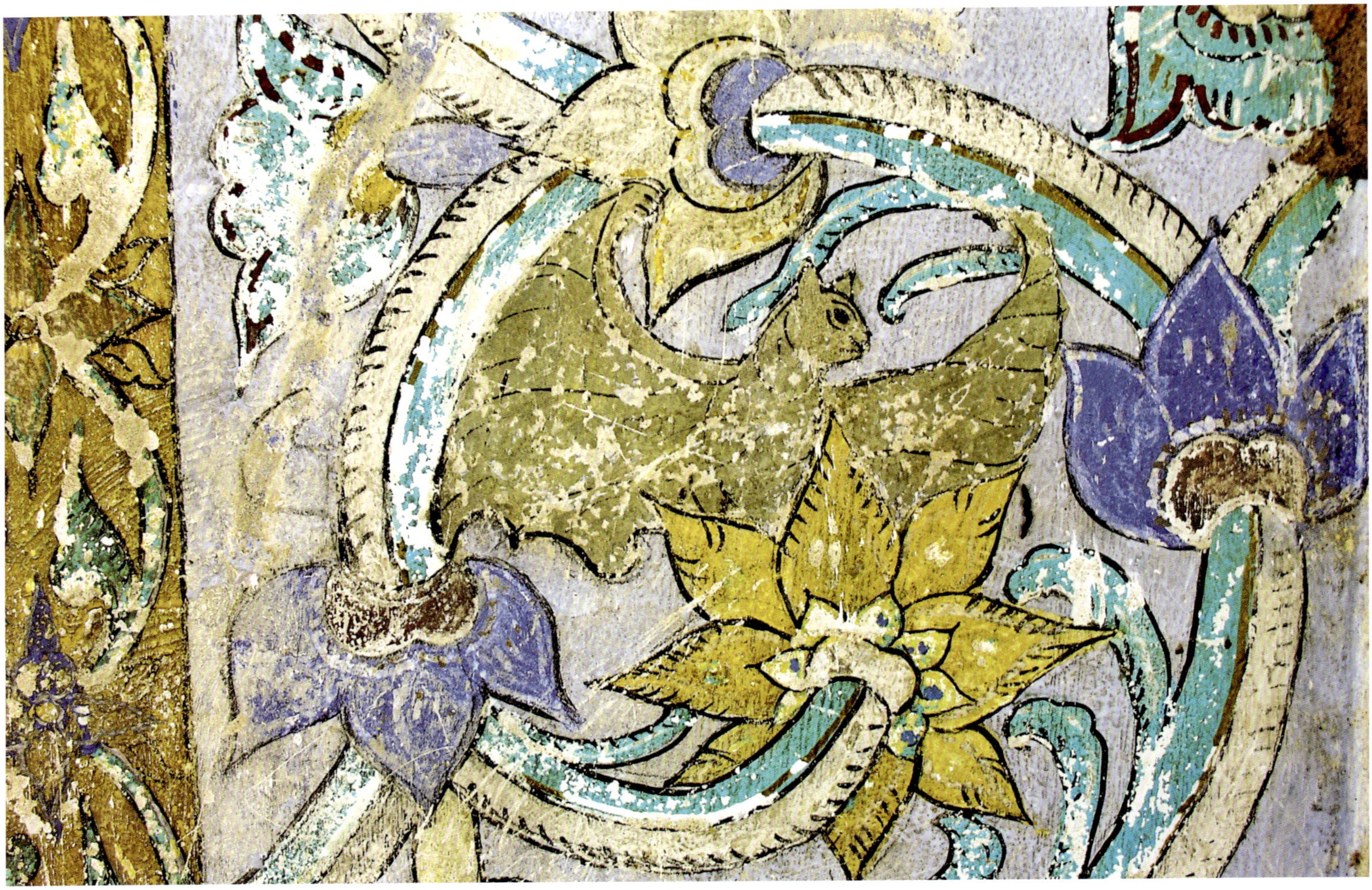

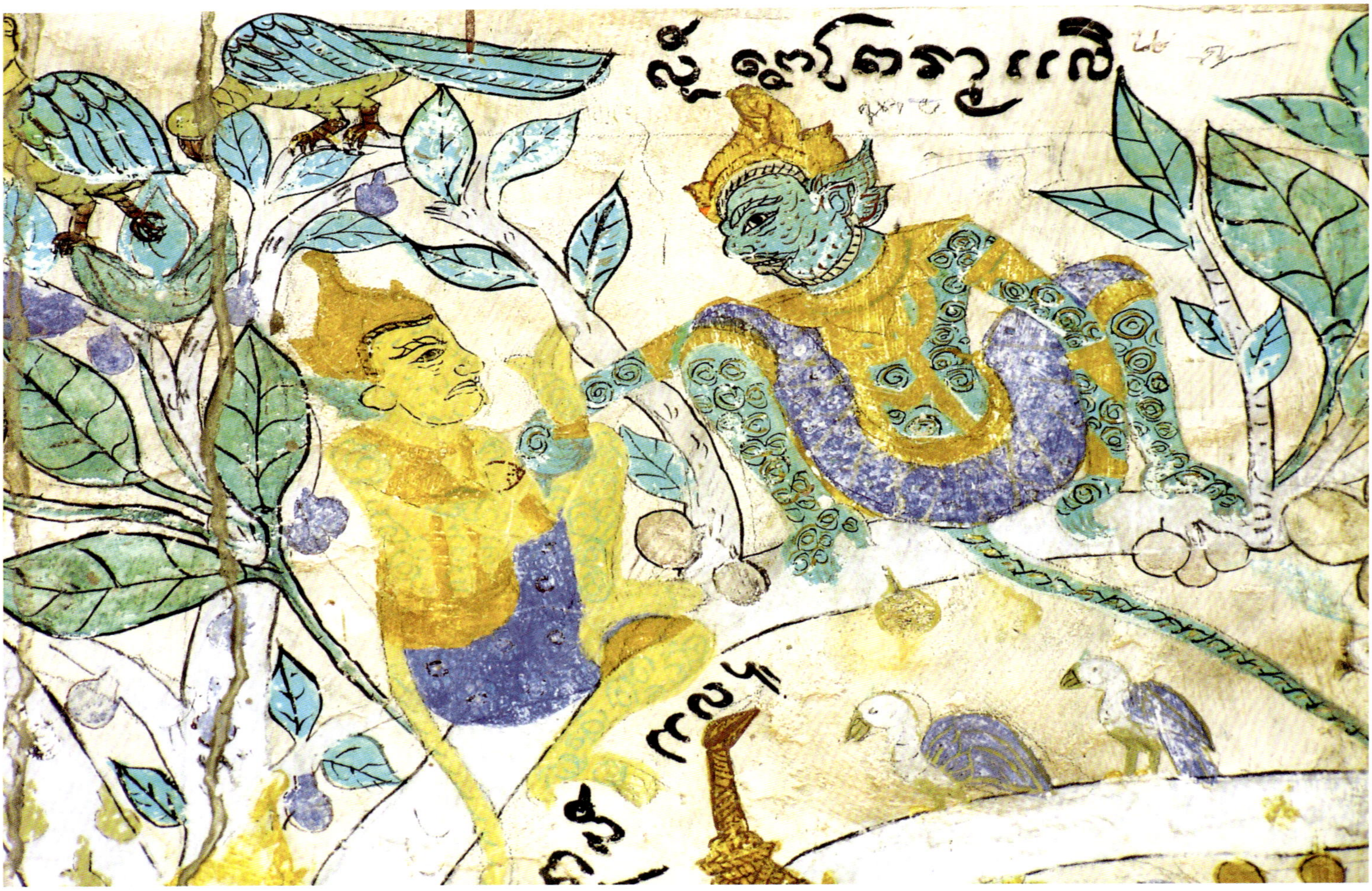

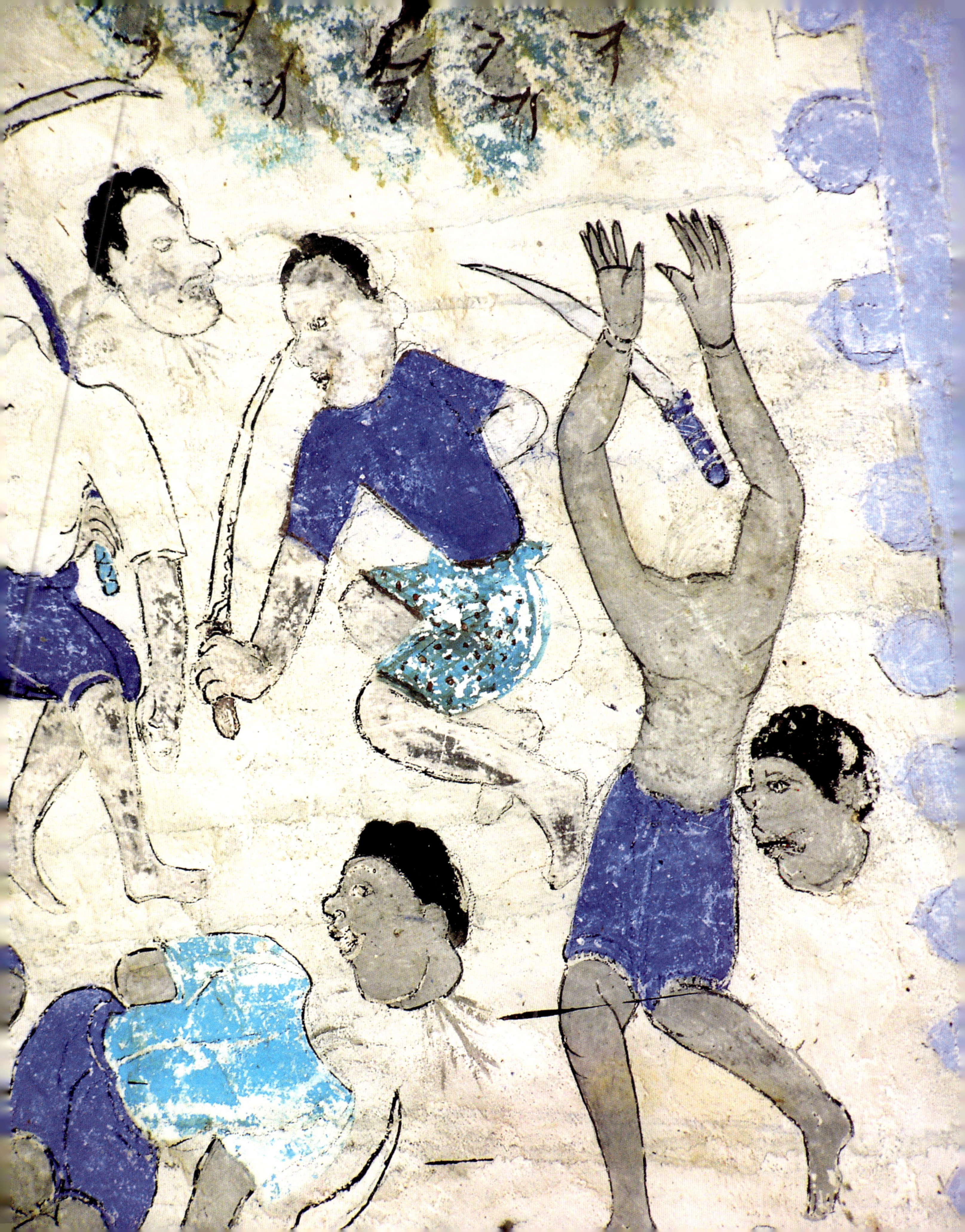

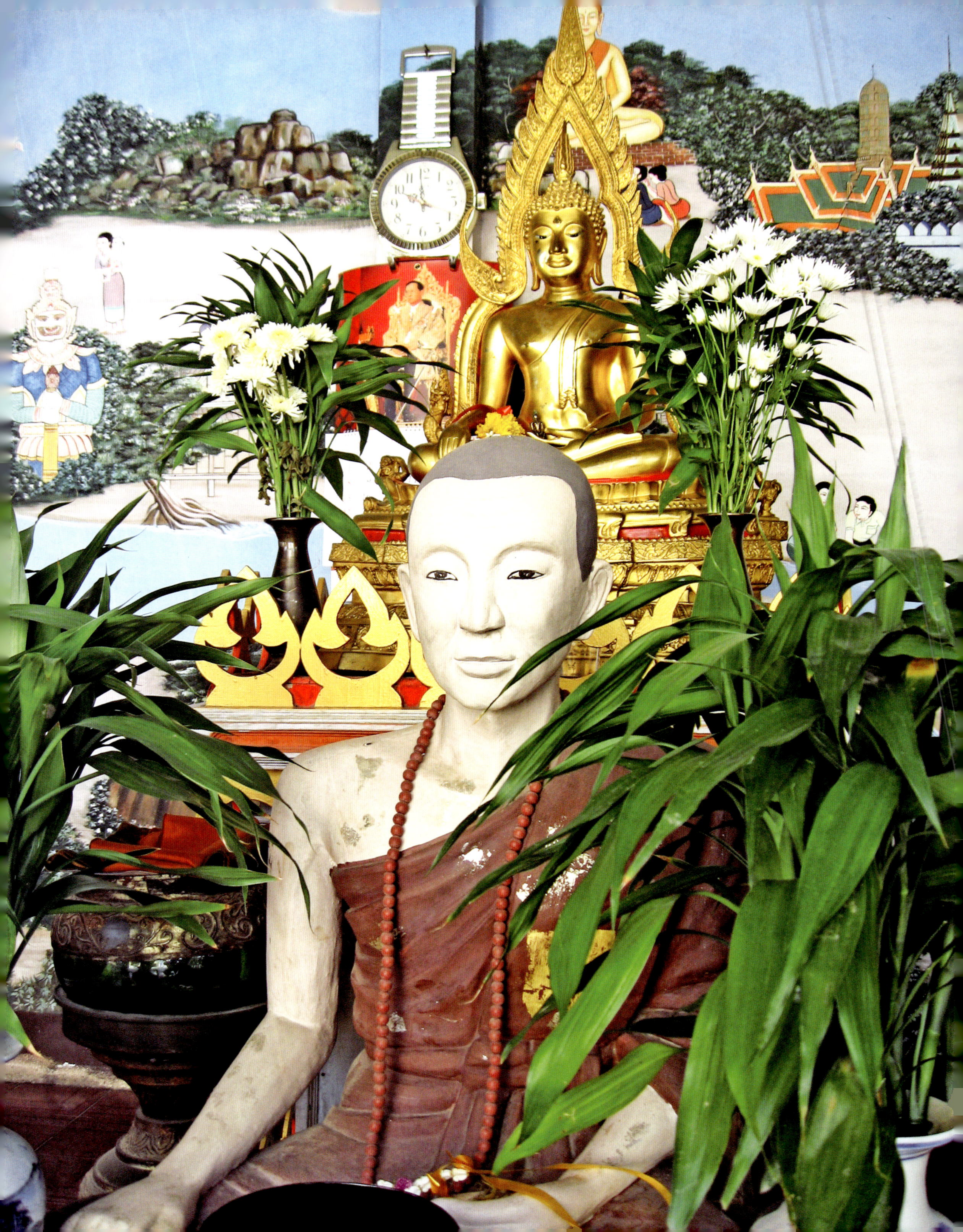

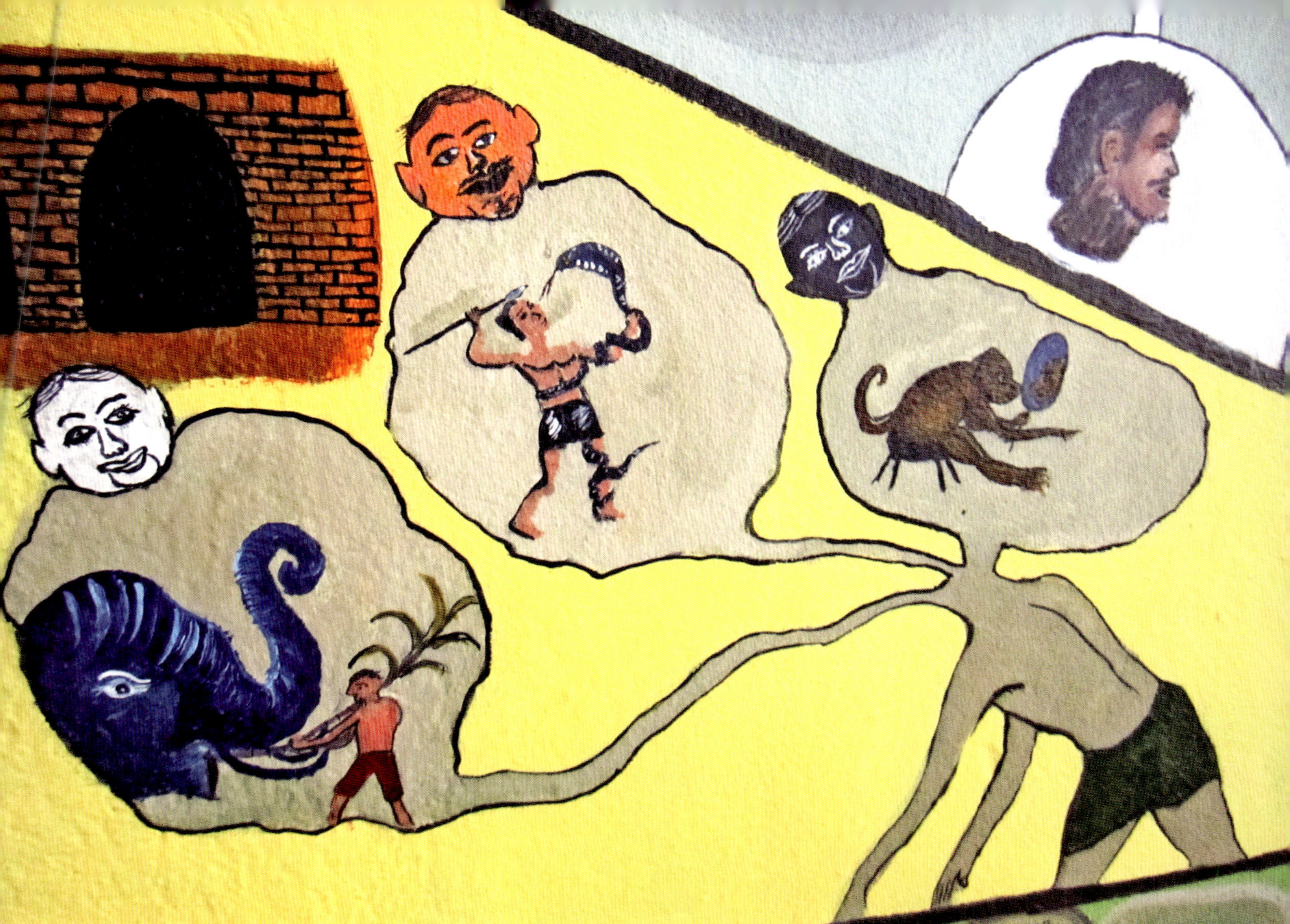

7. TEMPLE ART

While much of temple artwork depicts scenes from the Buddha's life, or tales from his previous incarnations, other artwork details village life. Thais are a communal people, with a focus on the group rather than the individual, and murals will reflect this. Examples include depictions of people joining in a funeral procession, helping the departed on their way, with loud live music to scare away evil spirits (Pg. 196). Or villagers participating in a Songran tradition, the Thai New Year celebrated in mid-April, when one acknowledges the dust and dirt collected on their feet during the year by bringing a bucketful to the *wat* to build a small *stupa*, decorated with colorful banners (Pg. 200-1). During November's Loi Krathong festival, celebrated since the thirteenth century, Thais launch a decorated banana leaf float with a lit candle onto the waterways with a plea of forgiveness to the water goddess Phra Mae Khongkha. Originally an Animist rite, then a Brahmin festival later adopted by Thai Buddhists, the candle honors Buddha, and the floating symbolizes the release of one's past sins and negativity.

Wat Umong has a museum of moral folk art painted directly onto the walls by visiting monks. Two figures, each half visible as a skeleton, recalls the Buddhist concept of impermanence, reminding that all existence is in a constant state of flux (Pg. 209). Also featured is a variation on the Tibetan Wheel of Becoming, presided over by Yama, the god of death (Pg. 214-7). The center circle depicts the three poisons, ignorance (the pig), desire (the cock) and hostility (the serpent). The next circle addresses souls in rounds of rebirth, depicted in five realms: the *deva* or god realm, hungry ghosts, *Narok* or hell, the animal and the human realm. The outer rim depicts the 12 aspects of dependent origination, including sensation, shown as a man with his eyes pierced by arrows.

Temple door guardians, or *tawarabans*, are an overlooked art form. Some are hand carved, or of inlaid mother-of-pearl. Others are hand-painted with gilded gold leaf. In Hindu mythology, Shiva was protected by an army of *devas; tawarabans* serve the same function in Buddhist temples today. Diptych figures include *asparas* (Thai angels), *kinnarees*, *yakshas* and other divinities. Human figures are of a semi-divine nature, for example, celestial beings such as Mae Thorani (Pg. 224).

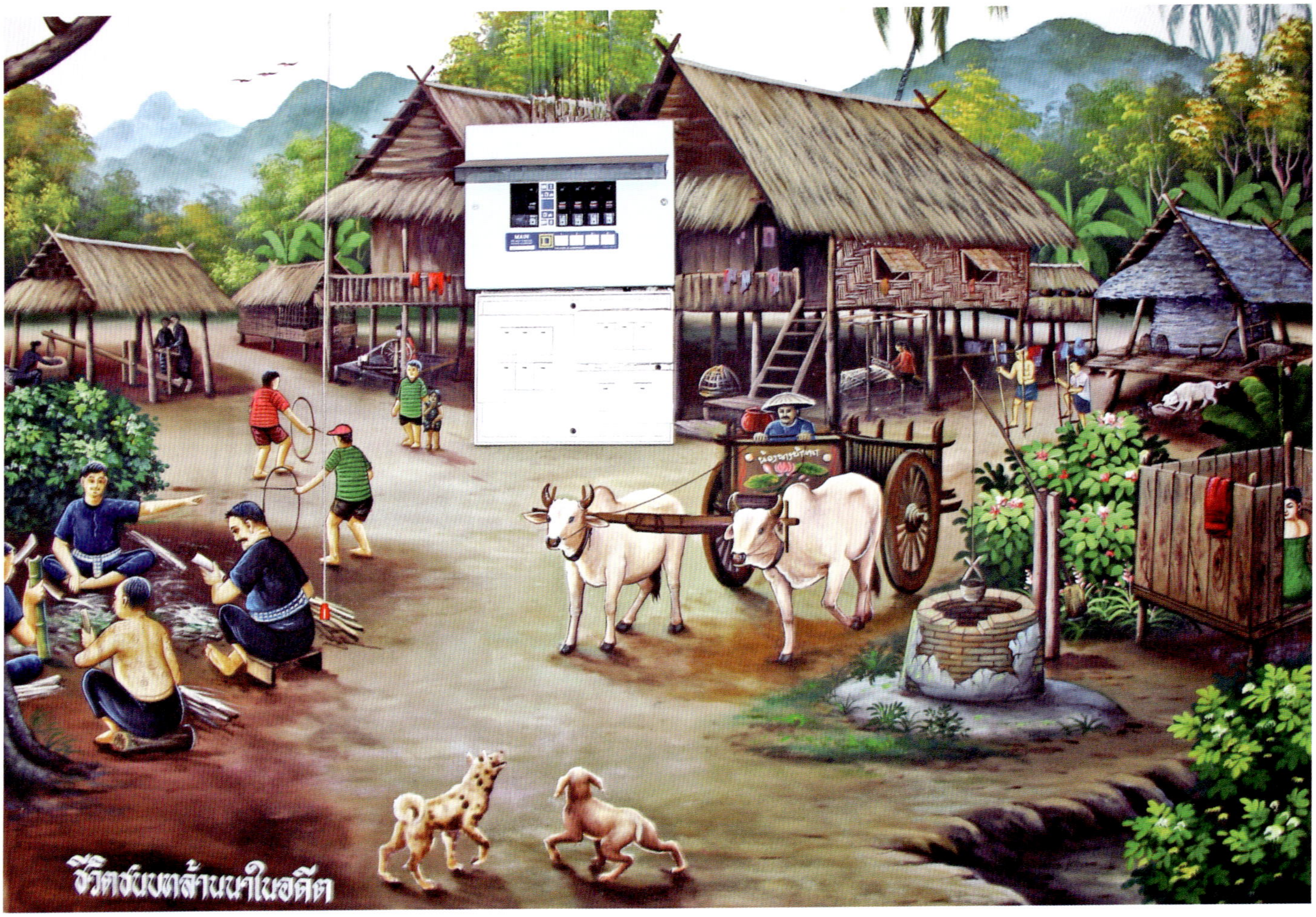

ชีวิตชนบทล้านนาในอดีต

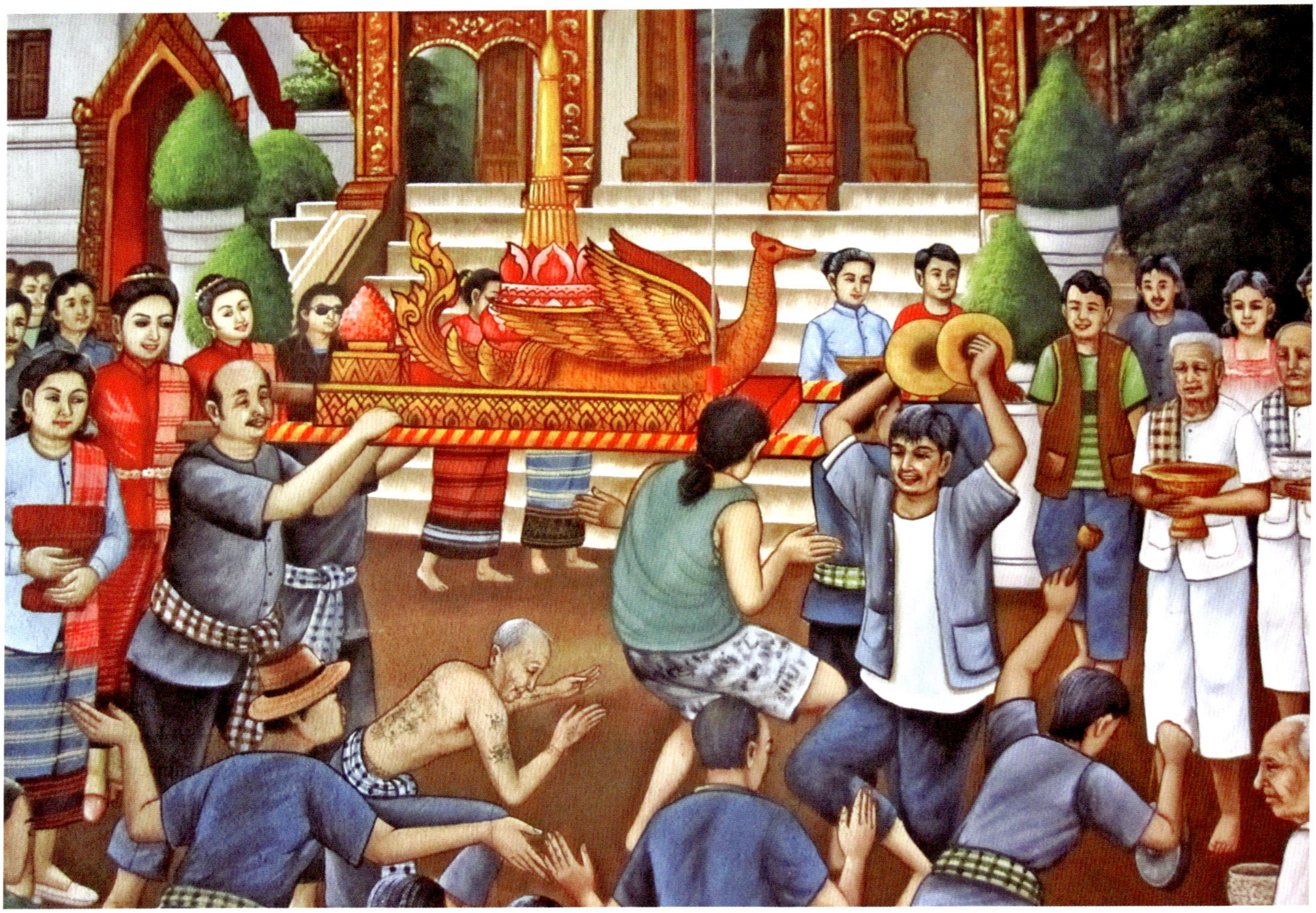

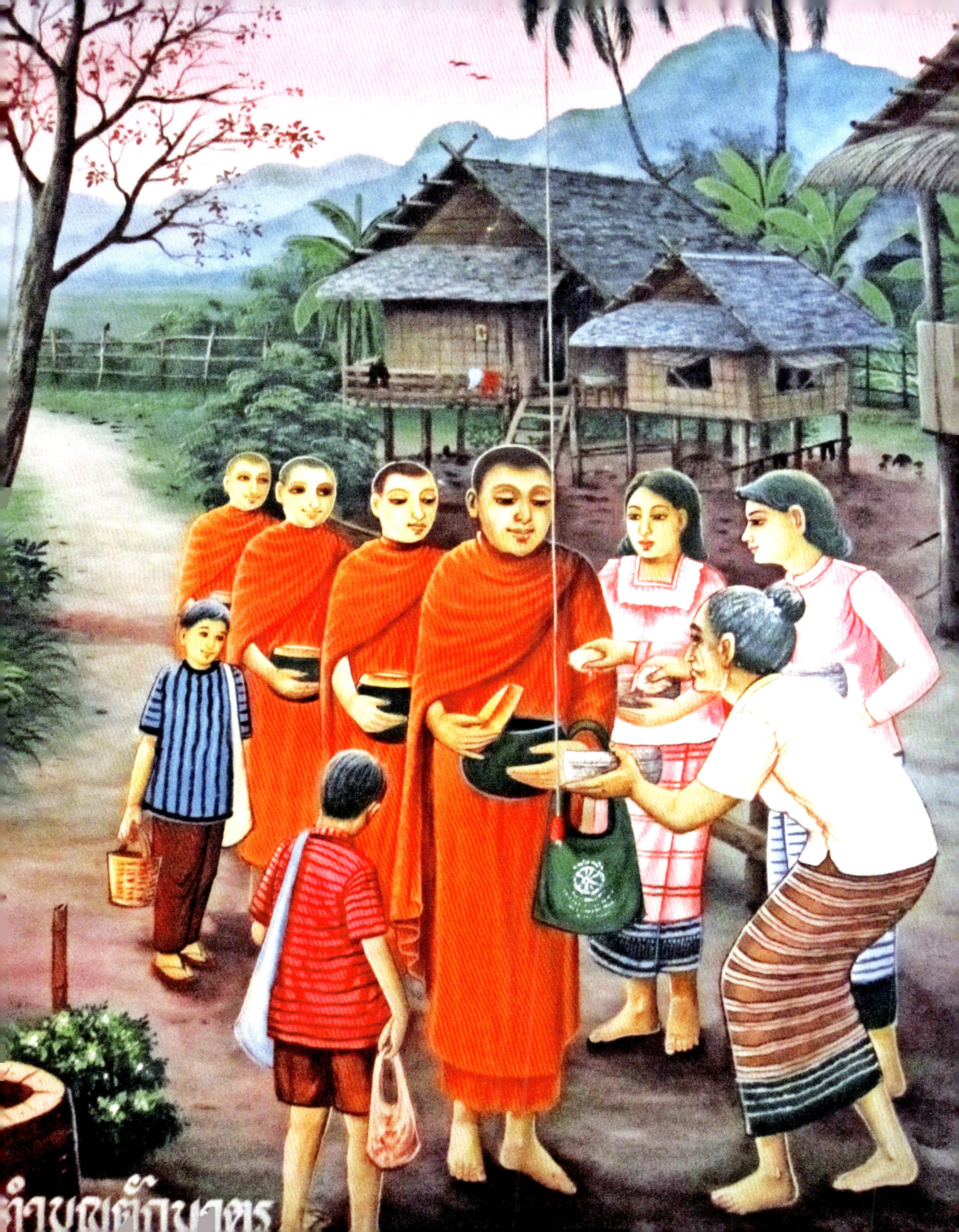
ทำบุญตักบาตร

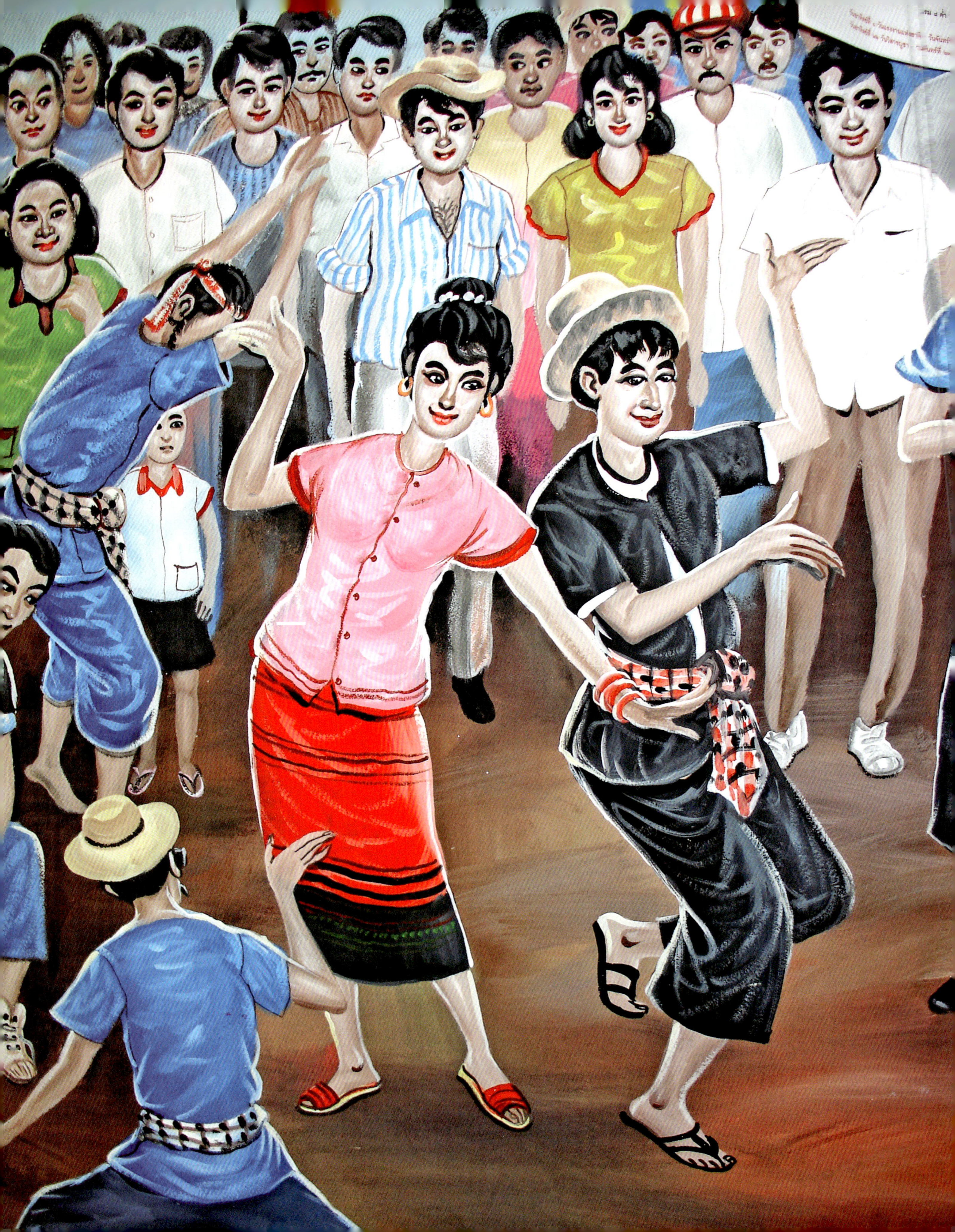

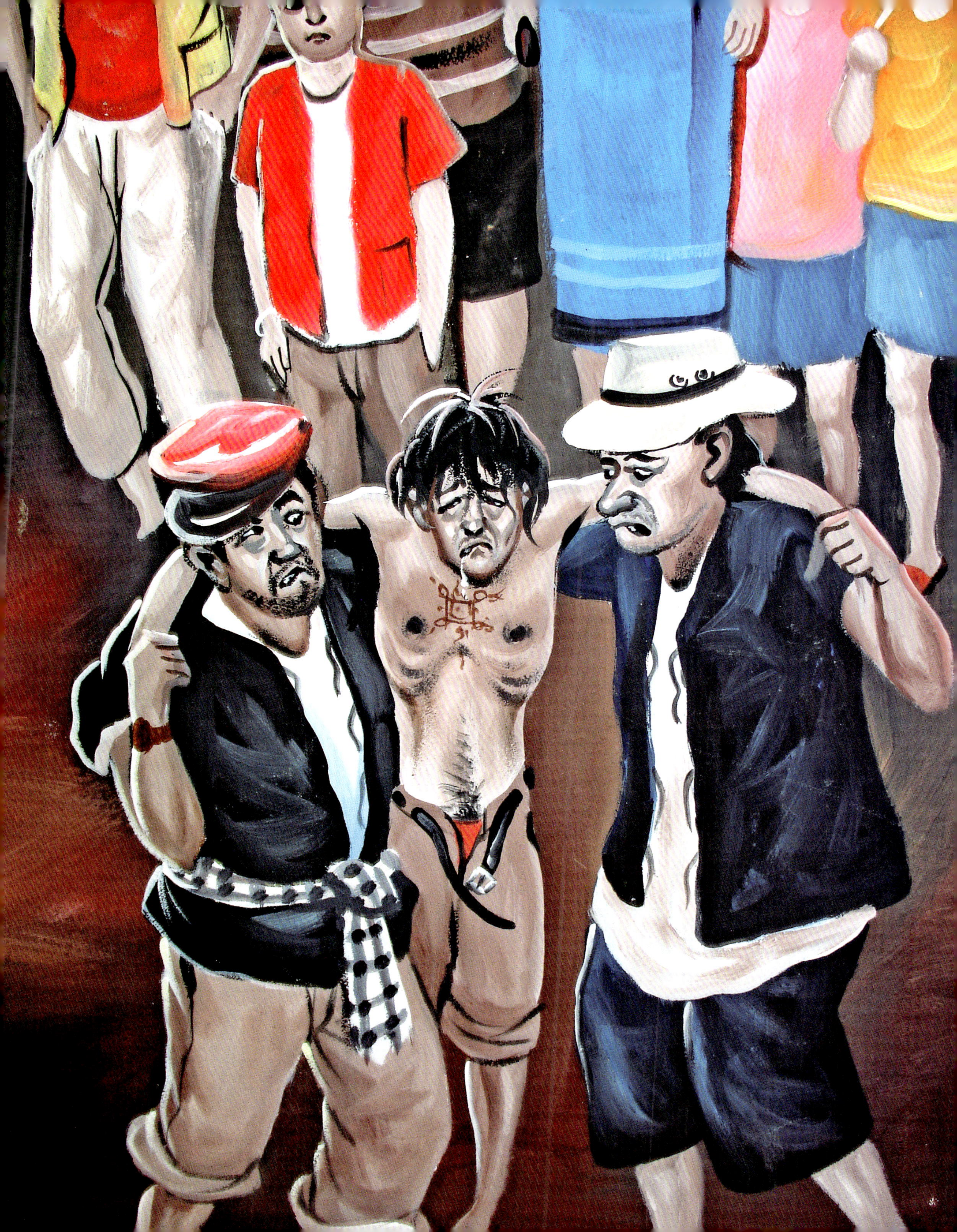

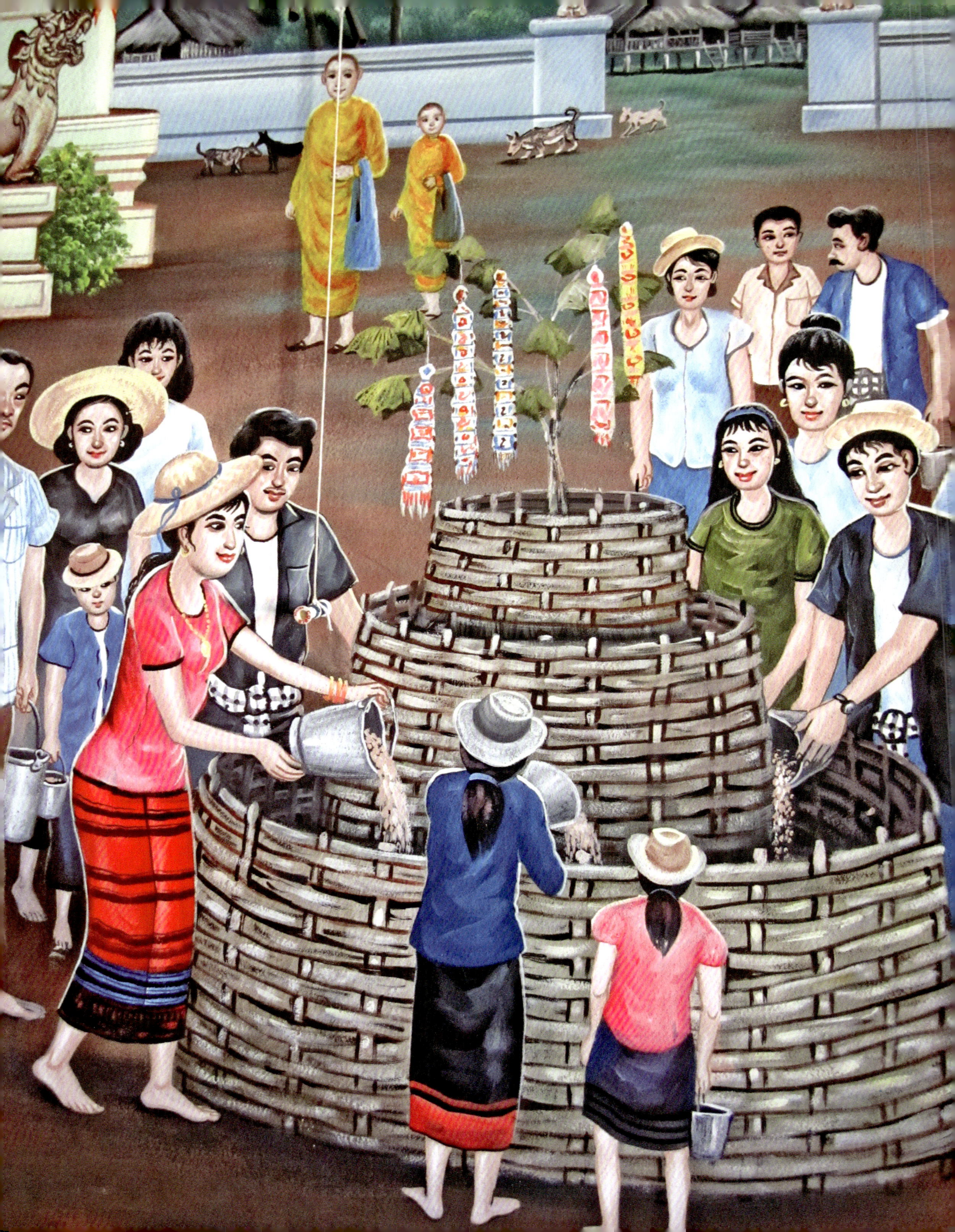

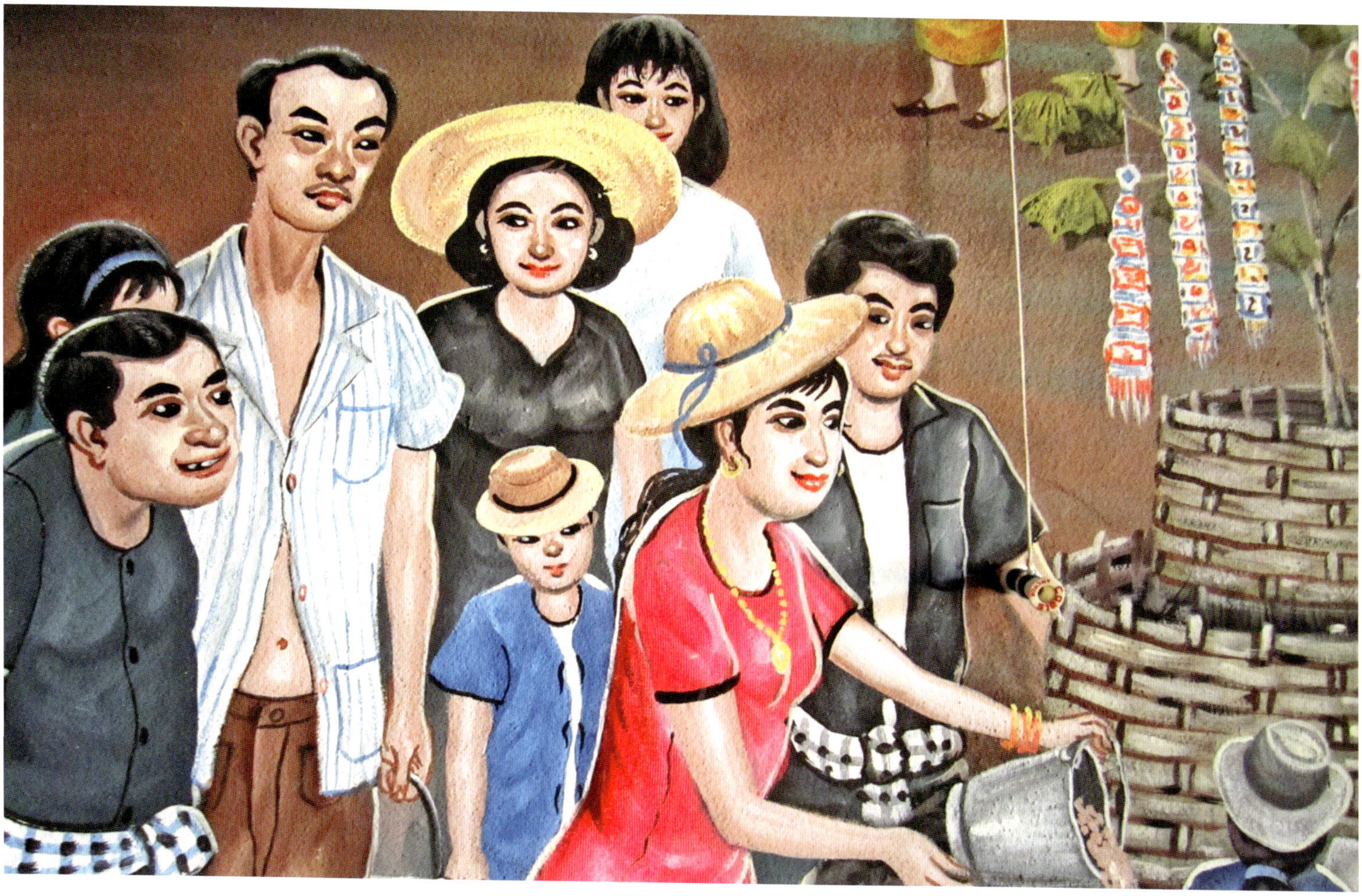

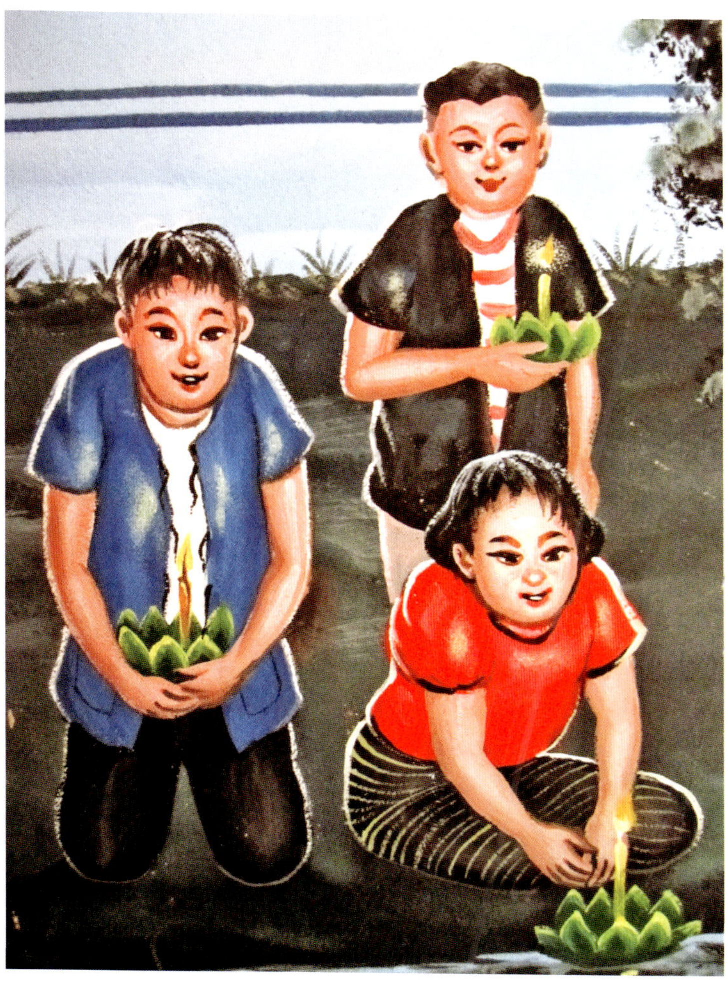

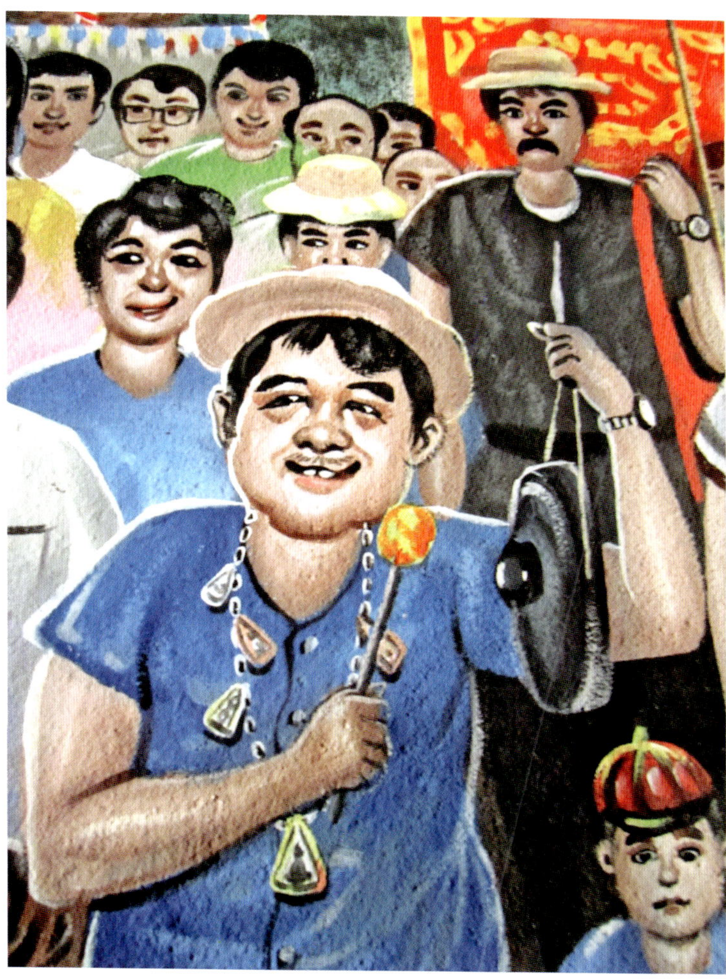

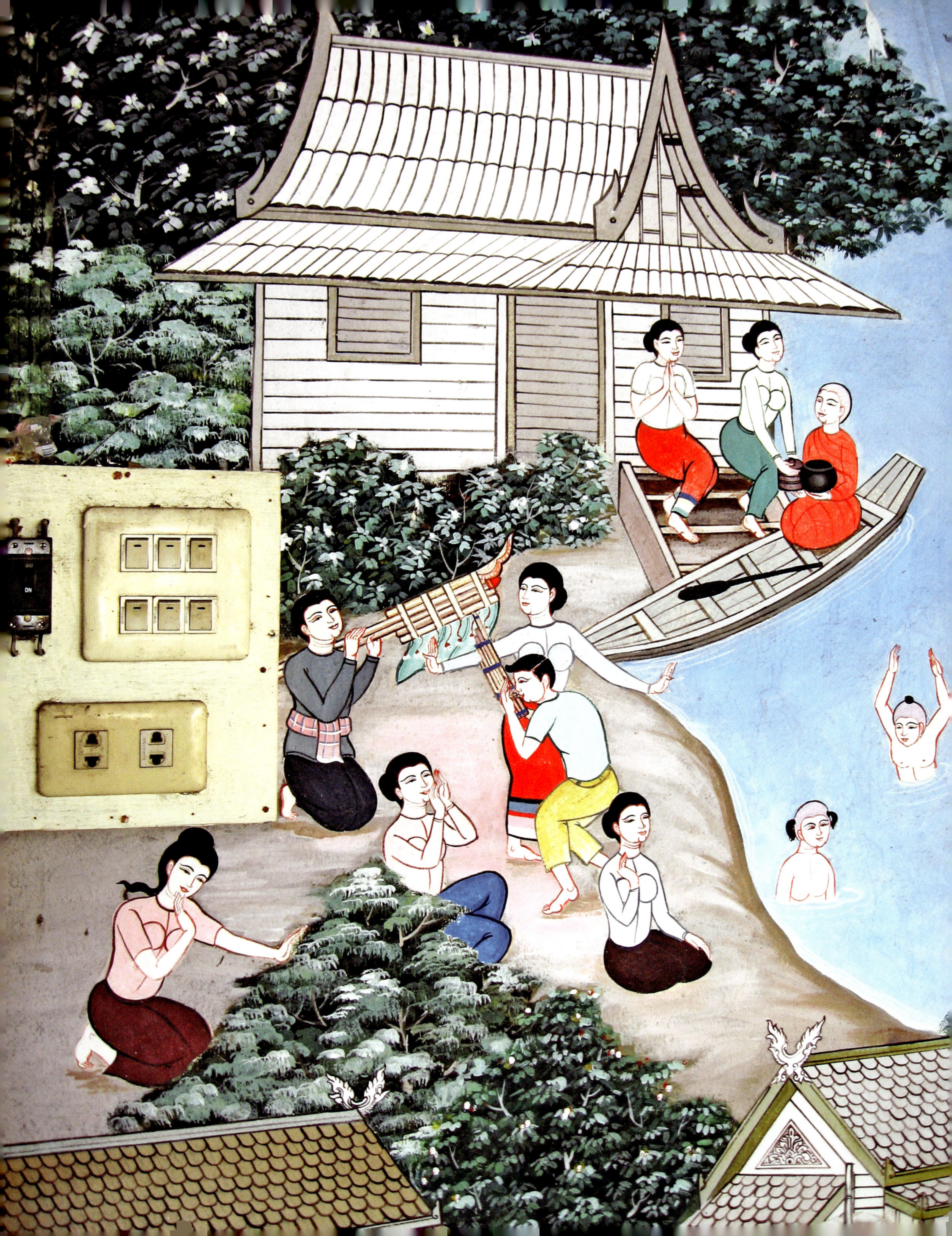

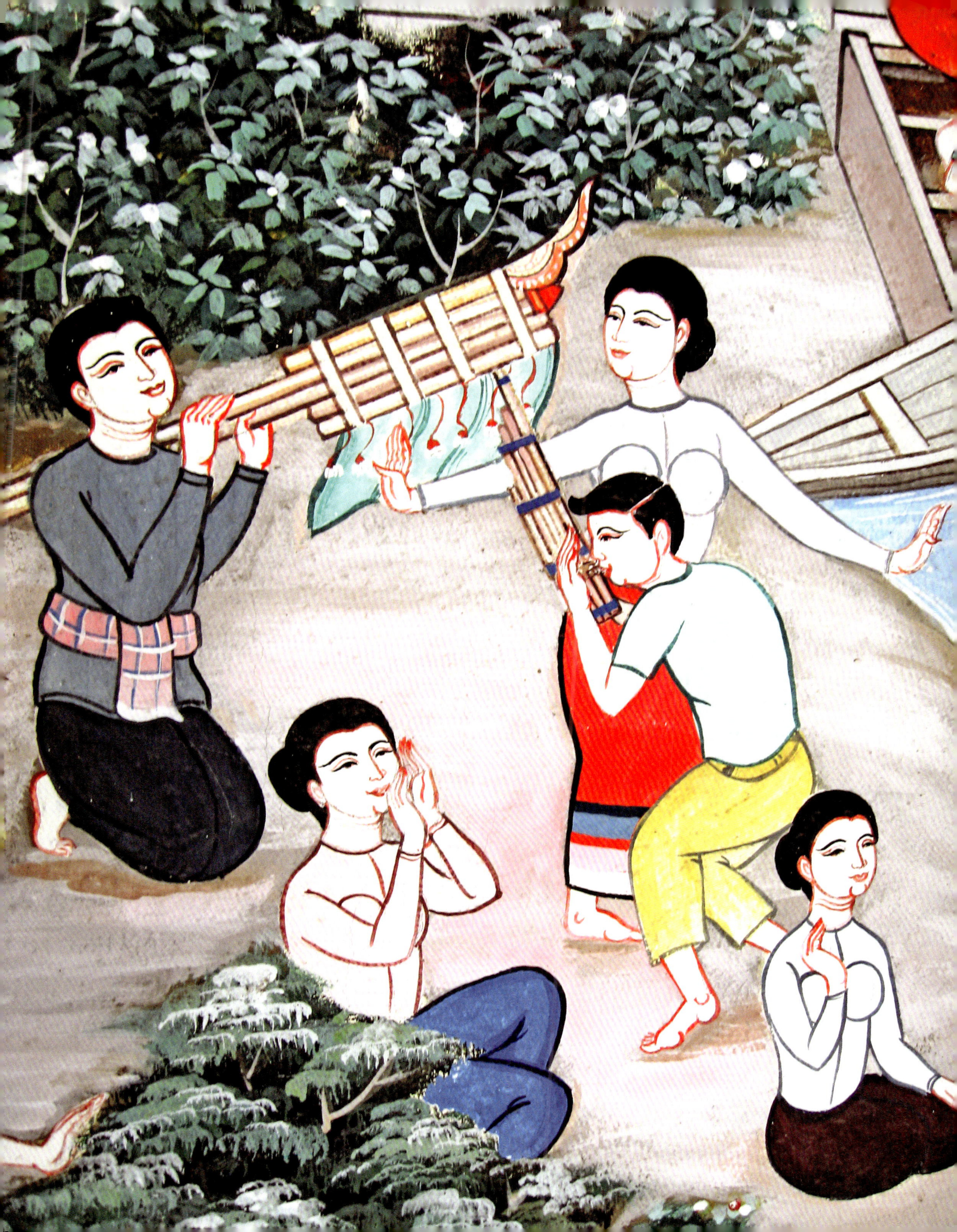

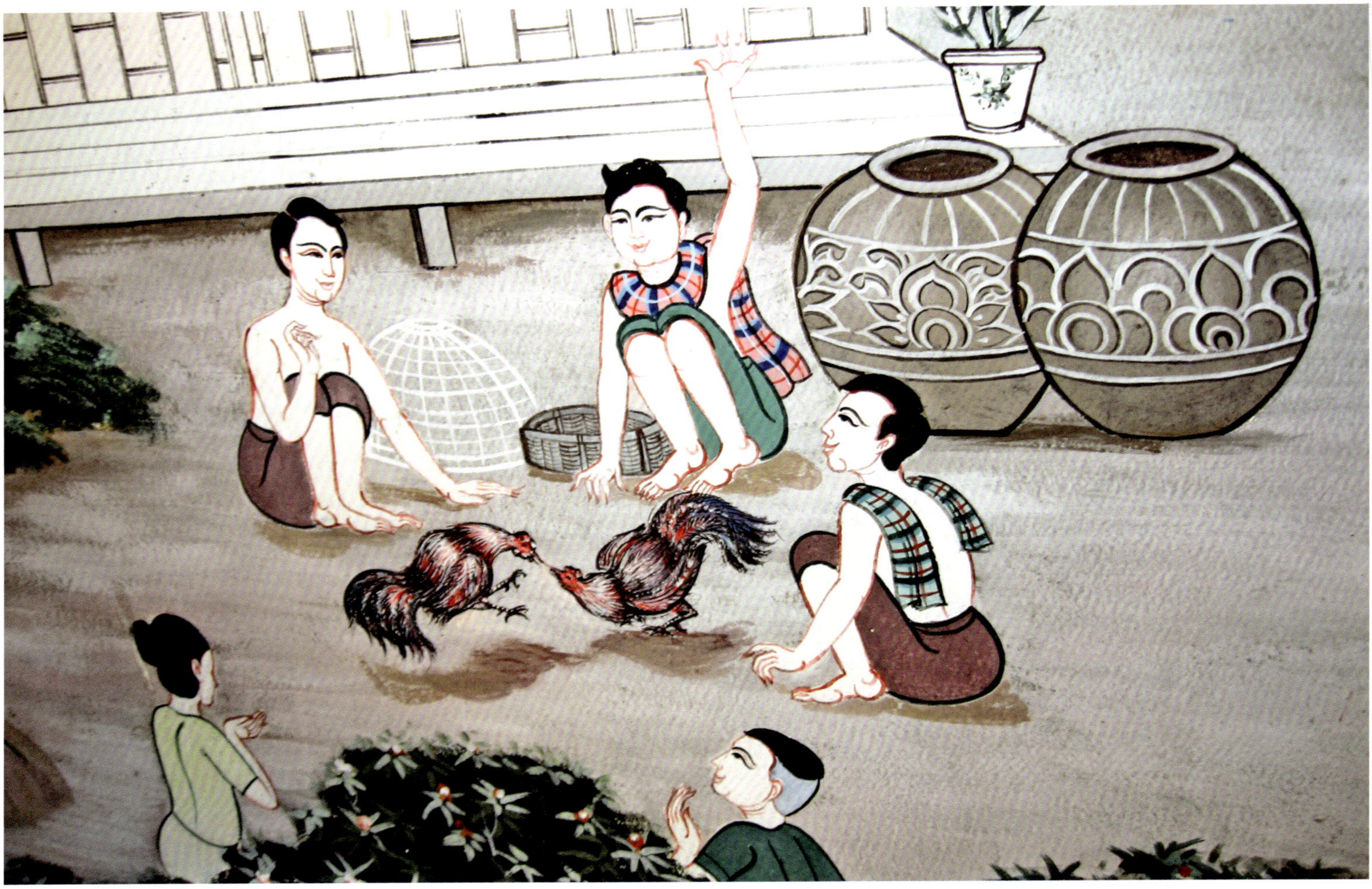

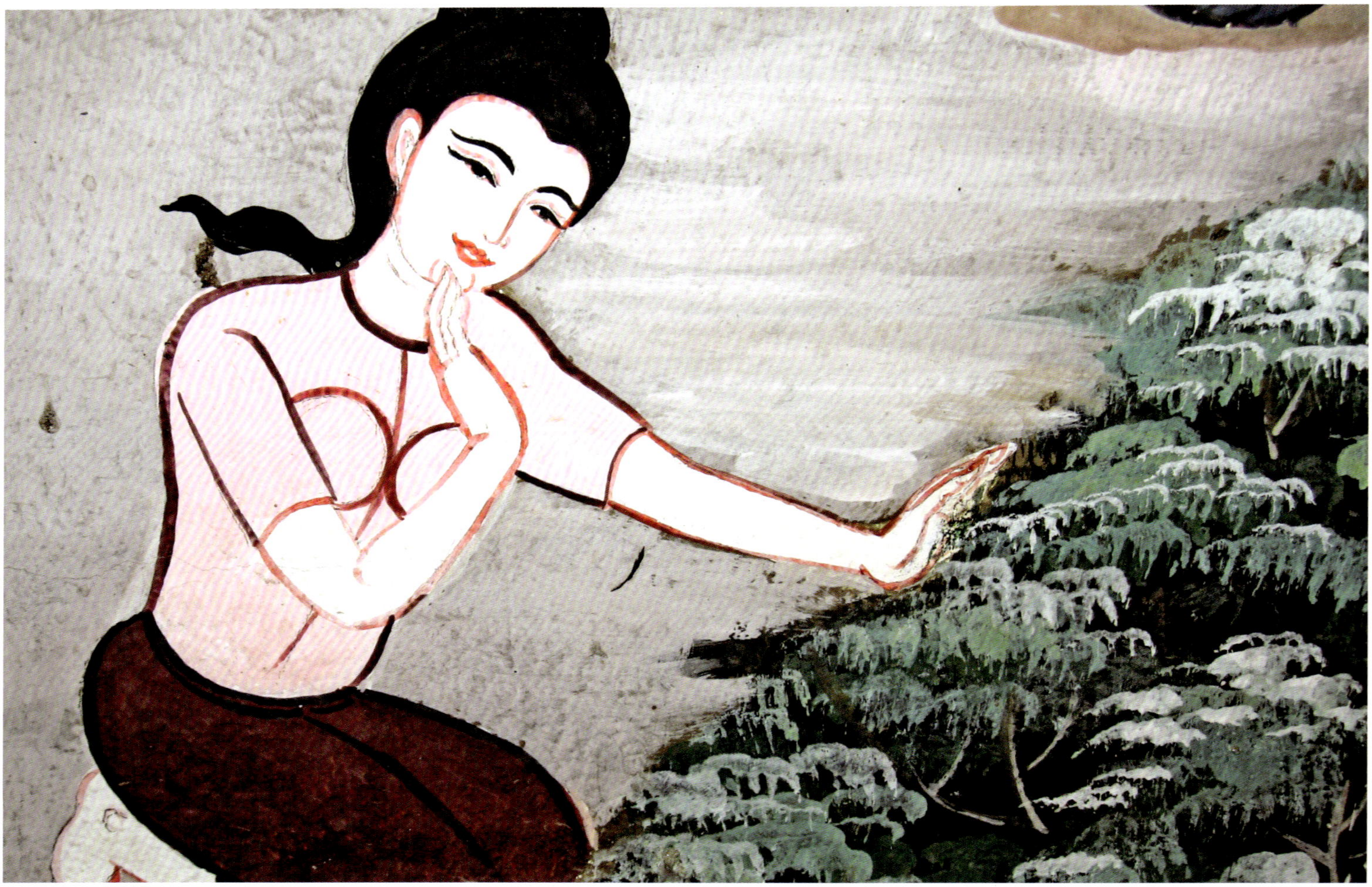

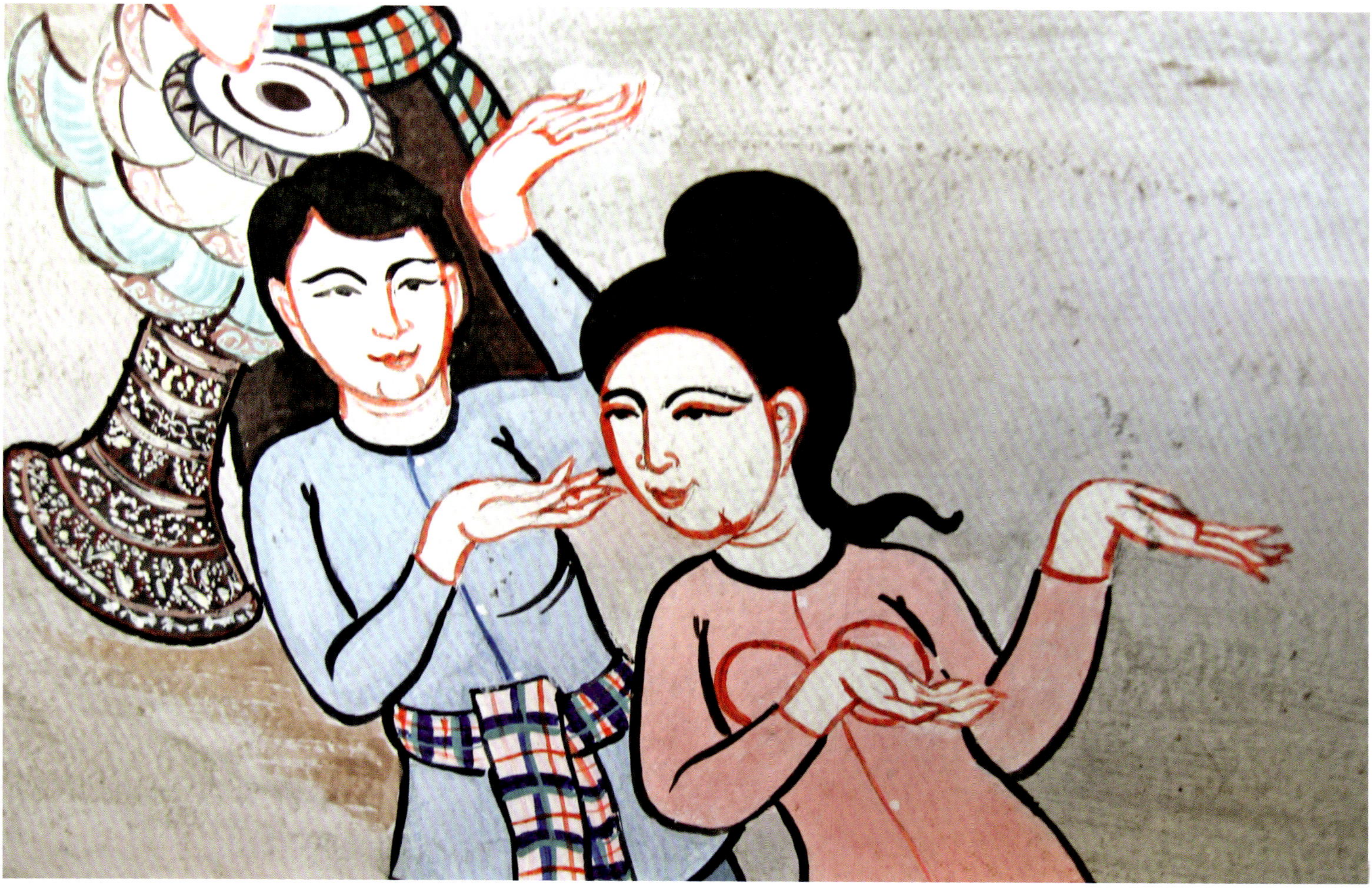

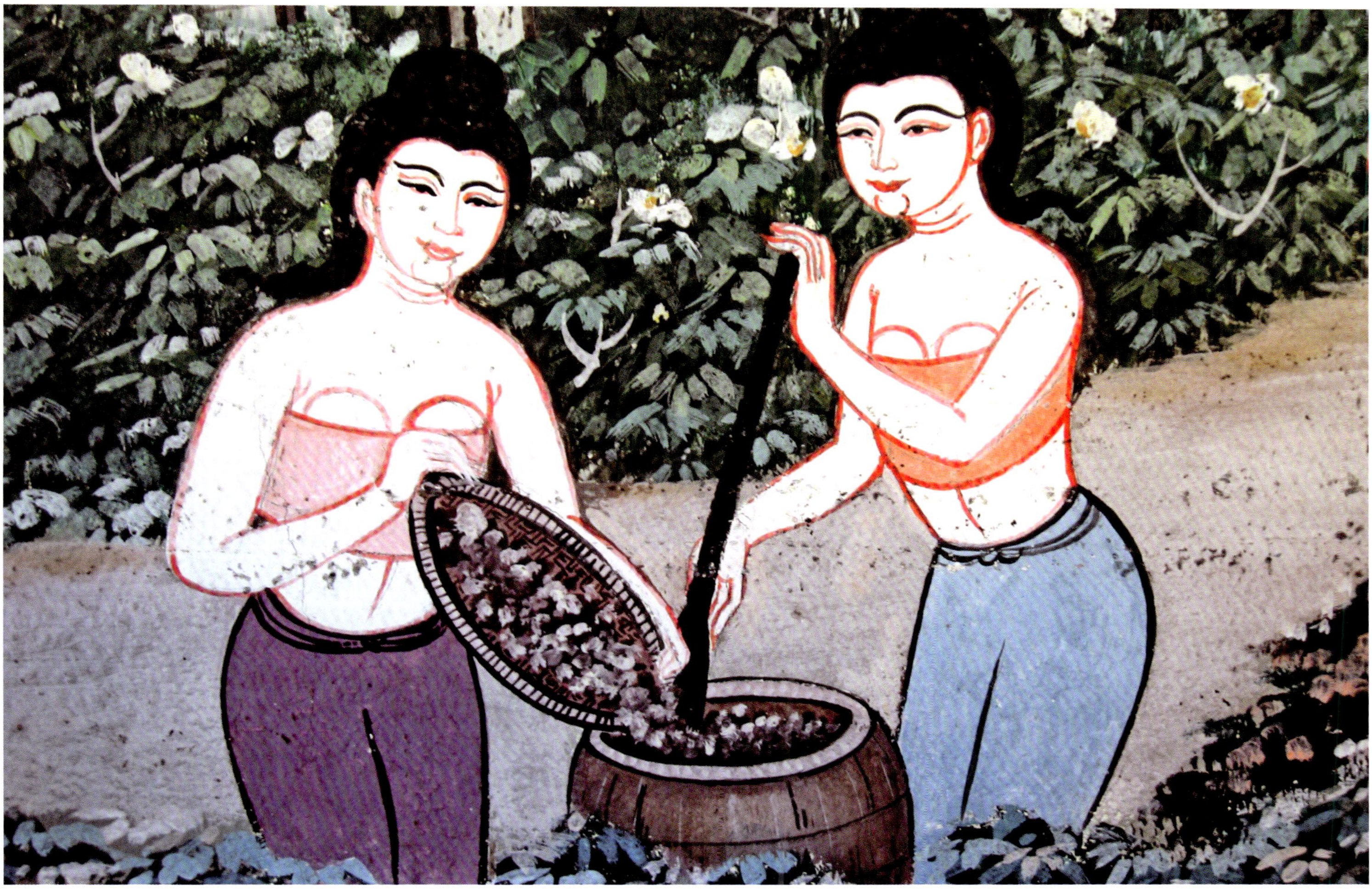

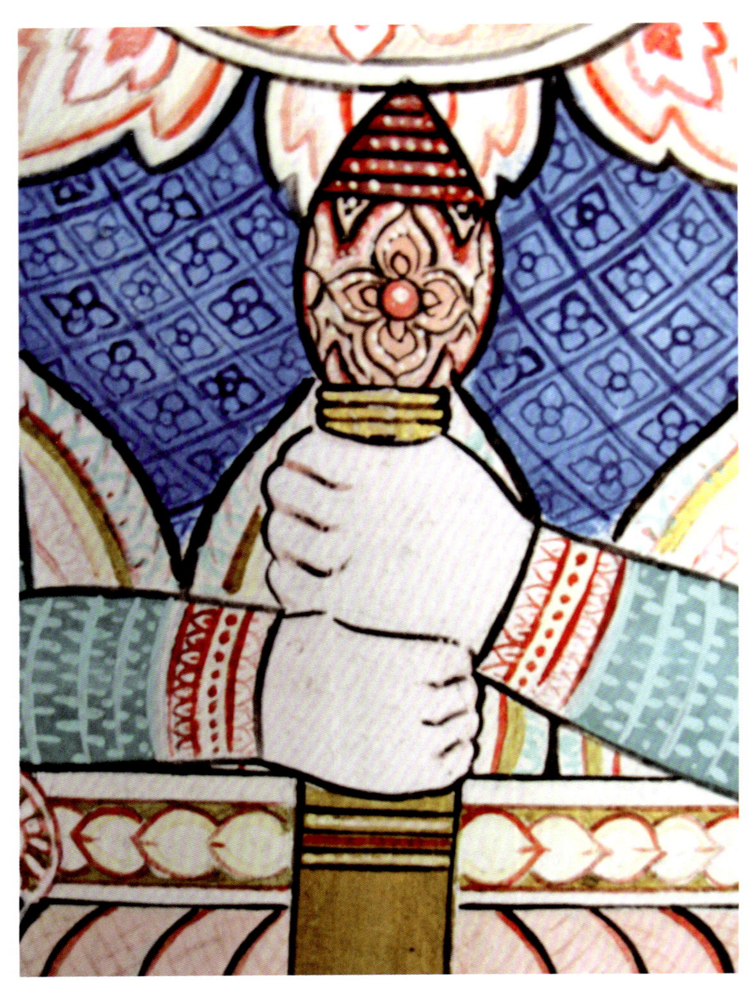

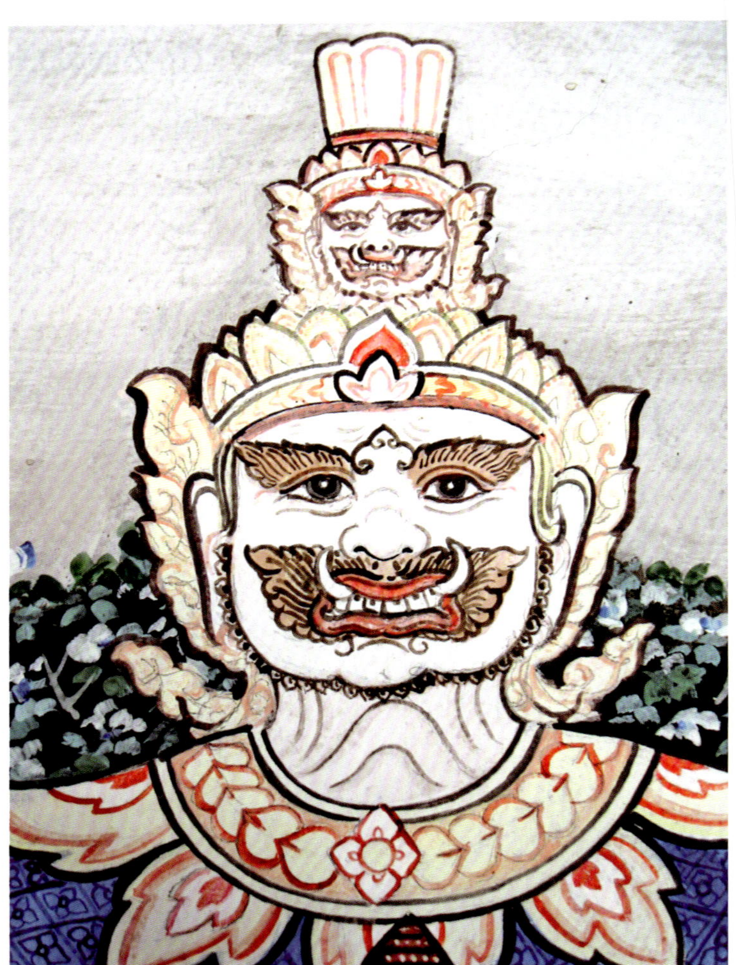

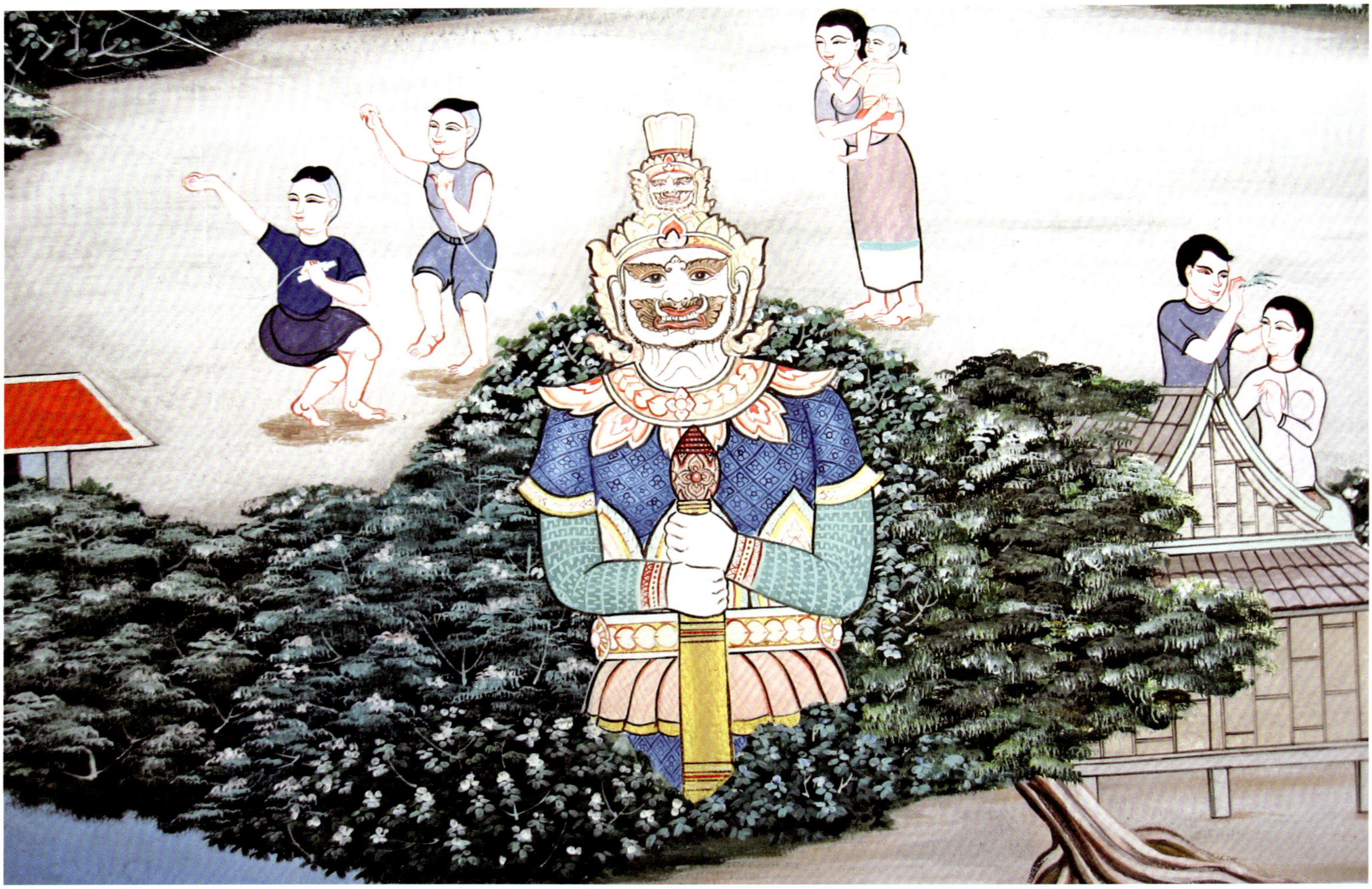

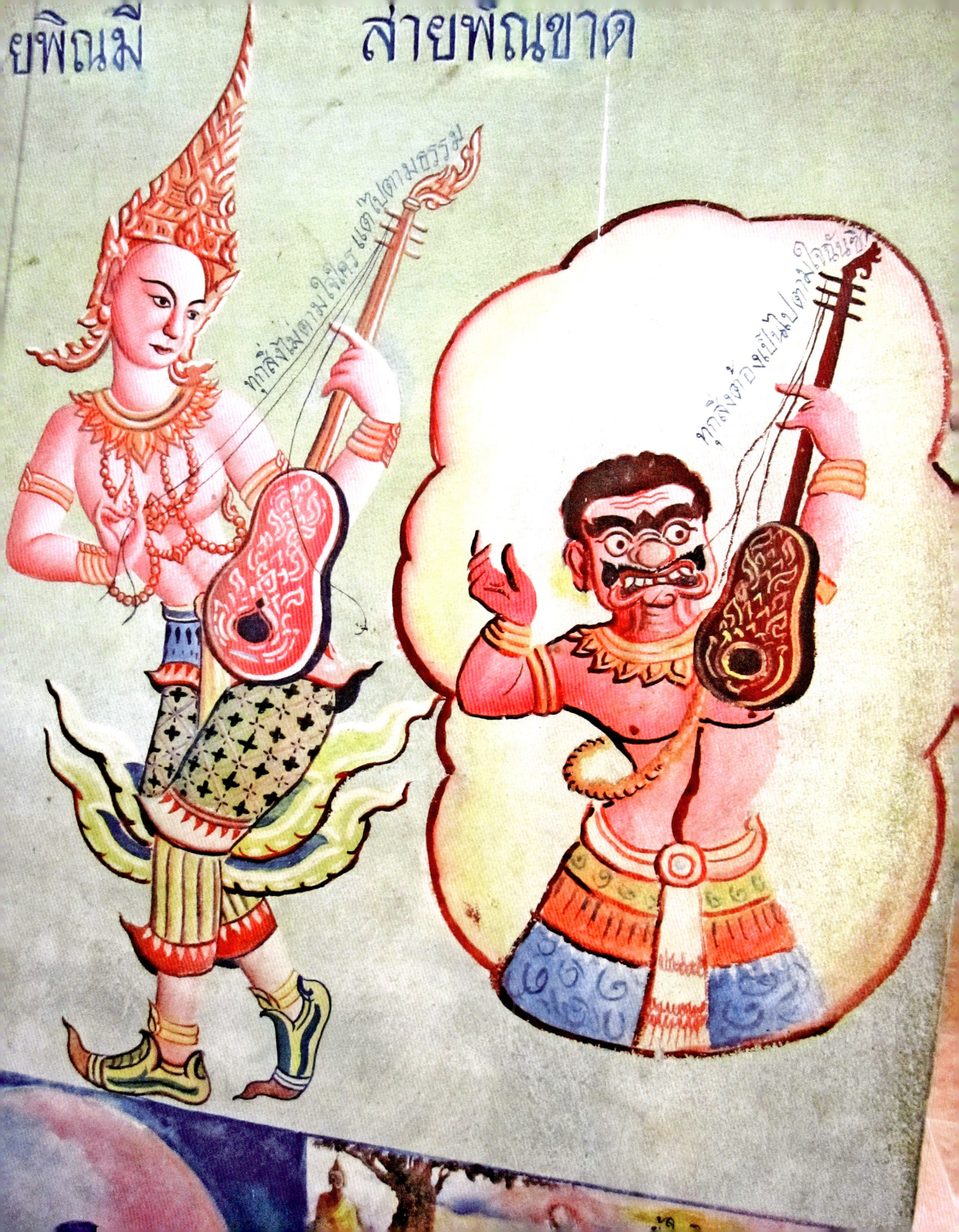

ยพิณมี
สายพิณขาด
ทุกสิ่งไม่ตามใจใคร แต่ไปตามธรรม
ทุกสิ่งต้องเป็นไปตามใจฉันซิ

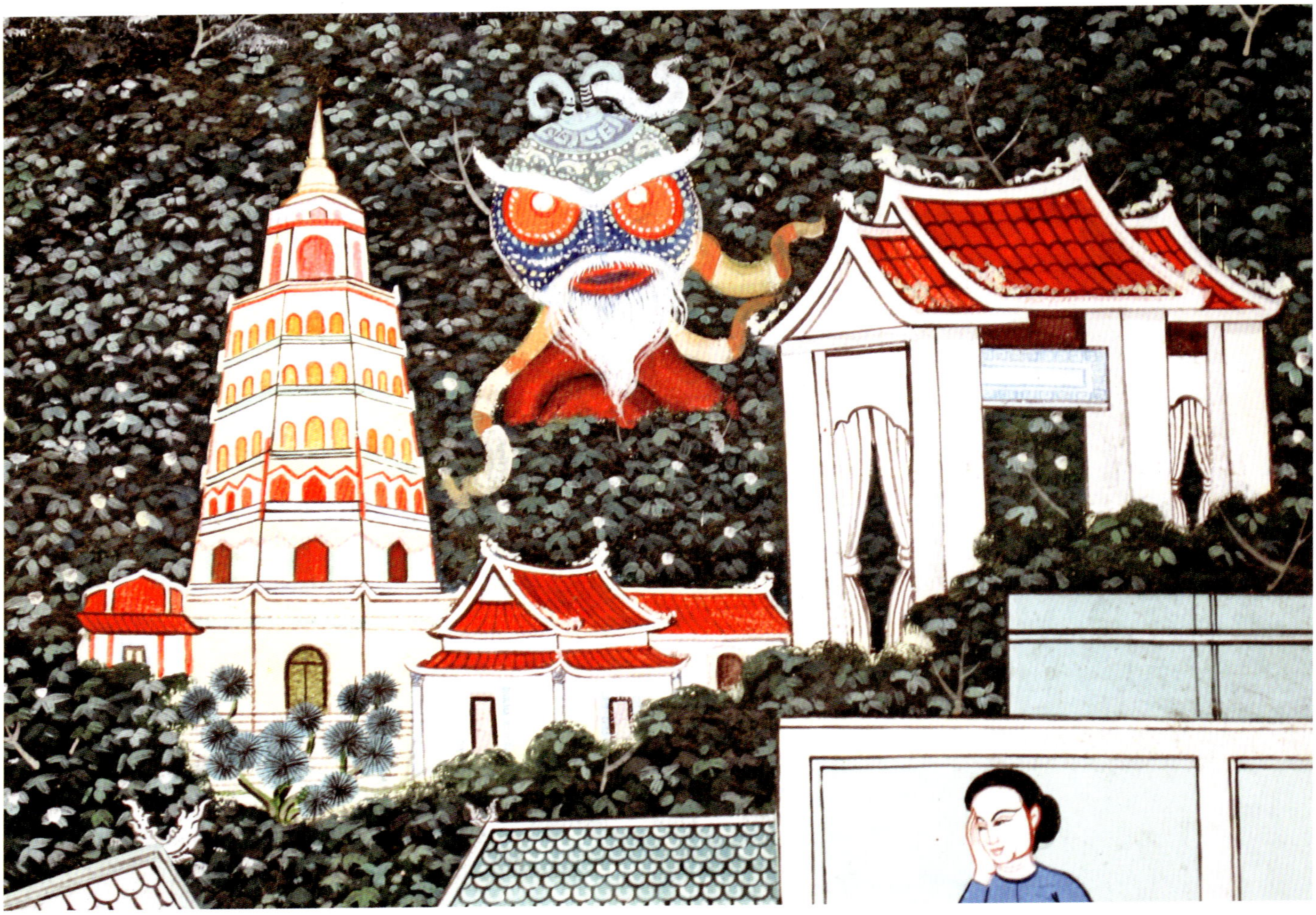

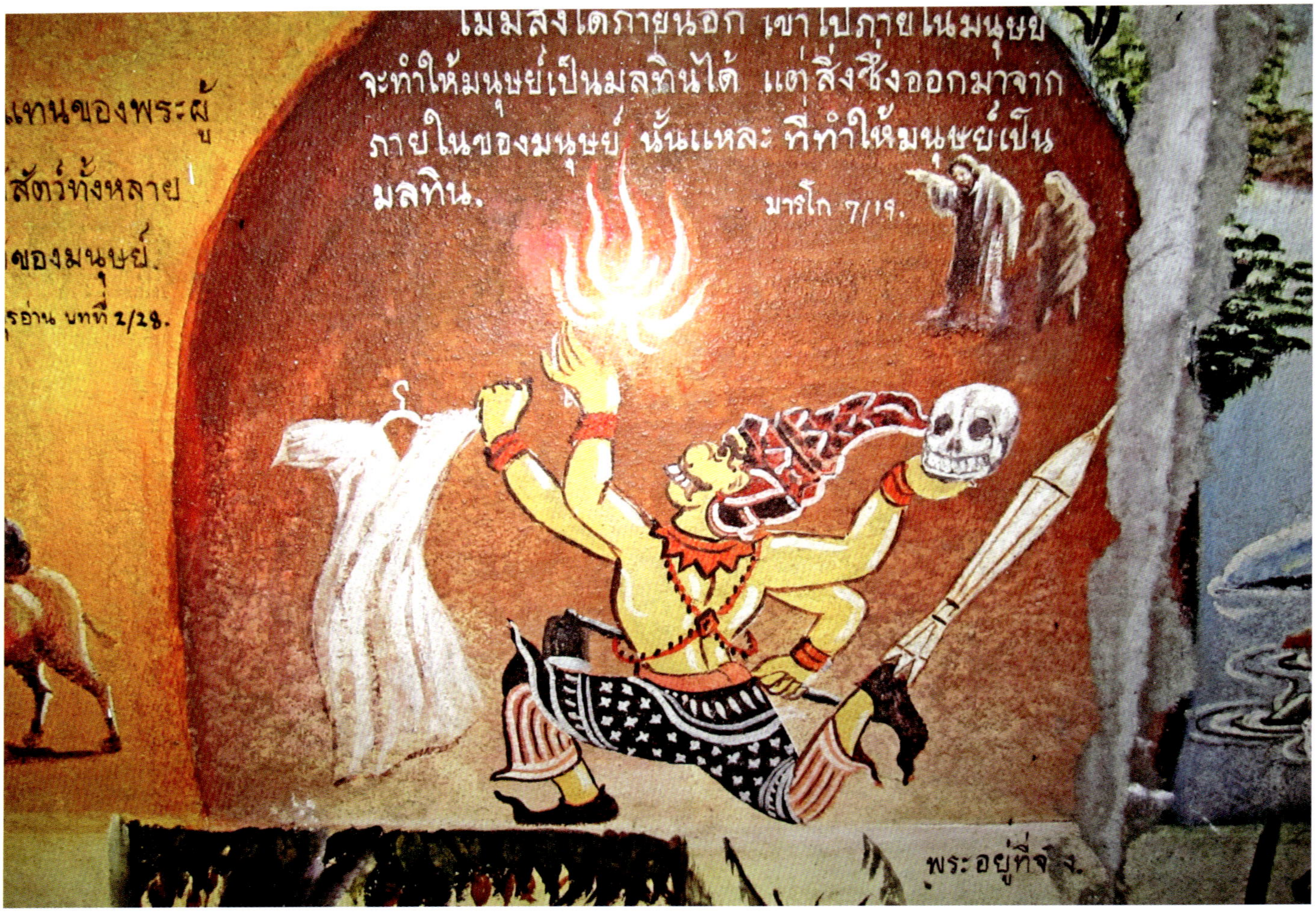

ไม่มีสิ่งใดภายนอก เข้าไปภายในมนุษย์
จะทำให้มนุษย์เป็นมลทินได้ แต่สิ่งซึ่งออกมาจาก
ภายในของมนุษย์ นั้นแหละ ที่ทำให้มนุษย์เป็น
มลทิน.
มาระโก 7/15.

แทนของพระผู้
สัตว์ทั้งหลาย
ของมนุษย์.
รอ่าน บทที่ 2/28.

พระอยู่ที่จ

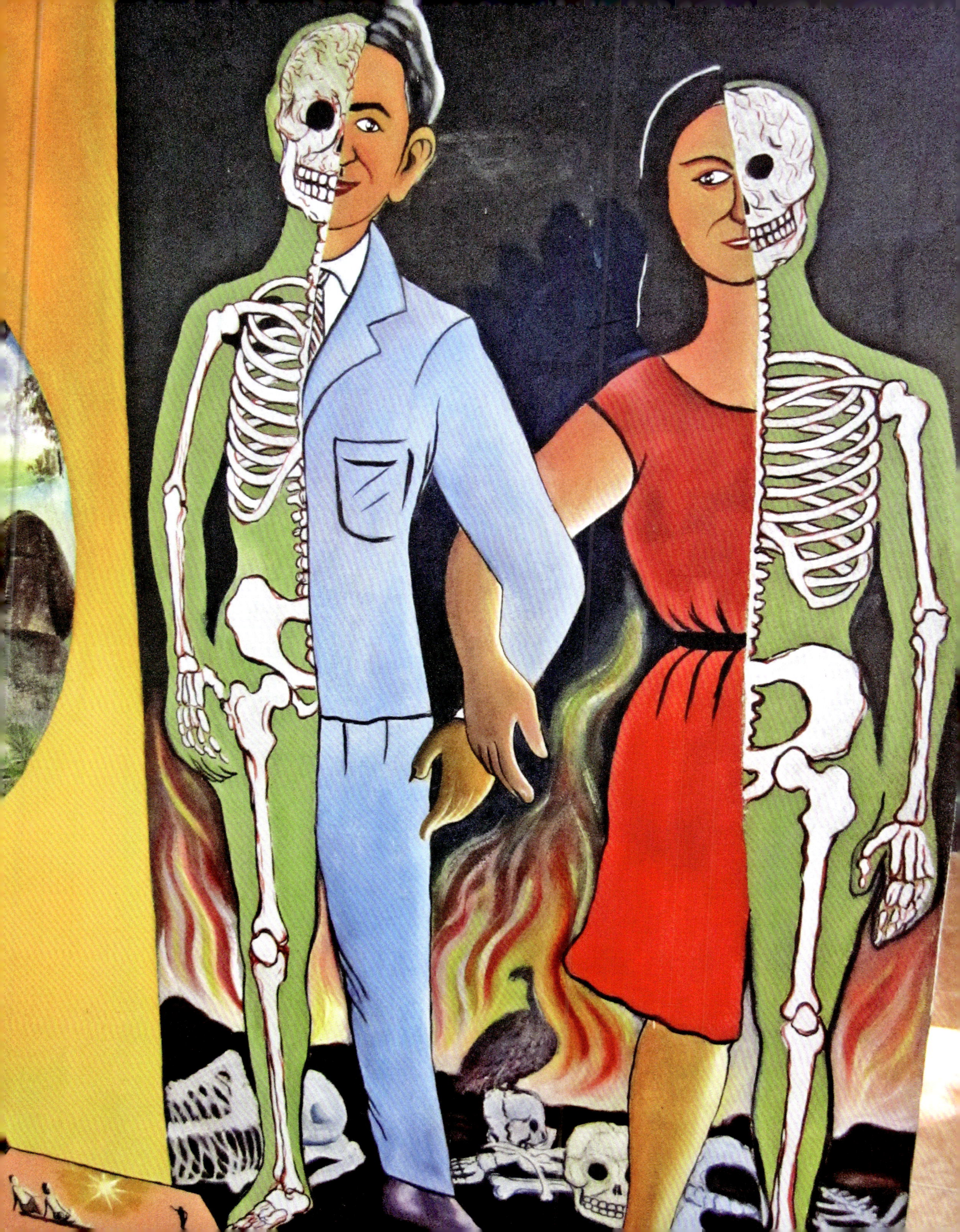

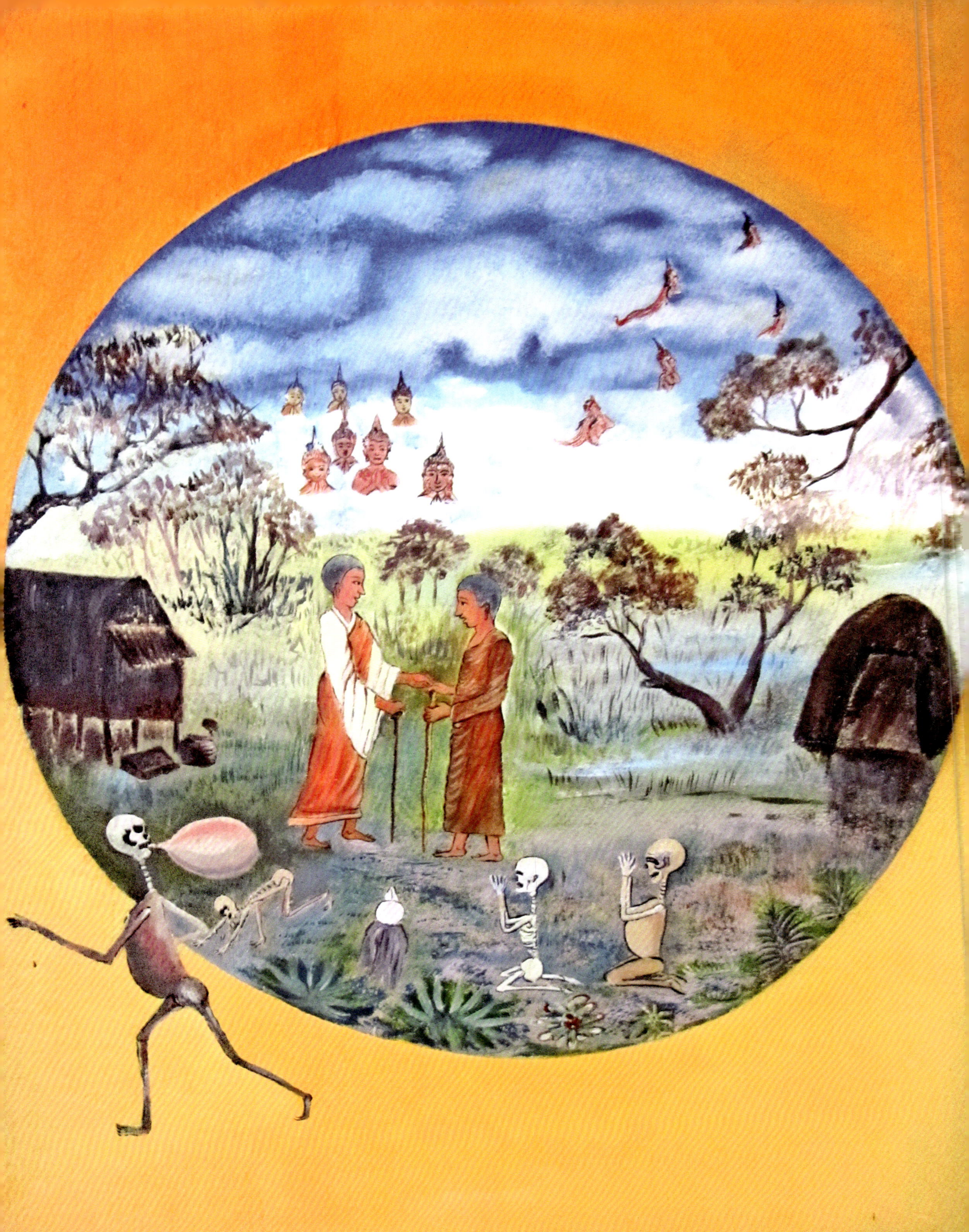

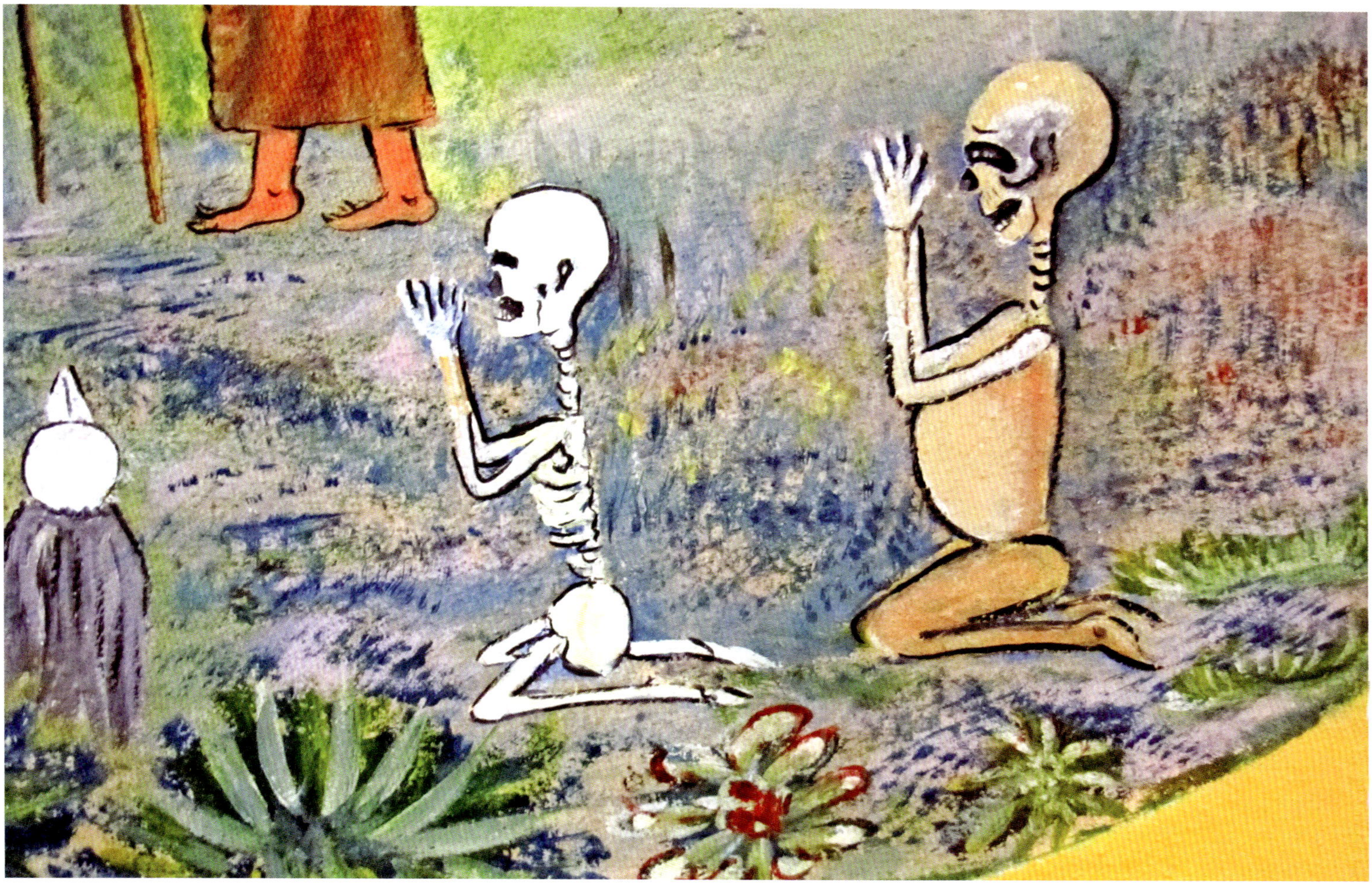

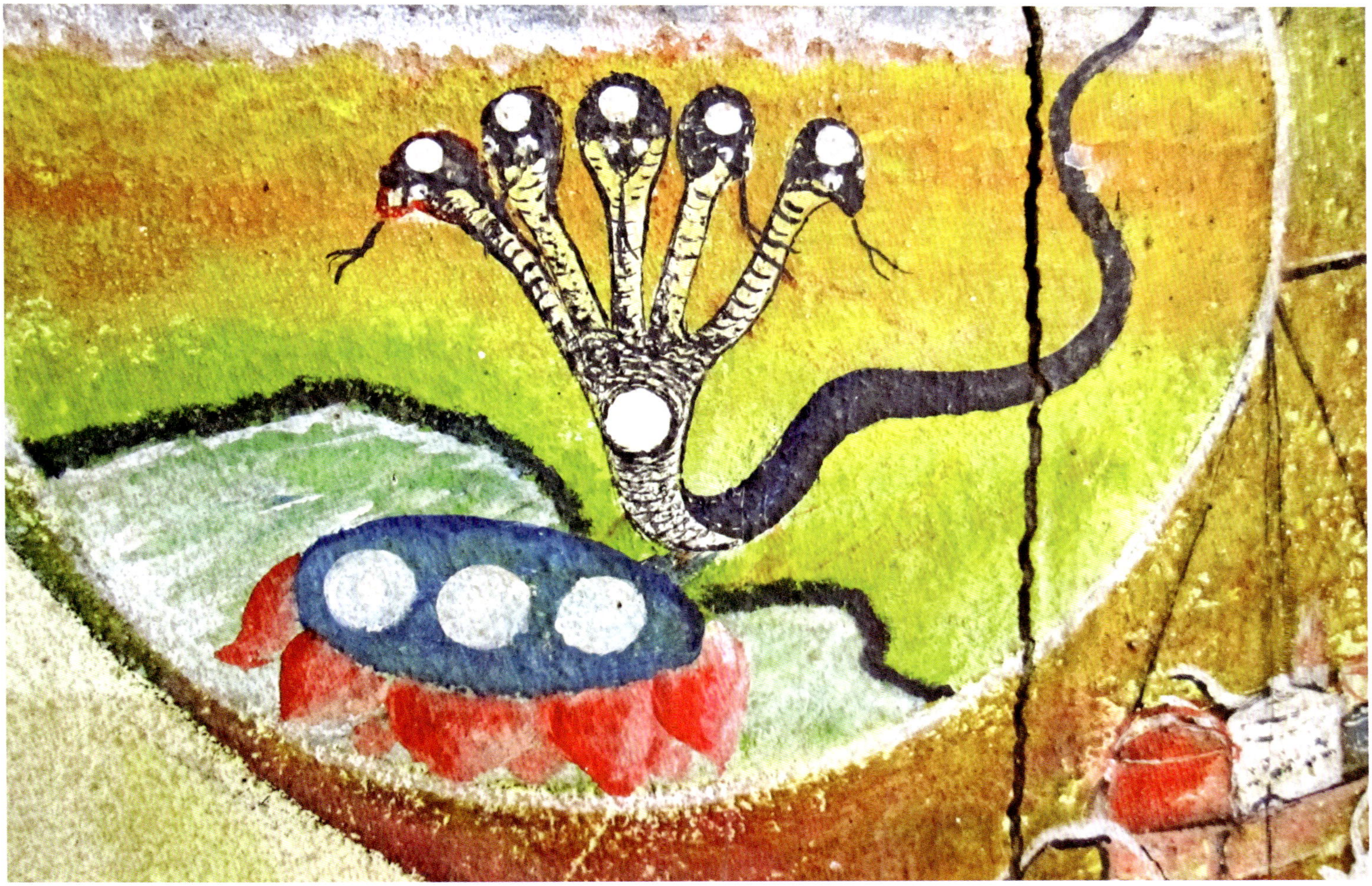

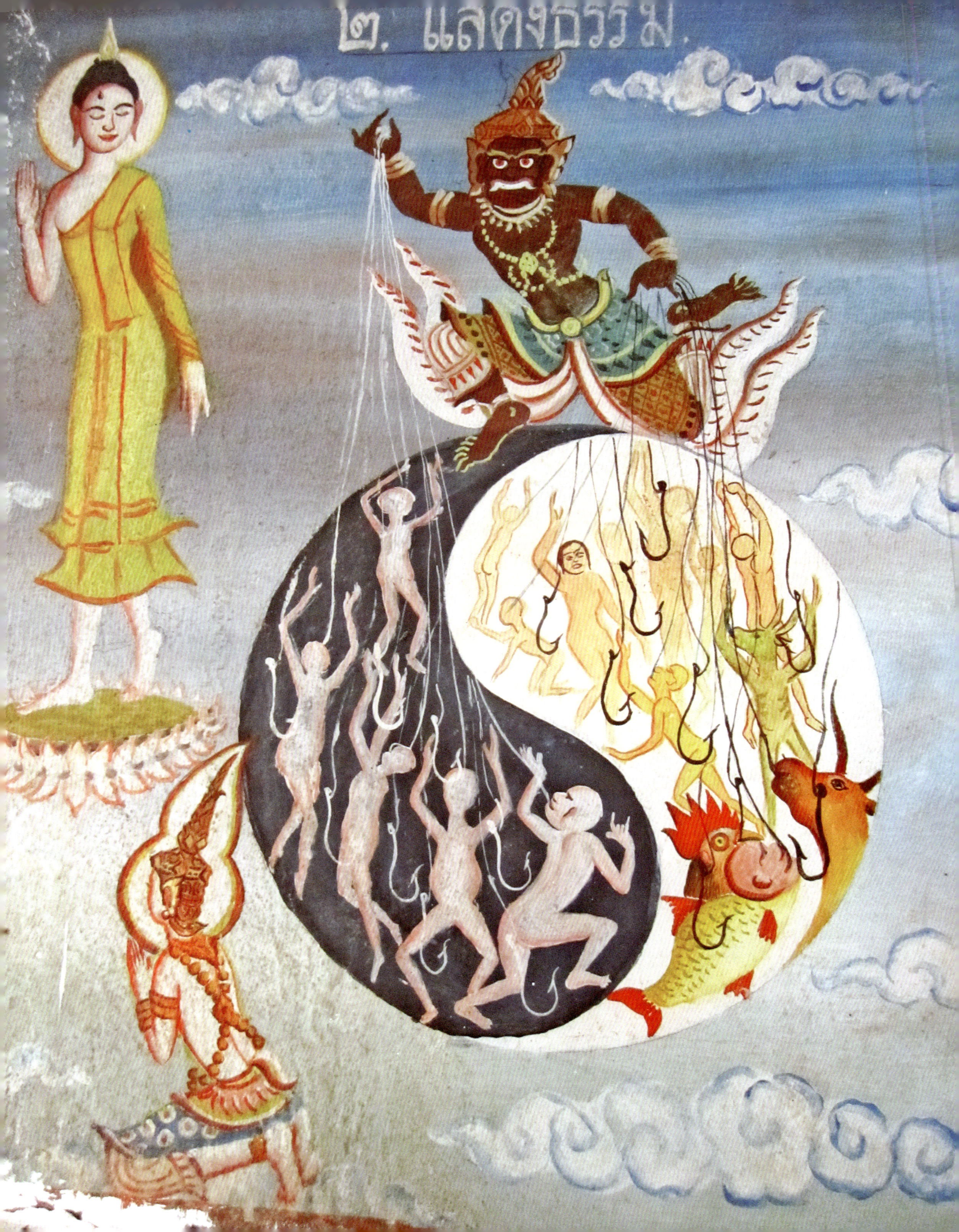
๒. แสดงธรรม

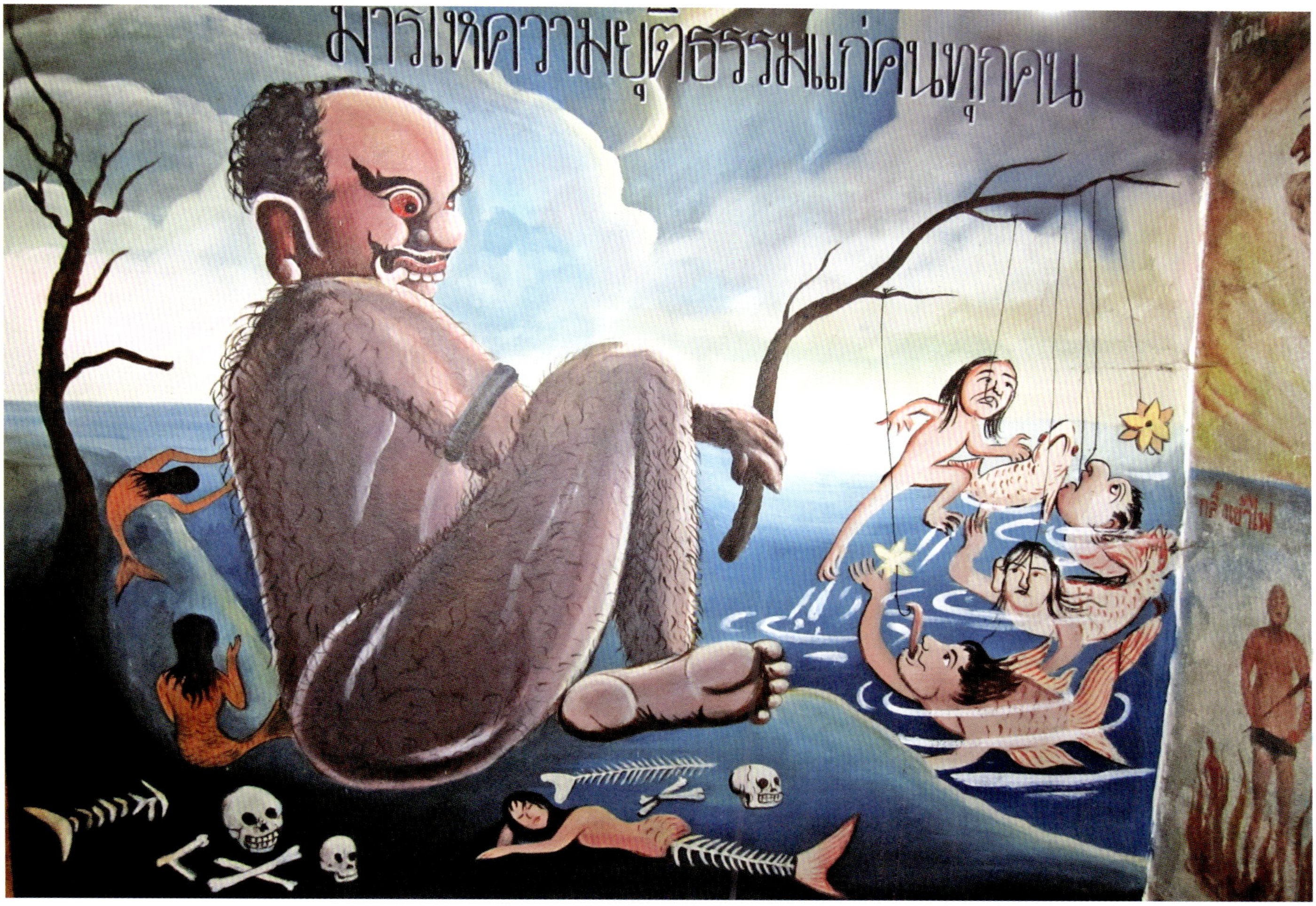

มารใหความยุติธรรมแก่คนทุกคน

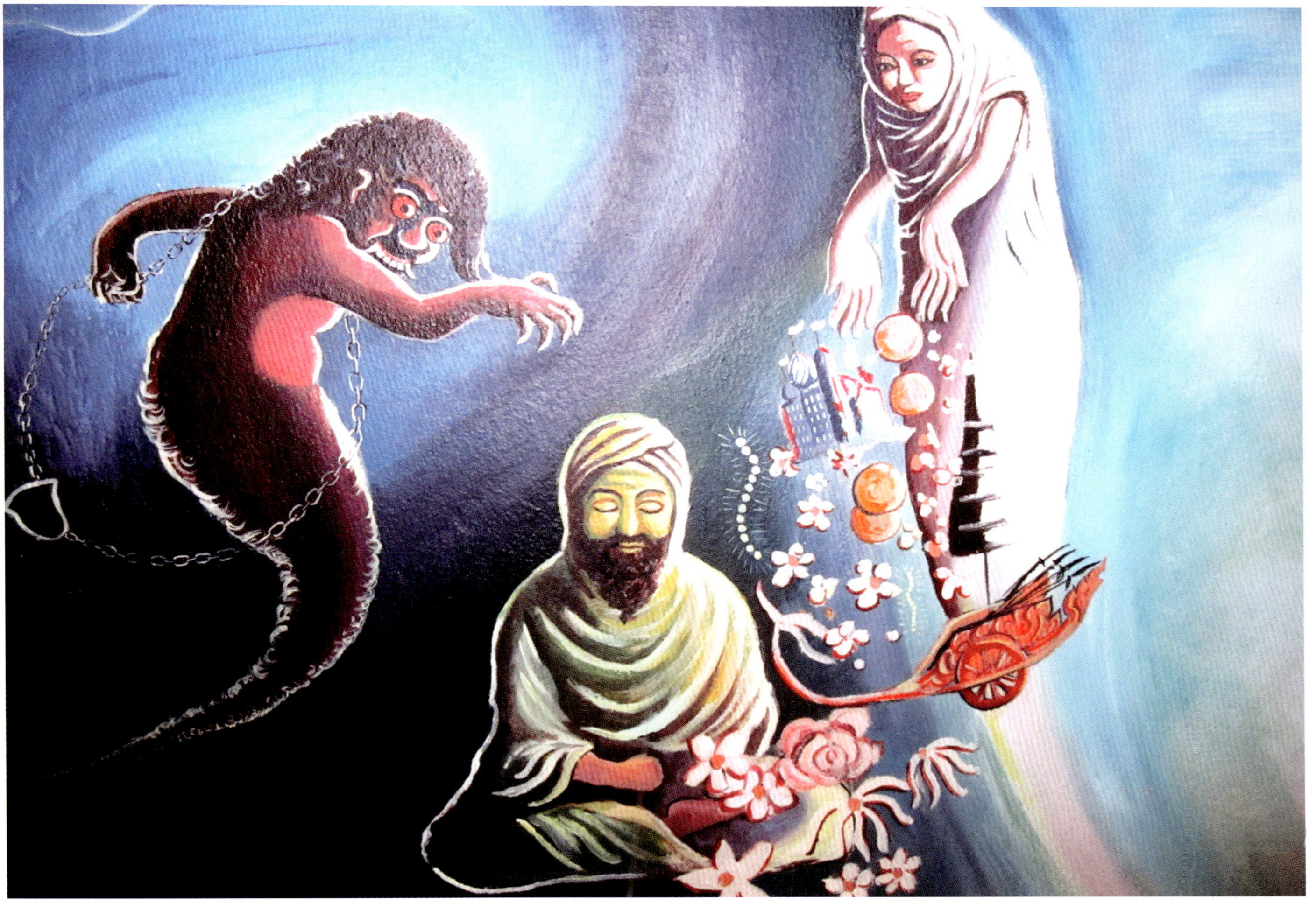

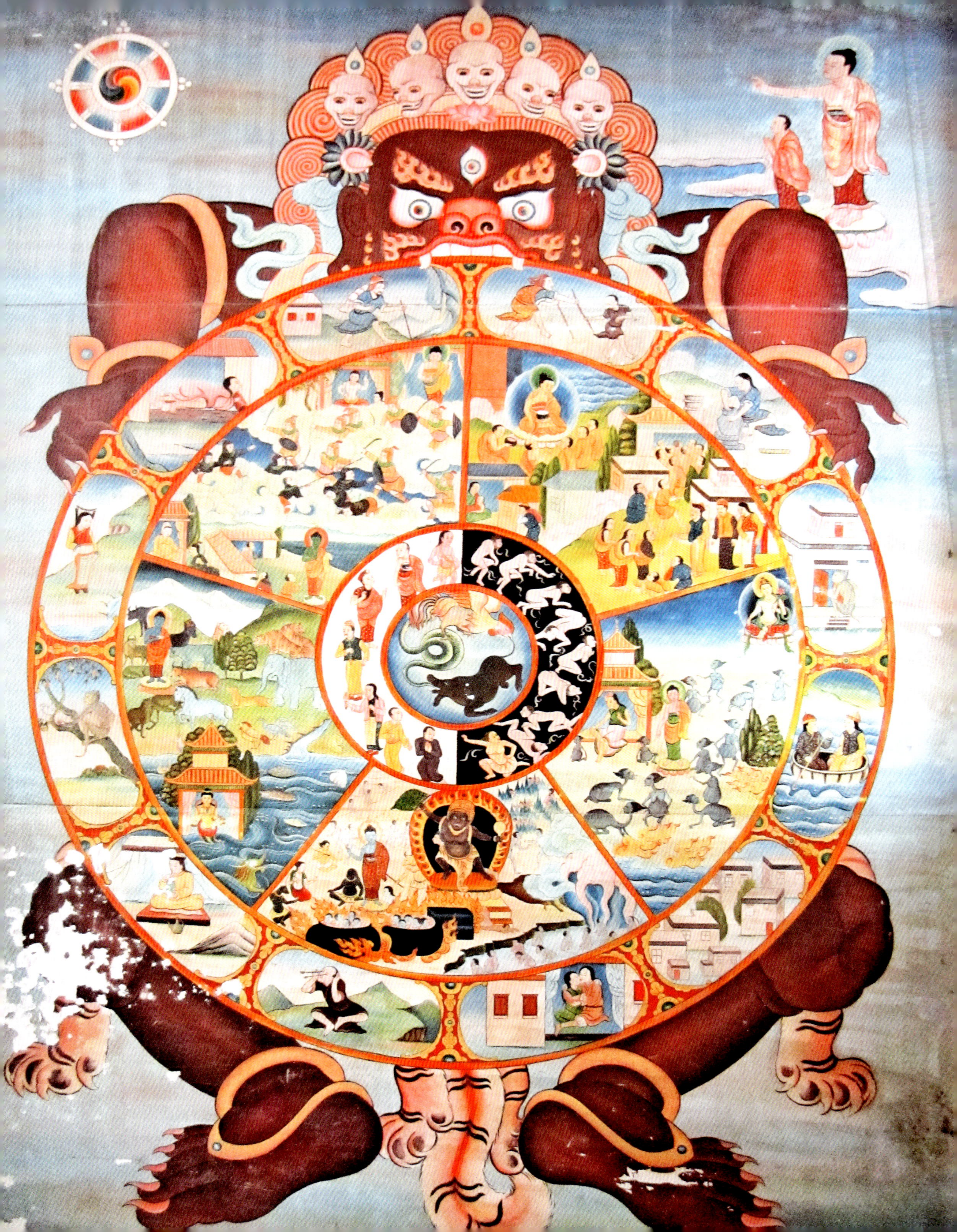

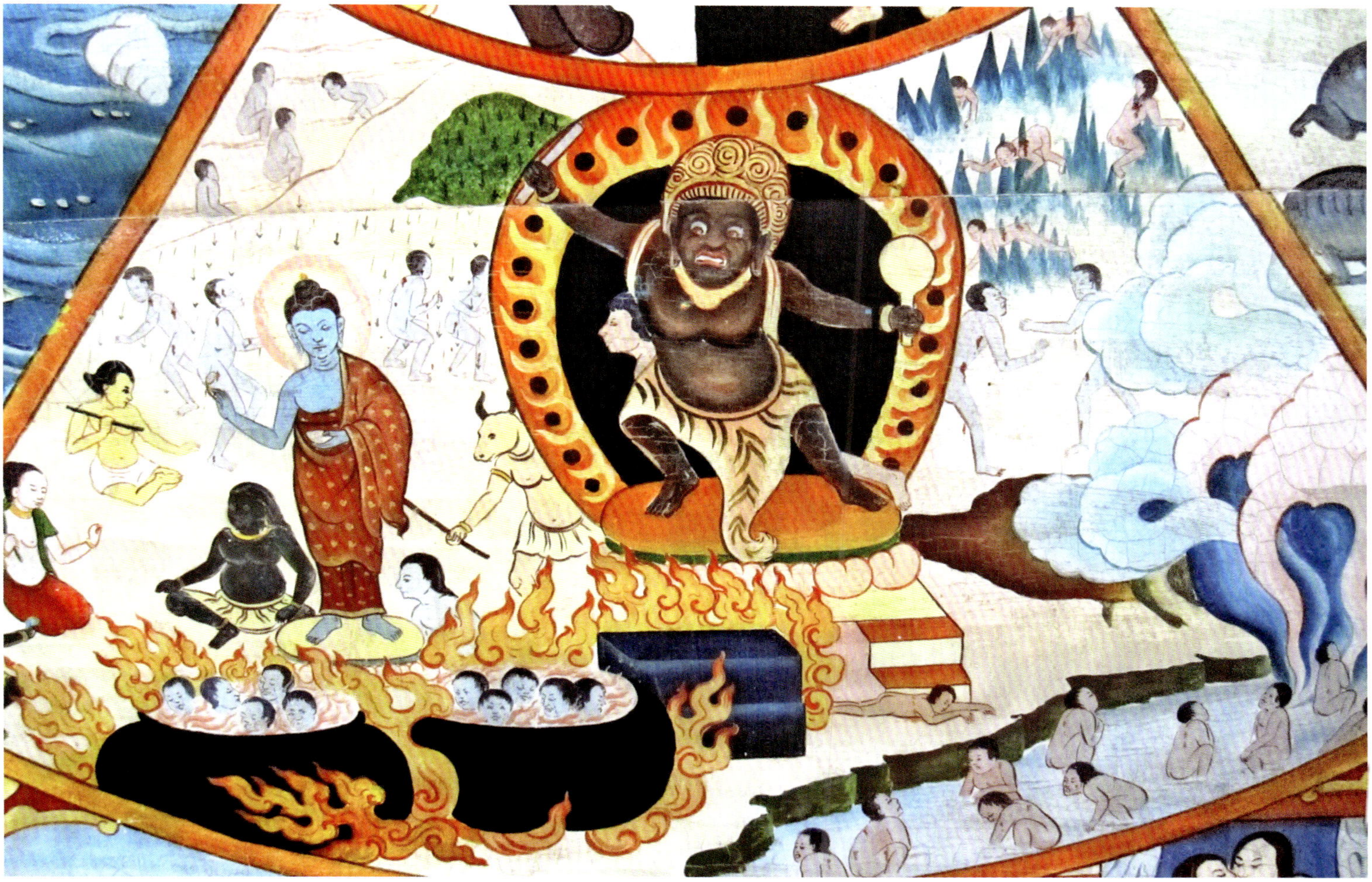

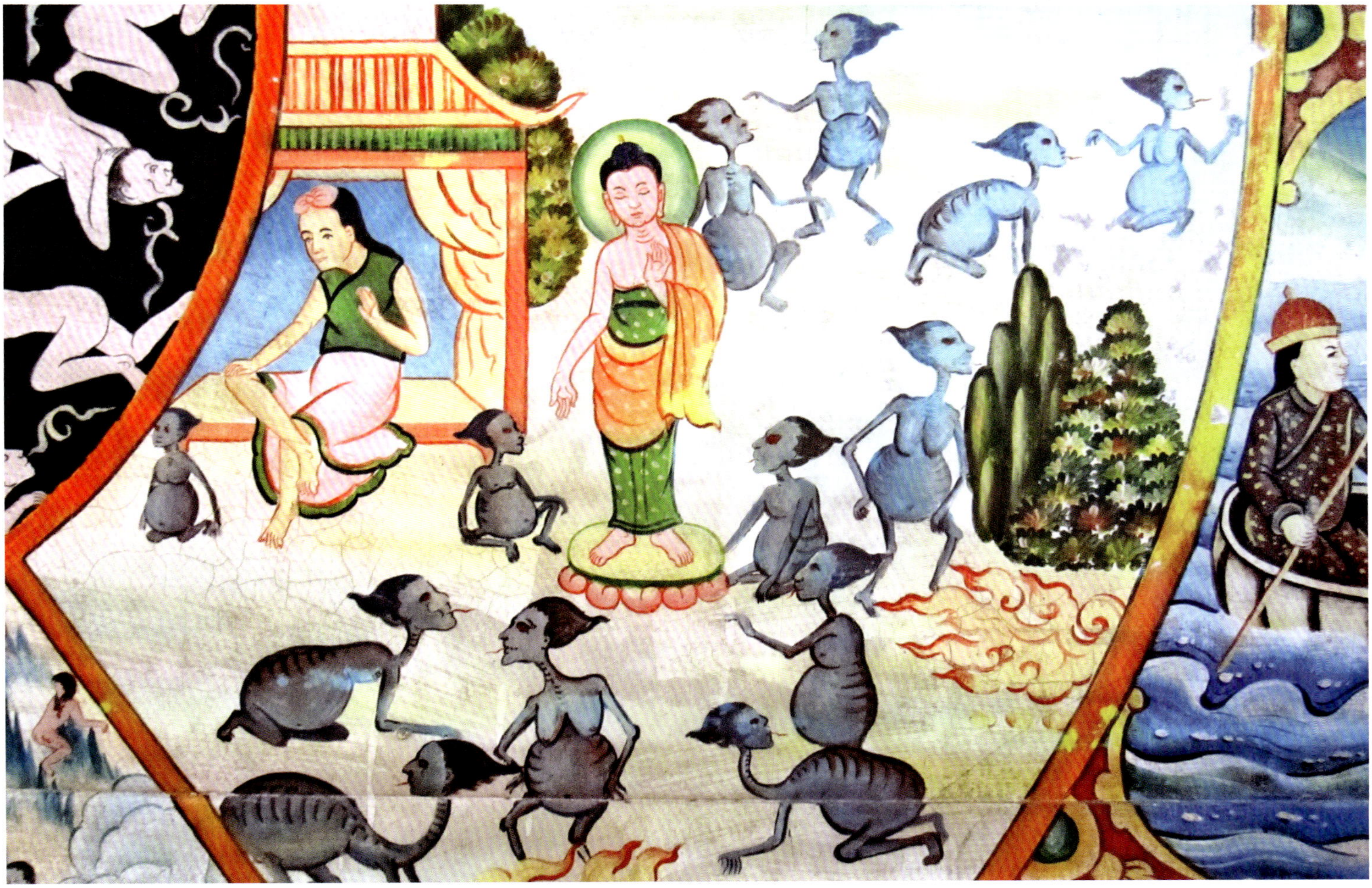

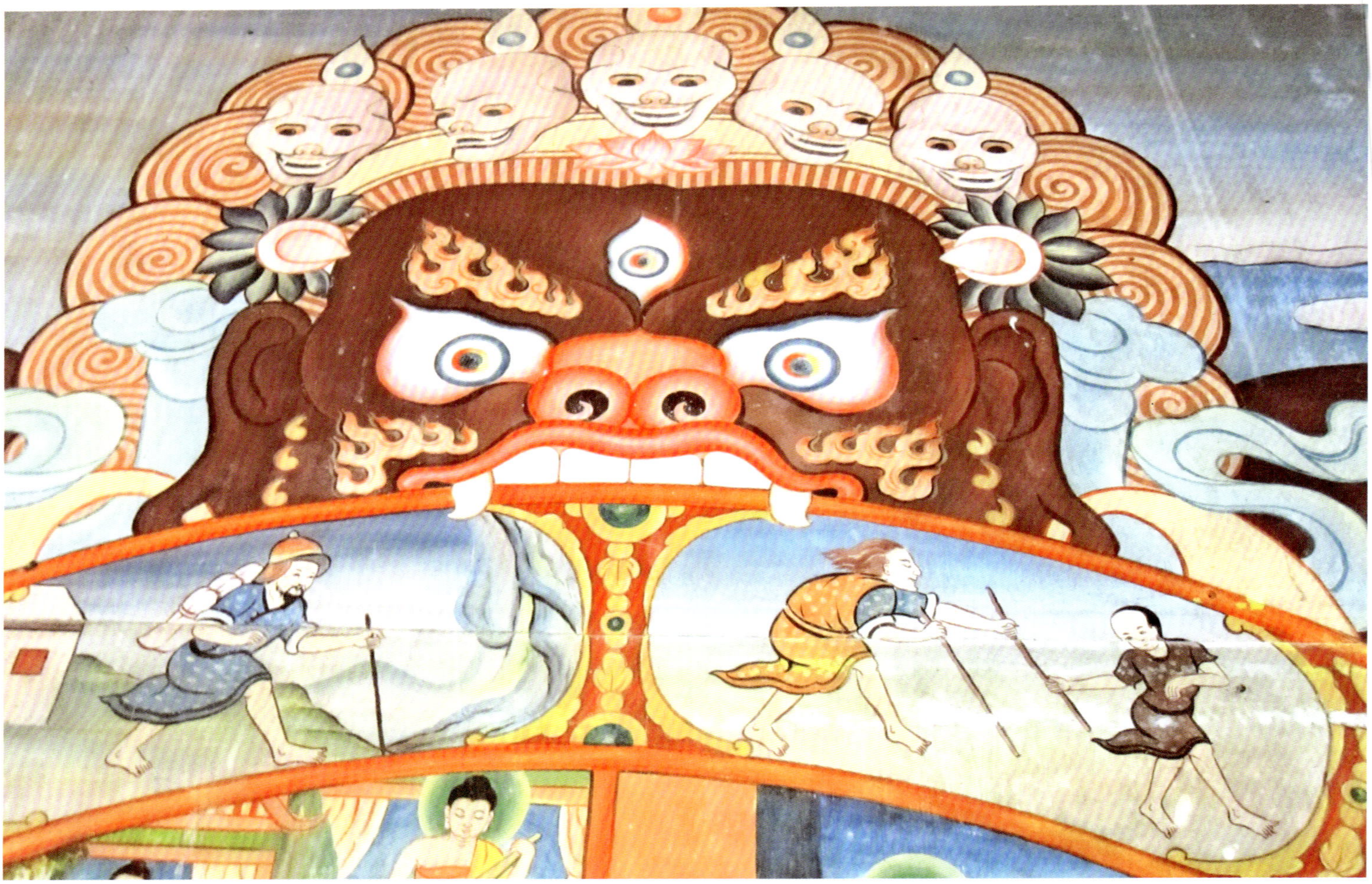

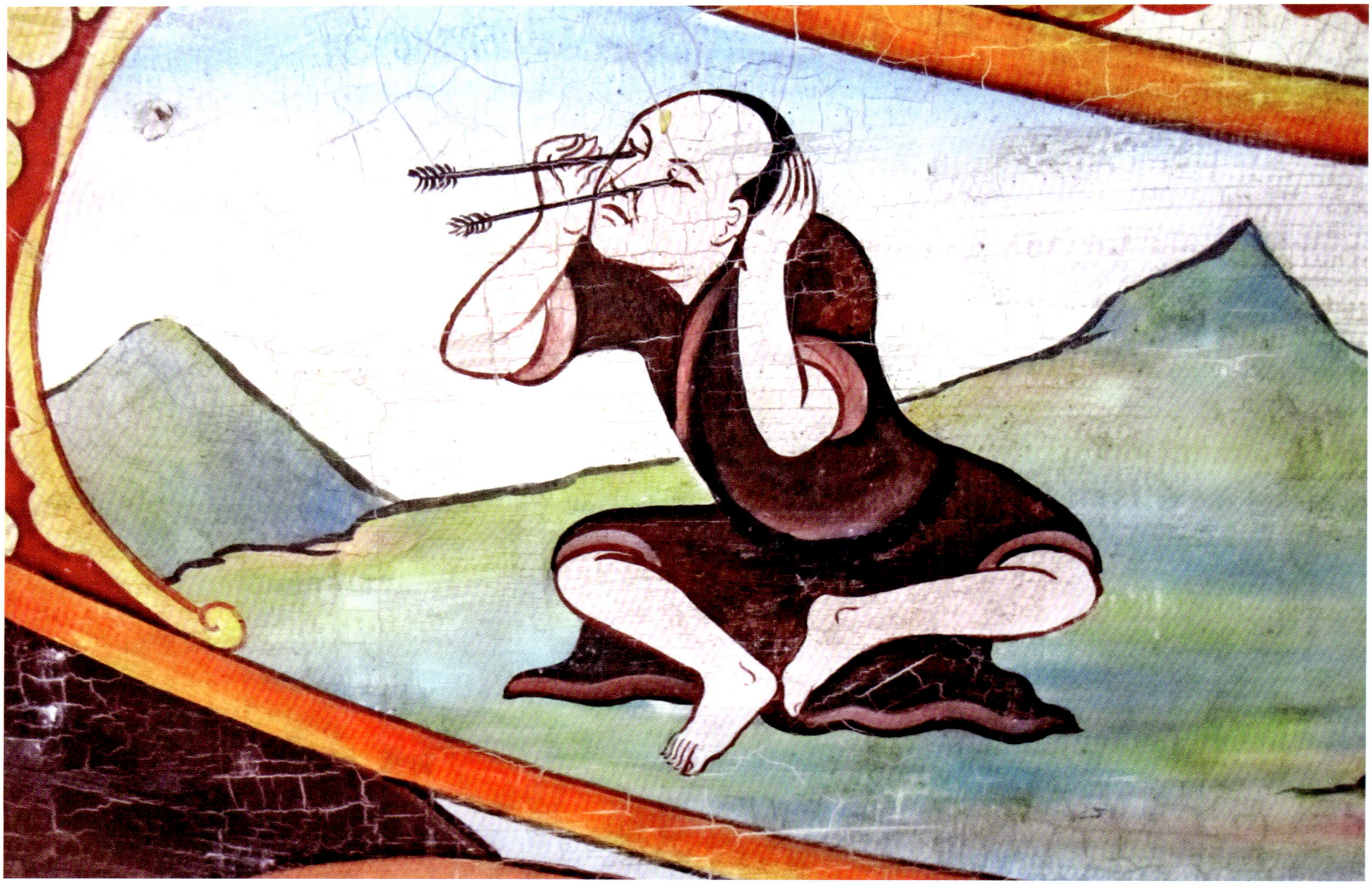

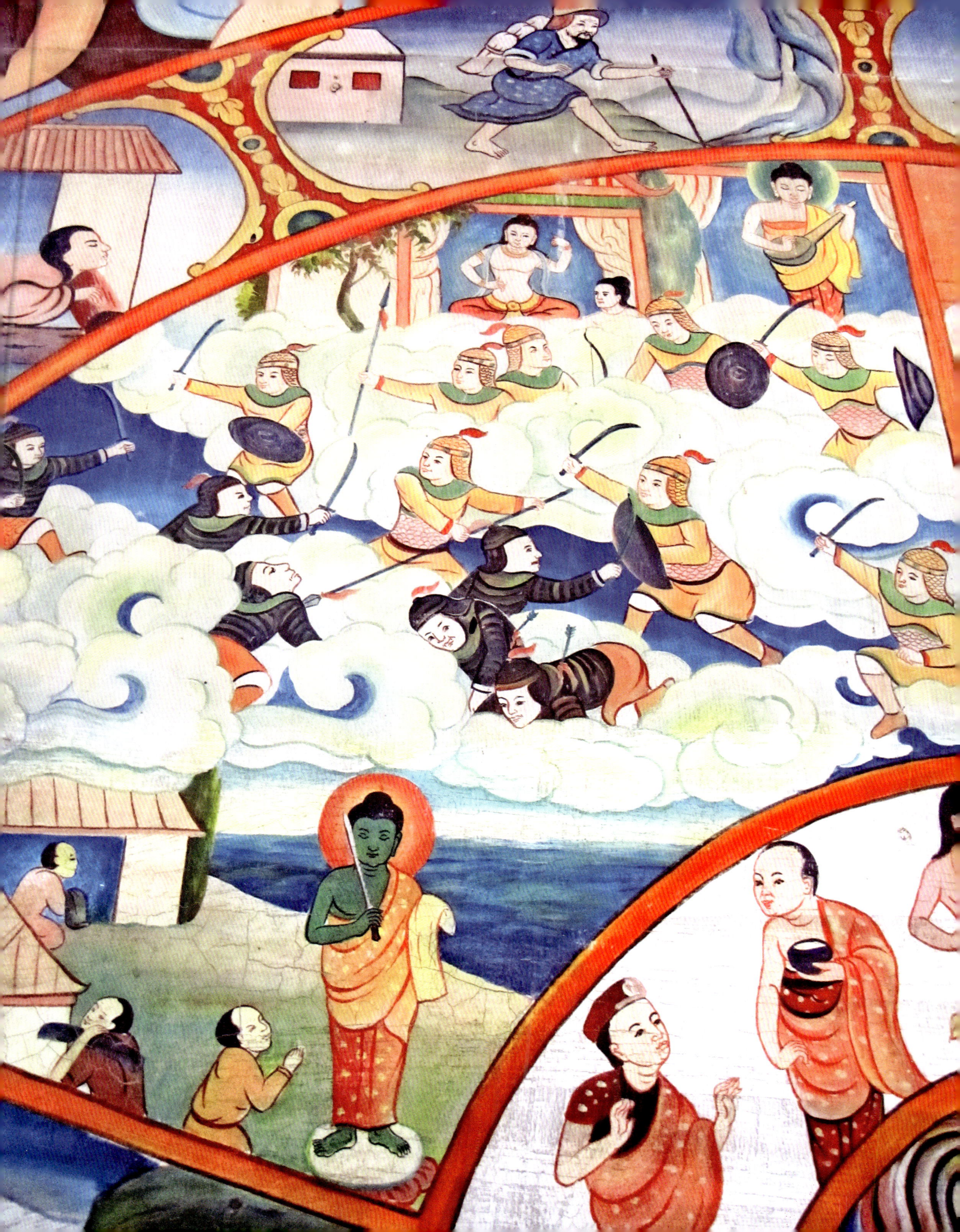

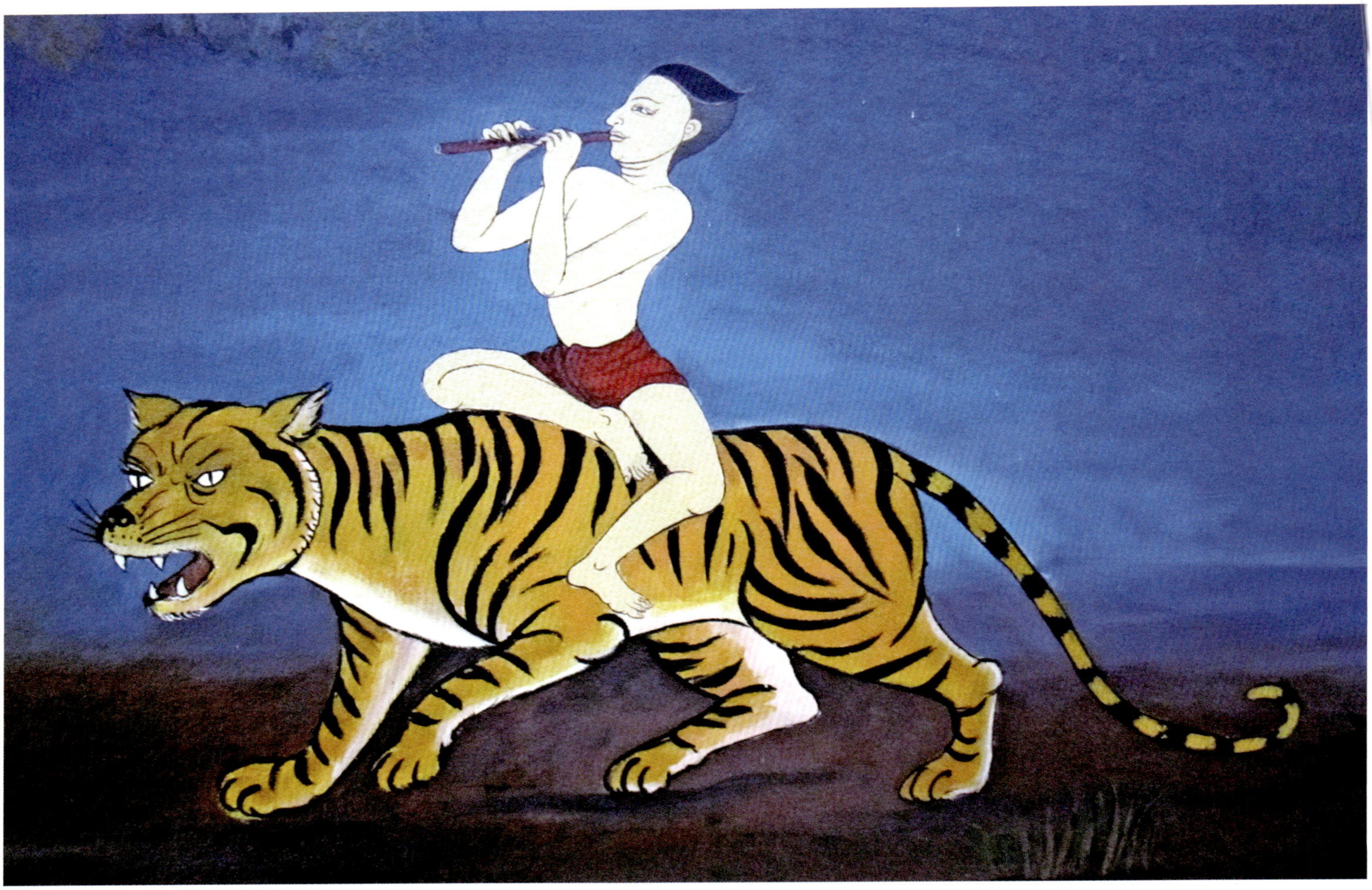

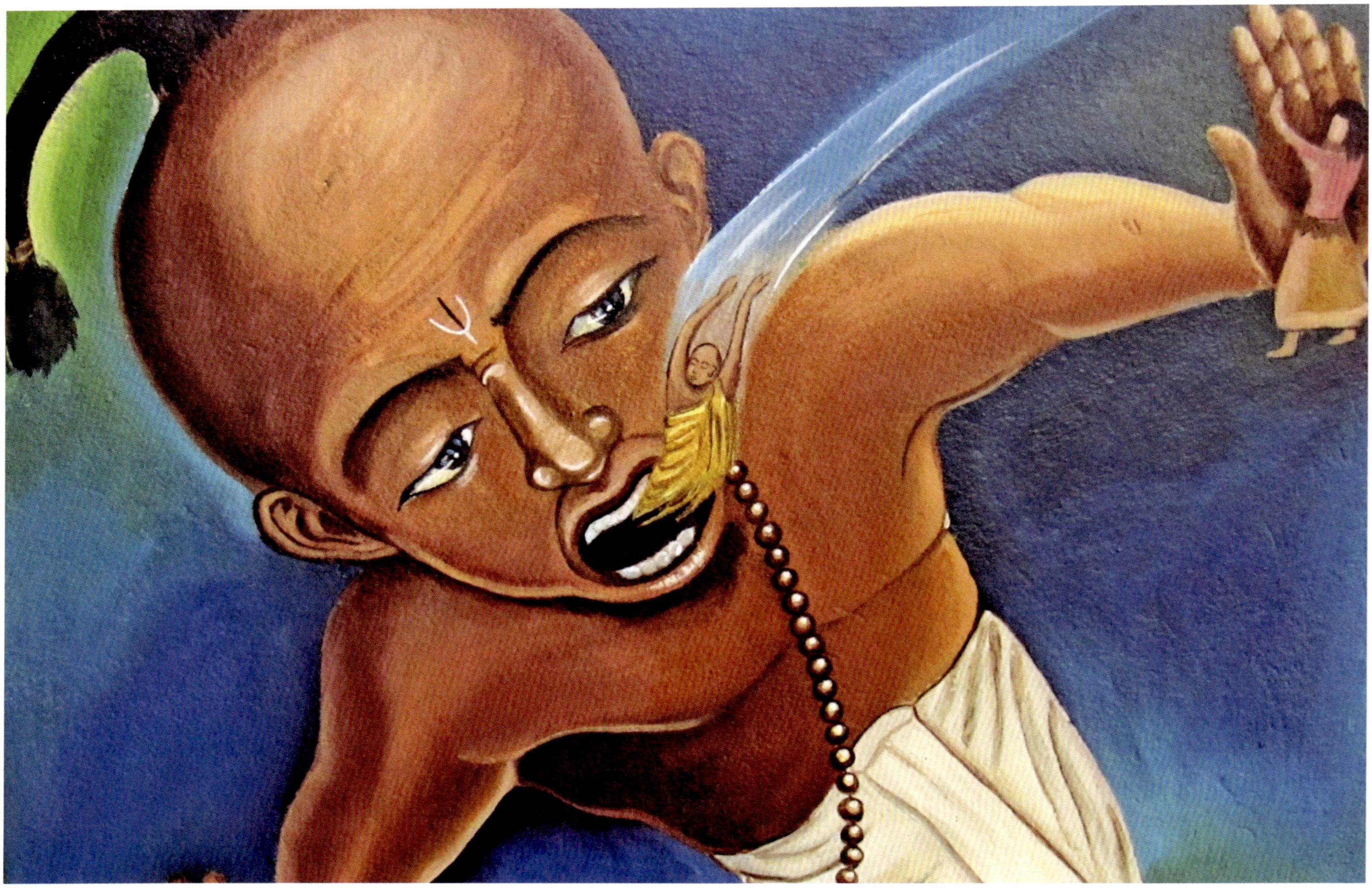

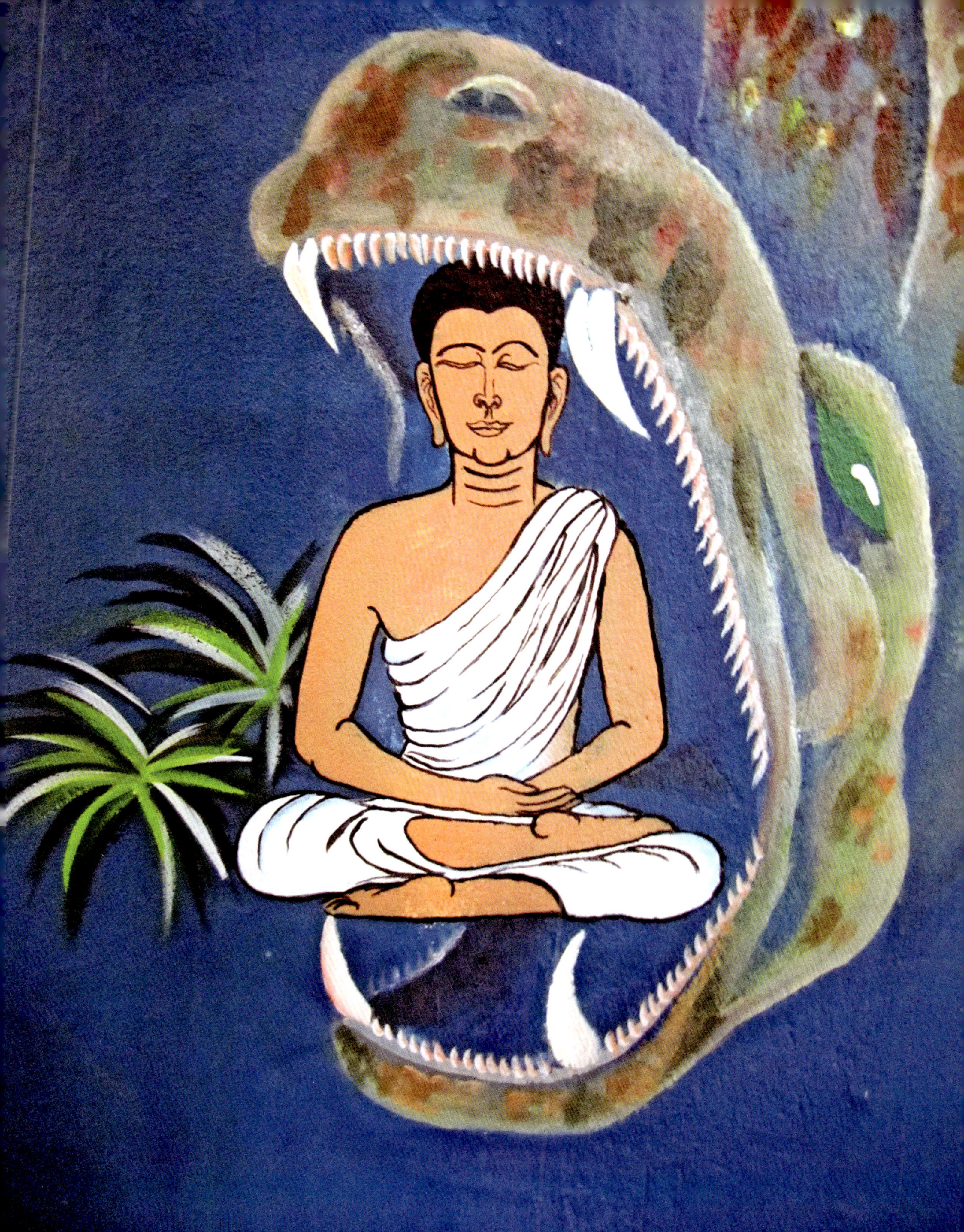

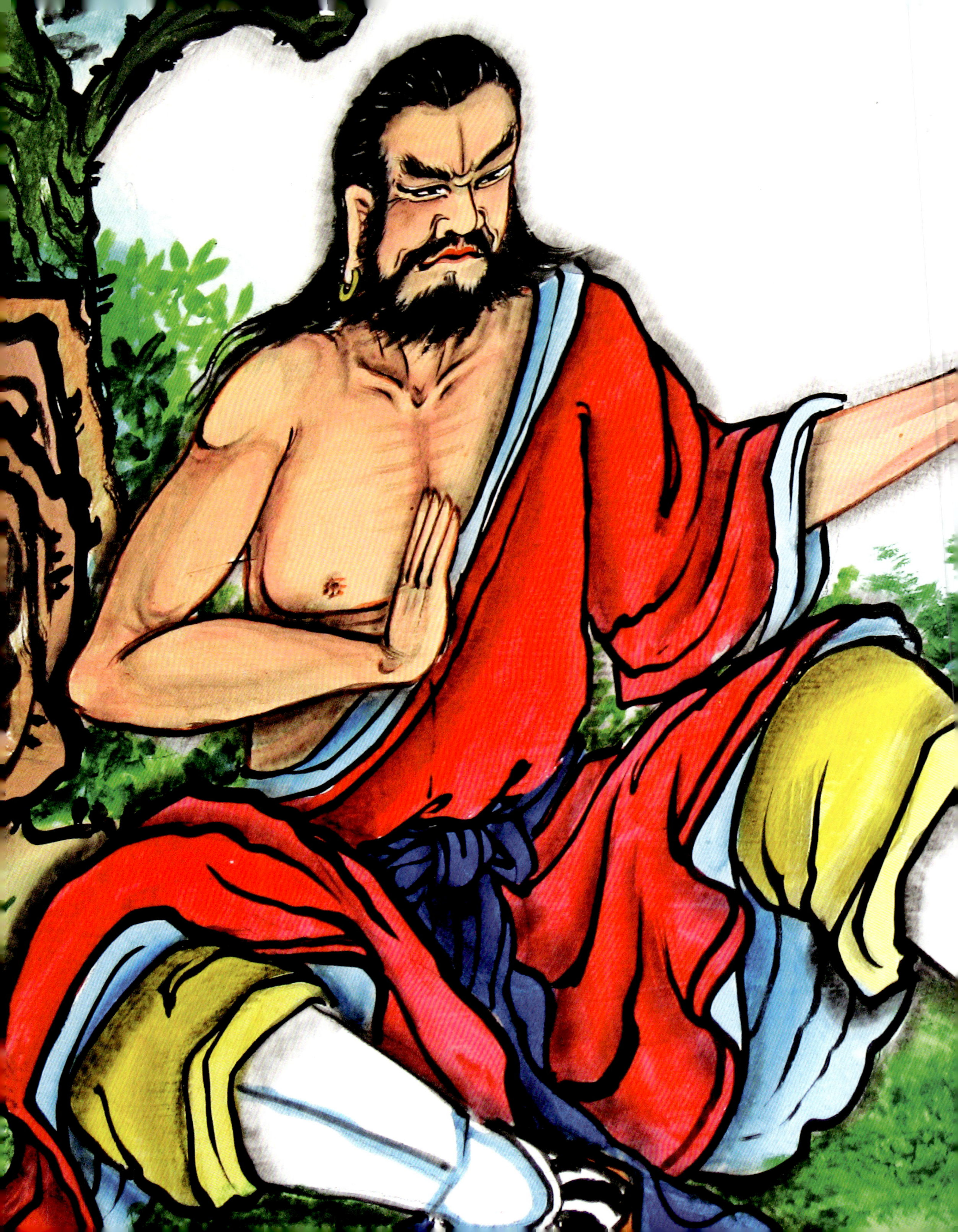

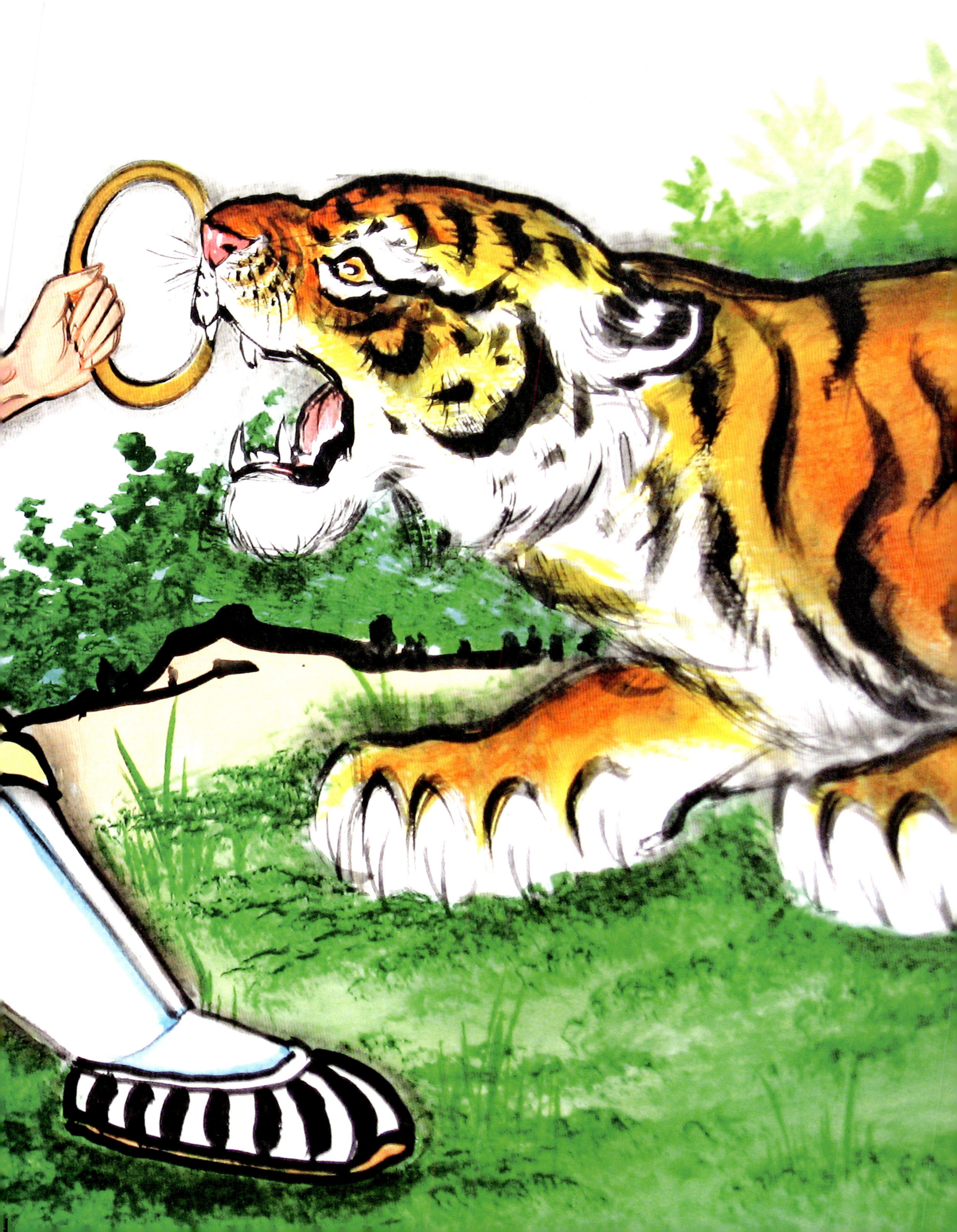

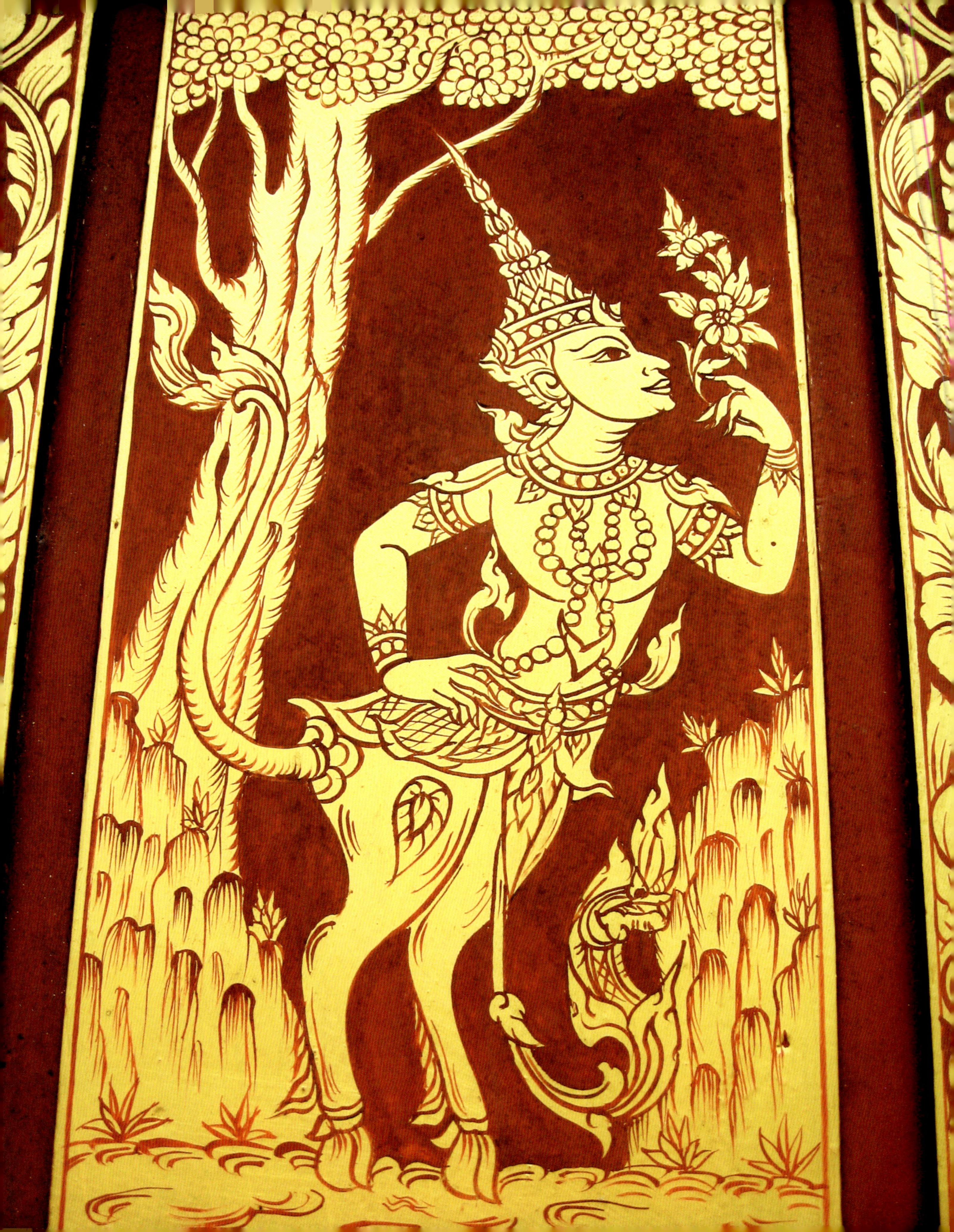

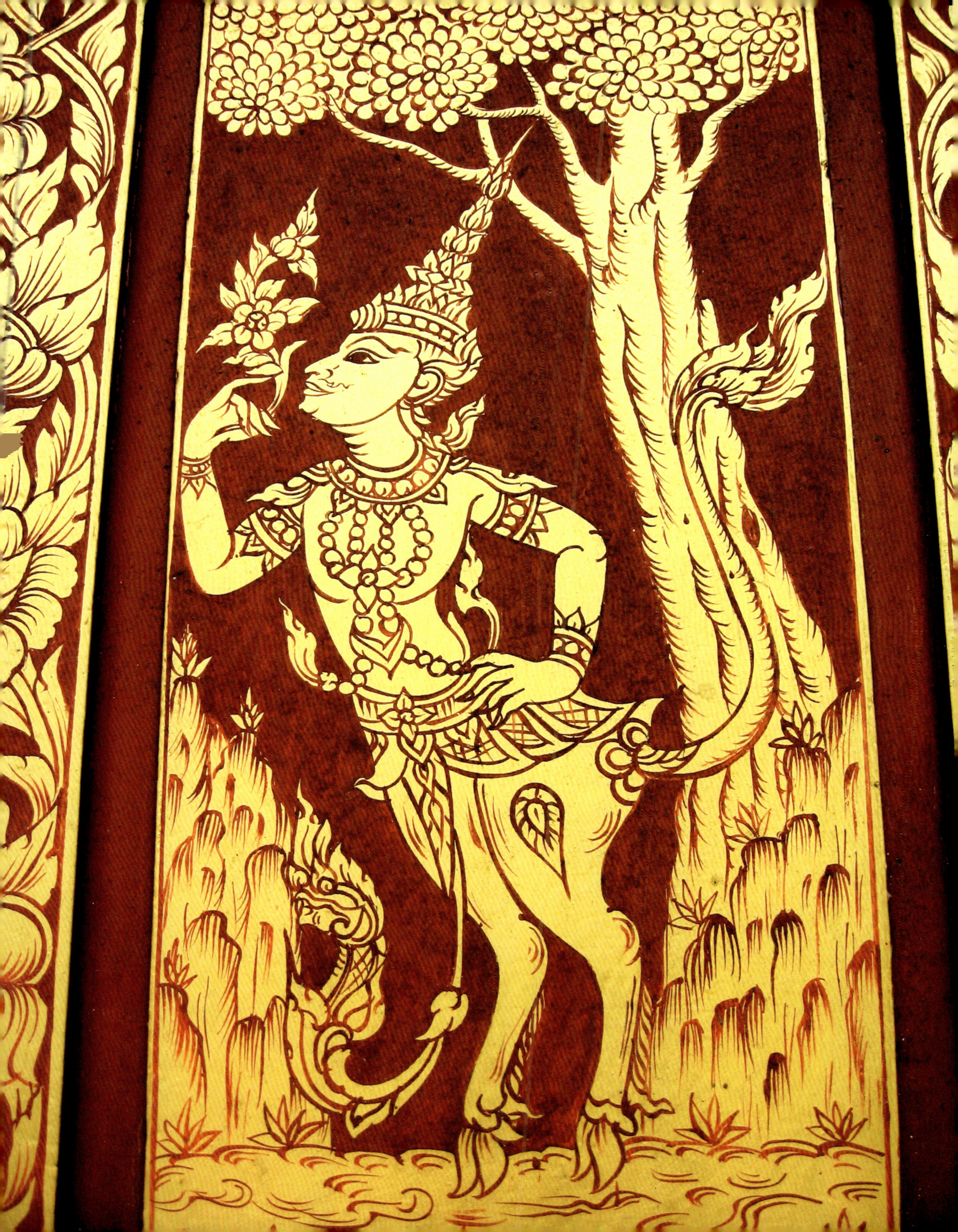

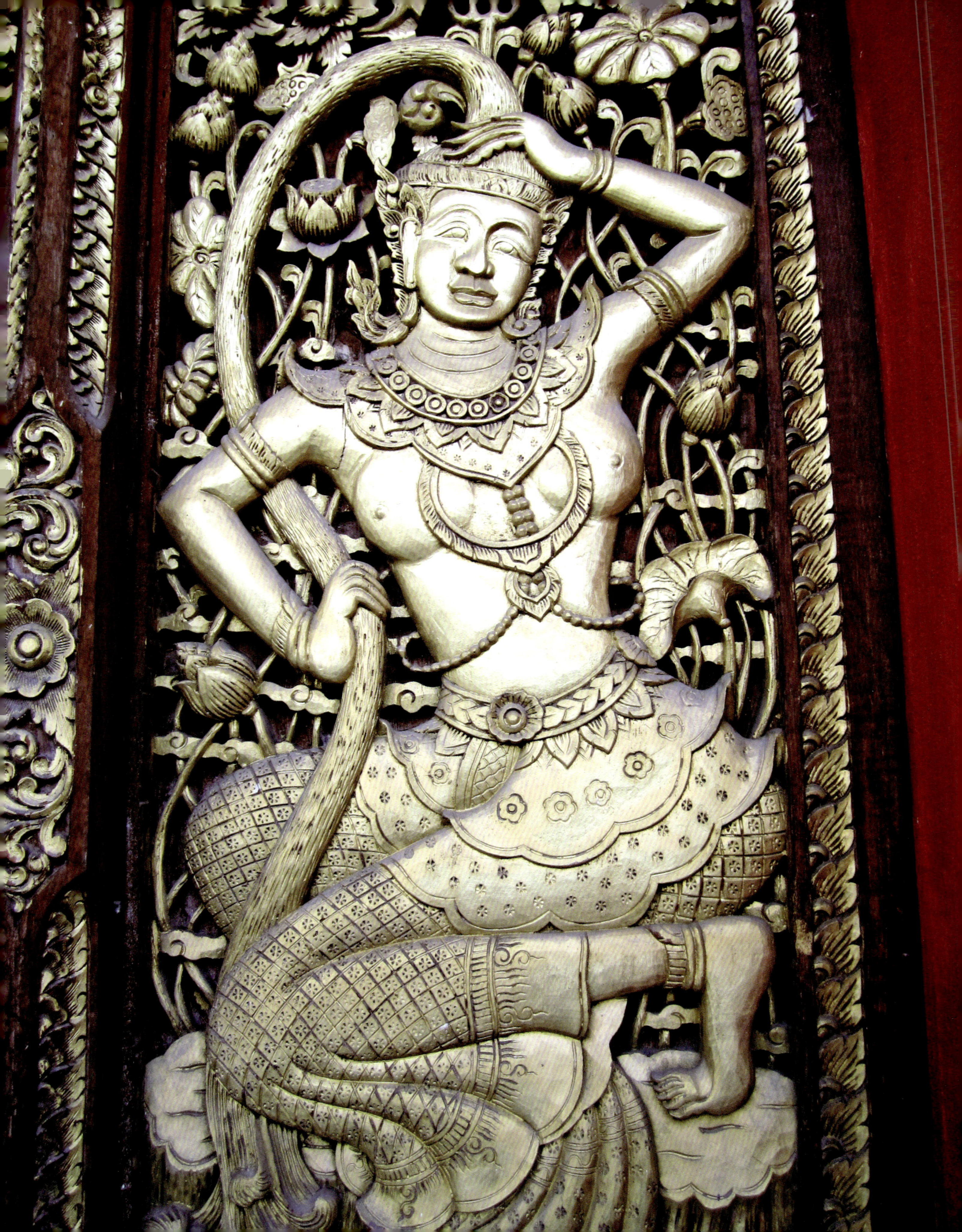

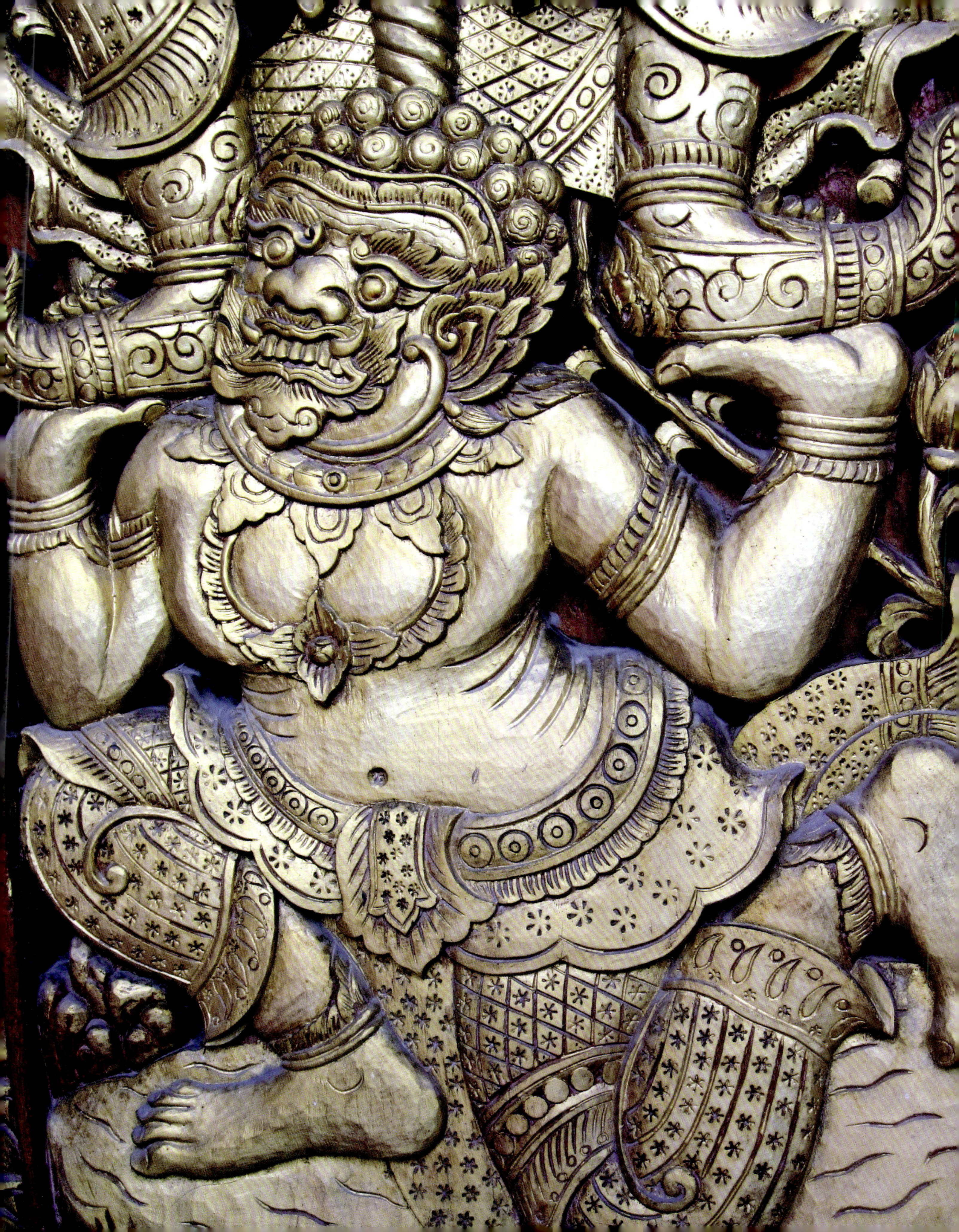

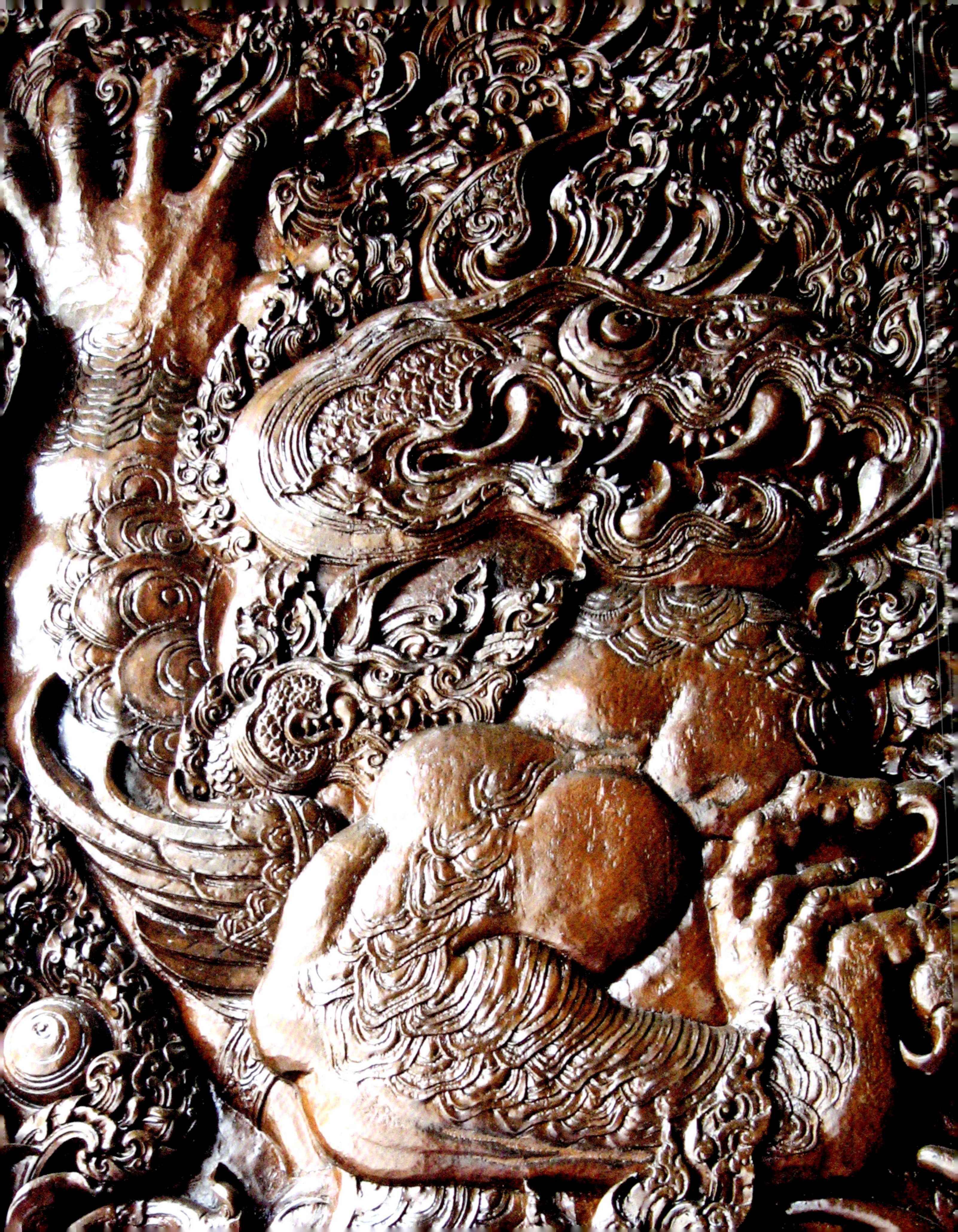

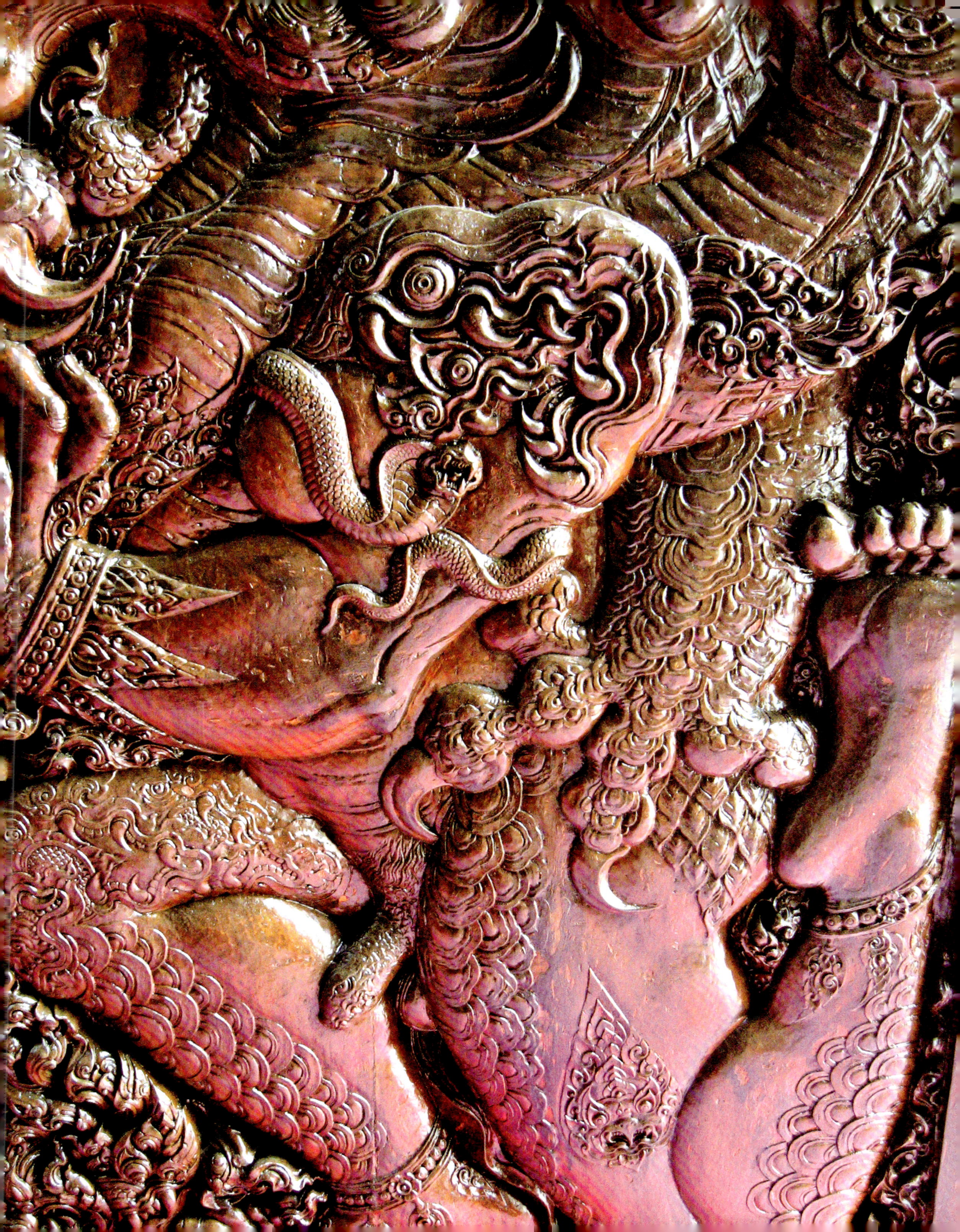

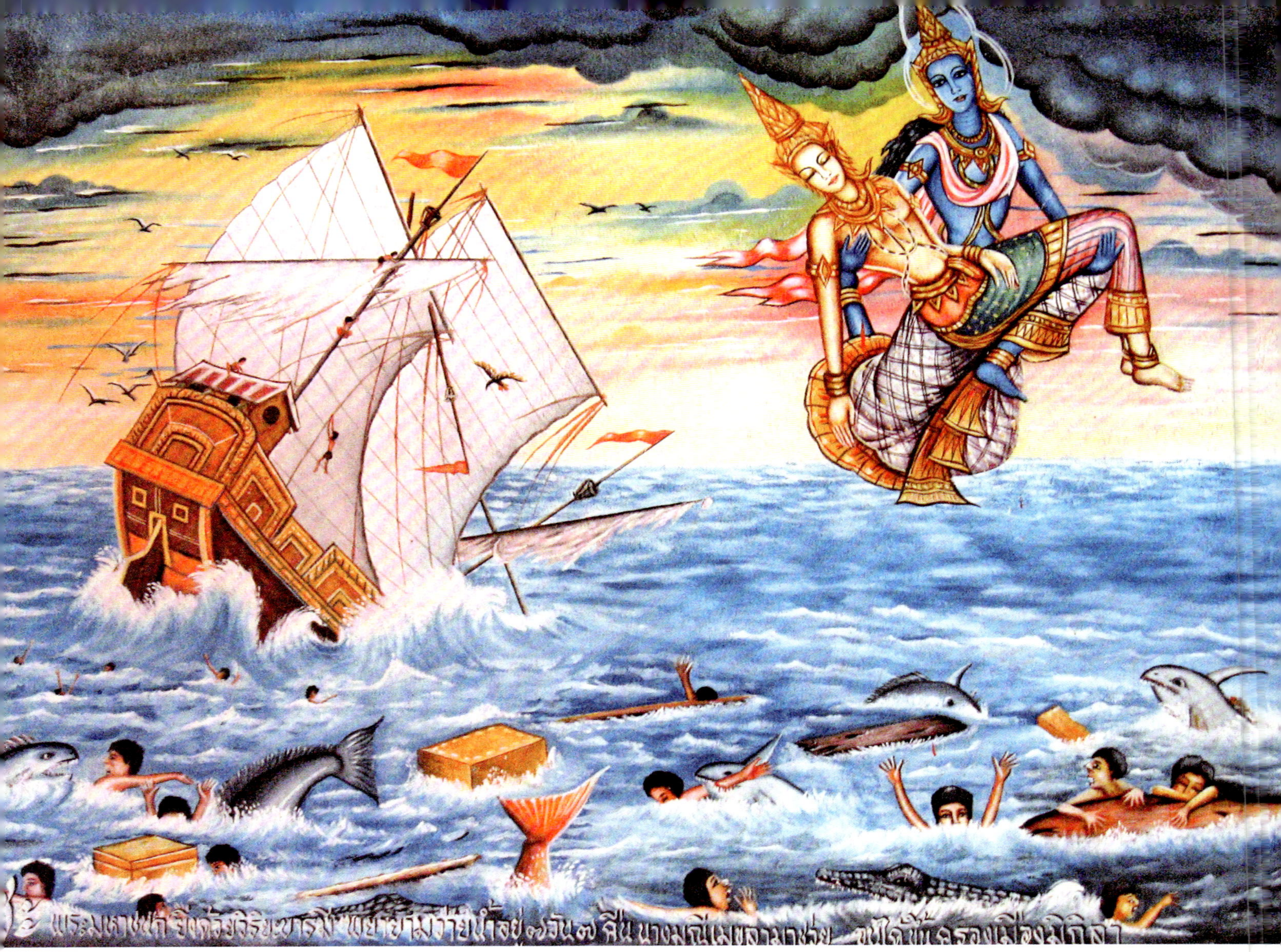

BUDDHIST MURALS

As Theravada Buddhist texts were written in Pali and Sanskrit, Buddhist temple murals needed to provide a visual narrative of the Buddha's teachings and related mythologies. One source was the *Ramakien*, the Thai version of the Indian *Ramayana*, where Hindu mythology was adapted to Thai beliefs, telling the story of the mortal hero Phra Ram and his divine origin. The finest mural example is at Wat Phra Kraew, the Temple of the Emerald Buddha, in Bangkok, detailing all 178 scenes of this epic. Another source is the fourteenth century *Triaphum*, The Three Worlds, depicting a vivid metaphysical three-planed universe of Buddhism and the creation myth. These are both usually detailed as individual scenes in one large mural.

Scenes from the Life of the Buddha are another source, showing Siddhartha's farewell to his wife and son and the Great Departure on his mount Kanthaka with Channa holding onto the horse's tail (Pg. 231), The Defeat of Mara, The Miracle of the Mango Tree, The Miracle of Parileyyaka Forest when the Buddha is attended by a monkey and an elephant (Pg. 233), Sujata's Gift of Rice and Bowl (Pg. 234), The Descent From Tavastimsa Heaven, and The *Mahaparinirvana* as the Buddha reaches complete nirvana leaving his physical body (Pg. 229).

The final source is the *Jakata* Tales, detailing the Buddha's past lives, particularly the last ten. In the *Mahajanaka Jataka*, the goddess Manimekhala rescues Mahajanaka from a shipwreck (Pg. 228). In the *Vidhurapandita Jakata*, the demon Punnaka carries off Vidhura in order to kill him (Pg. 232). The *Vessantara Jataka* is divided into 13 scenes, detailing when Sakka pours water on the hands of Phusati to ratify her ten wishes (Pg. 230), and the eight Brahmans request the white elephant (Pg. 232), and the gods send two deities to comfort Wesandon's abducted children (Pg. 238-9). Another depicted scene is the Legend of Mogallana overcoming the Naga King Nandopananda (Pg. 237). Scenes of *Narok* from the *Nimi Jataka* show adulterers climbing a tree of thorns: note Phra Malai observing, sent by the Buddha to make a report of various heavens and hells (Pg. 244-5). And from the *Triaphum*, people boiled in cauldrons of oil and thrown into pits of fire from a deeper abyss (Pg. 246-7).

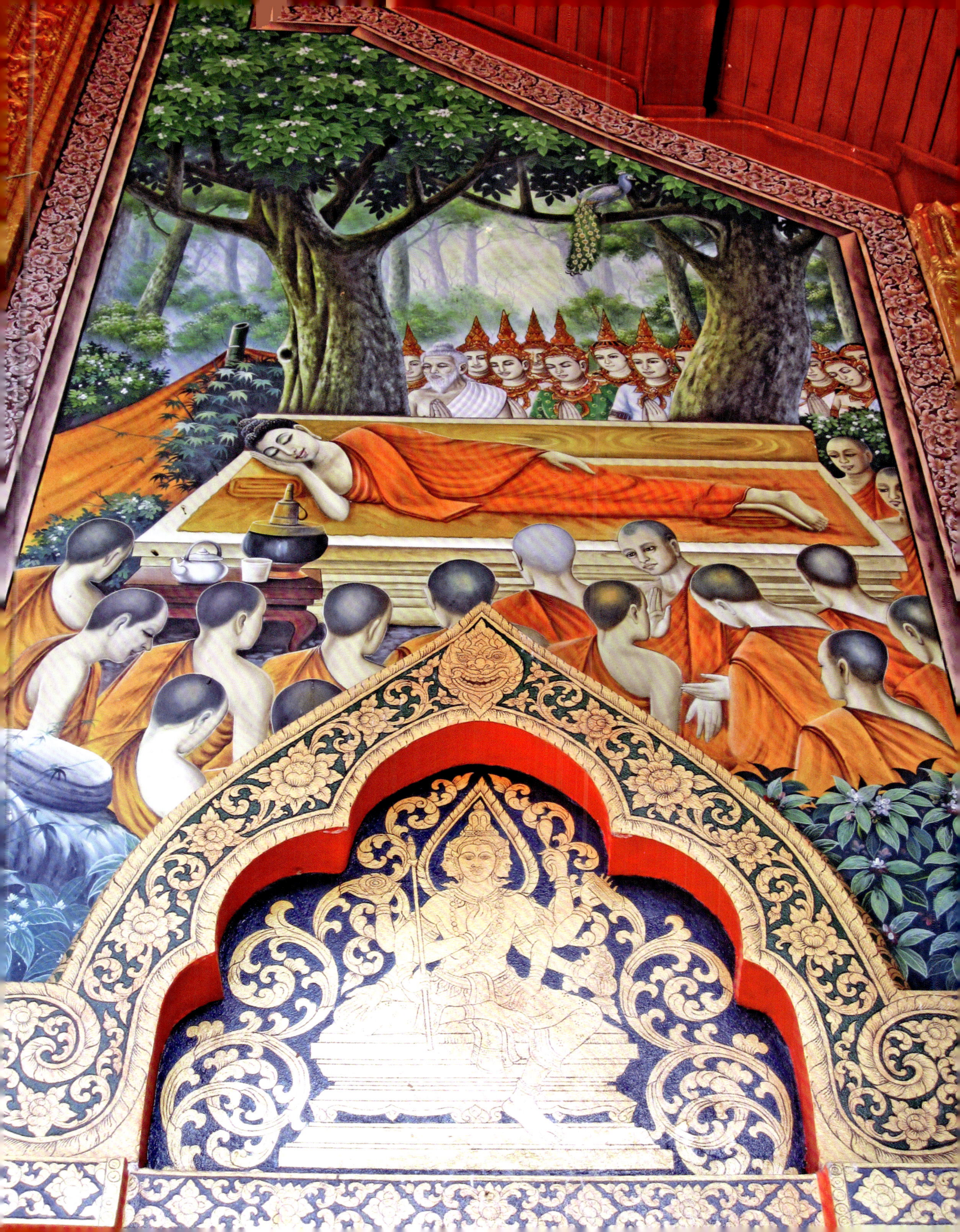

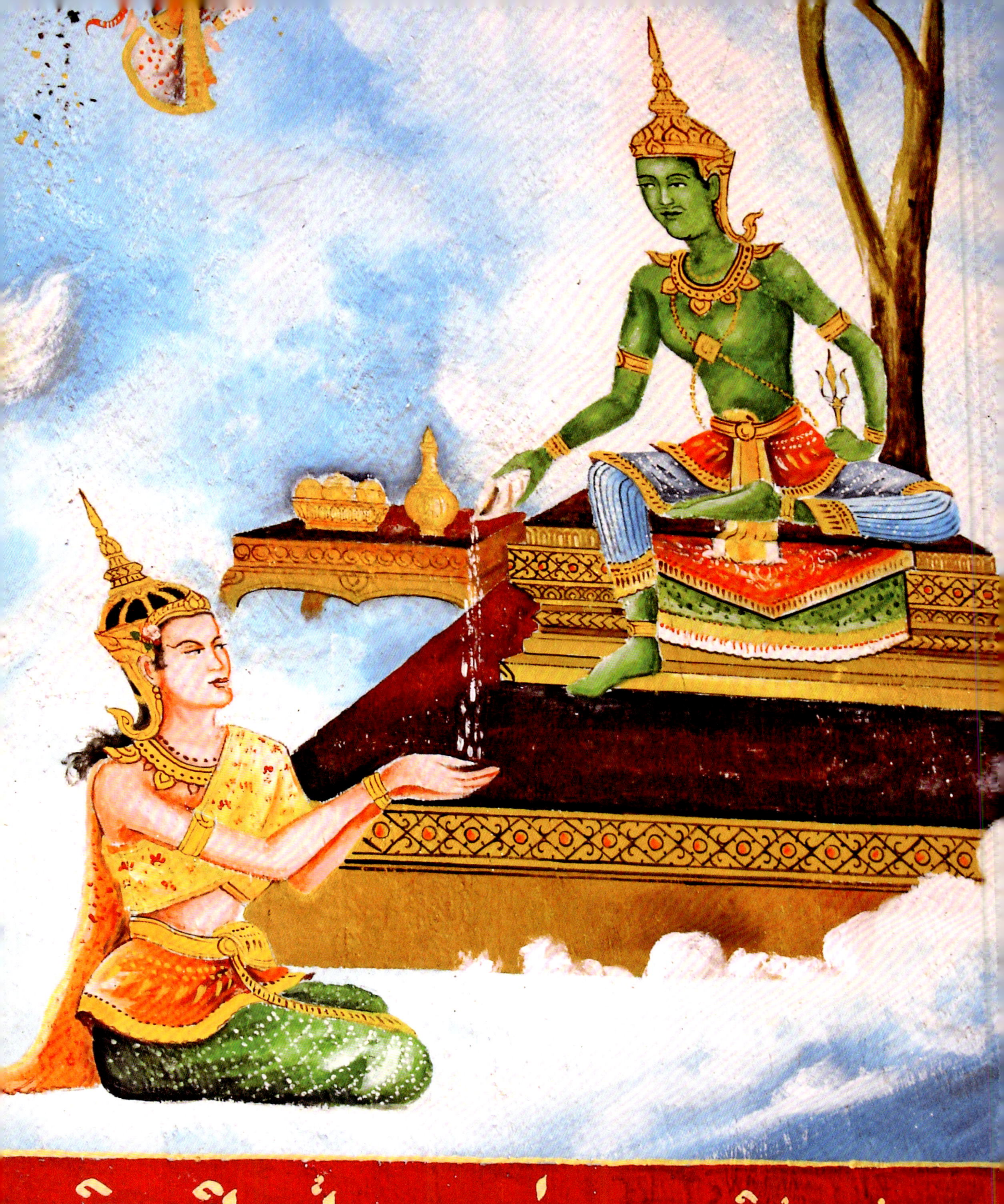
เจริญศิลป์การแว่น อุทิศ บูชาพระ

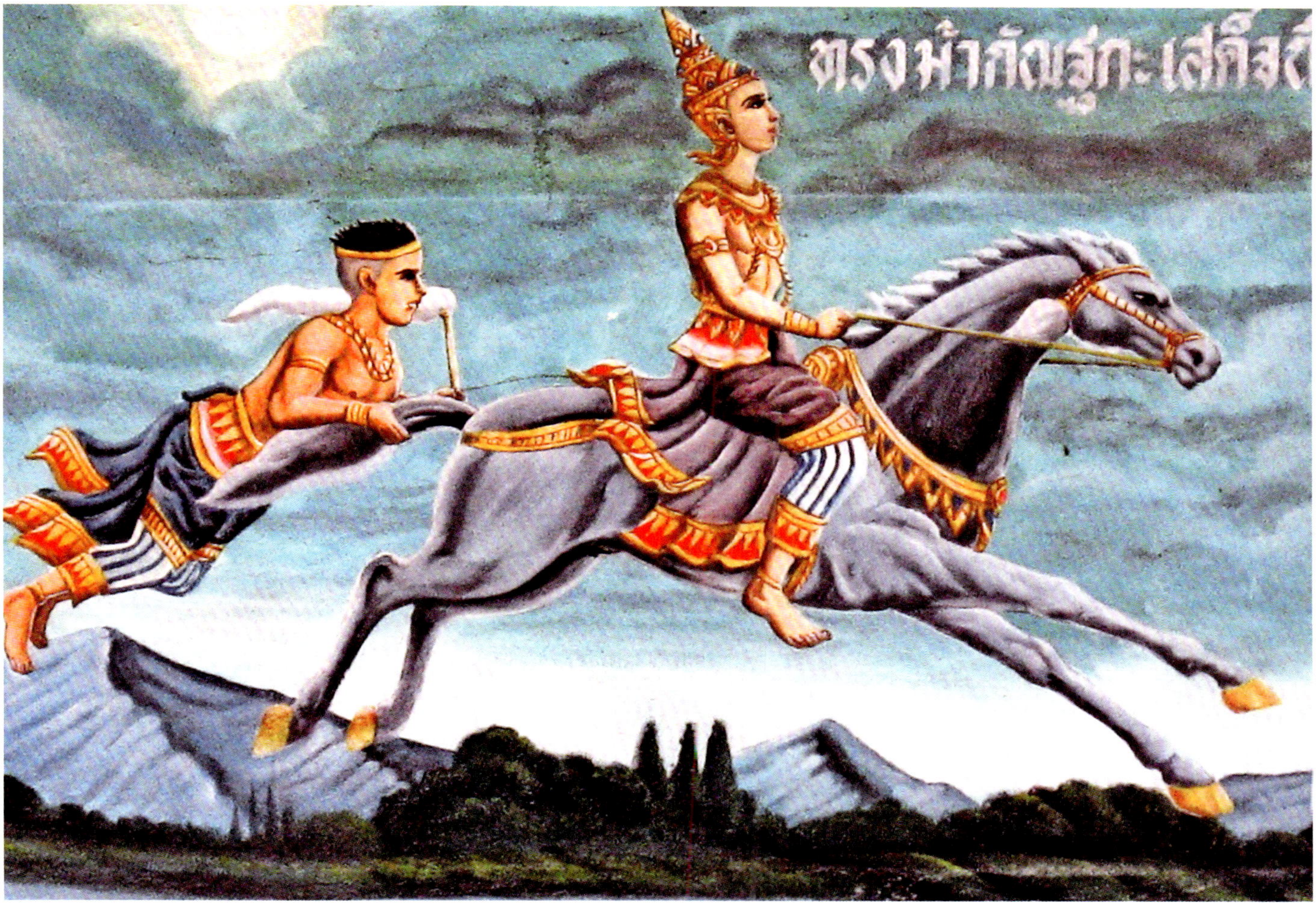

ทรงม้ากัณฐกะ เสด็จ
เจ้าชายสิทธัตถะ หนีบรรพชา 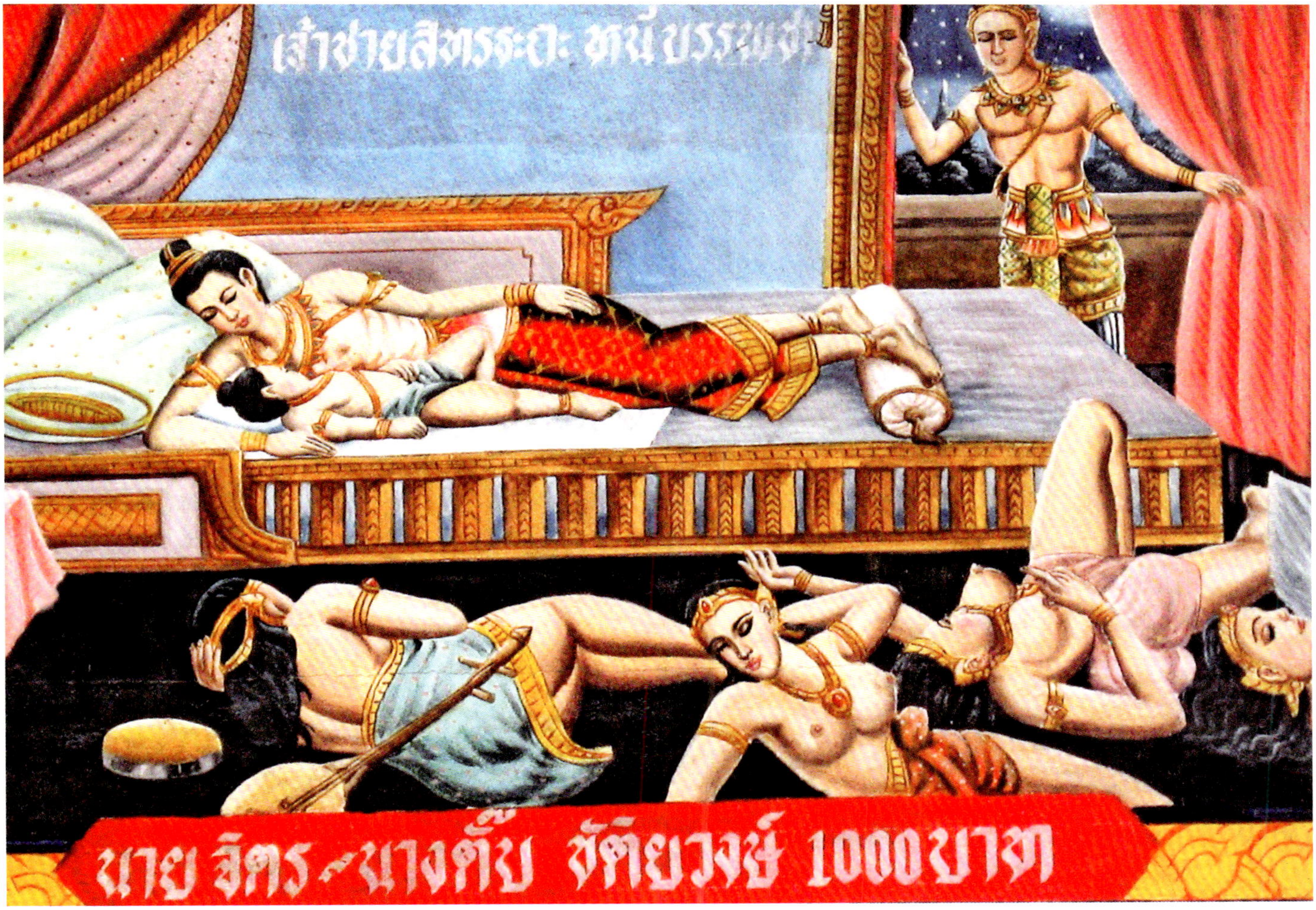
นาย จิตร - นางตั๊บ ขัติยวงษ์ 1000 บาท

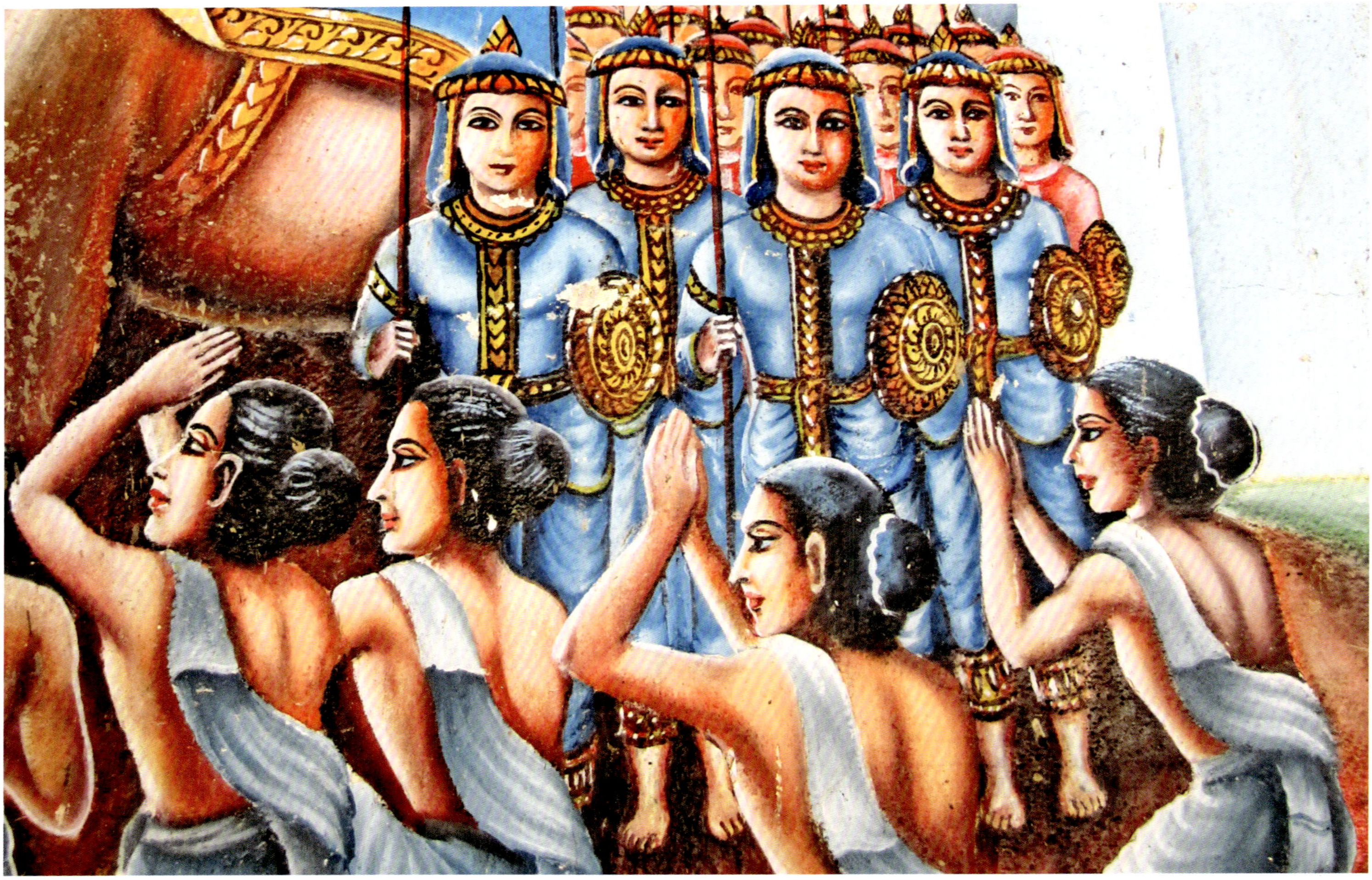

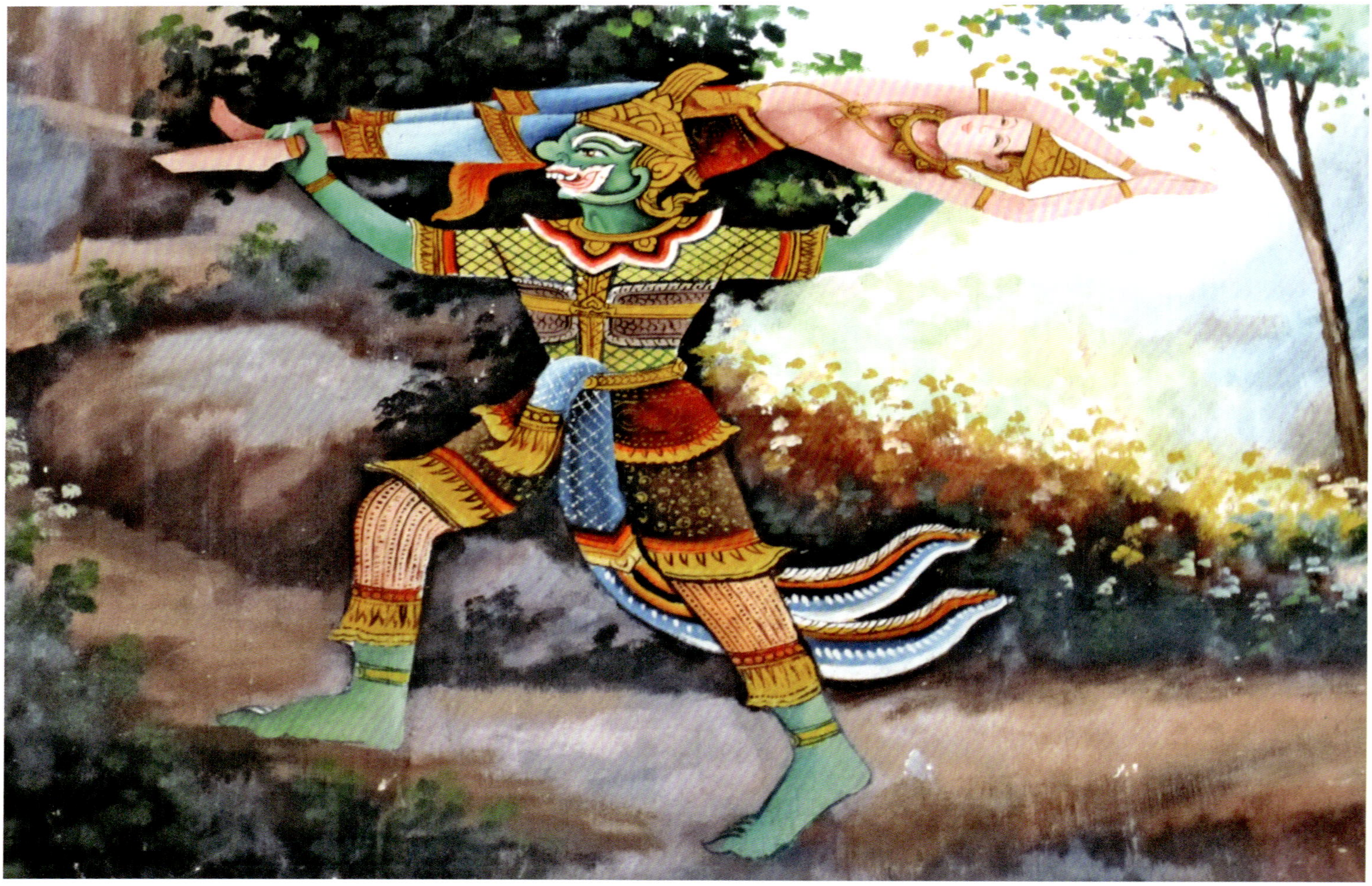

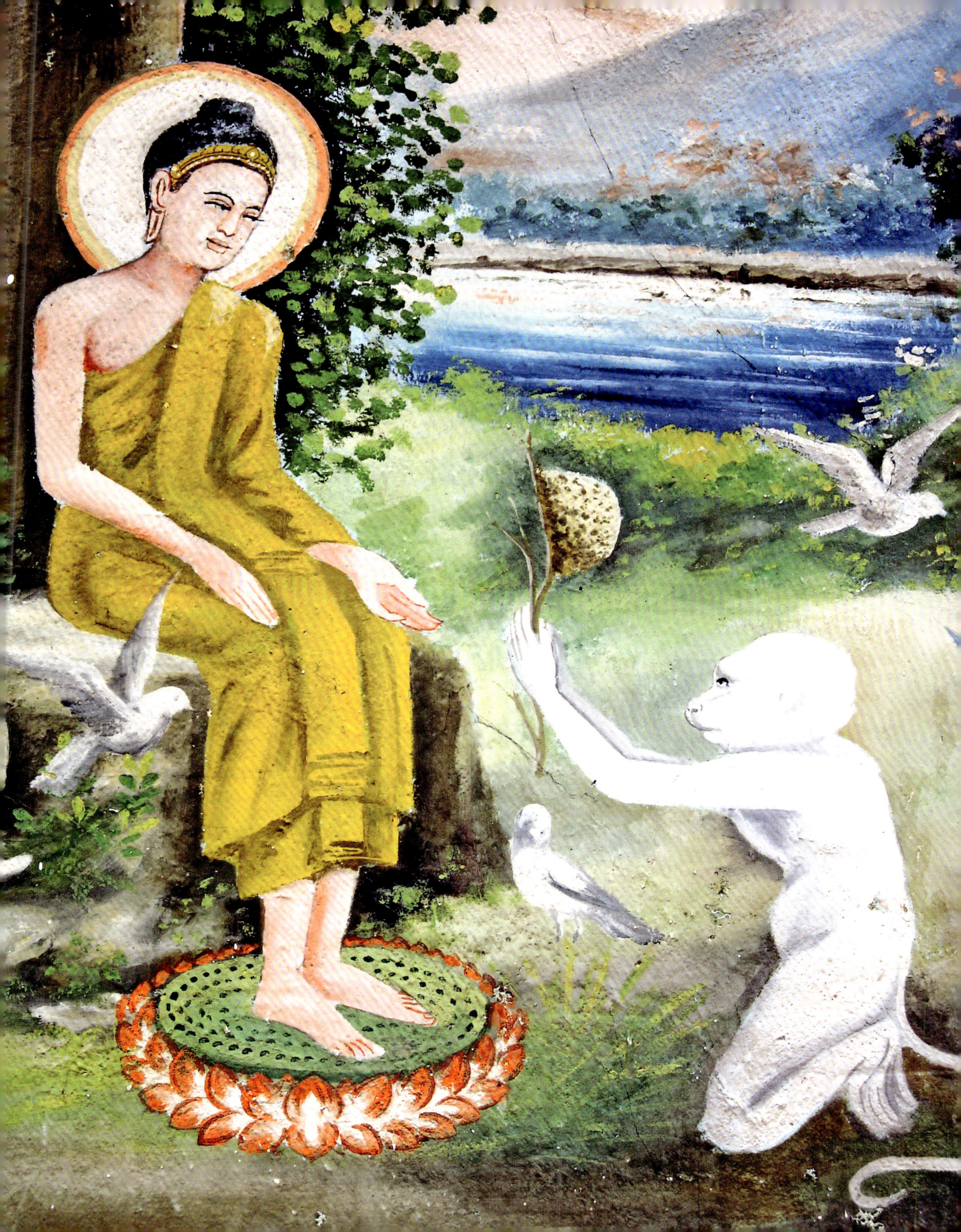

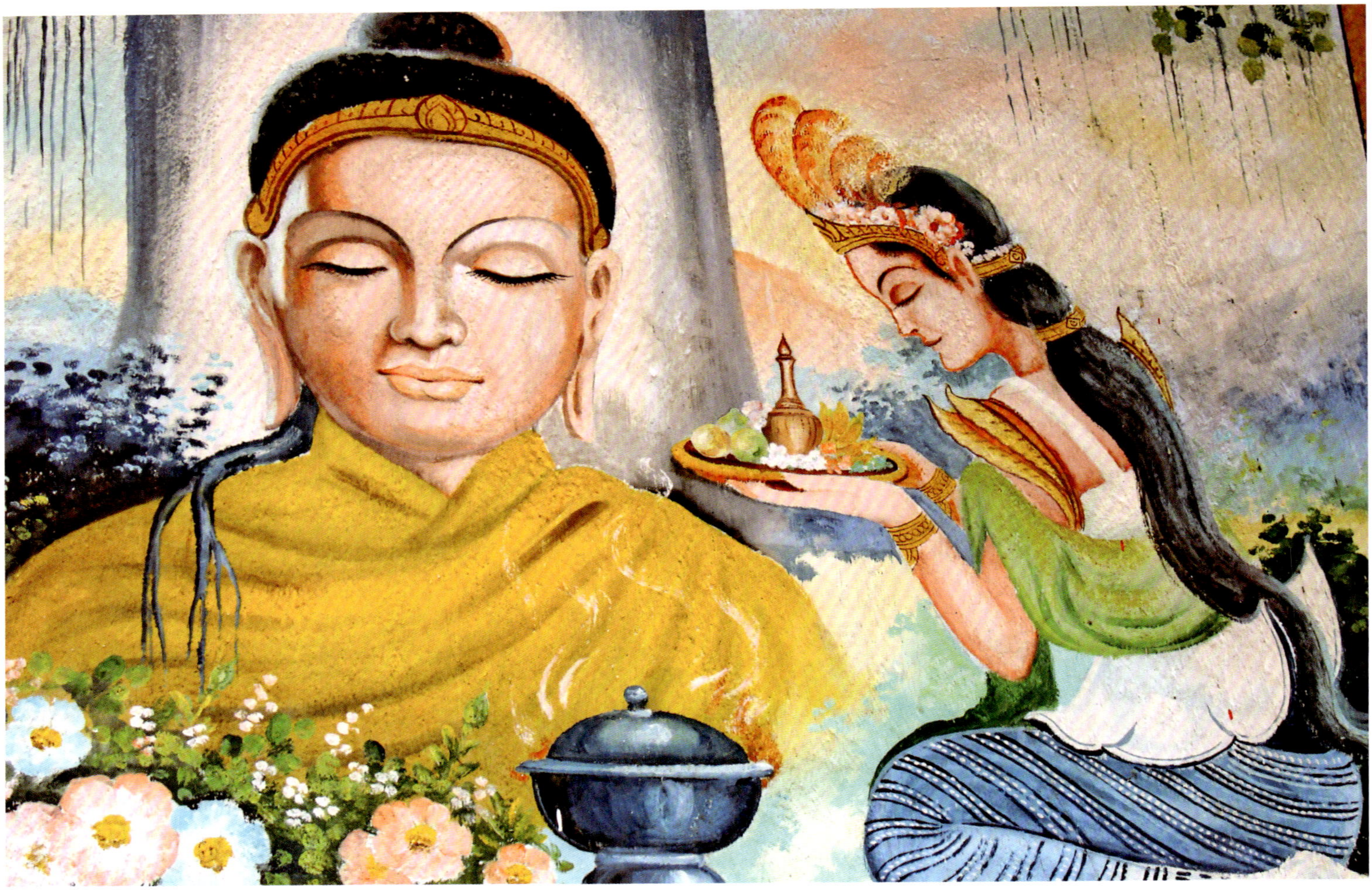

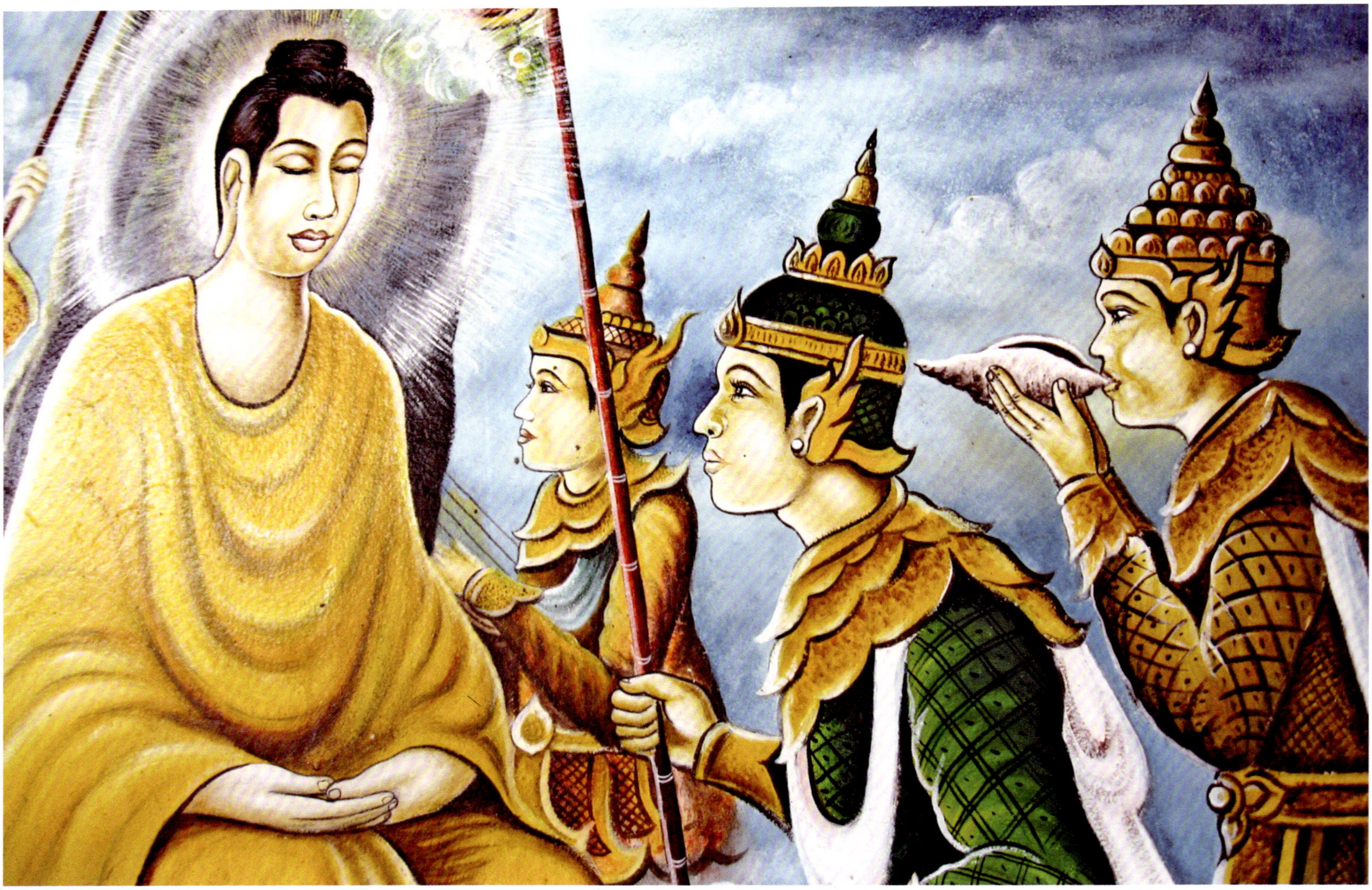

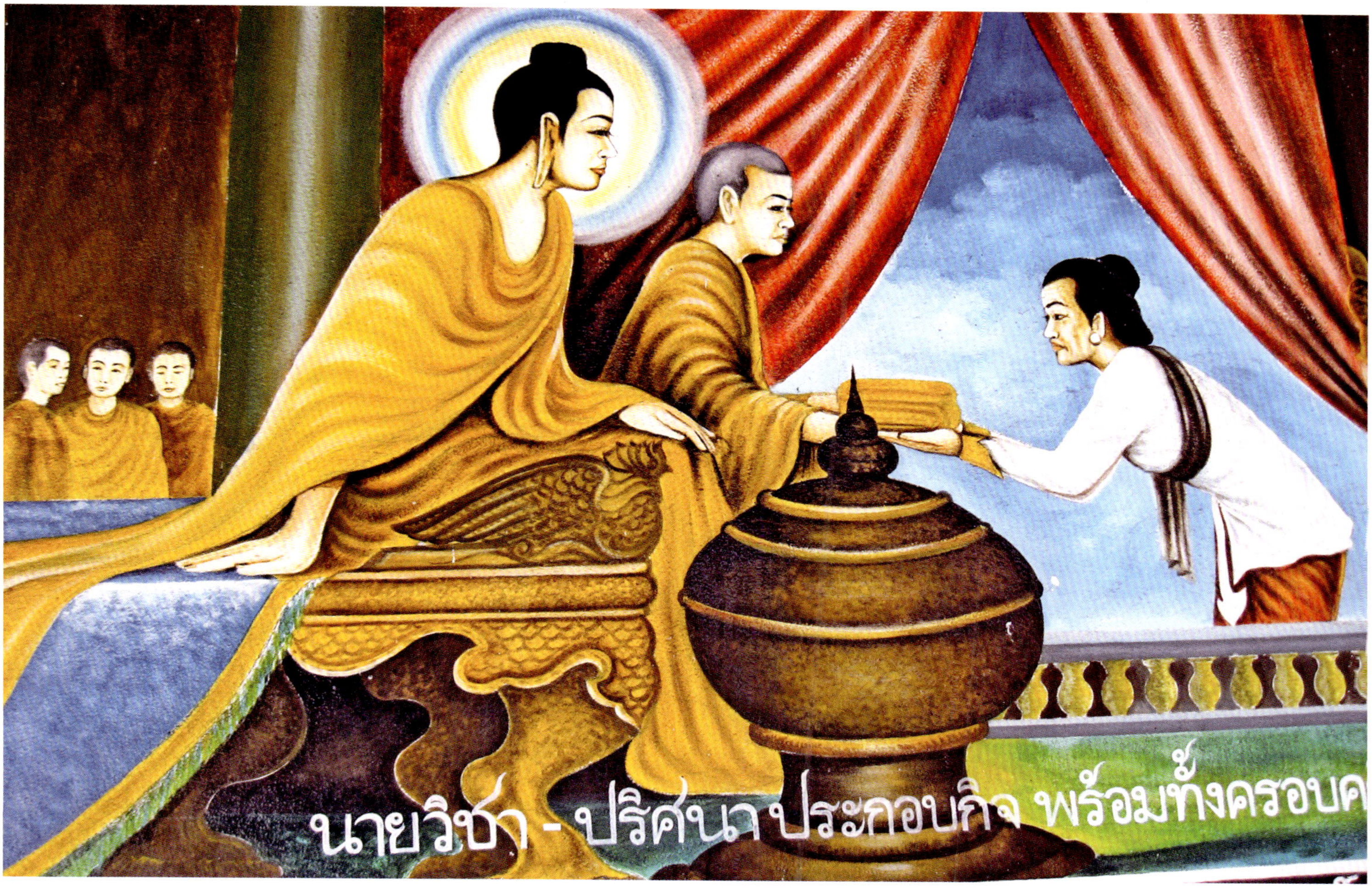

นายวิชา - ปริศนา ประกอบกิจ พร้อมทั้งครอบค

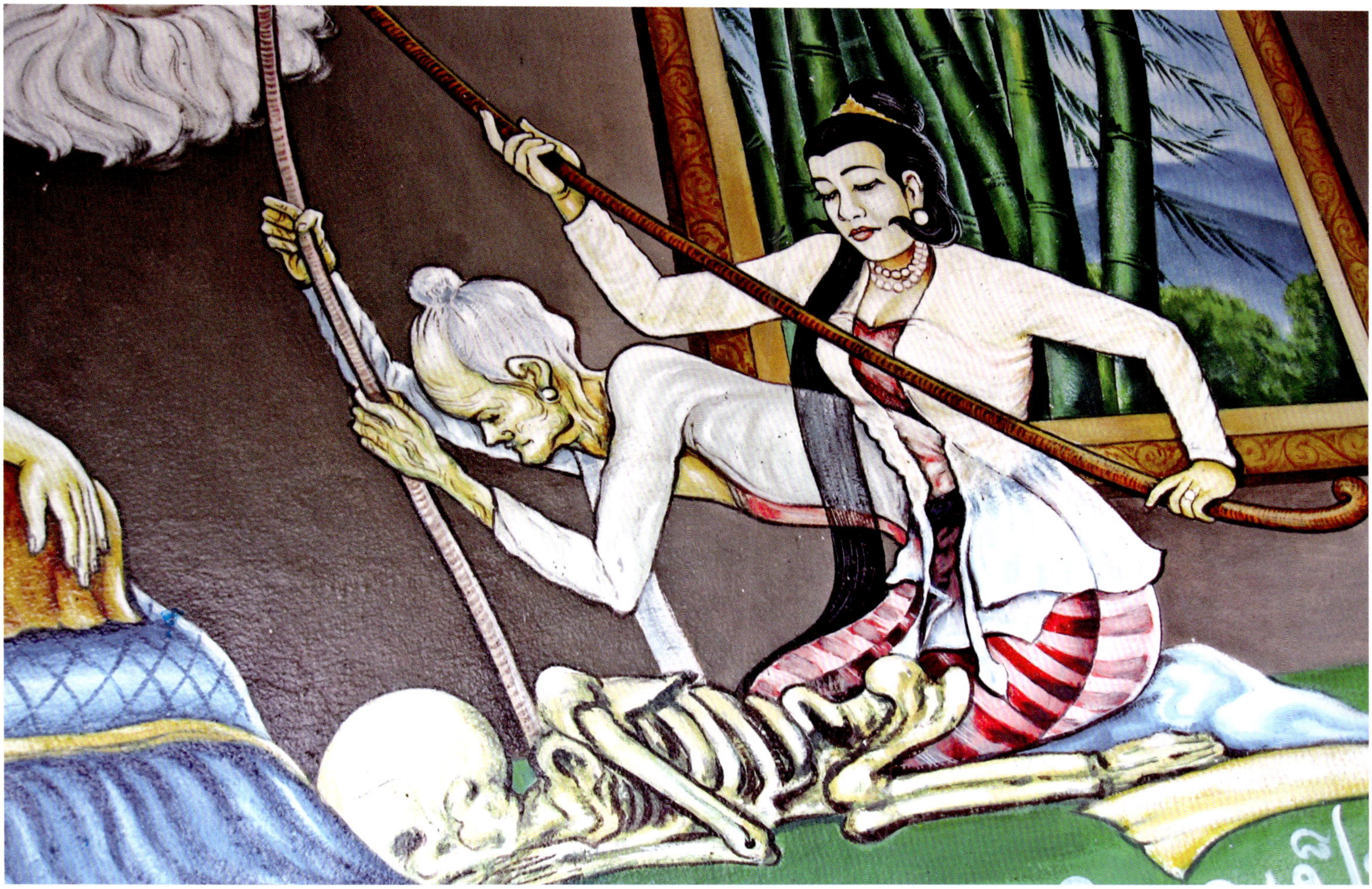

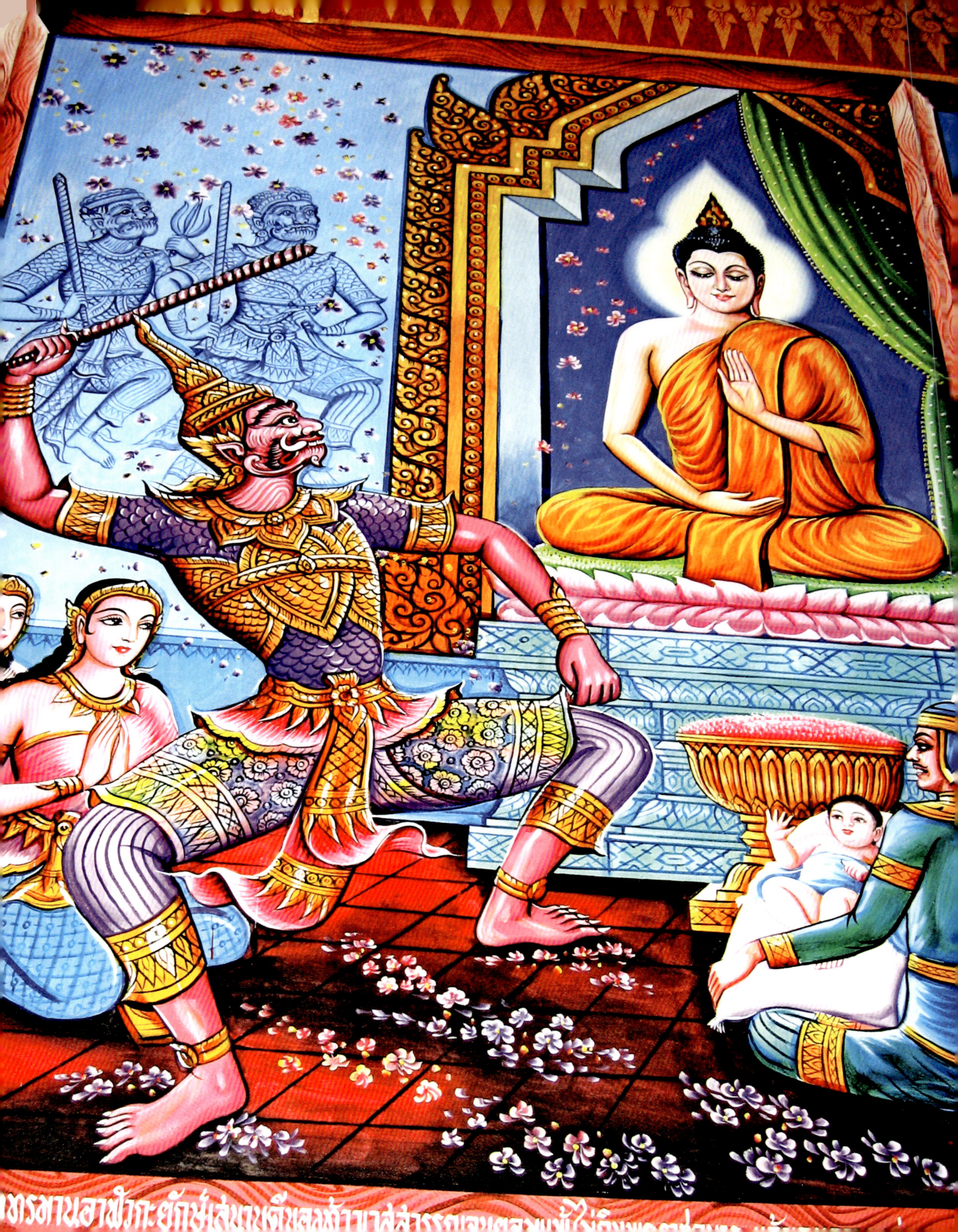

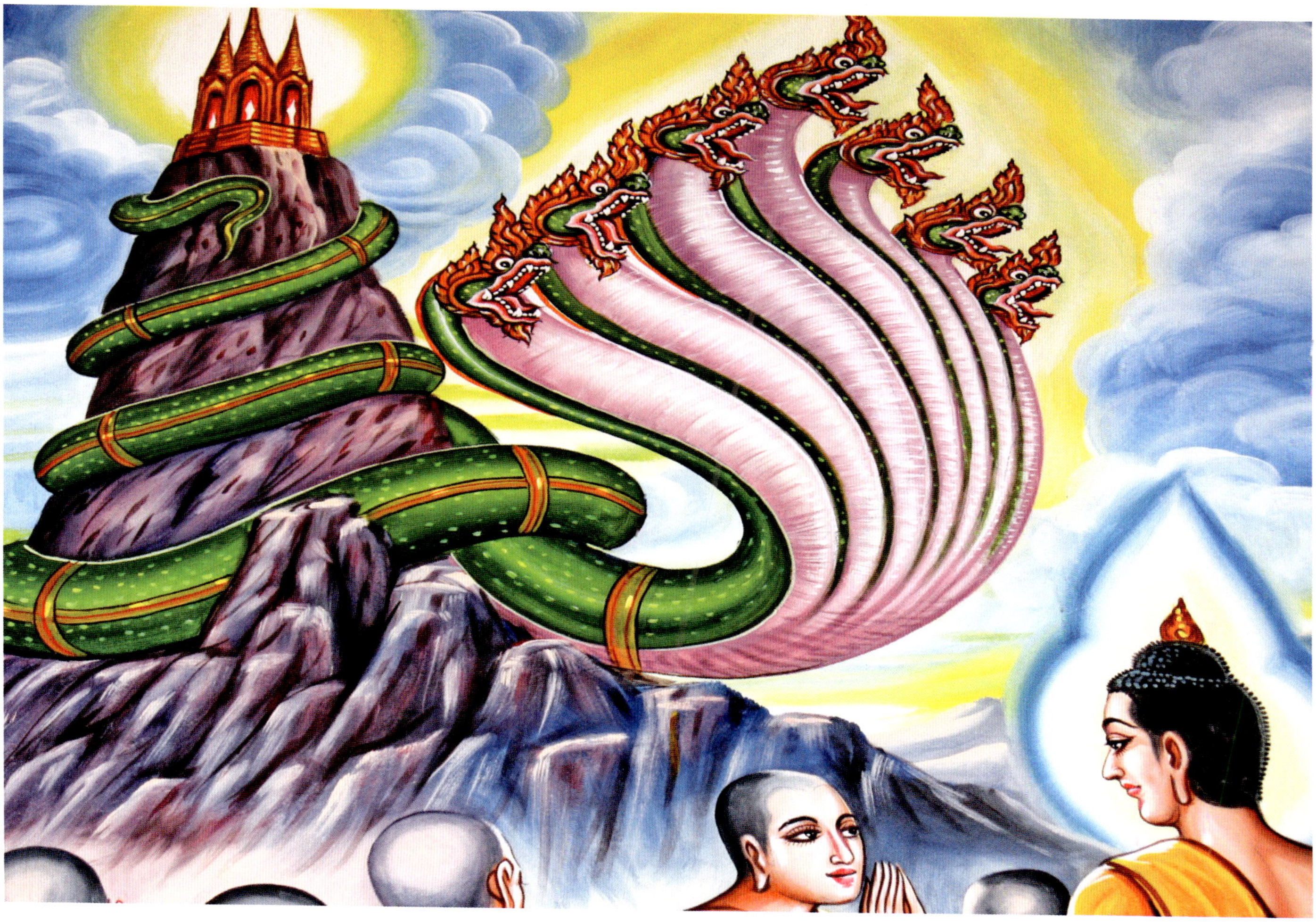

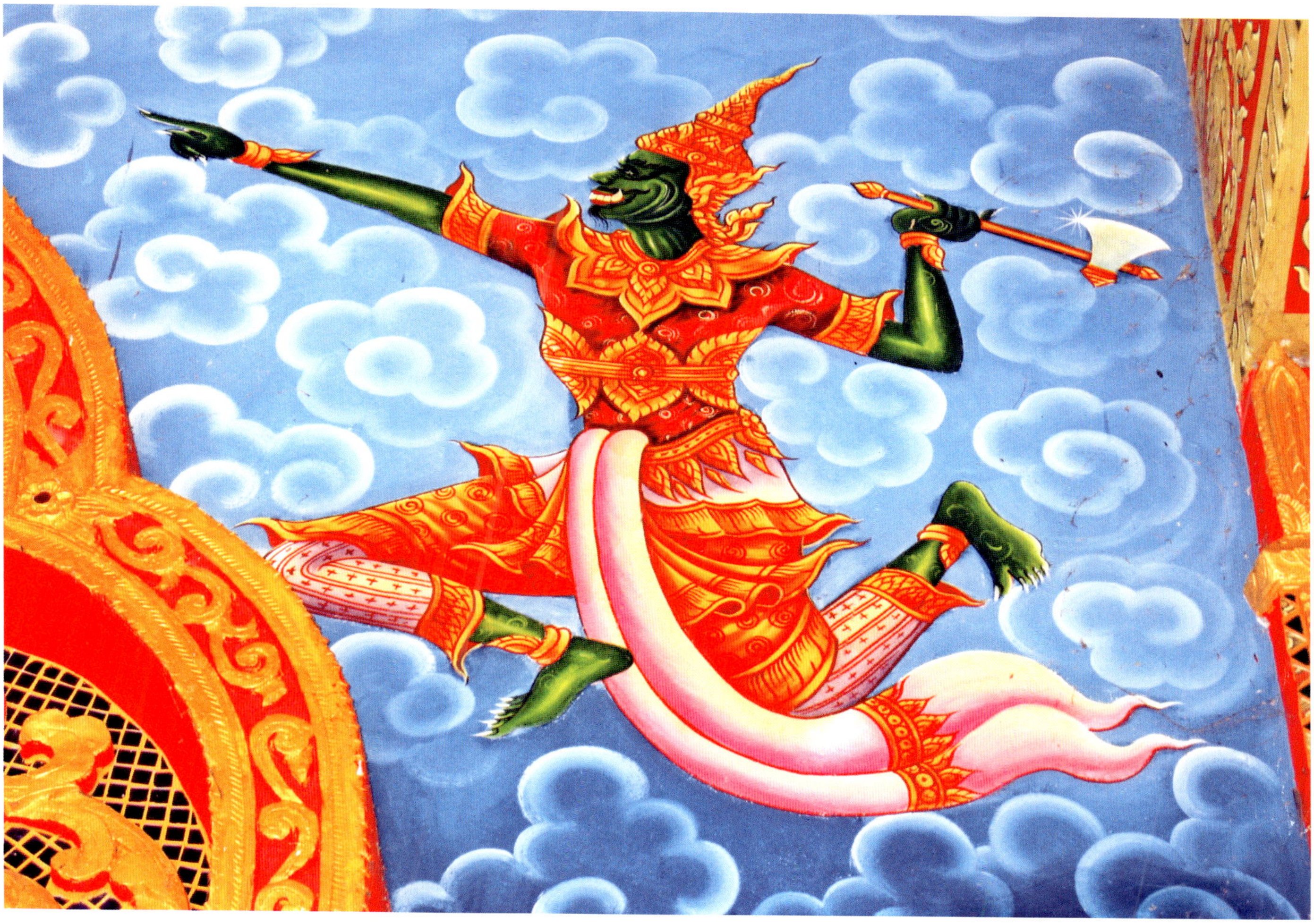

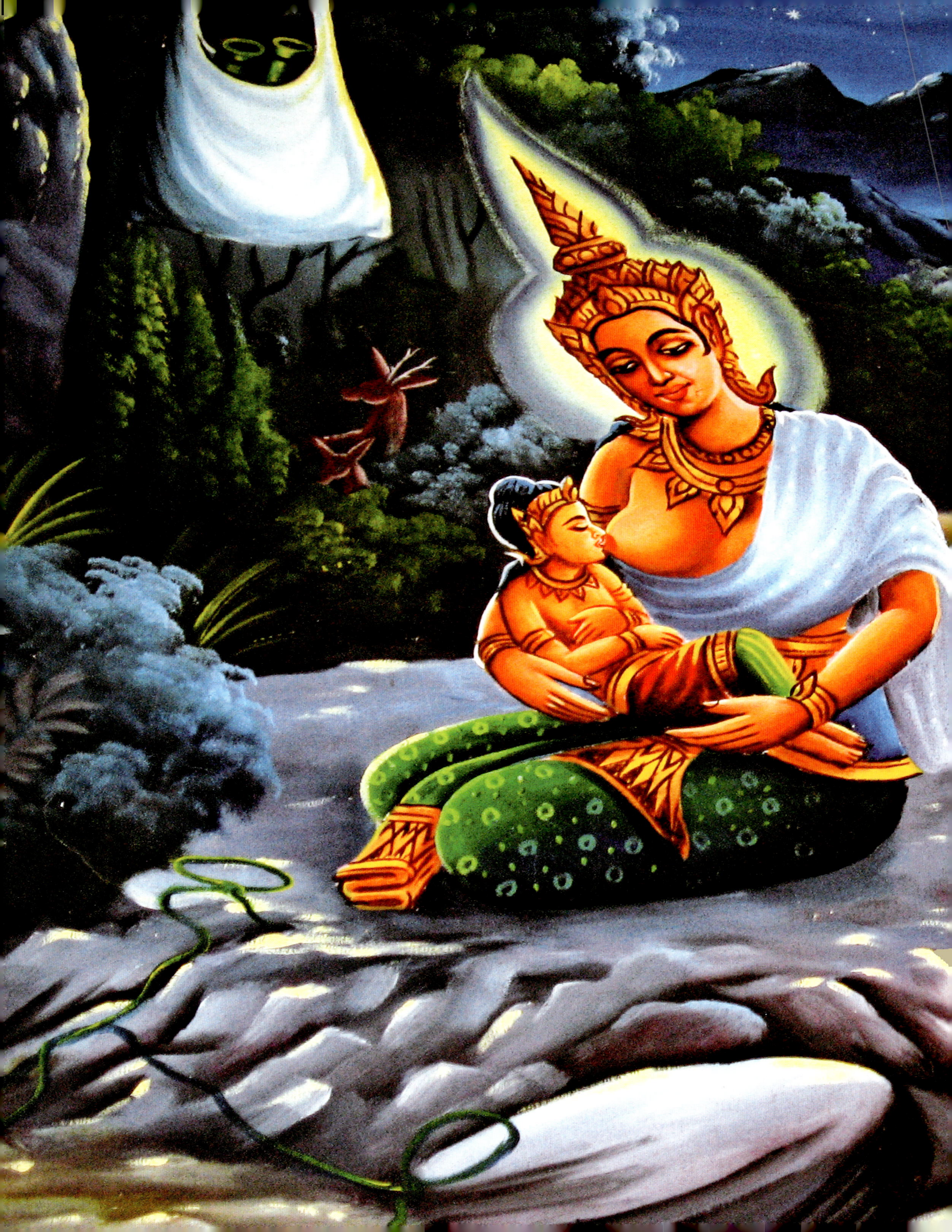

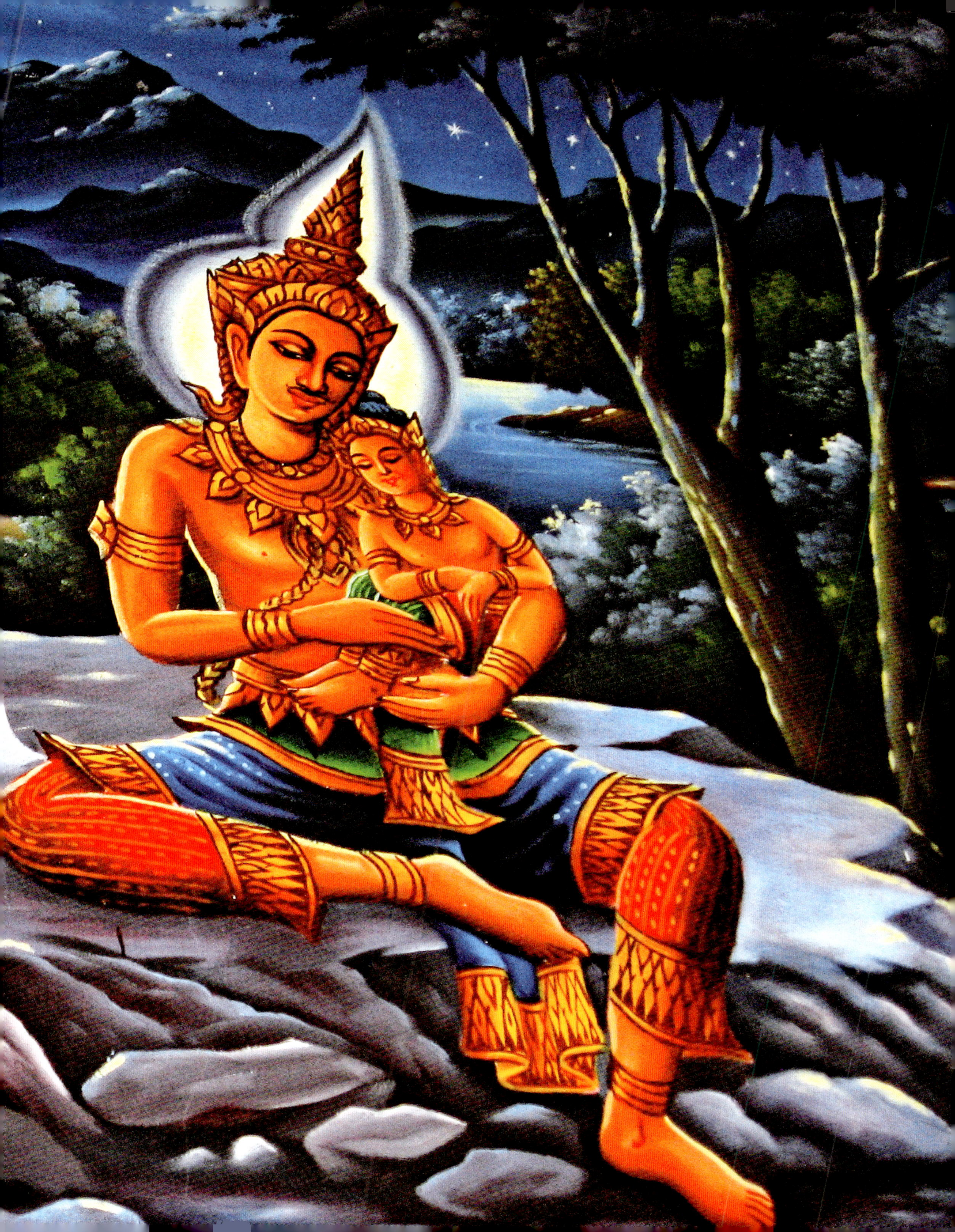

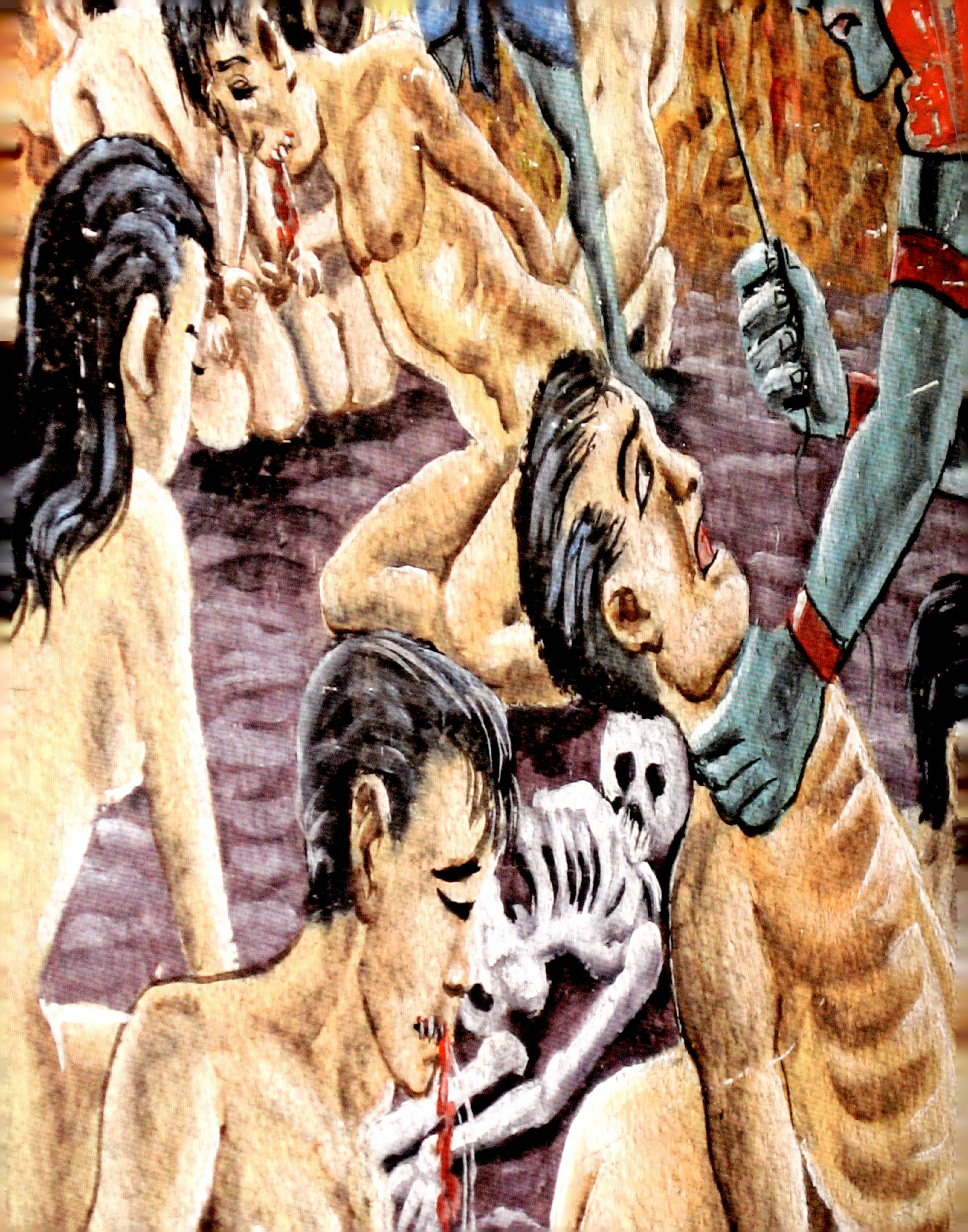

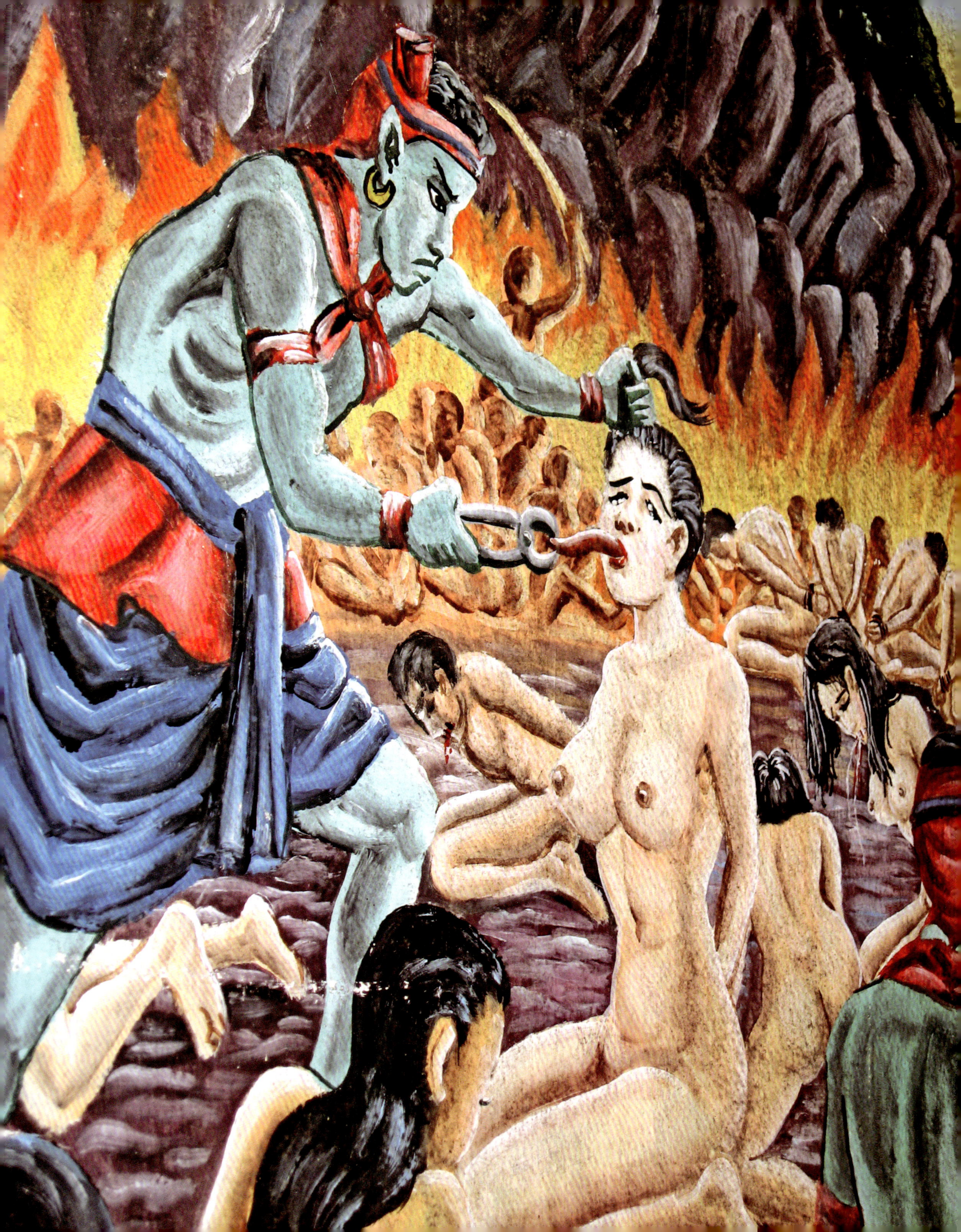

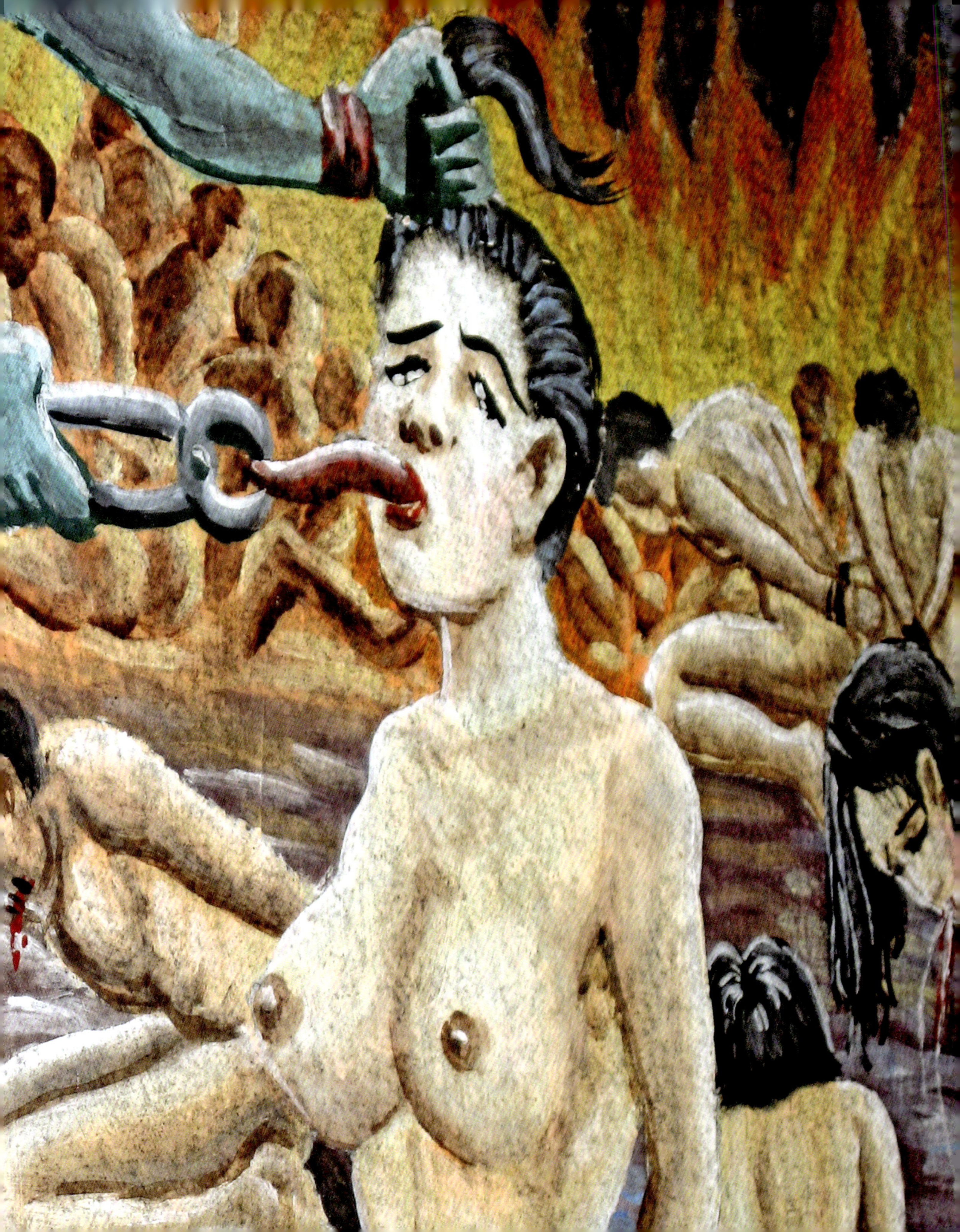

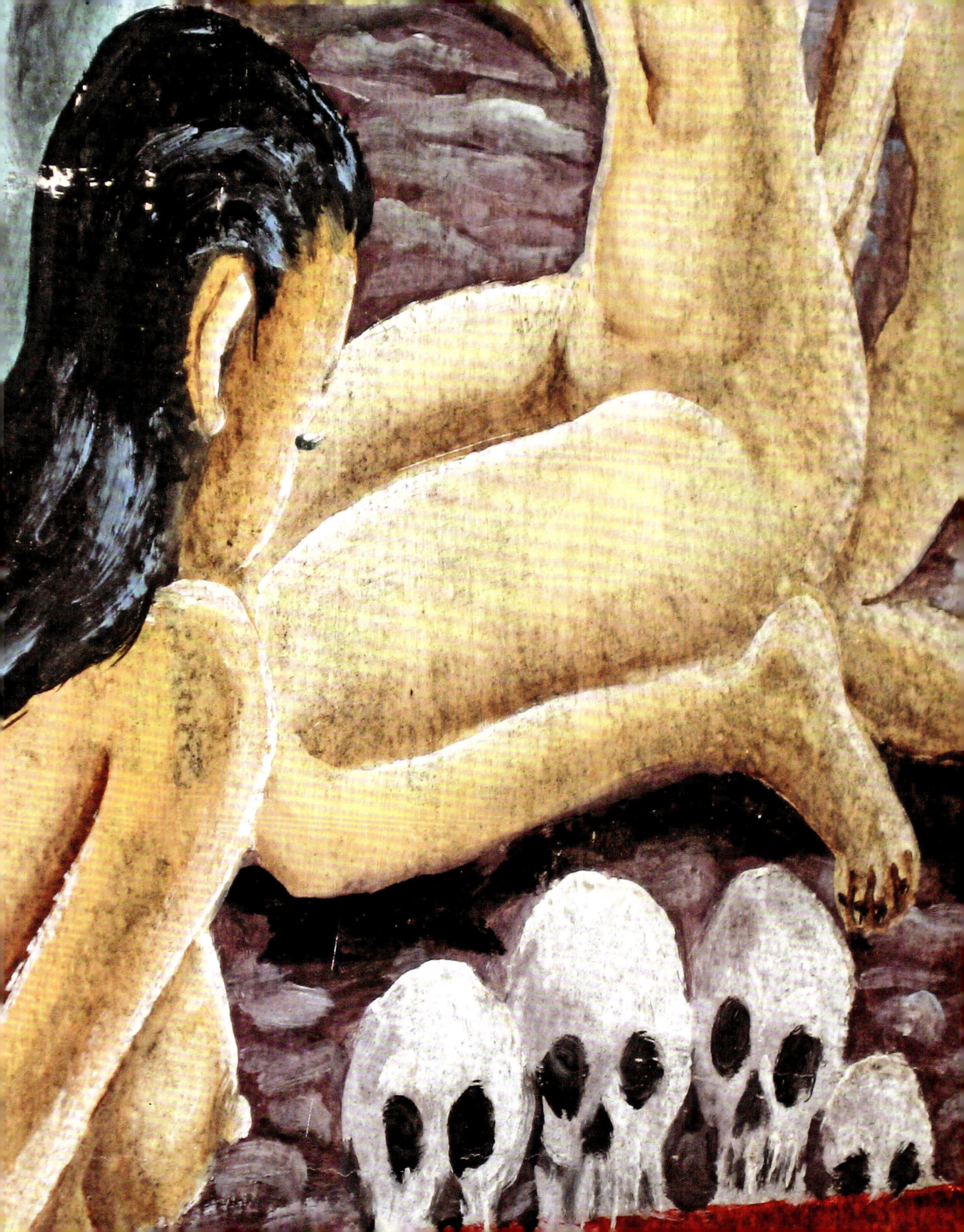

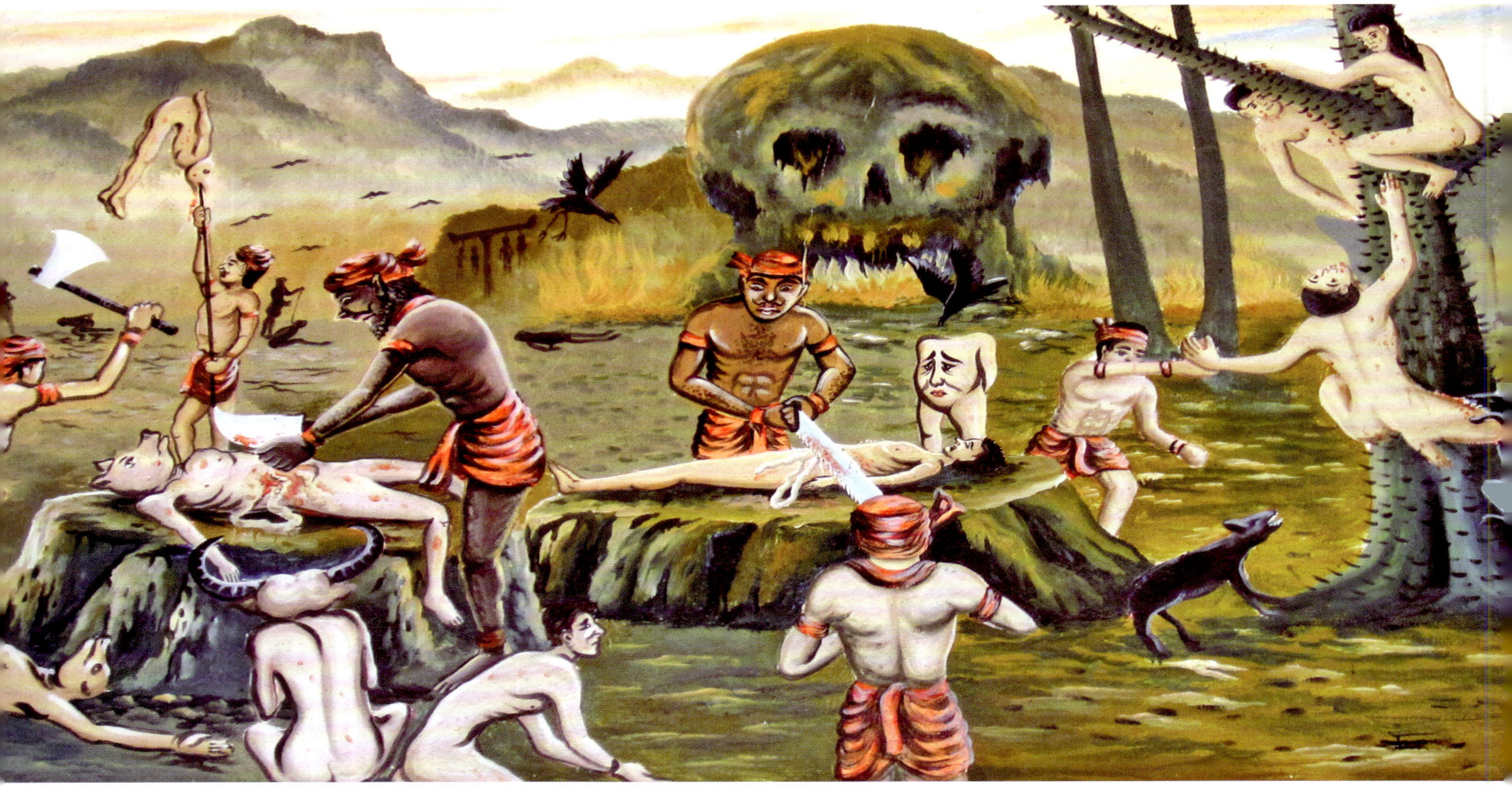

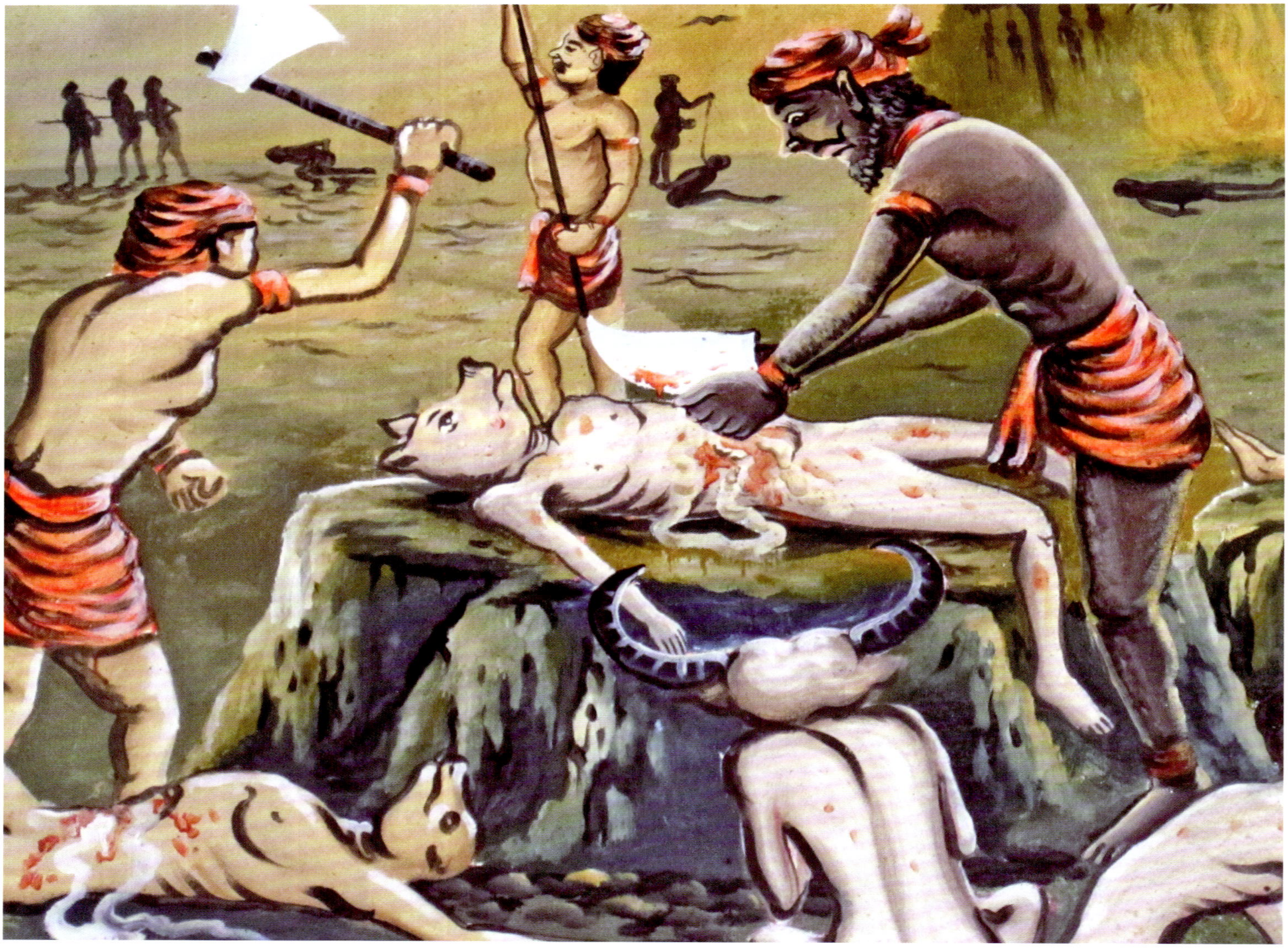

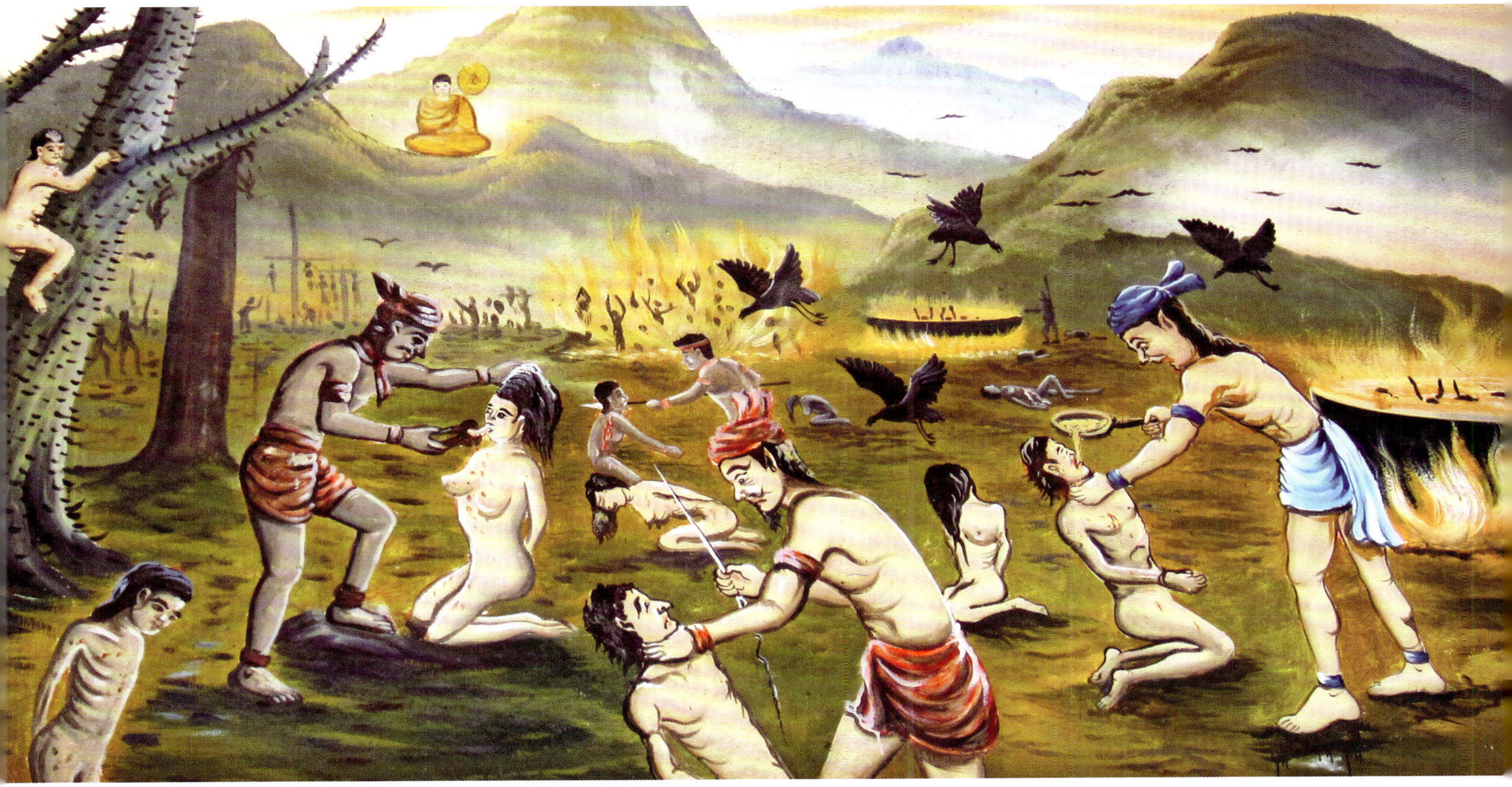

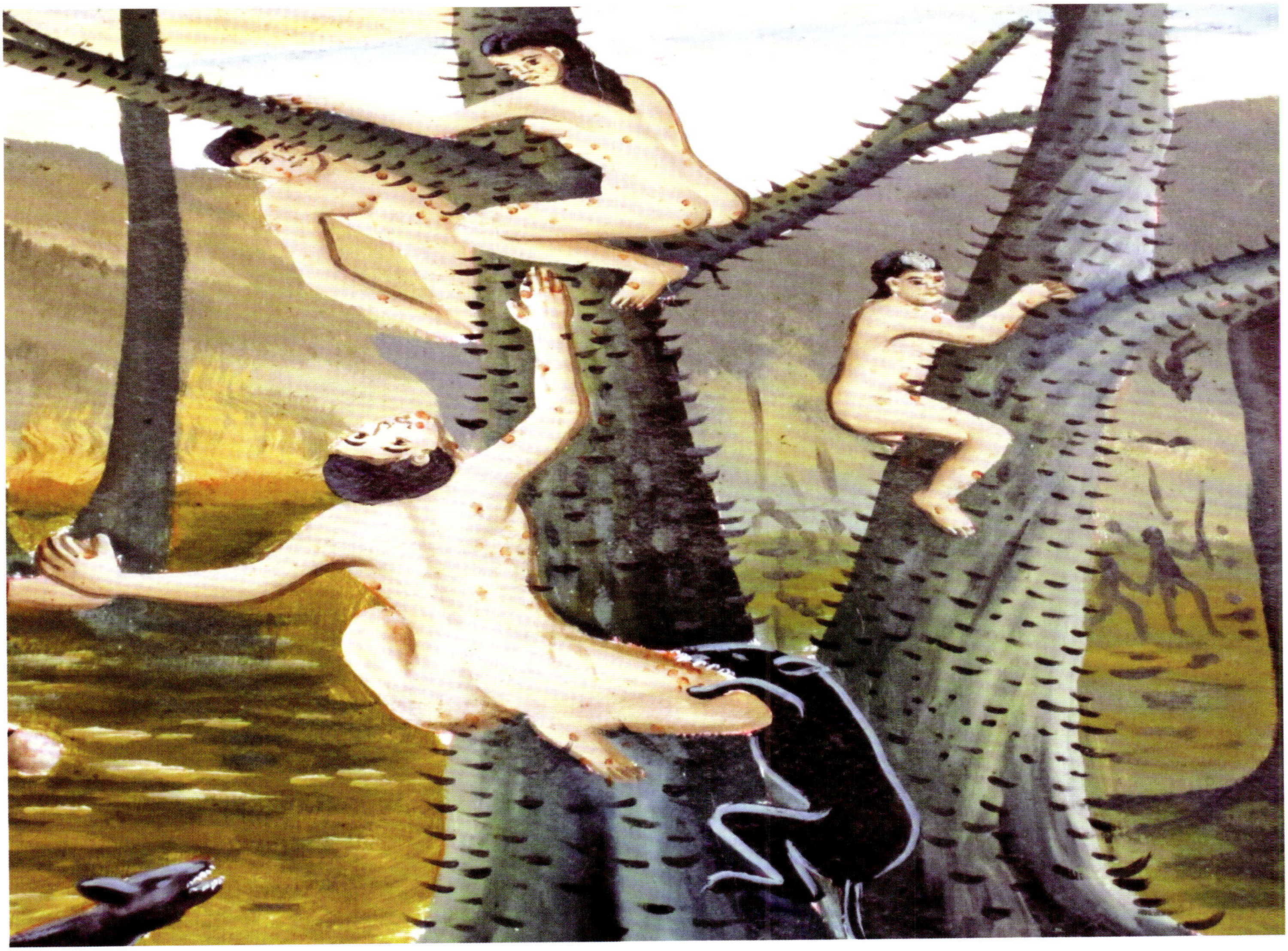

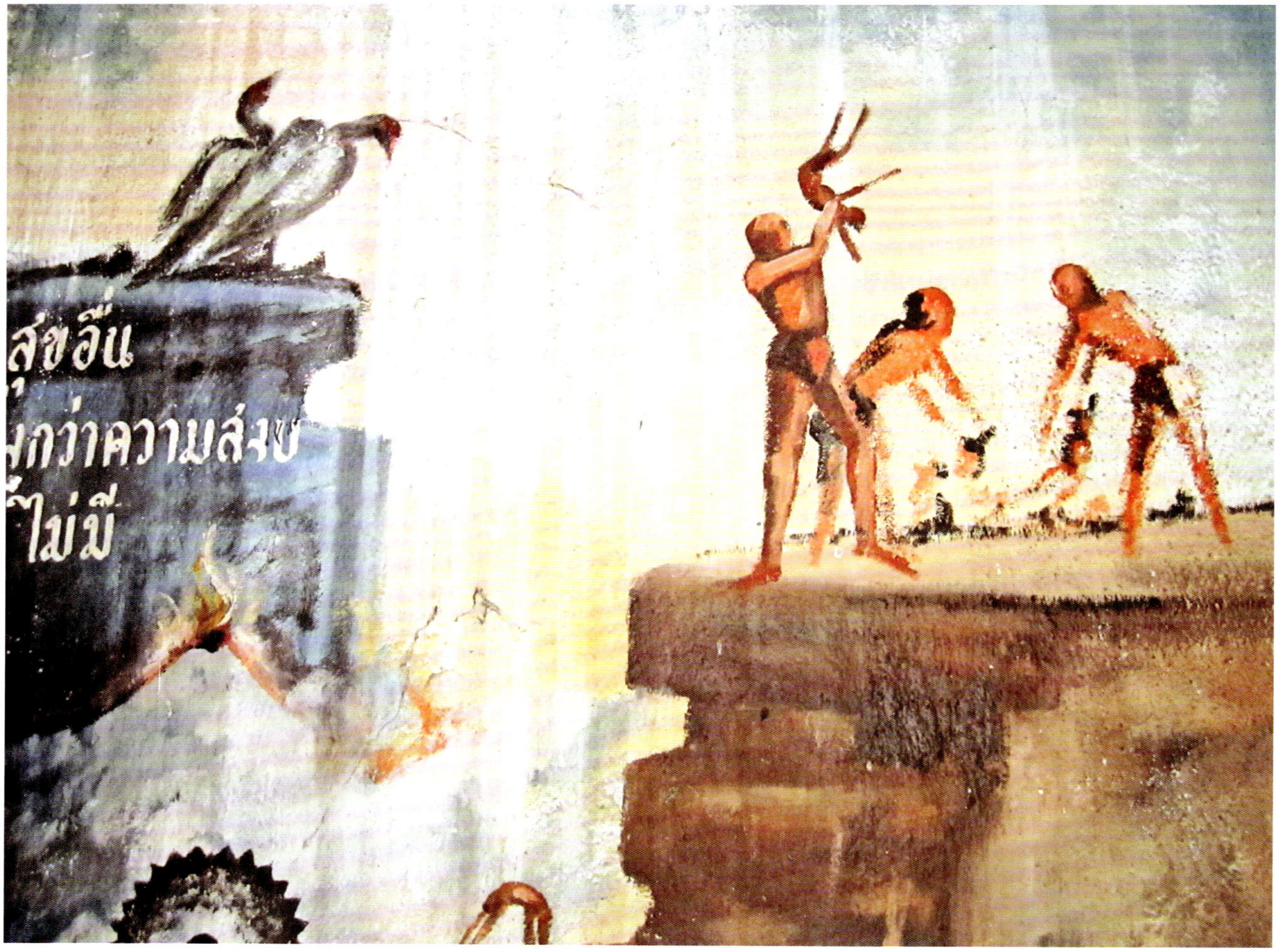

สุขอื่น
กว่าความสงบ
ไม่มี

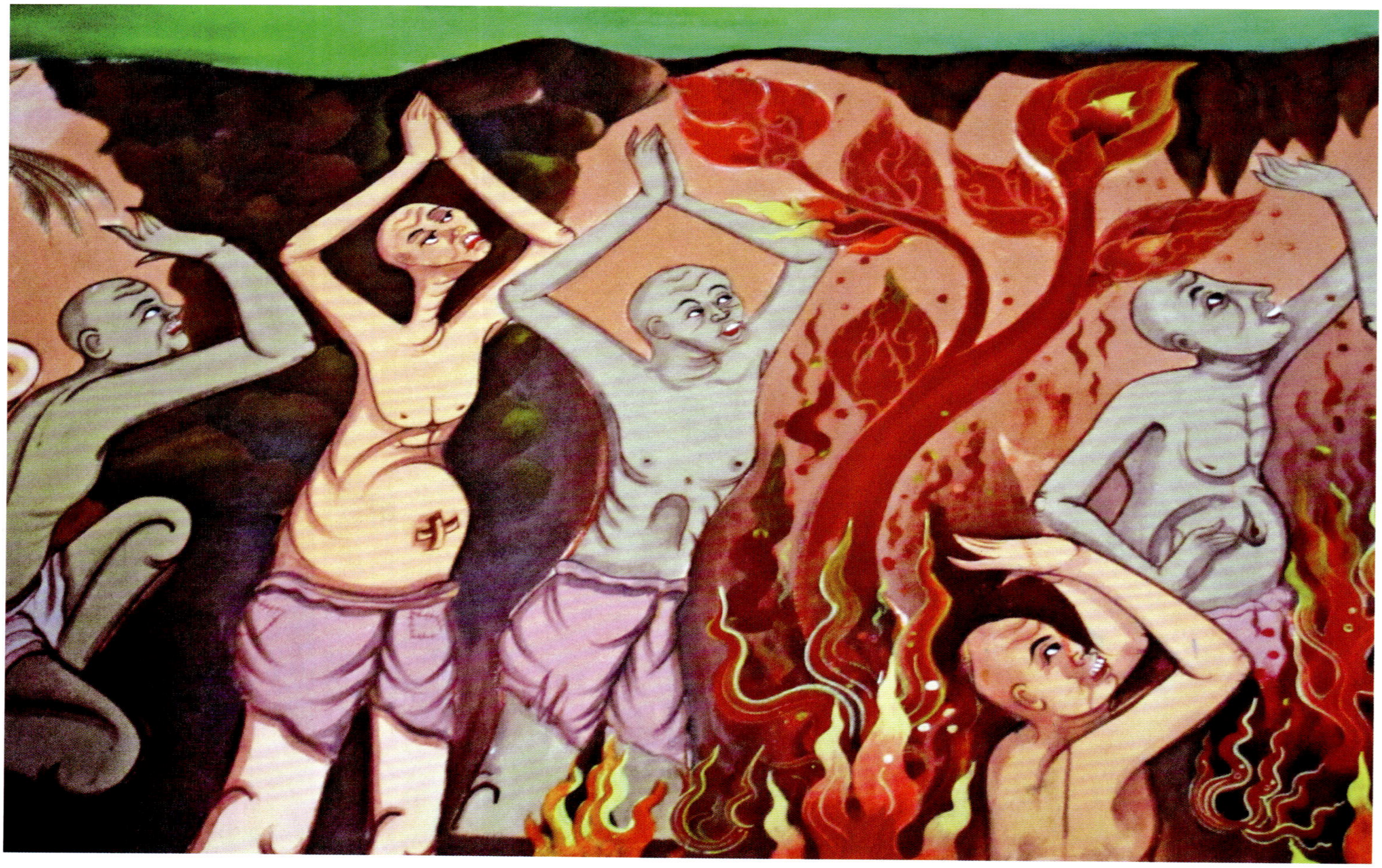

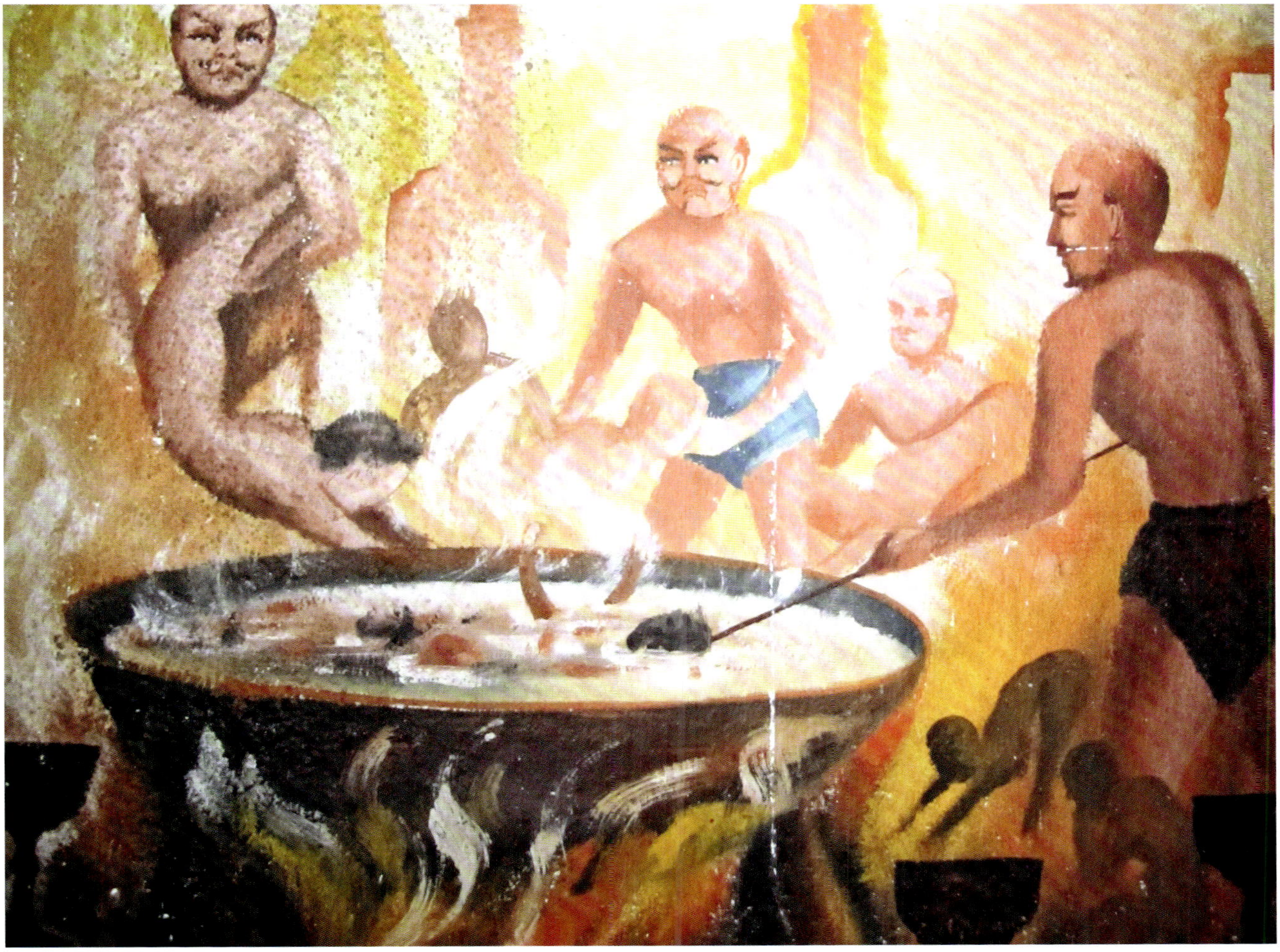

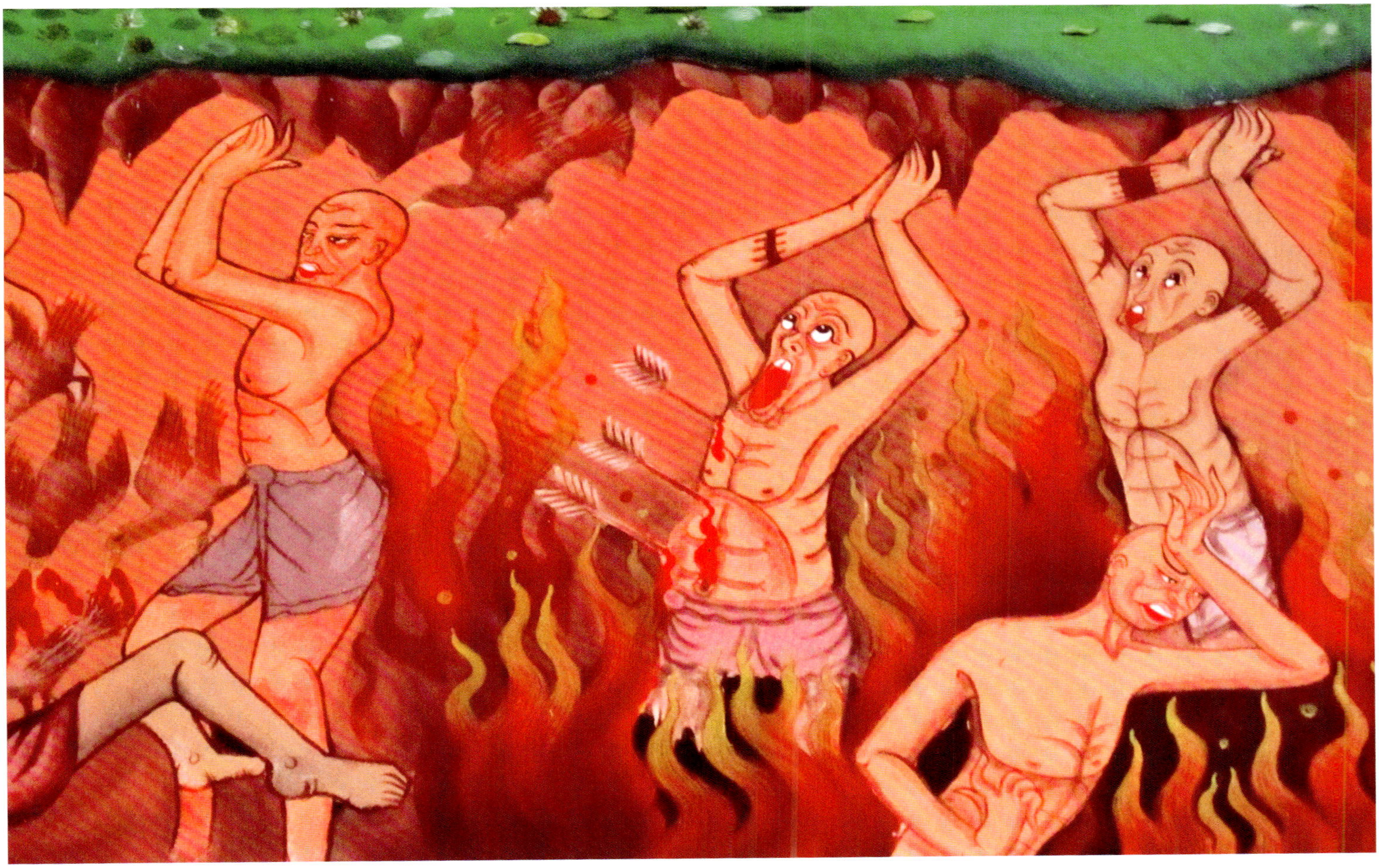

PHOTO CAPTIONS

Photographs are captioned in a clockwise direction from top left, by 2-page spread, as in the example immediately below.

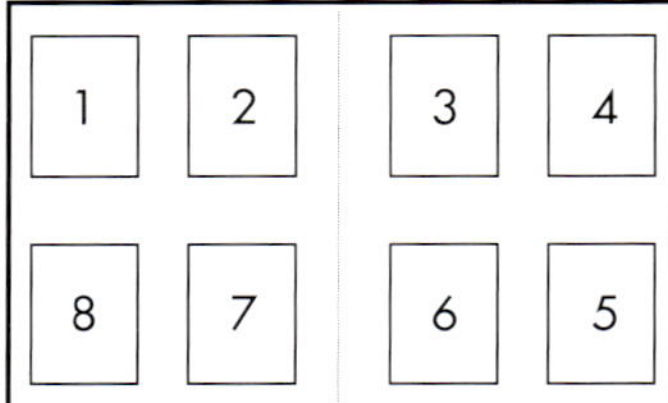

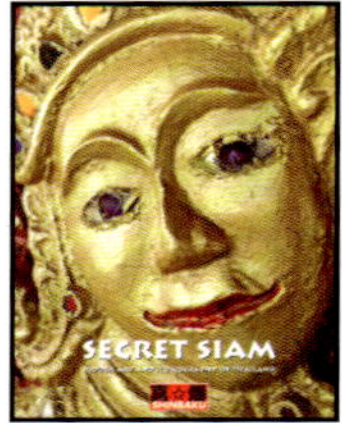

Title page

1. *Apsara* on main *viharn* platform, Wat Suan Dok, Chiang Mai.

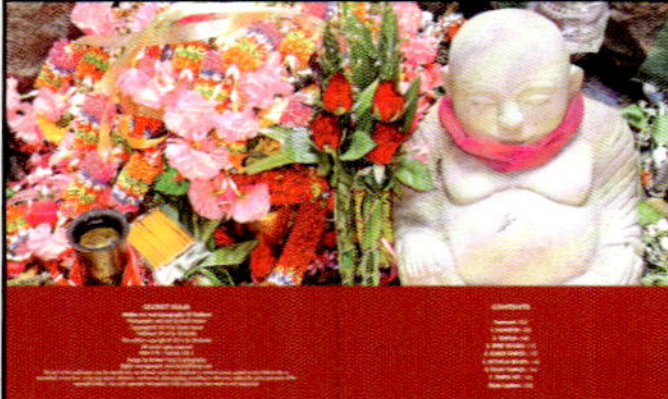

Pages 2-3

1. Shrine inside the *arogyasala*, the chapel of the hospital of Ku Santarat, Maha Sarakam province (from early thirteenth century).

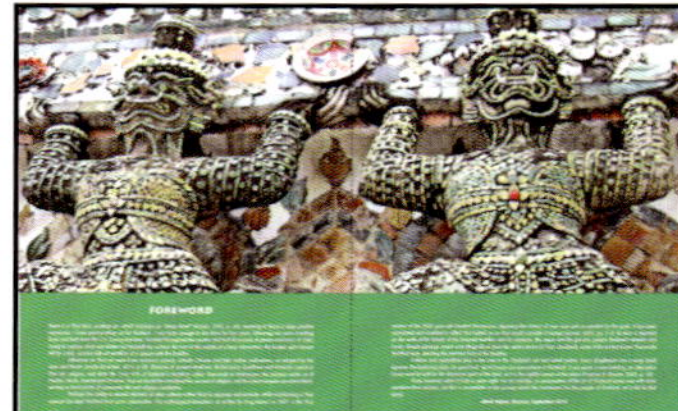

Pages 3-4

1. Guardian protector *yakshas* support the towers of Wat Arun, the Temple of Dawn, Bangkok.

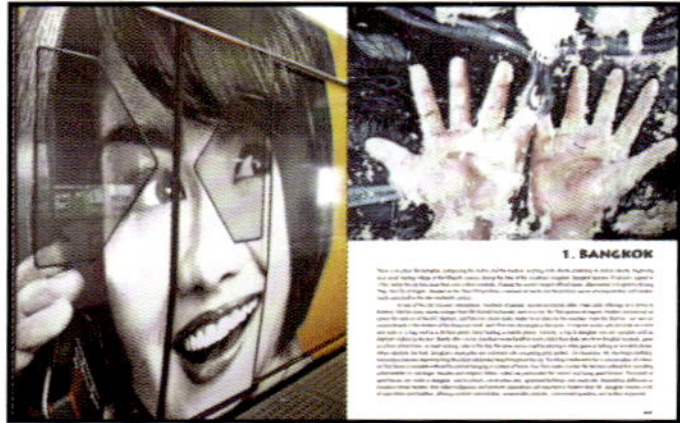

Pages 6-7

1. Advertising on BTS Skytrain, Bangkok.
2. Schoolyard mural, Bangkok.

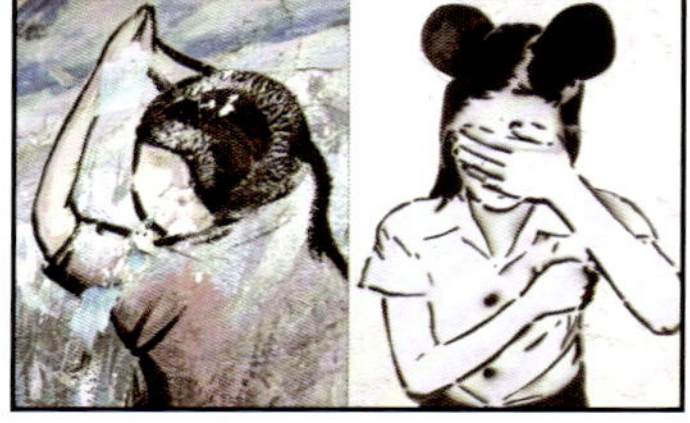

Pages 8-9

1. Girl *wais*, schoolyard mural, Bangkok.
2. Schoolgirl in uniform with mouse ears, Bangkok. Appropriation of artist Banksy's graffiti art style.

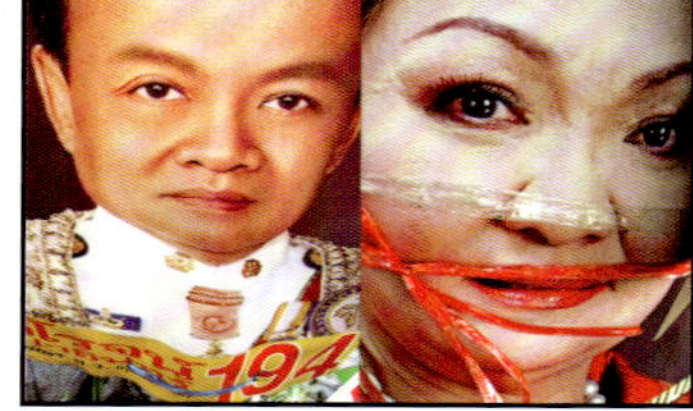

Pages 10-11

1. Political poster, March 2006, Bangkok.
2. Political poster, March 2006, Bangkok. Former Thai Rak Thai PM Thaksin Shinawatra was ousted in a military coup in September 2006.

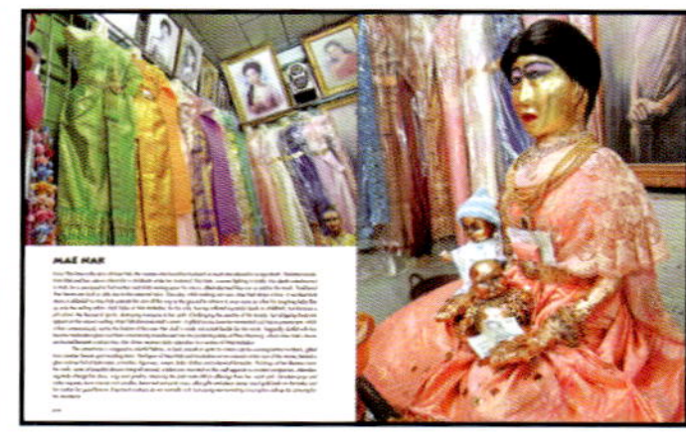

Pages 12-13

1. Dresses offered as gifts at Mae Nak Shrine, Wat Mahabut, Bangkok.
2. Statue of Mae Nak at Mae Nak Shrine, 2012, in human hair wig with baby; both figures have gold leaf sheets applied for good fortune.

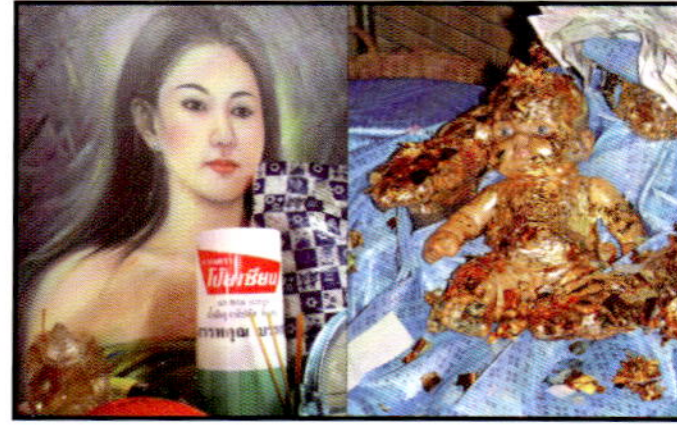

Pages 14-15

1. Gifted painted portrait of Mae Nak, Mae Nak Shrine.
2. Male baby doll with gold leaf applied, Mae Nak Shrine.

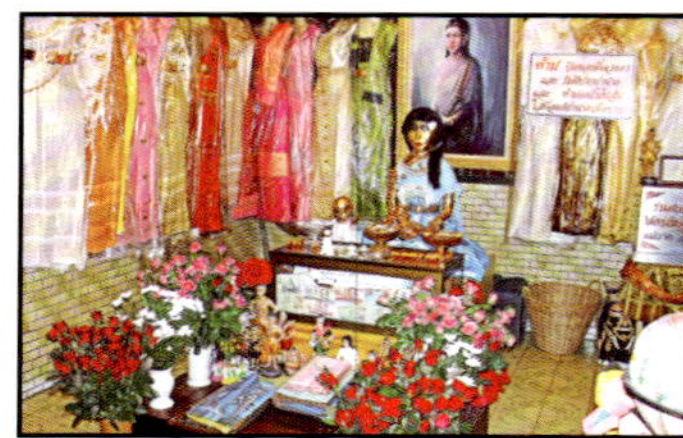

Pages 16-17

1. Mae Nak at Mae Nak Shrine, 2005. Red and pink roses, figurines, and baby toys fill her shrine.

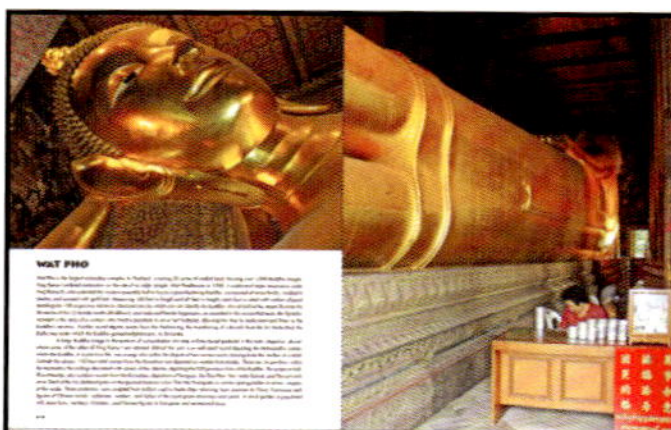

Pages 18-19

1. Reclining Buddha, 2005, Wat Pho, Bangkok.
2. Reclining Buddha (rear view), Wat Pho.

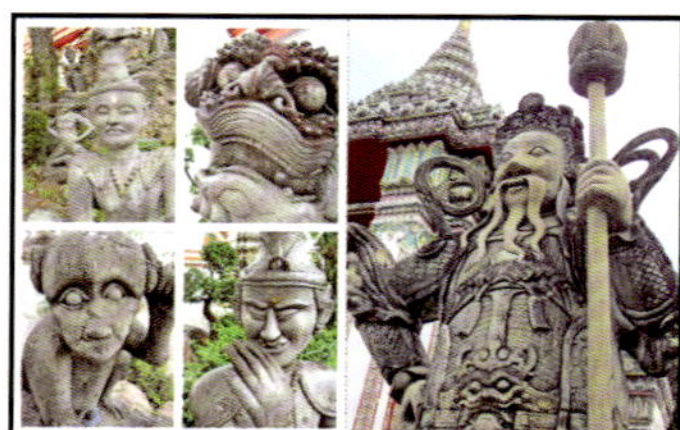

Pages 20-21

1. Stone statuary figure, Wat Pho.
2. Chinese-style stone lion guardian, Wat Pho.
3. Chinese *Lan Than* warrior guardian, based on historical combatants, Wat Pho.
4. Chinese stone statuary figure, Wat Pho.
5. Stone monkey (notice blue genitals), Wat Pho.

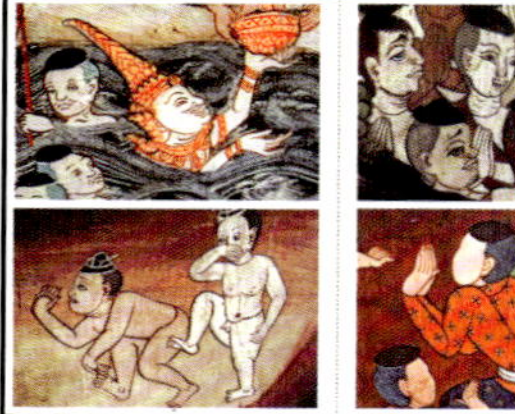

Pages 22-23

1. Human warrior; mural detail, Wat Pho.
2. Praying figures; mural detail, Wat Pho.
3. Faceless followers; mural detail, Wat Pho.
4. Naked figures; mural detail, Wat Pho.

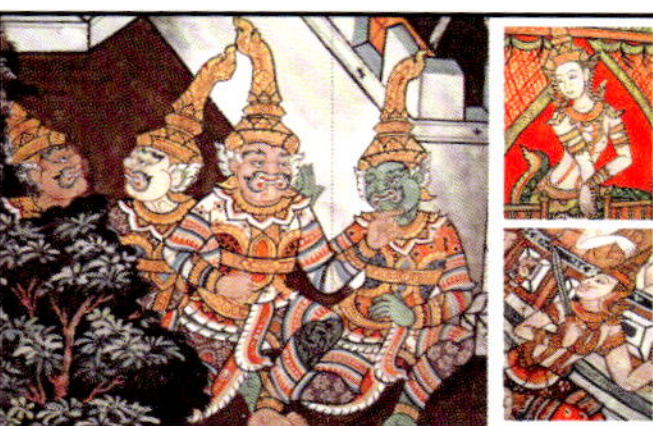

Pages 24-25

1. Giants; mural detail, Wat Pho.
2. Celestial mermaid; mural detail, Wat Pho.
3. Human warrior; mural detail, Wat Pho.

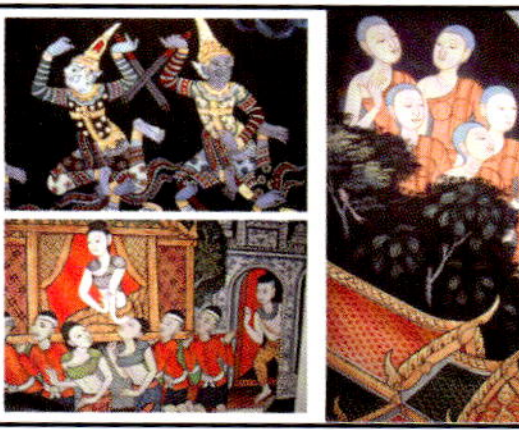

Pages 26-27

1. Giants; mural detail, Wat Pho.
2. Ten of the 13 Buddhist nuns, called *bhikkhuni*; mural detail, Wat Pho.
3. Beautiful and wealthy Phra Nunda Theri, carried by her attendants; mural detail, Wat Pho.

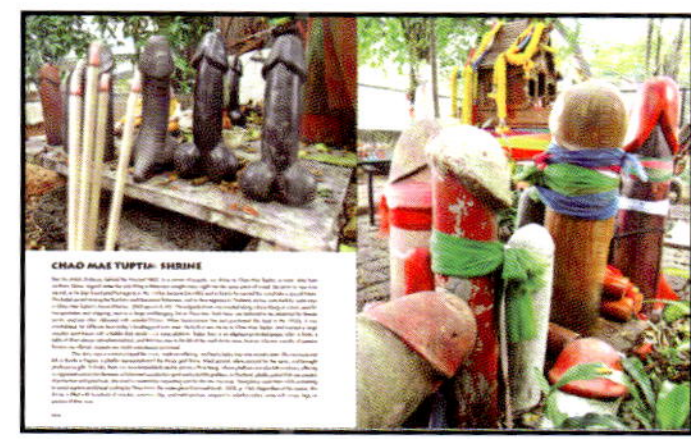

Pages 28-29

1. Joss sticks and stone phalluses on stone altar, Chao Mae Tuptim Shrine, Bangkok.
2. Concrete and wooden phalluses beside garland-adorned traditional wooden Thai spirit house, Chao Mae Tuptim Shrine.

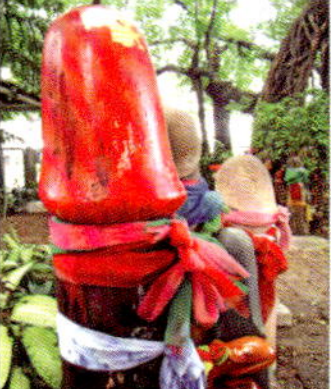
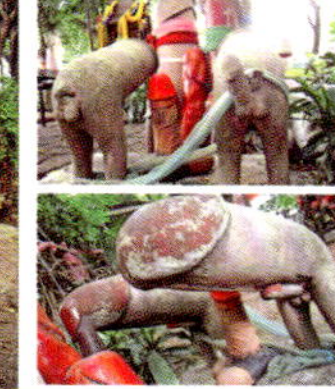

Pages 30-31

1. Wood and concrete phalluses, Chao Mae Tuptim Shrine, Bangkok.
2. Rear view: Concrete penis on legs with penis and testicles in place of anus, Chao Mae Tuptim Shrine.
3. Front view: Concrete penis on legs with second penis and testicles, Chao Mae Tuptim Shrine.

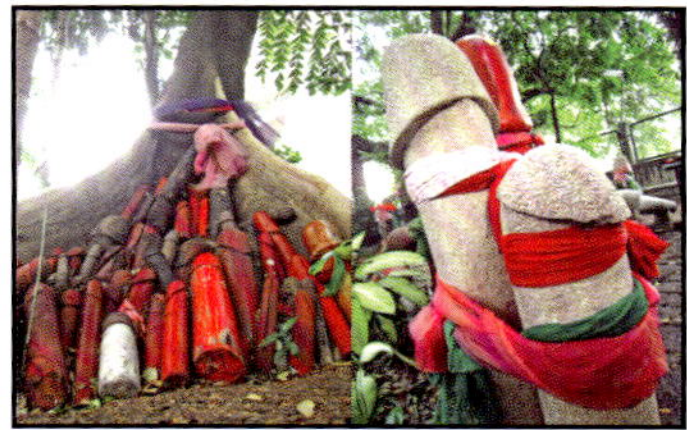

Pages 32-33

1. Sacred Ficus tree with phallus offerings, Chao Mae Tuptim Shrine.
2. Concrete and wooden phalluses, believed to be a symbol of good luck and protection against evil spirits, Chao Mae Tuptim Shrine.

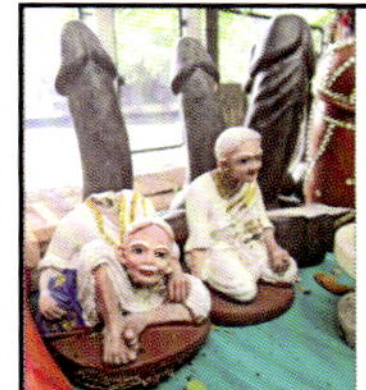
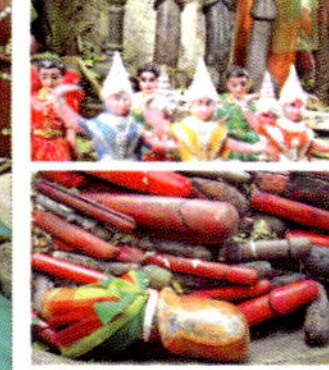

Pages 34-35

1. Grandparent figurines on side table, Chao Mae Tuptim Shrine.
2. *Khon* dancer and servant or attendant figurines arranged in front of phalluses, Chao Mae Tuptim Shrine.
3. Wooden phalluses, Chao Mae Tuptim Shrine.

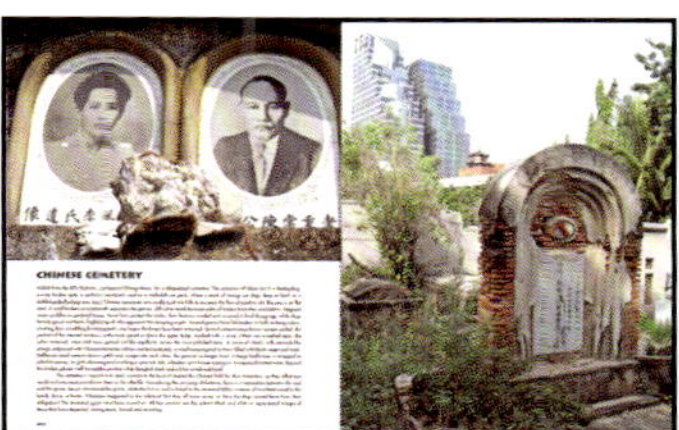

Pages 36-37

1. Mausoleum portrait, Chinese Cemetery, Silom Soi 9, Bangkok.
2. Dilapidated gravestone next to neglected crypts, Chinese Cemetery. Silom Soi 9.

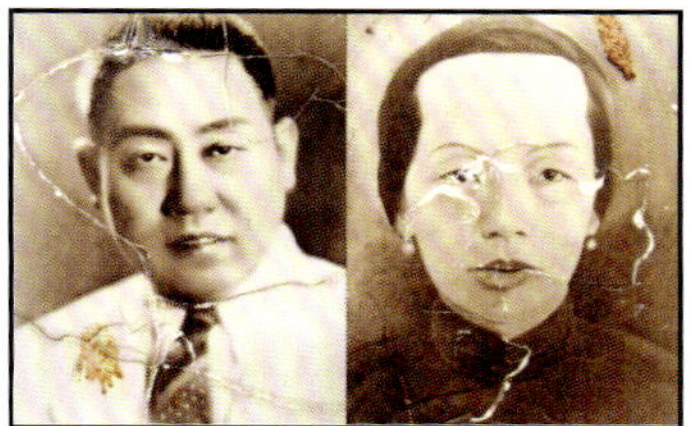

Pages 38-39

1. Mausoleum portrait, Chinese Cemetery, Silom Soi 9.
2. Mausoleum portrait, Chinese Cemetery, Silom Soi 9.

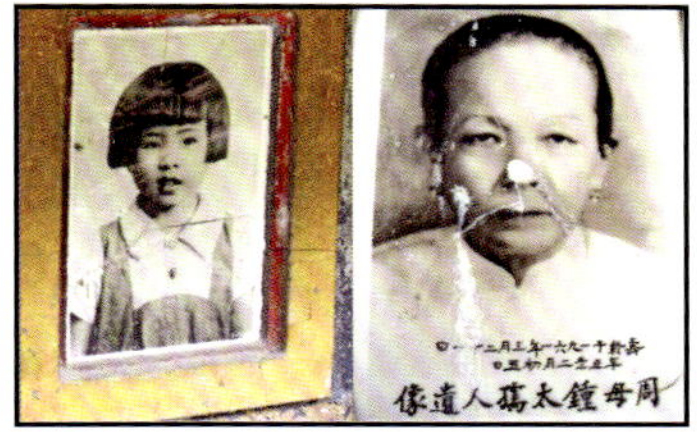

Pages 40-41

1. Mausoleum portrait, Chinese Cemetery, Silom Soi 9.
2. Mausoleum portrait, Chinese Cemetery, Silom Soi 9.

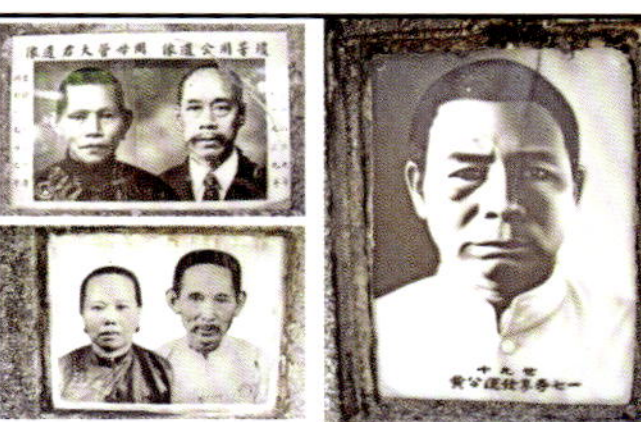

Pages 42-43

1. Mausoleum portraits, Chinese Cemetery, Silom Soi 9.
2. Mausoleum portrait, Chinese Cemetery, Silom Soi 9.

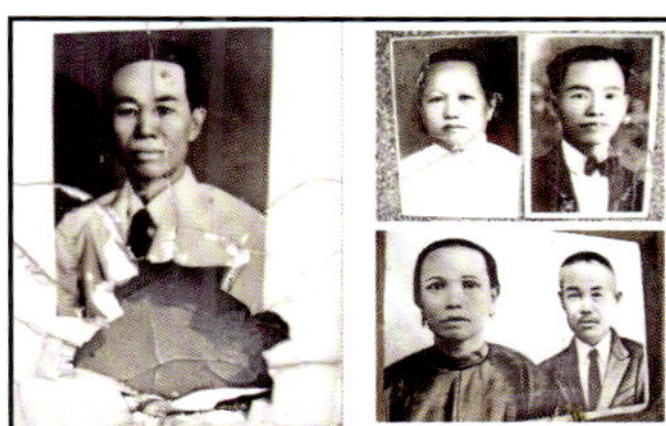

Pages 44-45

1. Mausoleum portrait, Chinese Cemetery, Silom Soi 9.
2. Mausoleum portraits, Chinese Cemetery, Silom Soi 9.

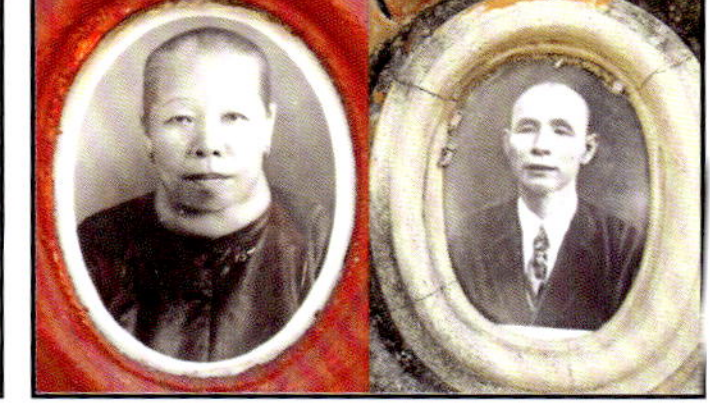

Pages 46-47

1. Mausoleum portrait, Chinese Cemetery, Silom Soi 9.
2. Mausoleum portrait, Chinese Cemetery, Silom Soi 9.

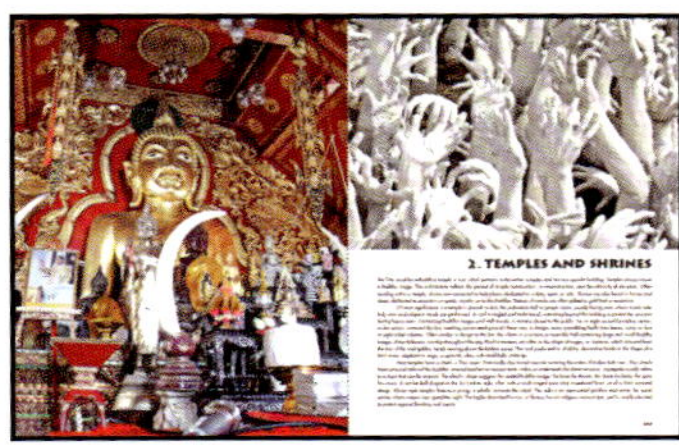

Pages 48-49

1. Buddha image in the *viharn*, Wat Klang Wiang, Chiang Rai.
2. Hands reaching up from Hell at the unconventional Wat Rong Khun, the White Temple, Chiang Rai.

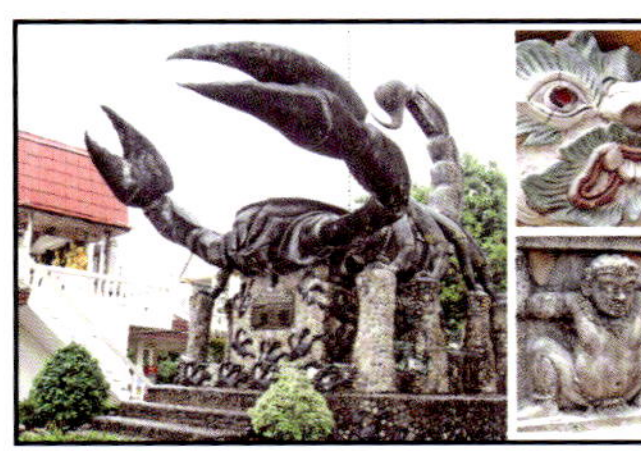

Pages 50-51

1. Scorpion statue, Wat Phra That Wai Dao, Mae Sai. The defensive claws of the scorpion point towards Tachileik, Burma.
2. Guardian dwarf protector, Wat Mahawan, Chiang Mai.
3 Temple support figure, Khon Kaen.

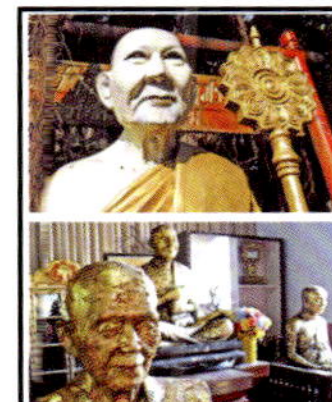

Pages 52-53

1. Revered monk statue, Mae Sot.
2. Temple entrance divinity, Burmese/Lanna-style, Wat Montien, Chiang Mai.
3. Revered monk statues, gilded with gold leaf, Wat Phra Singh, Chiang Mai.

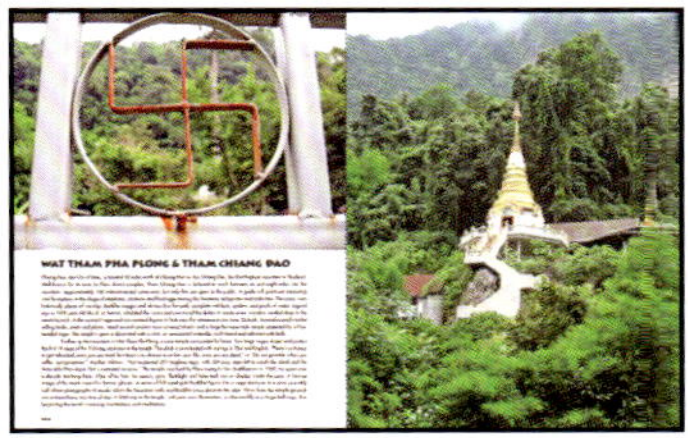

Pages 54-55

1. Swastika gate adornment, Tham Chiang Dao cave complex. Auspicious Sanskrit symbol.
2. Wat Tham Pha Plong, Chiang Dao.

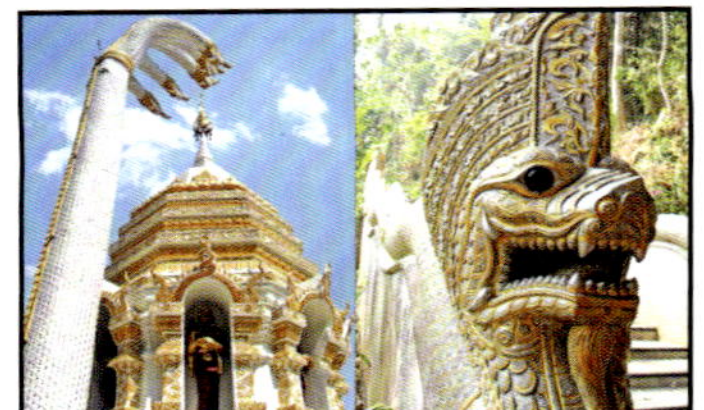

Pages 56-57

1. *Naga*-protected temple, Chiang Dao.
2. Crowned *naga* at the base of the 510-step climb up the mountain to Wat Tham Pha Plong, Chiang Dao.

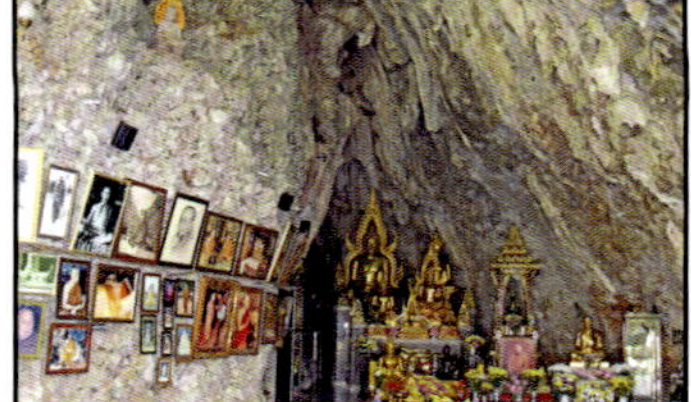

Pages 58-59

1. Cave assembly hall with portraits of revered monks, Wat Tham Pha Plong, Chiang Dao.

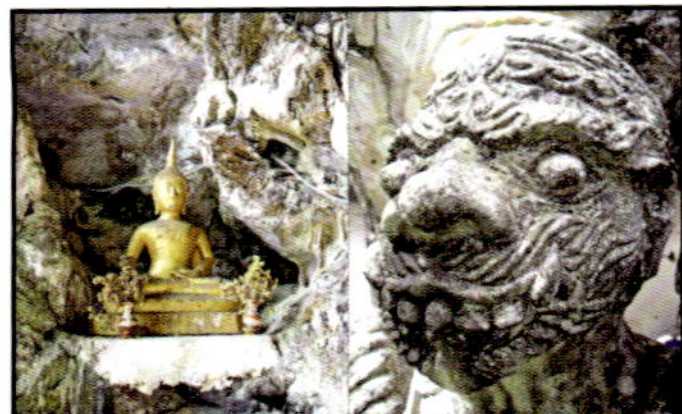

Pages 60-61

1. Buddha shrine, Wat Tham Chiang Dao cave complex.
2. Stone guardian *yaksha*, Wat Tham Pha Plong, Chiang Dao.

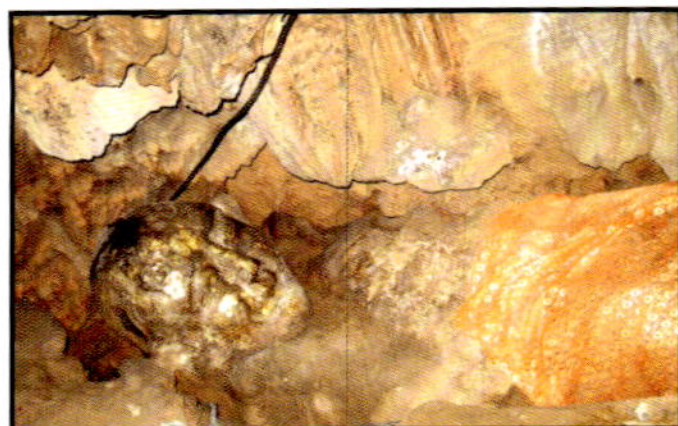

Pages 62-63

1. Petrified monk relic, Tham Chiang Dao cave complex.

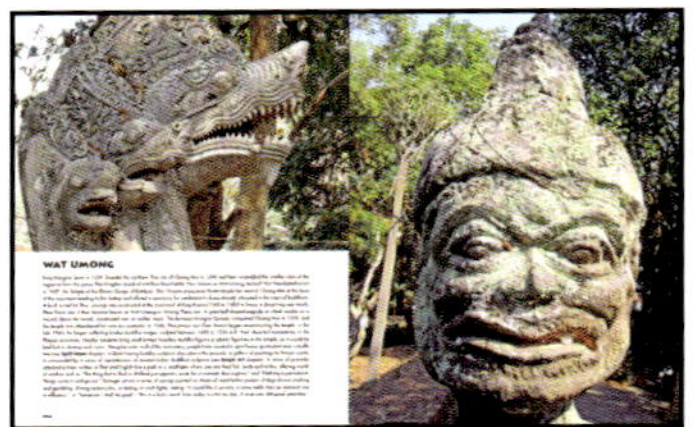

Pages 64-65

1. Crowned *naga* staircase adornment, Wat Umong, Chiang Mai.
2. Stone guardian statue, Wat Umong.

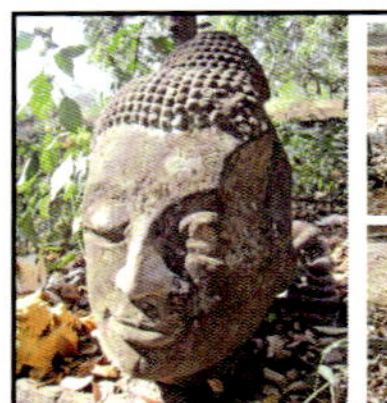

Pages 66-67

1. Damaged Buddha head, Wat Umong.
2. Damaged Buddha figures, Wat Umong.
3. Damaged Buddha heads, Wat Umong.

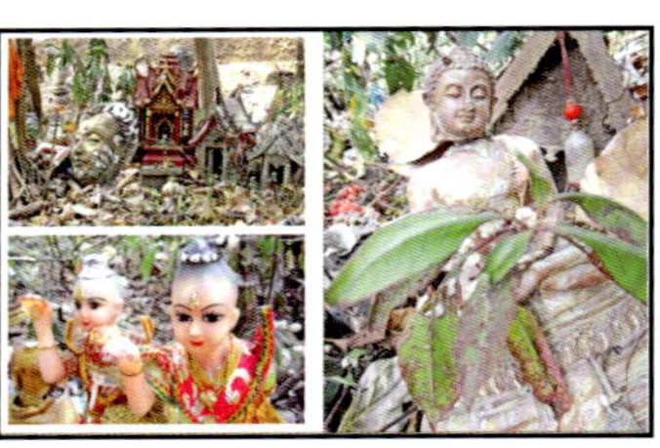

Pages 68-69

1. Spirit house cemetery, Wat Umong.
2. Abandoned *nang kwak* figurines, Wat Umong.
3. Broken Buddha figure, Wat Umong.

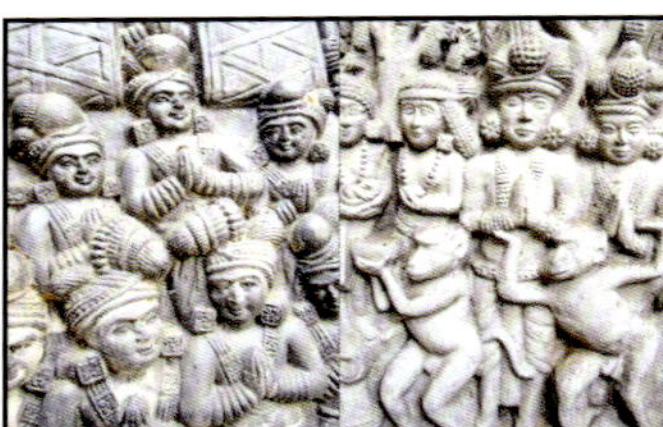

Pages 70-71

1. Stone carvings; reproductions of Indian works of art, Wat Umong.
2. Stone carvings; reproductions of Indian works of art, Wat Umong.

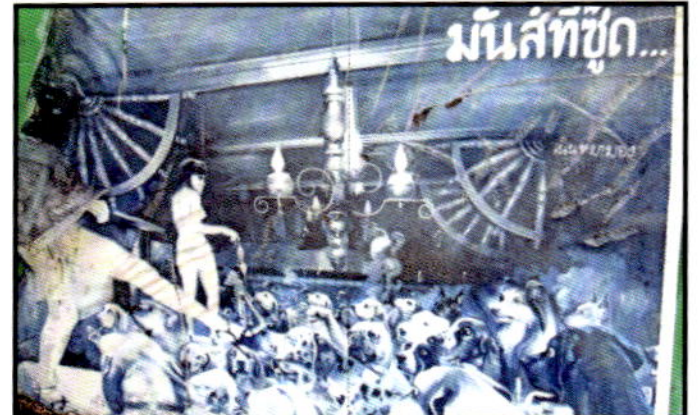

Pages 72-73

1. Strange dog poster with proverb underneath, painted on metal, written in Thai and English, Wat Umong.

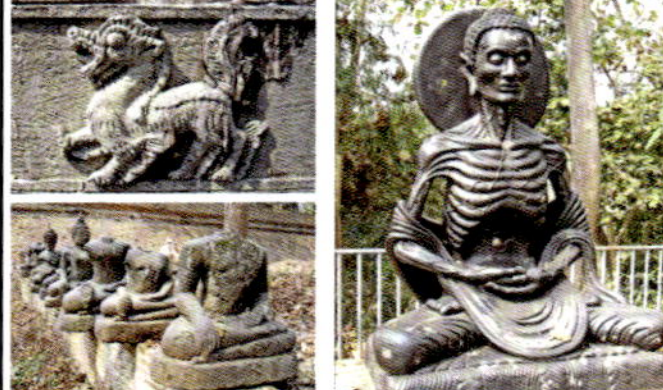

Pages 74-75

1. Mythical creature; temple adornment, Wat Umong.
2. Damaged Buddha icons, Wat Umong.
3. Black Fasting Buddha icon, Wat Umong.

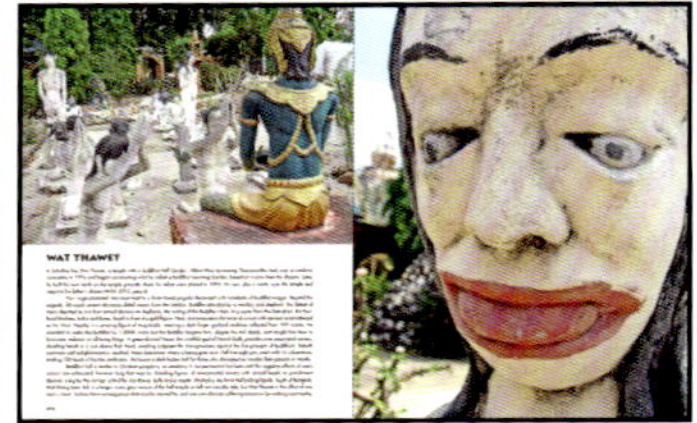

Pages 76-77

1. Yama, the god of death, decides the path of rebirth for souls based on virtues and sins; Wat Thawet, Sukothai.
2. Cement dead soul, Wat Thawet.

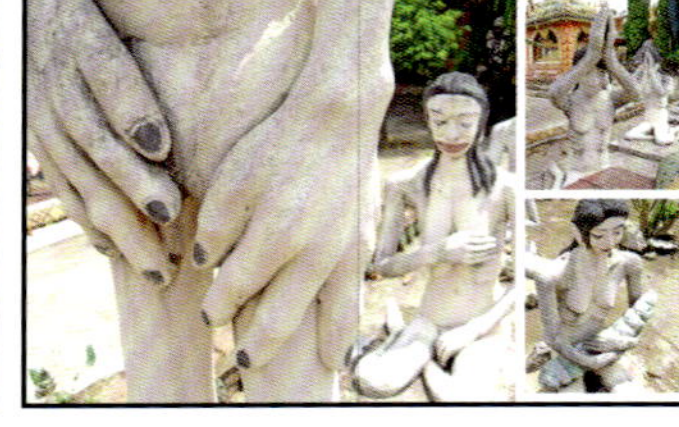

Pages 78-79

1. Genital-less dead soul, Wat Thawet.
2. Dead soul with hands raised in *wai*, Wat Thawet.
3. Dead soul holding cocoon, Wat Thawet.

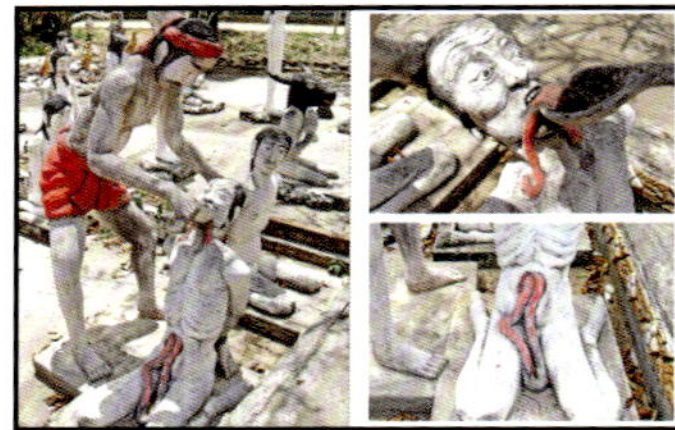

Pages 80-81

1. Alcoholic soul being fed boiling liquids, Wat Thawet.
2. Alcoholic soul being fed boiling liquids, Wat Thawet.
3. Entrails of alcoholic, Wat Thawet.

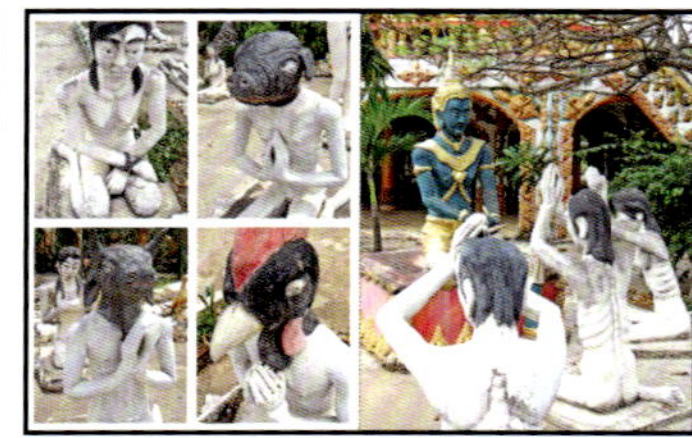

Pages 82-83

1. Dead soul with bound hands, Wat Thawet.
2. The corrupt receive a pig's head, Wat Thawet.
3. Yama with his "Book of Destiny," Wat Thawet.
4. Dead soul with a cock's head, Wat Thawet.
5. Dead soul with a goat's head, Wat Thawet.

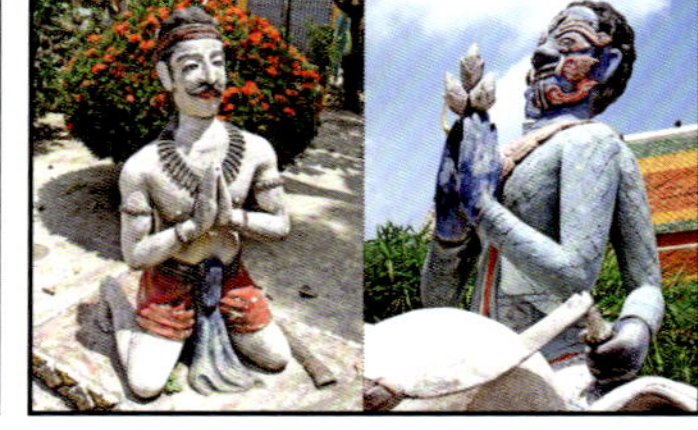

Pages 84-85

1. The killer Anguimala, Wat Thawet.
2. The demon Mara with lotus flower, Wat Thawet.

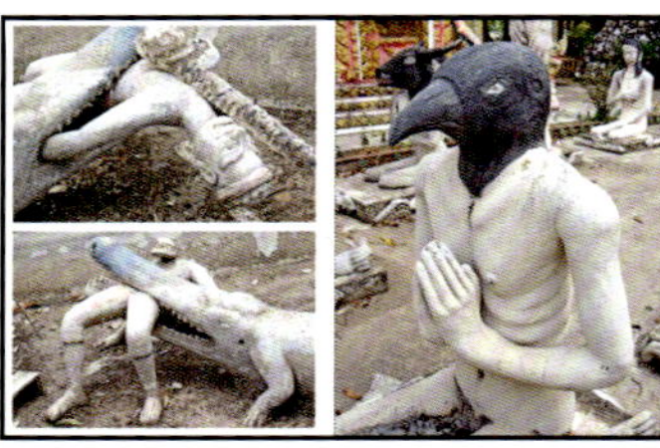

Pages 86-87

1. Crocodile eating deal soul, Wat Thawet.
2. Crocodile eating dead soul, Wat Thawet.
3. Rice thieves get a crow's head; Wat Thawet.

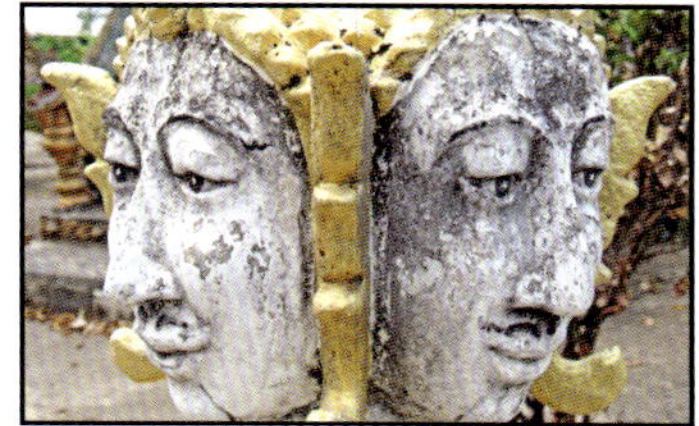

Pages 88-89

1. Brahma, Hindu creator of the universe, with two of his four faces visible; Wat Thawet.

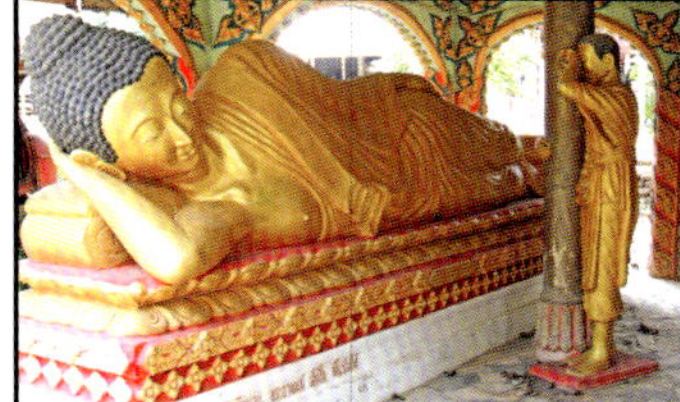

Pages 90-91

1. The *Mahaparinirvana* as the Buddha reaches complete nirvana leaving his physical body, with mourning disciple; Wat Thawet.

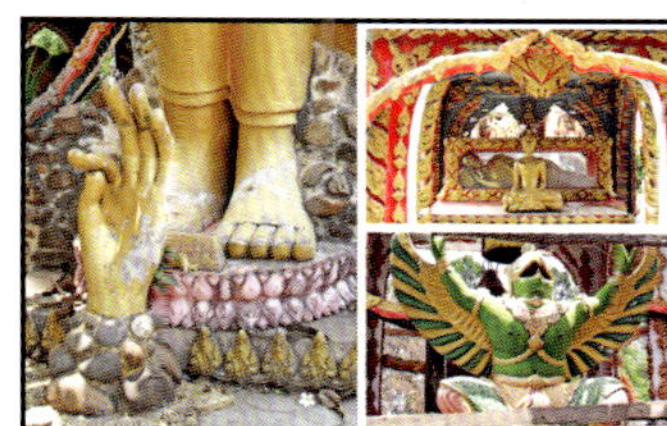

Pages 92-93

1. Hand in the teaching gesture, *vitarka mudra*, and feet of the Buddha; Wat Thawet.
2. Reclining Buddha in case with seated Buddha, Wat Thawet.
3. Garuda in bell-tower, Wat Thawet

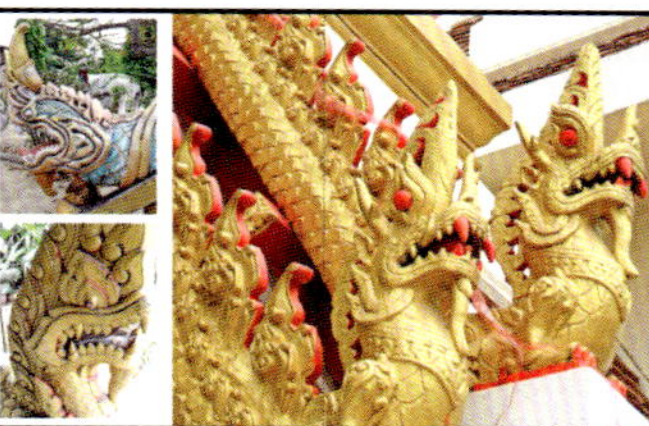

Pages 94-95

1. Crowned *naga* on balustrade, main pagoda, Wat Thawet.
2. Crowned *naga*-like *makara* with crocodile-type feet on balustrade, Wat Thawet.
3. Crowned *naga* on steps to *viharn*, Wat Thawet.

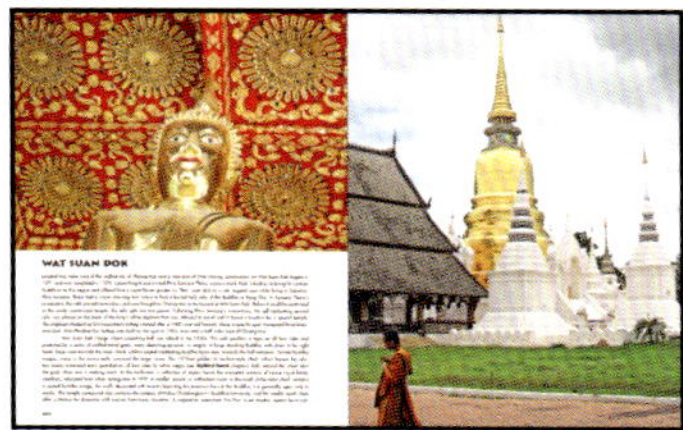

Pages 96-97

1. Buddha statue in main *viharn*, Wat Suan Dok, Chiang Mai.
2. Main golden 157-foot *chedi* with four smaller white *chedis*, pictured with novice; Wat Suan Dok.

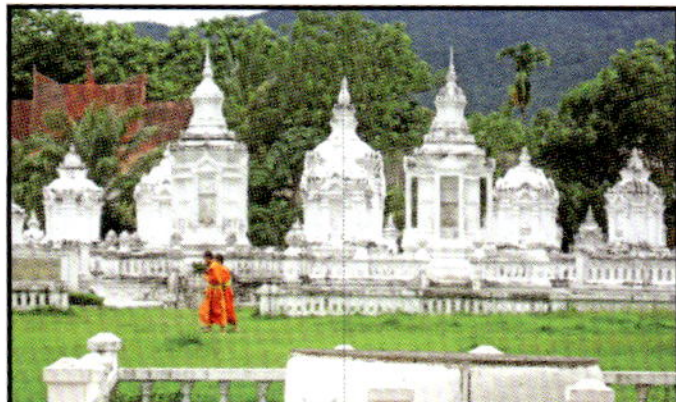

Pages 98-99

1. White-washed *chedis* housing the remains of Lanna royal family members, pictured with two novices; Wat Suan Dok.

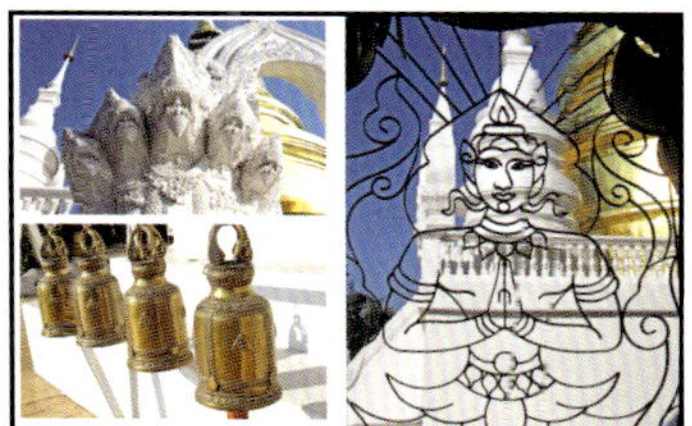

Pages 100-101

1. Five-headed crowned *naga*, guarding the entrance to the *chedi*, Wat Suan Dok.
2. Bells at base of *chedi*, Wat Suan Dok.
3. The main *viharn* is open-air and has a series of *apsara* gate guardians in place of walls; Wat Suan Dok.

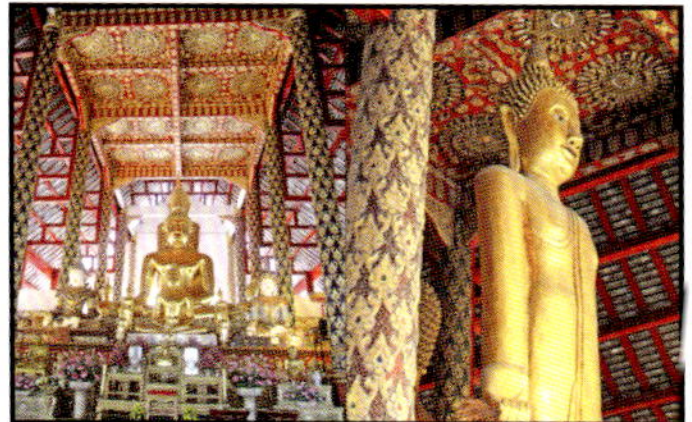

Pages 102-103

1. A seated golden Buddha, a meditating Buddha, and two crowned seated Lanna-style Buddhas face east in main *viharn*, Wat Suan Dok.
2. Standing Buddha holding a bundle of straw facing west in main *viharn*, Wat Suan Dok.

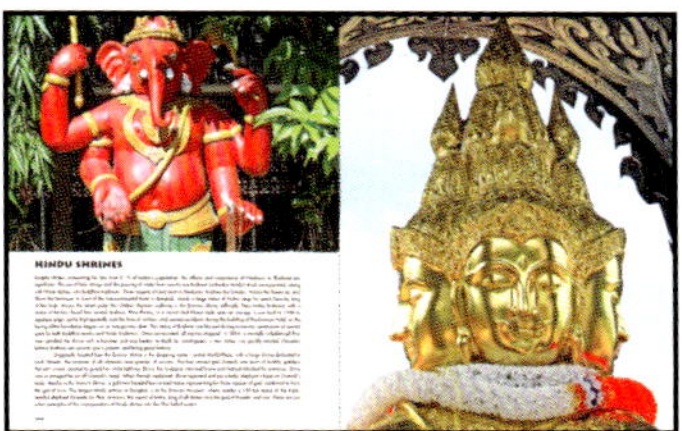

Pages 104-105

1. Four-armed red Ganesh, destroyer of obstacles, with spoon and trident; Chiang Mai.
2. Shrine to Brahma, the god of creation; Chiang Rai.

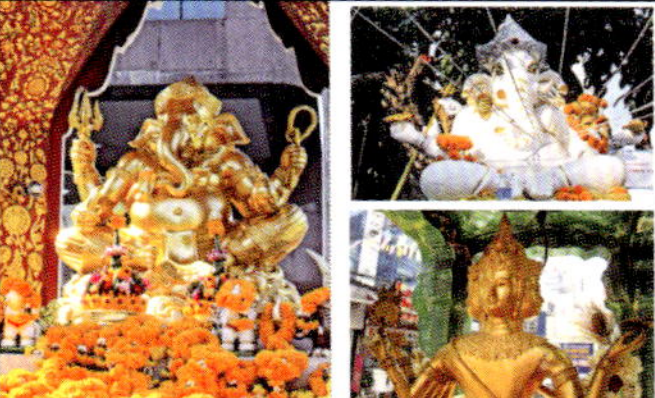

Pages 106-107

1. The Ganesh Shrine, Central World Mall, Bangkok.
2. Ganesh statue with Brahmin sacred thread, Wat Mahawan, Chiang Mai.
3. Shrine to Brahma on busy Sukhumvit Soi, Bangkok.

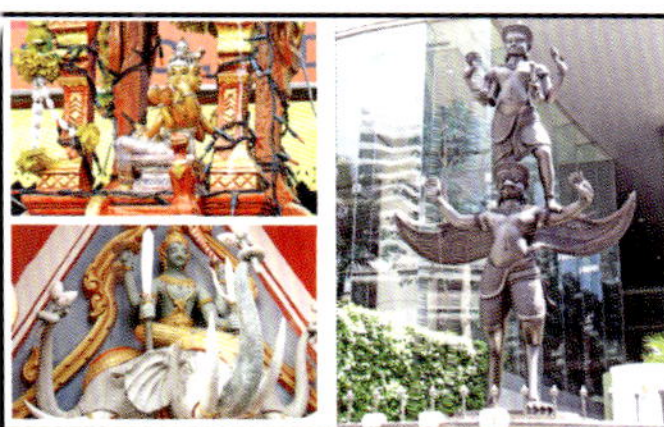

Pages 108-109

1. Brahma shrine next to spirit house, Chiang Mai.
2. Indra, king of the *devas*, riding his elephant mount Erawan, Wat Plai Laem, Koh Samui.
3. Vishnu on his steed Garuda, Intercontinental Bank, Bangkok.

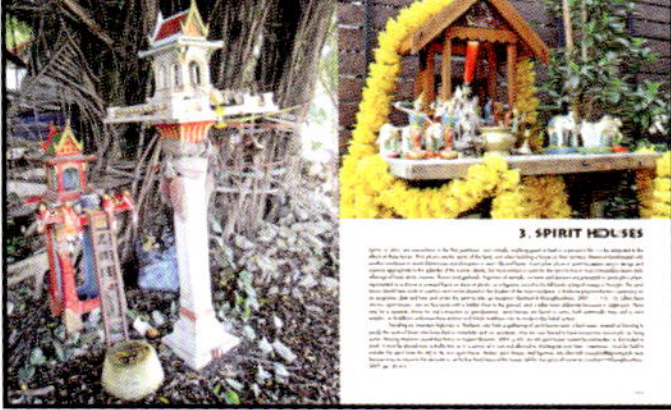

Pages 110-111

1. Two spirit houses under Bohdi tree, Koh Samui.
2. Spirit house with garlands, Bangkok.

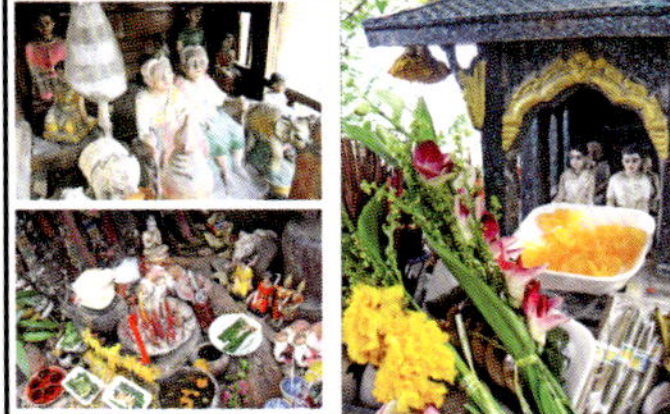

Pages 112-113

1. Grandparent figures found in ancestral shrines, Soi Lang Suan, Bangkok.
2. Spirit house with offerings of flowers, fruit, desserts and cigars, Koh Samui.
3. Offerings in front of sacred tree shrine, Sala Daeng, Bangkok.

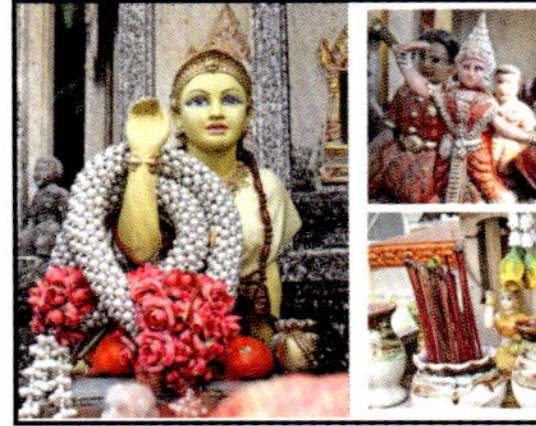

Pages 114-115

1. Beckoning lady figurine with jasmine flower garland, Chiang Mai.
2. *Khon* dancers and servants in spirit house, Chiang Mai.
3. Incense sticks, and attendants on the veranda, with spirit of the land figurine inside the spirit house; Chiang Mai.

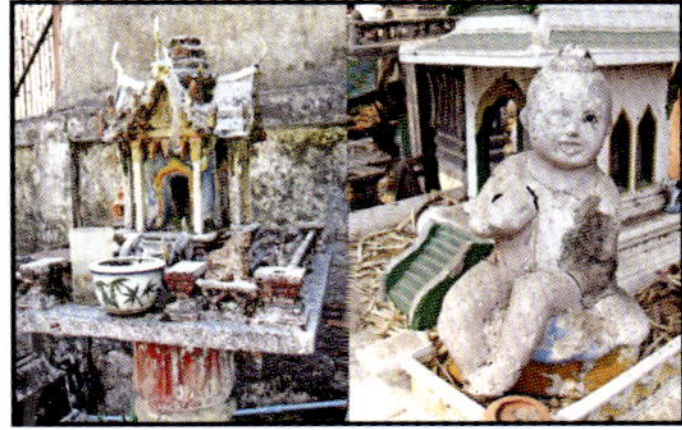

Pages 116-117

1. Unattended spirit house, Mae Sot.
2. Spirit house cemetery, Suthep Soi 4, Chiang Mai.

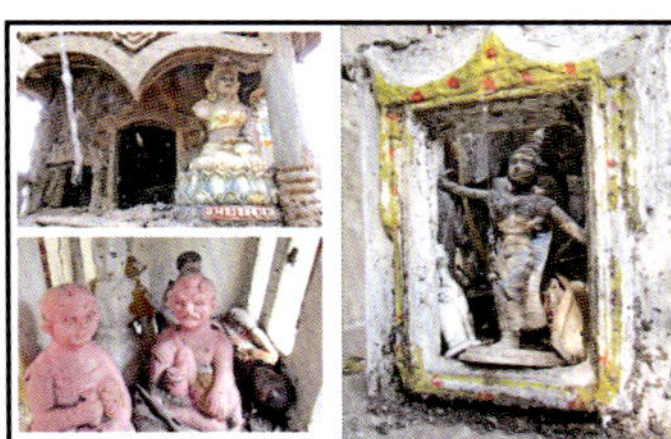

Pages 118-119

1. Broken female figure and retired abode; spirit house cemetery, Chiang Mai.
2. *Khon* dancer in old spirit house under Bodhi tree, outside Wat Umong, Chiang Mai.
3. Abandoned spirit house and figurines; spirit house cemetery under Bodhi tree, Chiang Mai.

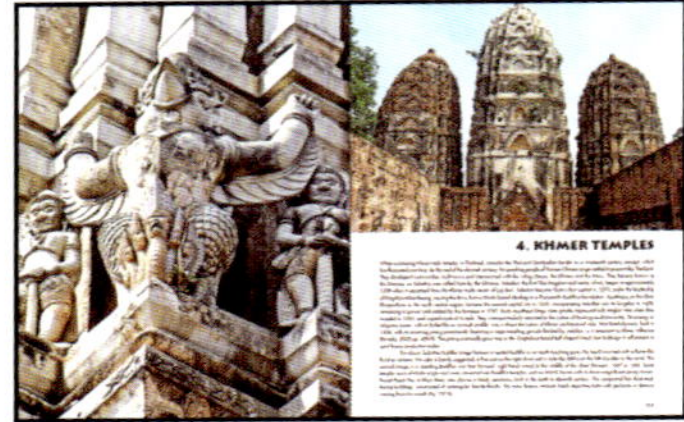

Pages 120-121

1. Original stucco *garuda* with crowned five-headed *naga*, flanked by *yakshas* (1424); Wat Ratchaburana, Ayutthaya.
2. Three-*pranged* twelfth or thirteenth century Hindu temple converted to a Buddhist temple, Wat Si Sawai, Sukothai.

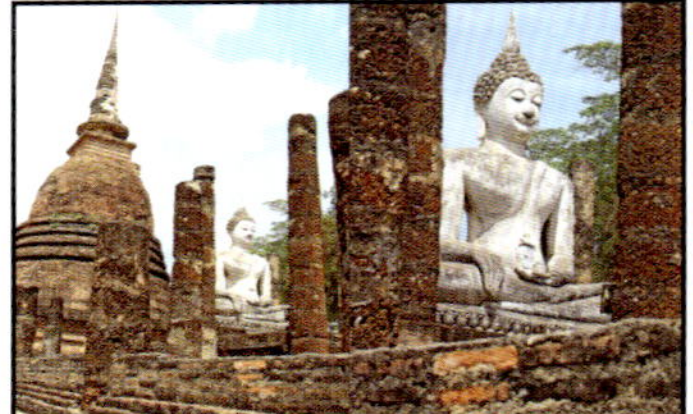

Pages 122-123

1. Seated Buddha in front of a Singhalese-style *chedi*, Wat Sa Si, Sukothai.
2. Stucco seated Buddha, late fourteenth century, Wat Sa Si.

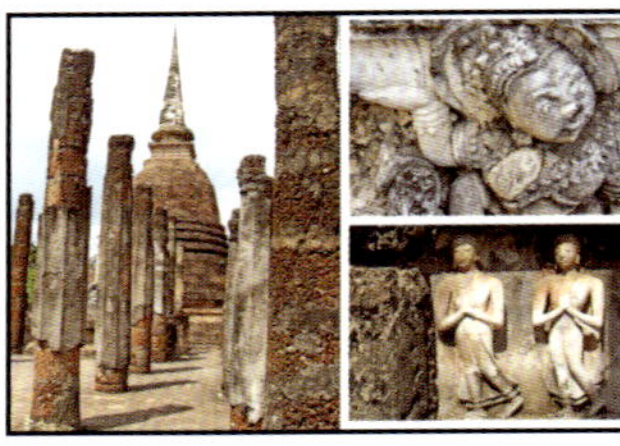

Pages 124-125

1. Temple surrounded by a reservoir, Wat Sa Si.
2. Temple support adornment, Wat Mahathat, Sukothai.
3. Temple disciple adornment, Wat Mahathat.

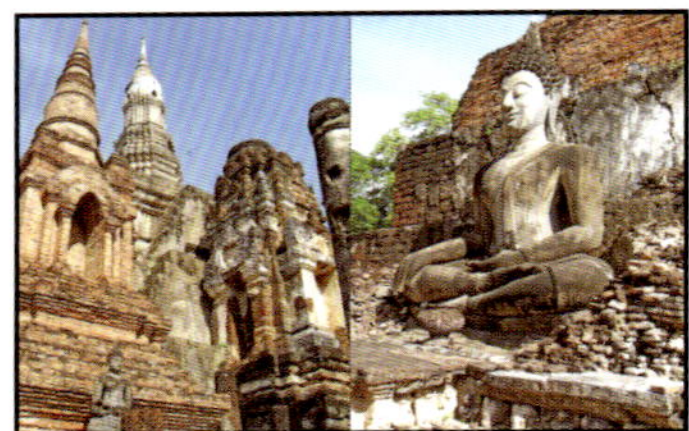

Pages 126-127

1. Temple ruins, established in the thirteenth century and rebuilt in the fourteenth; Wat Mahathat, Sukothai.
2. Seated Buddha, Wat Mahathat.

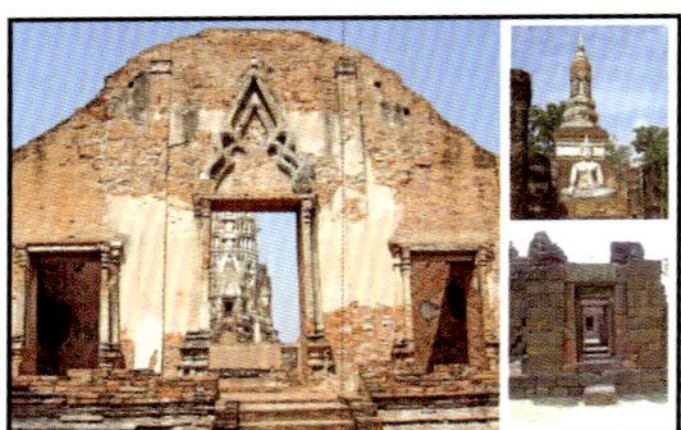

Pages 128-129

1. Temple ruins, Wat Ratchaburana, Ayutthaya.
2. Seated Buddha in front of lotus bud *chedi*, Wat Traphang Ngoen, Sukothai.
3. Bayon-style site, built by Khmer King Jayavarman VII, Wat Ka Santarat, Maha Sarakam province.

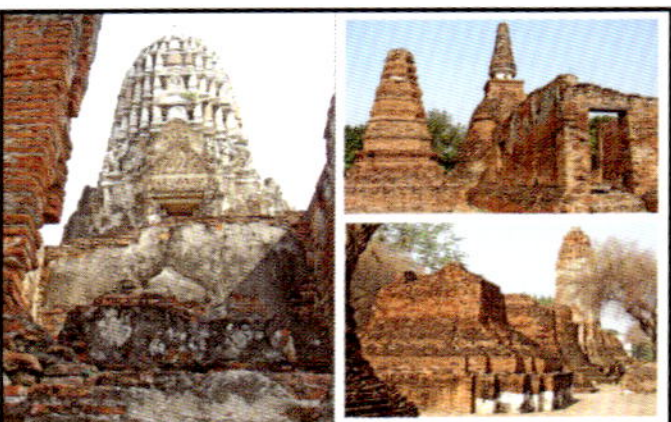

Pages 130-131

1. Main *prang*, built during reign of King Borom Rachathirat II on the cremation site of his two older brothers, Wat Ratchaburana, Ayutthaya.
2. Brick temple ruins, Wat Ratchaburana.
3. Brick temple ruins, Wat Ratchaburana.

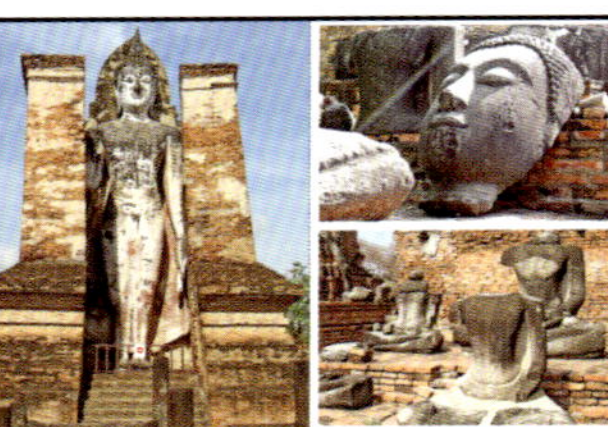

Pages 132-133

1. Standing Buddha, Wat Mahabut, Sukothai.
2. Temple ruins, Wat Ratchaburana, Ayutthaya.
3. Temple ruins, Wat Ratchaburana.

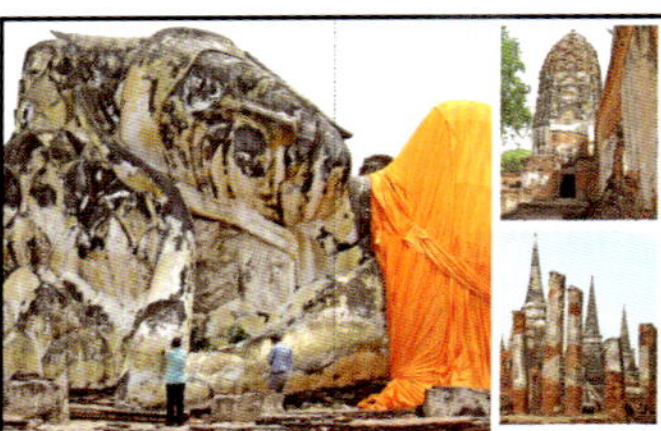

Pages 134-135

1. Reclining Buddha, temple established in 1374; Wat Maha That, Ayutthaya.
2. Central *prang*, Wat Si Sawai, Sukothai.
3. Temple ruins, Wat Maha That, Ayutthaya.

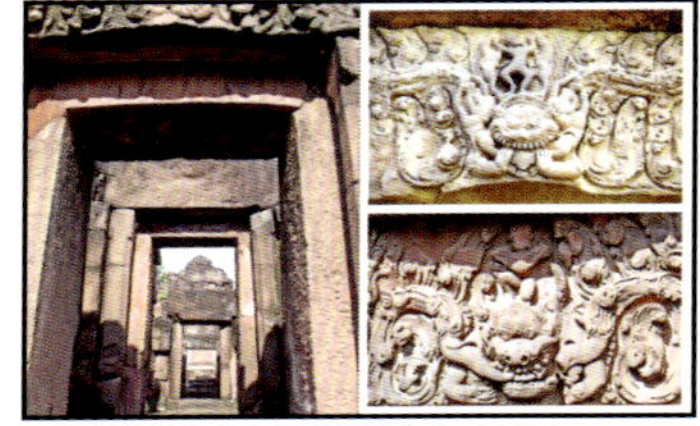

Pages 136-137

1. A laterite wall surrounds the temple compound, eleventh century; Prasat Pueai Noi, Khon Kaen.
2. Kala with demons emerging from his mouth; decorative lintel, Prasat Pueai Noi.
3. Guardian demon with garlands in its mouth, Prasat Pueai Noi.

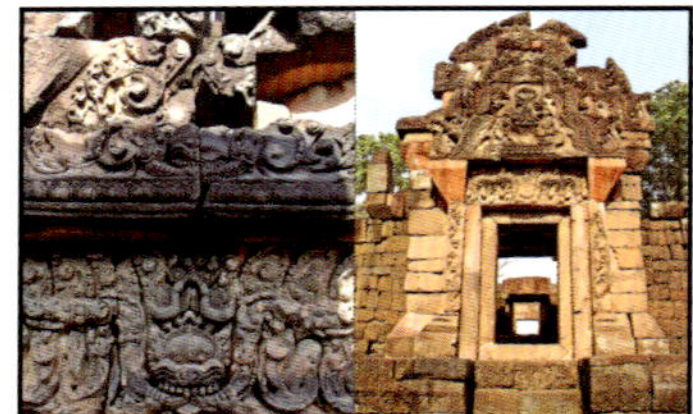

Pages 138-139

1. Two-tiered decorative lintel to ward off evil spirits (notice the two *hongs* or mythical ducks on bottom guardian's head), Prasat Pueai Noi, Khon Kaen.
2. Doorway entrance, Prasat Pueai Noi.

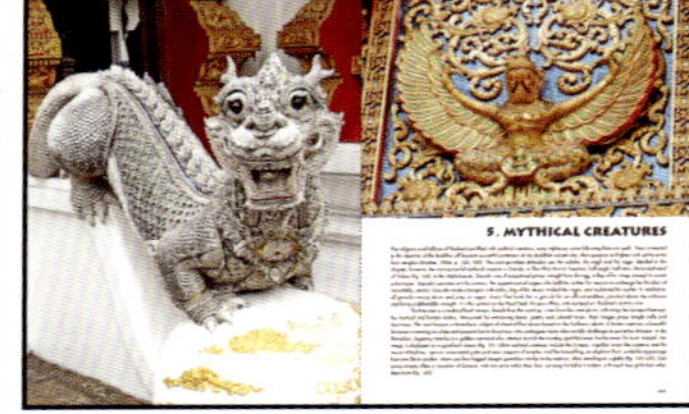

Pages 140-141

1. Lanna lizard-like *mom*, front paws on globe; temple entrance guardian, Wat Buppharam, Chiang Mai.
2. Golden *garuda* protector above temple entrance, Chiang Mai.

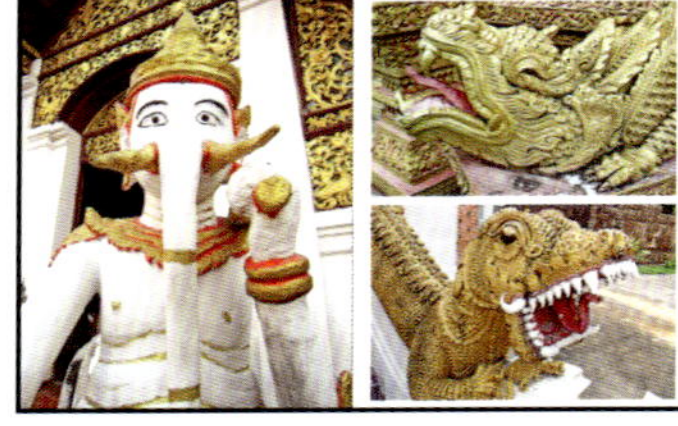

Pages 142-143

1. Seated two-armed Ganesh holding attribute, Wat Buppharam, Chiang Mai.
2. *Makara* without *naga* on balustrade, Wat Prathat Doi Wao, Mae Sai.
3. Lanna *mom* on balustrade, Wat Pan On, Chiang Mai.

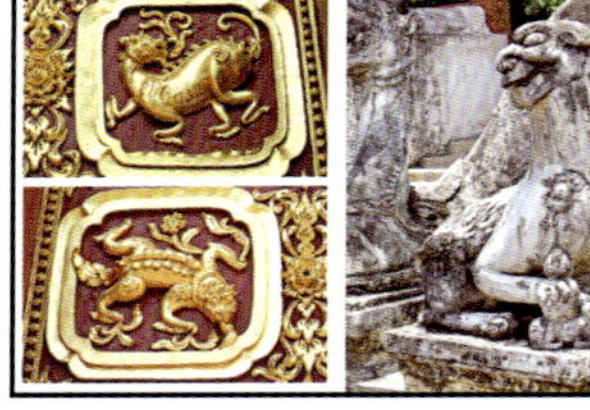

Pages 144-145

1. Mythical creature; temple adornment, Wat Montien, Chiang Mai.
2. Stone Chinese lioness with cub and ball under right paw, Wat Phra Singh, Chiang Mai.
3. Mythical creature; temple adornment, Wat Montien, Chiang Mai.

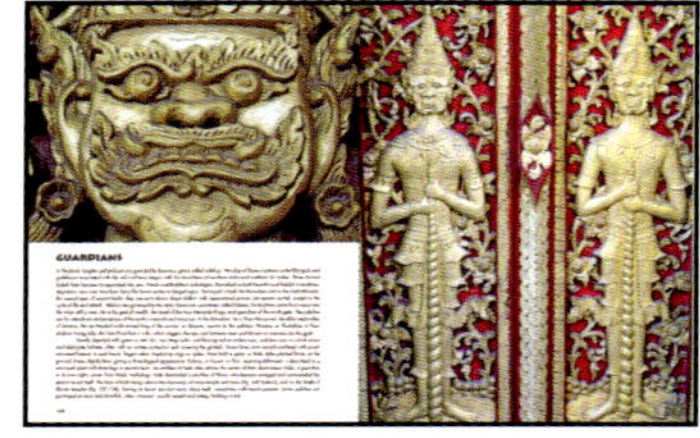

Pages 146-147

1. *Yaksha* temple door guardian, Wat Chetawan, Chiang Mai.
2. *Yaksha* temple door guardians, Wat Chetawan, Chiang Mai.

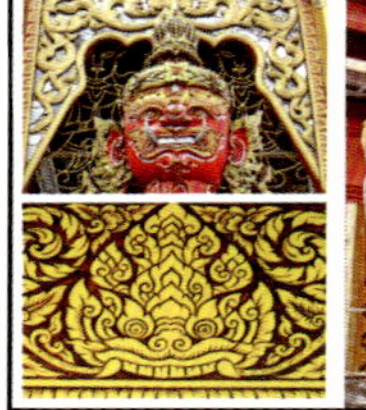

Pages 148-149

1. *Yaksha* temple gate guardian with Rattanakosin helmet, Wat Sai Mun Mueang, Chiang Mai.
2. Painting of Kala above temple door, Chiang Mai.
3. Green-skinned *yaksha* temple gate guardian, Phrathat Doi Kham, Chiang Mai.

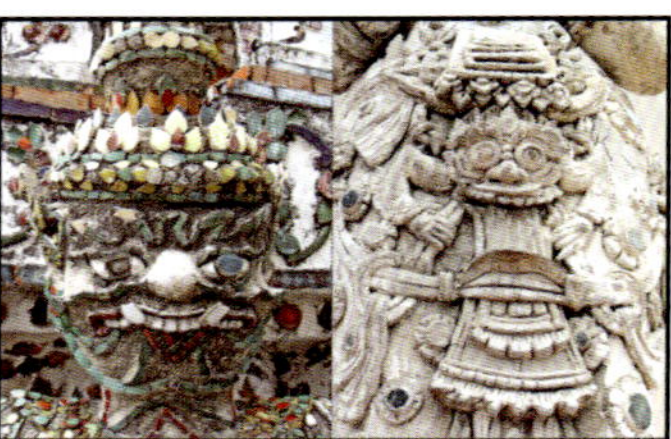

Pages 150-151

1. *Yaksha* decorated with porcelain plate fragments, Wat Arun, Bankgok.
2. Guardian emblem on divinity figure, under renovation; Wat Montien, Chiang Mai.

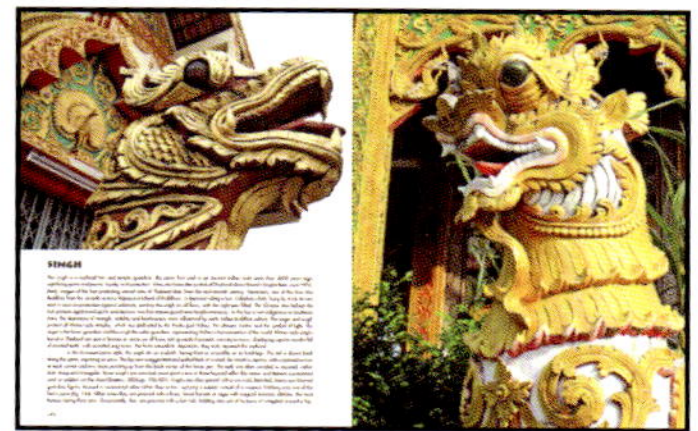

Pages 152-153

1. *Singh* guarding temple entrance, golden peacock above door, Wat Prathat Doi Wao, Mae Sai.
2. Burmese-style *singh*, nineteenth century, Wat Chetawan, Chiang Mai.

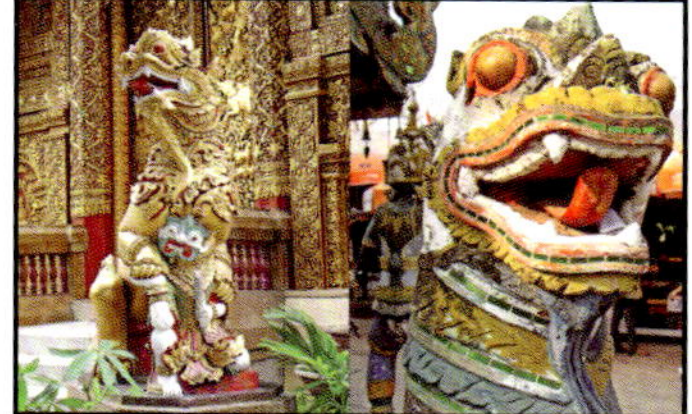

Pages 154-155

1. Lanna/Burmese-style *singh* with dwarf guardian protector, Wat Mahawan, Chiang Mai.
2. Cement *singh* with mirrored tiles, Phra That Doi Kham, Chiang Mai.

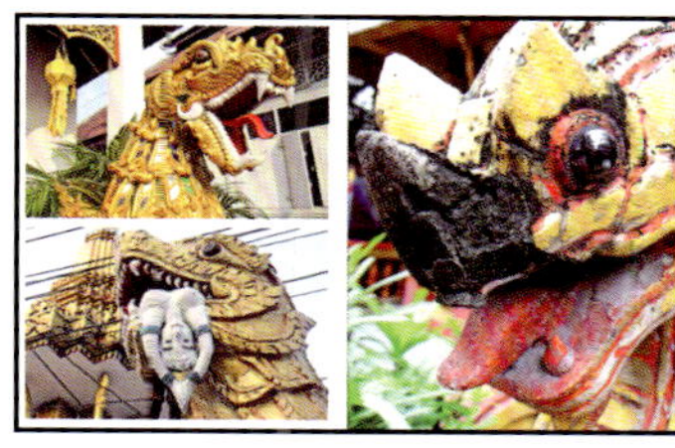

Pages 156-157

1. Golden *singh* with mirrored tiles, Wat Sai Mun Mueang, Chiang Mai.
2. Painted cement *singh* at market square entrance, Chiang Mai.
3. Painted *singh* with female figure in its mouth, Wat Puak Pia, Chiang Mai.

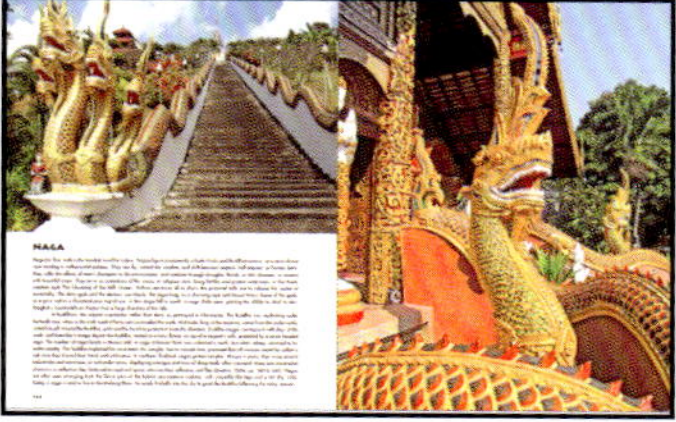

Pages 158-159

1. *Naga* balustrade on long staircase, Chiang Mai province.
2. *Naga* with flame and beard on balustrade, Wat Chang Kong, Chiang Mai.

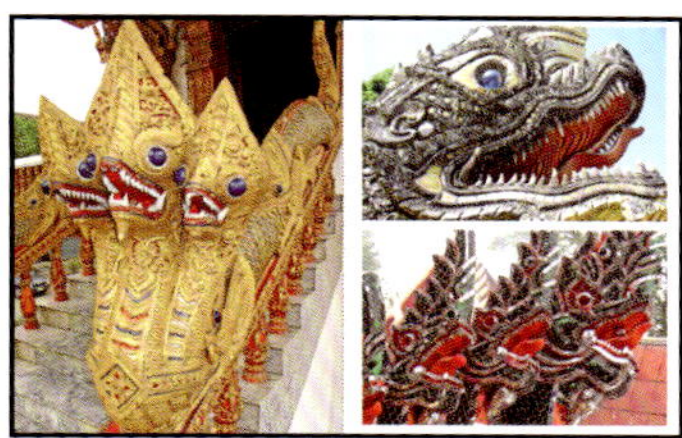

Pages 160-161

1. Crowned three-headed *naga* with *makara*, Wat Phra Singh, Chiang Mai.
2. *Naga* with light-bulb eyes, Wat Phra That Chom Chaeng, Phrae.
3. Reflective mirror-tiled *naga*, Wat Phra Yai, Koh Samui.

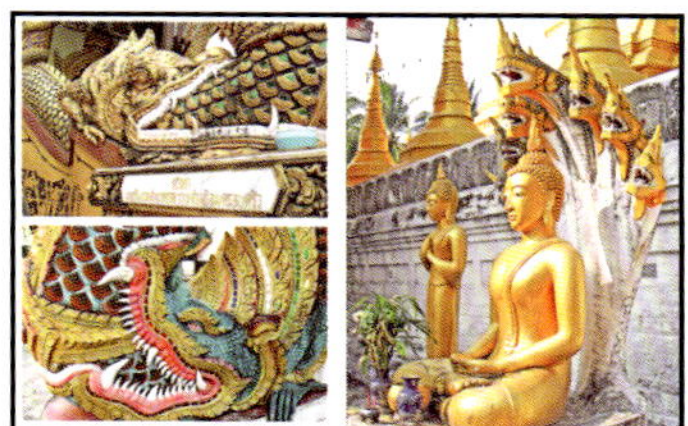

Pages 162-163

1. *Makara* with *naga* emerging from mouth, Wat Prathat Doi Wao, Mae Sai.
2. Seated Buddha with 7-headed *naga* canopy, Wat Chumphon Khiri, Mae Sot.
3. *Makara* with *naga* emerging from mouth, Wat Phra That Chom Chaeng, Phrae.

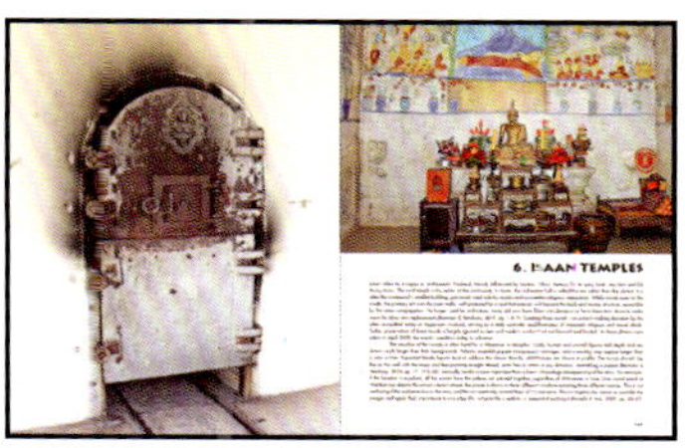

Pages 164-165

1. Cremation oven door, Wat Sa Bua Kaelo, Khon Kaen.
2. Altar inside the *ubosot*, Wat Sa Bua Kaelo.

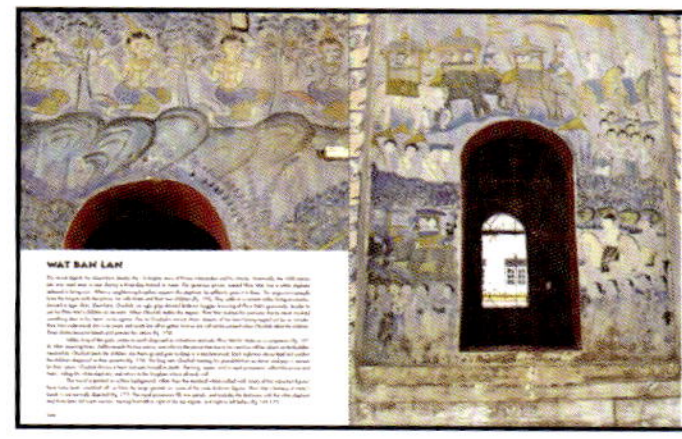

Pages 166-167

1. Phisati's four celestial attendants; mural detail, Wat Ban Lan, Khon Kaen.
2. One of two panels depicting the royal procession's return to the palace with Pha Wet and family to crown him king; Wat Ban Lan.

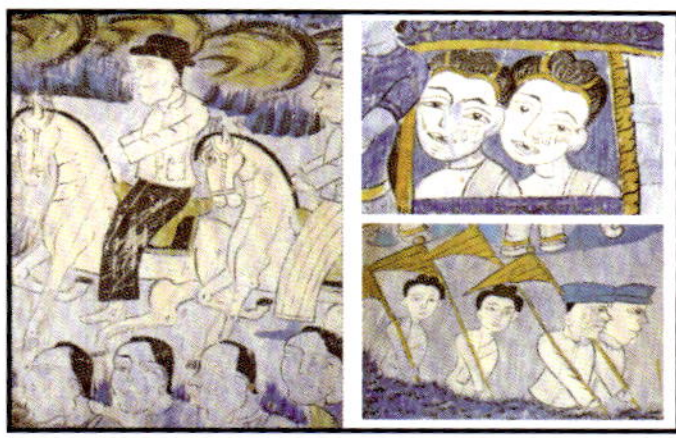

Pages 168-169

1. Riders on horseback; mural detail, Wat Ban Lan.
2. Royal family members; mural detail, Wat Ban Lan.
3. The royal procession; mural detail, Wat Ban Lan.

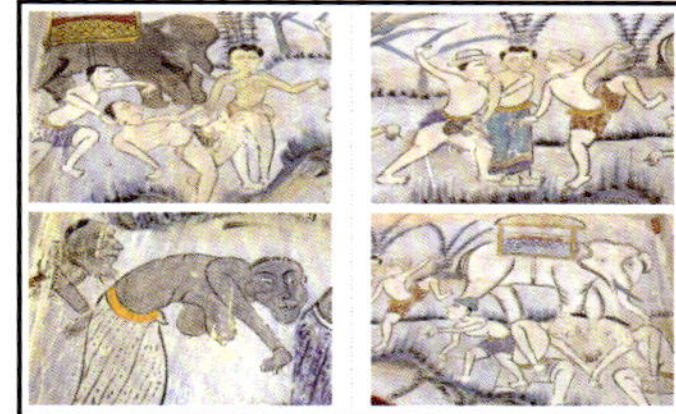

Pages 170-171

1. Brahmins return to their city; mural detail, Wat Ban Lan.
2. Brahmins return to their city; mural detail, Wat Ban Lan.
3. Brahmins with white elephant; mural detail, Wat Ban Lan.
4. Old women; mural detail, Wat Ban Lan.

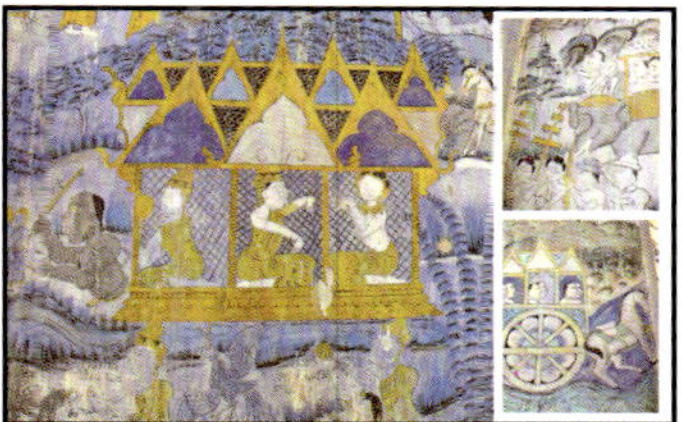

Pages 172-173

1. Pha Wet gives his children to Chuchok, and Matsi tells Pha Wet of her nightmare; mural detail, Wat Ban Lan.
2. The royal procession; mural detail, Wat Ban Lan.
3. The royal procession; mural detail, Wat Ban Lan.

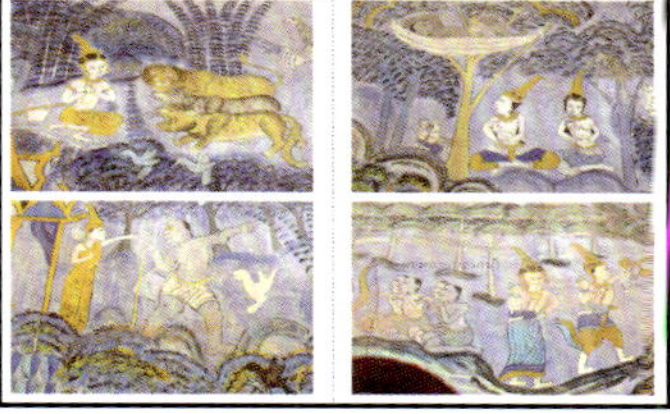

Pages 174-175

1. Deities become a lion, leopard and tiger; mural detail, Wat Ban Lan.
2. Chuchok asleep, deities comfort the children; mural detail, Wat Ban Lan.
3. Pha Wet and family sent into exile; mural detail, Wat Ban Lan.
4. Chuchok tricks hermit to reveal Pha Wet's location; mural detail, Wat Ban Lan.

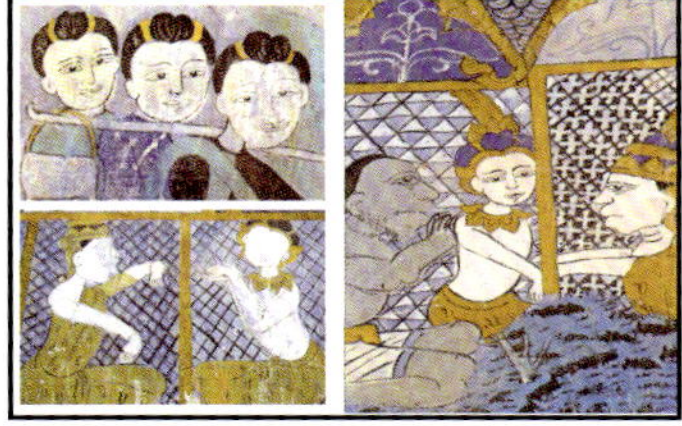

Pages 176-177

1. Village women carrying water; mural detail, Wat Ban Lan.
2. Pha Wet gives Matsi to Sakka, who is disguised as a Brahmin when he requests her; mural detail, Wat Ban Lan.
3. Matsi tells Pha Wet of her nightmare (notice scratched-off faces); mural detail, Wat Ban Lan.

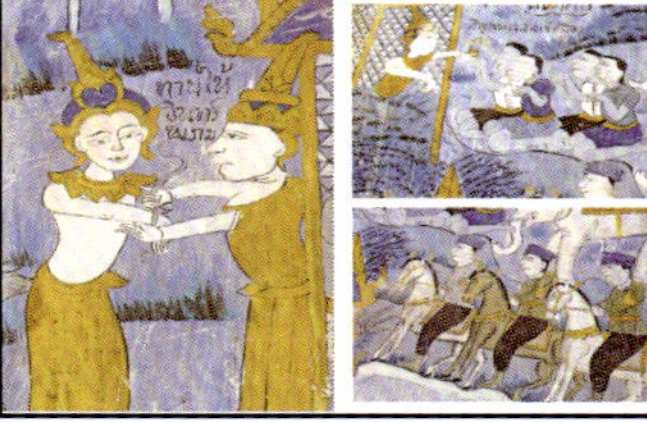

Pages 178-179

1. Pha Wet binds Matsi as a gift to Brahmin; mural detail, Wat Ban Lan.
2. Pha Wet gives alms to villagers; mural detail, Wat Ban Lan.
3. Soldiers in royal procession; mural detail, Wat Ban Lan.

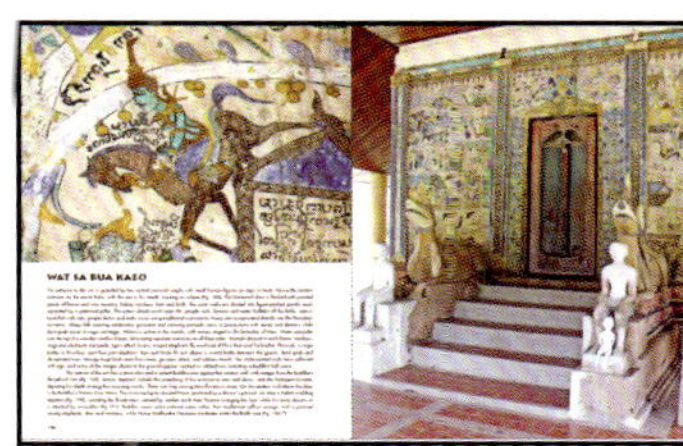

Pages 180-181

1. Phra Ram on horse; mural detail, Wat Sa Bua Kaelo, Khon Kaen
2. Entrance to *ubosot*; *singhs* and human figures on balustrade, Wat Wat Sa Bua Kaelo.

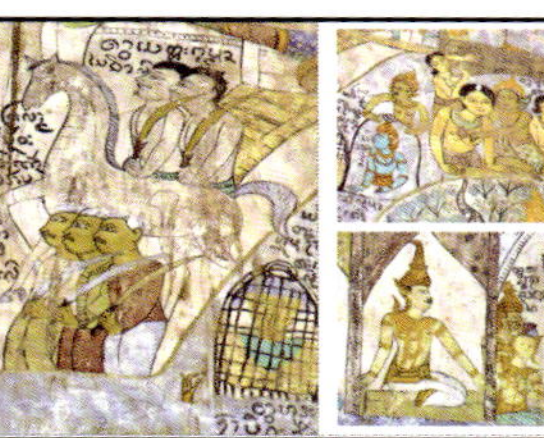

Pages 182-183

1. Soldiers; mural detail, Wat Sa Bua Kaelo.
2. Mural detail, Wat Sa Bua Kaelo.
3. Phra Ram in palace; mural detail, Wat Sa Bua Kaelo.

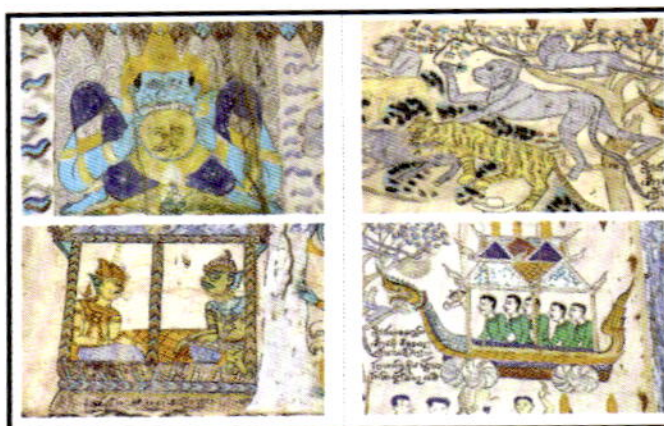

Pages 184-185

1. Rahu eats sun; mural detail, Wat Sa Bua Kaelo.
2. Wildlife; mural detail, Wat Sa Bua Kaelo.
3. Mural detail, Wat Sa Bua Kaelo.
4. Figures in *naga* carriage; mural detail, Wat Sa Bua Kaelo.

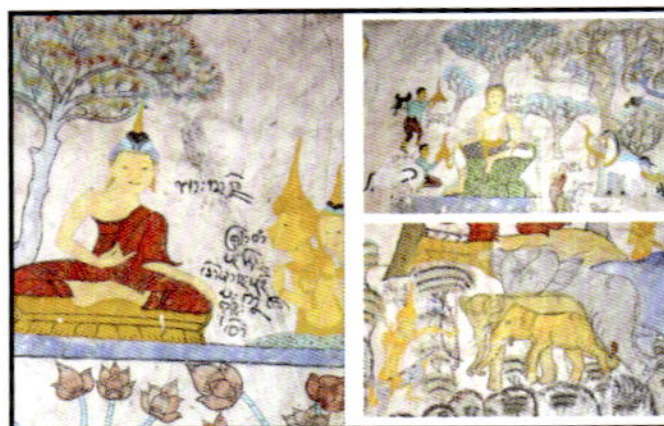

Pages 186-187

1. Buddha's sermon; mural detail inside *ubosot*, Wat Sa Bua Kaelo.
2. Buddha under the Bodhi tree; mural detail inside *ubosot*, Wat Sa Bua Kaelo.
3. Sin Sai and elephants; mural detail inside *ubosot*, Wat Sa Bua Kaelo.

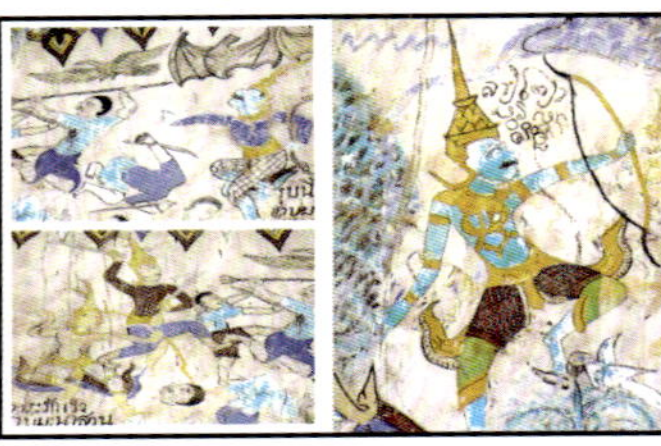

Pages 188-189

1. Battle scene, Sin Sai story; mural detail, Wat Sa Bua Kaelo.
2. Phra Ram with bow after Thotsakan abducts Nang Sida; mural detail, Wat Sa Bua Kaelo.
3. Battle scene, Sin Sai with sword and bow; mural detail, Wat Sa Bua Kaelo.

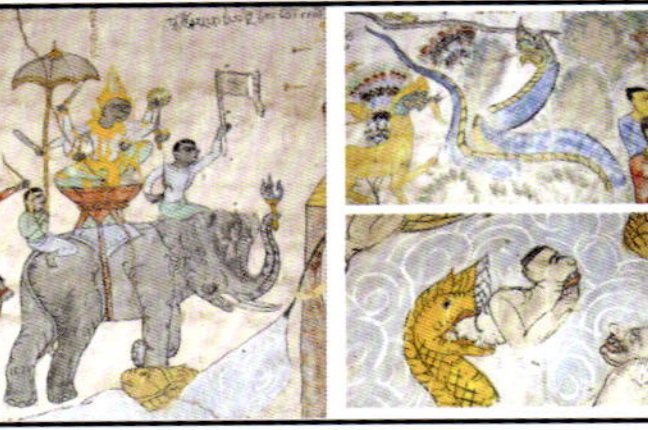

Pages 190-191

1. Mara on elephant, mural detail, Wat Sa Bua Kaelo.
2. A *naga* battles a *khochasi* in Buddha's Victory Over Mara; mural detail, Wat Sa Bua Kaelo.
3. Mara's soldier eaten by *naga* warrior, mural detail, Wat Sa Bua Kaelo.

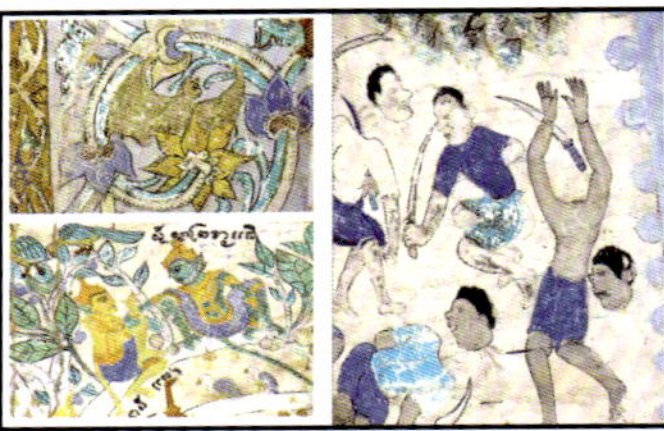

Pages 192-193

1. Bat and foliage on pillar, Wat Sa Bua Kaelo.
2. Battle scene, Sin Sai story; mural detail, Wat Sa Bua Kaelo.
3. Mural detail, Wat Sa Bua Kaelo.

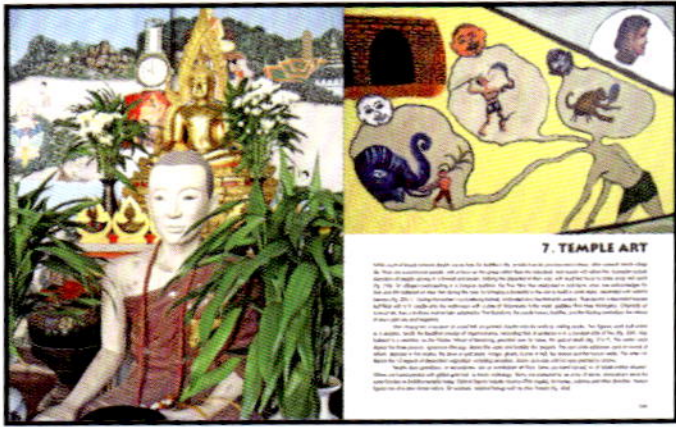

Pages 194-195

1. Statue of revered monk in front of mural, Wat Chumphon Khiri, Mae Sot.
2. Temple wall painting, Wat Umong, Chiang Mai.

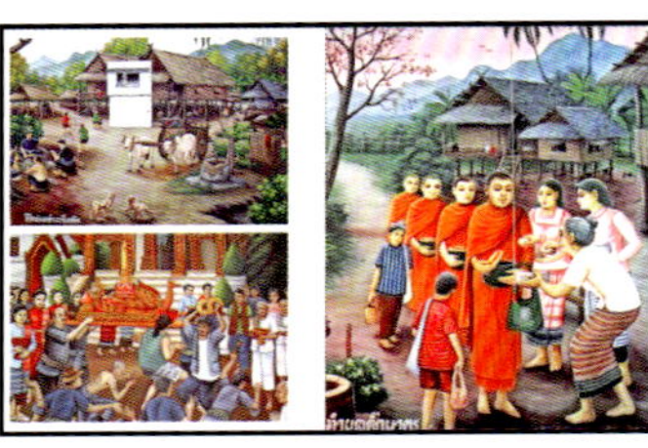

Pages 196-197

1. Mural of village life (notice electrical fuse box in center of frame); Wat Chetawan, Chiang Mai.
2. Mural of daily *tam boon* offerings to monks, Wat Chetawan.
3. Funeral procession with musical accompaniment; mural detail, Wat Chetawan.

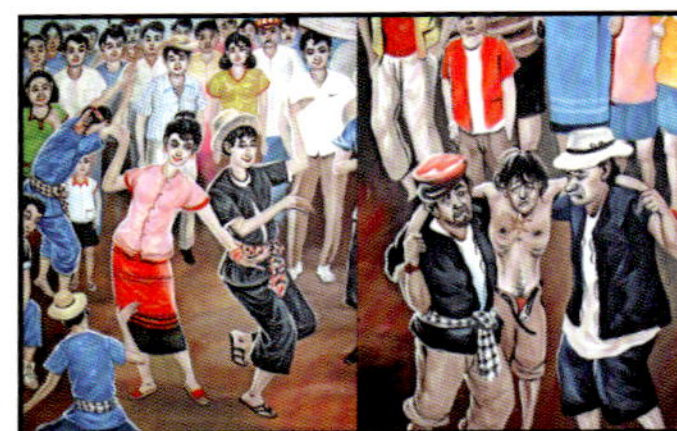

Pages 198-199

1. Villagers dancing; mural detail, Wat Chetawan.
2. Drunk villager is carried away; mural detail, Wat Chetawan.

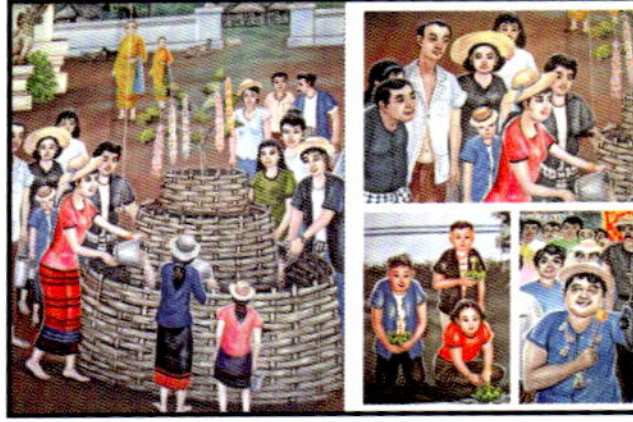

Pages 200-201

1. Mural of Songkran tradition, Wat Chetawan, Chiang Mai.
2. Songkran tradition; mural detail, Wat Chetawan.
3. Villager with Thai gong; mural detail, Wat Chetawan.
4. Launching Loi Krathong floats; mural detail, Wat Chetawan.

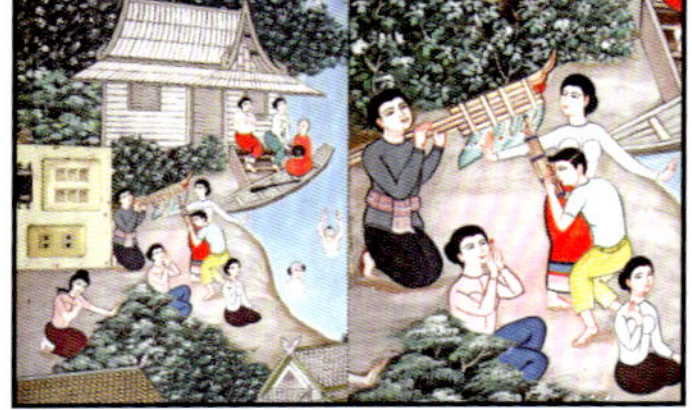

Pages 202-203

1. Mural of Isaan village life (notice light switch at left of frame); Wat Chumphon Khiri, Mae Sot.
2. Villagers playing the *khaen*, a Lao mouth organ; mural detail, Wat Chumphon Khiri.

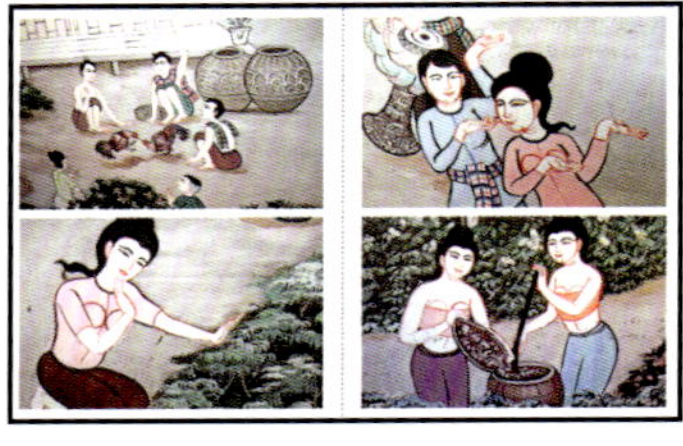

Pages 204-205

1. Isaan villagers and roosters play; mural detail, Wat Chumphon Khiri.
2. Isaan couple dancing; mural detail, Wat Chumphon Khiri.
3. Isaan woman dancing; mural detail, Wat Chumphon Khiri.
4. Isaan women working; mural detail, Wat Chumphon Khiri.

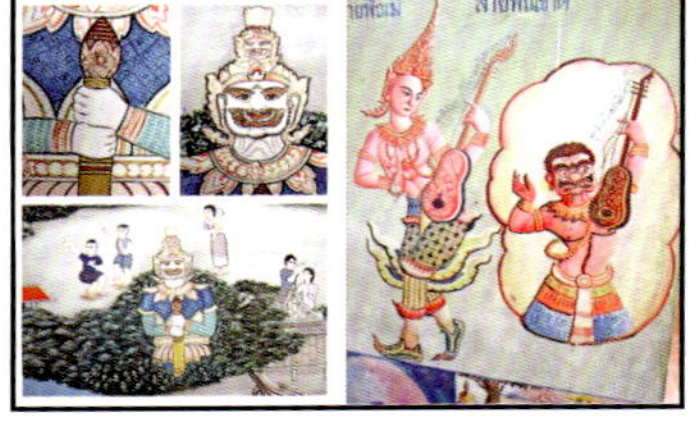

Pages 206-207

1. *Yaksha*; mural detail, Wat Chumphon Khiri.
2. *Yaksha*; mural detail, Wat Chumphon Khiri.
3. Wall painting of *deva* and demon, Wat Umong, Chiang Mai.
4. *Yaksha* protecting villagers; mural detail, Wat Chumphon Khiri.

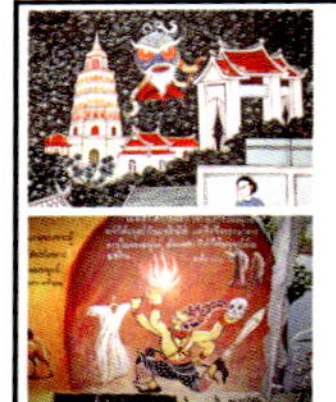
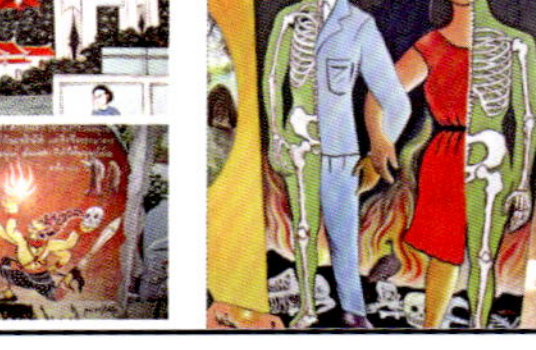

Pages 208-209

1. Chinese spirit; mural detail, Wat Chumphon Khiri.
2. Mural depicting the impermanence of life, Wat Umong.
3. Demon; mural detail, Wat Umong.

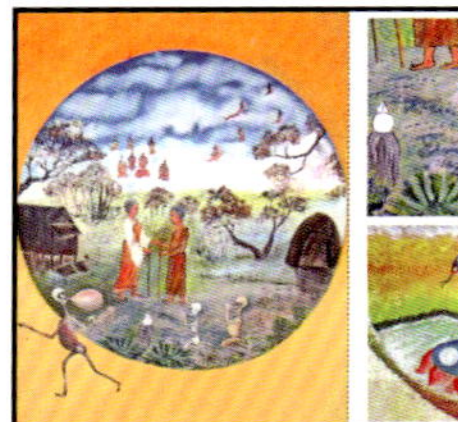

Pages 210-211

1. Mural of ascetic meeting the Buddha, Wat Umong.
2. Spirits; mural detail, Wat Umong.
3. Five-headed *naga* and lotus; mural detail, Wat Umong.

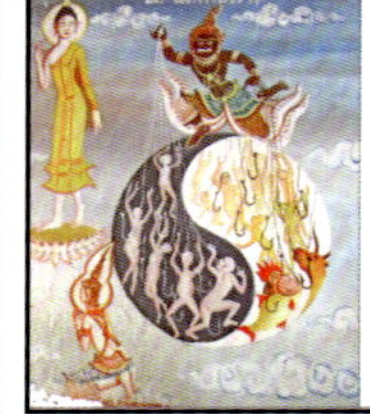

Pages 212-213

1. Mural of demon with Buddha observing, Wat Umong.
2. Mural of demon fishing, Wat Umong.
3. Temptations; mural detail, Wat Umong.

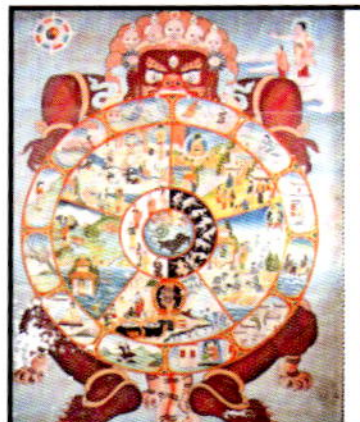
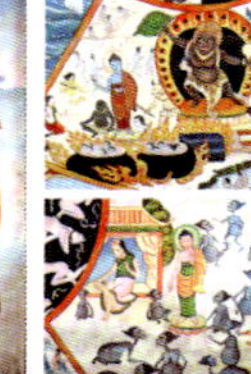

Pages 214-215

1. Mural of Tibetan Wheel of Becoming, Wat Umong.
2. The *Narok* or hell realm; mural detail, Wat Umong.
3. The realm of hungry ghosts; mural detail, Wat Umong.

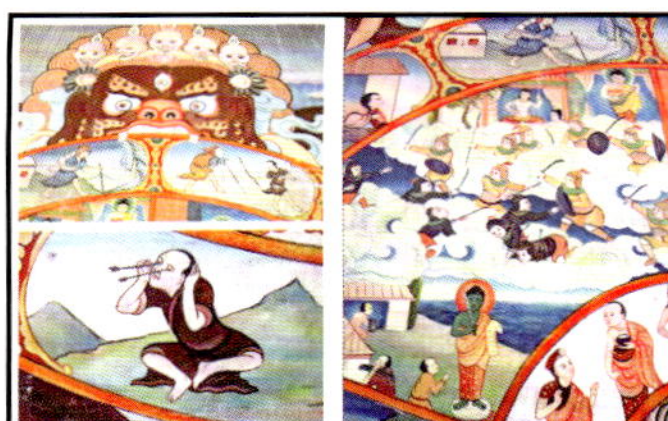

Pages 216-217

1. Yama, the god of death; mural detail, Wat Umong.
2. The realm of mankind depicted as warfare; mural detail, Wat Umong.
3. Loss of sensation; mural detail, Wat Umong.

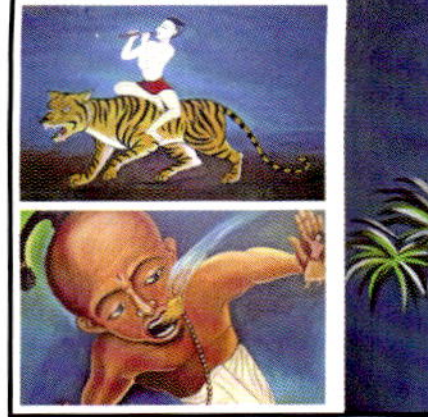

Pages 218-219

1. Wall painting of boy with flute on tiger, Wat Umong.
2. Wall painting of the Buddha with *naga*, Wat Umong.
3. Wall painting of boy, Wat Umong.

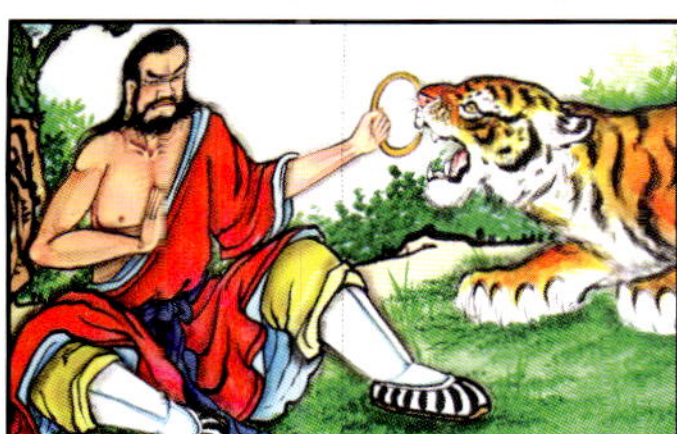

Pages 220-221

1. Mural of Chinese man and tiger, Pung Tao Gong Ancestral Temple, Chiang Mai.

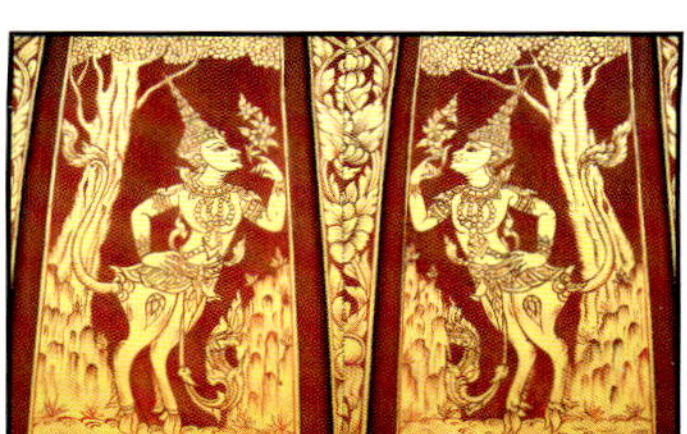

Pages 222-223

1. Centaur temple door guardian, Wat Mahawan, Chiang Mai.
2. Centaur temple door guardian, Wat Mahawan.

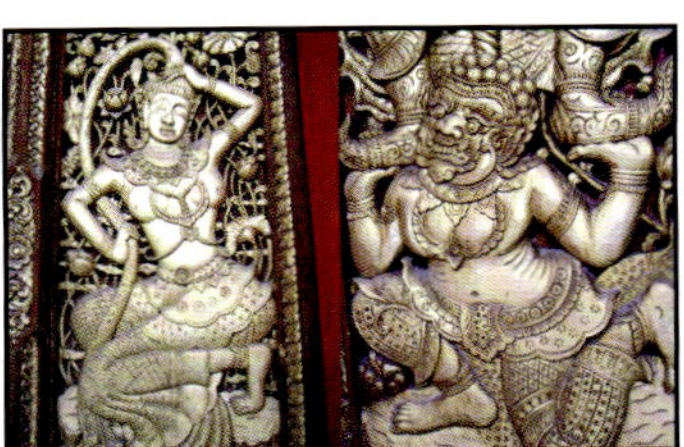

Pages 224-225

1. Mae Thorani, Mother Earth, temple door guardian, Wat Chetawan.
2. *Yaksha* temple door guardian treading on demon dwarf, Wat Chetawan.

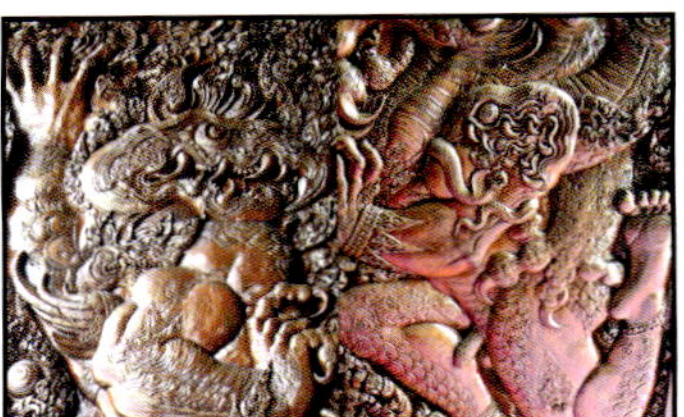

Pages 226-227

1. Modern wood carving as temple door guardian, Wat Phra Singh, Chiang Rai.
2. Modern wood carving as temple door guardian, Wat Phra Singh.

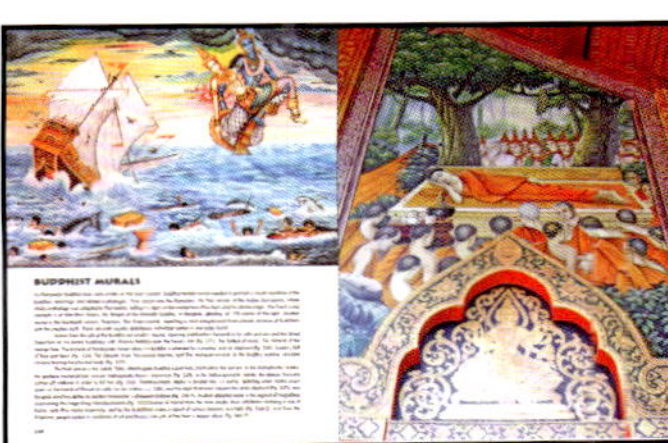

Pages 228-229

1. Mural of Mahajanaka rescued by Manimekhala, suggesting the power of perseverance; Wat Phra Singh.
2. Illustration of the *Mahaparinirvana*; Buddha reaches nirvana with demi-gods and disciples in attendance; mural detail over door, Wat Chetawan.

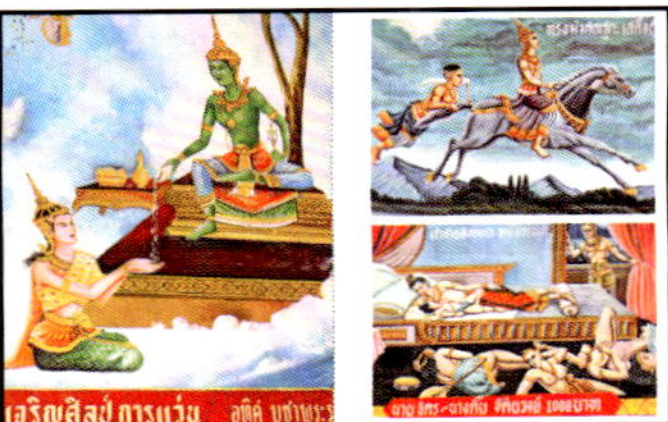

Pages 230-231

1. Sakka grants Phusati's ten wishes; mural detail, Chiang Mai.
2. Siddhartha leaves the palace at night to begin his ascetic journey; mural detail, Mae Sot.
3. Siddhartha's farewell to his family; mural detail, Mae Sot.

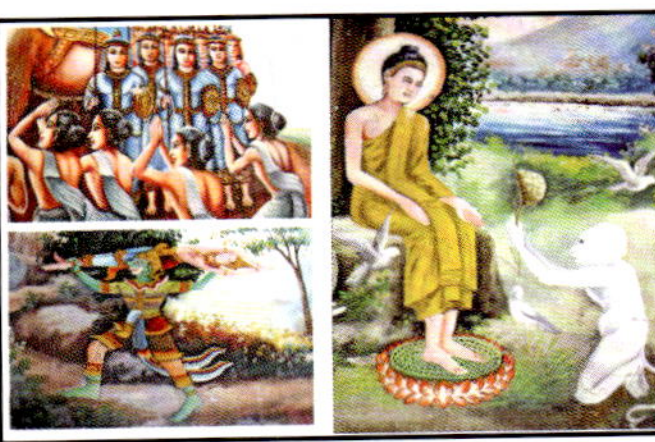

Pages 232-233

1. Brahmins request Pha Wet's white elephant, angering the villagers; mural detail, Wat Mani Phraison, Mae Sot.
2. A monkey offers the Buddha honey; mural detail, Chiang Mai.
3. The demon Punnaka captures Vidhuru, but is later converted to righteousness by him; mural detail, Wat Chetawan.

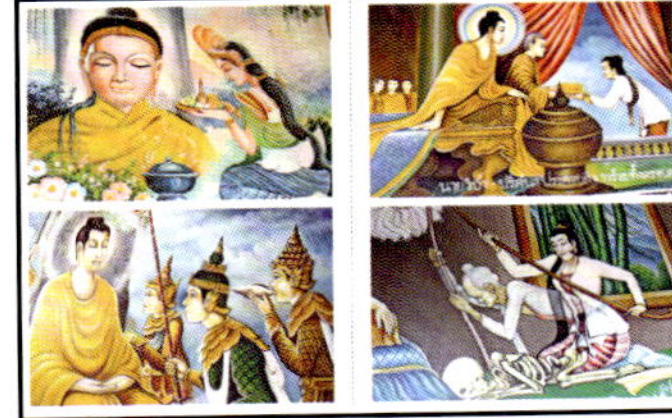

Pages 234-235

1. Sujata brings Siddharta a gift of milk-rice; mural detail, Chiang Mai.
2. *Tam boon* for the monks; mural detail, Wat Mani Phraison.
3. Stages of life; mural detail, Wat Mani Phraison.
4. The Life of the Buddha; mural detail, Wat Mani Phraison.

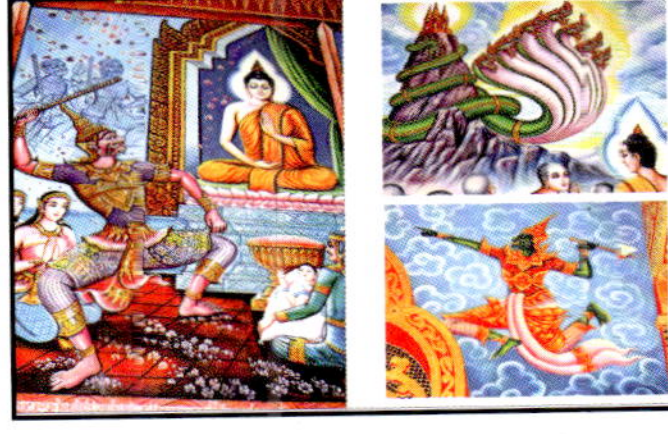

Pages 236-237

1. Panel from The Life of the Buddha, Chiang Mai.
2. The *Naga* King Nandopananda coils himself around Mount Sumeru; mural detail, Chiang Mai.
3. Mara, the demon of desire, tempts the Buddha; mural detail, Chiang Mai.

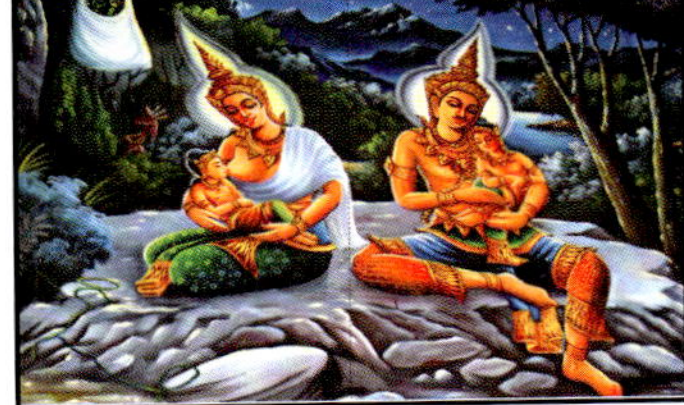

Pages 238-239

1. Pha Wet's children, tortured by their new guardian, are nursed at night by deities who transform into their parents, from the *Vessantara Jataka*; mural detail, Viharn Lai Kham, Chiang Mai.

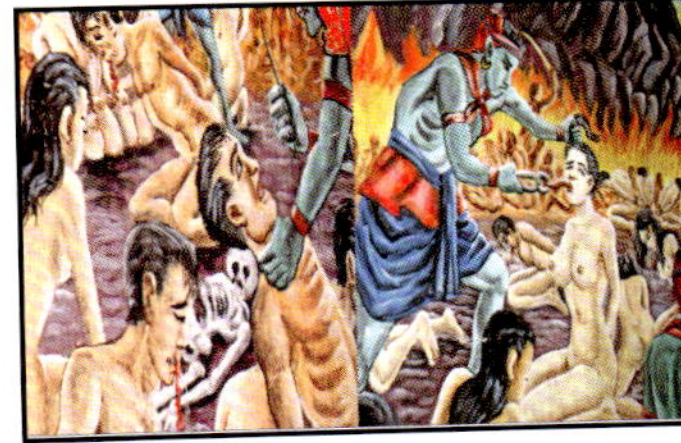

Pages 240-241

1. Tortures in *Narok* or Hell; mural detail, Mae Sot.
2. Tortures in *Narok*; mural detail, Mae Sot.

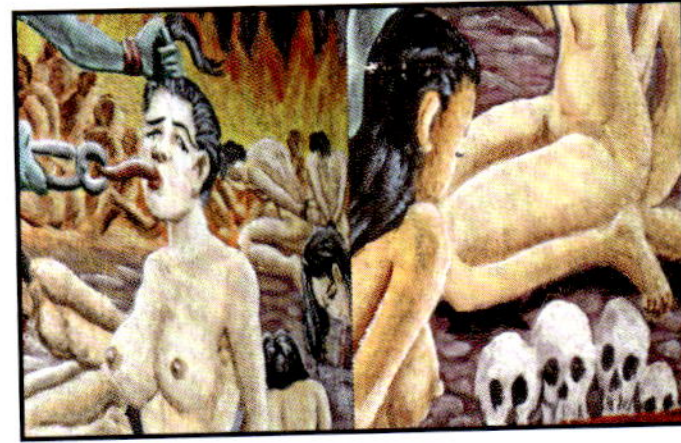

Pages 242-243

1. Tortures in *Narok*; mural detail, Mae Sot.
2. Tortures in *Narok*; mural detail, Mae Sot.

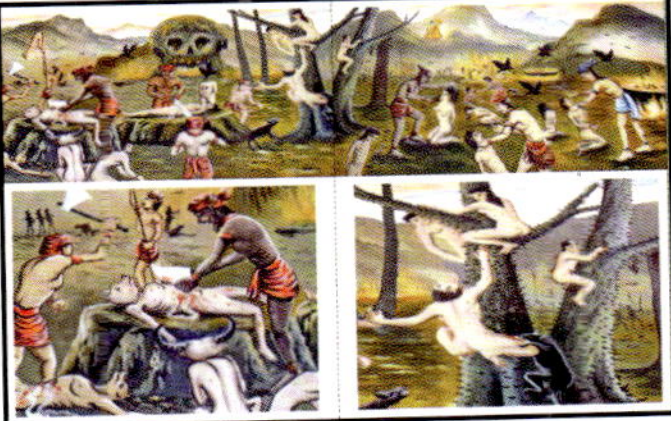

Pages 244-245

1. Hell scene; mural detail, Wat Mahabut, Bangkok.
2. Phra Malai travels to Hell; mural detail, Wat Mahabut.
3. The corrupt are tortured in *Narok*; mural detail, Wat Mahabut.
4. Tree of thorns for adulterers; mural detail, Wat Mahabut.

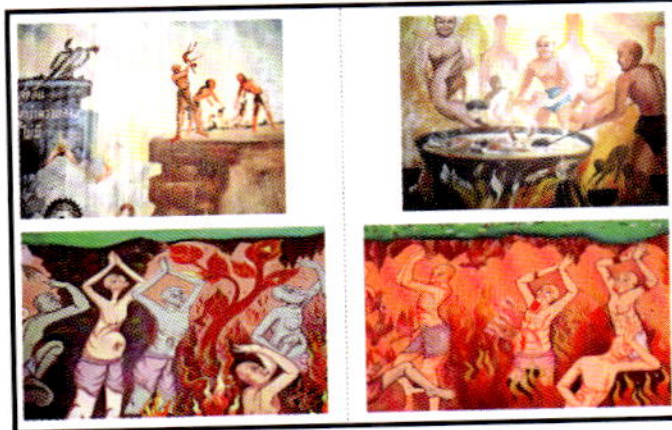

Pages 246-247

1. Tortures in Hell; *Narok* mural detail, Wat Muen Larn, Chiang Mai.
2. Boiling cauldron for alcoholics; *Narok* mural detail, Wat Muen Larn.
3. Tortured souls; *Narok* mural detail, Chiang Mai.
4. Tortured souls; *Narok* mural detail, Chiang Mai.

REFERENCES

BIBLIOGRAPHY

Brereton, Bonnie Pacala, and Somroay Yencheuy (2010). *Buddhist Murals of Northeast Thailand.* Chiang Mai: Mekong Press.

Cadet, John M (1995). *The Ramakien.* Chiang Mai: Browne International.

Campbell, Joseph (1974). *The Mythic Image.* Princeton: Princeton University Press.

Campbell, Joseph (1990). *Transformations of Myth Through Time.* New York: Harper & Row, Publishers, Inc.

Cornwel-Smith, Philip, and John Goss (2005). *Very Thai.* Bangkok: River Books.

Freeman, Michael, and Alistair and Shearer (2000). *The Spirits of Asia: Journeys to the Sacred Places of the East.* London: Thames & Hudson, Ltd.

Jumsai, Manich M.L. (1977). *Thai Folk Tales: A Selection out of Gems of Thai Literature.* Bangkok: Chalermint Press.

Jumsai, Manich M.L. (2002). *Thai Ramayana.* Bangkok: Chalermint Press.

Kawasaki, Ken, and Visakha Kawasaki (1995). *Jakata Tales of the Buddha.* Kandy: Buddhist Publication Society.

Krairiksh, Piriya (2012). *The Roots of Thai Art.* Bangkok: River Books.

Mathur, Suresh Narain (2008). *Hindu Gods and Goddesses.* New Delhi: Diamond Books.

Moore, Christopher G. (1992). *Heart Talk.* Bangkok: White Lotus.

Nathalang, Siraporn (2004). *Thai Folklore: Insights Into Thai Culture.* Bangkok: Chulalongkorn Press.

Rama I (2003). *The Story of Ramakian: From the Mural Paintings Along the Galleries of the Temple of the Emerald Buddha.* Bangkok: Sangdad Pueandek Publishing Co., Ltd.

Rawson, Philip (1967). *The Art of Southeast Asia.* London: Thames & Hudson, Ltd.

Reichart, Peter A., and Pathawee Khongkhunthian (2007). *The Spirit Houses of Thailand.* Bangkok: White Lotus.

Roveda, Vittorio, and Sothon Yem (2009). *Buddhist Painting in Cambodia.* Bangkok: River Books.

Roveda, Vittorio (2005). *Images of the Gods.* Bangkok: River Books.

Roveda, Vittorio, and Sothon Yem (2010). *Preah Bot Buddhist Painted Scrolls in Cambodia.* Bangkok: River Books.

Stratton, Carol (2004). *Buddhist Sculpture of Northern Thailand.* Chiang Mai: Silkworm Books.

Warren, William, and Barry Broman (2005). *Spiritual Abodes of Thailand.* Singapore: Marshall Cavendish International.

Warren, William, and Luca Invernizzi Tettoni (1999). *Thailand The Golden Kingdom.* Bangkok: Asia Books.

Ziv, Daniel, and Guy Sharett (2005). *Bangkok Inside Out.* Jakarta: Equinox Publishing.

INTERNET SOURCES

Cowell, E.B., & W.H.D. Rouse, translation (1907). *The Jataka, Vol. VI.*
Retrieved from http://www.sacred-texts.com/bud/j6/j6013.htm

Crocker, J., translation (2002). *The Wetsandon Jakata.*
Retreived from https://digitalcollections.anu.edu.au/html/1885/41898/wetsandon.html#chuchok

Wild, F. (2013). *Wat Thawet: A Small Buddhist Hell Garden Near Sukothai.*
Retrieved from http://www.unusual-travel-destinations.com/Wat_Thawet.html